HOLLAND PARK

—— since 1958 ——

an Ofsted outstanding and DfE designated te[...]hool

A place of scholarship; determinedly [...]ic with outstanding A level and GCSE results.

A place of ambition, endeavour, drive and creativity, with outstanding success in placing students in top flight universities.

A place of self-effacing confidence.

A place to find oneself and hear the still small voice.

A place where the potency of academic prowess embraces the human beating heart.

A place which believes that lives and futures can be altered and that chance can be marginalised.

HEAD: Colin Hall

ACADEMY HEAD: David Chappell

AIRLIE GARDENS, LONDON W8 7AF

www.hollandparkschool.co.uk
admissions@hollandparkschool.co.uk

THE GOOD SCHOOLS GUIDE

London South

www.goodschoolsguide.co.uk

The Good Schools Guide is a registered trademark

Sixth Edition published 2019 by Lucas Publishing Ltd
The Good Schools Guide, 4/4a Bloomsbury Square, London WC1A 2RP
www.goodschoolsguide.co.uk
978-1-909963-22-1 The Good Schools Guide London South sixth edition
A CIP catalogue record for this book is available from the British Library
Copyright © 2019, Lucas Publications Ltd

Printed by Cambrian Printers Ltd

Every care has been taken to ensure that all information was correct at the time of going to press.
The publishers accept no responsibility for any error in detail, inaccuracy or judgement whatsoever.

Acknowledgements

Writers

Alison Pope
Bernadette John
Beth Noakes
Carolyn Murphy
Charlotte Phillips
Carolyn Thomas
David Hargreaves
Emma Jones

Emma Vickers
Grace Moody-Stuart
Jackie Lixenberg
Janet Breeze
Judith French
Kate Hilpern
Lisa Freedman
Mary Ann Smillie

Mary Langford
Mary Pegler
Melanie Bloxham
Sophie Irwin
Susan Hamlyn

Design: David Preston

Typesetting: Theresa Hare, Optima Information Design

Editorial review: Beth Noakes and team: Janita Clamp, Melanie Sanderson, Kathryn Berger, Amanda Perkins, Melanie Bloxham

Advertising sales: Charlotte Hollingshead, assisted by Jo Dodds, Publishing Matters

Project management: Katja Lips

Everything held together by: Shari Lord

Junior League of London for excerpts from *Living in London: A Practical Guide*

Photography: Thanks to all the schools who supplied photographs.

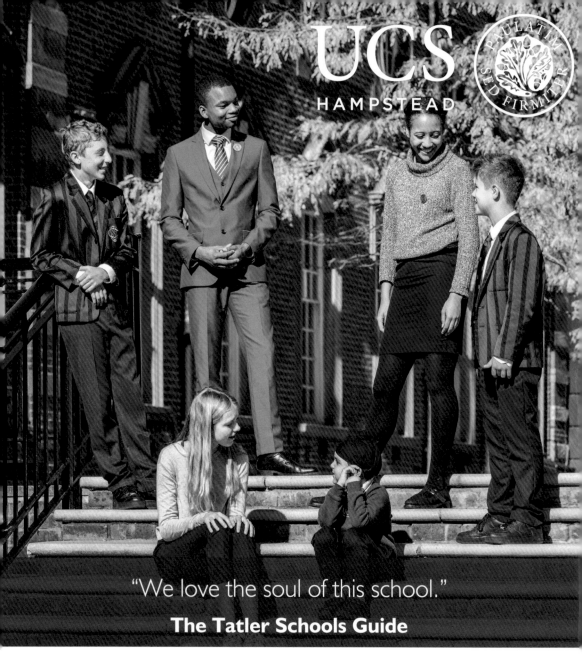

The Good Schools Guide charter

We take our independence very seriously and the separation of commercial and editorial content is absolute. No school can pay to be included in (or choose to be excluded from) The Good Schools Guide, and we do not charge schools for reviews.

In recent years we have helped to defray our costs by selling advertising space and licensing schools to reprint their own reviews for a fee. We make these offers only to schools are that already reviewed by the Guide on merit. Whether or not they choose to advertise has no bearing on their inclusion in the Guide nor on the content of their review. Schools that we have not chosen for inclusion are not allowed to advertise.

Our printed guides and website offer advice on a vast range of education matters. We also have a fee-paying personal consultancy service for parents (Good Schools Guide Educational Consultants). We receive no commission nor any other payment from any school for these services. If you have any questions or concerns about our commercial policy, please contact editor@goodschoolsguide.co.uk.

WITH OUR SUPPORT, SHE WILL THRIVE

BROMLEY
HIGH SCHOOL

GDST
GIRLS' DAY SCHOOL TRUST

We are an outstanding GDST and HMC girls' school with an exemplary reputation for academic results, sport and music. In a green and leafy environment with space to grow, our girls aged 4 to 18 make rapid progress academically and socially.

Register online **www.bromleyhigh.gdst.net**
for an Open Day or Taster Day

LEARNING AND ACHIEVEMENTS ARE EXCEPTIONAL (ISI 2016)

Contents

Key to symbols

The age range of a school is shown by the colour of the title bar.

Junior School

Senior School

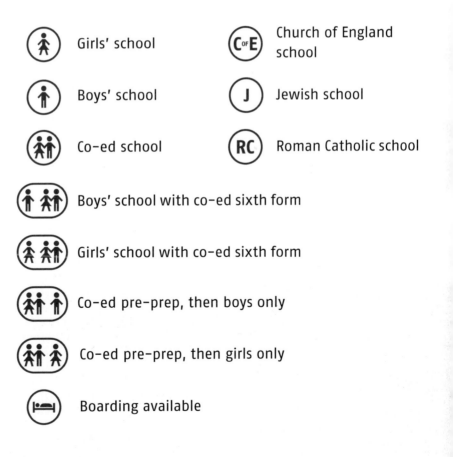

Girls' school

Boys' school

Co-ed school

Boys' school with co-ed sixth form

Girls' school with co-ed sixth form

Co-ed pre-prep, then boys only

Co-ed pre-prep, then girls only

Boarding available

Church of England school

Jewish school

Roman Catholic school

EXCELLENT
ISI inspection 2018

spirit

Every Heathfield girl has an irrepressible spirit. Uniquely hers, it drives her passion, voice and character. As well as providing an excellent academic education and top-class pastoral care, Heathfield identifies your daughter's distinctive strengths and encourages her to live her ambitions, embrace her spirit and talent so that she develops as the best possible version of herself. **Live life like a Heathfield girl.**

WE HOLD TERMLY OPEN MORNINGS.

PLEASE EMAIL registrar@heathfieldschool.net

TO BOOK A PLACE OR TO ARRANGE A PRIVATE TOUR

Heathfield
School
Ascot

Boarding and Day for Girls 11-18
heathfieldschool.net
+44 (0) 1344 898343

GIRLS
FIRST

London South map

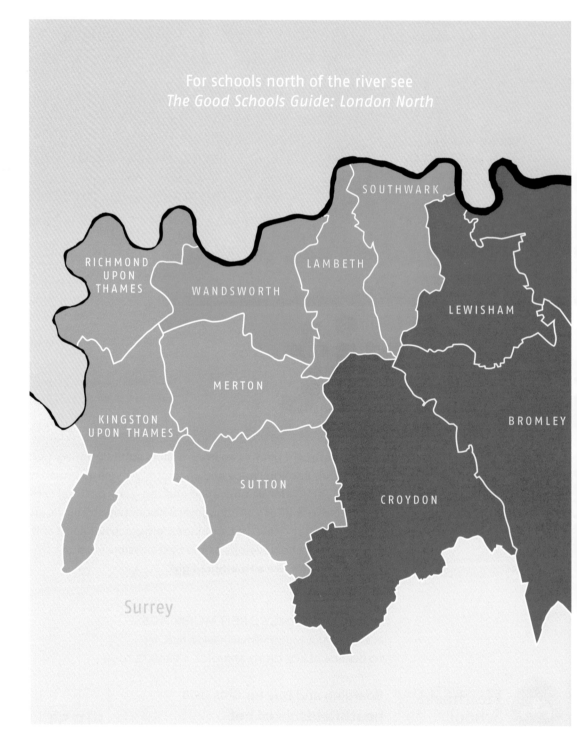

For schools north of the river see
The Good Schools Guide: London North

SOUTHWARK

RICHMOND
UPON
THAMES

WANDSWORTH

LAMBETH

LEWISHAM

MERTON

KINGSTON
UPON THAMES

BROMLEY

SUTTON

CROYDON

Surrey

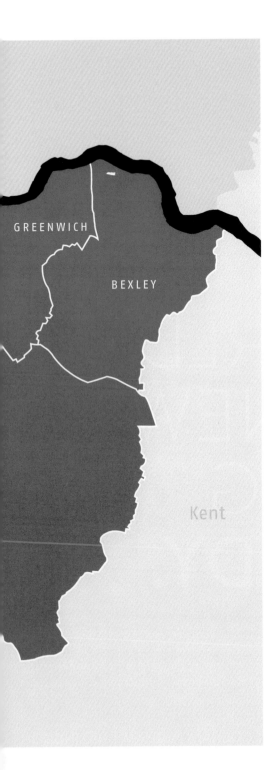

CENTRAL SOUTH 55

Lambeth
Southwark
Wandsworth

SOUTH WEST 171

Kingston-upon-Thames
Merton
Richmond-upon-Thames
Sutton

SOUTH EAST 301

Bexley
Bromley
Croydon
Greenwich
Lewisham

SCHOOLS FOR SPECIAL EDUCATIONAL NEEDS 397

London South SEN schools

ACS
INTERNATIONAL
SCHOOLS

THE WORLD NEEDS NEW THINKING.
GET READY.

COME AND SEE CURIOSITY AT WORK.

At ACS we prepare our students to be ready.
Ready to ask new questions and demand
better answers. Ready to innovate and create.
Ready for cultures that crossover, boundaries
that blur and ideas that interconnect. We ready
them for a world that demands a new kind
of learning – and a new kind of citizen.

- Girls and boys aged 2–18
- International Baccalaureate (IB)
- Advanced Placement Programme (AP)
- Bursaries and scholarships
- Extensive busing

COBHAM | EGHAM | HILLINGDON
Visit acs-schools.com/opendays

Introduction

Welcome to the sixth edition of the Good Schools Guide to London South. We offer you our knowledge, inside information, experience and opinions on the capital's best schools south of the Thames. Here's our round-up of recent developments on the London educational scene on both sides of the river.

London continues to be a superb place to educate your child, and our London reviewers have once again been inspired by the sheer dynamism, diversity, achievements and aspirations of all the capital's great schools – from local primaries to world famous names. We hope you enjoy reading about them.

London's schools made their regular appearances in the higher echelons of 2018's national A level and GCSE results tables. Looking at the relative performance of London schools, big hitters such as KCS Wimbledon and Westminster are in good company with selective state schools such as Queen Elizabeth School, Barnet, Wilson's Grammar School, Sutton, Tiffin and Tiffin Girls, plus non-selectives such as St Marylebone and Camden School for Girls.

As ever, parents push hard to get into the best and most fashionable schools – so planning well ahead will make your life much easier. This book is here to help, as are the Good Schools Guide Education Consultants (see pages 48-50).

State schools are facing a real-terms funding cut of about 10 per cent over the next few years. Some teachers are reportedly asking for parental contributions to meet basic workplace expenses such equipping science labs; whatever they say, and whatever the social pressures, these are not compulsory. Perish the thought, say the independent schools, as they push fees up ahead of inflation again.

For state schools, look carefully at how each of them is dealing with the funding cuts. According to a survey of some 400 London state school heads by London Councils, nearly half of schools surveyed have increased class sizes, half have narrowed their curriculum and half say they have had to cut teaching staff. Try to scrutinise whether the cuts in the schools that you are looking at are falling in areas that are vital for your child.

Schools also report difficulties in recruiting and retaining staff. High house and rental prices are putting teachers off applying for jobs in London and causing others to move away from the city. Good management – staff feeling really valued – and disciplined, motivated pupils, so that it is a pleasure to teach them, can help to teacher stem defections: make sure that when you visit you get to chat to some teachers well away from their superiors.

The government's ideological support for grammar schools means that there is money around for the (few) London grammars – for as long as this government lasts.

Arts subjects are undoubtedly suffering from the double whammy of exclusion from the EBacc and funding cuts. London textiles teacher Andria Zafirakou of Alperton Community School, 2018 winner of the Varkey Foundation global teacher prize, announced she was planning to spend her million pound prize money on recruiting painters, musicians, dancers, actors, illustrators, film makers and comedians to become artists in residence in London schools to inspire a generation of children.

Languages are another area where it is worth making sure that your child will be offered the opportunities you want for them. Some London secondary schools are showing a decline in take-up and provision, and a high performing sixth form centre in East London doesn't even offer language A levels, saying there is no demand. Pretty disgraceful for such a cosmopolitan city.

With independent school fees now well beyond the reach of most families, around a third of pupils receive some form of financial help. The Independent Schools Council (ISC) annual census for 2018 revealed that although the lion's share was non-means-tested scholarships and discounts, almost £400 million provided means-tested fee assistance for pupils at ISC schools, four per cent more than last year. Some of these means tested bursaries include help for families earning up to £140,000 a year – which shows you how high some fees have got (see pages 48-50 for GSG help on finding out about bursaries).

More than 200,000 children and young people in London have some level of special education need or disability. In the last 10 years there has been a 20 per cent increase in the number with high-level needs and the types of need are increasingly complex. There are concerns that the level of funding given to schools for pupils with high needs is insufficient to provide the quality support they need.

Special schools are inundated with referrals to a point we haven't seen previously – we see heads with application paperwork stacked literally desk high. One head of an autism unit said the number of applications per place made her school now 'harder to get into than Harvard'. Our education consultants include SEN experts (see pages 48-50).

Glimmers of hope? We hear that the Church of England is recognising a chasm in its school provision and is investigating opening special schools. And with council bean counters noticing the huge sums being spent on independent special schools, and we are now hearing of budgets being allocated to open new in-borough provisions.

The English school system

London has an abundance of good schools – state and private. Many families mix and match, and may have a child or two in each system at different stages of their schooling. A choice of school may depend on logistics as much as ideology. But for those not familiar with English schooling the systems can seem baffling.

State schools

Many families head for London hoping for a place in a good local state school. There are huge advantages: at primary level in particular, your child's friends will almost all be local. You will soon feel part of the local community. You won't spend hours in a car trying to navigate London traffic or have to squeeze onto a rush hour tube or bus. In central London especially, many are used to young children arriving without fluent English and have systems in place to help. And of course they are free.

Primary schools

Primary schools start at 3 (if they have a nursery class) or 4 and most run through to 11, though there are some infants' schools (3-7) and junior schools (7-11), often but not always linked with automatic entry from one to the other. Increasing numbers of senior schools are opening linked primary schools, and will eventually become all-through schools.

The cut-off date by age is 31 August in both state and private schools in England (though some private schools may be more flexible). This means that if your child's birthday is on 31 August they will start in the reception class when just 4, whilst a child with a 1 September birthday will actually be just 5 when they start.

Virtually all British state primary schools are co-ed and non-selective academically (the exception is the London

Oratory Junior House, which takes only boys – and tests for academic and musical aptitude), though faith schools mostly select by church attendance.

State primary schools may not have the specialist teachers, small class sizes or facilities enjoyed by private prep schools but the quality of teaching shouldn't be inferior. If you're lucky enough to live close to a good primary school and have a good state comprehensive down the road then your children's education is sorted. However, state primaries don't prepare children for 11+ entrance exams, so if you are aiming at a selective secondary school you will probably have to rope in a tutor in year 5 or so (see Tutors and Tutoring, page 444).

Secondary schools

There is a much greater variety of state secondary schools: single sex and co-ed, selective and non-selective, plus those that select a proportion of students for academic, music or dance prowess

The vast majority of London secondary schools are non-selective, but a few academically selective grammar schools remain, in areas such as Kingston, Sutton and Barnet. The BRIT school in south London for 14-19 year olds is the only state performing arts school in the country, with entry by audition.

State primaries may not have the small class sizes, but the teaching shouldn't be inferior

Some students move on after GCSEs to a sixth form colleges for 16-18 year olds. These tend to offer a wide range of subjects and to have an atmosphere more akin to a college than a school. Some are academically selective, others offer vocational courses to those with a more practical bent. East London Arts and Music is a sixth form for students aiming for a career in music, games design or film and TV.

Academies and free schools

Increasing numbers of state schools – particularly secondary schools – are becoming academies. These are state funded but often run by academy chains, and the current government is encouraging all schools to become academies over the next few years.

Free schools were originally intended to be set up by groups of parents and some of the early ones were, though many were set up by religious groups, and now most have academy chain backers.

Both of these types of school are outside local authority control, can decide on their own admissions criteria (though they should abide by the national code), do not have to teach the national curriculum and may employ unqualified teachers.

Private schools

Families moving to London may find it logistically easier to apply for private school places because, unlike state schools, they do not require you to have a local address before you make your application.

Prep schools

Many areas of London are well-equipped with prep schools (boys', girls' and co-ed). They are likely to have small classes, specialist teachers and a relatively biddable intake – if not the sports facilities you will find in a country school. Don't assume the teaching will be better than at a state school – both sectors include those who would be better off in a different profession.

They are likely to start at 3 or 4 and go through to 11 or 13 – historically, girls have moved on at 11 and boys at 13, though increasing numbers of boys' and co-ed senior schools now have a main intake at 11. Some are divided into pre-preps

- Flexi, weekly and full boarding
- 120-acre campus
- Just 20 minutes by train from King's Cross
- 'Pastoral care uniformly "phenomemenal"'
  — *Good Schools Guide*

Queenswood

1894

A LEADING INDEPENDENT BOARDING
AND DAY SCHOOL FOR GIRLS AGED 11-18

Open mornings
Wednesday 13 November 2019
Saturday 14 March 2020

BOOK NOW

Brookmans Park, Hertfordshire AL9 6NS | 01707 602500

(3-7) and preps (7-13), though usually with a fairly seamless transition between the two; others don't start till 7.

As the name suggests, prep schools prepare your child for entrance exams to secondary schools, and advise on which are likely to be most suitable. A prep school is judged at least partly by its leavers' destinations, so it will do its best to ensure your child moves on to a decent secondary school, even if it has to dampen down your expectations.

Independent senior schools range from the ferociously selective to those that provide a gentle haven

A stand-alone pre-prep, that goes from 3 or so to 7 years, may be a good bet if you are arriving in London at short notice. Some of the children who join at 3 may move on at 4 or 5, so places do come up. The disadvantage is that they are, inevitably, obliged to spend quite a part of the upper years preparing children for 7+ or 8+ entrance exams.

Senior schools

Independent senior schools range from the ferociously selective such as Westminster and St Paul's to those that provide a gentle haven from hothousing or social integration – with admissions policies to match. A glance at the league tables will give a clue as to the degree of selection they operate.

Historically, girls' independent secondaries have started at 11 and boys' at 13, but increasing numbers – especially boys only schools that have turned co-ed – are switching their main intake to 11, with shrinking numbers of 13+ places. Thirteen plus schools with linked junior schools will often offer 11+ places in their junior schools with guaranteed transfer to the senior school, mostly aimed at state school pupils and those whose prep school finishes at 11.

Some independent schools go all the way through from 3 or 4 to 18, which can provide welcome continuity and freedom from 11+ or 13+ selection tests. However, few

THE EATON HOUSE SCHOOLS' PROMISE

Eaton House Schools has a rich traditional heritage coupled with a modern outlook. We offer a nurturing pathway for both boys and girls within separate schools to some of the top academic London day and boarding schools across the country and our pupils win many scholarships. Our main entry points are at 3+, 4+, 7+, 8+ and 11+ years.

With personalised teaching and wellbeing at its core, pupils blossom academically and emotionally at the right pace for each child, growing into confident, rounded, intelligent and inquisitive young people. This adds up to the promise of a superb education for your child.

Come and visit us and discover for yourself what makes us so special.
Belgravia | Clapham
020 3917 5050 | sfeilding@eatonhouseschools.com | www.eatonhouseschools.com
Book an open day on www.eatonhouseschools.com

EATON HOUSE SCHOOLS
✠ Celebrating 120 years of excellence ✠

guarantee that a child who is struggling academically will be able to stay on with their peers, and teenagers may well decide at 16 (particularly if they have been in the same single-sex school since 4) that the grass looks greener elsewhere.

Independent sixth form colleges

Independent sixth form colleges, sometimes called crammers, were originally set up to prepare students for university entrance, particularly Oxbridge. They still specialise in this field, generally offering a variety of routes that include full two year A levels and shorter courses for those who need to improve on past grades. Some also offer one or two year GCSE courses. Classes are small, the focus is on exam practice and extracurricular options are limited. They are useful for those arriving in London at short notice and students who have rethought their options or need to boost their results.

MPW
Mander Portman Woodward

TAILORED
NOT UNIFORM

When it comes to a good education, one size does not necessarily fit all. At MPW, one of the UK's best known names in fifth and sixth-form education, we offer a distinctive alternative to traditional schools.

- A levels and GCSEs in over 45 subjects
- Personal tutors providing individual academic and pastoral support
- Oxbridge-style tutorial groups with nine students or fewer
- Excellent results and progression to top tier universities
- Best in class inspection reports from the ISI and Ofsted

The ISI again awarded MPW London the highest grade in every category in their most recent inspection.

Discover MPW for yourself – visit **www.mpw.ac.uk** or call us to book your visit.

London
020 7835 1355

LYCÉE FRANÇAIS CHARLES DE GAULLE DE LONDRES

Excellence in International Education since 1915

Ages 3-18 | French, Bilingual & British Curricula | Brevet & Baccalaureate | GCSE, IGCSE & A-level

"Pupils thrive academically and socially in a vibrant and purposeful learning environment."

OFSTED

For over one hundred years, we have been at the forefront of **international education.**

Nurturing skills and inspiring ideas.

Fostering confidence, solidarity and ambition.

Helping pupils to develop into accomplished world citizens.

Together, we will **explore your talents and widen your horizons.**

♀ South Kensington

South Kensington Primary School
Nursery to Year 6

Collège-Lycée (Year 7-13)
and British Section (Year 10-13)
French, Bilingual and British curricula

♀ Ealing

André Malraux Primary School
Nursery to Year 6

♀ Fulham

Marie d'Orliac Primary School
Nursery to Year 6

♀ Clapham

Ecole primaire de Wix
Reception to Year 6

f 🄾 in 🆇 ▶   www.lyceefrancais.org.uk

Applying to a state school

It can be nerve-wracking deciding where you would like your child to take their first steps into school, or spend their teenage years.

The primary schools you are considering are likely to be very local. The main admissions criteria for non-faith schools are generally siblings and then distance – which can be less than a few hundred metres for the popular ones.

Secondary schools are far more varied in their character and in their admissions criteria. These may also include academic selection and/or auditions for performing arts aptitude. You may be able to apply under more than one of these.

Timing

Applications are made through your local authority in the autumn of the year before your child starts school or moves on to secondary school. The cut-off date for secondary admissions is 31 October of year 6. For primary schools it is 15 January before the September start date.

If the primary school has a nursery class for 3 year olds you apply direct to the school when your child is 2; however, you will still need to reapply for a reception (4 year old) place via the local authority.

Academically selective grammar schools, and some that partially select by aptitude for eg music, now do their admissions tests/auditions in the summer term of year 5 or the September of year 6, so that they can give out initial results before the October closing date for applications. This will usually involve registering with the school during the year 5 summer term – so check dates carefully.

It can be nerve-wracking deciding where you would like your child to take their first steps into school

How do state schools offer places?

There are some general rules that most schools adhere to.

- Education, Health and Social Care plan naming the school. These children come first in line and must be given a place.
- Looked after/previously looked after children. These generally come next.
- Siblings. These often, but not always, come third. Check before you move house after your first-born has got a place.
- Exceptional medical or social need. This generally involves a letter from a doctor or social worker explaining why St Cake's is the only school that will cope with your child's needs. Very few children get a place by this route.
- Distance. Generally as the crow flies, but sometimes by the shortest walking route. Sometimes faith schools designate parishes, other schools may designate particular areas as their catchment. Some have specific feeder primary schools. Some grammar schools limit the distance applicants may travel to school by eg giving preference to those from specified postcodes. Your local authority should have information on how close you probably have to live to any individual school (except faith schools) to be in with a chance of a place.

However, London has a plethora of different types of school with different – and sometimes multiple – entrance criteria.

Grammar schools

These are academically selective by entrance exam (usually some combination of maths, English and reasoning tests). Increasing numbers give preference to children who live relatively locally; some also prioritise a certain number of students on pupil premium. You will be told if your child has reached the qualifying standard before the closing date for applications, but not if he will actually be offered a place.

Faith schools

These may demand that you baptised your child before she was 6 months old and have attended a specific church weekly for the past five years. They are no longer allowed to give points for eg brass polishing and flower arranging, felt to advantage middle class applicants.

Free schools and academies

These may set their own entrance criteria, though they should abide by the national admissions code. They, like most faith schools, also decide which applicants to accept (local authorities make that decision for community schools) and thus are vulnerable to accusations of cherry picking easy-to-teach pupils.

Aptitude

Some schools select part of their intake by aptitude for eg music, dance, technology or languages.

Fair banding

An increasing number of non-selective schools use fair banding to divide applicants into ability bands, taking an equal number from each band via other criteria eg distance. This generally involves computer-based reasoning tests and is not pass/fail.

Filling in the form

You can list six choices of schools in London and we recommend using all of your choices. It's vital in include at least one where you are more-or-less sure of getting a place – even if it isn't your first choice. If you don't, you may only be offered an undersubscribed school some distance away. For faith schools, you will probably have to fill in a supplementary application form and get it signed by your religious leader. If a new free school is opening in your area, you will quite likely in its first year be able to apply direct to the school in addition to your six other choices.

NB Put your school choices in order of preference – if you qualify for a place at more than one, you will only be offered the school highest on your list. The schools don't know where else you have applied, and don't know if you have put them first or last – only the local authority knows that.

Moving to London

As long as you have a right of abode in England, you can apply for a state school place here. However, you can't apply till you have an address in the country and are living here (except for Forces/diplomatic families and those applying to state boarding schools).

If you are applying for a school place not at normal admissions times – ie reception or year 7 – admissions will probably be handled by individual schools, though you will have to complete the in-year admissions form. Your local authority should be able to give your information on which schools have spaces, but it's worth contacting schools direct too.

Don't want the school you are offered?

You can appeal for a place at a school you prefer, but do it quickly. In the meantime, accept the school you have been offered (otherwise the local authority is under no obligation to find you a school at all). Ensure you are on the waiting list for any schools you would be happy with. And do visit the school you have been offered: you may find that contrary to local reputation, it is up and coming and will suit your child very well.

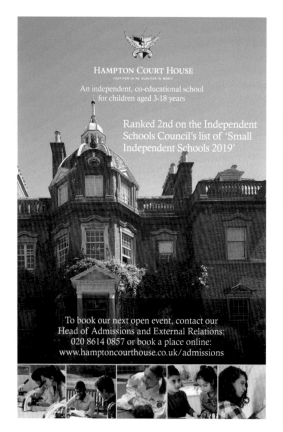

Independent school admissions

Prep schools

London prep schools have never been more popular. Their fearsome reputation for preparing children for entry to London senior schools with a champion's regime of revision, tests and extension work may well suit the bright, robust child but can cause others to flounder.

If a school particularly interests you, request a private visit and make sure it includes time to see the head and watch the school at work. Try to get a balanced view of the school – chat to pupils, staff, other parents and don't allow the marketing manager to dominate your visit. Before (and after), browse the website, prospectus and marketing literature – they'll all be glossy with happy, smiley faces, but do you like the tone and the events they put centre stage? Same old faces, same old names or a good smattering of faces, across the ages? Some preps are very traditional – blazers and boaters are often a clue; others more relaxed – sweatshirts could be a signal. You can probably tell without visiting whether or not your family ethos is likely to be a good fit.

Entry requirements at 3 or 4 vary considerably from 'first-come, first-served' (which may mean name down at birth) to mini-assessment days complete with interview and observations to see just how well Harriet integrates with her peers and playmates. Few will expect children to read and write on entry but such is the pressure for places at favoured schools that, to the dismay of many heads, parents have been known to enlist the help of tutors for their 3-year-olds. In general the play and learning that goes on at home or nursery school should be adequate preparation. At 7 or 8, nearly every prep school operates a formal assessment process, and for many London day schools, the pressure is on.

As their name suggests, the main aim of 'preparatory

They'll all be glossy with happy smiley faces, but do you like the tone and events they put centre stage?

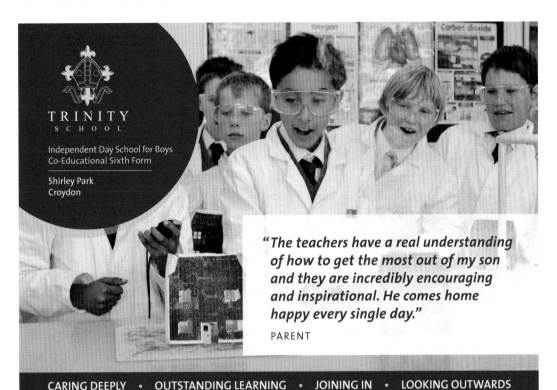

schools', or prep schools, is to prepare children for entry to fee-paying senior schools at 11 or 13. Traditionally, pre-preps take children from 3 or 4 and prepare them for moving on to preps at 7 or 8. There are fewer stand-alone pre-preps than there used to be as their main market, the boarding prep, has declined in numbers. Today, many pre-preps and preps are linked schools, with a more-or-less seamless transition between them and sometimes their senior school too. In London, with fierce competition for 7+ places at top prep schools, quite a few stand-alone pre-preps survive. Their raison d'être is preparing children for these competitive exams, which can mean the pressure starts in year 1 with regular practice papers. Some, whilst having linked prep schools, also send large numbers of children elsewhere.

Preps tend to stand or fall by their senior school destinations. Parents, whether they are aiming to get their 3 or 4 year old into the pre-prep of a chosen all-through school, or their 8 year old into a prep that sends many of its pupils to the top day or boarding schools, are generally looking ahead. Yet all-through selective schools rarely guarantee that children they take in at 3 or 4 or even 7 will have a seamless transfer upwards. If your child is felt to be struggling, you may well be advised to look elsewhere. Equally, a child who fails to gain a place at the pre-prep stage may well have developed sufficiently to sail in there or elsewhere later on. So a school that helps your child to become a happy and confident learner is the best investment.

Senior schools

If your child is already at a prep school then the process of selecting and applying to the 'right' senior school should mainly be taken care of – it's a large part of what you're paying them to do.

It used to be the case that parents rarely challenged a prep's advice about which senior school would best suit their son or daughter, but heads tell us that 'managing parental expectations' is now a significant part of their job. A prep school's reputation stands or falls on the destinations of its pupils at 11 and/or 13; prep school heads spend a large part of their time visiting senior schools and getting to know their pupil profiles. Experienced heads can spot which children should be aiming for which senior schools fairly early on and if this conflicts with parental ambitions then he or she will advise accordingly. No school will 'under sell' an able child, so if you disagree with the advice you have been given you should be able to have a frank discussion about the reasons behind it. The decision about which senior school to apply for should be at least as much about where a child would fit in and be happy as it is about academic ability.

Many prep school heads are concerned that pre-tests don't suit late developers who may not have come into their own academically

State primary to independent senior

Plenty of children from state primary schools do move on to independent secondaries, often with scholarships or bursaries. It is not the state primary school's job to prepare children for independent school entrance exams, so most parents take on a tutor for a year or so to ensure their children are used to, say, writing a story in half an hour, and timing their answers. Neither can you expect a primary school head to advise on likely senior schools, so you will

need to make your own judgement on which schools are
likely to be suitable for your child.

Applying from abroad

The first step is often an online UKiset test which measures
academic English language skills. Most schools will also ask
overseas applicants to sit their own entrance test, and are
generally happy to send tests abroad, though they may ask
applicants to attend interviews in person.

Pre-tests

An increasing number of senior schools offer provisional or
definite places based on the results of 'pre-tests' taken in year
6 or 7 (age 10 or 11). Senior schools use these tests as a filter
and to give an early indication of demand for places. Many
prep school heads are concerned that pre-tests don't suit late
developers (often boys) who may not come into their own
academically this early.

   Pre-tests are age-standardised and include multiple-choice
tests in maths, English, verbal and non-verbal reasoning. If
your son or daughter is offered a place after completing these
tests, he or she may be required to sit the common entrance
examinations in year 8 – though some top schools, including
Westminster and St Paul's, are abandoning the CE in favour
of prep school assurances of 'continued good conduct and
academic progress'.

11+ and 13+ tests

The 11+ test is taken in year 6 for entry in year 7 and comprises
papers in English, maths and sometimes reasoning. Many
London schools set their own papers, though the London 11+
Consortium of 12 girls' schools sets one common exam – a 75

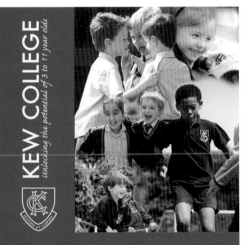

minute cognitive ability test – and shares results.

The 13+ common entrance – a set of exams common to most independent schools – is taken in year 8. Core subjects are English, maths and science and candidates may also sit papers in history, geography, modern foreign languages, Mandarin, ancient Greek and Latin. Tests are taken at the candidate's own school and are marked by the school to which they are applying. Many independent schools set their own tests for candidates (perhaps from abroad) who have not been prepared for common entrance.

Most London independent girls' and co-ed day schools accept pupils from age 11, as do increasing numbers of boys' schools. There are still some traditional boys' schools such as Westminster and St Paul's and boarding schools such as Eton and Harrow that start at 13+. Thirteen plus schools with linked junior schools will often offer 11+ places in their junior schools with guaranteed transfer to the senior school, mostly aimed at state school pupils and those whose prep school finishes at 11.

Interviews

While state schools are prohibited from interviewing any but potential sixth form (or boarding) students, the interview is an integral part of nearly every private school admissions process, and tends to send the applicant's parents, rather than the actual applicant, into a spin. Parents feel considerably more responsible for their child's social presentation than for his or her ability to do long division or conjugate French verbs. And, while a school may breezily describe the interview as 'just a chance to get to know the child better', this hardly quells fears about sending young Daniel or Daniella into the lion's den.

HAMPTON SCHOOL

CLOSER THAN YOU THINK!

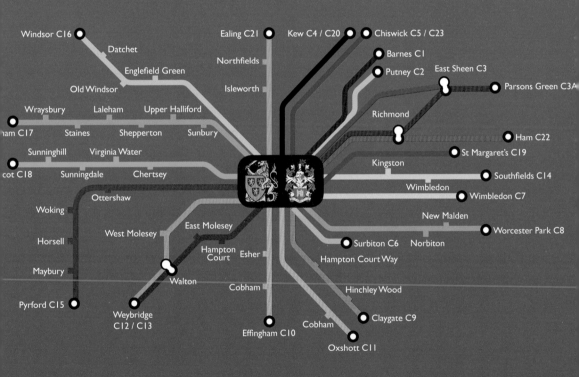

Windsor C16 •
Datchet
Englefield Green
Old Windsor
Wraysbury   Laleham   Upper Halliford
ham C17   Staines   Shepperton   Sunbury
Sunninghill   Virginia Water
cot C18   Sunningdale   Chertsey
Ottershaw
Woking
Horsell
West Molesey   East Molesey
Maybury   Hampton   Esher
Court
Walton
Pyrford C15 •   Cobham
Weybridge
C12 / C13
Effingham C10   Cobham

Ealing C21 •   Kew C4 / C20 •   • Chiswick C5 / C23
Northfields   • Barnes C1
Isleworth   • Putney C2   East Sheen C3
                                    • Parsons Green C3A
Richmond
                                    • Ham C22
                                    • St Margaret's C19
Kingston
                                    • Southfields C14
Wimbledon   • Wimbledon C7
New Malden
                                    • Worcester Park C8
• Surbiton C6   Norbiton
Hampton Court Way
Hinchley Wood
                    • Claygate C9
Oxshott C11 •

VISITOR EVENTS THROUGHOUT THE YEAR

(by appointment, see website for details)

Hampton School, Hanworth Road, Hampton TW12 3HD T 020 8979 9273
E admissions@hamptonschool.org.uk
www.hamptonschool.org.uk

Oversubscribed at every point, the selective London independent school tends to concentrate on the academic. The majority usually only meet the child after a written exam (generally used as a first edit), and the interview itself will probably contain a significant component of maths, comprehension or reasoning. The aim here is to probe intellectual strengths and weaknesses in order to select from the central bulk of candidates or to pick scholarship material. Finding out a little about a child's character is only of secondary importance.

Even the most academic schools, however, are not necessarily just looking for those guaranteed to deliver a stream of A*s. Some use interviews as an opportunity to create as balanced a community as possible:

'I didn't want all extroverts or all eggheads,' said one ex-junior school head. 'Most children who sat our exam scored between 40 and 65 per cent in the written paper, so I was looking for an individual spark. At the age of 7, particularly, the interview is a crucial counterbalance to the exam. Those born between September and December always scored higher marks in the written paper. At interview we would go back to the list and bring in some younger children.'

'I always tell parents if they're paying to coach 3-year-olds they might as well burn £20 notes,' said a school head with the task of selecting 40 4-year-olds

Parents, stand back!

Concerned parents often do their best to control the outcome of the interview, but professional preparation is seen as a waste of time, both by those who interview and by teachers. 'I always tell parents if they're paying to coach 3-year-olds, they might as well burn £20 notes,' said a junior school head who has the daunting task of selecting 40 4-year-olds from 200 applicants in a two-tier interview. 'The only useful preparation is to talk to them, play with them and read them stories.'

Further up the system, the advice is equally non-prescriptive. The head of a west London pre-prep does her best to relax the 7-year-olds she sends to prep school interviews by providing them with as much factual information as she can beforehand. 'I try to prepare them for what they'll find. I usually describe the head — because I'm a smallish woman they might expect all heads to be like me — and I'll tell them what the school looks like. Beyond that I just say, "Look them in the eye, answer carefully and be honest." Children sell themselves.'

Some pre-preps and prep schools provide mock interviews, some will carefully guide children on what books or hobbies that might show to best advantage, but most interviewers say they always know when a child has been coached, and honesty – at least in theory – is the quality they're looking for. 'I tell children,' says one private tutor who prepares children for 11 plus, 'to say what's in their heart, not what their teacher told them to say.'

'I am looking for sparkly eyes and interest. If a child sits there like a pudding, you usually don't take them'

Parents, step forward

Although the school interview is nominally about the child, the school is also interviewing parents and it's they who may need a little preparation while their child can happily be him or herself. A balance between steady, respectful (schools are ever keen to avoid the parent from hell) and interesting (but nor do they like dull ones) is best.

Is it fair?

Personality, of course, will always be the most variable aspect of any interview and all interviewers have a personal bias.

They may hate boastful children, or those who say their favourite leisure activity is computer games; they may prefer Arsenal fans to Tottenham supporters; but some schools do make a strenuous attempt to counteract the sense of one adult sitting in judgement on one child. One senior school sees candidates individually before sending them off to a lesson where they can be observed by another teacher as they work in a group.

The best interviewers can and do overcome the limitations both of the written examination and of the child. 'Children, even very shy ones, like to talk about themselves, their friends, their families and their pets. I get them to describe what they did on Sunday, or I turn my back and ask them to describe something in the room. Sometimes I even get a child to sing or dance. I am looking for sparkly eyes and interest. If a child just sits there like a pudding, you usually don't take them.' Some schools get over the 'what to talk about' dilemma by asking children to bring along a favourite object. If, however, the child pitches up with a copy of Proust or boasts a collection of Roman ceramics, parents shouldn't be surprised if the interviewer is somewhat sceptical.

Although most heads are honest in their report about a child – after all, their reputation depends on it – the interview can also benefit them. 'Occasionally, a prep school head knows perfectly well that a child is not suited to our school, but the parents just won't listen. Coming from us it doesn't sour the relationship with the school.'

How to judge a new school

Start a normal business and you can begin with baby footsteps, holding fire on major investment in resources and employees until you are confident you're on to a winner.

Founders of new schools, however, don't have that luxury. In addition to substantial premises, other chunky overheads include a head, senior management team (possibly compatible, possibly not), a full pack of teachers (ditto), not to mention the pupils.

With such a potent cocktail, the scope for fast track failure even in an apparently well set up new school is almost limitless. So why should prospective parents be prepared to take the risk? And how can they judge whether it will be worth it?

Talented team?

How confidence-inspiring is the head? With a massive extra workload and just one shot at getting things right, 'he'll do' or 'give her a try' just aren't enough. If you doubt the head's ability, give the school a miss. But bear in mind that some of the best heads aren't charismatic orators: their most important attributes are appointing able teaching staff and keeping them happily on board.

Check out the teachers. A good new school will thrive on teamwork. Do they radiate inspiration? And when you talk to them, do you wish you had been taught by them? Teachers in free schools and academies don't have to be qualified. Unqualified ones may be fabulous – or they may just be cheap to employ.

Great governors?

In an established school, all parents need know about the governors is that they are happy with the head – and vice versa. In a new school, however, the governing body's ability to choose a talented senior team, help get over inevitable initial difficulties and, most important of all, replace people fast if they have made the wrong choices, is vital.

You are looking for governors who are good as individuals and even stronger as a team, leading from the front and putting in the time to observe, listen (to you) and learn. Invisibility on open days or other school presentations is a serious warning sign that all is not well.

If your school has an academy sponsor, they will be involved in the governance. Some, like ARK, have stellar reputations. Others are close to disaster areas. Check out not just your school but the others they run. Their Ofsted reports may say more about them as a group than an individual prospectus ever can.

Parent power?

Is drop off time a turn off because of the attitudes and behaviour of other parents or their children? As a group, you are all important in working together to set the school on the right course. It takes extra energy and commitment and you need to know that other parents will chip in. Are they people you could work with? And are their children proud to be there?

Premises

Many new free schools open in uninspiring 'temporary' buildings, with the promise of a move to a fabulous purpose built (but often unspecified) site in a year or two. If the year or two is stretching out indefinitely with no sign of building work finishing (or even starting), beware.

Do your homework

Read the prospectus and study the school website very carefully. The latter should have the most up-to-date information and links to policies on matters such as admissions, discipline, child protection, SEN. How geared up is the school to deal with 'a touch' of dyslexia? Do the less co-ordinated ever get picked for matches? What happens if it becomes successful and oversubscribed and its catchment area shrinks? Will your second child still qualify for a place or will you, and similar other pioneers, be penalised? If you still have questions, ask the school directly or talk to other parents.

Now read on...

For the altruistic, enjoying the inner glow that comes with helping improve education in your local area may be enough. For others, the hope that a brand new school will do your child proud is a more tangible benefit. Whatever your reasons, good luck.

The Good Schools Guide Education Consultants

The Good Schools Guide has been trusted by generations of parents to provide expert, honest and unbiased information about schools. Our education consultancy provides the same high standards of expertise, independence and professional integrity to individual families.

Every day our highly-experienced consultants successfully help clients from all over the world to find the right schools for their children. However urgent the deadline, however complex the circumstances, call 0203 286 6824 (UK) or +44 203 286 6824 (international) to find out how we can solve your educational dilemmas.

Our consultants

All our consultants have visited and reviewed countless schools, many also have professional backgrounds or specialist qualifications in education. Between them they have direct experience of every aspect of both the British and international education systems, not to mention invaluable local knowledge about schools in London and all areas of the UK. Our team includes experts in SEN, school appeals, scholarships and bursaries, grammar schools and relocation to the UK from abroad.

Consultancy built around your needs

Our consultancy packages range from a 30-minute telephone consultation to a fully bespoke service tailored to meet complex, urgent or other specific circumstances. Additional services include accompanied school visits, providing translators and educational assessments and arranging specialist tuition. Our main consultancy services are outlined overleaf; for full details please visit www. goodschoolsguide. co.uk.

London Service

Designed to meet the needs of families new to London who need guidance, not just on schools but on residential areas, commuting, family services, nurseries, playgroups, tutors and much more.

State School Service

This service, run by the GSG expert in state education, is for parents who are interested in state schools only. It can give advice on admissions criteria, catchment areas and grammar schools.

Special Educational Needs

Our team of SEN experts is unique. We have specialists in eg dyslexia, autism, speech and language difficulties and we have extensive knowledge of both mainstream and special schools which cater for children with these difficulties.

Academic assessments

If you are not sure what academic level your child is at, particularly if you are coming from overseas, we can arrange academic assessments.

Scholarships and bursaries

We have amassed information on scholarships and bursaries to create a unique central resource, with information on the fee assistance available at hundreds of independent schools.

Contact us

Phone us on +44 (0)203 286 6824 or send a brief email to: consultants@goodschoolsguide.co.uk outlining what you need. Tell us the age of your child and where you live plus your contact details. We will contact you within 48 hours, discuss how best to help you and ensure we match you with the right consultant. Consultations can be by phone, email or face to face, and we can find a consultant to speak to you within an hour if necessary.

How much?

Ours is one of the most competitively priced tailor-made education consultancy services in the UK. Check our website for current fees.

Our guarantee

The Good Schools Guide has an international reputation for providing unbiased, independent advice on educational matters. We have no commercial links whatsoever with any school. This gives our education consultants the freedom to consider a huge range of schools in order to find the best one for you. You can have complete confidence that if our consultants recommend a school it is because, and only because, they consider it to be suitable for your child. You can also be assured that we maintain the highest possible standards of privacy and all dealings with clients are completely confidential.

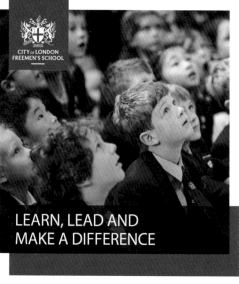

MERCHANT TAYLORS'
School

Central South

Lambeth
Southwark
Wandsworth

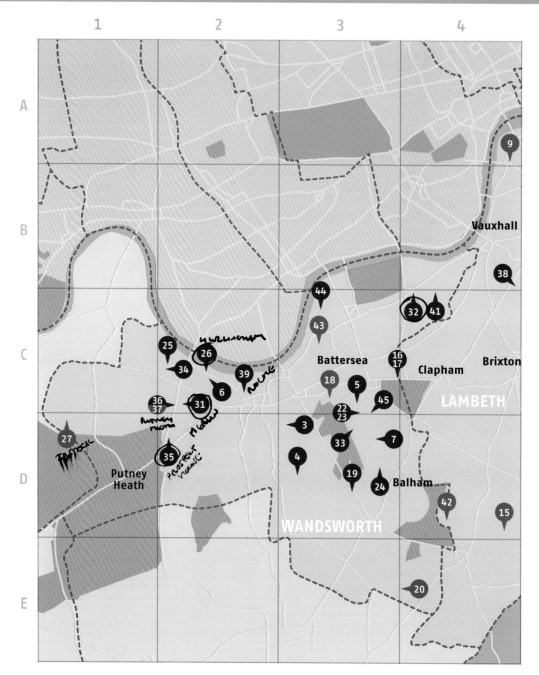

CENTRAL SOUTH

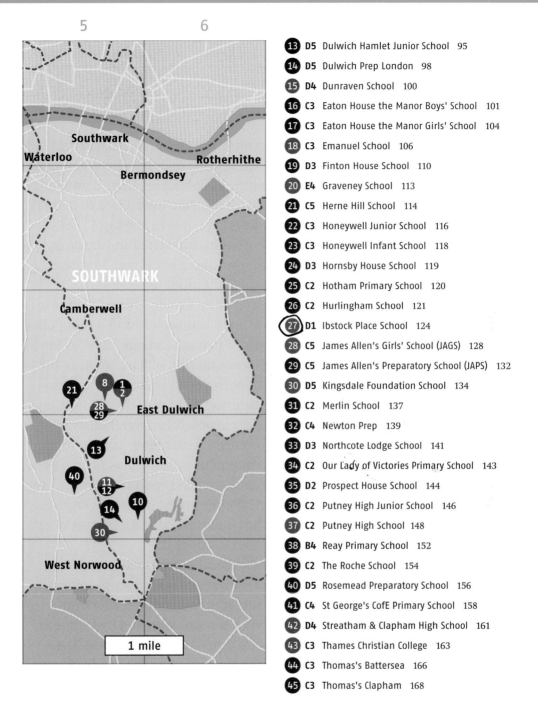

5   6

Southwark

Waterloo

Rotherhithe

Bermondsey

SOUTHWARK

Camberwell

East Dulwich

Dulwich

West Norwood

1 mile

Central South London and its state schools

Lambeth

Lambeth is a skinny borough running from Vauxhall and Kennington in the north via Brixton and onto Herne Hill, the eastern parts of Clapham (more High Street than Common), then south to Streatham and West Norwood. Hard to believe in some parts, but not so in others, it is in the top 10 of London's most deprived boroughs and state funding cuts have hit the borough hard, provoking widespread protest.

At secondary stage, Catholic families are well-served with La Retraite for girls, and co-ed Bishop Thomas Grant in Streatham, the latter, unusually, out-performing its single sex rival at GCSE. With the lack of strong academic choices for non-church goers causing some tearing of hair, we hear that children well-served by Lambeth primaries often scatter to the four winds. As a result the newly re-modelled Dunraven qv in Streatham, a dynamic, purposeful comprehensive out-performing the borough average, is extremely sought after; this has led to the establishment of a new linked primary and an excellent sixth form. Admission is by entrance test, using ability banding. Durand Academy, mired in controversy, is now to be taken over by the Dunraven Education Trust after the Harris Federation refused to adopt it.

Other options are diverse. Local parents advise taking a look with an open mind – there are some exceptional facilities, wide choice of subjects and strong leadership. Admissions for most are via a test co-ordinated by Lambeth and taken at the destination school closest to home. The Lilian Baylis Technology School partners with the South Bank University, Shell and IBM and in 2017 out-performed Dunraven. Attainment at Platanos College, Clapham is good, so popularity is surely set to rise. Head north for the Oasis Academy South Bank opposite Westminster Bridge in a remodelled office block, which has hit the Ofsted jackpot and opened a new sixth form in 2018. City-Heights E-ACT

Academy, yet to draw crowds, is growing from the ground up, partners with Dulwich College and has a language specialism. Meanwhile, Elm Green in Tulse Hill – set up as the first 'parent promoted' school in the country and with GCSE results tracking half the national average – has yet to hit its stride: its new MAT relationship with Rosendale School can do no harm.

Sailors get to mess about on the river at the London Nautical School but results dipped below the waves in 2017 at GCSE, whilst Lambeth Academy – often promoted to those seeking 'in year' admissions – has this year been recognised as seriously lacking in teaching capability. Pupils who have been signing up for Trinity School on Brixton Hill for three years are now enjoying their shiny new building. Approval has been given for a Gypsy Hill Federation senior school, which would be open to federation pupils and 10 per cent from the local area, but news of an opening has gone awfully quiet.

Lambeth presents an unusual picture with a few primaries the 'chosen ones' and a slew of others undersubscribed. Former pick of the primaries, Paxton in Crystal Palace, part of the Gypsy Hill Federation, has slipped in performance terms, eclipsed by Heathbrook, Durand, Jessop and Streatham Wells, to name but a few. Other popular choices are the delightful Clapham Manor and Henry Cavendish in Balham, and Sudbourne. Catchments are such that you won't get fit walking to school, so some relief that a few more schools join Ofsted's finest this year: namely, Granton near Streatham Vale and Henry Fawcett in Kennington.

Rosendale, not to be confused with the nearby independent Rosemead, has a large intake, attractive location close to Dulwich village, is recognised as a Confucius school teaching Mandarin, has an award-winning head and features prominently on local wish-lists. The stylish renovation and expansion of Julian's School, both in the heart of West

Norwood and on a dual site in Streatham, caused a stir in this upwardly mobile locale. Hillmead in Brixton deserves to be sought out, newly 'outstanding' in all categories and hats off to Herbert Morrison whose staff have worked tirelessly to pull it up by the boot-straps: from 'requires improvement' straight to 'outstanding' in all categories. Faith schools seem relatively thin on the ground. For Catholic families there is the excellent Corpus Christi and St Andrew's and for CofE: Christ Church, Streatham, Archbishop Sumner, St Andrew's and St Luke's. Iqra Primary does exceptionally well by its Muslim community.

Southwark

Southwark comprises the picket fences, finger-posts and green spaces of Dulwich, trendy East Dulwich, bursting at the seams with young families on the run from south west London house prices, arty Camberwell, Peckham and on northwards to Borough and London Bridge. Shad Thames stretches east from Tower Bridge and has a high concentration of warehouse conversions (think A Fish Called Wanda) and new mixed use buildings of flats, shops and cafes.

Given the highly visible presence of the famous independent schools of Dulwich College, JAGS and Alleyn's School, it's somehow all the more galling that Southwark's state schools are very often underwhelming. For the effortlessly academic, and those who may respond to tutoring, an Oyster card and a spirit of independence could bring the grammars of Kingston and Sutton within reach.

Closer to home is the reinvented Kingsdale qv in West Dulwich, remaining exceptionally oversubscribed. In 2016 the school began to capitalise on its popularity by opening its doors to a huge intake, rather than make staff cuts due to dwindling funding. Class sizes of 20 are a thing of the past, but GCSE results now top the borough and concert audiences are in for a treat. There are no distance criteria; places are allocated via ability banding; maths, music and sports scholarships are a savvy way to boost entrance prospects. The Charter School qv is popular with Dulwich families, performs well and has a no-nonsense attitude to discipline. Pupils there will no doubt benefit from The Charter School East Dulwich, a brand new secondary free school whose first intake is making do in temporary accommodation whilst awaiting what promises to be a grand building, the redeveloped community hospital. Harris Girls' Academy is performing fairly well, as is City of London Academy a bus ride away to the north. For secondary pupils in the north, progress is slow but a green light has been given to a new Haberdashers' Aske's Borough Academy on the site of the old fire station on Southwark Bridge Road. Secondary faith schools include St Saviour's and St Olave's CofE, and the star by far, Sacred Heart RC.

There are a few exceptional primaries in the north towards the Thames including Riverside and Boutcher CofE. Inspired leadership at Angel Oak Academy near Burgess Park has been rewarded with top marks from Ofsted. Further south competition hots up considerably for places. Among the most notable is Dulwich Village CofE Infants qv, every parent's nostalgic dream of a village school where you either need a terrifically desirable address, good stamina for church going or both. Dulwich Hamlet Junior qv (no automatic transfer) is not so oversubscribed. Nearby, somewhat hidden from view, Bessemer Grange is doing so well it is luring some parents away. Pupils at The Belham, a free primary run by the Dulwich Hamlet team in trendy Peckham – the icing on their already organic cake – have skipped over the road to their fabulously renovated school. The new Harris primary built on the site of the former East Dulwich police station filled a much-needed gap despite seeming to replace one architectural eyesore with another. With a brilliant first Ofsted report, it is now tougher to get a place here than at Dulwich Village Infants.

East Dulwich stalwarts, Heber and Goodrich, are tricky to get into even from neighbouring streets, despite so-so results and reputations, whilst Goose Green remains popular despite being one of the lowest performing primaries in the borough and the subject of thinly disguised negative press. In Camberwell, Lyndhurst School is worth finding, and one to watch is Crawford Primary after being taken under the wing of the Gypsy Hill Federation. Mog fans and German speakers have taken to the new Judith Kerr free primary in Herne Hill and seem to be winning in their fight to save their playing field. Expansions of Victorian red-brick primaries in this neighbourhood are keeping some architects in business. Ivydale in Nunhead recently took ownership of their brand new key stage 2 building inspired by a children's book called The Fox in the Forest.

Catholic primaries are currently top of the faith school leader board, namely the two St Joseph's in Bermondsey and Surrey Quays. Appealing CofE choices are not so plentiful but would definitely include St Mary Magdalene and The Cathedral School of St Saviour and St Mary Overy in the shadow of Southwark Cathedral.

Wandsworth

One of the largest boroughs, Wandsworth includes Putney and Southfields to the east and Earlsfield, Battersea, Clapham, Balham and Tooting to the west. Putney, along the south bank of the Thames, has a chain of attractive open spaces with extensive sporting grounds, especially rowing clubs – this is where the annual Boat Race (between Oxford and Cambridge) begins, packing the banks of the river and every possible pub and garden with cheering crowds. Battersea, dominated by Battersea Park and the formerly derelict Battersea Power Station, is now the location of the new American Embassy. The Thames frontage is the scene of incredible numbers of glittering high rise blocks, finished and under construction, many sold as investments to absentee overseas buyers. 'Between the commons' and elsewhere in these villagey neighbourhoods are row upon row of Victorian and Edwardian houses primped to perfection, a heartland for affluent professional families.

Apart from proximity to central and west London and the choice of green spaces, a big draw is the excellent choice of good state primaries (see below). If one can successfully drop into the right street for the right primary, all well and good, but a word to the wise is that come 11+ it's a different story. Lack of suitable secondaries means many either look well outside the borough or jump ship to independents or even grammars. Most parents consider a broad range of options, and as many applications as their offspring can stand.

There are two clear local winners in terms of popularity at secondary level: Graveney qv and Chestnut Grove. Although the two have always been mentioned in the same breath, Graveney leads academically (25 per cent of places are selective) hence applications most recently stood at 12 to one, so back-up plans are advisable and in fact Chestnut Grove (40 per cent art and language aptitude places) has been left behind in the new Progress 8 and Attainment 8 measure as well as GCSE grades for maths and English. Time to switch allegiance? Putting in an impressive performance is Harris Academy Battersea, outperforming some notable local independents and boasting the best performing sixth form in the borough. Special mention also goes to Ashcroft Technology College (21 technology places), 'outstanding' in every category and just a fraction behind Graveney this year at GCSE. A proportion of places in some secondaries – Graveney, Burntwood and Ernest Bevin – decided by the Wandsworth test, now taken in September by all year 6 children and a source of much angst. Other options include

St Cecilia's CofE with its music specialism (15 music places).

Those wonderful primaries, a particularly fine choice of faith schools, a veritable crop of Ofsted 'outstandings' and impressive performances, draw takers from all quarters, the irony being that, for the moment at least, Wandsworth parents are less likely than other Londoners to gain their first choices. Exceptionally popular are Belleville qv, with an expanded intake and Beatrix Potter qv in Clapham; Clapham Honeywell qv, Hotham qv – whose bilingual class is the most in demand; Brandlehow qv in Putney, recently downsized with a shrunken catchment to match; but also Hillbrook in Tooting, Earlsfield primary – now with the Ofsted ranking to match parental approval – Penwortham and Eardley in Streatham and Sheringdale in Southfields. Whilst those on everyone's lips maybe oversubscribed by up to six to one, preferences further down the list should still be better than most. Those moving to the area should scrutinize carefully the borough's 'priority areas' for various schools even down to which side of the street you need to live on.

Of the new free schools, pioneers have made a dash for Floreat Wandsworth, aiming high and focusing on character and good manners – so, no pushing please amongst the six applicants for every place this year. Tooting Primary, sponsored by Graveney, and Rutherford Primary in Balham are not tempting numbers to the same extent as established favourites. Oasis primary academy has recently opened on the former hospital site on Putney Common. Notable faith schools include Our Lady of Victories qv, Our Lady Queen of Heaven RC, Holy Ghost, Trinity St Mary's CofE, St Mary's CofE, St Michael's CofE, St Boniface RC, St Anne's CofE and Christ Church CofE among many others. St Mary's Putney is the most oversubscribed. Gatton Muslim School in Balham has expanded and Mosaic Jewish primary school has got off to a terrific start and offers as many open as faith places.

Alleyn's Junior School

Townley Road, London SE22 8SU

020 8557 1519 | juniorregistration@alleyns.org.uk | www.alleyns.org.uk

| Independent | Pupils: 243 |
| Ages: 4–11 | Fees: £18,363 – £19,125 pa |

Linked school: Alleyn's School, 67

Headmaster: Since 2015, Simon Severino (40s) MA (Oxon) PGCE. His degree subject was in geography and his first teaching job was at Culford Prep School, from there to Dulwich Prep London where he rose to deputy head, and then headmaster of St Andrew's Prep in Eastbourne.

When he arrived, although appreciative of the quality of the school, he was determined that there would be no resting on laurels and has instigated greater rigour in the classrooms appropriate for the 'bright cookies' the school attracts, and stimulated the co-curricular. There are now more clubs on offer, right down to the infants, more performance opportunities and more ways in which to express themselves. Friday mini lectures for children and parents have proved popular – guest journalists, authors and musicians so far. He has also worked hard to integrate with his parent body, introducing headmaster's coffee mornings. He likes the 'human scale' of this school, where no one will get lost, and the fact that with the infants and juniors under one roof there is a community feel and 'Infants have their heroes and role models'.

Parents described him to us as 'a good listener, which enhances his leadership skills' and 'approachable, thoughtful, calm, gentle, yet authoritative.' We found him friendly and confident in his vision for the school, which he seems to have implemented at high speed, and open to anything that is fed back to him: 'we're happy to admit when we get things wrong'. He lives within a stone's throw of the school and his wife teaches at Dulwich Prep London. He has two children, a boy and a girl. Out of school he enjoys family time, being in the garden and his Arsenal football club season ticket.

He describes this as a school where children will be 'pushed and challenged, yes, but not a hothouse' and an aim is for children to leave 'comfortable on all stages', whether that be musical, sporting or academic. A fan of co-educational schooling, he feels it gives 'a greater spectrum of ways of being and a greater number of niches' in which to fit.

Entrance: There is one class with 18 or 20 places (half girls and half boys) at 4+. Parents become aware of their child competing for one of just nine or 10 places, with about 10 applicants for every place; many choose to apply elsewhere too with these odds. At 7+ there are 24 or 25 places, and a six-to-one chance of getting in. Nine plus is a more unusual entry point and competition for these four or so places is stiffest of all.

The school is quite clear that selection is for academic potential. Four plus assessments are based on EYFS curriculum, 7+ and 9+ are based around the requirements of the national curriculum. Pupils identified with SEN will be assessed by a member of the learning support department.

Children come from a range of different schools and nurseries. There is a particular concentration from the wider local Dulwich area but children come from all over south London – Blackheath to Beckenham to Clapham to just north of the Thames.

Exit: Year 6 pupils sit the same 11+ assessment as external candidates for Alleyn's Senior School, but it is simply used for benchmarking, the opportunity to gain academic scholarships and as a target to work towards as they have guaranteed places. Less than a handful exit to other senior schools, seemingly tempted by single sex schools such as JAGS, Dulwich College or the City of London schools.

Remarks: The big news is that year 6 pupils no longer sit Sats. No more need to take so much time out of the timetable for any preparation, and with a guaranteed place at the senior school to progress to, the greatest pressure the children would seem to face here is on their initial entry. This frees up time for a year 6 diploma instead, which includes citizenship and life skills.

Class sizes rise gradually from 18-20 in reception to 22 in years 3 and 4 and 24 in years 5 and 6. As we tour the classrooms everything seems utterly spick and span, beautiful displays, activities set out on every table for forthcoming lessons; even the courtyard playground is laid out ready for break-time with dressing up clothes, crates for imaginative play, a box of hats, in addition to the pirate ship play equipment.

Meanwhile, the atmosphere in classrooms is fun and relaxed; all of the teachers take the time to talk to us, seeming to have an excellent rapport with their classes. Parents observe: 'Small groups where children work at a similar pace work well' and a mother said of her daughter, 'Her confidence in maths has been nurtured in a way that has been a joy to see.'

The year 6 children we meet are eager, polite and full of beans, quite delightful and terrifically proud of their school. There seems to be little about the school they don't know: even the fact that the school has a 'qualified nurse, not just a first-aider'. We particularly like the modesty of the school mascot, an elderly ceramic cat named Edward after the founder, who wears a tiny coloured ribbon around his neck according to which house has the most points.

French from the start. The English coordinator has introduced a rigorous approach to grammar along with weekly DEAR sessions (Drop Everything and Read), which have gone down well with parents. There is now setting in maths from year 4. There's a refurbished ICT suite with a high pitched roof. The school appears particularly ambitious for science with a dedicated lab and a specialist teacher. Various years experience food tech at the senior school.

The school mascot is an elderly ceramic cat named Edward after the founder, who wears a tiny coloured ribbon around his neck according to which house has the most points

More than 20 out of a total of 59 staff have been at the school for more than 10 years. One parent said: 'They encourage the children to step outside their comfort zone and create a safe place to take a chance, experiment or to fail without fear of embarrassment or humiliation.' Another told us: 'The teachers are extremely approachable, down to earth, and there is a high level of communication with parents.' We met an enthusiastic full-time librarian, building displays around the curriculum. There are over 7,000 books in the library and of course dressing up for Book Week.

As if anticipating our disbelief, a parent stressed: 'There really is no exam pressure.' Holiday homework is occasionally given but it is usually optional. Parents are urged not to pressure children if they are too tired for homework at the end of the day – music to our ears. A parent who had just gone through the junior to senior step up felt that the school works hard to ensure a smooth transition.

There is a forest school in reception and around 50 school trips a year. Year 6 and the chamber choir visited a professional recording studio; citizenship was brought to life at Commonwealth Day celebrations at Westminster Abbey, where one pupil talked to Prince Harry and another received a wave from Theresa May. A recent ski trip was the school's first for a while. Year 5s go wild with a bushcraft trip and Isle of Wight watersports trip, and year 6 have long enjoyed a Normandy residential. What do our guides like the most about their school? 'Lots of responsibility' and 'all of the trips and going away'.

The school makes the most of the on-site sporting facilities shared with the senior school including the recently refurbished swimming pool, a sports hall, Astro and acres of playing fields. Sport is compulsory and a significant part of the co-curriculum. All children can play in teams from year 3 and there are sports tournaments for all in years 1 and 2. School has offered girls' cricket and football in the co-curriculum for many years, and these two sports are now in the formal curriculum.

There is a large, busy playground between the music block and the playing fields where the older children let off steam, plus some picnic benches in the shade for quieter moments and a small, wooden adventure playground.

The music school is housed in a block dating from 1899, with all children having at least two class music lessons a week and many having individual lessons too. This is an exceptionally musical school, due in no small part to the fact that all children in years 2, 3 and 4 are part of the 'strings scheme', learning the violin or cello, and all year 5 follow the 'brass and woodwind scheme' in curriculum time. No wallflowers: the whole class is in the year 6 choir. And as if this isn't enough, there are 15 different musical and ensemble clubs. In Roald Dahl's centenary year, the year 6 play was a version of James and the Giant Peach with a 1960s spin.

There are over 60 clubs each term taking place before school, at lunch time and after school until 4.30pm. Virtually all are without charge. Great for working parents: after-school care is provided for children up until 6.00pm for a reasonable price.

Red-brick and purpose built with its entrance towards the rear of the main school, the building was opened in 1992 by Terry Waite, CBE. Classrooms are bright and spacious on two floors. Parents describe the atmosphere as 'relaxed, informal', perhaps particularly in the infants, where the children wear sweatshirts rather than blazers and striped shirts or dresses, but we observed this throughout the school. The head feels the school is 'tolerant and accepting, understanding of differences' which means that children can 'feel comfortable being themselves'.

Teaching focuses around thoughtful 'learning dispositions': empathy, courage and self-belief, thoroughness and focus, responsibility, resilience, imagination and reflectiveness. One mother told us her daughter 'particularly enjoys engaging with the older children through the house system'; another said her child 'feels incredibly safe and nurtured at school'; another, 'the school celebrates that every individual is special and different. They are being taught to be kind to each other in the school as well as to the people outside of the school.'

Around 10 per cent of children with SEND including dyslexia, dyspraxia and processing difficulties. The head of learning support works with a learning support assistant and a speech and language therapist – support is included within the fees.

Children reflect a diverse London population – 20 per cent are bilingual. Parents describe each other as 'friendly, laid-back and unpretentious' and feel children who will get the most from the school are 'those who enjoy busy schedules'. Another described parents, like their children, as wanting to get stuck in and involved in the community.

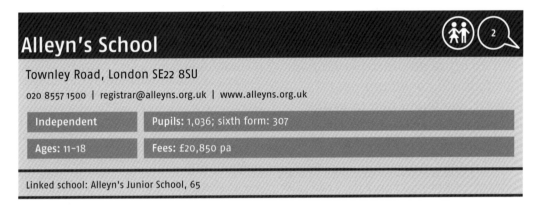

Alleyn's School

Townley Road, London SE22 8SU

020 8557 1500 | registrar@alleyns.org.uk | www.alleyns.org.uk

Independent	Pupils: 1,036; sixth form: 307
Ages: 11–18	Fees: £20,850 pa

Linked school: Alleyn's Junior School, 65

Headmaster: Since 2010, Dr Gary Savage MA (Cantab) PhD FRSA (40s). Having studied history, he topped this off with a PhD on the French Revolution. With a CV comprising the best names in education – he was under master at Westminster School, master-in-college and head of history at Eton – some parents wondered whether he would introduce a fearsome new academic regime on arrival, but one immediately realises this would not be his style. Instead he set out to 'engage the community to have more academic confidence'. And how? 'Let them breathe more, set the tone and create opportunities.' To this end he has introduced the sixth form governors' research project prize; and, fittingly for an arts-loving head, the headmaster's review prize for years 9 and 10, where they write a critical review of a play, book or exhibition, hoping to inspire all 'to enjoy London critically'. His message to teachers has been to take their own enthusiasm and 'impassion kids, not just teach the syllabus'.

He grew up in Suffolk, attending his local state school, and still supports Ipswich Town football club. Married for 25 years; he and his wife, who works in TV, spend much of their down-time in Berlin. With an office decorated in Hague blue featuring a vibrant neon artwork from one of the pupils, we found him to be charming, passionate,

energising and the most stylish head (spotted emerald green tie) we've yet to meet.

The parent view is equally impressed; the adjectives they find to describe him are 'dedicated, determined, approachable, hard-working'; 'caring and committed' and 'impressive, forward thinking, open-minded and inspirational'.

Academic matters: In 2019 at A level, 68 per cent of grades were A*/A; 88 per cent 9-7 at GCSE. Notably strong performances in A level French, art, art history, Greek, drama and philosophy.

There are six year 7 classes. Typically around 23 pupils per class rising to around 24 for year 9. Classes are smaller for GCSE courses in years 10 and 11. Upper school (sixth form) teaching sets vary from one to 14 depending on subjects.

The vibrancy of the science co-curricular dazzles, with a scientist and broadcaster, working as a scientist-in-residence, going into classes and curating a programme of Friday science lectures, not to mention the rooftop observatory, but we noticed A level biology and chemistry performing a notch below humanities subjects for the past three years. The head comments that science entrance to university is strong. Computing and DT are currently low points. At GCSE the sciences are far stronger. Maths is setted in years 8 and 9 with stunning IGCSE results.

The Alleyn's Learners' programme in years 7 to 11 aims to empower pupils to understand how they each learn so that they can utilise this as they progress to GCSE. It's all about 'developing life-long learners as well as well-rounded people,' says the head.

One period per fortnight for Spanish, German and French initially. Those choosing three creative subjects also study philosophy and history of art. Triple and double science depending on aptitude. The school is alert to what might be too much pressure. No early GCSEs in year 9 and no more than 10 subjects. One parent blessed with academic all-rounders said: 'possibly too light (if anything) on homework, rather than too heavy, but very acceptable workload.'

With an office decorated in Hague blue featuring a vibrant neon artwork, we found him to be the most stylish head (spotted emerald green tie) we've yet to meet

There are three pathways in the upper school – one four A levels, another three A levels plus an AS in maths, photography, English lang or a language, the third three A levels plus the EPQ. Sixth formers may be tempted by choices including psychology, art history, classical civilisation, politics, informatics, Greek and drama and theatre studies. We hear of students finding their academic passions in which case hard work ceases to be a chore. Sixth formers are given the platform to succeed with university applications: a subject specialist to comb over personal statements, extension societies. They are encouraged to have opinions and learn to hold their own (and rise to our more left field questions with ease). A large cohort of Oxbridge applicants strengthens aspirations and builds success.

Over 100 academic and support staff members have been with the school for over 10 years. A parent told us: 'I believe the teaching staff are very skilled, the teaching is varied and interesting. The school manages to engender a very strong work ethic'. And pupils comment: 'People do work hard and to a high level; the quality of teaching means you never feel under-prepared.'

We have heard of the odd dyslexic child from the school heading elsewhere due to an increase in pace towards GCSE (although the school has no record of anyone leaving for this reason), but the school currently supports around 150 pupils with identified SEND and points out: 'We very carefully track the progress of our boys and girls with dyslexia, to ensure they receive the support they need, and they do very well indeed at both public exam points'. Classroom differentiation and six week courses in small groups focus on study support and some one-to-one is provided. A mother with two dyslexic children said: 'They have felt hugely supported and encouraged by staff and fellow pupils and are thriving.' A tiny minority with EAL needs.

Games, options, the arts: The school is situated in the midst of 30 acres of lush playing fields with the Shard and the City just a glimmer in the distance. Every pitch imaginable, plus a newly refurbished 25m pool. The school is proud of its sporting heritage and parents feel it is 'taken seriously, but enjoyable'. An extensive sporting co-curricular: almost 400 girls and boys attend football club. By the third week of term when we visited, 300 pupils had already represented the school at a match. A similar number play netball and hockey. Water polo makes more than a splash. As ever, some sports dominate and some feel their particular passion is sidelined. Teaching staff have known sporting success: the deputy head, a former GB hockey captain still coaching at national level, is typical. DofE and CCF are popular – one often sees pupils in camouflage conducting exercises on the sports fields.

Similarly, most art teachers are practising artists. The art studios on the top floor didn't show any stunning displays at the time of our visit, instead there was an appealing art college air with paint spattered easels and overalls in rows.

Some 550 individual music lessons per week, taught by 40 visiting music teachers. A significant number of grade 8+ musicians attending junior conservatoires on weekends. All manner of choirs including gospel, jazz and barbershop.

In years 7 and 8, pupils follow a carousel of two terms drama and one term dance. Students appreciate how lucky they are to have the Michael Croft Theatre, a wholly professional flexible space where lower, middle and upper schools put on a production each year. 'Music and drama are outstanding. Lots of opportunities for a range of talent,' said a parent. House music competitions are hotly contested. Musical alumni include Dobrinka Tabakova (composer in residence BBC Symphony Orchestra), Benjamin Wallfisch (Oscar-nominated film composer), Florence Welch (of Florence and the Machine) and Jessie Ware.

Most clubs included in fees. The school buzzes until the final bell at 5.15pm when everyone is expected to be off site. Fantastic mentoring culture sees sixth formers instigating and leading clubs and societies, where they give talks in whatever their passion and career aspiration, such as law, politics and medicine.

Background and atmosphere: If the school seems both snazzy and contemporary, 'part of a global

'21st century', it is, but it's also one with a heritage – busy celebrating the 400th anniversary in 2019 of the charitable foundation on which it stands. Traditional elements, such as the well-supported alumni society, thrive. Commitment to bursaries and playing a role in London Academy of Excellence, Tottenham, continue the community spirit of the founder.

Buildings of every type dot the campus. A splendid, lofty, panelled Great Hall bears portraits of former headmasters and is used for assemblies. The Edward Alleyn building, red-brick and plenty of glass giving views of the playing fields, houses classrooms, a lecture theatre and a coffee shop sixth formers refer to as Costa. State of the art lower school building is now home to years 7 and 8, with pupils and teachers raving about the open spaces and ambiance. Its versatile atrium has proved its versatility with a year 8 architectural exhibition as well as a number of pupil and parent gatherings.

One parent talked of 'a unique energy I didn't feel in any of the other schools we considered'. Others feel the atmosphere is 'quite simply happy', 'and most important of all not obsessed with exams.' One family felt 'it is an overwhelmingly kind community where you are allowed to be yourself and to excel in your own way, without necessarily conforming to any norm.'

Pastoral care, well-being and discipline: The head's latest speech saw a recommitment to well-being, providing a safe environment in uncertain (political) times. He confirms his aim is for a 'holistic, kind, relaxed school at ease with itself'. Parents universally single out the pastoral care for praise: 'Unbelievably amazing!' said one. Another: 'My over-riding impression is that there is very little bullying, and kids (and young adults) are taught and encouraged to be respectful of one another.' This is repeated at every turn. The co-ed nature of the school means there are relationships between pupils, but everyone seems to take the environment totally in their stride as a preferred norm and there are always people to talk to: 'you never feel stranded', tutors 'have your back,' they tell us.

Pupils and parents: Will you fit in? Families are often 'city people, third sector, journalists... Londoners,' says the head. Accordingly this is a cosmopolitan bunch: pupils speak over 30 different languages at home, with a tiny few overseas nationals. One parent ensured we're entirely in the picture regarding parents: 'decent, obviously quite posh'. Prepare to be part of a community – 'involved' crops up frequently.

What kind of child would be happy here, we ask parents? 'Curious, independent and confident – but it is also a great school for children who are less confident because the school culture is so kind and accepting,' is representative. Upper school students wear business attire; our female guide negotiating the stairs niftily in platform wedges approved of the degree of latitude given.

Entrance: By far the largest entry point is 11+ when there are 135 places on offer and over 700 applicants annually. Prospective 11+ pupils can now come along as part of the admissions process for an Experience Alleyn's afternoon, which is designed to offer a taste of life at the school with lessons in sport as well as academic classes. At exam time, candidates are assessed in English, maths and reasoning (verbal, non-verbal and spatial), and a confidential report is sought from the current school. Candidates who fare well are invited to return for a small group activity and one-to-one interview. Over 300 are interviewed and the school takes a balanced split from state and primary applicants and those with different aptitudes. Adjustments for demonstrable SEND.

One third of the intake is drawn from Alleyn's Junior School pupils who are all guaranteed a place. Pupils come from both preps and primaries, most very local, so Dulwich, Herne Hill, Streatham, Clapham and Wandsworth. But the huge Foundation coaches that line the road at pick up time shuttle children from far further afield including Bermondsey, Croydon, Beckenham, Chislehurst and Kensington and Chelsea.

> A parent talked of 'a unique energy I didn't feel in the other schools we considered'. Others feel the atmosphere is 'quite simply happy'

No longer has a formal 13+ entry point. For the sixth form there are 15 to 20 places on offer; all candidates sit general papers that test their skills in critical writing, qualitative and quantitative reasoning regardless of their A level choices. The competition will be 100 strong.

Exit: Almost all to first or second choices of university. Most popular destinations recently: Bristol, Leeds Manchester, Durham, Cambridge, Oxford, Imperial, UCL, Edinburgh and Exeter. Others to BIMM Music Institute and Royal College of Music. In 2019, 13 to Oxbridge.

Money matters: More transparency than we often see regarding the financial commitments involved for prospective parents: spelling out the cost of school lunches and sports gear. Most scholarships are worth around 25 per cent of fees for the academic, sporting and musical. Application fees are waived for any children receiving free school meals. All bursaries are means-tested, with a focus on fewer but larger bursaries. Some 84 pupils currently receive bursaries and 70 per cent of these are fully funded. There even may be help with uniform, travel and school trip costs.

Remarks: A vibrant, 21st century school built on solid values where excellent grades seem just part of a broader and deeper education towards confident young adulthood.

Allfarthing Primary School

St Ann's Crescent, London SW18 2LR

020 8874 1301 | info@allfarthing.wandsworth.sch.uk | www.allfarthing.org.uk

| State | Ages: 3–11 | Pupils: 406 |

Headteacher: Since 2017, Tom Holmes, previously deputy head at St Mary's in Richmond. Has also worked at Honeywell and at a primary school in Surrey.

Strikes just the right balance between humility and authority and was an instant hit with the parents – no mean feat, given the turbulent journey they'd been through following the departure of the previous head, who'd reigned for 25 years. 'The school was very academic and had an amazing reputation, but she left and there followed a number of headships that either didn't work out or were temporary and which led to the school dropping from outstanding to good, with a feeling of discontent among the parents,' explained a parent. 'When Mr Holmes came in, it felt like a breath of fresh air – teachers looked happier, everyone saw the sense of direction that had been lacking and there was more focus on mindfulness and teamwork.' Another said, 'Sports and the arts have picked up pace dramatically since his arrival – a great way for children who aren't academic to find confidence.'

Many also love the fact that 'he greets every child by their name on the gate each morning.' Pupils call him 'kind,' 'always around and interested,' and 'strict when he needs to be, but always fair and never shouty.'

His first job was threefold: replace the high level of supply teachers with permanent recruits; up the ante on English and maths; and make some quick wins – introduce houses, year 6 mentoring, tighten up systems, be more visible etc. The remaining jobs, he says, have been slower burners – including ensuring the school meets every child's needs and expanding SEN provision. 'Essentially, I've shaken the bones of the place,' he says.

He is keen on sport eg touch rugby, cricket and cycling, and lives in Twickenham with his wife Kathryn and daughter Lottie.

Entrance: At 3+ into the nursery or 4+ into reception. Priority goes to siblings and then those living closest to the school. Attending the nursery does not guarantee a place in the infant department. Don't be put off the 400m catchment zone banded about every April – it's not as brutal as it seems, insists the head, with a zone of 1200m usually being the reality by September (mainly due to the transient nature of Wandsworth and parents opting for private schools instead). For occasional places in older age groups contact the school to check availability and put your name on their waiting list.

Exit: Something of a scattergun when it comes to secondaries, with no more than three or four to any one school – 'which is why I'm very keen to support parents to find the right school for their child, be it state or private,' says head, whose knowledge of local schools is 'impressive,' according to parents. Popular state choices are St Cecilia, Burntwood, Ashcroft, Graveney, ARK Academy and Bolingbroke Academy; odd one to Kingston or Surrey grammar schools. Around 30 per cent to independents such as Emanuel, Whitgift (which starts at year 6, leading to an annual exodus of a handful of children at the end of every year 5 – 'always a shame,' according to remaining parents), Ibstock Place, Wimbledon High School and Trinity. Odd one to Lady Margaret's, KGS and Streatham & Clapham High School.

Remarks: Situated on rather a busy corner, the tall Victorian building offers large, bright classrooms; eyes are immediately drawn to displays of children's work and art designed to capture imagination and interest. Reception and nursery classes have indoor and outdoor classrooms, ample resources laid out thoughtfully. Huge Astroturf area (which can be netted across to host two separate games),

Sports and the arts have picked up dramatically since head's arrival a great way for children who aren't academic to find confidence

playground equipment, table tennis tables, outdoor classroom (although children told us, 'it's not used that much, except in summer') and nature zone, with beds for the children to learn about growing food, composting and studying minibeasts. Separate playground for younger ones (up to year 3) but they get to use the bigger (more exciting) one during lunchtimes. Large inner-city mix 'from high-earning bankers to very working class and loads of different ethnicities – fabulous diversity,' as one parent put it. Around 30 languages spoken; around a quarter on pupil premium.

Standards are high and monitoring and assessing of progress is meticulous across the age groups to ensure underachievement is picked up and addressed swiftly. School's results in maths are impressive. Ditto with English; lots of drama and speaking and listening activities are incorporated into the curriculum. Everyone learns Spanish from year 3. Parents report good traditional teaching with interesting history and geography projects alongside whizzy IT – all classes can access iPads, chrome books and trolleys of laptops. School very well in national assessments and has an above-average added value score. 'The teachers are amazing,' we heard more than once from parents – 'they're big classes, but they get to know which kids need extra support or challenges in every subject.' We saw children fully engaged in every classroom; not a yawn in sight. Homework at the talking end in lower years (less a case of 'talk to your child about Vikings' than 'Here's what we're going to be doing on Monday – can you help them prepare'). Plans in place for a homework club.

SEN support delivered inside the classroom for core lessons, plus small group or individual teaching when needed. 'The school has been instrumental in turning our two children with SEN around – one in particular needed lots of help and we didn't have to fight for any of it. It was recognised it was needed and they delivered, both on the academic and emotional side,' said one parent. Another told us, 'It was the school that recognised my child's problem. At first, I was in denial but they talked me through the process and the support they could offer, which has involved lots of one-to-one work but all the while never excluding him from the class. The patience they have is astounding as he's very active and needs a lot of attention.' Speech and occupational therapists visit the school

as required. School has partnership with Place2Be to ensure strong mental health – pupils, staff and parents are involved, with the option for children to drop in anytime.

Two multi-purpose halls (and soon to be a third) provide space for PE, assemblies, dance, drama, art and lunches cooked on site in the recently refurbished kitchens (although the number of lunchboxes suggest it's not as popular as it could be). On site sports include lacrosse, football, hockey, cricket, gymnastics and tag rugby; older pupils walk to Southfields secondary school for swimming lessons. Sports days are held on the local common.

Music has rocketed in recent years and features highly on the daily curriculum; super purpose-built accommodation with a dedicated music teacher. Opportunity for all from year 4 to learn an instrument, with many achieving grade 6 before moving to secondary school. Each child chooses a string or wind instrument for group lessons in year 3. The chamber choir, guitar ensemble and wind ensemble all perform locally, sometimes with audiences in the hundreds. Encouraging setting for musical families, currently something of a rarity for a state primary. Children told us they'd like more drama – 'it's mainly an after-school club when you're older,' one said, although there are all the usual class assemblies and plays. Art on the up, with each class getting involved in an annual themed project, the results of which are displayed in reception.

'The school has been instrumental in turning our two children with SEN around – one needed lots of help and we didn't have to fight for any of it,' said one parent

Remarkably good Friends of Allfarthing Group raises money for all sorts of activities (including every class teacher having funds to spend on two workshops and one trip a year on top of what's already offered) and equipment through traditional and creative ways. Monthly book club lottery raises funds for the library and other book purchases. All tastes taken into consideration for before- and after-school clubs, which run daily, with parents and pupils suggesting some of the choices available. Wrap-around care offered onsite by an outside company from 7.30am to 6pm – again, well used. A few rumbles among parents about costs, compared to other local schools, but all grateful for the provision. Plenty of local trips and three residentials – one each for year 4 (one night), year 5 (two nights), year 6 (four nights).

Pupils – whom we found polite, confident and articulate – are encouraged to voice their opinions through the school council and class reps, on school rules, sensible behaviour and other issues that benefit everyone's participation and enjoyment. Behaviour kept in check, also thanks to the 'good to be green' system (warning cards lead to red cards for misdemeanours; three red cards leads to an after-school detention; 'less than 10 a year, though,' says head, and only one exclusion in last two years). Bullying minimal, report all – anti-bullying week is a big deal here and worry boxes in each classroom are well used. Praise as big (if not bigger) a focus as punishment, with house points and a mention in celebration assemblies considered high currency by pupils.

Overall a popular school with supportive parents, smiley, focused and engaging teaching staff and a terrific head who is working hard to continually improve and develop provision. As one parent put it, 'This is a school that really knows your child – no cut-and-paste jobs on the reports here.'

Beatrix Potter Primary School

Magdalen Road, London SW18 3ER

020 8874 1482 | Info@beatrixpotter.wandsworth.sch.uk | www.beatrixpotterschool.com

| State | Ages: 3–11 | Pupils: 415 |

Headteacher: Since 1988, Stephen Neale MA Dip Ed Tech Dip Ed (mid 60s). Brought up in Kingston upon Thames, Mr Neale makes use of his south London roots to put local history into the heart of the curriculum. Not content with a display of Beatrix Potter's childhood connections to Wandsworth, Neale has staged a re-enactment of the school's wartime evacuation by steam train to Surrey and established a partnership across the globe with the Royal Newfoundland Regiment whose veterans lie in Earlsfield cemetery opposite. Unconventional but not irreverent, his conversation delights in describing his pupils' success, not solely their academic results. 'The outcomes, Sats in particular, don't tell the whole story,' he remarks. They have accolades as wreath-layers at Remembrance Day, as mascots in the O2 tennis championships and as ambassadors for the UNICEF rights-respecting school.

Married to a Polish opera singer with one grown-up son, Neale eschews the headmaster's traditional jacket and tie for an inscrutable look of Hawaiian shirt and tweed jacket. He had recently returned from giving a talk at the British EduTech show on 'fake news', which he links to studying historical evidence. 'Can we teach fake news to children? It's about what it is you are given, how to be wary of what you read'. Parents are impressed by the breadth of the teaching, 'The head and the deputy head are doing a million things', one remarked, though they felt he could spend a little longer on the commonplace, like proofreading the school newsletter for spelling mistakes. 'It makes you shudder,' said one mum, 'The teaching in the school is better than that'.

Entrance: By Wandsworth Education Authority admissions criteria to fill the two class intake, with priority to looked-after children, EHC plans which name Beatrix Potter School and a two stage catchment area. Many come from the school's own nursery. A long waiting list for places, but opportunities arise when families relocate.

Exit: Children move to approximately 20 different senior schools; independents include Emanuel School, Dulwich College, JAGS, Alleyns, Wimbledon High School, Whitgift School. Wandsworth state secondary schools include some with a selective year 6 test: Ernest Bevin College, Burntwood Academy and Graveney School as well as Chestnut Grove Academy, St Cecilia's CofE School and St John Bosco College. One mum felt there could be more emphasis on preparing children for the LA's test: 'The head says, "enjoy school", but that's what parents want…more emphasis on that exam in year 5'.

Remarks: Overlooking Wandsworth cemetery and the railway tracks of Earlsfield Station, the 1920s schoolhouse has a quaint suburban feel, despite having been enlarged and modernised on three sides in recent years. Named after the famous children's author/illustrator of talking rabbits and dancing mice, whose books were written for the children of her Wandsworth governess, the school honours Beatrix Potter's memory in images of Peter Rabbit on its insignia and uniform. 'The stories are a bit twee for most children,' explains the head. The teaching, on the other hand, cannot be accused of old-world whimsy, with consistently solid results in

Stephen Neale eschews the headmaster's traditional jacket and tie for an inscrutable look of Hawaiian shirt and tweed jacket

English and maths; each class of 30 benefits from a class teacher and TA in the lower years and a floating TA according to need in the older years.

We saw topic-based work on Victorian weaving looms linking DT and history, and watched year 5 children enthralled by a video demonstration of paper-weaving. The close connection with the Commonwealth war graves has engendered a wealth of creative output in drama, art and writing; 'The First World War poems were GCSE level', boasted the head. In addition, a SENCo team, including art therapist, works within the classroom with the six per cent of children who have additional needs, including ADHD, dyslexia and ASD-type difficulties. 'It's not about attainment', said one mum. 'The differentiation is amazing, they give my son work appropriate to his level'. The school is well resourced with gadgetry: a hall full of desktops and chariots of pink and blue iPads for tech on the go; Google funds virtual reality headsets to help with writing skills; and the children are regulars on Skype, promoting international citizenship with other schools.

A dedicated art room announces 'Art Makes Children Powerful', borne out by the highly decorated wall displays and Lowry-style paintings we saw in the year 2 classroom. Sports are on the up, with football, hockey, netball, cricket and rugby on the school's three hard courts and tennis at a local club (not Wimbledon). 'My son was sent by the head of PE to try out for Chelsea,' added one mum.

Most of the classrooms are on the ground floor, with direct access to the outside play areas, some off new corridors, others forming part of the characterful 1920s school building, with heritage parquet flooring and half-tiled walls. Reception and nursery have their own wing, decorated with Biff and Chip characters from the Oxford Reading Tree, hand-made by a talented caretaker. Outdoor play areas are divided by key stage, and include a train track, tepee and climbing equipment for all sizes and abilities; there's also a bandstand for open-air concerts and plays. Three hard courts with netball hoops and a trim trail are used for PE and the children spread into the fields beyond for sports day. A small pond in the front garden is undergoing a slow metamorphosis into a nature reserve, to attract some live Jeremy Fishers and Tiggywinkles.

After-school activities include sports and art clubs, karate, yoga, gymnastics, Chinese, Spanish and Russian. School trips take advantage of the London museums, and there are residentials to PGL and abroad. A second invitation awaits for a lucky few children to visit the Newfoundland friends in Canada.

Staff range from 'oldies to late 20s', as the head puts it, and turnover is slow for London, mostly due to retirements. Additional therapy experts are brought in if needed. One year 6 pupil told us, 'The best thing about this school is the teachers because all the teachers have helped me when I was struggling'. Parents said they were happy communicating to the class teacher face to face, and saw the head at the gate most afternoons; they were less impressed by the typos and date errors in the newsletter, 'he takes it as a badge of honour that the English and punctuation is a mess,' said one. Another added, 'We all laugh about it, but I've been in tears because I'm going to miss my kid's sports day...none of the dates match'.

Nevertheless, the school thinks big in terms of pastoral care: as a holder of the UNICEF children's rights respecting award, it displays values taken from the UN Convention on Rights of the Child proudly in the hall – equality, respect, dignity, non-discrimination and participation. To implement these each class, even the youngest, composes their own charter, and there are seven different school councils, including peer mentors and anti-bullying ambassadors. The head is mindful of today's cyber pressures. 'The ones who get into big trouble are those that are vulnerable,' he sighs. 'We don't ban kids from looking up something on the computer, all schools have parental controls, but parents are still awful at safeguarding their own children'. Parents praised the pastoral care particularly. One mum, who had raised an issue about friendship groups with the head, remarked, 'It was dealt with more seriously than I had expected. I had mentioned it in passing. It was resolved by a peer mentor from year 5 or 6'. We queried the air of concentration in each class and were assured it was the norm: 'they are really well-behaved children,' smiled the deputy head.

A small pond in the front garden is undergoing a slow metamorphosis into a nature reserve, to attract some live Jeremy Fishers and Mrs Tiggy Winkles

Sure enough, in each classroom, we were met by an articulate and charming student guide who explained the lesson in progress. Dressed in royal blue or red jumper, white polo and dark skirt or trousers, the children are representative of the local demographic; some from the residential streets of 'nappy valley'; some prison employee families and others from local social housing. 'The parents are very diverse,' we heard from one mum, 'and from a wealth of backgrounds...they celebrate everything'. We met a family who had moved into the catchment area specifically for the school. A posse of parents was busily organising the film club meeting when we visited, showing the Peter Rabbit film (naturally). 'We're all in the PTA,' they chorused. 'There's a steering committee, but it's not limited to a certain group of people'. The mood was buoyant; comments like 'family school' and 'no cliquishness' filled the air.

A modern school with a sharp sense of history, where teaching reaches out from local issues across international borders. The head leads a committed team of teachers and keen parents, to educate beyond the tick boxes of the curriculum and give children an appreciation of their role in the wider world. No flopsy bunnies here.

Belleville Primary School

Webbs Road, London SW11 6PR

020 7228 6727 | enquiries@bellevilleschool.org | www.belleville-school.org.uk

| State | Ages: 3–11 | Pupils: 947 |

Executive Headteacher: Since 2001, John Grove BEd MA (50s). A true local, born and educated in the borough; even his MA comes from Roehampton University on the far flung edge of Wandsworth and his previous job was head of West Hill Primary. Asked to take over this then struggling school, he used his immediately apparent mental energy and vision to change Belleville into a superstar amongst primaries, and his relaxed, calm exterior exudes confidence. His only sadness about his new role – he is now executive head of the multi-academy trust that includes three other schools – is that he now has less contact with the children and thus their parents, but this is belied by the ease with which the little ones interact with him and the number of parents who greet him on the street. Dedicated to discovering new and better ways to run his own schools, he covers the globe (from Finland to China), investigating educational methods that can be put into practice at Belleville.

Entrance: Consistently oversubscribed, the furthest offers by distance at the moment are under 500 metres for the school and just half that for the two nursery classes. Because the distance is measured from the Webbs Road site, this can mean that a child whose bedroom overlooks the Meteor street premises is unable to skip across the street to school. The long waiting list continues for all age groups as parents of children who find a place here tend to be reluctant to move. Admissions criteria follow Wandsworth Council's guidelines but a change has just been made to give places to the children of members of staff (all employees, not just teachers). Four form entry with an additional bulge class in some year groups and a very high proportion (can be over 25 per cent) of siblings.

Exit: The majority to state secondaries, with Bolingbroke Academy way out in front and about 10-15 per cent offered selected school places at the Sutton grammars and Graveney and a proportion off to independents, including major London players such as Alleyn's, Dulwich College, Emanuel and Streatham & Clapham High.

Remarks: Dominating the crest of the hill, reminding one of a mediaeval castle looking over its fiefdom (in this case the pushchair-filled Northcote Road), Belleville's Victorian brick building is a strong, confident presence. The wandering pigs, a noted nuisance to late 19th century residents, have long since gone, replaced by rows of well-tended, now extremely expensive, Edwardian houses.

A classic example of 19th century school design with three identical floors, allowing a steady upward progression from nursery at ground level to the heights of year 6, housed under the ornate beamed roof. Inside it's any colour as long as it's blue, but the building is far lighter than you'd expect (one of JG's improvements being to uncover the boarded-up windows) and the graphically designed, framed examples of school activities and pupils' work give the public spaces a much more cohesive feel than we normally see.

The head's first aim was to improve the standard of teaching by increased teacher training and support, and the goal of constant assessment and

Head has invested time and effort investigating and introducing Singaporean maths teaching methods (Belleville is a Maths Hub)

improvement remains his number one priority. It is blindingly obvious that he has hit the target, not only because of the exit results but also because his senior team have almost all been with him for over 10 years and new (about one third experienced, one third trained here and one third NQT) teachers increasingly stay put. The school is now a National Teaching School, which explains the emphasis they place on regular courses for their staff and, intelligently, they bring in all the newly qualified teachers they hire for three weeks of intensive courses in the term before they let them loose in the classroom.

JG has also invested time and effort in investigating and introducing far Eastern and, in particular, Singaporean maths teaching methods (Belleville is a Maths Hub), but the rest of the curriculum is no poor relation and children achieve strong results in all the core subjects. They are grouped by attainment for reading but are kept in mixed groups in other subjects, although they offer additional challenge and 'booster' classes outside school hours. Specialist teachers for PE, languages, art, music and ICT.

Local musicians, artists and actors are encouraged to come into the school part-time and we witnessed the enthusiasm of the year 6 Djembe drumming session although, due to the decibel level, we were pushed to distinguish the various compositions. According to the excellent website, they will also be designing a clay pot in art, inspired by Grayson Perry – should be colourful.

The inclusion director has a dedicated SEN team and a full-time learning mentor. At present there are approaching 100 children identified in house as needing additional support, with fewer than 10 having an EHCP. A bonus from the addition of the site on Meteor Street is that they now have a stair-free premises so that they can handle a wider range of physical needs. A very clear anti-bullying policy, particularly necessary in such a large school, as well as a straightforward Safeguarding Code of Conduct with a charming bee motif.

An amazing 37 different languages spoken by children of 22 nationalities, the French contingent numerically miles ahead (Brexit may alter this) with about a third of the pupils this year having English as an additional language. However, the diversity of their backgrounds was obviously not affecting the children that we met, who appeared completely at home in their blue surroundings, and the little ones were unabashed by the head and the stranger with him – in fact they cheerfully poked their heads round his open door and chattered about their day.

There could be a clue about JG's attachment to his beloved Chelsea FC in the blue strip (odd, that) worn by Belleville's football teams, proud of being borough champions. Cricket teams hold the same title, the year 5/6 gymnastics team are regular finalists at the London Youth Games and, judging by the cups in the cabinet, sport is taken seriously. All children take part in some sporting activity (unsurprisingly not such a large selection as at some of the local independents) for at least two hours a week from year 1 and there are after-school clubs for the seriously keen. It was a toss-up whether the teacher or the children were being more enthusiastic in a PE class we saw and the inter-house trophy is a wondrous, shiny creation.

Parents praise the mass of extracurricular clubs, finding breakfast and homework club particularly useful, but on offer as well is at least one club for each letter of the alphabet (barring Z), ranging from Arty Party to yoga dance, although these are subject to a charge (free sessions for children on free school meals). The PTA raises substantial sums, enough for minibuses (in the past) and 100 new iPads, about to be collected by a happy ICT teacher.

However, the most important new fact about Belleville is that it is growing. Now part of a multi-academy trust with Alton Primary, Churchfields Primary and the rather quirky Belleville Wix, where they teach the English curriculum to one third, half and half English/French to the second third and the remaining third belong to the French Lycée and follow the French curriculum in French – unlikely though it sounds, apparently it works.

There could be a clue about head's attachment to his beloved Chelsea FC in the blue strip worn by Belleville's football teams, proud of being borough champions

There could be a danger that the Meteor site is seen as a second division version of Webbs Road, but we felt that it was simply the same message in a different package. In our opinion Belleville is a very professionally run and well-oiled machine doing its best to overcome the naturally corporate nature of such a large-scale organisation. JG has great faith in the logic of managing a sizeable group of schools, saying that 'if you can get it right for one child, it is simply doing the same thing for more of them'.

Brandlehow Primary School

Brandlehow Road, Putney, London SW15 2ED

020 8874 5429 | info@brandlehow.wandsworth.sch.uk | www.brandlehowschool.org.uk

State	Ages: 3–11	Pupils: 358

Head: Since 2015, Ellie Loughnan (40s). She has been at the school for nearly two decades, arriving as a newly-qualified teacher and proceeding through the ranks to deputy head and SENCo before taking over as head. An outstanding communicator and team player, she's relentlessly positive, dealing with pupil behaviour ('I'm so proud', 'brilliant') and parental waywardness (such as taking over teachers' parking spaces) with equal upbeat grace. She's also a hugely capable administrator, managing the recent tricky downsizing of the school and building works with calm efficiency. Parents feel lucky to have her. 'Though it seems a bit of a cliché, she really does take time to find out what makes every child "succeed",' said one. 'She's great,' said another. Despite her undoubtedly heavy workload, she still makes time to run half marathons for charity, and is actively involved in the local junior football league.

Entrance: Unlike many London schools coping with the latest baby boom, Brandlehow has been reducing its yearly intake from 45 to 30, a decision intended to more accurately reflect the school's physical capacity. While ensuring a less cramped time for those already past the gates, not the best of news for those considering queuing outside. However, in the throes of expansion to return to two-form entry. After the multitude of siblings who come first in line, newcomers will generally have to live within 75 metres, an increasingly costly option as the school itself has created something of a micro property boom. Tour mornings available for those wanting to look and yearn.

Exit: Leavers well prepared for what lies ahead from year 4. The immediate area is not packed with first-rate secondaries, but well-informed parents investigate selective and non-selective state options (Wimbledon College, Graveney, Ashcroft, Lady Margaret, St Cecilia's, Burntwood, Tiffin). Quite a number, too, opt for private (Putney High a popular local choice, with others off to Latymer Upper, Emanuel, The Hall Wimbledon and Fulham Prep) or make the traditional leap to the country at this tricky juncture.

Remarks: One of the country's top performers in year 6 tests, with nearly every child reaching the government targets and progress at the top end of the improvement range in reading and maths. This, of course, is partly due to pupils' 'cultural capital' (with only the smallest percentage on free school meals), but equally down to its stimulating curriculum and 'relentless pursuit of excellence'. Teachers are well-trained and popular, lessons meticulously planned (says Ofsted) and aspirations high. Daily reading encouraged at home, weekly and bi-weekly homework (spelling, times tables, etc). Modern languages (French) from year 3. This is a carrot-not-stick sort of place and praise is lavishly sprinkled, with awards for in-school achievement ('handwriting heroes', 'world-class writing' and 'homework halos'), and a 'wall of wonderfulness' for those taking the initiative and doing 'incredible' work not set by the school. Pupils clearly respond well to the approach. 'My kids really enjoy school,' said one happy parent, reflecting a widespread thumbs up.

Those who struggle with specific difficulties are identified early and given appropriate support, overseen by a head who herself offers coaching in SEND and ADHD. Well-organised in-school offering, including specially trained teaching assistants, aided by external experts provided by the local authority.

Newcomers will generally have to live within 75 metres, an increasingly costly option as the school itself has created something of a micro property boom

Head regards parents as 'active partners in a child's education' and involves them closely, giving regular updates through Parentmail, detailed curriculum outlines online, and regular access to children's work through dedicated Book Look events, when children discuss what they've been doing in the run up to parents' evenings.

Sport an undoubted strength, and pupils split into four houses ensuring athletic prowess evenly spread for competition. Tennis, cricket, athletics, swimming (years 4-6), and outdoor and adventurous activities all taught as part of the curriculum, plus plenty on offer in the play-ground (Astroturf pitch, table tennis, hopscotch, climbing frame, basketball net, gym equipment, etc) and in-school clubs (lacrosse, tag rugby, yoga, badminton). Competitive sports day held annu-ally at Wimbledon Park track, with a trophy for 'sporting excellence' plus proper medals for those triumphing in everything from long jump to jave-lin. Dedicated PE uniform, in which pupils have proudly represented Wandsworth in the London Youth Games and fought their way to 10th place in London primary school rugby.

Music (timetabled once a week) and other arts strongly encouraged (with lively artwork through-out), and curriculum enriched by a multitude of free, teacher-led clubs (including coding, chess, Irish dancing, photography) before and after school, with paid options extending the range for budding linguists (Mandarin, Spanish, French) and musicians (violin). Plenty of trips, from a farm and aquarium to Barnes Literary Festival and Wandsworth Recyling Plant. Year also punctuated by exciting events, such as Book Week (with dress-ing up and guest poets), Rockstead concerts, and Science Week, where visitors recently helped pupils dissect a squid, learn first aid, and discover how to become a doctor.

Gardening a major focus (with classes named on a horticultural theme – Maple, Sycamore, Holly, Lavender, etc). Not one but two gardens, incorpo-rating a meadow, frog colony, pond, composting heap and miniature orchard, as well as raised beds. Green-fingered enthusiasts can also enjoy weekly gardening club, and regular family gardening ses-sions on weekends.

Safety, physical and emotional, a top priority, with staff posted at gates morning and evening, and reminders to parents to report back concerns. 'It's better for us to know about something that happens at school while children are still here,' says the head, suggesting parents advise kids not to wait to till they get home. Worry box in each classroom and all encouraged to be able to name three grown-ups they would feel happy to talk to if something bothered them. Practical measures taken, too, to address hardy perennials such as nits, with a hair-tied-up policy to fight the insect enemy. Strong international outlook, with former teacher posting regular updates about his cycling circum-navigation of the globe, letter links with partner school in Rwanda, and the school recently playing host to a dozen visiting Norwegian pupils.

Regular meet-and-greet coffee mornings allow parents to vent concerns (the divisive issue of cake,

apparently, being one), which are all carefully responded to in writing by the head. Lunches, cooked daily on site by the school's award-winning chef, satisfies even the pickiest, with three hot options (honey-and-ginger stir-fried vegetables, fillet of cod provençale, recent plats du jour) plus salad bar. (This is a school where after-school snacks are generally confined to bananas and rice crackers.)

Gardening a major focus (with classes named on a horticultural theme: Maple, Sycamore, Holly, Lavender, etc). Two gardens, incorporating a meadow, frog colony, pond, composting heap, miniature orchard and raised beds

Though the school doesn't brag of it, its cen-tral core is a rare grade 2 listed building by Erno Goldfinger, one of only two Modern Movement pri-maries by the mid-century maestro. Built in the 50s of pre-fabricated concrete (and part destroyed a decade ago), it has since been surrounded by a flurry of cedar-clad classrooms to accommodate increasing numbers. These low-rise buildings cluster round attractive, open and well-equipped grounds (picnic tables, Giant Connect), with quiet reading areas and dedicated sport pitch.

Parents generally well-spoken, well-quali-fied professionals, with dual-income families well catered for in before- and after-school clubs (where there have been complaints about the sharp-elbowed booking up spaces, which then go unused). Half from a wide range of minority ethnic backgrounds (about a quarter speak English as an additional language, though few are beginners) and South Africans, North Americans and Australians find the can-do atmosphere particularly compat-ible. Busy PTA helps fundraise (Christmas Fair, children's disco, etc), reorganise the library and run the multitude of cake sales (so many, they have to be rotated).

Though not financially favoured by the local authority, the recent challenging climate has left the school relatively unscathed as parents give gen-erously (a recent summer fair raised over £11,000, and head has been clever at finding additional revenue sources elsewhere (a Co-op scheme, for example, has aided library improvements), and is now embarking on a £3m expansion scheme.

Broomwood Hall

68-74 Nightingale Lane, London SW12 8NR

020 8682 8830 | broomwood@northwoodschools.com | www.broomwood.co.uk

| Independent | Pupils: 662 |
| Ages: Girls 4-13; boys 4-8 | Fees: £16,125 – £19,785 pa |

Linked school: Northcote Lodge School, 141

Principal: Lady Katharine Colquhoun BEd (50s). Has a rather regal manner but her vision has seen this school mushroom from humble beginnings to a thriving empire with over 600 pupils (as well as 200 boys at Northcote Lodge – the brother school down the road). 'She's remarkable,' one parent told us. 'Inflexible at times, and you have to toe the line with her, but she is seriously impressive.' Lady Colquhoun knows she has an able team behind her and believes the ability to delegate, which she learned as the eldest of five children, is her secret.

Lady Colquhoun has made the transition from headmistress to joint principal with her husband, Sir Malcolm. She still teaches literature to prep school girls, whilst he deals with administration and property. School has a board of directors which oversees both Broomwood Hall and Northcote Lodge.

Headmistress since 2001, Carole Jenkinson BSc PGCE (50s). Varied career, including time as ski rep, with stints at International Tribune in Paris and British Council. Started her teaching career at Northcote Lodge. Universally respected and admired by parents; everyone we spoke to described her in glowing terms. She exudes calm wisdom. Very knowledgeable about senior schools of every hue and spends a significant proportion of her time visiting potential schools up and down the country. Teaches maths to year 7 and verbal reasoning to year 4, so has a good grasp of each girl's abilities and character before recommending suitable senior schools. Now head of all three Broomwood Hall schools: two lower schools in Garrad's Road and Ramsden Road, and the upper school in Nightingale Lane.

Entrance: Lower schools hugely oversubscribed, non-selective and located in the heart of Nappy Valley. For reception class, parents must register their child in advance on the provisional list and are invited to register formally and pay the £100 fee once they have visited. Automatic entry to registered siblings and children of alumni; all others selected by random ballot. Currently forty reception places at Garrad's Road and 80 at Ramsden Road. Not a huge international contingent – still predominantly well-to-do British families with some Europeans and Americans.

Three forms per year in the prep, rising to four per year from year 7. Maximum 18 per class. Vast majority come up from lower schools. Those coming from elsewhere must register on the provisional list and provide a report from previous school. Parents have a tour and time with the headmistress, and prospective pupils spend a morning in the school where staff assess their academic ability in a classroom setting.

Girls in the prep come from as far afield as Fulham, Chelsea and Dulwich. A Fulham parent we spoke to felt that those who were not from the immediate area were made to feel like outsiders by parents – 'the Wandsworth brigade can be quite intimidating for non-locals as they stick together like glue.' The school itself bends over backwards to integrate the new recruits. Morning and evening minibus to Fulham and Chelsea. Places vacated by 11+ leavers are quickly snapped up.

Exit: Most lower school girls to the upper school and most boys transfer to Northcote Lodge. A few disappear at this stage to country preps (such as Cheam, Ludgrove and Cothill) and some opt for neighbouring day schools (Dulwich Prep, Dulwich College and King's Wimbledon among them).

Some 25-45 per cent leave at 11, mostly to south London day schools (eg JAGS, Alleyn's) or to boarding (eg Benenden, Downe House). More and more stay until 13 and then tend to head to co-ed boarding (eg Bradfield, Bryanston, Marlborough). Usually around 20 per cent of girls awarded scholarships. Plans to open a co-ed senior school in 2020, initially for 13-16 year olds, on the Garrad's Road site.

Remarks: The Garrad's Road site is an arts and crafts style Edwardian mansion. Large, pretty garden with lots to keep children occupied – hopscotch, vegetable patch, climbing frame, sandpit and out-side classroom for reading on summer afternoons. Ramsden Road is on two sites – The Old Vicarage, a rambling, red-brick former parsonage, for the first two years and 50 Nightingale Lane, around the corner, for the next two years. Both feel homely, with tartan carpets throughout. The upper school, also in Nightingale Lane, boasts an amphitheatre where girls perform plays.

Schools have a relaxed, country feel; on the day we visited, pancake races were in full swing in the playground at Garrad's Road and children and teachers were having a ball. Teachers engaging and inspiring; these are lively places to work. Good mix of long-serving and new staff, with some having chosen teaching as a second career. The parents we spoke to felt the lower schools give a solid academic grounding as well as a joyful start to school life.

Reading is of paramount importance and the libraries are well-stocked and well-used. School rewards hard work in all areas: copious numbers of cups awarded to pupils (including for good manners and friendship). Head believes children must learn that they will only win a cup when they have tried really hard and must learn to accept that they will not win every time.

Girls certainly keep their heads down in the upper school, although there is also great fun to be had along the way. Setting in English and maths throughout school. The upper school is ahead of the pack when it comes to technology. Girls bring in their own iPads and older girls learn computer coding (which they love).

Some 60 upper school pupils receive some form of SEND support. School feels able to support mild dyslexia and dyspraxia but wouldn't be the right place for anyone with severe difficulties. Currently 30 children with English as an additional language.

Tea is served at the end of lessons, followed by supervised homework – viewed as a godsend by busy parents; children say they like being able to relax once they get home

A very well-run, flourishing school that knows where it is heading. For those who want a modern education underpinned by traditional values, there is arguably nowhere better south of the river. Tea is served at the end of lessons, followed by compul-sory supervised homework at school. Viewed as a godsend by busy parents, and children say they like being able to relax (save for rote learning) once they get home. Some parents, admittedly, would prefer homework to be done at home so they can keep a

closer eye on their child's progress. Clubs, including flower arranging and glass painting, finish at 6pm.

Drama is a real strength; everyone is in two plays a year, one of which is biblical, 'so they know their Old and New Testament stories by the time they leave.' Flamboyant productions. Bright art and DT studios, complete with impressive equipment. Talented head of lower school music writes plays and composes scores for productions. Eighty per cent play a musical instrument. Four choirs.

Principal is keen on instilling good manners. Children hold doors open for adults and look you in the eye when they talk to you

Substantial amount of sport on the weekly timetable. Full-size hard tennis court in the Garrad's Road garden used for PE. Cricket, foot-ball and rugby pitches 10 minutes away on foot. One parent we spoke to felt this is 'possibly not the right school for a really sporty child,' though others disagreed and said there were plenty of matches going on. Some pupils currently performing at pre-county level. 'We've definitely become a sportier school,' says head. Currently winning or drawing three-quarters of matches; school excels at cross-country and netball.

Principal believes old-fashioned values hold true and is keen on instilling good manners in her pupils. Children hold doors open for adults and look you in the eye when they talk to you. Girls are required to have a comb in their backpacks at all times; ear piercing strongly discouraged. Pastoral care is a great strength of the school. A trained counsellor is at the upper school regularly to help girls with eg potential eating disorders, exam phobia or bereavement.

Delicious food. Girls are encouraged to make conversation at meals and to hold their knives and forks correctly. Leiths has written a bespoke cook-ery course for Broomwood and all girls in year 7 have weekly cookery lessons. During the summer term pupils put on their aprons and cook a three-course meal for their parents. Always a great success and highly anticipated.

Good communication between schools and home. Lots of social events, including leavers' dinner – a swish black-tie affair for parents, pupils and teachers. Massive amounts of fundraising for a school it has built from scratch in Ethiopia. Parents are very supportive of the enterprise, though one or two grumbles about not enough money being given to local charities. Drop off and pick up times involve huge numbers of mothers, either in gym kit or walking the family labrador, though schools note that more and more mothers work. Some joint upper school ventures with Northcote Lodge (debates, clubs and field trips) – but one mother we spoke to felt that the girls and boys hardly mix and that this is a missed opportunity.

Schools turn out well-adjusted girls, fully prepared both academically and socially for the next stage. Parents emphasise what a great job they do in producing confident, happy and successful girls. As the school handbook firmly explains: 'We don't expect parents to become heavily involved in the minutiae of the learning process; we do expect you to leave your daughter's education to us and let us get on with it.' If you do that, your daughter will be in safe hands here.

Head acknowledges that parents are more demanding than a decade ago but understands 'that the significant financial output for school fees means they inevitably want to know they are getting value for money.' Welcoming, gentle schools full of delightful, cheerful, well-behaved children.

The Charter School North Dulwich

Red Post Hill, London SE24 9JH

020 7346 6600 | info@charternorthdulwich.org.uk | www.charter.southwark.sch.uk

| State | Ages: 11–18 | Pupils: 1,239; sixth form: 337 |

Head teacher: Since 2013, Christian Hicks (40s), who grew up in West Norwood and was educated at nearby Dulwich College, then collected a BA in German studies and European literature at Bristol, an MA in English and American literature at Newcastle and an MA in effective learning at the Institute of Education.

Very likeable, open and seemingly far less ego-bound than some heads. Mr Hicks lives in Beckenham with his teacher wife and three young children – two boys and a girl. Out of school he thrives on learning new things, recently taking up magic and completing the Yorkshire Three Peaks Challenge. What could be more useful in a demanding headship than a head for heights, stamina and the ability to pull rabbits out of a hat?

Despite his own alma mater, he is committed to the principle of comprehensive, inclusive education. Previously deputy head of Blackfen girls' school in Bexley and before that deputy head of the Royal Docks Community School in Newham. His move was not without ambition. The Charter School is never far from the dazzle of the spotlight, its every move noted and often written about in national newspapers by the influential parental and local body. The Charter School East Dulwich opened in 2016.

Head jokes about his tough remit of improving on the already vastly improved academic standards. Has high expectations of his pupils, aims to challenge, inspire and be highly visible: he isn't too grand for break duty and is on the door with his headship team every morning and afternoon to greet, send off and confiscate any attempts to flout the uniform. He sees one of the most vital parts of his role as 'getting the right people on the bus' – the hiring and firing of an exceptional team of teachers.

Academic matters: Unfazed by the ending of modular assessment at GCSE, 79 per cent of pupils gained 9-5 in both English and maths in 2019; 39 per cent of all GCSEs in 2019 were 7-9 grades. At A level, 72 per cent of grades were A*-B and 23 per cent A*/A.

Standard-ish curriculum at GCSE, including French, Spanish and Latin plus Mandarin for those with an aptitude for languages at year 7. The school has been teaching Mandarin with some success and finds it accessible for those with dyslexia. GCSE English results have soared, maths is solid, and sciences are strong. History and art and design are both popular and successful. Weak spots most recently media studies and RE.

Relatively few taking computer science, but the school is ahead of the curve in making the transition from ICT and is looking forward to pupils who have been coding at primary school joining in future years. A group of girls recently won a competition to design an app for a local business, whilst prizewinning games designers met the Duke of Cambridge at an enterprise event at BAFTA HQ.

A few less deskbound options such as catering, PE and performing arts and a handful of BTecs on offer – science, business, social care, engineering and ICT, with most success in business.

Head assured us that school will 'really push children who have been successful at primary school' – hence this school does well by the more able, with some 20 per cent of pupils generally of International Bankers, Shell UK and more than 100 business mentors.

One parent tells us that assistance given to her son included 'mock interviews, workshops on CV writing, presentation skills and financial awareness workshops.' The CEO of the Science Council recently spoke to year 10s about STEM careers and a doctor from King's College Hospital runs an annual seminar on applying to medical school. Students also sampled uni life at Lille, London South Bank and Brighton and large groups are taken to both Oxford and Cambridge to inspire.

Someone here is in possession of an amazingly A-list little black book – a truly top-notch class of the great and good drop in to inspire regularly. Imagine the thrill of a Romeo and Juliet masterclass with none other than Joseph Fiennes; Jo Brand speaking to celebrate International Women's Day; Professor Sir Michael Rutter talking about his latest research to psychology students; not to mention professional Bollywood dancers teaching the samba. Nor are they short of invites: the day prior to our visit 30 pupils met Boris Johnson at City Hall at a reception to honour the contribution of African and Caribbean soldiers in the First World War.

Head emphasises the value of the growing DofE programme in fostering key learning aptitudes such as resilience. Around 300 day and residential trips every year, from Bletchley Park to Belgium, Berlin and Beijing. London theatres are made good use of with trips to the National, Unicorn and Young Vic recently. One parent said: 'The school also works closely with many charities and my son was lucky enough to take a charity trip to Kenya this summer.' The school is aware of hardship issues and helps with small bursaries where it can.

Head is clear about his expectations of staff: 'don't come here if you're not prepared to work hard for successful outcomes for the students'

achieving at least eight 9-7s. Stand-out performances include lashings of 8/9s, but we noticed the school proudly trumpets the achievements of pupils gaining three 3s if this means that they have achieved well and are on track for their next step.

Best-performing subjects most recently at A level are: further maths and maths, biology, chemistry, fine art, English literature, history and a few -ologies. Languages seem a complete turn-off. Head says school is not alone in this. Aiming for an all-round academics, school will run subject even with a single pupil if necessary. Equal numbers of girls taking maths and a strong showing in sciences too.

Twenty-one teachers have more than 10 years' service – hard to believe as they appear extremely youthful. As one parent noted, 'teachers are mostly young and cool.' In fact one was so young and cool that we witnessed the receptionist assuming he was a pupil. Head and parents point out the calibre of staff attracted here by the unusually leafy milieu for an inner city salary. Head is very clear about his expectations of staff: 'don't come here if you're not prepared to work hard for successful outcomes for the students.'

A thrilled father of three girls told us that 'science teaching at The Charter is fabulous; several staff have Oxbridge PhDs and the teaching is inspiring.' Others said: 'Our children are inspired by their teachers and are really motivated to learn' and 'the staff clearly work really hard and are extremely conscientious.' Average class size at key stage 4 is 20, with 30 the maximum and some as small as five for 'nurture groups.' In the sixth form the average is 18.

With regards to homework and pressure one parent said: 'There is a good balance of homework throughout the term and a very balanced approach to exams,' whilst another warned that 'it's very intensive.' Parents kept thoroughly in the loop. The school is quick to bring them in to discuss a student who is not attaining their individual target for each subject. Coasting is not permitted.

The school dazzles in its business and enterprise specialism, creating aspiration in thinking ahead to future careers – opening students' eyes to the wider world and maximising their situation in London is a real strength. The school has links with PwC, King and Woods Malleson, O2, King's College Hospital, the Worshipful Company

Someone here is in possession of an amazingly A-list little black book – a truly top-notch class of the great and good drop in to inspire regularly

Quite high numbers of SEN: around 20 per cent of students across the school cope with varying degrees of learning difficulties, so everything from specific learning difficulties such as dyslexia or dyspraxia to physical disabilities, autistic spectrum disorder or ADHD. Large learning support team of 23 staff, including specialist SEN teachers, higher level teaching assistants and learning support assistants, support students in mainstream classes but may also be able to offer small group withdrawals, extra literacy and maths intervention

Alleyn's Junior School

sessions, touch-typing, handwriting and reading clubs and input from a range of external agencies.

Games, options, the arts: Sports are compulsory – and the only time girls and boys are taught separately. Footballers enjoy links with professional clubs such as Millwall and Fulham FC. Cricket and rugby are on the up: the MCC coach cricket and the RFU rugby. The coaching team includes national class coaches in table tennis and aquathon. Students recently started play basketball competitively and are now enjoying BMX at Burgess Park.

Prior to lessons we noticed some boisterous boys in the corridor, but once lessons had commenced the atmosphere was quiet and calm

Successes across the board, with pupils competing regionally and nationally, particularly the girls: the school boasts a national champion in rowing; U13 girls' cricket team recently won the Lady Taverners' competition at the Oval; year 8 girls' rugby recently placed sixth in London; year 7 girls' netball team won the Southwark league. Over 500 pupils take part in after-school sports club every week.

The school appears rather boxed in by the neighbouring houses and plentiful sports ground of the neighbouring girls' school, but pupils use a playing field a five-minute walk away. Indoor sports hall is large and there is an on-site floodlit netball court, ball-court and Astroturf.

More than 200 learn a variety of 20 different musical instruments up to grade 8, with some lessons significantly subsidised and many trying an instrument for the first time. Two choirs and a jazz band, which may be led by teachers or pupils. Past students have gained places at the Royal Academy of Music. A favourite alumnus is rising star Kwabs – The Guardian calls him 'the new Seal' and he has a recording contract with a major record label.

All pupils study drama once a week in years 7, 8 and 9, enjoying purpose-built drama studios and a flexible theatre space. A highlight of the dramatic year is the whole school theatre performance – recently Guys and Dolls – featuring staff alongside pupils. A parent said of the art: 'I have been delighted with the art department. I feel the teachers really care about what they teach.' London galleries are frequented and facilities include a kiln, dark room, screen printing and Mac suite.

Lunchtime and after-school clubs include young historians, tennis, handball, track cycling, music theory, ukulele, African drumming and study skills. Pupils sign up on a first come first served basis. Most are free, with a small charge for tennis and swimming clubs.

Background and atmosphere: Smaller than most city comprehensives, The Charter squeezes into a plot a few strides from North Dulwich station and at the heart of Herne Hill. Built on the site of the defunct William Penn School, it opened in 2000 following a concerted campaign from parents in an area dominated by independent schools, but without a good state option.

Savvy parents realise that they have something of a find on their doorstep, but some nervousness persists locally around the legacy of the failed school, and the head is aware school has to work hard to ensure that no one child lets down the reputation of the whole amongst the local community. Ofsted has rated it outstanding twice.

Most of the buildings were remodelled rather than replaced. It is light and functional but now looking more than a little frayed at the edges, both inside and out. We wondered how a shy year 7 moving here from one of the cosy local primaries might make the transition. The head told us: 'This is a family school, a local school. When children move here they are often joining siblings or friends' – a third of every year group has school siblings. And everywhere in the mornings and afternoons one sees little gaggles of Charter pupils walking to and fro. Each year 180 new pupils join, but the school very often operates in year groups, with assemblies for each year. Lunchtime arrangements – a mix of indoor and outdoor seating under cover – see year 7s heading to lunch 10 minutes earlier to avoid being overwhelmed.

Sports are compulsory – and the only time girls and boys are taught separately. Successes across the board: the U13 girls' cricket team recently won the Lady Taverners' competition at the Oval

Prior to lessons we noticed some boisterous boys in the corridor, but once lessons had commenced the atmosphere was exceptionally quiet and calm, with each lesson we viewed in both arts and sciences equally industrious.

Parents talk of happy children who are able to be who they want to be here. When the head was writing his mission statement, pupils asked him to add 'happiness' because that is how they feel.

Pastoral care, well-being and discipline: The relatively relaxed school uniform – polo-shirts and pullovers mostly, so no ties and without the blazers of the other nearby state seniors – is deceiving as to the school's culture of high expectations. Given the issues of the school in its previous incarnation, it set out to be something of an innovator in managing behaviour and is known for its no-nonsense attitude to discipline, which it balances with care. Behaviour officers, not in evidence on our visit, have a remit to swoop into any classroom to remove a student who has overstepped the mark. The head says that 'any pupil who is disrupting the learning of others will be in school until 5pm.'

More serious offences such as smoking will result in exclusion – gross misconducts are half what they were five years ago, although slightly up recently. The emphasis is on inclusion and working with pupils to find a way back to contributing positively. There is a whole raft of rewards including VIVO Miles – like air miles for good behaviour – extra school trips, presentations and a phone call to parents from the head or head of year.

Known for its no-nonsense attitude to discipline. Behaviour officers have a remit to swoop into any classroom to remove a student who has overstepped the mark

Mobile phones are not allowed in school at all, except for sixth formers who must keep them out of sight. Any confiscated phones must be collected by a parent. No piercings other than one pair of ear studs; no hats, hoodies or outlandish hair colours.

Pupils should always have someone to talk to. There are strong relationships between staff and pupils, a tutor system, year 11 mentors for year 7s and a school counsellor. Even the staff get a buddy each.

Pupils and parents: A large part of the intake is from privileged Dulwich Village, Herne Hill and East Dulwich, but pupils encompass every kind of home life. More than 30 per cent of students are pupil premium students – the performance gap is significant but closing. On entrance, students demonstrate a wide range of ability but it is notable that by year 11, 56 per cent have risen to the two highest ability bands. A parent told us: 'This school is for children who want to learn, want to get somewhere in the world. It caters for all in that there is something for everyone.'

The school prides itself on its inclusivity and parents say it really 'celebrates diversity.'

Forty-seven per cent of pupils describe themselves as white British, with black British African as the second largest group (11 per cent of pupils). Surprisingly few EAL students and whilst there are many bilingual pupils, 93 per cent have English as their first language.

Parents come from all walks of life. Very effective PTA has just bought a 16-seater minibus for inter-school sports matches.

Entrance: Increase PAN for Y7 entry 2020 to 192 (from 180). The extra 12 places will be prioritised for Pupil Premium students.

The hoo-ha over the school catchment area is in the past. Admissions criteria are looked after children, then siblings, then distance criteria using safest walking distance as a measure, which places the catchment currently at no more than 1,600 metres from the school. Parents in East Dulwich may want to get out their pedometers. No feeders as such but largest cohorts from Dulwich Hamlet Junior School, Dog Kennel Hill School, Heber and Goodrich local primaries. Will increase from 180 to 192 year 7 places from 2020, with pupil premium students getting priority for the extra spaces.

The sixth form is more inclusive than many: pupils must have five 9-4 grades including maths and English, with varying minimum grades for different A level subjects.

Applications for places stand at seven to one. Crowded annual open days – often 2,000 attendees – are held in September for year 7 and November for the sixth form.

Exit: Nearly all to university, art or music college. Remainder to start gap year, apprenticeship or work. Recent destinations include Bristol, Durham, Birmingham, Edinburgh, Imperial College London and Leeds. Six (highest ever) to Oxbridge in 2019 and three to medical/vet school.

Many pursuing other dreams have exited to equally prestigious destinations, such as RADA, major London art colleges and the Royal College of Music. Two pupils recently gained sought-after City apprenticeships with KPMG and investment company M&G, whilst the Queen recently presented one girl with a Southwark Council scholarship to pay all her university tuition fees.

Remarks: A truly local comprehensive and for those on the doorstep it may be the stepping stone to very good things. Well connected, with increasingly impressive academic results driven by a talented staff promising much for children who want to work hard, and those who have previously found opportunities thin on the ground. For parents wondering whether there is life beyond school fees we recommend joining the open day throng.

DLD College London

199 Westminster Bridge Road, London SE1 7FX

020 7935 8411 | dld@dld.org | www.dldcollege.co.uk

Independent	Pupils: 434; boarders: 223 full; sixth form: 282
Ages: 14–20	Fees: £23,500 – £29,950 pa; Boarding + £18,000 to £28,000 pa

Principal: Since 2018, Irfan Latif BSc PGCE FRSA FRSC (40s). Educated at Emanuel School in south London, he went on to study chemistry at King's College London, where he also did his teacher training. Taught at Haberdashers' Aske's Boys' School in Elstree, followed by stints as senior housemaster at Whitgift School, deputy head (academic) at Bedford School, and five years as head of state boarding school Sexey's in Somerset. At which point, he was approached to head DLD. 'I relished the challenge of running a boarding school in London,' he says. A natural urbanite, decisive, fast-talking and energetic, he has quickly brought DLD into line – 'There were some pastoral issues in the past which needed addressing; things needed to change' – and is already planning ahead for expansion to 600 students.

Married to a teacher, with two school-age daughters, in his spare time he enjoys cooking, reading, music and adventurous travel. (He has, in the past, led a school trip to Everest base camp and is currently planning another one to Nepal.) He used to coach rugby, cricket and tennis, but his busy schedule now only allows time to give masterclasses in chemistry.

Academic matters: What DLD offers is intensive attention. Class size is kept to a maximum of 16, with most A level classes about 8-12. All are mixed ability. Teaching – in a day that extends from 8.50am to 5pm – is notably strong, as is 'value added' (in the top five per cent in the country). Staff are well qualified, many from Oxbridge, quite a few with doctorates. 'They know how to unlock potential,' declares Mr Latif. Many, too, have been at DLD for some time. 'I love teaching here,' said a long-serving art teacher. 'The student-teacher relationship is strong and I love the atmosphere.'

Over 30 subjects available, though some only when there is sufficient demand. 'If subjects aren't recruiting, we won't teach them, but I have resisted the temptation to consolidate,' says the head. Good sweep of languages (German, French, Spanish, Italian, Mandarin), plus EPQ and bespoke DLD diploma for those who want to work along similar research lines without external pressure. Unusually for an independent boarding school, DLD also offers the more vocational BTecs. ('My daughter really enjoyed her BTec in media studies,' said one parent. 'She gained hugely in confidence.')

As well as A levels and a two-year GCSE course, DLD teaches a one-year intensive GCSE programme for UK students who take a minimum of eight subjects (including maths, English, double or triple science, a humanity and a creative subject). Not necessarily the ideal option for those starting midstream. 'It's very structured,' said one parent whose daughter had done one year of GCSEs elsewhere. 'They go through the entire syllabus, starting at the beginning. She was looking for something more tailored.' Overseas students hoping to continue to sixth form can also take a one-year pre-A level course, with a smaller basket of GCSE subjects. 'As well as four to five GCSEs, we ensure their academic English is at the standard necessary to get them into a UK university and teach them about British culture and values, taking them on plenty of trips and visits.' In 2019, 26 per cent of A levels were A*/A, with 54 per cent A*-B, while 28 per cent of GCSEs were grades 9-7.

> '**We ensure their academic English is at the standard needed to get into a UK university and teach them about British culture and values**'

Strong 'learning support' department – 'We don't believe in labelling,' says the head – provides one-to-one attention, liaising with subject teachers and monitoring progress. The college also boasts a reigning Dyslexia Teacher of the Year. Site well adapted to physical disabilities, with a lift serving all parts of the building.

Games, options, the arts: Own basement gym and pool and weekly games afternoon, but the super urban location means no on-site playing fields. Main sports are football and netball played at nearby Archbishop's Park, in the lee of Lambeth Palace. Beyond that, 'London is our playing field,' says the head. Over 50 extracurricular activities provided on site, from creative writing to Model UN and DofE.

DLD has a particularly strong art department, offering graphics and photography alongside art. They have a 100 per cent success rate in placing students on art foundation courses (Central St Martins, Goldsmiths, Ravensbourne, Kingston) and students proceed to art-related degrees that range from fashion photography and illustration to interior design and animation. They are also regular prize winners in the Independent Schools Association's Art Competition. There is also an energetic music department offering an interesting range of music qualifications, including the subsidiary diploma in music tech and a foundation programme in music. Plenty of extracurricular music, too, with band club, Christmas concert, and DJ night. Drama, too, is lively, though not necessarily a reason to choose DLD.

Facilities for everything are excellent, with bright, well-equipped science labs, three large, light and airy art rooms, a spacious restaurant. A digital learning lab, a new library and a well-being centre have recently been built.

Boarding: Nearly 250 boarders – housed in smart, individual ensuite hotel-like rooms and shared well-equipped kitchen-cum-common room – are overseen by ample staff (seven on duty every evening), who operate a 'huddle' system to ensure everyone gets sufficient personal attention.

Those of compulsory school age remain on site during the evening with an early evening dinner at 6.30pm, followed by fun activities, such as marathon film nights, themed dinners and games, before a 9.30pm curfew. Sixth formers are allowed off site, but must be back by 10.30pm. At weekends, boarders are allowed out by prior arrangement. Those remaining in situ (the majority) are kept entertained with cultural trips and outings, including to football matches and the ballet.

Background and atmosphere: Launched as a small private sixth form college in the early 1930s, Davies Laing and Dick's original purpose was to tutor applicants for Oxbridge entrance and the Colonial Service exams. Still focused on helping individual students reach their potential, it is now one of 21 schools owned by private education company Alpha Plus and is primarily a boarding school, offering a safe bridge between school and university.

In 2015, DLD merged with Abbey College and moved from its long-time base in Marylebone to a bespoke, modern building a few minutes' walk

---

'My son came here because he was miserable at his previous school. Both he and I have been delighted with the support he's received'

from Waterloo and Westminster stations. Designed around a spacious central atrium used for meeting and group activities (drama productions, concerts, musicals), the centrifugal space extends upward in rings, with spacious classrooms offering London views of the former Eurostar hangar, the Thames and the Houses of Parliament. Good-sized outside garden-cum-playground on ground level; sunny, well-supervised terrace higher up used for barbecues and social events.

Pastoral care, well-being and discipline: Student well-being and mental health are central to the ethos – 'That's our raison d'être,' says the head – and staff have been carefully recruited to further this objective, with two counsellors, a life coach, a head of well-being, a head of co-curricular, an attendance officer, plus 40 staff trained in mental-health first aid. 'We're not too worried about league tables,' says the head. 'We want them to be comfortable in their own skin. If mental, physical and emotional needs are addressed, the grades will follow.' Parents appreciate what's on offer. 'The reason my son came here is that he was miserable at his previous school. Both he and I have been delighted with the support he's received.'

Discipline is structured but not authoritarian. 'In general, they're nice kids, very respectful.' There are, of course, still those who push the boundaries, and the head has dealt with four permanent drug-related exclusions since his arrival. Those not making sufficient progress, (ie not working hard enough), may also be asked to leave. Overall atmosphere is relaxed and informal. 'We treat them as young adults, with some independence, but not too much.' Staff are called by their first name, but the head is suited (if sans tie) and uniformly addressed as 'Sir'.

Pupils kept a close eye on inside and outside the gates, with double-guarded single entrance ('We're hot on safeguarding') and Reach tracking software used to identify movements of sixth formers. Years 10 and 11 not allowed out during the day.

Encouraging student involvement is also key, and a popular student council – 30 applications for 12 posts – is invited to senior leadership team meetings. Actively involved in charity, academic and well-being, members organise the summer ball and suggest ideas – such as last year's 'graduation' ceremony, which took place in a committee room at the House of Commons.

Pupils and parents: Large percentage of boarders from overseas (some 60 per cent) aided by well-administered visa system. A hefty cluster from China, but also significant numbers from Europe. International outlook celebrated in a United Nations of flags ornamenting the atrium, and global feast days – such as Turkish New Year – prominently displayed on noticeboards. DLD's well linked-in location means day pupils also come from far and wide.

Entrance: DLD is the only central London 14-19 college to offer on-site boarding, so, unsurprisingly, the demand is global, with over 50 nationalities represented. UK sixth form entrants – mainly escapees from boarding schools and London independent day schools 'looking for a different experience, something more academic or a different structure' – require at least five GCSEs at 5+. Overseas applicants must prove a minimum standard of English. All are interviewed to establish their motivation, work ethic and something about their home life. Below sixth form, by school report and interview.

Exit: One of Mr Latif's objectives has been to raise the academic bar, introducing an assistant principal with dedicated responsibility for UCAS and careers. Results have been encouraging. One

successful Oxbridge applicant in 2019, four to medicine and dentistry, and four off to the US (including TUFTS, UCLA and Columbia). Russell Group numbers are also up, with about 80 per cent proceeding to leading research universities. 'Our job is to create aspirations, encouraging pupils to believe they can do it if they put their mind to it.'

Money matters: Not the cheapest place on the planet, not even in London, but fees reflect up-to-the-minute accommodation and pupil-teacher ratio. Ten scholarships, three a year, awarded to those from the local area.

Remarks: This unique educational environment seems to capture all the best things about a college environment, combining them with the pastoral care and motivational structures that are more typical of school provision. All this takes place in small classes, with one-to-one help when required, in a state-of-the-art, purpose-built building in the heart of London, where students have the option to board on-site. The result is an informal atmosphere with an underlying structured regime where everyone is kept up to scratch. A fantastic place for the very bright, as well as remotivating the disaffected, although not for young people who want a more traditional boarding school experience.

DUCKS Kindergarten and Infants School

87 College Road, London SE21 7HH

020 8693 1538 | ducks@dulwich.org.uk | www.dulwich.org.uk/ducks

Independent	Pupils: 236
Ages: 6m–7	Fees: £13,890 – £15,855 pa

Linked schools: Dulwich College, 89; Dulwich College: The Junior School, 93

Head: Since September 2018, Miranda Norris, previously deputy head of Junior School, Dulwich College (Singapore). She has also been director of studies at Wetherby Prep, taught at the British International School in Jakarta, Indonesia and been deputy head of juniors at Dulwich College Suzhou.

Entrance: Into the kindergarten, six places for babies aged 6-18 months; 18 places for toddlers and up to 40 places for 'ducklings' of between 2 and 3 years. The infants' school comprises nursery from 3+ to year 2. There are usually five to 10 places available at the nursery, then 10 to 15 reception

places, with places occasionally emerging higher up the school.

No assessment for entry into the kindergarten, but children entering at 3+ and above will have an assessment to ensure their learning is up to date and at a stage where they can take advantage of everything the school has to offer. Priority throughout is given to the children of college staff and DUCKS siblings. We imagine the younger members of the college staff could keep the baby room next to filled. Given the small size, keen parents will want to register early.

Exit: Girls and some boys exit to a wide range of destinations at the end of year 2, beginning locally with Alleyn's, JAPS, Sydenham High, Oakfield Prep and Rosemead, spreading to Streatham & Clapham High School and St Dunstan's College.

The majority of boys (around two-thirds) move on to the junior school. There have been grumbles about the numbers being offered places in the past. The school says that realistically the college may not be the right school for every child.

Remarks: The teaching staff is mostly female, some mothers with relatively young children themselves, hand-picked based on 'qualifications and enthusiasm'. Parents seem to feel this a place where children can be themselves free from pressure. One said, 'It has impressed me that the staff are willing to work individually with children at a pace suitable for that child in that subject.' Another told us, 'My daughter is not interested in academic subjects but the teachers have awakened an interest in learning in her.' One felt that the school enables children 'to develop at the speed that they require, unlike the hothousing that is encountered at some prep schools.' This means 7+ time won't be overly-pressured, which won't suit all.

Parents suggest that there is a good balance between the kind of learning through play where children are having so much fun they are oblivious to the learning and good, solid foundation skills teaching. 'Being taught how to count by jumping in puddles was a particular favourite of my sons,' said one mother. Another told us, 'My son rapidly caught up with his classmates in literacy skills, having moved to the UK from a country where phonics and literacy are started at a much older age.'

On our visit, the nursery children were busily and noisily involved in a variety of activities and play which only the trained eye would realise were carefully structured to deliver the early years curriculum – plenty of role play corners, freedom to go in and out, and excellent use made of glittery pasta. Their playground stretches up the grassy bank behind the school with forest school elements newly introduced at the top. Reception classrooms are large.

Head of the kindergarten says modestly that the school is not unique but doing what they do well. She cites her staff as following the children's interests in their teaching – she points out the artwork on the wall where a child has painted what he wanted rather than following the given theme, but it is still valued and appreciated. In the toddler room, decorated with a jungle theme when we visited, learning is very much child-initiated, with lots of sensory discovery.

No sightings of lunch, but pupils declared enthusiastically that the lunches are 'yummy' and 'tasty' – they are prepared on-site by DUCKS' own chef.

Achievements are celebrated in assembly, being invited to share a good piece of work with the head or with rewards including fruity tea. From year 1 the usual stickers, certificates, shields and trophies. Not a homework-free zone, but a parent said, 'just the right amount of homework and holiday work to keep the children ticking over.'

The peace and quiet of the setting lends itself to environmental themes, lots of muddy fun and gives rise to the names of the classes, all of wild birds

The school is committed to early identification of SEN – all pupils are carefully observed and assessed, if any SEN identified then they work with the parents to establish the best support for the child. There are nine children with identified needs currently. The school recently admitted its first pupil communicating with British Sign Language – children, parents and staff have all received training with a BSL instructor.

Aims for PE set realistically for the age group, looking to develop spatial awareness, love of physical activity and play as well as social skills. Rather boy oriented, tag rugby, football and cricket on offer, and everyone learns to swim. A parent explained: 'The PE teacher is one of a kind, immensely talented and patient. The children have sports three times a week as well as extracurricular sports clubs if they choose. My son has at least five hours of organised sport a week.' Everyone learns to swim in the college pool.

Music is taught by specialists and all of year 2 learns the recorder. 'The music teacher pulls together amazing productions given the young age of the children.' Very able children are able to join groups at the junior school.

After-school activities every day of the week run until 4.30pm at a cost of around £4 per session offering an appealing mix of down-time or, for those with the energy, 3D modelling, swimming, ballet, football, netball and more. When there is always so much to fit into every day, lunchtime clubs can be useful: 'I love that my daughter has had the opportunity to start ballet with her friends at lunchtime', said a mother.

DUCKS is so tucked away in Sydenham – one almost has to be in the know to venture in search of it when making the rounds of nurseries and pre-preps. If you are coming from Dulwich Village, Herne Hill or East Dulwich, it lies beyond a local curiosity, the Dulwich estate's antique toll-gate, which makes the road south of the college impassable to all but those willing to pay a pound a time to pass. Excitedly, we enquired as to whether DUCKS parents are given a toll-gate pass – not even staff are privileged with such a thing. Parents soon get the hang of the loop around.

A mere infant in terms of the almost 400 year old college, DUCKS recently celebrated its 20th anniversary. One might imagine that the school occupies only the large Victorian house fronting the road, but this is home only for the younger children: a good thing, as the rooms are slightly gloomy.

The majority of the classrooms are actually situated in a wooden-clad building looking over the playing fields and onwards to stunning views of the City and the glittering Shard. It looks very much like a cricket pavilion, echoing the actual pavilion used by the school until it burnt down in 1997 – the silver lining being the opportunity to create something which worked just for them.

The peace and quiet of the setting is a rare and unusual treat for any London family, and lends itself to numerous environmental themes, lots of muddy fun and gives rise to the names of the classes, all of wild birds. At the rear of the school are several soft surface playgrounds, segregated for various age groups, so plenty of space for letting off steam with no shortage of ride-on toys and a veranda ensuring children can play outside even on wet days.

The word used repeatedly by parents to describe the atmosphere here is nurturing. Parents told us, 'It is supportive of shy children but equally has the space and facilities for children who have boundless energy' and 'although not fiercely competitive, it does expect the children to stretch themselves.'

Whatever rumours of previous discord between staff and management have made their way to us,

there have been key new appointments, teachers spoke of their happiness working here and much may now be set to change.

No concerns voiced with regards to pastoral care. One parent said, 'Outstanding pastoral care, and the school is good at communicating any concerns about our children with their parents'. 'They discuss bad behaviour in circle time in what appears to be a very meaningful way for the children.' Years 1 and 2 are all buddies to lower school pupils, whilst senior boys from the college visit as part of their community service.

Something about the building suggests a place more akin to a nursery than a school, but parents surprised us, saying it would suit 'a child responsive to structure who is keen to learn' and 'those who prefer a more free and easy approach to learning would probably find things difficult.'

The school is proud of its pupils' cultural and linguistic backgrounds, celebrating them throughout the year. Currently 17 children in the kindergarten are at least bilingual and 29 children in the Infants' school are bi- or trilingual. Far fewer, just a handful, have EAL needs.

The school praises the parents, who embrace themes and initiatives keenly, even recently attempting to pry themselves from their phones and tablets for a 'screenless week'. One mother with an eye for telling detail said: 'This is not a school where working mothers and stay-at-home mothers compete, or where a parent can achieve kudos by the quality of party bags at their child's party.' Phew.

One summed it up with satisfaction: 'Outstanding. I have wanted for nothing.'

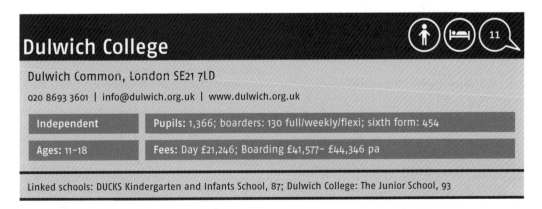

Dulwich College

Dulwich Common, London SE21 7LD

020 8693 3601 | info@dulwich.org.uk | www.dulwich.org.uk

Independent	Pupils: 1,366; boarders: 130 full/weekly/flexi; sixth form: 454
Ages: 11–18	Fees: Day £21,246; Boarding £41,577– £44,346 pa

Linked schools: DUCKS Kindergarten and Infants School, 87; Dulwich College: The Junior School, 93

Master: Since 2009, Dr Joseph (Joe) Spence BA PhD (50s), a graduate in modern history and politics; the Irish histories and literature of his postgrad line his study walls. Previously headmaster of Oakham School and for 10 years until 2002 held the prestigious position of master in college at Eton, housemaster to the King's scholars. His first decade at Dulwich College coincided with the college's 400th anniversary.

Grammar school educated, he describes his career path as the 'story of accident', a happy one. Immensely warm and charming, putting one at ease, the embodiment of the oft repeated 'Dulwich boys can talk to anyone'. He brings a sense of fun to those around him, appearing to wear his responsibilities lightly.

Married to a lawyer, with two sons and daughter, he still finds time to write, recently penning a new libretto for a concert at King's College Cambridge. 'My duty is to make sure that every Alleynian leaves with something intellectual... a passion which will be with him for the rest of his life'. Parents unanimously declare him to be outstanding, enthusing: 'a good orator, a great listener'; 'a great presence and a motivational leader'.

His vision for the transformations in progress – physical and philosophical – start with 'get the classroom right, then everything else', but quickly go beyond with the desire to create a generation of original thinkers. You don't have to be a scientist or an artist here – instead the aim is 'learning that is free from the syllabus', allowing boys to take risks in a dazzling programme of challenges, symposia, performances and adventures.

Academic matters: It's well known that improving the academics was top of the agenda. The college is now in the top eight per cent for value added nationally and the master is confident that the best is still to come. In 2019, 84 per cent of I/GCSE grades were 9-7. Plenty of A*s in sciences, English literature, maths, French and Spanish. At A level/Pre-U, 63 per cent A*/A, and 86 per cent A*-B. Maths is most popular by far, followed by physics, history, economics and chemistry. High percentage of A*/As in physics, plus history of art, English, further maths, history and art. A levels remain as the core upper school offer but individual heads of subject have the flexibility to offer Pre-U.

> *Liberal studies in the upper sixth with the girls at JAGS allows boys to try something new: modern poetry, yoga, book-binding, Italian cinema, even ballroom dancing*

Academic teaching is described by parents as solid lower down the college but inspirational higher up. Thirty-five per cent of teachers in residence for over 10 years. The master says candidly that now only a handful are perhaps not on message, and he won't see boys stuck with them, which chimes with parents, who say, 'very good standard of teaching, noticeable improvement'

and 'incompetence would not be tolerated'. They also describe staff as 'hugely committed'; 'they understand a boy's potential'; 'they set the bar high academically' and 'the daily report system is excellent'.

The master drives innovation. A key recent appointment is the director of science, formerly at lauded Brighton College, plus two new deputy heads. Turning things on their head, 'flip' lessons might give boys homework first, then they come in and discuss how they found it, or mini-whiteboards may enable a teacher to see at a glance whether boys have 'got it'.

Curriculum is largely as one might expect; choosing options is quite complex. Languages have a particularly strong focus throughout. French, Spanish, Chinese and Latin are taught in the lower school, later on there is the addition of German, Italian and Greek. Appealing language trips. Exchanges take place too, but with boys considerately settled in host families in pairs.

The only setting is for maths. All pupils study separate sciences up to IGCSE and the college doesn't necessarily encourage the collection of an excessive number of results. Intellectual boys wishing to stretch themselves further between years 7 and 11 can enrol on the scholars' programme, described by one as 'the highlight of my week'.

Quirkier A level options include critical and contextual studies and ancient history. Liberal studies in the upper sixth in conjunction with the girls at JAGS allows boys to try something new: modern poetry, yoga, book-binding, Italian cinema and even ballroom dancing.

Also for sixth formers, the Dulwich Diploma, which looks to offer the depth of A level with the breadth of the IB: the three components comprise academic study, including an extended essay or research topic of their choice – recent examples Who Killed Sylvia Plath? and Is Medical Research the New Imperialism? Whilst all of this adds up to a very full plate, parents say there are 'high expectations with excellent support through study skills sessions' and 'it's pretty intensive in terms of workload but not too high pressure'.

A team of four well-qualified learning support teachers are shared with the junior school, and provide support to individual boys with a diagnosed learning difficulty – 20 per cent. Eight per cent of middle and upper school boys receive EAL support.

Games, options, the arts: In year 7, whilst skills are built and some sports tried for the first time, rugby, football, hockey and cricket are all compulsory. By year 8 choices emerge, one being dropping rugby for fencing. Tennis currently squeezed for space with only three courts. No single sport is compulsory in the middle school but a plethora of teams make it tempting to get involved – skiing, rowing, fives, squash, cross-country and basketball, to name but a few. Years 10 and 11 may try golf, rock-climbing, self-defence, taekwondo and rugby 7s, whilst upper school choices aim to involve boys in sport, perhaps officiating or coaching as well as trying gentlemanly pursuits such as croquet, horse-riding and sailing. Boys are able to use the superb facilities at nearby Herne Hill velodrome.

World class performances from school's formidable debating team, who recently trounced the competition at the Oxford and Cambridge Unions

Seventy acres of playing fields recently reseeded, and rugby is the triumphant sport. Success, too, for the U14 rowers, who are national champions, and the school supplies four members of the U15 GB water-polo team. Boys we had lunch with laughingly said the only thing they didn't like was swimming as there was no point trying to keep up with the Olympic swimmers and water-polo players.

'Arts, music and co-curricular are outstanding'. We arrived just in time to be treated to a sensitive rendition of W H Auden's Stop All of The Clocks as part of that day's house poetry competition. The school has a rich theatrical tradition, a flexible theatre space, Chewetel Ejiofor and Rupert Penry-Jones are OAs, makes the very most of the London theatre scene, and each year produces three drama festivals and 24 performance pieces.

This term's Dulwich Creative week was produced with all of the finesse and confidence of a national arts organisation gone guerrilla and saw art hijacks where every pupil – astonishingly even the babies in the kindergarten – produce a clay self-portrait, which then came together into one installation. A surreal note remained overlooking the cricket pitches, giant polyurethane mushrooms by international street artist Christian Nagel. Art and DT facilities are light and bright, and where we found some of the most exuberant classes in full flow.

Numbers learning instruments peak in the lower school at 45 per cent of boys falling to 25 per cent by the upper school. Standard of musicianship varies from enthusiastic beginners to boys who are leaders of section in the National Youth Orchestra or principals at Glyndebourne and the ENO. The music department has upgraded: there is a shiny new Mac suite for music technology, a new acoustic percussion suite, and small and large practice areas. Another funky new facility is the electric 'shed', fully sound-insulated, a great place to let rip with the electric guitar.

World class performances from a formidable debating team, who recently trounced the competition at the Oxford and Cambridge Unions. Where next for the boy currently ranked number one in the world?

Long lunch hours ensure even the senior boys feel they have time for a sophisticated list of clubs and societies, which continue after school. Poultry society boasts its own hens; whether they are ever eaten is set to be a college myth. Our curiosity was piqued as to what goes on at the Gentlemen's Club (no-one seemed to know); presumably no cigars.

The careers office has a 2,000 strong network of former parents and corporate contacts: a recent event invited 40 such to the Dulwich Picture Gallery. Boys were instructed to read up on everyone's biographies then were sent off to network fiercely.

Boarding: Two-thirds of boarders are in the sixth form, majority from China and Hong Kong but also Eastern Europe. The boarding houses are on the campus, modernised period houses decorated with OA sporting team photos: quite basic in our view, small-ish rooms with less than luxurious en suite bathrooms, but unlikely to worry most boys intent on studying and playing hard surrounded by friends. Common rooms with large screen for movie nights, table football and all-important toasters. Now offers flexi boarding.

Background and atmosphere: Founded in 1619 by the wealthy actor and businessman, Edward Alleyn. He set up and endowed the Foundation, which distributes its surplus profits to a group of schools including Dulwich College, JAGS and Alleyn's. The college moved to its present site in the 1870s. The main buildings are stunning Italianate red brick designed by the son of the architect of the Houses of Parliament.

Sitting amidst vast manicured pitches, the college is a gracious and intriguing south London landmark. Closer up, the collection of modern buildings forming a large part of the teaching spaces, particularly in the lower school, are plain and nothing more than functional, quite possibly a bit depressing. The buildings housing the upper school feel fresher – Ned's place looks like a commercial café, and there is a huge common room, whilst a second one was sacrificed to create a popular 'work room' with banks of computers.

We donned hard hat and work boots to inspect the then almost complete Laboratory, costing over £21m, which is now open and should put the college's science offer ever more firmly on the map. Led by prestigious Grimshaw Architects – Cutty Sark, The Eden Project – It literally removes the divide between arts and sciences, including a 240 seat auditorium, as well as five IT suites and 18 glassy labs. The finishing touch, which should transform the feel of the college as much as anything, is the bright idea of removing the central car park, replacing it with landscaped recreational and thinking spaces.

The Dulwich College partnership schools overseas thrive, the latest in Yangon, Myanmar, but the master is clear that Dulwich is his absolute focus: he has delegated all but top level sign-off. Similarly, although he has championed outreach and partnership with a London academy group, a pie-chart of time devoted would see this account for only 10 per cent.

Sartorial traditions define the college – 'colours' blazers are boldly striped affairs awarded in recognition of achievement. 'Buy a big size,' advised the school captain – they will be de rigueur come OA reunions. You need a spotters' guide to identify old school ties, there are so many for every society and event. The master sees the Christmas fair attracting 3,000 local residents as a way to prove that the school isn't 'stuck up'. He is aware that the uniform gives off mixed messages, but wants the boys to wear it with pride and believes the school is and should be 'class, creed and colour-blind'.

Recent topics of pupil-led assemblies included homosexuality and discrimination. The school captain said: 'There is no Dulwich way. You don't have to conform'

School lunches seem due for a make-over, but boys won't starve. Students we spoke to in the lower school were amusing, boisterous; those higher up articulate, but not at all arrogant, and all with different interests. A regular visitor to the school said, 'The boys appear relaxed and happy, there's always plenty of banter and camaraderie in evidence'.

Pastoral care, well-being and discipline: A senior prefect told us he's a rarity, having been at the school all the way from year 1, but has relished meeting new boys – 'each intake year interests and friends shift' – and although the school is large, boys feel they know each other within their year. The transition points are handled thoughtfully, ensuring boys get to bond with each other, for instance on a Welsh adventure when joining the lower school.

Houses are named after great Englishmen, and wooden boards throughout the school see Drake, Spenser et al jostling for position – house competitions facilitate new friendships as well as much rivalry.

The partnership schools overseas thrive, the latest in Yangon, Myanmar, but the master is clear that Dulwich is his absolute focus

We were on the look-out for indifferent pastoral care, but found no evidence for it whatsoever, instead much praise. A parent – 'Boys know where they stand with the master, and whilst he's friendly and approachable, boys know he won't tolerate certain misdemeanours...hard line on bullying'. Another, 'He strikes the right note on being nurturing but also seeing that the boys get on with being independent'. 'A caring atmosphere which celebrates the individual,' said a parent of a child diagnosed with ASD. Gross misconducts such as possession of drugs or bullying would result in consideration for exclusion, whether fixed term or permanent, rather than an automatic exclusion.

Pupils and parents: The college is academically selective and socially inclusive, with a very culturally and ethnically diverse population, augmented by the boarders. Lots of multilingual children who may speak Chinese, Russian, Spanish or French at home. Boys mentioned pupil-led assemblies: recent topics include homosexuality and discrimination. The school captain said: 'There is no Dulwich way. You don't have to conform.'

A parent: 'It takes boys who are sporty, academic, musical, artistic and a mixture of all those things. If your child is gifted in one area, they will soar here. If they are a good all-rounder they will be encouraged to be a great all-rounder.' And it may come as a surprise to find that parents describe each other typically as 'a good bunch of mixed, non-stuffy parents', 'un-snobbish and not cliquey.'

Alumni include Chiwetel Ejiofor, Raymond Chandler, P G Wodehouse, Nigel Farage, Lionel Barber, Sir Ernest Shackleton.

Entrance: Not the ultra-elite intake of a few London schools, but still a top 15 per cent ability profile. At 11+, half of the 75 boys arrive from Dulwich College Junior School and half from a variety of local primary and prep schools including Hornsby House, Blackheath Prep, Rosemead, Dolphin School, Oakfield, Honeywell, Belleville, Corpus Christi, Dulwich Hamlet, St John's and St Clements. Parents are asked to send a letter from a registered professional regarding SEN needs to ensure appropriate assistance with the entrance exam. At 13+ the main feeders are Dulwich Prep London, Northcote Lodge and Fulham Prep. Non-refundable registration fee of £100 for Brits and £200 for overseas candidates.

A good number come from the immediate vicinity of Dulwich, but Foundation coaches brings pupils from as far away as Notting Hill, Canary Wharf, Wimbledon and Chislehurst.

Exit: Recent leavers to over 47 universities including Bristol, Durham, Edinburgh, Exeter, Imperial, KCL, LSE, UCL, Warwick and York; 24 securing their Oxford and Cambridge places and four going on to medical schools in 2019. Increasing focus on global destinations, particularly Ivy League.

Money matters: Nearly a third of boys have some financial assistance: two-thirds of these from scholarships (from a third of fees to 105 per cent), a third from bursaries (up to 100 per cent of fees). Dr Spence has stated his ambition for for college to provide financial support to up to 50 per cent of its pupils in year 7 and above. 'Superb value for money,' said one parent of three privately educated children. 'Quite simply, Dulwich College far outstrips the rest in terms of communication, professionalism and results'.

Perhaps most exciting of all in terms of evolution is the college returning to its early 20th century past in launching a New Dulwich Experiment, championed by the master, which will see up to 50 per cent of pupils coming from families who cannot afford to pay full fees, opening up admissions to some of the brightest pupils from all backgrounds. In some ways it is a protective measure against becoming a school for the global super-rich, and the master freely admits it is 'enlightened self-interest', but partly funded by OAs keen to give something back, it sits very well in this already socially enlightened place.

Remarks: A school with a long tradition, with all of the prestige that comes with it, but now with a thrilling new dynamism which is raising the academic ante in every way, creating glittering new learning spaces and delivering a stunning co-curricular vision. Far more inclusive than one might imagine, the new bursary scheme needs to be trumpeted far and wide to ensure the school is on the radar of the brightest from all backgrounds.

Dulwich College: The Junior School

Dulwich Common, London SE21 7LD

020 8299 8432 | junioradmissions@dulwich.org.uk | www.dulwich.org.uk

| Independent | Ages: 7–11 | Pupils: 221 | Fees: £21,246 pa |

Linked schools: Dulwich College, 89; DUCKS Kindergarten and Infants School, 87

Head: Since 2013, Dr Toby Griffiths (40s). Educated at Whitgift School and the University of Edinburgh; completed a masters in educational psychology and a doctorate in educational psychology at Oxford. Previously a six year stint as deputy headmaster at Lanesborough School in Guildford, where he was involved in the management and marketing of the school in a parent-facing role: a good precursor to being head. He has also taught at St Paul's Juniors, and eight years at The Dragon, where he was boarding housemaster and head of maths. Part of a teaching dynasty, his father taught at Whitgift for 38 years and his mother was a prep school head. He and his brother, also now a headmaster, were hockey blues together at Oxford. He considered teaching psychology, but from the moment he experienced the Dragon 'all bets were off' – he loves the junior school age group: 'their energy and enthusiasm, they seem so alive'.

Parents enthuse: 'He is approachable and responsive' and 'very much involved in every aspect of the college and knows the boys well'. Determined and no doubt extremely competitive: 'bring it on!' he said (with regards to a forthcoming school inspection).

The green spaces of Dulwich made moving to London easier. He lives nearby with his wife, Vicky, now working in the City. Their son is at the top of the junior school and daughter at nearby Sydenham High.

Entrance: Approximately 45 places available at age 7+, many taken by boys coming up from DUCKS, six to eight places in years 4 and 5. Register in the autumn preceding the desired year of entry. Assessments during January in maths, English, verbal and non-verbal reasoning. Not looking for perfection – understanding of differing educational experiences – but all round ability. Successful applicants invited for an interview and an activity morning; process now includes a taught element 'to see how boys react in a lesson situation and how well they learn something new'.

Dr Griffiths says the junior school has gone from being popular to very popular, with now over three applicants per place, and is increasingly seen as the 'start of the college'. Boys come from as far away as Greenwich, Orpington and Fulham, up to a 40 minute commute. The school lists an eclectic list of feeders at 7+ in addition to DUCKS: Herne Hill, Bertrum House, Broomwood Hall, The Villa Pre-Prep, River House Montessori and Babington House, though seemingly not many of the nearby state primaries.

Exit: Almost all (nearly 100 per cent) go on to the college. The head says that those who don't go on from the lower school are very rare, and only after extensive dialogue over several years regarding where they would thrive best, and then it is the parents' decision. We asked a parent if they felt their son was well-prepared for the next stage; they replied, 'absolutely. And if we didn't, we would feel comfortable raising any issues with the teachers and headmaster.'

Remarks: Once more sporty than academic, the balance has been redressed, and it is now much more of an all-round school. Dr Griffiths says, 'It had always been a through school, but at one time the boys from the junior school had taken their foot off the pedal whilst everyone else worked hard to get there [the college], so four to five years ago the bar was really raised to ensure primacy of the classroom'. It does mean that there is no need for exam pressure to dominate. Focus is on 'doing their best, not pass or fail'.

Big leap in scores of boys coming in recently. Teaching time has been increased by 40 minutes per day and all children now have two periods of French per week. No gripes about teaching reached our ears, quite the opposite: 'The boys seem fired up by what they learn. There has been a practical element to subjects which fires the imagination and creates interest.' Curriculum is taught by form tutors with specialist staff initially for French, art, DT, music and games, with additional specialists in later years.

Parents pretty united on homework, saying, 'We don't feel it is intensive at all. Obviously there is homework, but we feel that it is suited to our sons' capabilities. There is extension homework for those boys who are more academic and help for those who perhaps find it takes longer to grasp certain things.' No holiday homework – other than when preparing for the 11+ exam. 'Doesn't feel too pressured re exams or testing'.

Improved rewards system – commendation certificates, bronze, silver and gold, are presented in assembly. Reports for parents show effort and attainment, which is appreciated by parents who conclude, 'it will likely do much to encourage the children.' 'Very little pressure on the lead up to exams. In general, we haven't known when the boys are due to have any sort of assessment.

The headmaster tells us, 'We want boys to be and to try everything by the time they leave here – rugby player, actor, musician, chess player, mathematician, writer...'

Surprisingly low levels of SEN. All children are screened for dyslexia on entry to year 3. Some may be referred for further testing and diagnosis. There are four full-time learning support teachers shared between the junior and senior schools. In the junior school, teachers work with individuals and small groups to provide extra support where needed, perhaps in terms of how their working memory affects spelling, organisation, numeracy, creative writing or comprehension. Less than two per cent receive EAL support, but many from multilingual families.

This is the time for experimentation. The headmaster tells us, 'We want boys to be and to try everything by the time they leave here – a rugby player, actor, musician, chess player, mathematician and writer'. Should not have to choose between a swimming gala and orchestra practice – the sporty head says he won't let fixtures take over.

'With 70 acres of fields there is no shortage of sport and it is all first class,' cried a delighted parent. All boys play rugby, football, hockey and cricket, everyone has the opportunity to play a competitive fixture, whether extra or intra school. Aim is for boys to represent the school in every sport – 'everyone gets to go on the coach and shake hands with the opposition', so far managed it for football. 'Our sons are not in the A or B teams for sports, but they always get to play matches and be involved in the sporting community'. Fitness should be a given with gymnastics, swimming, rackets and athletics in addition. Stars include a year 6 national breaststroke champion and several county representatives in cricket and chess. A highlight for many is the trip to the college's outdoor centre in the Brecon Beacons. Everyone performs in the year 3 and 6 plays. The recent Bugsy Malone performed in the Edward Alleyn Theatre looked enormous fun.

Music department seen as first rate. All the boys in the junior school learn a stringed instrument in year 3 and a wind instrument in year 4, and perform in two major productions. Some 40 per cent then have individual lessons. 'Our younger son has decided to have extra violin and guitar lessons and we are not a musical family,' said a surprised parent. There are opportunities to play in ensembles and orchestras and sing in the choir. Pupils benefit from the wider college co-curricular activities.

These boys are readers – the library has 8,000 books and a full-time enthusiastically chatty librarian who insists that books are not just for book week, that she never tells everyone to 'shhh!' and that 'life's too short to finish a book you're not enjoying'. Art projects line the walls, currently takes on Mark Rothko and work inspired by a trip to Tate Modern to study Henry Moore.

Just the swim squad and chamber group up and at it early. At lunchtime a couple of by invitation clubs such as madrigal and chapel choir, but also each year has choices such as karate, tennis, book club, chess, sewing and various music ensembles. After-school clubs have been extended (there are 95 in all) and now run until 5pm, with after-school care available until 6pm. Boys can do their prep in the homework club or try Russian, dance, cycling, magazine club or French aviation.

The location on the southerly edge of the college campus in a peaceful backwater just a stone's throw from the useful South Circular and station makes drop-offs and collections pleasant. The building itself is modern and handily adjacent to the lower school, with a pitched roof, wide corridors upstairs and quite spacious classrooms. Year 3s have their own playground.

We were impressed that year 6 boys were entrusted to lead us solo on our tour of the school, with only a little assistance from Dr Griffiths on time-keeping – not every school entrusts its pupils, of whatever age, to speak as they see fit with a visitor wielding a pen. It speaks volumes. Parents, too, speak of this level of trust between boys and teachers. One said of their son, 'He truly looks forward to being at school. He has had very supportive form teachers – strict, but fair, so there is an obvious level of trust.'

Boys seem to feel listened to and have seen their ideas put forward to the school council come to fruition, such as more play equipment for the playground.

A parent told us, 'This school excels in its pastoral care. We couldn't ask for better.' Others agree, 'They know the students very well and truly try to understand not just individual students, but the different dynamics amongst various groups of boys.' And in the case of a problem with peers raised with the school, 'The boys were supported, but given opportunities to address the issues themselves.' Teachers are seen as responsive – known to answer emails out of school hours.

Competitiveness abounds – house allegiances start here – but there is room for inclusiveness: all year 6 boys are prefects, rather than an elite group. And every year 6 child has a buddy in the lower years.

Parents say, 'The boys feel like they belong in the school and with each other.' And, 'The atmosphere is one of feeling included. It is not an exclusive school.' Parents themselves sound unpretentious and appealing, describing each other as 'friendly, relaxed, supportive of their children', 'from all walks of life', 'welcoming, fun, and interesting.'

As for the college as a whole, appearances can be deceptive and there is a rich social mix. Many say there is no type for whom the school particularly caters, 'it's tough to see what kind of child the school wouldn't be suitable for.' Several say: 'He can't wait to leave the house in the morning.'

A few academic scholarships at 10 per cent of the tuition fees, plus means-tested bursaries may be available for the very able whose families fulfil the financial criteria.

Dulwich Hamlet Junior School

Dulwich Village, London SE21 7AL

020 7525 9188 | office@dulwichhamletjuniorschool.org.uk | www.dulwichhamlet.southwark.sch.uk

| State | Ages: 7–11 | Pupils: 360 |

Head of school: Since 2016, Claire Purcell BEd (40s). Having gained her degree at what is now Southampton University and her first teaching post in a Hampshire school, Mrs Purcell headed to the Hamlet, rising from class teacher and senior manager with a music specialism, via deputy to the new post of head of school over the course of 20 years. Extremely modest, she is, however, responsible for the incredibly rich musical life of the school. One parent told us of her son punching the air when she was made head. We would have liked to spend more time with her but our visit coincided with year 6 Sats. She is devoted to music and family and we hear plays the recorder and sings wonderfully too. She has two young children.

Executive head since 2007 is Sonia Case BA PGCE (50s) who has no plans to retire. Since the school became part of a multi-academy trust, she has been executive headteacher of Dulwich Hamlet Junior School and The Belham Primary School, an exciting reinvention of a Victorian school in Peckham which she is building from the ground up. She has an office at the Hamlet, but currently splits her time, spending three days at the Belham, whilst this school continues to spin along like a well-trained top.

Prospective parents would be advised to brace themselves for a particularly high number of dressing up days – Roman, Celt, Greek, Indian and Shakespeare

Mrs Case started life as an actress, including a role in the original series of Poldark, before moving into advertising and has worked in education for over 24 years. Prior to leading Dulwich Hamlet she taught at three state primaries in Bromley. Parents describe her to us as 'a driving force', 'dynamic', 'passionate' and she 'encourages readiness to learn by expectations of excellent behaviour'. We found her to be vibrant and full of fizz with a real passion for where the right style of teaching can make a difference to individual children. She has two daughters and two grandchildren.

Entrance: The main feeder school for Dulwich Hamlet is Dulwich Village Infants' School. No automatic entry from one school to the other. Unlike the infant school there is no faith stipulation governing admissions. The school is oversubscribed but not to the tune we had imagined from its local reputation, and there is always some movement on the waiting list after first offers are made. Stories of houses being rented nearby to get in persist, but a hard line is taken by the local authority and are perhaps more focused on the infants' school than here.

Other admissions come from local prep schools such as DUCKS, JAPS and Herne Hill and some other local state schools.

Exit: The majority of children fall into the catchment for the nearby Charter School and head straight there, whilst a percentage of both boys and girls move into the independent sector, to Dulwich College, Alleyn's, St Dunstan's or Sydenham Girls' School. Some children attend schools further afield

such as the Grey Coat Hospital school or grammars in Bromley and Kent. According to parents, those preparing for selective entry elsewhere sometimes use tutors, more for exam technique than academics.

Remarks: The school consistently ranks near the top of league tables with regards to academic attainment. Ofsted, declaring it outstanding in every category, has long since moved on to other more variable territories. It does well by children across the board, but also by high attainers.

Teachers have two surprising qualities; they are young and quite often male. Mrs Case delights that they are enthusiastic and fresh from training, full of the kind of multimedia experience and latest thinking that invigorates what she describes as a 'glittering curriculum'. We concur that it is pretty sparkly and ambitious. A parent told us about a year 6 English lesson which involved tightrope walking. We visited shortly after Shakespeare week, where each year took a different aspect of A Midsummer Night's Dream and created a film to be viewed by the whole school and parents. Students study for LAMDA exams. Stem week answered questions such as 'can you eat a candle?' and 'how do you get the fizz in pop?' Prospective parents should brace themselves for a particularly high number of dressing up days – Roman, Celt, Greek, Indian and Shakespeare. Drama often comes into lessons with role-playing techniques used. There are currently striking papier-mâché sculptures of Ted Hughes' Iron Man around the school and we saw year 5 pupils creating blueprints of wild flowers inspired by Victorian women artists employed by Kew Gardens. Displays within classrooms are 'learning walls' whilst those in the public spaces, on lovely felt boards, exhibit the children's work.

A couple of parents said to us that the teachers have 'all been so different but have continually excited and stimulated my children'; they are 'approachable and accessible' and 'most are imaginative in their teaching and enthuse the children'. Setting of children is minimal as Mrs Case points out that removing the brightest would disadvantage those who would benefit from a higher level of discussion, but there is setting for maths from year 3 to enable more teaching resources where needed.

Parents describe sport as having improved dramatically since the school has had access to neighbouring sports fields. There are also courts adjacent to the school in use most days for either netball or tennis with specialist coaches. At least half of the students in each year group have represented the school, participating in football or netball tournaments, and many attend sport clubs before or after school. The cricket team – girls as well as boys – won the British Land cricket trophy, playing the final at Lord's. Years 4 and 5 are strong swimmers, both having won their Southwark schools' swimming galas this year. A parent said of sport: 'the school balances a competitive spirit with inclusivity'. There is a minibus for away matches provided by the PTA. The cross-country team represents the school nationally.

The school excels in its musical provision. All children receive music lessons conducted by specialists, and then nearly three-quarters learn musical instruments up to grade 5 taught by peripatetic music tutors. Whatever the instrument, there's an ensemble for it – woodwind, brass, strings or guitars. Steel pans are very popular. The fusion ensemble developed an original composition, Londinium, which was presented with an award for innovation and performed at the Royal Albert Hall as part of the primary proms. There are two choirs, who have sung at The Scoop on the Southbank, the Young Voices Concert at the 02 and the Bromley Music Festival. Recorder playing is taken to a new level here, with an annual recorder festival featuring a workshop, performance from professionals and inter-school concert. We were lucky enough to hear the early music ensemble play at Dulwich Festival; the standard seemed so high they could provide the incidental music to Wolf Hall.

Parents are asked to make a voluntary contribution of less than £100 per annum to help fund the extracurricular, such as trips and specialist workshops. The school offers a wide variety of fun after-school clubs including cookery, knitting, magic, Lego robotics, yoga and clay, with some charges.

The school presents as a picture postcard Victorian school, with patterned brickwork and scalloped roof tiles, at the heart of picturesque Dulwich village, encircled by sunflowers in the summer, thrilling many a parent and passer-by with nostalgia. The school has had many incarnations, but the main building dates from 1897. On the sunny spring morning of our visit, the nearby village hall promoted a barn dance, whilst the petite row of shops sell ice-creams, children's shoes, beautifully curated art and school stationery: it's an idyllic slice of middle class 'village London'.

Through the gates it doesn't disappoint, in fact, the rear outlook looking across the Griffin Fields, which the school leases for sports, is a hidden delight. Between the admin building and 'village building' housing the traditional high-windowed Victorian school hall is an Astroturf playground. There is free play, but also structured play at lunch time such as teacher-led football. We liked the Astroturf shady veranda of an attractive wooden classroom built with 'bulge' funding, for those wanting to escape the hurly-burly.

Space at the front of the school is newly transformed into a garden with raised vegetable patches, bug houses and composting and what will be a wild flower space for curriculum work. Lunches with an international menu can be eaten either in the refurbished dining hall or at circular picnic tables under a shady canopy in the playground. Above the dining hall are DT and food technology facilities which outclass those of several of the nearby prep schools. A couple of the celebrities familiar to everyone who lives locally were parents here and opened the transformed building. Year 5 participates annually in a project run by the Architectural Association. There is a large library and break-out space for year 5. And the whole school hall now boasts a sophisticated sound system paid for by the PTA. Given the school's focus on design and media, the ICT room uses Macs.

It presents as a picture postcard Victorian school, with patterned brickwork and scalloped roof tiles, at the heart of picturesque Dulwich village, thrilling many a parent and passer–by with nostalgia

Pupils describe the school to us as 'fun and happy'. Despite the affluent catchment area, there is apparently more of a social mix than one might imagine. Certainly a wide range of languages is spoken within the school, from Urdu to Japanese and Hindi. A word which crops up several times from parents is 'inclusive'. The school has a full-time inclusion manager, and there is small room for one-to-one teaching. The school is also a Dyslexia Friendly School, though one parent mentioned being disappointed the school had not highlighted her child's dyslexia to her. Parents say that bullying is not unheard of but they trust the school to resolve such matters swiftly. They say: 'the general atmosphere seems to be caring' and 'they will go out of their way over the smallest issues to ensure every child is happy and included'.

The children of parents hopping onto the local trains and buses to commute are well provided for with a large dedicated classroom and qualified staff offering breakfast and after-school care. A parent described her peers to us as 'high powered with equally high expectations', which we are told is a fair portrait. Most seem grateful and appreciative, as one mother shared: 'I frequently find myself telling my kids I wish I could have gone to a school like theirs', whilst another concluded: 'quite simply a joyful experience'.

Dulwich Prep London

42 Alleyn Park, London SE21 8AT

020 8670 3217 | admissions@dulwichpreplondon.org | www.dulwichpreplondon.org

Independent	Pupils: 852; boarders: 20 flexi (from year 4)
Ages: 3–13	Fees: £13,605 – £20,088 pa

Head: Since September 2019, Louise Davidson. Degree in economics and social economic history; worked in banking, PR and marketing before post-grad teacher training at Cambridge. Her first post was teaching maths and science at King's Junior, Canterbury. Studied and taught special needs at Edinburgh University, became SENCo at a London school, leading to headships at state primary schools across the country and then Leader in Education roles.

'I am confident that I can hold my own in a 10k, play and coach football (including in goal), swim and teach swimming.' Keen on family travel and adventures. Her husband runs an international genocide prevention charity; three children – the youngest has joined Dulwich Prep London.

Ruth Burtonshaw BSc Phd PGCE Dip, dyslexia and learning, and an early years specialist, is head of the pre-prep.

Entrance: Admission is selective. Multiple points of entry but majority start in the nursery at 3+ (girls and boys), at 4+ (boys only) or at 7+ (boys only). Limited number of means-tested bursaries to new applicants in years 3 and 4, determined by academic assessment.

Exit: Don't think that entrance to DPL is a do-not-pass-go ticket straight to Dulwich College, but a large proportion of pupils do gain entrance. Other recent leavers to eg Whitgift, Trinity, Alleyn's, Tonbridge, Westminster, Harrow, King's Canterbury, Eltham College and Bryanston (73 scholarships, half of the academic, offered in 2019). Conversation regarding choice of senior school starts as early as year 4 and school claims that every boy achieves his first (guided) choice of destination. Only two or three boys a year choose to leave at 11+.

Remarks: Founded as Dulwich College Prep School (DCPS) in 1885 but is completely independent from Dulwich College and is an educational trust with its own governing body; and now, to clear up the confusion, has a new name Dulwich Prep London (DPL). Situated in west Dulwich, a few minutes from the train station, the buildings, mostly fairly modern, crowd around the playground. Four distinct sections divide up the 800+ pupils, each with its own library and classrooms. It really works – 'the boys are quite protected from feeling lost in a huge place, and they're fully prepared for moving on,' said a parent.

The main curriculum is fairly traditional. French from year 1 and everyone tries their hand at Latin. Spanish offered as alternative to French. We found the lack of fashionable forward-thinking options such as Chinese or Russian surprising when even the local state primaries are giving them a go. Head says Mandarin was offered as a club, but there was little interest.

Setting in maths from year 4, extended to all examined subjects by year 7. This really works, with parents confirming there is sufficient flexibility for boys to move within the year to find the right level and to be encouraged by their ability in different subjects. Young, male teachers were particularly noticeable in the classes we visited, in amongst the boys or sitting on desks. Relations looked easy in lessons ranging from European history, via maths, to music technology. Energy fairly resounds and parents of pupils at the lower school, particularly, describe it as 'buzzing'. Homework is, as ever, controversial. One mother commented that whilst the boys love the varied topic work, parents find it 'never-ending' at weekends.

Art teaching clearly inspiring. We were wowed by the boys' 3D acrylic sculpture, after Jackson Pollock

Almost 20 per cent are identified with a learning difference, mainly mild to moderate dyslexia. The school (with highly-trained specialist staff) will endeavour to do its best by all, but any with significant difficulties may be guided to a more specialist school such as Fairley House. We saw great learning integration in the older years with dyslexic boys using laptops alongside their peers; parents confirm that boys don't feel singled out in any way if they need extra help. Nonetheless, some comment with feeling on just how tough it can be and wish for a little more two-way communication with teachers.

Well-resourced sport, with fixtures both after school and on Saturdays. Seven full-time PE teachers, specialist coaching from year 4, more than 70 teams and achievements at national level, particularly in rugby and swimming. Every boy has an opportunity to play. Parents say coaching is less good at the lower levels, and whilst clubs offer exciting opportunities from rock-climbing to kayaking, 'alternatives to the obvious sporting options are very limited in the younger years.'

Drama features both an annual year 6 and upper school play. Year 7 classes have drama and each year 8 class is off timetable for two weeks to produce an original production. Art continues to year 8 with clearly inspiring teaching, new facilities and technologies. We were wowed by the boys' 3D acrylic sculpture, after Jackson Pollock, and the excitement in the room as they made sophisticated digital animations. Music is rich, appealing and widely pursued, with over 20 ensembles and choirs and concerts of every type at venues in and out of the school. Ninety per cent of the boys from year 2 upwards study an instrument, many reaching grade 8.

Clubs (only a few additional charges) and activities run at lunch-time for boys from years 1-4, but also 4-5 pm from year 5. Current options include Lego, Warhammer, movie-making, beekeeping, street dance, juggling, Greek and golf. Wide array of trips – no stone unturned on the London museum circuit; further afield during school holidays (often built into the fees) eg Pompeii and Normandy. All this plus a thought-provoking lecture series – recently featuring a holocaust survivor, notable writers, broadcasters and adventurers.

Parents from the nursery year to higher up the school all comment on the benefit of a single sex school where teachers are free to focus on knights, dinosaurs, bloody battles etc. If there's one thing this school seems to do brilliantly it's the ability to really 'get' boys and how they learn and put this into practice. There is wiggle time (dancing around between lessons), marble parties or even a pool table as a whole class reward – 'the motivation and excitement are huge.'

The school motto is 'one for all and all for one' and the houses are named after North American Indian tribes from Chippeway to Objiwas. The winning tribe raises their flag weekly up the pole in the playground and if this is all sounds incredibly macho, we hear the boys sometimes choose to sing ABBA as their victory song. Meanwhile others, who choose the calmer activities from book club to weaving and needlework, do so without fear of ridicule. Some parents transfer from a co-ed environment for exactly this reason.

While the head's emphasis on character and kindness rings true – right on cue we witnessed children relating a contemporary version of the Good Samaritan – a couple of parents commented that it can take a while to find your niche. 'If you're not good at sport, you're not popular in the playground.' This is a school which aims to develop 'resilience'. When asked which kinds of boys would be happiest here, parents suggested: 'a self-starter, bright and athletic' and 'you've got to be robust'.

No surprises that the majority of parents are highly affluent, most living within an expanding 10 mile radius of the school. However, we hear that there is a healthy mix from the scarily ambitious to the more laid back, so there is a good chance of finding like-minded souls.

Asked which kinds of boys would be happiest here, parents suggested: 'a self-starter, bright and athletic' and 'you've got to be robust'

School has one boarding house called (not so aptly in our opinion) Brightlands; this can accommodate 25 weekly or flexi-boarders from year 4. Rather a sombre looking house with a garden, next to the pre-prep. Recently redecorated, with a young and welcoming housemaster plus family, but we spied scary paint colours downstairs and 1950s style curtains in the dining hall and we wondered how this rated, as a home from home, compared to the boys' weekend surroundings. Definite fun, though, is one week a year when years 5, 6 and 7 stay from Sunday to Thursday; you can win the Tomahawk Award for life skills such as button-sewing and bed-making as well as trying a spell away from home.

The pre-prep early years department is a stunningly designed new-build – all wide open flowing spaces, blending indoor/outdoor. Classrooms give onto a huge covered sandpit for wet days and a splendidly green view of playing fields, woodland and the grounds of Dulwich Picture Gallery. Nothing locally compares to the rural feel of this setting, a great comfort for any parent who didn't expect to raise their children in one of the world's biggest cities.

Girls are the minority in the nursery but are carefully selected and more than hold their own. Parents of girls have little need for concern – except getting them in, applications are oversubscribed. Rainbow Club, staffed by regular teaching staff, offers care and activities pre and post school, from 8am to 4.45pm. The head assists in girls' applications to local private and state schools. Almost all the boys move up to the prep.

Dunraven School

94-98 Leigham Court Road, London SW16 2QB

020 8696 5600 | info@dunraven.org.uk | www.dunraven.org.uk

State	Ages: 4-18	Pupils: 1,700 (including primary); sixth form: 250

Headteachers: Guy Maidment BA PGCE NPQH, previously deputy head at Camden School for Girls, is head of secondary.

Head of primary is Michaela Christian, previously at Fairlawn Primary School in Lewisham.

Academic matters: Results are a testament, says head, to the commitment of 'a fantastically creative and hardworking staff team.' At GCSE in 2019, 28 per cent of grades were 9-7 and 52 per cent of pupils got 9-4 in both maths and English.

Expectations are high. 'We start from the premise that the children will do well, and might do even better than we think.' Younger pupils are kept aware of how well the older ones are doing, and the benchmark is set higher each year; school was rated outstanding by Ofsted in 2014.

The curriculum in key stages 3 and 4 is broad and balanced, thanks to what's called the Dunraven Baccalaureate: English, maths, science, humanities, languages, and all the arts, because 'the kind of learning opportunity you get through the arts is invaluable.' Other subjects are also offered, notably DT, ICT and PE/dance. Visiting teacher from Westminster comes in every week to teach Latin, which is proving a popular option at GCSE and A level, but we thought the language provision could have been broader. French and Spanish are offered, with the G&T students given the chance to do both; but there used to be Mandarin. The impressive sixth form, housed in its own new purpose-built centre, is the most successful in Lambeth, and offers a wide range of academic and vocational courses – A Levels, BTecs, GCE applied and the AQA baccalaureate. In 2019, 26 per cent A*/A grades at A level (51 per cent A*-B). All Dunraven year 11s can apply to study there and most do, but places are sought after and are not guaranteed. Strong enrichment programme of activities, both on and off site, includes theatre and opera visits, excursions, exchanges, competitions, and residential trips abroad.

SEN provision is excellent and enlightened. The school has its own on-site speech therapist and parents were full of praise for the SENCo, who was described as 'fantastic', 'works like a Trojan', 'highly empathetic'. 'We felt that our child was properly supported throughout her time here,' was a typical remark. Hosts a specialist centre for children with speech, language and communication needs.

There were parental murmurs about their child being unable to study all his/her preferred subjects at GCSE due to timetabling issues (a problem not unique to Dunraven), but the majority of feedback was overwhelmingly positive. 'My child left with a love of all his subjects, based on great teaching,' was one comment. 'There is rigour in all that Dunraven does,' was another, and everyone we spoke to praised the 'constantly rising level of academic achievement.' The children agree: 'The teachers are good and you learn stuff,' said a cheerful year 7 boy, who'd been temporarily sent out for being cheeky. 'You make friends, you learn, every class is suited to you,' added a strikingly poised year 10 girl.

Games, options, the arts: You can do almost any sports here: in addition to football, rugby, cricket and basketball, there are opportunities for badminton, fencing, swimming, diving, the martial arts, boxercise, trampolining and ice-skating (using facilities at Crystal Palace). Engagement with games remains good throughout KS4. Drama, dance, art and photography are all popular, and the Soul Choir enlivens many a local church concert. Music is also strong, and the excellent Play It Live initiative, part-funded by the local authority, enables the children to work regularly with professional musicians.

Background and atmosphere: The school is approaching its 100th anniversary. Originally founded with a bequest from the Earl of Dunraven, it expanded onto its present site in 1960, moved into the Philippa Fawcett College in the 1970s, became grant-maintained in 1993 ('a very important decision for the school'), and became an academy in 2011. £25 million mixture of rebuild and refurb (under the last government's Building Schools for the Future initiative) now complete, including new sixth form centre. Some very inventive touches, including the use of recycled shipping containers for new buildings, which look incredibly smart and cost half of what was originally planned. Primary school opened with reception class in 2013 and has expanded with a new class each year. The aim is provide a seamless progression from 4-18.

Play It Live initiative enables the children to work regularly with professional musicians

Smart blue and grey uniforms, own clothes for sixth form (with a requirement to be 'respectable'). Students work purposefully, and – during our visit, at least – an air of orderly quiet prevails. The pupils we met were polite and helpful. Even the malefactors hanging around outside the classroom who'd refused to go in, for reasons they were unable to articulate, knew what was expected of them. After chatting to us about how much they liked their school really – 'It's fun here...there are nice trips... a good after-school club, something to do every day' – they filed in equally to begin geography.

Pastoral care, well-being and discipline: Considering the size and diversity of this school community, we were impressed by how calm and purposeful the students were. The emphasis everywhere is on courtesy and consideration, and the pupils confirm this: 'The people are nice. The teachers are good and you learn stuff.' Parents praise the staff as 'incredibly supportive', and any bullying is dealt with swiftly and effectively with 'restorative justice' sessions and behaviour contracts. Very low turnover of staff tells its own successful story.

Pupils and parents: An inclusive, socially and ethnically mixed intake that reflects the diversity of the area.

Entrance: At primary level priority to looked after children, then siblings, then by distance (straight line home to school). NB applicants must complete Dunraven's online supplementary information form as well as applying through the LA. They will have an automatic right of entry to Dunraven Senior when they reach year 7. The head positively radiates excitement: 'This provision will eliminate the trauma of secondary transfer. Everyone will benefit. We'll be able to offer expertise and opportunities to enrich the primary experience, and their different pedagogical approach will increasingly influence us.' Heady times indeed.

Entrance tests put secondary applicants into one of five ability bands; the school, which is heavily oversubscribed, then takes 20 per cent from each band, allocating places in line with its (non-academically selective) admissions policy.

Exit: At 16, the majority (65 per cent) progress to Dunraven sixth form; a few move to local sixth form colleges, training etc. At 18, nearly all leavers go on to university, with an increasing number of top university successes every year, including Oxbridge (two in 2019, plus one medic), Bristol, Durham, Leeds, Manchester and Camberwell College of Arts. The rest take a gap year, or have a lead into work of some kind. Head says, 'The aim is to get to the end of Y13 with a real choice and a sense of control about your next step.'

Money matters: ESFA-funded academy, and in receipt of many grants and awards in recognition of its academic success and work for the community.

Remarks: A dynamic, exciting, successful school community. Proof that you can have a comprehensive school that works for everybody.

Eaton House the Manor Boys' School

The Manor House, 58 Clapham Common Northside, London SW4 9RU

020 7924 6000 | admissions@eatonhouseschools.com | www.eatonhouseschools.com

Independent	Pupils: 510
Ages: 3–13	Fees: £17,079 – £20,514 pa

Linked schools: Eaton House Belgravia, 110; for Eaton House the Manor Girls' School see *The Good Schools Guide London North*

Head: Since 2016, Sarah Segrave (40s), who has a BA in education and history from Durham and an MA from the Institute of Education, and was previously head of the girls' school. She joined the Eaton House schools in 1993 as one of the founding teachers. She taught history, Latin and was housemistress at the prep, became head of the pre-prep then in 2010 head of the girls' school. It was difficult to leave the girls behind, but feeling that she 'lived and breathed Eaton House' and wanting someone who knew the schools to take on the role of prep head, she stepped forward. The new role also combining the position of director of education for all four schools on the site was the final draw. She aims to move forward but hold onto the traditions of the school.

Married to Nick, with two children at the school, she lives in Earlsfield. Far from travelling in with her husband who looks after IT for the group of schools, she's more likely to have left the house at 5am. Parents describe her as 'professional yet very approachable' with which we concur, and hearing of her exceptionally long days, dedicated and extremely hard-working too. A parent observed, 'she's introduced a lot of positive changes'.

Boys were diligently working with the breeze wafting in from the common in every class we saw

Pre-prep head: Since 2017 is Nicola Borthwick, previously deputy head of the girls' school.

Nursery head: Since 2005, Roosha Sue.

Entrance: In the words of the head, 'entrance has sky-rocketed' and entry is now three forms throughout. Entrance to the pre-prep at 3+ is non-selective; simply register for a place as early as possible. Boys migrate from the pre-prep more or less automatically via continual assessment, although if the head feels the school isn't right for a boy families would be advised and this is the case for one or two each year. Entry at 8+ and 11+ into the prep is selective via testing in maths, English and verbal reasoning and by interview. External entrants should register no later than the autumn prior to entrance. There are three applicants for every place at 8+. Boys enter from both local state and independent schools.

Exit: Over the past seven years boys have headed to a list of 35 different schools, the most popular being Eton, Dulwich College, Harrow and Charterhouse, most at 13+, but an increasing few at 11+.

Remarks: About a third of the staff have been at the prep for over 10 years. The head describes them as the school's 'best asset and biggest strength, very passionate about what they do with incredibly high standards'. Parents tell us: 'very good teachers, inspiring yet demanding'; 'teachers ensure the subjects/topics are fully understood, taking

extra time where necessary'; and 'great cohesion between subjects in the curriculum', citing a combined geography and art project involving a trip to the British Museum and a week's work about James and the Giant Peach involving art, reading, writing, sport and drama. There is an emphasis on boys as readers, supported by excellent reading lists.

In the first two years boys are taught by their class teacher; subsequently all subjects are taught by specialists and there is setting for English and maths. Reasoning in addition to the usual curriculum including Latin and French.

Prep class sizes average 16, maximum 18; hence some of the classrooms up under the roof are small rather than spacious. Boys were diligently working with the breeze wafting in from the common in every class we saw. Our guide was so enthusiastic that a Latin class was unmissable; he raced us up three flights of stairs moments before our departure. Science is taught in a charming old lab, where one could believe Faraday actually worked, and a sparkling new lab about to have its wrapper removed; we found a science teacher already in residence, thrilled by the pristine equipment. There is also a new DT lab complete with three 3D printers and a laser cutter. The art studio has the most stunning view of London's skyline towards the Thames, perhaps inspiring a wonderful paper scale model of London landmarks, our favourite a beautiful Greenwich Observatory.

This is a school with excellent academic outcomes, very good value added, ambitious parents and consequently a school of 'really high expectations'. The head has ensured that targets are set clearly and there is greater transparency, so that children and parents know how they are doing across all subjects. 'Good shows', to which we want to add the word 'jolly', are for excellent work. A smiley face outside the head's office shows the times when she is free for visits to share them. Exam weeks are dotted with sport. Parents speak of boys taking it in their stride and that 'homework is manageable,' particularly lower down the school. There are currently 16 children with SEN, mostly mild dyslexia and dyspraxia, for which they receive up to two one-to-one periods of support a week.

The head was rethinking the scholarship programme, for which boys are selected in year 7 and commences in year 8. We got the sense that conversations about destination schools with parents were tackled with diplomacy and frankness in equal measures to ensure everyone has a realistic choice without underselling themselves. Parents given insight but their choices are supported: such those who decide they would prefer their child to attend an ultra-academic school where a child will be in the bottom 10 per cent versus another school where he might gain an academic scholarship.

One of the louder and more exuberant schools we have visited at the start of the day: 'friendly and happy,' offered a parent

There is one hour of ICT a week, boys use Learn Pads and there are banks in classrooms as well as an ICT room. The head is looking at the most engaging and productive teaching methods to get the boys from A to B. She challenges her staff, saying: 'Has your lesson made a difference to a child today?' and continues to teach herself to see the children from different angles.

Sport is 'highly competitive,' say parents, with boys battling it out. Football, rugby and cricket are their major sports and hockey, cross-country, swimming, karate, tennis and athletics are minor sports, but more than one parent told us they'd like to see more fixtures, national tournaments and tours. The U12 footballers came fourth in English Schools FA Cup and there have been sports scholarships to Dulwich College, Bedales, Radley and Whitgift.

Two music lessons per week and weekly drama – two major productions per year. Some 70 per cent play instruments, beginners to grade 5. Staff get involved in the Battle of the Bands. 'The boys are encouraged to join the vocal ensemble and the choir,' said a parent.

There is an early morning room from 8.00am and a supervised homework class until 5.00pm without charges. In addition there are a great number of clubs that run before school, during the school day and after school such as DT, chess, running and Spanish.

The Eaton House group of schools, first founded in 1897 on Sloane Street, also includes the girls' school next door and a school in Belgravia. This is a large operation now, but the division into three schools with autonomous heads means that the staff know children really well.

We are used to the maze-like experience of schools that have adapted old buildings to suit over many years, but this school nonetheless could confuse a Minotaur. The children giggle sweetly at our disorientation and trip adeptly from one part of the school to the next.

Behind the period façade, the elegant Georgian house dating back to 1792 facing the green of Clapham Common and housing the boys' school has classrooms often high up in the rafters, lots of lino – more practical and less elegant than it appears, and behind this a functional quadrangle of classrooms forming the pre-prep. Then there's the new-build delights – the science lab and two bright modern dining halls complete with eco-friendly

exterior 'living wall' in the style of the girls' prep building. At the time of our visit the builders had been in situ for a whole 10 years. The children have, of course, weathered it stoically, but everyone was looking forward to the scaffolding coming down and the playgrounds being reinstated.

The pre-prep classrooms are in a block formation, large and bright off wide lino-floored corridors, rather standard issue after one has seen the new buildings: boys must have a sense of graduating when they attain the staircases, views and quirks of the prep school classrooms. But we found the nursery teachers enjoying their very spacious, purpose built classrooms with in-and-out spaces close to the dining hall.

One of the louder and more exuberant of schools we have visited at the start of the day and in the playgrounds: 'friendly and happy,' offered a parent commenting on the atmosphere. A pupil summed it up as a school: 'where teachers are encouraging and the children are kind'.

Revisiting pastoral care has been very high on the head's agenda – 'if children aren't happy they won't flourish.' She wanted to rethink what she saw as a bit of a feeling that 'boys will be boys being acceptable'. The school rules have been rewritten collaboratively with pupils; they previously made no mention of bullying. Assemblies are an important place for discussing PSHE-like topics, so now there are junior and senior assemblies pitched to the different age groups, a recent one tackling the topic of stress. Boys are asked if they know whom to go to for help and encouraged to talk to whomever they feel the most comfortable with at any time. Boys have also been introduced to the idea that this is a 'telling' school and talked about whistleblowing in society. A mother told us: 'The head of pastoral care is really wonderful'.

The art studio has the most stunning view of London's skyline towards the Thames, perhaps inspiring a wonderful scale paper model of London landmarks

Parents from all walks of life, many dual nationalities – German, French, Spanish, American families and almost 40 children from overseas. Parents describe each other as 'relaxed, friendly, sociable and down-to-earth'. A mix of working and non-working mothers who make newcomers welcome.

No bursaries, but the school has been very supportive of families who have found themselves in financial difficulties during their prep career.

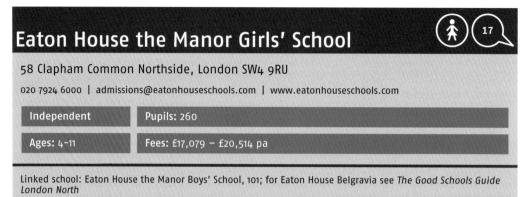

Eaton House the Manor Girls' School

58 Clapham Common Northside, London SW4 9RU

020 7924 6000 | admissions@eatonhouseschools.com | www.eatonhouseschools.com

Independent	Pupils: 260
Ages: 4–11	Fees: £17,079 – £20,514 pa

Linked school: Eaton House the Manor Boys' School, 101; for Eaton House Belgravia see *The Good Schools Guide London North*

Head: Since 2016, Oliver Snowball (early 40s). BA (in English literature), MA (in theatre studies) and PGCE. Previously a teacher of English and drama at Tunbridge Wells Girls' Grammar School, then at various points head of drama and senior housemaster at Kent College Pembury. Most recently deputy head and interim head at Kent College Prep.

Energetic, immaculately turned out, friendly and engaging, with an almost paper-free glamorous (if hot on a summer's day) office/greenhouse, Mr Snowball seems to have hit the ground running with his vision for the school and is clearly engaged with contemporary educational debate. Firstly, he has introduced a focus around seven character traits that he feels will help children perform to the best of their ability. They include grit, optimism, empathy and trust. The head and teachers model the attributes and discuss them in assemblies. The challenge is to make the results tangible, but it is clearly working well with girls, jotting down on post-its when they have demonstrated attributes, and staff able to feedback evidence to parents. More creativity and thoughtful planning went into the Adventure Book – an A4 book which is a girl's own space to explore ideas just for herself without any right or wrong.

A parent who has seen a lot of change at the school told us she has generally been impressed with it all. Others say: 'I think that Mr Snowball sets a very warm, supportive and nurturing tone for the school. He also seems to be a genuinely kind person, with time for the girls as individuals.' Another mother agreed: 'He learnt my daughter's name and face very quickly and always congratulates her on good work she has done or outside achievements when he says good morning.'

He is married to Claire with two children and the family is enjoying the novelty of London, being 'resident tourists'. Without quite so much country air at his disposal he has inevitably found himself joining the local joggers around the common.

Entrance: Currently non-selective at aged 4; offers made around a year before entry, with sibling priority. Any later entrants are required to spend a day at the school during which they sit a maths and English assessment. Rows of scooters attest to the vast majority travelling from within a two to three mile radius, with many from the neighbouring streets.

Exit: Girls head to both a broad and notable mix of day and boarding senior schools, from Godolphin & Latymer, JAGS and Putney to Benenden, St Mary's Ascot and Woldingham.

Remarks: Standard curriculum. French not Spanish, as befits this corner of London perhaps, and Latin and critical thinking for the senior girls. Mr Snowball is pleased to see the children responding well to more 'curve-ball' open ended type questioning in lessons which will serve children well as the 11+ landscape potentially moves away from simply testing maths and English. His focus will be on improving independent thinking, creative and analytical skills, and whilst wanting to stretch the upper abilities will try to ensure the middle range are not forgotten. One mother shared her delight with the way academic learning alongside well-matched trips have inspired her daughter: 'This week she came home talking about the Roman walls around Londinium and London Bridge's timeline, and wanting to look up related topics in books or on maps.' Another parent: 'The trip to 10 Downing Street was amazing. Teachers are very enthusiastic, which rubs off.'

Parents believe the main emphasis of this school is on the academics and arrive looking for a top London exit. The head comments: 'We are an academically rigorous school; we are not a hothouse' (his office aside). Parents would seem to agree, but there is more talk of the pressures of homework – which begins in year 1 – than we often encounter, and the head says that he will be reviewing it at the end of his first year, given his belief in family and down-time. One parent: 'There is probably more homework than there needs to be at times but it's a good learning process.' Another: 'I would say quite a lot of homework, but not more than they can handle. My daughter does a lot of sport outside school, and the teacher is always prepared to let her complete homework the following evening if necessary. There is a certain amount of exam pressure, but we live in a very competitive area.'

There are a tiny number of children with identified SEN in the school currently – mainly dyslexia, mostly with mild tendencies, but one or two with mild dyspraxia and ADHD. One full-time and one part-time member of the learning support team offer one-to-one sessions, regular review meetings with parents and external specialists.

Of the 25 staff only three have been at the school for more than 10 years, with a couple of NQTs bringing the latest ideas into practice. All female except for the head of music. The head describes them as 'passionate and dynamic', 'incredibly impressed with their work ethic, the best I've seen at any school' and 'open-minded to new initiatives'. We created quite a stir by commenting on them, revealing the girls' knowledge of all of their neighbours' daily habits. Smart new science lab, and lovely charcoal drawings of characterful Vikings on one classroom wall. The art room is light and bright with lovely work in evidence of a cubism project, designs for Harry Potter book jackets and Giacometti sculptures tying in with the Tate exhibition.

This is a school of keen readers, but the library didn't do too well out of the rebuild: behind a closed door in the new basement, it's a tiny and, we felt, uninviting space with a modest collection of books to choose from. When we enquired as to whether girls would come here at lunchtime, they were understandably bemused.

'My daughter came home talking about the Roman walls around Londinium and London Bridge's timeline, and wanting to look up related topics in books or on maps'

Not, as yet, the most fiercely competitive sporting school. All girls have a PE, games and swimming session each week at the nearby Clapham leisure centre and everyone learns ballet. All girls from years 3 to 6 play netball, hockey and rounders or athletics in the summer. The new netball courts on Clapham Common are useful, but the girls can also make use of the huge new basement sports hall and gym for indoor football, hockey, fitness and netball. Recent sporting success from year 6

has boosted year 5's performances too. This year, the U11 netball team won the IAPS Smaller Schools tournament and the U9 A and B teams won their respective hockey tournaments involving a number of other London prep schools.

One parent told us: 'in my opinion, music and drama, although taught and appreciated with enthusiasm, get a little squeezed out.' The head (with his theatre studies background) agrees that there is room to develop. There is no head of drama – form teachers currently direct productions – but the school will introduce expertise from outside when needed. The girls we met were very much enjoying rehearsing Bugsy Malone. A parent suggested: 'I think the girls and boys could have a little more interaction, eg in drama.'

Everyone learns the recorder and over a third of girls currently learn piano, violin, flute, drums, guitar or voice, ranging from beginners up to grade 4. There are three choirs: the non-audition junior and senior choirs and Bel Canto by audition for potential soloists. There is also an orchestra and children perform in music assemblies and concerts.

A fun and sophisticated mix of clubs, running until 5pm, some with an intellectual bent such as Plato's Child, a mix of English and philosophy for year 5s, plus book-making, curiosity club, introduction to psychology and yoga. Some are joint with the boys next door and many with additional charges. There is also an early room club from 8.00-8.30am for parents in need of an early drop off.

The school seems to be perceived as very much 'traditional', but we'd add without being remotely stuffy. Mr Snowball can see why it has that reputation: there is the very distinctive green and red uniform of blazers and boaters, a sense of formality, he shakes hands with every child on the way in and the way out and there is the calendar of events from harvest festival to sports day. But as he's demonstrated, the school is as modern and fresh as the new buildings in terms of the contemporary educational thinking they engage with. These buildings, opened in 2008, are light, bright and full of unexpected views, green roofs and the odd living wall – a very pleasant space in which to learn.

This is very much a girls' school – 'There is a lovely feel of girl power about the place!' said a mother – but given the school's buildings and structure, with the boys' prep next door, it seems instead to have the atmosphere of one big family with brothers and sisters and family friends educated alongside each other, sometimes in adjacent classrooms. There is one combined residential trip with the boys in year 3.

When we asked parents about the school's feel, a typical response – whether talking about the girls' school or Eaton Manor as a whole – was: 'The school has a relaxed atmosphere, although most parents have a common goal to get their children into a top secondary school.' Every classroom we stepped into certainly seemed focused on the task in hand but also calm and relaxed, plenty of discussion in science and quiet pottering about in art. One mother observed 'It's 'pretty competitive' but also, 'She sees the school as her second home. She feels very comfortable with the other girls and teachers.' One parent got into the spirit of things in answer to our wondering about whom this school might suit: 'Bright, busy, friendly, kind, chatty, confident, open, ambitious girls, prepared to pack a lot of stuff in and work hard.'

Rules are straightforward: to be kind, be polite, be careful, be tidy and be smart. A parent said: 'The teachers are extremely kind but they are no-nonsense in my experience.' The house system has

recently become 'more substantial'. Housemistresses will know the girls right through their life at the school. Girls in the upper years are 'big sisters' to the KGs (reception), which they seem to love. Year 6 girls feeling both nervous and excited about next step very much appreciate old girls coming back to talk to them about their senior schools.

Predominantly British with a few girls coming from families where one or both parents are western European, Asian or American. Approximately 10 per cent of girls are bilingual or trilingual. Only a couple of overseas nationals. A handful receive EAL support.

No bursaries or scholarships currently, but watch this space as scholarships are being introduced.

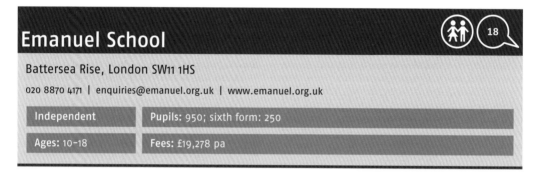

Emanuel School

Battersea Rise, London SW11 1HS

020 8870 4171 | enquiries@emanuel.org.uk | www.emanuel.org.uk

Independent	Pupils: 950; sixth form: 250
Ages: 10–18	Fees: £19,278 pa

Headmaster: Since 2017, Robert Milne previously deputy head (pastoral) at King's College Wimbledon, where he also taught English and coached a variety of sports. Started off teaching English at Oundle, moved to King Edward's Birmingham as housemaster of a day house and thence to Magdalen College School as head of English.

Academic matters: Both A level and GCSE grades have been steadily improving year on year. In 2019, 47 per cent of A level grades A*/A (82 per cent A*-B), and 71 per cent 9-7 at GCSE. Grades in chemistry and physics at GCSE are streets ahead of the rest. Strong results in maths but mathematicians sometimes outclassed by a huge cohort of historians who really shine at A level too. Politics and economics are also popular. Linguists in handfuls.

GCSE: all pupils study English, maths and one language from French, German, Latin and Spanish – French and Spanish are far more popular than German. Either double or single sciences; the decision on the final route is made during year 11. Pupils choose a further three subjects from a wide range: art, economics, classical civilisation, DT, drama/theatre studies, geography, history, RS, music and PE. Not complete freedom to choose. A levels add in business, further maths, politics and

psychology. The majority of pupils are now expected to take three A levels and the EPQ.

Around 30 teachers have been at the school for more than 10 years. The most recent ISI report offered a host of 'excellent's when referring to both the teaching and attitudes of the pupils to learning, noting the good rapport between staff and students, though almost every parent we asked about the teaching staff began carefully with 'on the whole'. One said: 'There are some exceptional, inspiring teachers across the school who can transform a child's understanding.' Another: 'Overall, I would say the teaching is very good with some excellent examples thrown in'. Some offer praise without reservation: 'My wife and I are astonished by how much she loves the academic lessons too; we can't remember that school was this much fun when we were teenagers.' Interestingly innovative, the school has been keen to try the Harkness method where teaching is done in a small group, with a maximum 16 of students sitting around an oval table with tablets for instant online access: it's felt to encourage participation and the exchange of ideas.

A little more than average numbers with a learning difference, but a well-qualified head of learning support with two assistant practitioners,

Every pupil carries a conduct card. Chocolate as a reward has been dropped for the sake of blood sugar levels

both with qualifications in the support of dyslexia. The school does not screen all on entry, only if making 'poor progress'. Those with an ed psych report will have a 'learner profile' created to advise class teachers of learning preferences, some small group withdrawal. A few extras on offer such as an early morning spelling club and homework club every day of the week. Pupils talk of the value of touch-typing lessons and a Cogmed course, designed to help with working memory. Some 12 pupils currently have EAL assistance.

As befits the happy and relaxed atmosphere of the school, children don't seem to feel too intensively pressured. A typical report: 'Children seem to be prepared for exams without being over stressed.'

All departments seem plugged into national competitions. Year 10 students entered and were shortlisted for the Cambridge triple helix science writing competition. A DT student was recently awarded a prestigious Arkwright Scholarship. Maths students are regularly successful in both the UKMT Maths Challenge and the Hans Woyda competitions. Science students compete in the annual Science Olympiad, over half taking home a medal. Two students have won prizes in the Peterhouse essay competitions in recent years, both of whom were later awarded places at Cambridge. This is also a well-connected school which has no problem attracting an impressive line-up of speakers, such as Samira Ahmed, Sir Bob Geldof, Professor David Starkey, Alastair Darling and Lord Coe. Rowan Williams came to talk to the literary society about the Christian symbolism in the Narnia series. Sir Tim Berners-Lee, possibly the most famous OE, returned to the school.

A member of staff is responsible for Oxbridge applications and arranges university visits for all of year 10. Oxbridge candidates attend seminars held jointly across the Westminster schools group. Work experience begins in years 10 and 11. The sixth form makes use of OEs coming back to the school to give them advice on everything from surviving the first year at uni to spending a year in industry. There is an annual careers convention attended by more than 70 guests, working the parent body as much as former pupils.

Games, options, the arts: A parent told us: 'Emanuel does punch above its weight in sports for the size of the school. That is down to the encouragement the children get from the games staff.' Sport is a major feature of the school, with rugby followed by rowing the most popular. One parent said: 'If you don't like rugby you can have a problem'. However, school is planning to introduce boys' football, starting with years 6-8, from 2020, gradually becoming the core spring term boys' sport alongside rowing (girls row in the summer). Teams are kitted out in striking navy and gold stripes.

Facilities are extensive: apart from 12 acres of on-site games fields there is also access via a private gate to facilities on Wandsworth Common plus 14 further acres near Raynes Park. The sports hall includes a climbing wall. There is a large pool and a boathouse at Barnes for 75 boats. Rowing is historically the most successful sport at Emanuel with over 50 international and Olympic rowers in the record books and recent medals for girls and boys.

The school has also been awarded top 100 cricket schools status by The Cricketer Magazine (girls' and boy's teams); rugby teams successful. Plenty of netball and hockey stars too, locally and at county level. Some would like to see more done outside of these core sports: there are naturally fewer matches and opportunities outside of the major sports.

Some 300 individual instrumental lessons a week, of all grades with many reaching grade 8. Recently, two pupils gained places to attend the junior Guildhall School for Music and junior Royal Academy of Music. It is common for students to gain choral scholarships to Oxbridge colleges as well as win places at music colleges. A good rehearsal and concert space.

Rowing is historically the most successful sport at Emanuel with over 50 international and Olympic rowers in the record books and recent medals for girls and boys

Drama is a highlight with many OEs entering careers within the field of drama, film and television. Recently one boy starred in Dickensian. Recently, the senior play was Brief Encounter; the junior play was The Lion, the Witch and the Wardrobe and the year 7s bonded over The Witches. A parent: 'I look forward to every concert or school production as it saves me a trip to the West End.' An enlarged theatre of around 100 seats was opened by Ralph Fiennes and Mike Leigh.

Passports at the ready – too many international trips, sports tours, departmental exchanges and adventures to mention covering what seems like the entire of Europe and further afield to India and

Dulwich College

the US. Partnership with schools in Tamil Nadu and year 10s off to volunteer in the Gambia alongside local young people. Over 40 clubs and societies: choir, computer club, drama club, technical drama club and Eton fives are all after school. Many others take place before school and at lunch time including one for Dr Who fans.

A new initiative sees lower sixth students spending Friday afternoons teaching and mentoring local primary school pupils – especially those from more deprived areas – sports and arts as well as academic subjects.

Background and atmosphere: A school with a history – founded in Westminster in 1736 using funds bequeathed in 1594 by Lady Dacre. The school's magazine, Portcullis, has recently reached its 300th edition. Unusually, it was co-educational from the start with just 10 boys and 10 girls. The boys then moved to Wandsworth in 1883 to the current building, originally a Crimean war orphanage. The school became a voluntary aided grammar school in 1944 until it resumed its independent status in the 1970s. In 1995 it became co-educational once more. The school is growing and will continue to do so up until it has about 960 pupils. There is a courtyard in the middle of the main building dedicated to three Queen Elizabeths. The first on the throne at the foundation; the second who planted the central tree, Queen Elizabeth, The Queen Mother; the third her daughter who made a royal visit in 1994.

A smart new bridge provides access from Spencer Park, showcasing the school at its best angle – called the Memorial Bridge in memory of the Clapham Rail crash in 1988. The railway line provides only a gentle rumble of trains going past. Despite this, the school has the feel of a green oasis – the buildings' outlook onto the sports fields at the rear, particularly the outdoor café under the cricket nets, is very appealing on a sunny day. The library, at the heart of the old building, is remodelled to blend modernity with aspects of the school's heritage, including an archive area and 'family photo wall' of OEs. Large and well-stocked, with a spiral staircase and mezzanine, it lends out up to 500 books a week; teen fiction such as The Fault in Our Stars leads the way. This is a Christian school with Christian values and the chapel with stained glass windows remains on the first floor. Sixth formers have their own modern block with plenty of corners to hang out and a café akin to Starbucks.

The main building is impressive, but far more institutional and shabby inside than we expect – it even smells rather like a hospital. New developments – a £10m humanities building including a film studio and a separate 'temple to maths' including a maths café, grand foyer and lecture theatre – suggest the fabric of the school is starting to match the head's ambition.

Parents report: 'Whenever you visit the school there is always a very happy atmosphere among the students and great camaraderie'; 'there has been an increase in the number of highly academic children at the school but I still feel that the school is not a pressure cooker'. Another: 'There is a definite atmosphere of letting everybody have a go at everything without judgement – it doesn't matter how good or bad you are'. 'It's fun and pretty cool,' added a student.

Pastoral care, well-being and discipline: A system of form tutors who see pupils every day combined with a house system and easy access to the head of year ensures that any problems that arise should be spotted and dealt with quickly. We hear they are quick to respond. Parents agree the school is supportive and caring. There are two chaplains, and a fully trained counsellor.

The library has been remodelled to blend modernity with aspects of the school's heritage, including an archive area and 'family photo wall' of OEs

A detailed anti-bullying policy is in place, updated to include cyber-bullying, giving pupils, staff and parents clear guidelines as to what to do and a fairly long list of sanctions if pupils are not behaving with courtesy and co-operation. Every pupil carries a conduct card. Chocolate as a reward has been dropped for the sake of blood sugar levels. We hear one report of the school's rigorous discipline procedures seeming quite severe to newcomers. But there are also 'lots of parental talks to help support children.' Useful in a co-ed school, we're told by a parent: 'Their sex ed offering is similarly "full on", which I fully support'.

Pupils and parents: Coming from all over London and occasionally beyond as the school is within seven minutes' walk of the transport hub of Clapham Junction. Many parents work in the media or creative industries. The Fiennes family is connected with the school. The majority of pupils are white European in ethnicity, and reflecting the local area 26 pupils have French as their first language. Ten per cent are from overseas. Parents tell of us of making friends here, something that happens less at senior school. There is even a choir for mums and dads and socialising in the pub in Barnes whilst watching the rowing. They describe each other as 'committed and unpretentious'; 'friendly, mostly working parents'; 'down to earth and genuine.'

Entrance: Registration for entry from 2020 no longer capped. One of the few London senior schools offering the opportunity to avoid all of the hoopla and stress of 11+ with a 10+ entry point, it is apparently still as competitive to enter, as at 10+ there are only 40 in a year group rising to 130 in year 7.

At 10+ and 11+ there are papers in English, maths and verbal reasoning. At 13+ English, maths, science and a language. At 16+ an English essay and three subjects of the applicant's choice (in subjects they intend to study for A level) and a reasoning test. Pupils with SEN will be considered for extra time if appropriate.

Some 70 per cent enter from state primaries at Y6 and Y7, higher than we often see, but it is a wide community. Students come in from over 200 feeder schools such as Belleville, Fulham Prep, Honeywell, Hornsby House, Hurlingham, Maple Walk, Orchard House, Our Lady of Victories, Thomas' Clapham and Wimbledon Park. Biannual open days plus several week morning tours per term.

Exit: Some 15 per cent leave after GCSEs. Current popular university destinations are Exeter, Durham, Sussex and Essex, with long tail of others heading off to pursue everything from PPE to product design, both in the UK and abroad (one to US in 2019).

Money matters: A generous number of scholarships and bursaries and unusually lunch is included in the standard fees. One in five have a scholarship. Fifteen children currently received 100 per cent assisted places, which the head hopes to roll out to 20.

Remarks: One to keep a decided eye on as it makes its upwards progress. Something of a boarding school atmosphere – open seven days a week in a day school format.

Finton House School

171 Trinity Road, London SW17 7HL

020 8682 0921 | admissions@fintonhouse.org.uk | www.fintonhouse.org.uk

| Independent | Ages: 4–11 | Pupils: 340 | Fees: £16,242 pa |

Headmaster: Since 2016, Ben Freeman BEd (design technology) PG Dip (educational leadership) (late 40s). Still very much 'the new kid on the block' (his own words), Mr Ben, as he is known here, is not just new to Finton House but new to Wandsworth and the buzzing metropolis of London. Previously head of Windermere Prep for eight years, a school that had already munched its way through two heads in quick succession before he arrived, he was brought in to rescue the situation having been teaching at Malsis Prep school in North Yorkshire (which no longer exists).

The fresh air of the English countryside runs through Ben Freeman's veins. Born and brought up in the Wirral, he was educated at Rossall School and then the University of the West of England, Bristol. He cut his teeth teaching in a secondary state school in Bristol but was lured to Malsis to set up its DT department. By the time he left he was deputy head. Married to Sarah, who is training to be a teacher and ran the outdoor education at Windermere. She has three grown up children. The landscape of Ben Freeman's life so far has been one of natural beauty – sea, hills, lakes: it's no wonder that one of his passions is the outdoors. Walking and sailing as well as skiing are his means of relaxation and he is keen to instil in his pupils a love for everything outdoorsy. He regards his two main focuses here to be developing the technology so that the teachers are using cutting edge digital platforms in the class room, and making sure the children live a healthy life, a combination of plenty of exercise, practising mindfulness and well-being, eating healthily and limiting screen time.

Most parents are pleased with a more down to earth approach he brings to the school. 'He looks the children in the eye when he greets them in the morning,' said one mother, 'rather than looking over the top of their heads at the parents.' Some find him inscrutable. A troubleshooter in the past, there seems to be quite a bit for him to get on top of here too. A tricky period when the school lacked a proper head, issues with SEN provision, a lack of balance between boys and girls and the usual challenges of a very competitive field for the 11 plus transfer. Some parents suspect that he is out of his depth but he comes across as genuine and concerned to do the right thing for pupils and parents.

Entrance: Names down at birth if you want to be sure of a place. First come, first served, though siblings continue to be given preference. Even numbers of places offered to boys and girls (between 25 and 30 places for each in reception). Tours on request: those on a waiting list are offered week day open mornings, parents with a definite place are shown round individually and meet the head.

Occasional places do come up further up the school, especially in years 3 and 4 when some pupils move here from the state sector. A child attends the school for a taster morning and informal assessments.

Each year the school says it welcomes two or three children with special needs; they have to apply along with everyone else and places are offered on a first come, first served basis. When a child with SEN receives an offer, then the parents meet with the SENCo and head of special needs to ensure his/her needs can be met before the place is confirmed. Some state funding for children with an EHCP.

Exit: Most leave at 11, though some boys still leave at 7 or 8 (occasionally to KCS but more often to board). At 11 they go to a range of south London schools, with Emmanuel, Wimbledon High, Alleyn's, JAGS, Whitgift and Woldingham currently the most popular destinations. One or two choose to board at, eg Benenden or Heathfield; some of those needing to bridge the gap before boarding at 13 go to Northcote Lodge (for boys), Broomwood Hall (for girls) or boarding preps. A handful of scholarships (12 in 2019), several academic as well as art, music, sports and design technology. School prides itself on advising parents carefully so as to limit the number of applications to three schools only. 'The senior schools know the applications are genuine and our success rate is high,' affirms the head of academics.

Remarks: Tucked into a corner of a warren of narrow Wandsworth residential side streets, which, at 8.30 in the morning teem with 4x4 SUVs negotiating their right of way, Finton House is a cosy, intimate and smart little school. The playground is a sea of navy cord (girls in wide culottes, boys in cute shorts or long trousers), and blue and white crest emblazoned blazers. Overwhelmingly white middle class, 'Wasp like,' said one parent, this has long been the first choice of school for the established well-heeled English resident of Wandsworth. Traditional families that tended to move to the country after their decade in the smoke, and for whom the grinding competitiveness of the 11+ was never much of an issue, gave their children a nurturing, but solid foundation here. The school, which is non-selective, was regarded as unpressured and positively inclusive. There is a history of accepting children with a wide range of special educational needs: historically there has been a child in each class in every year with an EHCP.

The character of the school is changing, however. Fewer families move to the country, more stay for the duration and will be negotiating the 11+ to one of the London secondaries. Always diverse in terms of ability, the school is becoming slightly more diverse socially, though the number of international families is still surprisingly few compared to other schools in the area. It is more common now for both parents to work (though one mother we spoke to remarked that there were very few nannies in the playground), and boys are more likely to stay until year 6 (although there were only five in the top year when we visited). School is actively working to keep the boys. One parent commented on the importance of inclusivity academically as this goes some way to making the school feel diverse. As the academics become more streamlined the school is starting to feel more homogenous. A dedicated parent body, with a system of class reps as well as committees for major events (helps to reduce cliquishness, we were told).

Many of the teachers (of whom the majority are women) have been here for well over a decade. Longevity of staff is seen as a strength by some, a weakness by others who regard some old timers as complacent and out of touch. A broad range of ability was evident in the class assembly in which some pupils were able to recite large tracts of memorised text beautifully, while others were reading their one line from a prompt. However all are rewarded for their effort, enthusiasm and interest with celebration certificates each week. Lots of singing – 'everyone sings at Finton' – whether it be the song for the celebration book – 'for working hard and being kind you have exercised your mind!' or singing Happy Birthday! to a classmate and the plethora of songs during assemblies.

Overwhelmingly white middle class, this has long been the first choice of school for the established well-heeled English resident of Wandsworth

Broad curriculum all the way through to year 6. Specialist DT (from year 1), art, music and computing teachers all the way through. Sport is taught by trained PE teachers from reception. Drama included as part of the curriculum and taught by class teachers and the English department. Seventy per cent of pupils play at least one instrument. Class music lesson and a recorder lesson from year

3. Plenty of groups and ensembles – everyone can have a go.

The ethos of being supportive and inclusive of children with special educational needs continues, though a number of parents feel this has been heavily diluted. The school has traditionally had a good relationship with Wandsworth council and will support a family trying to obtain an EHCP. Mixed reports about how the funding is managed, dissatisfaction in some quarters, primarily centred on poor communication. The deputy head oversees two SENCos, one of whom is responsible for learning support, the other for SEN. They are supported by five part-time specialist teaching assistants and in addition there is an occupational therapist and a speech and language therapist. Each class has a teaching assistant assigned to it, and a child with greater needs may have someone else in addition to this. Occupational therapy room complete with gym mats, beanbags and climbing ladders. Most classrooms have an amplification system so that all pupils can hear. Just under 40 per cent of children in each year group receive some form of additional support.

DT feels vibrant and ambitious, the room filled with little wooden robots (a whole school project) as well as teaspoons fashioned into characters

Three classes per year of about 20 between reception and year 4. Historically the numbers have dropped considerably in years 5 and 6 – fewer than 20 in each class, though numbers not as low in the final year now as they used to be. Occasional places at the top of the school unfortunately cannot be filled as the numbers are capped owing to planning restrictions. Homework can be pretty intense, especially if your child struggles academically. One parent talked about the pressure of homework as early as year 1.

A healthy bursary fund set up in memory of much loved former head, Sally Walker, offers bursaries (four on 100 per cent, but there are 80 and 70 per cent bursaries too) for children arriving in years 2 and 3 (often from the state sector). School carefully manages their exit at secondary to enable the experience the child has benefitted from at Finton House to continue. Frequent fundraising extravaganzas are organised by the parents and wholehearted support of the governors means this is likely to continue to grow and be a great feature of the school. Nor do you 'have to be destitute' to apply for a bursary, says Mr Ben. Question mark as

to how the bursary fund is going to be used with the decline in spaces in years 2 and 3.

The school is blessed with a spacious playground, complete with climbing frames, Astroturf, and Wendy houses. A separate, modern wing for reception, the Emma Thornton building, houses DT, cooking, science, music and learning support. Light and airy – even in the basement. DT feels vibrant and ambitious, the room filled with little wooden robots (a whole school project) when we visited as well as teaspoons fashioned into characters. Materials used are mainly wood and textiles; year 6 were making go-carts. Lovely smells of old fashioned carpentry workshops, and tools like saws, drills and glue guns adorn the place.

Wonderful art room at the top of the school in the eaves. Parents we spoke to praised the inspirational art teacher and we witnessed her in action – the children completely absorbed in colourful Indian art forms and the use of glitter. The year 6 project was concerned with drawing and printing bugs. Lovely circular seat where children can be invited to read, draw or just rest, as a reward. Busy library overflowing with books and children reading them when we visited (it didn't seem staged). iPad and laptop stations on each floor are used discriminatingly in the class room.

A flagpole flies the flag of the house with the most house points that week. There are inter-house competitions in cricket, football, netball and rugby as well as hockey, rounders and swimming. Sport takes place at Trinity fields and Tooting hard courts. Cupboards displaying a plethora of silverware, cups and shields line the basement. The music department is carpeted and warm (a good place to retreat to practise); lots of percussion instruments and, on our tour, singing filled the space. The five boys in year 6 (when we visited) double up with year 5 boys for team sports.

Lots of positions of responsibility for children at the top of the school. The head boy and head girl have to make speeches in front of the school, prefects regularly meet Mr Ben and are in charge of house points and there are several house captains as well as games captains and one swimming captain. Subject monitors – those who show a passion or talent for a particular subject – as well as three library monitors. Children remark on how much Mr Ben gets involved – whether it be cheering teams on at the swimming gala, greeting them in the playground, or commending them on individual pieces of work. Parents delighted with the prize day he introduced at the end of the academic year.

An excellent foundation for the all rounder but, despite the cosy size, don't expect it to be as 'fluffy round the edges' as it used to be.

Graveney School

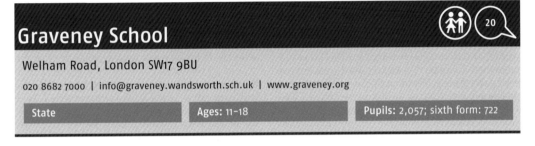

Welham Road, London SW17 9BU

020 8682 7000 | info@graveney.wandsworth.sch.uk | www.graveney.org

| State | Ages: 11–18 | Pupils: 2,057; sixth form: 722 |

Principal: Since 1989, Graham Stapleton MA (60s). Read history at Trinity College, Cambridge, and started teaching at the school 40 years ago when it was Battersea Grammar School. Married with two grown-up children, his hobbies include reading (20th century American novels and historical fiction) and listening to soul and jazz. He has the air of a history professor about him. No immediate plans to retire as he wants to stay and oversee the new Tooting Primary School. 'Fantastic and inspiring', declared one parent. 'He really cares about each and every student'.

Becoming CEO of the Graveney Trust.

Academic matters: School is regarded as one of the top 200 state schools in the country. Thirty-five subjects available at A level – English literature the most popular and film studies recently added to the list. In 2019, 58 per cent A*/B grades at A level, with 30 per cent A*/A; 72 per cent of pupils obtained 9-5 grades in both maths and English at GCSE, with 45 per cent 9-7 grades. Focus is on the academic subjects. Some 85 per cent of students take triple sciences. RE is a compulsory GCSE. All students study a foreign language – French, Spanish or German (with Latin and Mandarin available as twilight subjects – before or after school) – and many take one to GCSE.

Pupils are divided into ability bands as soon as they enter the school in year 7. They are banded largely by English scores and then set for maths from year 8 onwards. Extension programme for those nominated by teachers (includes PE, music and art as well as English, maths and science). Some concern from potential parents about what school is like for those who don't get into the top band (extension group), but anecdotes from current parents say that the next band (upper) is also very high achieving. 'Whichever band your child is in, the teachers will push them to achieve their best', said one mother. 'They seem to have a knack of finding out what motivates your child and then encouraging them'. There is movement between the bands so no need to panic if your child is not in the extension group. However, some parents complain about the high number of students in the extension classes – up to 33 in some cases.

Large number of students with special needs (55 with EHC plans) – 'because we have such a good reputation', explains the principal. SENCo and various learning mentors look after these students.

Games, options, the arts: Everyone is encouraged to take part in team sport and play for their form or house. Sports include rugby, football, volleyball, netball, cricket, tennis, athletics and basketball. One parent complained that there is only one time-tabled session of games per week but principal stresses that all students are encouraged to take part in one extracurricular sports club after school. Even PE classes are streamed, so students get chance to play with others of similar ability.

Students orderly and well behaved. Pupils all stood up when principal entered class – emphasis on good old-fashioned manners

School puts a special emphasis on music. All children eligible for free school meals get free music tuition. Around 350 learn an instrument at school (taught by peripatetic teaching staff) and more learn outside school. Each year around five students are members of the London Schools Symphony Orchestra and some students go on to study music at university or music college. School orchestra has 40 students, and choir has 70. All encouraged to take part in a musical event or production. Over 200 sixth form students recently took part in a production of Singing in the Rain.

Background and atmosphere: School is spread out over two campuses so despite its size (around 2,000 students) it doesn't feel overcrowded. Formerly a teacher training college, the original Georgian building (now rather scruffy) houses the art department. Other buildings have been added on over the years. School was due for refurbishment before government budget cuts so now looks rather tired. However, new RIBA award winning sixth form block plus new classroom block now open.

When we visited at break time, students were orderly and well behaved. Pupils all stood up when principal entered class – emphasis on good old-fashioned manners. No lockers, so pupils have to carry everything round with them, complained one parent.

School meals fantastic – delicious food and good selection, though some grumbles about the lengths of the queues. Newish lavatories for boys and girls (replacing the 'rather ghastly' previous ones).

Pastoral care, well-being and discipline: Teachers really do seem to care about each and every student. When we visited we came across the head of art berating an A level student for not completing his coursework. Afterwards she confided, 'He'll get an A* but he needs to understand that he has to put in the work.' This attention to detail is followed through at all levels. We also met a year 11 student being mentored by the principal to ensure that he gains the all-important five 9-4 grades at GCSE. 'Are you making sure your homework is handed in on time?' he enquired. 'Mostly', mumbled the student. Pastoral care is very good and students with difficulties are mentored by students higher up the school who have been through the same experiences.

Pupils and parents: Parents include middle class arty types and a good cross-section of the local community. Pupils in the extension group (those selected by ability) travel from further afield whereas others live locally and walk to school. Pupils are proud to belong to the school. 'Now I'm

at Graveney I believe I can do anything', a year 9 student told us proudly.

Alumni include Naga Munchetty, BBC TV presenter, Amol Rajan, BBC media editor and Kyle Sinckler, England rugby international.

Entrance: For year 7 entry all applicants take the Wandsworth year 6 test. This selects 25 per cent of places by ability (63 pupils out of 2,000 who sit the exam), with 75 per cent selected on proximity to school. Sibling policy now applies to all pupils, including ability places (although it does not guarantee a place in the extension group: pupils still have to take the test to see which class they go into).

Students need five GCSEs at 9-4 including maths and English to stay on into the sixth form. Most do and are joined by an extra 150 (over 1,000 apply for these open places). Sixth form popular with pupils from the private sector, especially from single-sex schools. 'I think they want a more culturally diverse environment', says the head, 'and of course at that age they want to meet the opposite sex'.

Exit: Up to 20 per cent leave after GCSEs, perhaps because they haven't achieved the crucial grades. Those with poor end of year 12 results are also advised to find alternative courses. Around half to Russell Group universities, including eight to Oxbridge plus five medics in 2019. Some to music, art or drama colleges.

Remarks: Pupils who manage to get in are assured of a top class education in a socially mixed environment. Local parents often turn down places at schools like Alleyn's and Dulwich if their children manage to get a place here.

Herne Hill School

The Old Vicarage, 127 Herne Hill, London SE24 9LY

020 7274 6336 | enquiries@hernehillschool.co.uk | www.hernehillschool.co.uk

| Independent | Pupils: 270 |
| Ages: 2-7 | Fees: £6,780 – £15,465 pa |

Headteacher: Since 2016, Ngaire Telford (pronounced Nyree) 50s, a lady who radiates positivity and affection. She originally trained and taught at secondary school level in New Zealand, but fell in love with early years teaching after coming to the UK and being posted to a primary school in the

Old Kent Road as a supply teacher – a baptism that might have frightened off a lesser soul. Took a 10 year career break to have four children of her own, all of whom went to Herne Hill School, thereby introducing her to the place. After teaching reception here part time, she became head of early years in 2009, then deputy head, and took on the headship in September 2016. 'It really is a dream job for me, because this is such a lovely place to work.' Married to Duncan, a management consultant.

Tall, slender, elegant, beautifully dressed and full of joie de vivre, she is the very embodiment of a fulfilled working mother. Parents love her. 'She is simply the most inspiring head teacher I have ever met,' wrote one. 'She knows every child by name, she knows all their little quirks and is genuinely interested in their well-being and that of their family.' 'Mrs Telford's leadership is brilliant,' wrote another. 'Leads by example with her warmth and commitment'. 'Calm, focused, fun and very glamorous! I don't know how she manages to run the school like a family but also with such rigour.'

Interests include running, singing, and early music, particularly Bach, which may account for her remarkable equanimity.

Entrance: First come first served, and early registration is advised. There are three entry points: kindergarten (2+), pre-reception (3+), and reception (4+). School takes up to 60 children into kindergarten, but won't have more than 40 in school in any one session (although this is set to change following purchase of a new building to expand current provision). Total year group number in pre-reception and reception currently capped at 70, so places at these entry points limited by numbers coming up from kindergarten. However, every year there are children who move on at 4+ to the Dulwich Triangle schools, so it's always worth applying.

Gentle and informal assessment process. School looks for self-esteem and confidence, the ability to engage with the teacher, and the child's listening and communication skills. For those applying to reception, it's a bonus if they can write their name, but 'not the end of the world if they can't.' Some sibling priority, but points are taken off for parents who took their first child out to start reception elsewhere.

Exit: About a third of pre-reception children leave for state schools such as Dulwich Hamlet, and independents such as JAPPS, DUCKS, etc. However, school does not prepare for 4+.

After year 2 everyone leaves, most to the six local independent schools that offer 7+ entry: Dulwich College Junior, Alleyn's Junior, JAPS, Sydenham High, Dulwich Prep London and Rosemead. Head meets with all parents individually to plan (and sometimes manage) expectations, and school's track record of success is long-established. 'Everyone gets a place somewhere, most get multiple offers. Choosing is the hardest part.'

Remarks: Housed in the former vicarage of St Paul's Church, Herne Hill School began life in 1976 as a nursery school when the vicar's wife couldn't find one she liked for her own children. It became a pre-prep 10 years later in response to parental requests, and now it's one of the most highly regarded providers of early years education in an area not short of same. The beautiful original red-brick mansion is still the hub of the school, but the garden has been developed into an excellent children's playground complete with Astroturf. Tasteful new buildings provide space for the school's growing needs and numbers: the Oak Building, built underground to avoid taking up playground space, contains a splendid all-purpose hall with bleacher seating, beautifully-resourced kindergarten rooms and the kitchen. Since 2002, school has been owned by Swiss businessman Dominik Magyar, who works closely with the head and has brought the buildings and resources to their present very high level.

Forest school sessions are given weekly to all children in pre-reception and above in the rather magical woodland area at the back of the school

Preparing children for 7+ entry is a major part of the school's raison d'être, but the curriculum here is imaginative and the approach is child-initiated. As head observes, 'Learning needs to be about doing what children love, and they won't be 6 and 7 again!' We loved the Talk For Writing unit, where children learnt ancient Greek letters whilst studying Theseus and the Minotaur, and the maths room that was a riot of colour and creativity. French taught by native speaker, and the children spoke with beautiful accents. 'Fantastic teaching staff!' was the verdict of every parent we spoke to, and the standard of work on the walls, both in accuracy and inventiveness, bore this out. 'Lessons are fun yet challenging, and I have nothing but praise for every teacher we have encountered,' wrote one mother; 'my daughter has adored each one and has come on in leaps and bounds.' A father added, 'Insanely good teachers – where do they get the energy?' Staff-pupil ratio of 1:6 ensures everyone gets the attention they need. The learning support coordinator has her own room, cheerful and well-equipped, and supports a range of needs such as dyslexia, AD, EAL with a variety of interventions including one-to-one sessions.

Unsmiling and unshaven after the demands of putting 70 children through their paces for the leavers' show dress rehearsal, the music director nonetheless directed a bravura performance from the piano, although the play itself struck us as something of a propaganda exercise – we were a little startled when all the children carolled 'We're learning through play!' Parents admit themselves completely entranced by it all. 'The school's music teaching must be about the best in the country judging from the Lloyd-Webber-esque quality of its productions – the amazing choral and wind instrument performances teased out of pupils is staggering,' enthused a parent.

Forest school sessions are given weekly to all children in pre-reception and above in the school's own rather magical woodland area at the back of the school. 'I'm an outdoors girl myself,' explained the head, 'and the learning you do outdoors is so important.' Woodwork recently added to the curriculum, taught by an early years specialist.

Wide-ranging and inclusive sports provision by dedicated sports teacher on and off site includes gymnastics, football, cricket, velodrome club and swimming at Crystal Palace. Outside lessons, there are lots of optional activities available including baking, art club, slime club and jigsaw club, but the children are equally welcome just to relax and play with friends. 'We're quite big on unstructured time here.' Regular trips to eg Kew Gardens, Godstone Farm, The Polka Theatre, Leeds Castle, Battersea Children's Zoo.

'Love, Care, Excellence' are the school's founding principles, and parents raved about the pastoral care. 'There is a real emphasis on nurturing each individual child and promoting kindness and respect for each other,' wrote a mother. 'The team there create a wonderful atmosphere for young children, whose childhood is extended somehow by experiencing school in such a supportive and friendly environment,' was another comment. Mindfulness and reflection actively promoted. Yoga is taught twice a term – 'the breathing exercises

help get rid of the butterflies,' said a young performer we met before the dress rehearsal. All the year 2 children either sit on the school council or act as a playground buddy to younger pupils, and the Big Brothers and Sisters Club arranges for them to read and play with the little ones. 'We feel it's a very special school,' said a mother, 'founded with real love, and it genuinely nurtures very happy children.' The school is non-denominational, but children attend harvest, Easter and Christmas services at St Paul's Church in the grounds.

After a change in the catering provision, the lunches are now superb – the best we've ever eaten in an early years setting. Dishes are freshly prepared on site, beautifully presented and genuinely appetising – we liked the jerk chicken, carefully toned down to appeal to young palates but delicious nonetheless. Puddings are low on sugar but popular and nourishing – we enjoyed our compote with yogurt and granola. Parents, most of whom are hard-working professionals, are as grateful as the children, and make full use of the breakfast and after-school clubs, where children from reception to year 2 can stay until 6pm (4.45pm for the pre-schoolers). Most families live within walking distance, but some come from as far as Brixton, Crystal Palace, East Dulwich and Nunhead.

When choosing to bring their children here, parents have to factor in the need to send them elsewhere at 7. The school has made such a success of being a stand-alone pre-prep, however, that we're inclined to think Herne Hill has got it right and that it's all the other schools who've got it wrong. 'Sending our children here enabled us to look for the right school for them at the right time,' as one parent put it. In the words of another, 'Superb school, sublime class teachers, very happy kids. I wish I still went to school.'

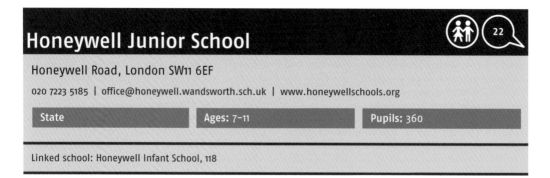

Honeywell Junior School

Honeywell Road, London SW11 6EF

020 7223 5185 | office@honeywell.wandsworth.sch.uk | www.honeywellschools.org

| State | Ages: 7–11 | Pupils: 360 |

Linked school: Honeywell Infant School, 118

Head of junior school: Since 2001, Mr Duncan Roberts BEd NPQH (50s). Previously deputy. Inspiring and popular head who is well respected by teachers, parents and pupils. Good sense of humour. Keen sportsman who enjoys swimming,

football and playing water polo and instils in the children 'the importance of both winning and losing with dignity'. One parent described him as 'a born leader, but also a team player,' while another told us that 'he gets on with everybody.' Has two young children.

Retiring in December 2019.

Entrance: Once through to the infant school, each child is allocated a place in the junior school, though still necessary to reapply via the borough. Places do become available further up the school, so it's worth persevering. Incredibly popular.

Exit: At 11, roughly half to the state sector, including Bolingbroke Academy, Graveney, Burntwood, Grey Coat, Tiffin and Lady Margaret's. Those going down independent route head for Alleyn's, Dulwich, Whitgift, JAGS, Emanuel, Wimbledon High, Streatham and Clapham High.

Much support and guidance given to parents when selecting a secondary school. Head knows that a lot of tutoring goes on at top of school and concedes that the right tutor can help with fine-tuning. As one parent told us, 'It can get pretty competitive around here at the start of year 6, though I think it's more the parents getting stressed than the children. The school manages to keep the kids pretty grounded, but it can be fairly tense at times.'

Remarks: School is situated in a prosperous, middle-class area and the intake mostly reflects this. Head observes that a good proportion are 'advantaged children.' Thirty pupils per class. Around 17 per cent have English as an additional language but bilingual children catch up quickly, with weekly sessions for those needing extra support.

Excellent SATs results, with some pupils gaining level 6 (head isn't complacent, though). The progress of each child in the school is monitored very closely and immediate action is taken if anyone is seen to be treading water. The current focus is on improving the standard of reading comprehension. Low turnover of staff. One assistant for each year group from year 3. French taught to all pupils. Well-resourced school and heavily involved in teacher training.

A total of 75 SEND children and support is given both inside and outside the classroom – in groups and individually. Playground can be a noisy affair in this large school. Lego club has been set up for quieter souls who find the hustle and bustle of break-time too much, as well as a cordoned off quieter zone, but some parents still feel 'it's a bit of a jungle out there.'

Sport is a major strength and is taken very seriously from year 3. Inter-house competitions recently introduced so 'everyone can take part' and house points hard fought for. Welcomed by parents, as some felt that previously only the sportiest were given the chance to play. School participates in every tournament going – often with great success. Huge number of trophies on display to prove it. Swimming from years 3 to 5. Not just predictable sports here – cross-country and orienteering offered, and lacrosse played at the highest level. Before and after-school clubs are very popular. All tastes catered for, including tennis, Mandarin, knitting and baking. Early morning running club on the nearby common for pupils, parents ('mostly mums') and teachers.

Playground can be a noisy affair in this large school. Lego club has been set up for quieter souls who find the hustle and bustle of break-time too much

Gold Artsmark awarded to for high level of provision in the arts. Huge orchestra with 60 members, as well as string orchestra. Individual tuition on a variety of instruments (recorder, violin, flute, cello), with regular concerts and performances for parents. The head's attitude is 'now you've got your grade 1, let's all enjoy it.' Recorder compulsory for year 3. Two choirs, so something for everyone, including one dedicated to popular music (scores from West End musicals). School hires drama facilities for year 6 production involving all 90 children. Recent productions include Bugsy Malone and We Will Rock You.

This is a school which makes the most of being in the capital – lots of trips, visiting speakers and workshops. Year 6 outdoor pursuits residential trip to the Isle of Wight is a high point in the final year.

Supportive, vociferous PTFA. Whether they're hearing readers, producing a snappy school magazine, fundraising or coming in to talk about their experiences, they're a force to be reckoned with. Excellent wrap-around care on offer, including holidays. Communication between parents and staff has improved recently with the sharing of teachers' email addresses.

School has strong links with the community and actively supports local charities. The importance of being a good citizen and of giving back to society – 'either in time, effort or finances' – is instilled in the pupils. Good manners are high on the agenda and behaviour is very good. Head stresses that school wants Honeywell pupils to be decent citizens, as well as achieving academically. No uniform (apart from PE kit), after lengthy consultation with the school community, and some pupils could do with smartening up.

A first-rate state primary that offers the lot. Produces independent, confident children ready to cope with the next stage. Old pupils are always coming back to visit. As one parent told us, 'My girls loved Honeywell. I genuinely believe that it gave them the best possible start.'

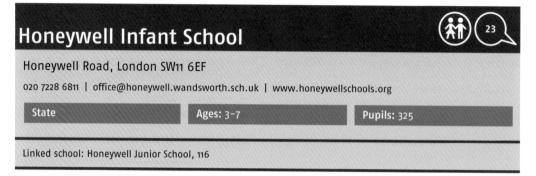

Honeywell Infant School

Honeywell Road, London SW11 6EF

020 7228 6811 | office@honeywell.wandsworth.sch.uk | www.honeywellschools.org

| State | Ages: 3–7 | Pupils: 325 |

Linked school: Honeywell Junior School, 116

Head teacher: Since 2004, Jane Neal BEd NPQH. Previously deputy head, she has been at the school for well over 20 years. Two children. Softly spoken and reflective. Proud of her school and devoted to those in her care. 'She's seen it all over the years and not much ruffles her feathers,' said another. Passionate about early years learning and keen on reading, walking, cooking and children's theatre.

Entrance: At 3 to nursery, although there's no automatic transfer to infant school at 4. Nursery offers 50 part time places, plus 14 full time places (39 maximum in a class). From reception, three parallel classes, with 30 per class. Usually one assistant per class from reception. A handful leaves at the end of nursery. All must reapply to get from nursery into reception. Criteria for offers to infant school – looked after children, siblings, those with exceptional medical or special need, proximity to the school (as the crow flies). Once through to the infant school, each child is allocated a place in the junior school, though still necessary to reapply via the borough.

Exit: All to junior school. Transfer over to juniors is generally smooth, thanks to system of reading partners (pupils) and induction sessions (parents). As one parent put it, 'There's just enough mixing of the two schools for the move to the big school to seem like a natural progression.'

Remarks: Infants on the same site as the juniors, though each has its own head, both of whom specialise in their own age group. Schools share a governing body, staff room and some facilities. Infants get to see the highlights of junior school but lead separate existence day to day. As the head says, 'we get the best of both worlds.'

A total of 40 SEN children offered group and individual support. A small number of children with statements. Nurturing environment, especially in the early years. Forensic attention to detail when assessing the needs of each child – the school isn't just paying lip-service to treating each child as an individual. Excellent results at each stage. Head is aware that the middle achievers deserve special consideration too, not just the high flyers and the ones who are struggling. School is currently focusing on how to make maths more 'girl friendly.'

Loads of outside space and vast amounts of equipment for the pupils. The head told us: 'The children can do all the things here that they can't do at home.' Pupils have their own playground as well as the shared playground garden, complete with tepees, toadstools, fairy-tale bridge and enchanted forest – inspiring, imaginative and the envy of other schools. All-weather surfacing means that it's now used come rain or shine. Staggered use, so each year group gets the chance to use it. Jolly ICT suite, just for infants, complete with jazzy multi-coloured keyboards.

Forensic attention to detail when assessing the needs of each child – school isn't just paying lip-service to treating each child as an individual

Good manners are high on the agenda and behaviour is very good. Head stresses that school wants Honeywell pupils to be decent citizens, as well as achieving academically. No uniform, after lengthy consultation with the school community, and some pupils could do with smartening up.

A very welcoming school. Happy staff and happy children, who are having an exciting time. Bright classrooms, with huge windows and colourful displays at every turn. Learning is made fun at Honeywell. The school produces articulate, confident children who work independently from early on. One parent told us: 'Honeywell's strength is that there is a feeling of community about the school. Everybody is looking out for each other.' As ever, the school is hugely popular but isn't resting on its laurels. Children get off to a flying start here and parents are willing to move heaven and earth to get their offspring a place.

Hornsby House School

Hearnville Road, London SW12 8RS

020 8673 7573 | school@hornsbyhouse.org.uk | www.hornsbyhouse.org.uk

Independent	Pupils: 430
Ages: 4–11	Fees: £14,865 – £15,960 pa

Headmaster: Since 2012, Edward Rees BA (40s). Previously deputy head at Dulwich College Junior School, also an ISI inspector for the past 10 years. He grew up in Hampshire and became a keen cricketer while attending Charterhouse, playing in the past for the MCC. Today he lives in south east London and is married with a son and a daughter. Parents say he is a sociable and hands on head, always willing to talk, and quick to respond to issues or concerns they may have. The school was founded in 1988 by educational psychologist Bevé Hornsby, best known for her pioneering work in the field of dyslexia.

Entrance: At 4+ into reception. Non-selective, places are offered on a first-come first-served basis from a waiting list, in order of the age of the child at the date of registration. Priority is given to siblings. Thereafter occasional places; prospective pupils sit assessment tests in English, maths and reasoning. Not as many places as there used to be at 8 as the majority of boys and girls stay though to 11+. At 8+, the school offers a few means-tested bursaries. Always worth applying for as it is not overwhelmed with applications.

Exit: At 11+ pupils move mostly to London day schools; around half of the girls to JAGS or Streatham & Clapham High whilst half of the boys go to Whitgift. Others to eg Alleyn's, Dulwich College, King's Wimbledon (via new 11+ entry), Emanuel, plus state schools Graveney and Tiffin. A few to boarding schools eg Benenden.

Remarks: Over the last decade, Hornsby House has earned itself a good local reputation for offering a lively all-round education to pupils of varying abilities. A wide and carefully planned curriculum runs through this inclusive school, enabling children to develop at their own pace. All subjects are taught to mixed ability classes, with setting in mathematics for older age groups. Modern foreign languages are taught via a range of exciting topics and projects, French for reception to year 4, then Spanish for years 5 and 6. Parents feel teachers provide plenty of back-up work when needed plus extension activities for the more able pupils. Full-time SENCo with part-time specialists can offer support to children with milder specific learning difficulties, either individually or through small group work. There is an additional charge for one-to-one specialist teaching. The buildings are wheelchair accessible and staff are always willing to work with speech and occupational therapists as necessary. The school prides itself on developing potential in sports and the arts as well as academics, alongside helping parents to choose the right secondary school for their child. Proof is in the pudding: around a third of pupils are offered awards for music, art, sport or academics each year.

Whole-hearted teaching team with bags of energy; good mix of male and female, predominantly youngish, although there are some long servers. High staff ratio: two deputies, subject specialists, and all year groups have assistant teachers; reception classes have two each. A number of gappers add bounce to the sports and arts staff team as well as working as playground and classroom assistants. Many of these popular jobs go to past pupils; the gap year mentor remembers most of them from when they were in reception themselves.

Pupils commemorated the 25th anniversary of the school by constructing a fabulous mosaic in conjunction with artist in residence Tamara Froud

Fairly compact site, cleverly designed by architects: it boasts lovely, light modern classrooms which sit side by side with the original Edwardian buildings. Whiteboards have disappeared in favour of the latest interactive technologies, all looked after by full-time technicians. Computing is very much on the curriculum. Minecraft, a newish club, helps with coding skills; pupils also use visual programming software. Art, drama, music and science have their own specialist rooms and teachers. Abundant arts and crafts on offer; Hornsby has been rewarded for all its hard work in art, DT and drama with Artsmark Gold. Pupils commemorated the 25th anniversary of the school by designing and constructing a fabulous mosaic in conjunction with artist in residence Tamara Froud. Drama teacher supported by an assistant puts on a variety of productions throughout the year across the age groups so everyone gets a chance to perform. Much looked forward to annually are the major year 4 and 6 productions. Music provision has developed in leaps and bounds since our last visit: two open choirs, chamber choir by audition and a small orchestra. Music room packed with instruments, mouth organs to African drums; pupils also benefit from workshops run by visiting musicians. Everyone learns the recorder and ukulele in class and individual tuition is available on some 11 other instruments. Considering the facilities and staff enthusiasm, some parents feel the orchestra is not particularly well supported.

Despite a lack of on-site space, sport is one of the jewels in Hornsby's crown; pupils use all the local facilities and are taken on sports tours. Main sports football, hockey, rugby and netball; all have successful teams, some impressive winning streaks and are always striving to improve. Cricket for all in the summer, proving very popular with the girls: definitely a few old girls who say they wish it had been on the agenda in their day. Anyone with physical difficulties or injuries can join in at their own level with the help of one of the stalwart sport

> *Parents and children like the open kitchens and serving hatch; children can see food cooking and what they're eating*

assistants. Large underground kitchens and dining hall, which doubles up as extra space for gymnastics and dance. Parents and children like the open kitchens and serving hatch; children can see food cooking and what they're eating. 'Absolutely yum,' said two little ones.

All is brought together by the school community's positive, can-do attitude, and the house system which sees children of all ages working together on different projects. There is also a good choice of lunchtime and after-school clubs. Year 3 upwards get the opportunity to go on residential trips around the UK and France. Most families live locally; many are part of the strong Parents' Association, with some going on to become school governors. Parents we spoke to all commented on the friendliness of the children and the pleasant character of the school. In the final year pupils work towards the leaver's qualification the Hornsby House Certificate. This involves achievements including taking on leadership roles, displaying resilience during the year 6 trip to a Scottish activity centre, taking part in a charity event and speaking confidently in public: an ideal finale to the junior school years.

Hotham Primary School

Charlwood Road, London SW15 1PN

020 8788 6468 | info@hotham.wandsworth.sch.uk | www.hothamprimaryschool.org.uk

State	Ages: 3-11	Pupils: 413

Headteacher: Since January 2017, Sarah Martin.

Entrance: The nursery class admits 36 full and part time children each year. Reception class of 60, including bilingual class.

Waiting list for places in most year groups, which is an indication that someone is doing something right, considering four state primary schools in very close proximity, one of which is virtually next door. Admissions policy is administered by Wandsworth local authority so out of head's hands.

Exit: To a range of 15 different secondary schools. Maybe two or three a year go into the private sector but the majority are state school bound. Ashcroft (formerly ADT) is popular, but some also to Lady Margaret's, Richmond Park Academy, The Ark and St Cecilia's. Some to private schools on scholarships.

Remarks: At first glance this looks like a typical Victorian primary school. It even has the original boys' and girls' entrances. The classrooms have high, light, draughty windows and are accessed by corridors and stairwells decorated with those funereal tiles so beloved of that era. The whole place cries out for a lick of paint and some TLC. Outside, the obligatory grey, hard playground is surrounded by a high wall.

However, what lies within tells a very different story. Take a closer look at that playground, for example – well-tended, well-planted flower beds all around the edge, each one the responsibility of one year group. Look further still and you come across a hidden, secret garden containing bird boxes, trees and plants to represent the four seasons, wood piles to provide homes for dozens of creepy crawlies and a quite amazing human sundial which looks very like a mini Stonehenge. All this surrounds a small classroom usually inhabited by the man affectionately known as Mr Hotham. Retired, he then returned part-time to give extra help to those in need and seems to embody the spirit of the school.

The classes are large (26-30 on average) but all supported by TAs. Twenty per cent of the pupils need EAL help, with full support on offer. Special needs pupils include those on the autistic spectrum, some dyslexic, some have cerebral palsy, some with language delay, some have ADHD. All are supported within the classroom as the school can see 'no point in doing anything else'. It's a 'place where we all learn from one another' and the wish is to see pupils become 'independent learners, to use their initiative and solve problems by using their fantastic, inquisitive minds'.

A bilingual stream has been introduced into the reception class and is making its way up through the school. In the bilingual class, around 15 per cent of the week is spent speaking French, and this proportion increases by year group so that by the last year the children will spend about 50 per cent of their time using French. Four French speakers on the staff and years 5 and 6 go on school trips to France. There's a link with a school in Paris.

Take a closer look at that playground, each well-tended flower bed around the edge is the responsibility of one year group

Music is very strong, with choirs performing in Wandsworth events. All year 4s learn the clarinet. Swimming is taken seriously in KS2 when all children are taught in four ability groups over a six month period. Teams in football, cricket, netball, cross-country, swimming. After-school clubs in gym, yoga, photography, art, French. Very active PTA – recently completely refurbished the library. Polite, happy children in smart red, white and blue uniforms. Excellent handwriting throughout (would put many a private school to shame). As one parent remarked, 'Despite the presence of two excellent faith schools in the vicinity, Hotham gives a brilliant start to its kids. Its multicultural mix seems to work well.' Has recently won the Green School of the Year Bike-It award and two of the staff were finalists in the annual Teaching Awards.

This is a solid primary school offering a solid education to its local community from the nursery ('the best in the borough', according to one parent) to the final year, where discussion groups in the class are animated and passionate. One book which should not be judged by its cover.

Hurlingham School

122 Putney Bridge Road, London SW15 2NQ

020 8874 7186 | admissions@hurlinghamschool.co.uk | www.hurlinghamschool.co.uk

| Independent | Ages: 4-11 | Pupils: 350 | Fees: £17,850 pa |

Headmaster: Since 2010, Jonathan Brough BEd (Cantab) NPQH (40s), married to Harry, a high powered city lawyer. There really was no way out for JB, born with a double dose of the teaching gene. His father made a slight push to suggest an unlikely career as an air traffic controller and his mother, a home economics teacher, might have liked him to be a food technologist but teaching won the battle early on. Now, he has occasional thoughts of what might have been, brought on by Bake Off, but he is clearly extremely happy about the choice he made. Before arriving in Putney, he ran a selective single sex school (the City of London Girls' Prep) and says that he 'was extremely fortunate that the vacancy at Hurlingham came up at just the right time'.

Admitting to being a 'stereotypical bookworm', with a preference for new hardback novels, he's a bit of a theatrical groupie, having ventured onto the boards in his student days. However his first love is his school and this 'finger in every pie' head is totally involved in the nuts and bolts of his scholastic kingdom, either when rehanging a stray duffle coat on its peg or unconsciously revealing an in-depth understanding of a particular child and its parents. His declared wish to be at the cutting edge of all things educational and proving his point that 'a non-selective school can be just as good (if not better) for gifted and talented pupils than any selective institution' is a big hit with local parents.

Entrance: Into three forms at reception from a range of nurseries but first priority goes to siblings and children from the newly acquired Lion House nursery and pre-prep, now officially under the Hurlingham banner, and then to those living within 1.2km of the school. Non-selective.

Exit: Most popular destinations currently Epsom College and Ibstock Place; followed by Kings College, Lady Eleanor Holles (LEH), Putney High, Whitgift and Woldingham.

Remarks: Only a few strokes away from the start of the Boat Race under Putney Bridge, the busy road outside explains the slightly bossy instructions about delivering and collecting your children. TfL should take lessons from this military-style operation that takes place twice a day in the semi-underground car park. Child in back seat clutching belongings on lap is swooped on by teacher and bundled into school whilst parent, with eye firmly on rear mirror, waits for the signal to move swiftly on.

We were secretly pleased to be told by JB that the ukulele was passé in Putney and that 'DooDs' (junior clarinet) and 'TooTs' (junior flute) were becoming all the rage

The proximity of the river also accounts for why the four school houses are called Herons, Kingfishers, Mallards and Swans. Apparently, the somewhat eccentric founder of the school was glancing from her waterside window (the school overlooked the river at that time) and spotted the ornithologically unlikely sight (particularly in the case of the kingfisher) of all four birds dancing in the water. As the myth goes, she immediately commanded that the children should, henceforth, be divided into colonies of birds but, in reality, the names were chosen by previous pupils.

Above the basement garage are stacked three floors of classrooms, a large multi-purpose hall and some rather skimpy offices; the deputy head's quarters resembling an engine, rather than a ballroom. An out of scale ante-room with panoramic school photographs on the walls leads onto an L-shaped hall. Here, via another ruthless planning schedule, the space metamorphoses from assembly room to karate studio to food hall to theatre, all in one action-packed day. We were intrigued that the props to achieve this were kept in a miraculous cupboard, crammed with tables to eat off and even a stage to act on.

Across the marginally dreary passage, dividing the admin and school hall from the rest of the school, you enter another world: literally every inch of every surface is decorated in some form or other, transforming this potentially uninspiring building. We particularly enjoyed the doors, in years 1 and 2, turned into illustrated book covers. After a lengthy inspection, we decided that our favourites were Lost and Found by Oliver Jeffers decorated with a plump, red scarf-wearing penguin and Whatever Next by Jill Murphy, represented by a teddy bear peering out of a box sporting a bright green colander as a hat. The doorways also fulfilled an additional function of making you feel that you were literally inside the book the children were studying.

In reception, three light, bright classrooms all open onto a playground, filled in the afternoon with small people engaged in a variety of outwardly jolly activities concealing a definite learning plan devised by the smiley, supervising teachers. Above this apparently relaxed operation are stacked three more floors topped with an Astroturf outside space. There is an orderly feel to this purpose-built place with extensive libraries on each floor, and the layout allows the school to divide easily into junior, middle and upper with a natural upward progression from year 1 to the more serious academic atmosphere of year 6 on the top floor.

Once inside the classrooms, three to a year throughout, the relatively young staff teach the same syllabus to all the pupils but adapted to each child's needs. There are no specific scholarship sets, only maths is setted from year 1 and English in the run up to 11+. Instead, the teachers rely on their knowledge of each individual to decide how much work they can handle. A parent remarked that her daughter was asked by her teacher, 'Do you ever learn your spelling words or do you just know them?' and on being told the latter was given an extra five, more challenging, words to learn every week. This attitude was echoed by another parent who praised the bespoke nature of the homework handed out and the fact that the teachers know the children 'very, very well'.

They seem to have found the secret recipe (maybe down to JB's flirtation with food technology) to getting the maximum out of each child without taking the fun out of learning, and parents talk of their children being 'massively enthusiastic about going to school'. JB teaches mainly extension classes, often in his own space, eliciting the comment: 'it was really good, we went and had our lesson in his office'. As pupils move up the school they are given increasing responsibility over organising their days, a popular move amongst parents who feel that they start senior school ahead of some floundering contemporaries. Homework diaries have to be filled in and they find their own way from lesson to lesson, more steps towards the increasingly independent life ahead.

JB is meticulous over preparing pupils for the 11+ and exams for their next school, giving them computer tests as well as maths and English and then advising on three sets of choices, optimistic, realistic and back-up. A surprised mother even told us that her son was so well prepared that he 'loved the exams'. Once 11+ is out of the way additional time is given to Latin and computing, which led to one ex-pupil at her next, high-flying school being charged with explaining technical skills to her new classmates. No child has failed the OCR qualifications that everyone takes in both subjects, fairly amazing as these are often used to test 16-year-olds and Hurlingham is a school of totally mixed abilities.

When we visited, an art teacher was busily cutting out glittery stars, the results of a competition to design Christmas decorations. The entries ranged from the wildly wacky and somewhat impractical to the more traditional, but the winner came from reception, proving that in festive design, imagination can trump technique. The walls featured large paintings of animals, one a particularly convincing horse, clearly the work of a pupil who had really 'got it' when it came to equines. Art squeezes into and onto every nook and cranny, including the ankle level window to the parking lot featuring, literally, hundreds of small, brightly painted pottery people. Music is also built into the life of the school with an 'inspiring' head of music who, despite his professional musical theatre background, makes a determined effort to include everyone in regular concerts, even if their finger work produces the odd rather squeaky note.

Music, art, drama and dance also feature in an after-school club (MADD) and we were secretly pleased to be told by JB that the ukulele was passé in Putney and that 'DooDs' (junior clarinet) and 'TooTs' (junior flute) were becoming all the rage. Unsurprisingly, the Christmas play from reception runs along the angels and animals route, but the rest take a hand in writing their own scripts. Books, presumably partly due to JB's addiction ('book club is a real treat for me'), play a huge part in the school with the head of English handing out free copies of books suggested by the pupils, and a discussion society that decided, with a bit of prodding, that it would be incorrect to read Finding Black Beauty without reading its inspiration first, however distressing you might find the fate of Ginger.

As pupils move up the school they are given increasing responsibility over organising their days. This is popular with parents who feel that they start senior school ahead of some floundering contemporaries

Very slightly divided parental opinions on sport, with one mother telling us that she thought that it was a pity that there were not more specialist sports available whilst another said they did a great job, particularly in being flexible over boys who are not keen on rugby being allowed to play hockey with the girls and fielding mixed cricket teams in the summer. All commented that a real effort was made to make it enjoyable even if sport was not one of your major talents, and the head remarked that you could feel a frisson of excitement through the whole school when year 2 marched out for their first match.

Special needs provision is comprehensive, ranging from sending children home with reading games to making life easier for a severely disabled child. The dos and don'ts of school life are made very clear at Hurlingham with six golden rules, deliberately written to show both sides of the coin, an example being 'We are kind, helpful and polite. We do not hurt the feelings of others'. To back up this philosophy, various tools are used from traffic lights in the lower school to Excellence and Order books further up. Postcards and giant golden stars announce good deeds as well as hard work and we are very pleased to report that the Excellence book was nearly full and the Order book barely started.

The organisational skills of JB and the rest of the staff in shifting over 300 different children in an endless pattern of activity – 'no two days are the same and they are never bored' – is admirable in itself, but the dedication to helping all children scale their particular peak, both academically and socially, is truly impressive. This is a kaleidoscope of a school where the whirling patterns are constantly formed into happy, successful children.

Ibstock Place School

Clarence Lane, London SW15 5PY

020 8876 9991 | registrar@ibstockplaceschool.co.uk | www.ibstockplaceschool.co.uk

| Independent | Pupils: 970; sixth form: 130 |
| Ages: 4-18 | Fees: £17,115 – £21,735 pa |

Headmistress: Since 2000, Anna Sylvester-Johnson BA PGCE. Previously three years as head at Arts Educational School. A far cry from her first job, aged 22, at SW London comprehensive teaching disaffected pupils, there only because of rise in leaving age. 'Quite an eye-opener.' Followed by a two stints at Lycée Français Charles de Gaulle, separated by spell at Green School in Hounslow, where she was head of English.

Married to local GP, with two grown up children (both Cambridge grads), Mrs S-J, a formidable, charismatic presence with ramrod straight posture, is the reason why school has shot from laissez-faire offshoot of a teacher training college to oversubscribed and highly successful all-through school today (with recently-added kudos of HMC membership).

Though parents don't see much of her, no complaints. With well-regarded management team mopping up day-to-day concerns, Mrs S-J is seen as the visionary seeing the school on to future glories.

Supportive and doesn't miss a thing, say staff. 'She trusts me to make the right judgement – am careful about not taking advantage'. Pupils value her good opinion. 'If she congratulates you, it's a big deal,' felt a sixth former.

Parents know their place. Mrs S-J is 'effective' with 'incredible' charm – but will not kowtow. 'Unlike a lot of heads, she has no glossy exterior towards people who she feels complain for the sake of complaining,' said parent.

Approach has its benefits. 'Children are judged on the basis of who they are as individuals, not what various competitive mothers may be trying to do,' said a parent.

That said, parents stress that this is not a school for bolshy families. 'We're just really grateful that the school's telling our child what they're good at,' said one.

Head of juniors since September 2018 is Kate Bevan. History degree from Exeter, PGCE from Cambridge and MA from Surrey. Spent most of her career at Danes Hill, in roles including head of history and director of studies.

Academic matters: Forget 'alternative' reputation. Results now are as mainstream as they come. In 2019, 73 per cent of GCSEs were graded 9-7; 60 per cent A*/A and 88 A*/B at A level.

While inspectors are besotted with school's liberal and humane approach (several mentions in the latest report), school stresses its 'fundamentally conservative' approach with focus on traditional academic subjects, 10 GCSEs the norm with mother language an occasional extra.

Lunchtime house maths quiz (questions in German and French – no native speakers or bilingual pupils allowed) – reinforced the message. If you want an easy academic option, this ain't it. Mixed ability groups in year 7 with subsequent setting for science, maths and English. Two hours of homework in year 7 rising to three-ish in sixth form. Subject support and free supervised homework club till 6pm help to colour in the gaps.

Firefly – online homework tracking from distribution to completion – is 'brilliant for disorganised children or parents with multiple offspring,' said parent. Not the place for more than mild SEN. About 100 have some learning needs, only 40 or so get formal support – a few touch-type, for example – and nobody has an EHCP. Similarly, while there are plenty of EAL pupils (some multilingual), only 10 have additional help with English.

Mind-expanding activities include senior school subject-related clubs ('Make' – takes things apart and rebuilds – and 'Why?' – your questions answered) and lots of debate, with year 8 geographers attempting to solve famine in Somalia in UN-style committee meeting (English Speaking Board qualifications offered from prep school upwards).

School is in top five per cent for progress, assisted by low pupil to teacher ratios (one to nine in seniors and one to 10 in prep), plus zest to uncover pupils' strengths. 'My child has transformed into a completely different creature,' said parent.

After gentle start in the pre-prep, pace becomes brisker in year 5 with introduction of timetabled tests – 'cycle', in school parlance – in maths,

English and reasoning, which give class places and clarify the likelihood of making the cut to senior school. (Parents are asked not to – and don't – share results.) School felt to tackle this tricky topic with honesty. 'Handle it very sensitively,' said parent. Ditto support for the anxious or disorganised. 'My child is a worrier – they spotted that quite early and spent time reassuring her,' said prep parent. All achieved with quality teaching. Old cynics have been replaced by younger enthusiasts (many in 20s). 'Almost exclusively exceptional,' said one prep parent. 'Have to be strict but they help, they're open,' thought senior pupil.

Attention to detail extends to dog ends of the academic year. After 11+ exams, prep pupils get a fiver to start a mini business – home knitted pom poms a recent highlight – while year 11s (known here as PVIs – pre-sixth formers) return after GCSEs for a summer school with left field options (creating balsamic vinegar capsules in a molecular gastronomy session) and conventional ones (making a clay bust in a day). Can convert pupils to formerly unenvisaged subjects. 'Didn't know I would take further maths,' said sixth former whose idea of bliss was work experience on an oil rig. Others raved about Mandarin, sport and art.

Games, options, the arts: Just contemplating the range of activities is exhausting, so numerous (around 70 clubs each for prep and seniors) that they stretch out of the week and into Saturdays. Why go anywhere else? 'I'm cancelling family's gym membership,' said mother. At least one club a week the minimum – one prep pupil was up to five, and counting.

Helped by compact campus (getting from A to B doesn't involve a trawl through the alphabet) though one parent felt stronger communications – particularly for new bods – about where to collect children would be helpful.

Arts remain the school's big thing, with addition of new, better facilities to do them in. Dance (ballet, street etc – nothing wrong with musical theatre but needs good foundations first, says head) is timetabled in prep with clubs for all ages. Though sheds senior boys along the way, some hang in there – several at pro standard.

Same richness applies to drama. Budding thesps have quick change performance space (smaller back up in prep school) which transforms from seating to scenery in minutes. Even the green room – all glass, light and views – is stunning.

Around 400 learn at least one instrument (string scheme for all prep pupils), with boys-only ensembles (and positive discrimination to ensure gender balance in selective IPS singers). Glitzy productions such as Cinderella. Also have ensemble in residence which performs pupils' GCSE compositions live – beats headphone and computer rendition any time).

Quality of art is stunning and relentlessly original, from prep school's pen and ink reimaginings of Rousseau's tiger that avoid listless copies seen elsewhere to sixth former's Pre-U work, a menacingly beautiful street scene with hurrying people interspersed by stitched outlines of ghostly others – a thought-provoking tribute to the 'disappeared'.

As to sport – it's 'out of this world, run very fairly and with great good humour,' said parent. Despite fluctuating interest and talent levels it's often very successful, helped by continuity – sports teachers work with both junior and senior pupils.

Traditional division of girl and boy sports is mutating into something more equal and interesting – girls' football already here; boys' hockey mooted (but surprisingly few takers so on the back burner for now), co-ed cricket and water polo highly successful.

Attention to detail extends to dog ends of the academic year. After 11+ exams, prep pupils get a fiver to start a mini business – knitted pom poms a recent highlight

School keeps a careful eye on anyone in danger of what it describes as 'choice anxiety', as well as offering tea (a bargain £2 for the full cake and sandwich experience). No wonder parents describe the choice as 'overwhelming,' but in a good way, they were keen to explain.

Background and atmosphere: Site of two halves, bisected by a road (instant Saturday detention for failure to cross by footbridge). To the left (facing Roehampton) there's the art 'hut', showing age, DT, sports hall and large sports field, all bordered by semi-public Roehampton university accommodation (pupil access strictly controlled). Needs something stiffer than white hydrangeas to transform, so school wisely doesn't attempt it. On the other side, it's beauty all the way. 'I don't remember my school being this nice,' said another visitor, staring up at the winding, intricately carved staircase. Nor us.

If leavers lack heightened aesthetic sensibilities, it won't be for want of trying. Mrs SJ's combines an eye for beauty with another for a bargain (binocular vision worth having) and is an auction regular (finds include the ancient font masking the hole where grab rail, demanded by health and safety, was briefly planted). Main building features a pitch perfect recreation of a de luxe Edwardian country house lifestyle (the Duchess of Sutherland, house's original owner, would feel she'd never been away)

James Allen's Girls' School (JAGS)

to the best of contemporary design. Cleaners regularly wash the light walls (impressively fingerprint free) and there's even talk of 'low level dusting.' Library bookshelves have ironwork frames built to the head's design, shelves made of extra-strong American white oak. Even reception pupils' sandpit is actually plastic beads – tens of thousands of them. Flow authentically but rubbish for sand castles.

Outside, even the smallest of spare spaces is densely planted (with occasional tactical use of artificial grass). Statement vases as well as statement wheelbarrows pep up paths and enhance armadillos (the curved music practice huts) with those signature white hydrangeas everywhere. Though slap bang in the centre of the site, pre-prep (reception to year 1 – gentler transition through EYFS) and prep (years 2-6) have a school within a school, think parents. Smart, well-equipped classroom blocks, library, art and ICT space and mostly soft surface play areas (pupils keen for upgrade to remaining asphalt). Spacious new refectory replaces previous cramped conservatory dining area. Remaining homeopathic quantities of the old Froebel school (display of earnest looking 1960s toys) don't impinge.

Prep uniform (navy cords for boys, Liberty print dresses for girls) is both sweet and practical (if a bit wanting in a heatwave, said pupils). Youngest wear emerald green jackets – ensures maximum visibility during school visits – navy duffle coat for older pupils. Wellies essential, say parents. Children will spend plenty of time outside. Teachers, too, have their uniform – males, anyway, all in shades of grey (required, apparently). Well, you can't have anyone clashing with those lovely cream walls.

Pastoral care, well-being and discipline: 'We're quite relaxed,' say sixth formers firmly, looking, well, quite relaxed. 'If you have a worry they will show you it's not the end of the world.' Parents agree. 'When I went around ... I saw incredibly happy confident pupils, at ease with themselves and each other who looked like they believed that the world was a good and exciting place,' said one.

It's a tribute to effective pastoral care headed by class teachers (for juniors), with vertical houses, each with academic and pastoral tutor, in senior school. No mollycoddling but 'they do look after us,' said one. Daily Pupil Notes record staff concerns. Effective, say parents, who rarely escalate issues to top level.

Little fazes staff. Transgender pupils are accepted without fuss, uniform policy is flexible (skirts and trousers could be worn by either girls or boys) and there's plenty of give and take ('teachers will always give your child a fair hearing if they think they've been unfairly treated,' said one mother). However, this isn't a place for boat rockers. Parents stress the importance of complying with school expectations, and advisability of paying close attention to home-school contract. Only two or three days a year when blazers aren't worn, for example (sustained scorchio levels only) and detentions are the rule for missing homework. Perks for seniors include arriving early for breakfast, though no common room till sixth form. Zero tolerance for mobile phones, which don't in any case work anywhere pupils might be tempted to use them (loos and library, for example).

Statement vases and statement wheelbarrows pep up paths and enhance armadillos (the curved music practice huts) with white hydrangeas everywhere

While one parent thought there was a little latitude for 'charming' naughtiness – if countered by unimpeachable work ethic and creative talent – tolerance for the merely disruptive felt to be low to zero. 'You fall into line and work hard.' Parents of those who don't (though admittedly we didn't encounter any) would almost certainly have a very different experience. 'It's not that kind of school,' said mother. 'To me this is a smart school that wants to keep itself smart and you have to abide by the rules.' Generally works a treat. 'The most well-behaved children I've ever taught,' says a smart young gent who's off to induct prep pupils into the mysteries of coding. Parents agreed, and were surprised to hear of the small number of pupils we encountered who failed to hold doors for their headmistress. Agreed that uncharacteristic. 'Low blood sugar,' felt Mrs S-J. Only other question mark was over quality of school lunches, particularly for prep pupils. 'Not always appetising and it can sometimes be cold,' thought parent. (School stresses that 'catering team at IPS work extremely hard to get it right and most pupils are positively glowing about the quality of our lunches.') Otherwise, 'I don't believe there's anything that hasn't been handled well.'

Pupils and parents: Catchment typical for area with a blend of well to do with sprinkling of self-effacing celebrities – not an oxymoron as 'don't make a big deal but you know who they are,' said parent. More local than most and friendly, too. 'Pretty nice people,' said mother.

Bonding helped by dynamic PTA selling secondhand uniform and running Christmas fair so successful that upmarket commercial organisations (multi ply cashmere variety) compete to pay for a stand.

Thinking (and living) local definitely a good bet given location – 30 minutes' walk from Barnes Station or a five minute trip on the (free) shuttle bus fleet that runs from 7.30am before school and until 6.10pm afterwards. Otherwise, 'a really challenging place to drive to,' said parent, though drop off parking logistics are eased by pleasant staff member who deals with the hard of understanding with smiling determination.

Entrance: Non-selective in reception (not fair to assess this young, says school), pupils accepted on date of registration. Occasional places in other prep years.

At senior level, substantial competition and growth in selectivity. Two-stage exam process (look for scores of 105/110). Everyone interviewed (50 staff involved), so anyone with exceptional qualities to offer but an iffy exam performance doesn't lose out.

About 60 per cent of junior pupils go on to senior school but 'no safe passage,' says school – compete on equal basis with external candidates. Informally, parents reckon that school will try to admit pupils, especially siblings, if parents keen – but worth considering how much they'll enjoy the experience. 'Unless they're the child that's happy to bump along at the bottom, they're not going to have a fun time,' said one.

Exit: Once accepted, senior pupils are supported through to 16+. Minimum of a year's warning for those who may not make the cut to sixth form. 'You've got to be academically minded and it's silly to be in an environment where you're not going to feel happy,' says the head. Post 16, some leavers into sixth form colleges (Esher and Richmond) for less

> *'To me this is a smart school that wants to keep itself smart and you have to abide by the rules'*

'crunchy' subjects, others to eg Hurtwood House to specialise in drama.

Very occasional unscheduled exits. Just one for drugs in past decade, says school (making it unique in SW London), though head stresses that 'no one is marched through the door. A mistake has been made and therefore we must assist.' Help with rehoming as well as taking in the casualties from other schools. 'We have to understand that we were all children once,' says Mrs S-J.

Languages popular, usually several to art foundation courses. Bath a popular university destination, followed by Durham and Exeter. Several to universities in the USA and Europe; three medics and four to Oxbridge in 2019.

Money matters: Music award available at 11+. Music, drama and sports scholarships at 13+ (no longer at 11+). Academic, creative arts and sports scholarships at 16+. Bursaries means-tested here as everywhere.

Remarks: Striking combination of space, style and success has led to regular appearances on more SW London parents' long lists than ever before. To flourish here, reckoned sixth former, 'you need to be hardworking, ambitious, have to want to do well, be positive, extrovert and not afraid to have fun.' A yen to commune with the odd white hydrangea won't come amiss either.

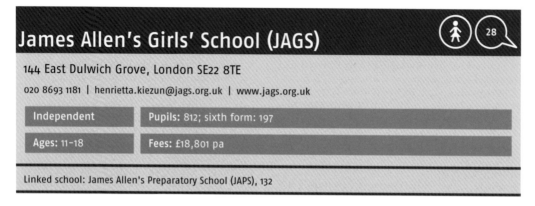

James Allen's Girls' School (JAGS)

144 East Dulwich Grove, London SE22 8TE

020 8693 1181 | henrietta.kiezun@jags.org.uk | www.jags.org.uk

Independent	Pupils: 812; sixth form: 197
Ages: 11–18	Fees: £18,801 pa

Linked school: James Allen's Preparatory School (JAPS), 132

Headmistress: Since 2015, Sally Anne Huang MA MSc PGCE. Previously head of Kent College, Pembury. Educated at Bolton School for Girls and Lady Margaret Hall, Oxford where she read classics and English. PGCE from King's College, London. Taught English and classics at Sevenoaks, where she was also housemistress. Sixth form housemistress at Roedean before becoming deputy head, a post she held for four years.

Head thinks that 'what JAGS does best is prepare young women for the modern world. That's the most important thing we do. We encourage intellectual curiosity, a sense of responsibility and purpose. We want the girls to lead purposeful lives.'

Girls adore her and are charmed by her easy manner and approachability. Seen as a very positive role model. Her open-door policy means pupils regularly pop into her bright red study at break time, often just to stroke her three dogs and say hello. Teaches one lesson a week of classics to top year at the prep school, so knows many of the girls when they arrive. Also teaches philosophy to year 7 and civilisation to year 10. Knows impressive numbers of pupils by name.

Liked by parents too, who appreciate her warmth and energy. 'She has refocused the school,' said one. 'Mrs Huang is already very popular. It was a difficult job stepping into the gargantuan shoes of the previous head but she has injected modernity into the school,' said another. 'A breath of much needed fresh air!' commented another.

Lives next door so regularly nips over at weekends to catch up on work. Husband Alexis is Chinese but grew up in south east London. 'Multicultural, ethnic diversity is very close to my heart and so was a definite attraction of coming to JAGS,' she explains. Two teenage sons. Interested in children's literature and is particularly keen on Marcus Sedgwick's novels. Loves theatre of all kinds, especially immersive theatre and frequently heads to nearby Globe. In the holidays, she is at her happiest walking her beloved dogs in Wales, where she has her home. Though brought up outside Manchester, she 'wants to be Welsh' and is an avid Welsh rugby supporter.

Off to become the first female head of St Paul's School in September 2020.

Academic matters: Strong results at A level, with 71 per cent A*/A 2019. Maths, biology, chemistry, history and English literature particularly popular. At GCSE in 2018, 91 per cent awarded 9-7. Girls normally take 10 or 11 GCSEs.

English department is particularly strong. JAGS was top of national league tables in Pre-U recently thanks to English literature results. No mean feat. Other Pre-U subjects offered are history of art and history. School is otherwise sticking to A levels rather than opting for IB. Head explains that 'a lot of the girls at JAGS are specialists so they might be better served with A levels and Pre-U courses.' Modern foreign languages also well taught, with French, Spanish, Italian, Russian, Japanese and German offered. Two of these must be studied until end of year 9. Bilingual girls can take a foreign language GCSE early but otherwise pupils take all subjects at end of year 11.

Inspirational staff. Quality of teaching described as 'fantastic,' 'incredible' and 'superb' by parents. Some NQTs taken on most years but more than half the teachers have been here over a decade. Head explains that 'recruiting here is great, due to the reputation of the school.' Males are well represented, making up around 40 per cent of the teaching body. Head observes lessons on a regular basis so knows her staff well and has been hugely impressed by the standard of teaching here. She acknowledges that recent upheavals in education have been a pressure on the teachers and she is also frustrated by the 'maverick' marking of A levels.

All the parents we spoke to raved about the exceptional quality of music. Gustav Holst was a music master here for 16 years and the main hall is named after him

When academic problems do arise, parents feel they are dealt with quickly and efficiently. Setting in maths and French from year 8, though sets are fluid with plenty of moving up and down as required. Surprisingly few take the EPQ but head hopes to encourage more to take it up in future years.

Historically class sizes have been large – reaching as many as 28 in the earlier years. Now, having moved to a five-form entry, the maximum class size is 25.

Small numbers with special needs. School can support girls with relatively mild dyslexia, dyspraxia, ADHD, limited sight and hearing. Two SENCos in the school. 'We don't have girls who need a lot of one-to-one attention here,' explains head. Girls must be able to keep up with the snappy pace so would not suit a pupil with profound difficulties, though adjustments are certainly made to support SEN pupils where possible.

Games, options, the arts: Music is high profile and taken very seriously. All the parents we spoke to raved about the exceptional quality of music. Gustav Holst was a music master here for 16 years and school's main hall is named after him. Orchestras, ensembles, choirs and bands galore. Huge new music centre includes classrooms, IT suites and performance areas. Large numbers learn an instrument and play to high levels. Girls regularly win places in national youth choir and national youth orchestra.

Masses of sport going on. Netball and athletics considered to be especially strong. School boasts its own pool which is well used, even on the cold December morning we visited. Twenty-two acres of grounds. Enviable amount of space for matches and practice. One mother we spoke to complained that the sports department tends to focus on the most able, 'often to the detriment of those who do not excel as much.' School, however, explains that girls who are less able on the sporting front can at least play for their house, so everyone does compete at some level. Another parent felt that the school should try to concentrate on personal fitness more for those who were unlikely to make teams and that the state-of-the-art gym seemed under-used. Extraordinary climbing wall to challenge all levels. Shares Dulwich College's boathouse, so increasing numbers taking up rowing.

Hugh amounts of collaboration with Dulwich drama department too. Middle school and senior school productions include a healthy mix of frothy musicals and more heavyweight plays, ranging from Grease and Thoroughly Modern Millie to Tristan and Isolde. Plays considered to be slick and high quality and the set we saw would have put the West End to shame. School encourages girls to get up on the stage as much as possible, including public speaking in assemblies, but for those less keen on the limelight there are plentiful opportunities behind the scenes too.

Increasing collaboration with close neighbour Dulwich. 'Mrs Huang is encouraging more integration with the boys, which is very popular, as you can imagine,' said one mother

The three art rooms as well as printing room reflect the popularity of this art throughout the school. All girls are encouraged to take one creative subject at GCSE, with roughly half opting for art. Displays of art and DT work around the school, including radios and board games, reflect the high standards. TeenTech Consumer Innovation Award recently won by two girls for a cycling jacket, with lights on the shoulders to indicate the direction you are heading in, was rewarded with a ceremony at Buckingham Palace.

Plenty of trips abroad: history department heads to China, RE girls to Israel, others do voluntary work in Romania, and the netball team has played in Barcelona. The cap on costs of trips has been lifted, with bursary girls being supported by funding from the school. Ski trips have been reintroduced. Head's belief is that not all trips need to have academic clout, that there is an awful lot to be gained socially and culturally from travelling abroad on school trips.

Background and atmosphere: Founded in 1741, by James Allen, master of Dulwich College, making it the oldest girls' independent school in London. Part of a foundation (including Alleyn's and Dulwich College) set up by Elizabethan actor Edward Alleyn. Increasing collaboration with close neighbour Dulwich, from music productions to cookery classes. 'Mrs Huang is encouraging more integration with the boys, which is very popular, as you can imagine,' laughed one mother.

Ethnic and socio-economic diversity is a fundamental element of the school's ethos. One mother commented, 'In the past it has felt more like a grammar school than a fancy private school. The head seems to be smartening the place up but keeping the diverse student population, which is an important part of the school.' Girls accept and enjoy the variety of backgrounds here. 'We never judge each other on background or clothes. Not at all. We are very inclusive,' explained one of the pupils.

Christian foundation though the school wears it lightly, as there are many girls here of different faiths and none. Charitable work is viewed as important. 'Girls are encouraged to have a social conscience,' according to one father. The Saturday literacy scheme is a typical example: year 10 and 11 girls help children from local primary schools with their reading at the weekend. JAGS also arranges Latin classes at Charter School next door. 'This sense of giving back makes us different from many other similar independent girls' schools,' states head.

Outward looking school that is keen to be recognised on the national stage: Arkwright scholarships awarded annually to budding engineers, girls also excel at the junior and senior maths challenges as well as literary competitions. Inspiring range of outside speakers.

Pastoral care, well-being and discipline: A nurturing school. Current head has done lots to improve pastoral care and girls have an array of people to turn to when they hit bumps in the road: form tutors, heads of year, assistant heads, as well as senior girls. Informal 'sister groups' within the school. The house system means girls in different year groups work together. The girls feel there is always someone there for them.

Three school counsellors, including one from the local church and a CAMHS counsellor specialising in mental health, sixth form counsellor, youth worker and school chaplain. Head assumed there would be many girls with mental health issues given the high achieving nature of the school but has been struck by how few there are with difficulties. She explains, 'We are managing it, but it is definitely there. Teenagers are under increasing pressure.' Girls are good at looking out for each other here and assemblies on self-esteem and a 'happy being me' programme aim to address problems head on.

Bullying is rare, and girls are taught the importance of being kind from early on. The way the girls interact with each other is crucial and the school will come down like a ton of bricks on anyone who misuses social media. Bringing the school into disrepute at weekends not tolerated. A girl would be asked to leave 'if she was having a negative impact on other girls', though current head has not had to expel anyone yet.

Pupils and parents: Over 50 languages spoken at home. Though some pupils are from affluent backgrounds, there is a sizeable proportion of the squeezed middle that is working very hard to pay the fees. Parents are doctors, lawyers, teachers, journalists, hairdressers, bus drivers and students, as well as media folk. Most families are dual income.

Pupils come from far and wide, though majority from south east London. Handful from north of river and Kent. Coach service shared with Alleyn's and Dulwich means travel from long distances is manageable. One pupil we spoke to travels for three hours a day and she is not alone.

Good relationships between parents and teachers reported. Parents rave about the improved communication and love the fact that they can now email staff directly. Head has been delighted by how 'rational, liberal and educated' the parents are at JAGS and feels under less pressure from parents here than at any of her previous schools. 'I didn't expect that. Parents here have a great sense of proportion.'

Entrance: Main points of entry are 11+ and 16+. At 11, around 500 apply for 120 places. Pre-selection assessment mornings in the autumn term, where girls are observed in a one-to-one context as well as group situations. The day consists of puzzle-solving activities, taster lessons taught by head and online tests in verbal, non-verbal and numerical reasoning. 'We know after this assessment day that there are some girls who will not thrive at JAGS.' Candidates are informed before Christmas whether they are to be allowed to take the entrance exams in January, but majority are called back. Written tests in maths and English. Offers are made in mid-February. No sibling preference. Nearly 90 per cent of JAPS girls come straight up to senior school. They have automatic entry.

For occasional places in other years, candidates sit tests in mathematics, English and reasoning (non-verbal, verbal and numerical); 13+ and 14+ candidates sit an additional modern foreign language paper of 30 minutes (if they have a second language).

Places in the sixth form are dependent upon entrance exams based upon subjects to be studied at A Level, GCSE results, school reference and interviews with head and head of sixth form.

Exit: Around 15 leave after GCSEs, often heading for co-eds such as Westminster or KCS Wimbledon. Every year some girls return within the first weeks of the autumn term, having missed the supportive environment of JAGS. 'We are happy to take them back, though we might not be able to accommodate their subject choices at this stage,' states head. A few new girls come in at this stage to replace the leavers and head intends to recruit more.

Innovation Award recently won by two girls for a cycling jacket, with lights on the shoulders to indicate direction, was rewarded with a ceremony at Buckingham Palace

Most A level leavers head for university though some choose one-year courses at the Royal Academy of Music. Others make a beeline for art foundation courses, particularly Kingston, Camberwell and Central St Martins. Popular university destinations include Durham, London, Edinburgh, Leeds and Bristol. Increasing numbers to Oxford and Cambridge recently – 13 in 2019. One parent commented that, in the past, girls have not always ended up at the top universities, but head is changing that. She is focusing on giving pupils the confidence to apply for elite universities. Girls choose a wide variety of courses from biomedical engineering to history of art, and medicine is a strength: 12 medics in 2019, plus one to dentistry and two to veterinary science.

Money matters: Art, music and sport scholarships available. At 11+ academic scholarships are worth up to £4,000 pa. Over 120 girls currently on some form of bursary, with over 50 on totally free places. A few 16+ scholarships of £1,000 awarded, based on GCSE results but girls keep it pretty quiet as bragging is frowned upon here.

Remarks: One father commented, 'JAGS is everything you would want from a school. Girls are genuinely happy. They are given the chance to be what they can be.' Another said, 'The head is taking the school onwards and upwards. It was great before, but Mrs Huang is changing things for the better.' JAGS produces articulate, ambitious, confident yet modest girls. Impressive on every front.

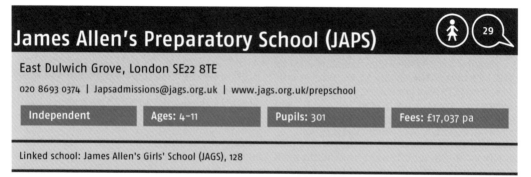

James Allen's Preparatory School (JAPS)

East Dulwich Grove, London SE22 8TE

020 8693 0374 | Japsadmissions@jags.org.uk | www.jags.org.uk/prepschool

| Independent | Ages: 4–11 | Pupils: 301 | Fees: £17,037 pa |

Linked school: James Allen's Girls' School (JAGS), 128

Headteacher: Since 2007, Finola Stack BA PGCE Mont Dip. Currently working towards an MA. Co-founded Finton House School in 1987, before moving on to Cameron House as head in 1994. ISI inspector. Revered by the girls. Highly articulate, Miss Stack goes to great lengths to express herself as unambiguously as possible. One parent described her manner as being 'quite restrained, which can seem chilly, though she is probably just being careful.' Parents describe her as 'kind' and 'sensitive,' and appreciate her professionalism. Finds time to boost those girls with low self-esteem. The consensus among parents seems to be that she is 'fair, reasonable and at pains to do her best for the girls and for the school...but she won't be bullied by parents'. Not a head that hides herself away in her study. 'Very visible,' commented one parent. Leads running club on Thursdays and regularly sports a tracksuit at galas and inter-house matches. Teaches RE. Three grown up sons. Her main interests are 'family, theatre and exercise.'

Head of pre-prep, JAPPS: Liz Channon, previously deputy head of Sydenham High Junior School.

Entrance: Entry at 4+ and 7+ in December and January each year. Highly competitive at both stages. Over 100 apply for 36 places at 4+. Open morning in October and school tours offered on Wednesdays. Reception teachers carry out assessments for 4+ entry through varied pre-reading, writing and number activities. 'Nothing to worry about,' reported one parent. 'The girls think they are just playing.' Written report from nursery requested. 'We're looking for academic potential. We're not looking for a specific type of girl. We offer places to a wide cross-section of girls with different dispositions and from a wide cultural base too.' School does not recommend tutoring as it creates a false impression of child's ability. 'We're not looking for the facts they know. We're interested in their thinking process. It is spottable.'

Maths, English and reasoning papers sat by prospective 7+ candidates. If girls meet the academic criteria, they are invited back for a reading test and interview with head. Report from current school requested. No sibling policy at any stage. Ms Stack comments, 'I do feel bad that sometimes sisters aren't accepted but we are entirely transparent in this. If we start muddying the waters, people will become confused about what we're doing.' All occasional places filled in double quick time.

Exit: Around 90 per cent moves on to senior school (JAGS), often with academic, music and sport scholarships. Automatic entry to JAGS provided that girls are up to scratch in maths and English in years 5 and 6. If not suited to the highly academic environment of the senior school they are encouraged to look elsewhere. Head takes great care with those who are moving on: 'If a girl has received good support at home and at school but is still not making the progress we anticipated, and it looks as though she will struggle at the senior school, then I'll work with the family to find the right school for her. It's a sensitive process'. All JAPS girls heading for JAGS must sit the entry exam on same day and in same circumstances as external candidates, so they have access to scholarships and bursaries. 'This in line with us being transparent. It also helps the senior school to see the nature of the cohort they are getting,' explains head. Has introduced taster days in languages, sports, science, drama and DT for year 5s from other local schools who are considering the senior school.

Remarks: Pre-prep runs from 4-7 and is housed in a converted Edwardian mansion in Dulwich Village. Two parallel classes per year, with 18 per class, rising to 24 in middle school. 'A wonderful start on the educational journey,' remarked one parent. 'I can't criticise the school,' said another. 'It's a lovely, gentle, happy place,' said a third. Beautiful garden with immaculate lawn, pear trees, lavender and a summer house. Heaven on earth for children. Plenty of time is spent outside just being little girls, pottering about, playing and riding up and down the path on wheeled toys. Sensory garden includes a house for a hedgehog and instructions written by the girls on the gate to 'look out for thorns!' 'A 4 year old is a 4 year old, however bright. Emotionally they are still very young.' No one is forced to grow up too fast here. How refreshing.

Praise and encouragement readily given. Girls are rewarded with gold leaves which they place on the gold leaf tree. On the day we visited, the tree was weighed down with leaves. One leaf celebrated a girl's ability to concentrate well, another was awarded for impressive show and tell presentations.

Even from early days, girls are given responsibilities and are listened to. They are taught to analyse problems and find solutions for themselves. Pupils from key stage 1 onwards have a school council. Girls recently suggested a Fun Friday when they can let their hair down. Everywhere we looked at the pre-prep, the girls were busy but not frantic. One father summed the atmosphere up as being 'comfortably dynamic.' A winning combination.

No worksheet-driven teaching here. Girls are competitive and lively and there was a distinct buzz in the air on the day we visited. For bright, sparky girls, it's hard to imagine a more exciting environment. Possibly a little harder for those who are less academically whizzy. French teaching singled out by parents as being exceptional – French, PE and music lessons taught totally in French as part of the immersion programme. Accents apparently spot-on by the time they leave. Plenty of differentiation but not rigid setting anywhere.

Teaching considered very strong throughout. We hear reports of some outstanding teachers and certainly witnessed a couple on the day we visited, including a dedicated science teacher busy preparing equipment for the imminent solar eclipse. By year 5, all lessons are taught by specialist teachers.

Everywhere we looked at the pre-prep, the girls were busy but not frantic. One father summed the atmosphere up as 'comfortably dynamic.' A winning combination

This school is constantly looking to ways to improve what it delivers. Recently introduced reading sessions after lunch break to encourage girls to read more avidly. Makes the most of its links with the senior school. Older girls come over to help with projects and to give extra mathematical support to the very gifted as well to run language clubs.

Currently 17 on SEND register, mostly for dyslexia, dyscalculia and dyspraxia – no global learning difficulties here. Academic and pastoral support free of charge. Pastoral care taken seriously with a successful buddy system in place to reinforce this. Librarians also provide a sympathetic ear for pupils who want to share worries with a non-teacher. The girls feel well nurtured here.

Huge amount of extracurricular activities on offer as school 'wants to work out what engages a girl.' Clubs currently include sessions on climbing wall, portraiture, gardening and coding. Mostly free of charge. Shares sport facilities with JAGS, including swimming pool, pitches, courts and athletics track. Plenty of matches against other schools. Good variety of sport offered including football, hockey and rounders. Everyone makes a team and sport here is inclusive, C and D teams fielded when possible.

Impressive design technology and art department. We saw one class trying to work out how thermoplastic is like chocolate

Head of music considered exceptional and utterly dedicated. Parents are transfixed by his enthusiastic conducting at carol concerts. Huge variety of instrumental lessons. Girls encouraged to perform as often as possible. Numerous choirs, ensembles, string and wind groups as well as orchestras. Community music centre planned. Parents report on the high standard of drama. Year 4 and year 6 put on annual productions, the latter performed in the senior school's theatre.

Impressive design technology and art department. On the day we visited, one class was trying to work out how thermoplastic is like chocolate. Girls were enthusiastic, engaged and enjoying themselves. Art studio jam-packed with animal masks, lino prints and still life drawings.

School makes good use of its London location. Further afield, year 2 heads for Lille for a day, year 4 to Swanage, year 5 to Cornwall on an outdoor pursuits adventure and year 6 to Paris. When classes are mixed up at the start of year 5, three days of bonding on a bushcraft course occur. Pretty primitive – no running water and the girls cook their own food. 'Some of our girls would never normally do something like that!' comments head.

Multi-ethnic families from all over central and south London send their girls here. Coaches dart back and forth to Alleyn's, Dulwich College and JAGS daily. Every class has bilingual children and EAL support given to those who need it. Extra French conversation classes for bilingual girls. 'Lots of smart mummies with multiple children dashing about on the school run. Some fairly glamorous types with shiny black 4x4s and sunglasses, as well as a smattering of tiger mothers,' commented one parent, though school feels this is an

133

'unrepresentative appraisal.' Increasing number of families where both parents work. After-school care on offer is activity-based rather than glorified babysitting.

Parents remark on the sense of community here and participate in the life of school. 'It's important that the girls see we're a community, with teachers and parents all working together,' says head. Parents fundraise for projects, such as for a pond in the sensory garden. Head feels majority of parents is supportive and positive about the school but alert to the fact that 'some parents have strong views.'

Though some locals claim this is an elitist school that produces sharp-elbowed girls, school feels this is not the case. Head believes that 'above all, it's important all children here should be challenged, engaged and learn to give back. Given the advantages they have had, they need to ask themselves what they can then do to benefit others'. This ethos runs throughout the school.

JAPS deserves its outstanding reputation. With its enviable facilities, energetic teaching and dedicated leadership, it's unrivalled in this part of town. These charming, articulate and happy girls seem ready to take on the world by the time they leave.

Kingsdale Foundation School

Alleyn Park, Dulwich, London SE21 8SQ

020 8670 7575 | info@kingsdale.southwark.sch.uk | www.kingsdalefoundationschool.org.uk

State	Ages: 11–18	Pupils: 1560; sixth form: 200

Head: Since 1998, Steve Morrison. He had previously been senior teacher and head of maths here in the 1980s.

Academic matters: Results are on an upwards trajectory, with around 80 per cent getting 5+ for both maths and English GCSE in 2019. Highest performing subjects usually maths, physics, chemistry, biology, computer science, Latin, textiles, food technology and statistics. At A level in 2019, 40 per cent A*/A, nearly two-thirds A*-B.

Although head is keen for the school to showcase its achievers, he says: 'we are not just interested in the children at the top end'. The school believes it does well by pupils across the board. Head says: 'We don't believe we've got it cracked, we believe we did not previously do enough because not every child achieved their potential'. The school is proud of its high performers in whatever arena – the boy who entered the school with little hope, whose mother died during his studies but who turned down the opportunity to train as a professional footballer to enter the sixth form when he achieved nine A*/9-8s and three A/7s at GCSE. He is now at Columbia University with a soccer scholarship. Or the boy who got five A*s at A level and is now reading medicine at Oxford. There are several more on the same track right behind. It speaks of individual talent, but also teachers who are able to nurture that talent with the right support and inspiration.

A broad and traditional set of GCSE options to rival many, includes triple science, Latin,

economics and psychology. 'No vocational shortcuts', says the head. Pupils have the opportunity to study two languages, or one, from year 7: a choice of French, Spanish, German and Latin, with other languages as clubs, such as Mandarin. We watched a small French class of only 12 students taking place in the library. Students study a condensed key stage 3 in science, so that they can spend three years on their GCSE courses. Science labs are light, bright and modern with both benches for group work and lecture style seating. It's also a hi-tech environment. Every child has access to an iPad for home and school use, subsidised by the school, as well as PCs, Apple Macs and laptops.

Staff ratio is one to 10. The head says: 'Pupils actually like the staff and staff actually like the pupils'. A parent said: 'A real strength of the school is the commitment of the teachers'. Our impression from talking to sixth formers is that for the motivated student the staff will be right behind them, as one girl said to us: 'all you have to do is ask'. Particularly in the approach to the summer examinations, the school is open seven days a week with evening revision classes, Saturday schools, Sunday schools and one-to-one sessions. As a pupil said: 'Kingsdale doesn't sleep and never leaves any pupil behind'. Ofsted in its latest inspection believed there is more to be done to challenge the most able pupils, with teachers required to provide more detailed feedback on pupils' work so that they can make progress.

A sixth former told us of a music trip to Brazil, working with young children: 'I've never done anything more amazing in my life'

Classes we observed were working quietly and diligently. When we enquired of a pupil about disruptive behaviour in the classroom she said: 'There was a lot to start with, but the teachers deal with it... it might make you laugh... but if you want to work you can'.

For nine successive years, it has been identified as a special school for inclusion. One mother said of her experience and that of her children: 'They've been treated like they have a voice. We've been listened to. It isn't a one size fits all school'. A mother of a child with both dyslexia and dyspraxia talked of receiving everything she asked for. The focus is on in-class support provided by teaching assistants rather than withdrawal. There is monitoring of reading ages and provision of reading clubs, touch-typing classes, hand-writing groups, and GSCE support groups. Learning mentors provide additional support across year groups. There is also a school nurse for medical matters.

Sixth form courses include a baccalaureate programme comprising A levels, one AS level and an EPQ, plus extracurricular including DofE, or straight A levels. Also on offer: an access to medicine course. Ambitions are nurtured with trips to Yale and Harvard as well as the UK's most prestigious universities.

Games, options, the arts: The school has little outside space, but there are some courts and pitches behind the main building. To the rear is the new sports hall, seemingly made of golden plywood. It contains courts for basketball, netball, volleyball, badminton and more, plus a mezzanine for dance classes: ballet, modern, hip-hop and jazz. On the wall are posters of inspirational Olympians and female sporting role models. With a dynamic female sports director, there are teams and fixtures for every sport and some sporting stars among them: one was recently signed for Manchester United, another represented England at the Commonwealth Games 3000m and gained a bronze medal; one is member of the team GB gymnastics squad and one coach is a former rugby U21 international player. There are 42 sports clubs on site and locally, including inline skating, yoga, tennis, American football, go-karting, archery, fencing and trampolining, fencing, BMX bikes and cycling at the Herne Hill velodrome.

Music is truly outstanding and adds a real vibrancy to the school. The head of music, at the school long before the current regime, is renowned for her ability to inspire and her ambition for the children who may not have picked up an instrument before coming here. Every year the school hosts the Dulwich Festival Youth Concert and steals the show from the massed independent school ensembles – most recently with a group xylophone rendition of an especially composed medley of Bond theme tunes. Ensembles for every instrument imaginable running at lunch times and after school, as well as steel pans, rock band, theory classes, jazz groups and chamber choir. The new music building is all curvy plywood and includes music practice rooms, teaching spaces and a recital hall with raked seating, plus a music tech suite. We heard a student's composition which sounded professional, akin to the latest pop release, and girls singing acoustically around a piano.

The art room displays accomplished textile GCSE projects, books rich with embroidered textiles and illustration. Within DT pupils study food and textiles technology and product design. A large, light DT lab with all of the usual workshop equipment, plus a laser cutter and CAD-CAM suite. The library seems rather gloomy, with dark blue carpet and a little low on books. The upper school library has computers that rise from desks.

One mother said of her experience and that of her children: 'They've been treated like they have a voice. We've been listened to. It isn't a one size fits all school

There are lunch time clinics for students who need additional help or are struggling with homework and plenty of academic clubs. The school works hard to offer opportunities for exciting trips that are accessible for all. There are annual language department trips to Europe and some more far flung: a sixth former told us of a music trip to Brazil, working with young children – 'I've never done anything more amazing in my life'. The 'trips of a lifetime' programme subsidises trips to destinations such as Japan, Namibia, Brazil, the USA and the French Alps.

Background and atmosphere: A local authority school which was cause for concern by the late 1990s, it was completely reimagined to the tune of £30m under a new management team and with the involvement of a design and innovation consultancy which placed the design of the new school at the heart of change, becoming a foundation school in the process. The design won multiple awards, including Building of the Year from the Royal Fine Art Commission for its architects, and is now the most popular state senior school in Southwark and wears this badge with pride.

Situated south of Dulwich and Belair Parks, the school is located in a particularly leafy part of south east London. Its location on a residential street lined with multi-million pound homes, next door to Dulwich Prep London, makes for a calm outlook, surrounded by mature trees and safe-feeling journeys home via the buses on the South Circular or nearby West Dulwich overground station. There could be a bit of discomfort around a state school so surrounded by the plushest of independent education's finest – we get the feeling that there is only minimal sharing of facilities – but since the revamp and the climbing academic standards there is much to feel good about.

There is a complicated system of admissions criteria – so complicated, the maths teachers are assigned to try and explain it to bewildered parents at open days

As you step through the sliding doors you find the most striking feature of the school: a huge, slightly humid central quadrangle, originally the school playground, now acres of green flooring enclosed with a glass roof – a central bed of tropical plants adding to the greenhouse effect. When it rains the noise on the roof is pleasantly loud. This futuristic central space is encircled by plywood banks of lockers on wheels designed to look like little houses, and most stunning of all a central 'egg' or pod, with fantastic acoustics and a steeply raked bank of seating for concerts and addresses. The usual dark school corridors have been cleverly done away with, instead wide, metal walkways encircle the quadrangle linking the classrooms on the first floor. Classrooms are light with brightly coloured walls. There is a freestanding lift linked to the walkways for wheelchair users. It's an exciting space. At lunchtime hot food is served here too, and there are tables outside. It's a versatile space that can be used for anything from art exhibitions to trampolining.

Pastoral care, well-being and discipline: A large school, but staff work to make it manageable, particularly for those joining year 7, with divisions between the upper and lower schools and induction days. There are buddies, junior and senior school

prefects and a house system. Around a quarter of the student population is from disadvantaged backgrounds. Some 26 per cent of pupils speak English as an additional language. The uniforms, fairly smart black blazers and house ties, seem to be worn with a bit of a hastily assembled attitude, especially by the girls higher up the school – plenty of micro skirts with knee socks and half-mast ties. Ofsted was most complimentary about the behaviour of pupils in its most recent inspection, saying pupils 'show respect and courtesy to one another and to staff'. The pupils we talked to were polite and passionate about their school, appreciative of their teachers.

With discipline in mind, the school's very design is partly about transparency. Teachers can see what is going on everywhere, without anyone feeling monitored. However, a girl eager to leave no stone unturned on the tour of the school told us as we crossed the playground: 'There are fights. Not daily. You won't get into a fight if you're well behaved'. The head tells prospective parents there have been no exclusions for five years, but following a recent incident, where a pupil returned to the school after the end of the day resulting in a stabbing, the head suggested that the incident concerned an excluded pupil. Our enquiries amongst parents and pupils as to what has been changed with regards to safeguarding at the school in response to this incident did not yield any firm information.

Most parents we encountered seemed excited by the school as a prospect. With such a large school there are inevitably diverse reports once pupils are there. One grandmother told us how quickly her shy grandson settled into the school and made friends – when he wasn't very happy with the school lunches he felt able to talk to the school about it: even better, they responded with changes. An easy-going mother was nonetheless disappointed to feel after two years that the teachers didn't really know who her daughter was at parents' evening.

There was a certain freshness and honesty about the pupils at the open day we attended who told us: 'Kingsdale isn't perfect. Kingsdale admits its imperfections as a way to improve'; 'pupils are well-supported and grounded with room to make decisions for themselves'.

Pupils and parents: From all walks of life and backgrounds and from all across London. Many join in little bands from their local state primaries in East Dulwich, Herne Hill, Crystal Palace, Gypsy Hill and Forest Hill. But as there is unusually no distance criteria, students come from Clapham, Greenwich and beyond. We met a sixth former who had attended a local prep but after attending an open day and winning a music scholarship could think of no reason not to take up a place here instead. And the odd refugee from the uber-competitive selective schools that dominate the local scene. The head's invitation is for prospective parents to 'show up when you like: someone will show you around.

Entrance: Admissions to year 7 via the local authority common application form – simply place the school as high up the list of preferences as possible for a chance of a place and await National Offers Day. Most recently applications stood at 11 to one. Pupils sit a banding test, in non-verbal reasoning, prior to the allocation of places, so that the school has an academically mixed intake. Numbers in each band will vary from year to year, so there is no way of assessing chances of a place. There is a complicated system of admissions criteria in terms of how places will be allocated – so complicated, the maths teachers are assigned to try and explain it to bewildered parents at open days. Fifteen per cent of places to those with music or sports scholarships; then siblings, staff children, medical or social needs, with the rest of the places by random allocation within bands.

Internal and external sixth form applicants who want to study A levels must get at least six 9-6 grades at GCSE including English language and maths.

A parent going through the admissions and scholarship process commented she wasn't sure she'd want the school in charge of evacuating the Titanic as everything was slightly chaotic. With so many applicants to places the school is possibly rather overwhelmed by the process, but gets there in the end.

Exit: Around 50 per cent of students achieve places at Russell Group/other top universities; occasional one to Oxbridge.

Money matters: Unusually for a state school, scholarships are available in music and sports at year 7 entrance. The awards comprise additional tuition and coaching, such as £1000 worth of instrumental lessons for music and a scholar's programme – the musicians might attend workshops with professional musicians and the sports scholars take vocational qualifications in sports leadership. No need to be already at a high grade of accomplishment on your chosen instrument and sports scholarships are simply looking for 'potential' – candidates will be assessed for component activities and team work. Sixth form scholarships are also available in maths, performing and expressive arts.

Remarks: For those able to stretch to the local independents, there may be more peace of mind, particularly for the most able and ambitious elsewhere. For parents looking for a vibrant school with a growing academic capability and a uniquely inspiring daily environment, join the crowds heading this way.

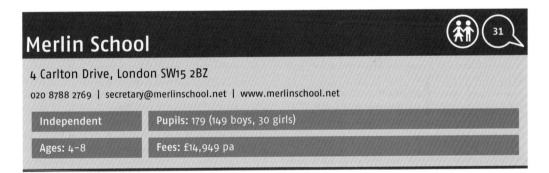

Merlin School

4 Carlton Drive, London SW15 2BZ

020 8788 2769 | secretary@merlinschool.net | www.merlinschool.net

| Independent | Pupils: 179 (149 boys, 30 girls) |
| Ages: 4-8 | Fees: £14,949 pa |

Headmistress: Since 2003, Kate Prest BA Music/ Ed PGCE (Oxford Brookes), formerly head of pre-prep at The Harrodian. Welcoming, personable, caring, with tremendous enthusiasm, Mrs Prest (late 40s) teaches music to all and knows every child by name. She champions creative thinking and teamwork in a school, which parents agree is 'like a big family, where all are made to feel welcome and are well looked after'. Apart from the head, her PA and a long-serving member, staff are known by Christian names. Mrs Prest is proud of the Merlin spirit of 'have a go', which underpins confidence-building, and parents agree confidence is a hallmark of Merlin pupils. Mother of three, children attended the school, with husband in the City and no plans to move on, Mrs Prest thoroughly understands London pressures, the intense competition and high expectations. As one parent commented, 'Mrs Prest and Science Sue hold the tide in this highly competitive environment. She reminds us children are only children once and their childhood is precious. It is important not to get sucked into the madness'. Mrs Prest moves energetically in and out of classes without interrupting activities, and pupils are respectful but not intimidated by her, enjoying her encouragement and praise. Parents value her realistic advice and are full of praise for her open door policy and emphasis on verbal communication, which works well in this relatively small school.

Entrance: Early viewing is advisable for this very popular, non-selective school. Prospective parents attend a half-termly open afternoon or fortnightly tour on a week day morning. Offers are made in order of date of registration – priority given to siblings. Occasionally places occur higher up the school. Children come from local nurseries: Putney, Fulham, Barnes, Southfields and Wimbledon.

Exit: Some leave at age 7, remainder at 8. Destinations are various and widespread, with a number moving on to The Harrodian at 8 where they are interviewed in November rather than examined in January. Other popular destinations recently include King's College Junior School and Shrewsbury House plus Bute House, Putney High, St Paul's Juniors, Feltonfleet, Latymer Prep, King's House, Prospect House, Rokeby and the occasional boarding school.

Remarks: Established in 1986 by Sir Alford Houstoun-Boswall, chair of governors and proprietor of both The Merlin and The Harrodian School in Barnes. Merlin is a well-maintained, converted Victorian house with large, high-ceilinged, light classrooms packed with colourful displays, and the original ballroom serving as the main hall. Four reception classes are 'at the heart of the school,' says Mrs Prest, close to her office and the front door but with timed access to the outside play area. Carpeted stairs abound leading up to the year 1s, specialist ICT room where all years have weekly lesson, and down to dining room, science room and music room in the basement. On the far side of the spacious Astroturf playground are purpose-built year 2 classrooms and, under cover, great resources for zoned play including dressing up and a bench where children can read or be quiet.

'Mrs Prest and Science Sue hold the tide in this highly competitive environment. She reminds us children are only children once and their childhood is precious'

Small mixed ability classes (averaging 17). Significantly more boys than girls but parents we spoke to had not found this to be a concern. Mrs Prest explained how children are mixed up and start their day with 'quickies', working independently on literacy and numeracy skills, and are team taught and moved about in their sets.

Eager year 2 pupils carried out a mathematical investigation using circles to identify right angles in their classrooms

Teachers really know the pupils well with setting from second term of reception for phonics and mathematics; English and maths sets for years 1, 2 and 3 support the tailored teaching. We watched eager year 2 pupils carrying out a mathematical investigation using circles to identify right angles in their classrooms. In all the lessons we saw engaged, focused pupils, happy to explain their reasoning. Traditional skills include times tables and handwriting with specialists for French, science, computing, drama, games, art and music. Cross-curricular topics are carefully planned and head explained the importance of 'seeing and doing, not just being told'. In choosing the Merlin, parents spoke of how they were attracted to the 'energy and the stimulating teaching environment'. Pupils are proud of their school. They described their teachers as 'fair, they make lessons fun'; some mentioned year 3s dissecting sheep organs and handling bones in science. Interactive boards visible in upper school with emphasis away from iPads and technology as so much is readily accessible outside school, and head wants her teachers in front of children.

All pupils benefit from the specialist art room. Creativity abounds with ambitious drama and musical productions which feature original scripts and music. Successes are celebrated in the school half-termly magazine. Extracurricular activities such as sport, chess, yoga and sewing are very popular but do not begin until year 2. Performing is encouraged with choir involvement in local festivals and Mrs Prest ensures all pupils learn to understand music terminology, read and create their own music, playing the recorder or glockenspiel. At the time of our visit, 40 were learning a musical instrument, with individual violin or piano lessons rotated in school hours.

The Merlin Code is understood and any silliness picked up and dealt with quickly. Our visit coincided with a windy, wet day but the pupils' behaviour was exemplary, as inspectors also found. Kindness is encouraged. Playground buddies were named in assembly and there is a bus stop in the playground for anyone feeling lonely. Sport with experienced sports master is inclusive with one weekly indoor PE session, one outdoor session and one off-site games session. Pupils enjoy their lessons in football, netball, hockey, cricket and rugby with fixtures for older pupils. The in house nutritionist ensures a high standard of catering and puddings are a great hit.

Qualified, caring head of SEN with her team ensure support is quickly put in place and early dyslexia screening for the youngest and full screening if suspected in older children is available. Regular staff meetings identify any possible problem ahead and the school provides those children who experience learning difficulties such as dyslexia and dyspraxia with additional one-to-one reading, small literacy and maths support groups. Specialist one-to-one sessions are organised at an additional cost. Other support groups include social skills and EAL club. Parents are made to feel welcome; we saw some listening to readers, all are invited so that they can see class assemblies and plays and the two parent reps organise fundraising events for charities. They agree that this would not be the right school if you want acres of playing fields and masses of sport, or drilling for examinations.

Some working parents might be put off by the school hours with school finishing at lunch time on Fridays and 4.30pm finish after clubs for the upper school.

Just as inspectors judged the school to be 'outstanding' in all aspects in a recent inspection, so parents are delighted with this warm school with its emphasis on allowing children to have access to a stimulating, creative environment where they do exceedingly well and have fun. As one parent remarked, 'The Merlin is aspirational and taps into each individual child'. Another added, 'They give pupils lots of confidence, spotting opportunities and putting them their way'. The first head chose the school name with its distinctive wizard hat logo prior to tales of Harry Potter. Over the years this has become more embedded and developed and there is a sense of magic about the school and what it achieves

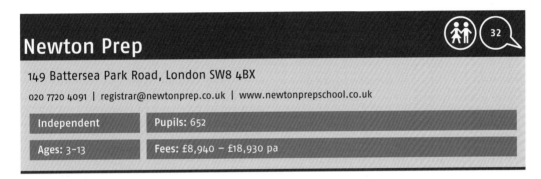

Newton Prep

149 Battersea Park Road, London SW8 4BX

020 7720 4091 | registrar@newtonprep.co.uk | www.newtonprepschool.co.uk

Independent	Pupils: 652
Ages: 3–13	Fees: £8,940 – £18,930 pa

Headmistress: Since 2013, Alison Fleming BA MA (Ed) PGCE (40s), a grammar school girl and theology graduate. Previously head of Dulwich College Junior School for four years, and before that deputy head at Highgate Junior School. A team inspector for the ISI and a governor of a local school. And, far more importantly, an ace head.

Forthright, articulate, warm and confident, Mrs Fleming inherited a large prep in good heart, good nick and with a massive new-build. She spent her first year listening, looking, learning and thinking. And now, subtly but decisively, change (all for the good, as far as we can judge) is happening. Her aims are to maintain the school's 'academically ambitious' ethos while developing its parental involvement and community links. In these aspirations, she appears to carry her own eclectic and inclusive school community with her. But there is far more of sound educational value afoot too.

Warm praise, especially from seasoned parents who have been part of the school under the last three regimes and who particularly value the increased headmagisterial presence around the school. 'She

is always smiling and approachable,' we were told. 'She is independent-minded and has lots of ideas,' another enthused. A third said, 'She is fabulous. Really enthusiastic and has a really good combination of strength, warmth, leadership and vision.'

Entrance: Oversubscribed at all stage. Nursery application process, by 'playdate', ensures an even balance of i) boys and girls and ii) of autumn, spring and summer birthdays. There's a waiting list and those who don't get in can reapply for reception. Sibling policy.

Informal assessment the autumn term before entry into reception. 'A gentle process.' Staff observe the children to see how they relate to adults, their peers and the world around them. Year 1 or 2 candidates spend a day in class and take tests in reading, English and maths. Admission at year 3 and above by competitive testing. Any applicant for year 3 is considered for a scholarship (currently worth £250 per term) or a place backed up by a means-tested, top-up bursary. A surprising amount of financial help available. Most of those admitted at nursery or reception move smoothly up but this isn't guaranteed.

Exit: Leavers' lists are encouraging largely because there is clearly no stereotyped Newton product and they go to a wide spread of schools at both 11 and 13. Good range of scholarships – art, sports, dance and academic – won too. Year 6s to eg Alleyn's, Emanuel, Francis Holland, JAGS, St Paul's, Wycombe Abbey. Year 8s to eg Whitgift, Bede's, Brighton College, KCS Wimbledon, Westminster. New role on the senior management team for a deputy head with responsibility for senior school transfer – a rare, if not unique position amongst prep schools. Watch the others scampering to follow suit.

Remarks: This part of London is not generally appealing. To find an enormous, sought-after prep school housed, partly in an Edwardian block of debatable attractiveness and partly in impressive and extensive new build, is unexpected. However, one only has to enter via the wall and tree lined esplanade to be transported into a very different and disarming world.

The newest bits are breathtaking for a prep. A splendid auditorium and equally impressive, acoustically perfect, recital hall. Many senior schools would drool. Vast airy dining room with seriously inviting food, eaten by all

First impressions are formed by the children. They are happy, confident, relaxed, articulate, polite and eager to share their school with a visitor. Second impressions come from the place itself. From nursery, through lower school and up to the subject-specific classrooms and studios of the top two years, each learning area is well-structured, full of colourful, stimulating and thoughtful displays and staffed by smiley, interesting teachers. We longed to linger – the language rooms ('souriez et entrez!') invite learning, the art rooms are full of creativity, the science labs and IT suites are sleek and the library is simply the best we've seen in a prep anywhere. Worth lingering especially here – exceptionally well-stocked, each child's reading is guided and encouraged and the children find that they have everything they need for research. A real understanding here that books can provide complementary riches, in so many ways, to the internet – which is equally well-used. Sofas, carpets, beanbags and cushions and hundreds of lovely books.

Learning and inventiveness hums. We ventured into the RS room and were instantly involved in a fascinating discussion about the compatibility or complementarity of religion and science.

The old building, seamlessly now melded to the new, is old school standard eg green and brown tiles, sensible corridors, parquet. The new build is high, broad, confident with big spaces of the kind you'd expect from a sizeable and prosperous high school. The newest bits are breathtaking for a prep. A splendid auditorium and equally impressive, acoustically perfect, recital hall. Many senior schools would drool. Vast airy dining room with seriously inviting food, eaten by all. Scooter and bike park: 'they really encourage us to bike or walk to school – you get a special badge for it'. Sports hall, gym and other spaces for muscle stretching. Two art studios full of lovely stuff. We liked especially the monster sculptures – custom-built in some cases ('our librarian really wants a dragon to hang in the library'), the earth-colour tribal shields, the batik, the ceramics, the marionettes.

Outside space is equally enviable – there is so much of it. A huge all-weather pitch and various other good-sized safe-surface areas, well-equipped and colourful – for the different age groups. So sports thrive and, as parents crow, 'it's not exclusive – they have a C team and everyone has a chance'. Most delightful is the 'garden' – tucked away between car park and road but a rus in urbe idyll once you're in, with shady leafy nooks, fruit trees, plots and beds, all well used by keen gardeners and for lessons of all sorts.

Around eight per cent have some sort of SEN – vast majority mild dyslexia, small numbers with eg ADHD or some speech and language delay in early years. Support is given either on an individual or small group basis by the director of learning development or by teaching assistants in classrooms, but head acknowledges that there is work to be done on the SEN side, which will be welcome to parents current and future. Music, under sparky head of dept, also rising to match the stunning new facilities. We anticipate the Newton's impressive lists of art scholarships might well be matched by music similar in coming years.

About 20 to a class except for two nursery classes of 24. Pupils from all over south west and central London; locals walk or scoot to school. All speak good English though around 50 (nine per cent) are bilingual eg French, Spanish, Italian, Urdu, Arabic, Russian spoken at home. Small group EAL sessions for those who need them.

Best is the creative and collaborative ethos and the sense of community. Inclusiveness is key, as parents testify – 'my children are totally different characters and it's been great for all of them' – and eccentricity is relished. There is little of the preciousness and snobbery one can sometimes encounter in other preps, and the pupils feel part of something bigger than themselves. As they told us: 'Our teachers are so approachable. You can always ask for help'. 'You're not babied by the teachers.'

'There's no fear between the year groups. Year 3s often come and chat to us in year 8.'

A parent summed it up, 'We're going to be really sad to leave.'

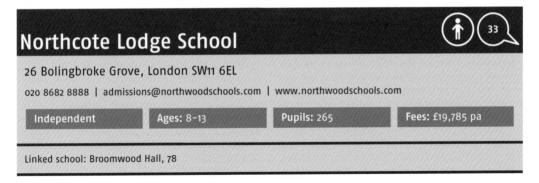

Northcote Lodge School

26 Bolingbroke Grove, London SW11 6EL

020 8682 8888 | admissions@northwoodschools.com | www.northwoodschools.com

| Independent | Ages: 8–13 | Pupils: 265 | Fees: £19,785 pa |

Linked school: Broomwood Hall, 78

Headmaster: Since January 2019, Clive Smith-Langridge, previously head of Packwood Haugh. Limbered up for the role by spending 16 years in marketing before switching to boarding schools (has also been deputy head at Walhampton). Brings essential savvy plus the experience of having captained a Chile cricket XI vs Brazil. Married to Sally; two daughters.

Entrance: At 8. At least 80 per cent from Broomwood Hall Lower School, the sibling school round the corner. The others mostly local, although school minibuses bring in some from across the river. Potential candidates must register for the main list some 20 months before date of entry although late registrations will be considered for the 'headmaster's list'. This is reserved for boys who show exceptional talent in art, academics, sport, design or music and who might be expected to enter for a scholarship at a senior school.

Parents and families attend an open day and meet the headmaster. A year before entry it's assessment time. A couple of hours at the school include tests in English, maths, verbal reasoning and ball skills, an interview with the head and some carefully observed playtime, including a snack. If your son is offered a place, you have to pay a deposit of £2,750, which is refundable when he leaves the school. They feel this encourages only those really serious about the school. There are no bursaries or scholarships.

Exit: Nearly all at 13, with around three-quarters to boarding school eg Harrow, Eton, Tonbridge, Sherborne, Bradfield, Marlborough or Wellington. The rest to London day schools, with vast majority to Dulwich College, others to eg Whitgift or Emanuel. However, planning to open a new co-ed senior school in 2020, initially for 13-16 year olds, in what is currently one of the pre-prep buildings in Garrad's Road.

Remarks: Many are thrilled to be spared the 'pressure pot' felt to be all around in this part of south west London; this is very much the school's aim. This makes some anxious that the school is not as rigorous academically as it could be, feelings the school is aware of and feels aren't accurate. One parent told us: 'The teaching is inspirational; they have really developed an inquiring mind as opposed to a child who is learning for learning's sake.'

'Caring' is the word that crops up most often when describing the atmosphere of the school: 'friendly, inclusive, caring and focused'

Until the final years, all homework (prep) is done at school and there are reports of happier home lives for it. There is a relaxed attitude to exams and revision: 'They appear to actively discourage any revision over the holidays, particularly in the younger years, and are very much of the view that holidays are to relax in,' a parent surmised.

About 20 per cent of pupils are monitored for an SEN and 10 to 15 per cent receive learning support, predominantly for dyspraxia, dyslexia, dyscalculia or dysgraphia, but the school says it is not the place for more severe learning difficulties. All boys are fluent in English and there are no EAL requirements. There is a full-time head of learning support and two part-time specialists; regarding one-to-one support, 'there's no stigma – it's just like a trumpet lesson'.

Sport takes place on Wandsworth Common, opposite the school, and is more at the forefront than in previous years, but we notice the lack of on-site sports facilities is still on parents' minds whether they are consoling themselves that they do just as well as other schools with more lavish facilities, or wondering why the fees can't fund it.

All boys play matches in the major sports and teams are competitive against much bigger schools. One mother said the school is 'very hot on ensuring good sportsmanship'. Plenty of minor sports such as golf, shooting, table tennis and running and there has been strong cross-country success. With no pool, swimming has been rather overlooked, but a swimming squad is emerging. One parent felt that 'grass roots athletics gets little attention'. The school is proud of the recent Welsh rugby tour. The school says: 'Every boy who wanted to go, did, and we had 76 per cent of the year group on tour'. Latest cricket tour to South Africa. Sportsmen drop in to inspire and coach, recently Ben Cohen, Ben Loosemore and Martin Brockman.

Over 60 per cent of the boys play an instrument, regularly taking ABRSM grades and sitting music scholarships for senior schools. Drama is on the up, resulting recently in a handful of drama scholarships to Whitgift, Harrow and Emanuel. Recent dramatic productions include Mary Poppins, Oklahoma and Grease, The Wizard of Oz and West Side Story. Every year boys take LAMDA exams, recently with 72 distinctions.

Boys wear tweedy jackets, soft blue shirts and look like miniature gentlemen, but frayed cuffs and stubborn mud stains speak of rough and tumble

Plenty of international trips: year 7s voyage to the Château de la Baudanniére with girls from Broomwood Hall, and there's also a joint post-CE trip. There is an annual ski trip to Italy, plus outdoor pursuits and PGL. After-school clubs from the sporting to art, cooking and coding four days a week. There are termly costs for clubs that might be inclusive in other preps. This is clearly a civilised enclave: the bridge club has a waiting list.

Founded in 1993 with just 14 pupils and two teachers for traditional Broomwood Hall boarding families who preferred to send their sons to a London day prep than a boarding prep at 8 years old. The original founders, Sir Malcolm and Lady Colquhoun, remain as principals of Broomwood Hall and Northcote Lodge. Scottish notes – tartan ties, St Andrew's Day celebrations with bagpipes

– nod to the Colquhoun's Loch Lomond forbears. Parents describe boys feeling part of a family, a community and proud to do so.

Housed in a pretty Dutch-style Victorian main house set back from the road, the school entry is flight of steps into a hallway with fresh flowers, plump carpets and oil paintings of the former headmasters. Boys wear tweedy jackets, soft blue shirts and look like miniature gentlemen, but frayed cuffs and stubborn mud stains speak of rough and tumble rather than any concerns over dry-cleaning. A teacher quips that the tweed jackets are 'standard issue' as he hangs his up. Year 4 classrooms are all in a row on the glass-roofed Shell corridor. Our guide told us: 'It's a big step up coming here, most people get nervous, but after two days I loved it! It's a family school, all children mix, it's nothing to worry about'.

'Caring' is the word that crops up most often from parents when describing the atmosphere of the school: 'friendly, inclusive, caring and focused,' elaborated one. When we enquire whether houses are fiercely competitive as we have seen elsewhere the boys are slightly baffled. Parents tell us: 'There is a competitive spirit but it is one with a great comraderie'. Such is the gentleness of the boys on the whole that the school is sure they will be 'less street-wise' than their peers when arriving at boarding school, and is addressing this in the weeks following common entrance, but feels 'it's a reasonable price to pay'.

We have never been quite so wowed by beautiful and relaxed good manners as we were on this visit. Not only did the boys unfailingly hold doors open for us and each other, but spontaneously congratulated each other on recent triumphs up and down year groups, and every boy who crossed our path said 'Hello' warmly. 'Discipline and manners are paramount, which we love,' said a mother.

With so many busy, working or indeed separated parents as a part of modern life, for some boys 'stability is school,' and it sets out to provide it. Once upon a time boys paraded so many reward badges, they decorated not just their lapels but right around the back of their collars. These have gone, replaced by a simpler award for the best performance relative to peers in a week, which now seem worth winning. Some instances of bullying find their way to us, but in each instance parents report it was swiftly dealt with. The boys we spoke to genuinely seemed to regard bullying as something they learnt about but had not experienced.

Most boys live locally but there are minibuses from Fulham and Chelsea. The stats show a homogenous, white British group, less racially mixed than one would usually see in a London school. When we asked parents to describe their peers they told us: 'fantastic, friendly and really good fun... but the demographic of the school is very narrow'. Social shorthands abound: 'largely old money, a lot of red trousers but friendly and caring'; 'supportive mums who aren't alpha parents'; and 'typical nappy valley'.

'Who might this school suit?' we asked parents. 'A child who will flourish given a supportive environment. A child who enjoys team sports and is sociable'. And, perhaps the most in tune with what we saw in action: 'a very happy school where the boys seem to buzz around enjoying their childhood.' School concludes: 'Northcote can cope with quirkiness and variety; we are failing if we only fit a particular type of boy'.

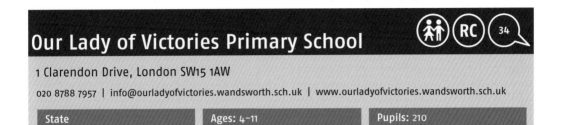

Our Lady of Victories Primary School

1 Clarendon Drive, London SW15 1AW

020 8788 7957 | info@ourladyofvictories.wandsworth.sch.uk | www.ourladyofvictories.wandsworth.sch.uk

State	Ages: 4–11	Pupils: 210

Head Teacher: Since April 2019, Anna Madden, previously interim head.

Entrance: Priority to Catholics in all categories; siblings only get preference if parents still regular worshippers. Ballot allocation decides places in inevitable event of oversubscription. Places sometimes come up in the older age groups (usually due to families moving away from London), so it's worth contacting the school for occasional vacancies.

Exit: At 11+, just over half of pupils move to popular Catholic secondary schools such as Cardinal Vaughan, The London Oratory, Sacred Heart, Ursuline High School, Wimbledon College, Gumley House. The rest go to local independents (Emanuel, Ibstock Place, Latymer, Hampton) or to Catholic boarding schools (Worth, The Oratory School, Reading and the IBVM convents).

Remarks: A first-rate primary school tucked into the residential streets of Putney, in the parish of Our Lady of Pity and St Simon Stock. Originally run by the Sisters of the Poor Servants of the Mother of God, the school was handed over to the Diocese of Southwark in 1978. Housed in the former convent (there are several modern extensions), its compact site is well kept and decorated with an array of colourful artwork by the children.

School is exceptionally well accomplished in all areas. The majority of children achieve above expected Sats levels by year 6, with everyone's progress assessed each half term. A well-balanced curriculum is delivered throughout and children achieve particularly well in maths and English. French classes from year 1. The school has won silver and gold awards in junior maths challenges.

Creative writing is strong and pupils do variety of science, history and geography projects each term. Older children practise verbal and non-verbal reasoning for the Wandsworth 11+ tests and are taught how to write timed essays.

The school has strong links with the parish. The choir sings in the church and at local care centres

The school has strong links with the parish – it celebrates a number of religious festivals and the local priest visits the school regularly. At holy communion, children process from school to church, a day rounded off with a visit to the ice cream van. The choir sings in the church and at local care centres. Music, led by a dedicated music teacher, is very strong. Lots of music lessons in school, concerts and the school's recorder group and choir attends annual Music for Youth festival. Pupils take part in the National Theatre's Primary Programme (workshops held in school and theatre visits), alongside trips to concerts and the ballet.

Impressive PE programme offers a range of sporting activities at Dover House Road playing fields and swimming at the nearby Putney Leisure Centre pool. Good range of clubs includes fencing, zumba and Latin. SENCo and visiting speech and occupational therapists supervise learning support. Regular in-house training days and some teachers attend training courses run by a school specialising in specific learning difficulties and differences.

Lots of fundraising for charity organised by the school and parents, with many of the events run by the children themselves.

Prospect House School

75 Putney Hill, London SW15 3NT

020 8780 0456 | info@prospecths.org.uk | www.prospecths.org.uk

| Independent | Pupils: 314 |
| Ages: 3-11 | Fees: £18,420 – £19,200 pa |

Head: Since September 2017, Michael Hodge BPrimEd (Rhodes), previously deputy head (since 2004). Montessori trained. Taught in London state system for eight 'wonderful' years. Either he, or a senior member of staff, greets pupils by name every morning at the front door. No longer teaches maths, which he misses, but always popping into lessons, where he invariably gets involved. When the headship came up, he saw it as an irresistible opportunity to 'take the school further.' Highly ambitious for the school. Repeatedly states that 'the children are the most important thing.' Knows close collaboration between parents, staff and pupils is fundamental to a child's success. A team player, who is well supported by strong senior management team. Greatly adored by parents and pupils alike.

South African, but after more than two decades here, his accent is almost imperceptible, though apparently resurfaces whenever the Springboks are playing. Keen cyclist and enjoys high-intensity gym classes. A dab hand at DIY. A born extrovert, full of good cheer.

Entrance: Non-selective co-ed. First come, first served. Open events two or three times a year, but bespoke tours also offered. One September intake only. School prefers children to start in nursery at 3, when there are two classes of 16. Nursery pupils need to commit to staying for two years minimum, starting with at least five mornings a week, rising to three full days or more by the summer term. All nursery children are visited in their own homes prior to arrival, followed by induction morning in summer term. Can start in reception, but only eight to 10 more places at this stage. In reception, years 1 and 2 there are 20 per class, rising to 22 thereafter. For occasional places, tests in maths, English and spelling. Must have visited school before offered a place. Sibling priority throughout.

Exit: The 11+ exam is the one part of the job that head dislikes as 'every year it becomes more and more competitive'. Pupils are now heading to schools further down the A3 than before. Vast majority to day schools. Perennial favourites include King's College, Latymer Upper, Putney High, Hampton, Kingston Grammar, St John's Leatherhead, Ibstock, Kew House, Surbiton High. 'If you're looking to leave at 7+ then this is not the school for you,' states head. 'At 11+, we support parents in choosing a school where their child will thrive.' Head speaks honestly to parents, giving them three years of data on their child.

Remarks: One of three schools in House Schools Group, along with Bassett House and Orchard House. Each has retained its distinct character but some sharing of ICT support and joint insets.

Housed in two large, former family homes. Began as a nursery in 1960s. In 2013, early years up to year 2 moved into separate site up the road, which boasts a stunning garden, complete with climbing frame, hedgehog house and place for fairies to flutter. Years 3-6 in original building. Two sites but very much one school. Both buildings possess bright, colourful classrooms with eye-catching displays.

Two identical productions of Peter Pan were staged recently, with different casts, so everyone could have a reasonable part

Two mixed ability parallel classes throughout school, which are shuffled annually. School adopts different learning styles including Montessori elements for younger pupils. French from nursery, Latin from year 5 and Mandarin post-11+. From year 3, three ability sets for maths and English.

High expectations for all. Academics are taken seriously, but learning is fun, with one class enjoying a Mad Hatter's Tea Party after studying Alice in Wonderland and lots of dressing up as Anglo-Saxons and Tudors. 'If children aren't enjoying their primary schooling then we are failing them, as life is tough enough later on,' believes head. No heavy emphasis on testing, but pupils are well prepared for 11+ when it arrives. Despite its south-west London location, definitely not a hothouse.

Everything carefully thought out, with what is best for the children at the heart of all decisions. Range of reading schemes in key stage 1 to avoid comparisons with others and to 'stop them getting hung up on one scheme'. Nursery pupils swap classrooms with parallel class regularly so they can all enjoy each other's resources. Fantastic displays in nursery, including a life-size gingerbread house. Paradise for little ones. Head of lower school, the very approachable Mrs Hudson, warmly welcomes new recruits to the Prospect 'family'.

'We do not want our children to be tutored', head tells us, though he knows it goes on. He believes tutoring is wrong if used to get a child into a school to which they are not suited.

Seven academic scholarships in 2018; regular music and sports scholarships. No scholars board despite all regular scholarships bagged. Head comments, 'What does it say to a child who isn't on the scholars' board? We're not that type of school.' Cups and prizes awarded, for traditional subjects as well as for endeavour and citizenship. 'Everybody is catered for and we celebrate that.'

Head understands that each child is different and is proud that school is targeting pupils' needs better. Approximately 45 pupils with some sort of SEND. Supports pupils with mild dyslexia, dyscalculia and dyspraxia. Children in key stage 1 requiring help with reading, phonics, fine motor skills and speech are supported in focused grouped teaching; further up the school it is maths and English. Support ranges from small group work to tackle specific areas through to longer term individual support. 'When children go for extra lessons, it is just seen as a part of their learning, not as a separate entity,' says head.

Most able academically are stretched through differentiation, extension activities such as algebra and participation in external events. Talented musician currently getting one-to-one input from head of music. School is good at encouraging children to think for themselves, question, investigate and apply what they learn. No one is allowed to rest on their laurels.

Family feel. Lots of community spirit. 'The children are polite and well-behaved, but they are not robots without any personality,' says head of lower school. Pupils do genuinely love it here and the ones we met were bright eyed and bushy tailed. One chap told us, 'The only bad thing about this school is that it ends. I wish it was my secondary school too.' Another piped up, 'The teachers are kind and friendly. They're also funny!'

Excellent, open communication with parents, from ad hoc emails to daily phone calls if needed.

Parents are encouraged to come in and talk through problems and school responds speedily to their concerns. Message books go back and forth daily, so everyone kept in loop. Staff have a daily briefing to share information on pupils so know who to keep a close eye on. Children not defined by past demeanours – 'we build on the positive.' The consequences for bad behaviour tend to be mild, such as missing 10 minutes of break. 'Not a big deal,' commented one child.

Learning is fun, with one class enjoying a Mad Hatter's Tea Party after studying Alice in Wonderland and lots of dressing up as Anglo-Saxons and Tudors

Parents feel staff are approachable, dedicated and know their offspring well. Healthy ratio of male to female teachers. No supply teachers – if a teacher is absent then other in-house teachers step in. Specialist teachers for maths, English, IT, French, music, PE, art and Latin.

Mr Hodge wants to be the kind of head that staff want to work for. He believes professional development of staff is vital and encourages an open discussion about their teaching, rather than critical appraisals. Wants them to be constantly improving their teaching as well building up their CVs, even if it means they move elsewhere as a result.

IT provision considered excellent and well-integrated into curriculum. Laptops, iPads (all years 5 and 6 have their own) and MacBooks everywhere. Homework apps. Head knows screen time can be used negatively so care is taken 'to educate them in how to use their devices properly.' Inevitably, some parents feel there is too much time spent in front of screens.

PE lessons take place at all-weather pitch onsite and gym is in hall. Pupils also use local sports facilities. Head wishes he had sprawling playing fields but knows this is the nature of inner-city schools. Sport offered includes football, netball, hockey, cricket, athletics, rounders, gym, tennis, swimming and dance. Judo, fencing and running clubs offered too. Sports day for all. Good number of matches for everyone but tournaments only for the most able. 'We do well. Football is especially strong,' states head. He expects the pupils to throw themselves into their sports and to give their best. 'You play to win. It matters, but it must not override the enjoyment of the sport,' explains head. A few parental grumbles about sport. One commented, 'It's not exactly a sporty school.' School disagrees strongly, saying 'there is a huge amount of sport both in curriculum time and after school'. Another felt the school needed to expand the sports department, and another lamented the lack of time dedicated to swimming.

Legendary director of music. Over 200 individual music lessons a week, with a diverse range of instruments though not drums. Large orchestra. Numerous ensembles: strings, woodwind, brass. Annual musicals and concerts galore. Glorious singing in evidence on the day we visited.

Two identical productions of Peter Pan were staged recently, with different casts, so everyone could have a reasonable part. Typical of Prospect House – it wants everyone to have the chance to shine in their own way. All-singing, all dancing musicals are order of the day here: Mary Poppins, Sound of Music, Oliver! and Bugsy Malone.

Vibrant art department. One art co-ordinator per key stage. Dedicated art room in upper school, complete with kiln. No exhibitions, partly as head is 'sick of asking parents to spend more money to buy their child's artwork.' Puppets being made on the day we visited, with puppet show planned. Year 6 hugely excited about clock-making in DT.

Clubs include coding, yoga, chess, puzzles, football and calligraphy. Cookery perennially popular. Weekly homework club, where children take it in turns to bring tasty morsels from home to share with the rest of the gang. Reasoning club at the top end to help with 11+ preparation. All clubs are charged for. One mother welcomed the fact that clubs are now 'crunchier' and 'more academically focused than before.'

Residential trips for all of key stage 2, starting with two nights, rising to five days for top year.

Destinations include Suffolk, Dorset and northern France. Day trips to perennial favourites: National History Museum, Hampton Court and Kew Gardens. Visits to local church to ask Vicar Ben questions about Christianity. Post 11+ programme is both fun and interesting, including a Bake-Off competition with prizes for cakes with best texture and taste, as well as sessions at the Globe, as part of a Shakespeare project.

Each site has own kitchen which provide freshly-cooked meals. Parents are delighted that packed lunches are no longer needed. Some choice at lunch 'but not masses as it encourages children to be picky eaters.' The youngest pupils were having a very jolly time at lunch on the day we visited, with plenty of chatter and empty plates all round. Smiley chef whose specialities include child-friendly dishes, including mild curry, Spanish chicken and pasta.

Mostly local professional families. Many children are bilingual, including Japanese, Spanish, Swedish and Dutch. Most become fluent very rapidly though some need support with English idioms and inference. Increasingly, dual income. No wraparound care offered which can be tricky for these working parents. 'We're working on this.' Thriving parents' association which organises Christmas fair, school discos and uniform sales.

Means-tested scholarships available for 7+ for those coming from state education. Family income must be less than £50,000. No sibling discounts.

A school that allows children to enjoy being children. Mr Hodge states, 'I want them to be happy. If they are happy, they will succeed.' He is achieving his ambition. This must be one of the most joyful schools in London.

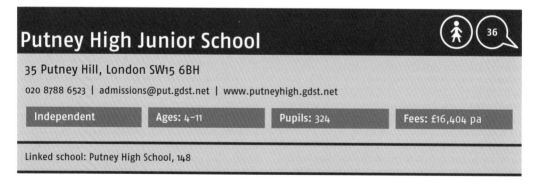

Putney High Junior School

35 Putney Hill, London SW15 6BH

020 8788 6523 | admissions@put.gdst.net | www.putneyhigh.gdst.net

Independent	Ages: 4–11	Pupils: 324	Fees: £16,404 pa

Linked school: Putney High School, 148

Head: Since 2017, Pippa Page-Roberts (40s), BEd Chichester. Previously spent 10 years at Kensington Prep as head of English, then director of innovation, so is very familiar with GDST ethos. Prior to that, stints at Kingswood School in Bath, and the Harrodian as head of English teaching years 3-9.

Half Italian and half Northumbrian, she is married with two stepchildren. Parents respond well to her approachable style, one parent saying she can imagine going out for a fun evening with her. Another parent told how, after intercepting a conversation at the school gate, the head reviewed the modern languages department.

With an eye to the senior school, she wants Putney High Junior girls to be self-directed and embrace the 'adventure of learning, hard work, fun and that it is cool to be clever.' She promotes transferable skills, 'whether they be 12th century or 21st', which she describes as collaboration, adaptability, problem solving, reflection and resilience – or 'stickability' and 'bounceback'.

She champions the power of pupil voice, asking the girls to help design an adventure playground (shortlisted for Education Business Award), encouraging their views when choosing the new uniform – as part of a rebranding exercise – and having an oracy festival for Y3 and Y4 (which they practise in the outdoor amphitheatre). A 'collaborative and democratic community' is enshrined as one of the school's six core values and, every Monday, she runs a school assembly focusing on those values.

She responds to the role of head with energy and vision. She has put in place a strong management team that includes deputy heads for both academic and pastoral. The leadership team members work together with other staff to produce a syllabus that stimulates and challenges, and an environment in which girls as young as 4 are used to being listened to properly. While cautious about revealing too much of future plans for the school, Mrs Page-Roberts is clear that there are schemes in the offing to ensure the school continues its positive trajectory. 'I want the girls to have loved this moment of their childhood,' she says.

Entrance: Age 4+ into nursery. Recently changed assessment process. Girls grouped according to birthday (max 12 in a group) overseen by six adults. There are three sessions a day, and each team sees every girl. Over 200 apply for 44 places (two classes of 22 in reception to year 2), and from Y3, four more places become available as class sizes increase to 24. Girls mainly local but some from Barnes, Sheen and Fulham, and the school will group girls from same postcode together in early years classes. No scholarships or bursaries in the junior school.

Exit: Nearly all to the senior school. The rest to boarding schools (Downe House, Cheltenham Ladies), to St Paul's or LEH, or to local schools elsewhere should the family move (eg Guildford High). Junior school girls sit entry exam to the senior school in Y5 to confirm whether have a place. Then, they all take the 11+ with the external candidates. Senior school open days familiarise the juniors with the senior school and ensure a smooth transition.

Remarks: The junior school girls benefit from sharing the senior school campus. There is a modern cafeteria, a good gym, tennis courts, a new performing arts centre, and years 3-6 have access to the DT studio. The junior school has its own all-weather adventure playground designed by the girls, to encourage risky play, an outside amphitheatre and an Astroturfed space for break times. Four go-karts sit in the corner, built from kits. The school arranges for the girls to be outdoors as much as possible, and while we were there some were busy outside the science classroom. Instead of a friendship bench, there is a Well-being Pod where girls can work in small groups or go to sort out their differences, our young guides told us.

An orator in residence works on presentation and public speaking skills, and there's an oracy festival for Y3 and Y4 (they practise in the outdoor amphitheatre)

The school building is sprawling, light and airy, and mainly Victorian with a newish wing called The Curve that houses the IT suite and the school hall alongside several classes.

Parents spoke of choosing the school for its broad syllabus. 'We liked it because it covered everything and when our daughter was 4, we didn't know what her passion would be,' said one. Year 1s were making mind maps for their creative writing work; all girls have library lessons, and reading and writing skills are covered in the history and geography syllabuses as well as English.

STEM subjects are big here, the maths department singled out for special praise by parents, and the school has recently appointed a head of e-learning who is an Apple 'distinguished educator'. From Y4, girls have their own iPads, and use both Google classroom and Firefly.

Girls are encouraged to make their voices heard. There's a gratitude wall, boxes called secret safes are placed around the school where girls can leave messages about anything that concerns them, and 'emotional barometers' in some of the classrooms help girls to monitor their emotional well-being and understand the impact it has on their learning. Staff are encouraged to take on individual research projects, and there is a CPD programme for them.

An 'orator in residence' works on presentation and public speaking skills, and parents praise the confident presentation of even shy girls, with the school putting up a team for junior Model United Nations General Assembly (MUNGA). Girls chose the names of their houses that are, somewhat predictably, Ava Lovelace, Marie Curie, Rosa Parks and Wilma Rudolph. They also select the charities for which they wish to fundraise.

Parents describe the teaching as 'exceptional'. One described her year 3 daughter learning a great deal 'but not being aware she is learning, she's just having fun.' Parents report a range of abilities and personalities. 'There is no such thing as a Putney girl,' says the head. The SENCo is part of the Learning Enrichment team, whose aim is support, stretch and challenge, and a SENCO. Parents speak of the 'tap on the shoulder' if their daughter isn't going to make it into the senior school; the head says, 'parents appreciate the honesty'

There's a strong commitment to music, with two music lessons a week, hymn practice assemblies on Tuesday, all girls sing in one of the choirs, and there's an orchestra in which 60 odd girls of grade 1 and above are members. Girls in Y5 and Y6 are encouraged to join the junior school choir that performs nationally and have an active role in choosing the annual year 5&6 musical production.

Whole afternoons of sports ranging from cricket and touch rugby to sports acrobatics, swimming and dance; they use the nearby Bank of England sports centre and Wimbledon Park.

The school offers wrap-around care with breakfast clubs from 7.30am and after school clubs until 6pm, as well has having a programme of co-curricular activities (over 70 clubs). There is an 'entrepreneur in residence', and Metro Bank comes in to talk to the girls about managing money.

They have taken part in a science conference at the Royal Institution, a maths conference at Oxford and an English conference in Howells school in Wales to celebrate Shakespeare's birthday. Girls visit parliament and go on extended trips to eg Dorset and the Isle of Wight. Children from local state schools are often invited to join in when speakers come round – this year Chris Riddell, Clare Balding and the Ocean Brothers.

There's a sense of oxygen around Putney High Junior, perhaps because of the outside space, perhaps because it is an environment curated to stretch the girls – gently but firmly. The emphasis is on developing good citizens, ambitious and unafraid of success, rather than demagogues or prima donnas. Parents love the energy of the head and her team.

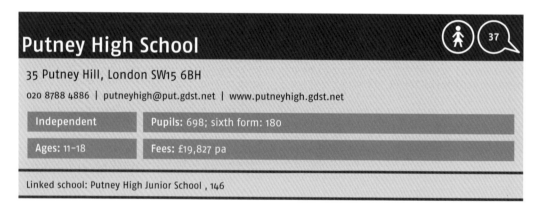

Putney High School

35 Putney Hill, London SW15 6BH

020 8788 4886 | putneyhigh@put.gdst.net | www.putneyhigh.gdst.net

Independent	Pupils: 698; sixth form: 180
Ages: 11–18	Fees: £19,827 pa

Linked school: Putney High Junior School , 146

Headmistress: Since 2015, Suzie Longstaff BA MA PGCE (late 40s), following a year as acting head and a previous six years as head of sixth. Mrs Longstaff read economics at Durham, did her PGCE at Homerton and gained an MA in education from Bath in 2015. She started her career at Shiplake teaching maths and ICT, then to Kingston Grammar as head of ICT and asst head of sixth. She joined Putney in 2009. It may be dawning on you that both her universities and all three schools are on – or virtually on – rivers and rivers all need rowers. Mrs Longstaff was Olympic cox for Team GB's women's VIII at Atlanta 1996 (her steering being described by one commentator as 'aggressive') and she has been captain of the Thames Rowing Club.

We found her warm, sparkly (on a very hot day), utterly charming, full of zest and fun and not remotely aggressive in her current role. Parents concur: 'She's brilliant.' 'She makes very good connections with both parents and girls.' 'A breath of fresh air.' 'Everyone likes her – she's open to change and very positive – and she comes to everything.' The girls echo this, describing her repeatedly as, above all, 'open' – and pay tribute to how she has made the school more relaxed. 'She walks around all the time, asking girls how they are.' We heard no dissenting voice. Mrs Longstaff is the mother of young twins who attend the school.

Internal appointments to headships are rare, can make waves and lead to choppy waters but Putney now has a keen eye on the course ahead and a steady hand on the tiller, steering with the lightest of touches.

Academic matters: Most popular and successful A level subjects are maths, biology and English Lit.

A wide range of options given this is not a huge school – economics and psychology are popular. In 2019, 70 per cent A*/A grades and 92 per cent A*-B. For GCSEs, 82 per cent 9-7 in 2019.

Innovative bilingual programme offered to native speakers of Mandarin, Spanish, French and German ie the languages taught in school. Greek, Arabic and Italian now on the timetable. Few takers of languages at A level in recent years but this now set to change as head is sticking her oar in to the somewhat becalmed waters and stirring them up with energy and commitment. 'I'd like to offer Russian too,' she says. There are now three German teachers – surely unique in a school of this size – and some truly exciting trips eg the Spanish-takers to Costa Rica – to promote these vital subjects. A school making a specialism of modern foreign languages has long been needed and Putney is set to assume the role.

Much enthusiasm for the teachers and their teaching 'style'. 'They discuss rather than teach so you want to join in,' we were told. Also for the school's flexibility when it comes to options at GCSE and A level. 'People are doing the weirdest combinations – you're allowed to do whatever you like.' 'Our daughters were not at all keen on homework but they have been inspired and now they really want to do it,' we heard, 'and even in the subjects they're not keen on!' Much praise for the very new head of careers – 'I talk to her every day,' one sixth former told us – and school has a strong offering in this area, organising a careers fair and making links with useful alumnae.

Lots of extracurricular stimulation in the form of high calibre outside speakers (Henry Marsh, AC Grayling for a start), inspirational trips and PIE – the Putney Ideas Exchange. We always like anything which celebrates ideas and this is genuinely exploratory, open-minded and, to some extent, pupil-led. Brilliant new interactive installation on the periodic table got even this science-phobe excited.

Average of 24 girls in years 7-9 classes, down to 15 for the GCSE years and around seven in the sixth form. Under three per cent have EAL needs -supported where needed. One sixth have some kind of SEN and the school has an unusually open approach. They will move classes to suit able girls with major physical disabilities if that enables them to attend and they welcome those who may need a full time LSA if that opens the curriculum to them. Mrs Longstaff's approach is, 'Great! How can we help?' and this is not just talk but borne out by the girls they have in school. Well staffed Learning Enrichment dept encompasses SEN.

Games, options, the arts: Rowing. Within a year of Mrs Longstaff's appointment, the school acquired the lease to a boathouse close to Putney bridge and now more than 125 rowers from years 8 to 13, backed by enthusiastic parents (and a pretty keen head), power up and down the Thames. But you don't have to do it, though everyone's eyes widen at the thrust given to sports since Mrs Longstaff took her seat. Unlike at many schools, here everyone gets a chance – lots of teams and a deliberate policy to delay team selection to ensure fairness for all. Some 85 per cent of them, we are told, represent the school in something that involves moving. Almost too much for some people. Some feeling that the sports staff now have too much power and girls' involvement elsewhere can suffer in a school where so much is on offer and there is so much eagerness to involve oneself in everything. Astro on site and smallish tarmacs but a few coach moments away are the main pitches and playing fields used by the school. Dance is big. Netball and lacrosse thrive and many other games and sports are on offer – acrobatics to zumba. And they win – masses. Top team GDST athletics recently.

Exceptional music. The head – prior to her rowing days – was herself a music scholar and is therefore very much in harmony with the needs of school music

Exceptional music, led inspirationally and with great success and financial investment – £30,000 recently spent on upgrading nine pianos, acquiring a baby harp and a new mobile recording studio when we visited. The head – prior to her rowing days – was herself a music scholar and, therefore is in sympathy with the needs of school music, as remarkably few are. Chamber groups win major competitions, girls leave with eg Oxbridge organ scholarships, and 'for several, grade 8 is a distant memory'. But lots of groups, choirs, ensembles of all kinds and our visit to the music centre with its many practice rooms was a not-particularly-well-sound-proofed joy. Drama similarly popular. Nice little studio theatre with battery of new lanterns and a good hall for shows. Also a delightful outdoor stage on the 'staff lawn' on which a junior production of Alice in Wonderland had just taken place – teacups lining the rim of the stage. 'We have theatre productions and concerts every two seconds,' one girl told us, quite seriously.

Impressive DT – 'someone made a really cool woven hedgehog home!' – and art: the catalogue of the sixth form art display which we just missed bore witness to genuinely original and skilful work in many media. Textiles – compulsory for half of each of the first three years – also big, popular

Putney High Junior School

and, at best, producing professional quality and highly desirable artefacts. 'There was this wonderful ballgown and someone made a leather jacket – very Alexander McQueen.' Not too much on display when we visited – not a lot of space for it – but also 'people do like to take things home'. Of course! School has all the mod cons – eg laser and 3D printers – as you'd expect – and use them with imagination and subtlety.

Latest resident, an orator (following on from orchestra, writer and entrepreneur in residence), tasked with encouraging all pupils to find their voice and communicate effectively via timetabled sessions and clubs.

Background and atmosphere: A Girls' Day School Trust (GDST) school. This one began life in 1893 – one of the latest of the many schools belonging to this venerable and highly respected organisation and, thus, relatively young, though celebrated its 125th anniversary in 2018 with, inter alia, a concert and a photograph exhibition of portraits of notable alumnae. The Trust itself celebrated its 140th anniversary in 2012 and, although each school is largely autonomous and free-standing, the features and advantages of belonging to this unique family of schools should not be overlooked – not least the attention now paid to attracting the right girls for its bursarial provision and the many opportunities now to compete against girls from sister schools in many activities.

Putney is on a compact site but clever use of space and imaginative building produces many surprises – among them the excellent sixth form centre opened by Jenny Beavan (one of its most celebrated old girls) in 2012. Study area, sixth form diner (open all day), internet cafe, outdoor balconies, huge sitting room, fitness room – few boarding schools offer more. This is an excellent resource and must be playing a major part in the school's growing success in retaining post-GCSE pupils. Opening in 2020 is a new science, music, drama and debating centre with state of the art, cross-curricular teaching facilities plus discussion and performance spaces.

Despite its relative smallness, nowhere feels cramped. Refurbished classrooms are light, pleasant spaces. All is orderly and well-maintained. Good, air-conditioned modern library with small stock in key subjects but a fast system of ordering books. Two small lawns, an excellent canteen with food everyone likes. 'I'm a vegetarian and I love it.' 'I'm seriously picky and it's great for me.' We would have been happy to stay to lunch.

Pastoral care, well-being and discipline: Parents and pupils enthuse about the new relaxed feel and the easier relationships developing both between staff and girls but also between girls in different years – fostered, in part, by a new house system. Parents

tell us of their daughters' growth in confidence and the great care and attention to detail taken by the teaching staff. 'They are very good at dealing with pupils as individuals,' we heard from several and this concurs with Mrs Longstaff's emphasis on 'individualised care'. Some sense among a few that not all staff have yet adapted to this change in culture – also, that some girls shy away from the school's 'open' take on matters to do with mental health and 'mindfulness' – but the structure and the understanding is there, if not yet fully embraced by all. 'What we need,' agrees Mrs Longstaff, 'is people opening up and engaging in a conversation.'

This is a 'busy' school – girls, parents and head repeatedly stress this. There's so much on offer and not enough time to do it all in a day school day

The staff structure is supported by a counsellor and a buddy system – year 10 girls pairing with newbies and backed up by year 11 Big Sisters – adds yet a further layer of help if needed. Discipline itself is rarely an issue – a real sense of friendliness, looking out for each other and kindness is palpable.

This is a 'busy' school – girls, parents and head repeatedly stress this. So much on offer and very little time to do it all in a day school day. But this has to be ambitious and right though it may not be easy for everyone to go with the flow. But the sense is that swimming against the tide won't work. Haul yourself onto the bank and look for the lifeguard. She'll be there.

Pupils and parents: Around 40 different home languages spoken as befits this diverse and cosmopolitan area. Most girls are white and middle class but this disguises a wider range of backgrounds and home cultures than is immediately apparent. 'Not as flashy and full of girls hopping out of 4x4s as some schools,' we were told and we agree. A down-to-earth, real world school. Parent-home connections very much fostered by Mrs Longstaff, who regularly meets representatives from the Parents' Support Association which works to pick up parental concerns or suggestions and act on them. Parents an appreciative, sensible bunch – most families living within half an hour or so, though some rather further. As one admitted, 'It's a schlep to get here but it's worth it.'

Entrance: Applications should be made online by early November of the year prior to entry via the school's website. All applicants are automatically considered for academic scholarships; music and sports require separate applications.

Vastly oversubscribed in the junior school (see separate entry.) Almost all junior school pupils move into the senior school. Some 650 external applicants for the 64 places at 11+ – the number of applicants at this level has doubled in the three years prior to our visit. They come from a vast number of preps and primaries. Exams in English and maths. Around 15 new girls come in at sixth form. They will need at least three at 8/9 at GCSE, three more at 7 and at least six at 6 including English and maths. Higher requirements for subjects to be taken at A level in some cases.

Exit: Some 90 per cent and rising now stay into the sixth form. Some go after GCSEs to eg boarding, mixed or IB schools but the number of leavers is falling – rightly. 'Quite a few left in my year and several came back, we heard.' The head doesn't bully the girls about this but 'I know ours is the best sixth form in London,' she says, endearingly. Thence to an impressive range of courses and places. Ten Oxbridge places plus four medics in 2019. Bristol, Edinburgh, Exeter and KCL also consistently popular and a good spread of subjects taken. A few now each year to US colleges, often to take courses in liberal arts. Several OG notables including Jenny Beavan – Oscar winning costume designer and

2016 GDST alumna of the year, Camilla Cavendish, Olly Grender, Nicola Hicks, Sandie Okoro, Ursula Owen, Olivia Poulet, Edina Ronay, Elizabeth Symons, Melanie Phillips, Sophie Raworth, Pippa Greenwood, Jemima Rooper, Madeleine Wickham (novelist Sophie Kinsella), Anita Corbin (who took the portrait photos for the 125th anniversary exhibition). And mostly a thoroughly worthwhile, sensible and unpretentious bunch of women.

Money matters: GDST scholarships in academic, music and sports at 11+. Academic worth up to 50 per cent of fees. Sixth form scholarships in art, academics, sports, music, drama and design. Unique travel and science scholarship open only to internal candidates. The GDST now has a substantial bursary pot and this money is not always used up each year. If your daughter is bright or talented but the full fees are beyond your means it's well worth looking into it. NB Bursaries are means-tested annually.

Remarks: A good all-round school with an enthusiastic staff and a top quality head. 'Openness' now palpable in the faces and relationships, and working its way through the school. Putney is no longer the also-ran of the London GDST schools. Under Mrs Longstaff, we feel, this school has caught the tide and is beginning to set the pace.

Reay Primary School

Hackford Road, London SW9 0EN

020 7735 2978 | admin@reay.lambeth.sch.uk | www.reay.lambeth.sch.uk

State	Ages: 3–11	Pupils: 250

Headteacher: Since 2014, Caroline Andrews BEd from Sheffield Hallam (early 40s). Taught at Chaucer Junior from 1996-2000, then at Wix Primary where she became ICT leader, followed by deputy then co-head. Established the first state French/English bilingual school along with French Lycée. Made head here in 2014. Hails from Nottingham. Husband works in TV. Has a young son at another school as she feels 'it wouldn't be fair for him to come here, with me as head.' Most of her spare time is spent socialising with family and friends. Travels to far-flung destinations as often as possible. Keen gardener and enjoys cooking, which she finds therapeutic. Parents are big fans. 'Down-to-earth,' according to one. 'She's brought a new lease of life to the school,' said another. Welcoming and friendly.

Entrance: School, rather than Lambeth, is now responsible for own admissions, so children in nursery are more likely to gain a place in reception than was the case previously, 'though there is still no guarantee as we have 30 places in reception and 40 in nursery.' Waiting list in operation for occasional places further up the school. 'When pupils leave, we can now move more quickly to fill the place,' says head. Oversubscribed: roughly six applicants per place.

Exit: Small minority goes down the fee-paying route, and those that do usually favour Alleyn's or Dulwich College. Popular state destinations include Graveney, Lambeth Academy and London Nautical. 'We invite secondary schools to come and talk to parents at the end of year 5, and then again before parents need to make the final decision in year 6,' explains head. After-school tutoring delivered by class teachers if requested, prior to 11+ exams. 'We do have a discussion with parents if we think the school they want is not right for their child, though. We don't want the children to be put under excessive pressure. They are well-supported and well-extended here anyway, so most would get places without tutoring in any case,' believes head.

Remarks: Three-quarters of pupils come from ethnic minority groups. Half speak English as an additional language. 'Though for very few is this a barrier to their learning. It's more of an asset,' states head. Nearly 50 per cent are eligible for pupil premium funding, much higher than national average. Most live less than 400 metres away. 'We have a hugely mixed intake. Some are from the high-rise blocks opposite and others live in million pound properties,' comments head. Very high attendance rate.

Housed in a purpose-built, high ceilinged Victorian building in the heart of Lambeth. A surprisingly peaceful oasis in this ultra-urban location. Great sense of space throughout. Huge double classrooms abound with plenty of room for breakout activities. Recently converted library with doors opening onto a courtyard where year 6 pupils can be found reclining on beanbags, devouring books on sunny afternoons. Separate playgrounds for different year groups, complete with a climbing wall and quiet area.

Head is confident that pupils' varying needs are identified quickly and that children do not fall through the net – 'that's the beauty of a one form entry school.' All classrooms have at least one additional adult on hand.

Learning is fun here and pupils were all full of beans on the day we visited. Much learning is done through project work, from nursery upwards. Shakespeare was being studied when we visited and one pupil was writing painstakingly with a quill pen and ink. Homework involves reading, spelling and times tables until year 5. 'Then,' says head, 'we up the ante, with past papers and test preparation. We believe that the children are so busy at school and are offered so many extracurricular activities that homework doesn't add much before that, especially in homes where English is not the first language.' Spanish taught from reception, with art and DT also taught in Spanish.

Pastoral care is a definite strength. 'We take mental well-being very seriously,' says head. School places great emphasis on outdoor learning in its beautiful nature garden, which includes a parent-built greenhouse, a tree-house, a pond for frogs and a bug hotel. Bluebells and blossom were in abundance on the day we visited, making it appear totally magical. One area is set aside for digging and another for making mud pies. Each class grows fruit and vegetables, including strawberries, tomatoes and lettuce. 'The garden is an area where children can get dirty and appreciate nature. Some children otherwise do not get an opportunity to play outside in this way,' explains head. She believes this area helps those who struggle to communicate, as some find it easier when busy in the garden. Weekly mentoring sessions also put on by local charity to help pupils build their social and emotional skills through activities and sport. One parent we spoke to said, 'Everybody looks out for each other here. The bigger kids look out for the smaller kids. The children nurture each other as much as the teachers do!' One parent mentioned an incident of bullying but was full of praise for the speed with which the school stepped in.

School places great emphasis on outdoor learning. Its beautiful nature garden includes a parent-built greenhouse, a tree-house, a pond for frogs and a bug hotel

School can support a range of special needs, particularly emotional, behavioural and social difficulties. Thirty-nine on special needs register and five currently have an Education, Health and Care plan. Most classrooms are on ground floor so easy accessibility for those with physical disabilities. Learning mentor offers one-to-one support for those who are need it, either socially or academically. She also supports families and makes home visits if required. Extra language assistance given to those who do not have English as their first language. Dyslexia screening available from year 2 onwards, as and when required rather than as a whole year group. Plenty of workshops for gifted and talented pupils and extra maths sessions laid on by local secondary schools. Art therapist and speech and language therapist regularly visit.

'We try to broaden their horizons through art, music and drama,' comments head. Gold Artsmark awarded in recognition of rich arts opportunities here. 'Children like the freedom of art and we want them to enjoy it. We value it as teachers,' explains head. Music is also an important part of life at Reay. Year 3 pupils learn recorder, year 4 the ukulele and year 5 has a class orchestra, with pupils playing instruments ranging from violins and double bass to saxophones. Some subsidised individual music lessons offered in top two years. Performances put on for parents, including at the Albert Hall. No choir at the moment though head stresses 'we have a lot of singing so the whole school feels like a choir.' Annual nativity play led by year 2 and a pantomime by year 6.

School has an all-weather sports pitch where children play cricket, netball, football and hockey. All year groups swim from year 2 onwards. Running club takes place in a nearby park. Pupils compete in local tournaments and participate in cricket schemes at the Oval. Extra sport laid on before, during and after the school day including yoga in French and basketball in Spanish. 'We have lots of space both outdoors and in the studio for sport and dance. We are very lucky,' says head. One parent we spoke to, however, felt that 'sport is challenge. I wish they did more. I feel like my son could certainly do with more of a run around than he gets.' Good range of after-school clubs from cooking and coding to street dance, run by a mixture of outside providers and in-house staff.

Wraparound care offered before and after school, so pupils can be looked after for over 10 hours a day. Breakfast club from 7.30am, with toast and cereal galore. 'Lots of us on the staff are working parents so we appreciate the need for a longer day,' says head. Reay pupils can also enjoy holiday provision at a neighbouring school.

Pungent aroma of fish and chips emanating from the dining room on the day we visited. Children have a choice of salads as well as fresh fruit and vegetables. Some take in packed lunches. Herbs grown in the school garden are used in the stuffing at Christmas lunch. Head hopes more of their garden produce can make its way onto the children's plates.

Trips aplenty to theatres, parks and sports venues. Residential trips for year 4 to Kent (along with pupils from other local schools) and year 6 spends four nights in France. Parents pay, but school subsidises trips as does the PTA. Whole school ventures merrily, in a long line of coaches, to a Sussex beach every summer term. 'We take picnics and it's absolutely lovely, though exhausting. Parents come too,' enthuses head.

A family-orientated school. Specialist sessions organised for parents on topics including how to support their children with speech development. Many parents volunteer at the school. Some give talks to older children about careers. 'Most parents are very supportive. We have an open-door policy and encourage parents to come in and sort out problems promptly. It makes life a lot easier,' explains head. She also stands at the gate every morning and afternoon so parents can bend her ear about any issues then. Active PTA that puts on regular events, including summer and winter fairs and a school disco. Communication with parents has improved recently.

A very friendly school, where kindness and good manners are considered important. 'We place an emphasis on the joy of childhood here. We want the children to work hard but also to enjoy their time at Reay,' says head. 'The children are proud of their school and we are very proud of them.' A happy, caring environment.

The Roche School

11 Frogmore, London SW18 1HW

020 8877 0823 | admissions@therocheschool.co.uk | www.therocheschool.com

Independent	Pupils: 291
Ages: 2.5-11	Fees: £11,970 – £15,690 pa

Principal: Since 2010, Vania Adams (50s). Another example of the educational gene with both her siblings university lecturers, she worked in broadcasting and publishing but decided to swap the office for the classroom. She still teaches 11+ English and loves 'getting stuck in' but also 'pops into' classes to spread her love of reading. She is also heavily involved in the annual production for the Shakespeare Schools Foundation, a major feature in the school's calendar. A warm, articulate, approachable woman with whom her pupils are totally at ease, this is definitely a carrot not stick headmistress.

She has taken over from the founders Carmen and James Roche but their influence and involvement, both in the governance of the school and the day to day (Dr Roche was helping one of the pupils when we visited), is still very apparent. According to parents the school is 'more organised and professional since VA's arrival but she has not changed its spirit.'

Entrance: The majority into nursery (24 children) here or their other nursery Keswick House (up to 50 children) or else into reception. There is a waiting list at 2 for both nurseries and the system is first come, first served but you can't jump the gun by a pre-natal move. Three reception classes with siblings automatically offered places. They are able to manage the full range of learning difficulties, provided that the child will be able to cope within the school's framework, and also EAL children if they are confident that they will catch up with their year group. The odd place on offer higher up the school, often attracting children who have not flourished elsewhere, as the head is very sympathetic to those who may have been the victims of an academic 'chuck out' policy and regards it as a challenge – result, a great success rate at 11+. A very flexible approach to bursaries, particularly for those already in the school, and there is a special pot so that no child misses out on a school trip or expedition.

Exit: The leavers' list can feature dozens of schools, explains the head, as they aim to ensure a good range of offers. In 2018, Emanuel, Streatham & Clapham High School, King's College Wimbledon and Wimbledon High were amongst those top of the list but there was a particularly wide range, from Eton to local grammar schools. A satisfactory number of scholarships including four to Dulwich College. VA says that she makes a huge effort to 'manage parental expectations', starting in year 4, 'encouraging parents to trust us'.

Remarks: In a tiny corner of London off the Wandsworth end of Putney Bridge Road and close to the river, you might easily miss the unassuming white façade with its discreet plaque. This is definitely not one for the parent who wants to expound on the glamorous outside facilities of their child's prep school but, once inside, an Aladdin's cave of educational possibilities opens up. Undoubtedly a small cave, but every inch has been used, including a booth for a front office that only functions because of the tangible goodwill of the people working there. All possible display spaces are commandeered for colourful mobiles, crammed notice boards and words of wisdom.

The nursery, housed looking onto a modest playground, contains puzzlers who look up politely and pirates who are too engrossed in their adventures to notice a strange visitor. One tidy tot puts away her toy on a shelf whilst a cheerful boy digs messily for treasure in a fake blue sea, all encouraged by smiley, qualified staff. Forest school is also part of the curriculum, taking place in Wimbledon Park or occasionally in more rural Richmond Park where one small, wise person pointed out to the teacher that the mushrooms were 'yellow, so they're probably poisonous'.

Once up the stairs (no barrier for one small girl moving up from nursery to reception: 'I'm going to do this on my own'), you find yourself in what is palpably the heart of the school. This is a space dominated by a library (complete with two librarians, albeit stuffed into a very small corner) and surrounded by classrooms with eight to 10 pupils in each, all heavily involved in either maths or English. The numbers are small because they group them in these subjects from year 1 although it is a flexible system and pupils move up and down regularly to make sure that the pace is correct for each child and extra support is available if necessary. The library is well stuffed with classics and modern authors, unsurprisingly, as reading is a 'big thing' with reading diaries, voluntary Book Club and even participation with 10 other schools in Battle of the Books.

We were treated to the whole of year 6's rendition of Leonard Cohen's Hallelujah, nearly reducing one not particularly religious GSG hack to tears

The top floor holds the multi-purpose hall and, although a non-denominational school, we were treated to the whole of year 6's rendition of Leonard Cohen's Hallelujah (complete with majorly enthusiastic synchronised waving), nearly reducing one not particularly religious GSG hack to tears but which, on a more positive note, had been the winner at the Woldingham Choir festival. The room also metamorphoses into the dining hall, served by a miniscule kitchen, a source of worry to one pupil who wished that chef had more room to work in. Year 6 lives up here too, engaged on our visit in a Philosophy for Children class on religion; lower down the school P4C is incorporated into topics in history, geography and RE.

To expand the space available they lease a building just down the road which now holds year 5, a surprisingly large art room, two music rooms and an extremely popular (high on the list of 'best things' when we asked) gym run by a physically imposing, newly promoted head of games. In an ideal world, the head would like this building to belong to the school and she is in talks about the possibilities of expansion, not that she wants more pupils, simply more room for them to occupy. However, as one parent remarked, 'although it is rather cramped and chaotic with children charging around, there must be a system as it all works'.

Games have been moved up a rung recently and parents notice that there have been improvements in both standards and the quality of the teaching, with netball fielding particularly successful teams and an original initiative making sport gender free (girls can choose rugby and boys netball if they so wish). Sport meets charity with Run For Us in Wandsworth Park which all take part in, including the head, who would normally prefer a good book or an exciting new play. Extracurricular clubs also feature sport as well as everything from carpentry to cooking to chess, which has a huge fan club.

It was a very nasty surprise to all concerned when the school was downgraded by Ofsted. Parents were uniformly 'astonished and shocked' and it would appear that the inspector was more than somewhat unprofessional in her approach, only squeezing in minutes observing lessons.

Nevertheless, VA accepts that there were some areas where improvement could be made and has brought forward the appointing of new legal and financial governors and a new early years co-ordinator. The rebuttal to the findings has to be the high regard in which parents (nearly 80 wrote testimonials for Ofsted after the event) hold the school and the three-fold increase in the sign up for places in 2019.

We simply wish that schools like this, where children hug the headmistress and the more academic move on to starry academic senior schools, had been around when we were young. The Roche Approach (Respect, Open-mindedness, Compassion, Humour and Effort), which might sound a tad jingoistic elsewhere, seems to be working beautifully.

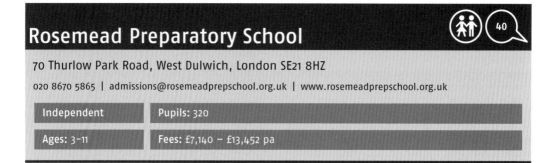

Rosemead Preparatory School

70 Thurlow Park Road, West Dulwich, London SE21 8HZ

020 8670 5865 | admissions@rosemeadprepschool.org.uk | www.rosemeadprepschool.org.uk

Independent	Pupils: 320
Ages: 3–11	Fees: £7,140 – £13,452 pa

Headmaster: Since 2017, Philip Soutar BEd, previously headmaster of St Wystan's School in Derbyshire, and before that deputy head at Ackworth Junior School. Degree from Exeter; main subject areas are science, PE (he's a golfer) and drama (interests include musical theatre and amateur dramatics), and has taught in junior and senior schools. Married to Lisa, a primary music specialist at Dulwich Prep London; they have two children.

Head of the pre-prep since 2005, Mary-Elizabeth Everitt BEd Goldsmiths College (40s). She started in the state sector, before teaching for 14 years at Dulwich Prep London. Friendly and quietly spoken, she is focused and clearly made of steely stuff.

Entrance: Describes itself as 'mixed ability'. Children may enter the nursery when they are two and a half; at 4+ into reception or at 7+ into year 3. Sometimes a few occasional places available at the prep. Assessments begin the November prior to entry, with a 90-minute informal play session for the nursery or reception entry and English and maths exercises for years 1-6.

Means-tested bursary scheme with no limit on numbers. No scholarships. Maximum class size is 22 in the pre-prep and 20 in the prep. No strict sibling policy, but will be taken into account. Unless your family is of Von Trapp proportions, the discount for four or more siblings is unlikely to assist you.

Exit: Pupils exit at 11+, with the school aiming to leave choices 'wide open'. We sense determined parents, as children make three applications on average, for which they are prepared with one-on-one interviews as well as practice papers. St Dunstan's the most popular destination currently (12 places in 2019, six with scholarships), then Streatham & Clapham High School, Alleyn's School and Trinity School. Improved numbers both in places offered and number of awards, particularly academic, art and sport (26 scholarships overall in 2018 and 20 in 2019).

Remarks: A traditional curriculum ticks all boxes, but there is modernising afoot, which is going down well. The school cites updating the texts used in English, and in maths a new online tutor sets tasks at an appropriate level for each child, 30 minutes in class and 30 minutes at home each week, with parents able to dip in any time online to see how they are doing.

A carefully thought through decision to switch from the traditional French to the more globally relevant Spanish has been pretty universally accepted and lessons have been doubled to twice a week. Spanish commences in the pre-prep with singing, stories and movement. History, geography and science have also been overhauled. Recent ICT facilities include class sets of Chromebooks and interactive screens. Humanities are supported by a wide array of trips, and highlights of the year are cross-curricular theme days and celebrations.

Reporting now looks at core skills such as concentration and organisation skills, as well as subject-specific scoring, all of which can be far more useful than a paragraph of commentary.

Some 18 per cent of staff in place for more than 10 years. Not a high turnover, but there is now one male teacher per year group at the prep. Reports from some parents are not spotless – but others impress upon us the warm atmosphere between staff and pupils.

With three classes per year in the prep, the class groupings sometimes change after year 3, once teachers have been able to assess how children work together. This can be a tad unpopular, as it isn't necessarily about friendship groups. However, classes are fixed by year 5. Setting for maths from year 3.

The anti-bullying policy has been carefully reviewed, with a buddy scheme throughout the school and year 6 visiting to read to the younger ones, and sharing special assemblies such as that for Chinese New Year.

Learning support, termed enrichment, has six staff, two of them full time, with one-to-one support for just under 10 per cent of the school. Very small number with EAL.

The fenced playground, high up above the street, is the venue for learning a variety of ball skills. Years 1 to 6 have a weekly PE lesson, a swimming lesson and a full games afternoon. There are two male PE teachers, and a female director of PE. With children taken to nearby Dulwich sports club and Rosendale playing fields for football, hockey, netball, rugby, tennis, cricket and athletics and making use of Crystal Palace's national training facilities for swimming from year 3, one parent commented, 'It's a small school with minimum on-site sports facilities, but they seem to offer a lot and children don't know or care that the sports grounds aren't owned by the school.' Rosemead regularly has children taking part at the ISA finals, both as individuals and in teams, and recently competed at national level in football.

Parents say, 'Children work hard, concentrate and give of their best.' And our visit backs this up. The atmosphere was calm and industrious, perhaps particularly due to year 6 exams looming.

How high pressure is it? A parent who has had three children through the school reported: 'I think Rosemead gets the balance right – one of the reasons we chose it... the amount of homework is about right, more than your average state primary, but not as much as some of the more high pressure private schools in the area.'

Parents commented to us in no uncertain terms that art has been a real weak spot in the past, but we visited the large, recently dedicated art studio and saw the specialist teacher in action – a highly talented former assistant from the pre-prep praised by staff and parents. The school now employs a local artist to take groups for sketching and painting, and pupils have been awarded large numbers of art scholarships to senior schools in the last few years.

The prep has more than its fair share of violinists, as all year 1 at the pre-prep learn violin in groups. Some 150 children have individual instrumental tuition, with several reaching grade 5 by year 6. There is a large school orchestra and two school choirs; ensemble clubs for cello, brass, strings and recorder; and an 'electric fusion band' which plays at the annual Dulwich Festival. A musical highlight is the major concert at the end of the spring term. One parent commented on the 'superb Christmas carol service in local church... very impressive'.

The pretty purple uniforms are a delight, but the stand-out feature of the pre-prep is the charming church building, sympathetically developed to create high ceilinged classrooms

Clubs – morning, lunch-time and after-school – offer mainly sporty and musical options, with a good show of language clubs for Spanish, French and Russian. Increasingly, this is a school for working parents and the school is well set up to offer a full day from 8am to 6pm.

Recently completed year 6 classrooms, together with a new library, bigger dining hall and ICT suites, stood out. Meanwhile, at the time of our visit, downstairs everything looked a bit shabby and utilitarian.

What will hold the school together as well as the head are the parents. Already established as an independent school for 70 years, in 1975 a group of parents took over the managing of the school and it became a limited company with an all-parent management team. It is now a non-profit making charitable trust.

Notable and somewhat off-putting is the location on the edge of Dulwich – a bit of a no-man's land on the traffic-heavy South Circular road – however, we did note that once inside we could not hear the traffic and the location between two overground stations is convenient for commuting quickly into town. The prep was actually a rehearsal space for the Old Vic theatre, hence the school hall resembling a proper theatre complete with fixed stage.

Two-thirds of families live close by, often walking to school; the rest come from all over south London, some from as far as Bromley and Elephant and Castle. This is a school for active parents who want to get involved – fundraising isn't just for external charitable projects but for valuable extras around the school. Talking of active, a team of Rosemead mothers recently rowed the Channel.

The school reports being bowled over by the response to their appeals for help: turning a piece of waste ground into a sunny little allotment for the pre-prep over the weekend, or creating a rota of volunteer librarians for the new prep library. All of which builds a real sense of community. Parents are a mixed and reportedly friendly crowd – we certainly saw gaggles lingering post drop-off – but particularly evidenced by the Easter family ski trip, which is not just for pupils but unusually everyone:

parents, siblings, grandparents, old boys and girls and their families too.

The pretty purple uniforms are a delight, but the stand-out feature of the pre-prep is the charming church building, sympathetically developed to create high ceilinged classrooms, with beautiful arches and bits of stained glass – a lovely space in which to work.

The pre-prep has assistants in every class and high staff ratios in the nursery. School commences in earnest at reception with some parents wishing for a greater emphasis on play: 'hardly any toys in the classroom, much like year 1'. Reception is very different in feel to the boisterous fun we saw in the nursery, but the head points out the gentle start with just 20 minutes of phonics a day compared with an hour in year 1.

It seems to be different things to different families – the pre-prep's church building brings back fond memories for some parents of what a first school should be like; more pragmatically, it could well be a port in a storm when faced with the ultra-competitive local options at 4+.

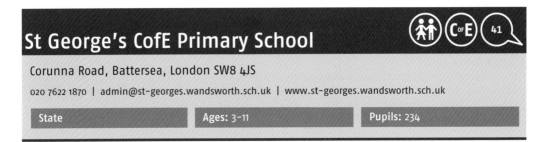

St George's CofE Primary School

Corunna Road, Battersea, London SW8 4JS

020 7622 1870 | admin@st-georges.wandsworth.sch.uk | www.st-georges.wandsworth.sch.uk

| State | Ages: 3-11 | Pupils: 234 |

Headteacher: Since 2015, Sarah Collymore (mid 30s); BA in primary education from Northumbria University. Went straight into teaching at 21 at a school local to her in Newcastle, but then decided to come to London with a friend and never looked back: 'We visited at Easter to view some schools – St George's being one of them. I rocked up one day and 12 years later, I'm still here.' Hired initially as a teacher in early years, at the same time as her predecessor Janet Hilary (former head) – this irrepressible duo took the school from special measures and on the verge of closure to Ofsted outstanding.

A Geordie lass who oozes warmth and likeability – the kind-natured, sincere head that every school should have. Dedication for 'her' children is tangible, and she is clearly popular with both parents and pupils alike – a few of whom came up to her in the playground whilst we were there to congratulate her on her new post as head. If one great head was going to leave, she was the only other

person for the job and the only one with enough experience to drive the school forward. And this is where she plans to stay: 'If you have the will and desire to serve a community that is where you stay. There is no question that my work is where what I do will make a difference.'

Mrs Collymore has been described as 'an outstanding teacher' in all the phases of primary education she has worked – from early years through to key stage 2, then to deputy head prior to becoming head. One parent told us: 'I feel very confident in Mrs Collymore's ability to lead the school.' Married with one stepdaughter (her husband runs an exclusion unit in a large secondary comprehensive), she laughed when asked what she does in her 'spare' time.

The passion and pure dogged determination that former head Janet Hilary put into the school cannot be overlooked. She clearly left an indelible mark on both the pupils and parents who we spoke to. One parent told us: 'I chose this school because I was aware of Mrs Hilary's work before becoming head of St George's, and I knew how she worked. Her skill was that she pulled parents and teachers together.' However, after 12 years in the post, Mrs Hilary felt it was time to move on and embrace other challenges. She was appointed executive principle for Floreat Wandsworth and Floreat Brentford, 'an opportunity I couldn't turn down.' But she did very much plan to stay in touch with St George's and maintain a close partnership with Mrs Collymore: 'We are the No 1 Ladies' Leadership Team after all!'

Entrance: After the customary priority for looked-after children, 50 per cent of the school places are offered for church attendance, mostly from the local St George's Church, although some have come from further afield. One parent told us she travels in from Brixton. 'I wanted my child to go to this school, so I drive him there every day.' The remaining half of the school's intake are siblings followed by distance, although alarmingly we were told that being on the same road doesn't guarantee a place: 'Because there are so many tall blocks, some of those residents won't get a place.' Cohort is predominantly eastern European/Russian, Caribbean, West African, South Asian, and an increasing proportion of South American pupils. A large majority comes from single parent families: 'Diversity is very healthy for us. It enriches us all.'

Exit: The largest share goes to the local comprehensive St Cecilia's CE, followed by St John Bosco RC, a new voluntary aided college. Other local comprehensives include Ark Putney Academy, Southfields Academy and Lambeth Academy. If you have a girl, Lady Margaret – 'virtually impossible to get in to' – as well as Grey Coat Hospital ('if it's good enough for the [ex-] prime minister...') are the schools of choice. One parent did say that she worries about the lack of decent secondary school education in the area, 'but try not to worry about it yet.' However, the head remains positive about the regeneration of the area and the new demographic buying into these properties. She says: 'I believe that in two years we'll have a secondary school of choice on the patch.' Recently, for the first time in the school's history, one of their students was awarded a scholarship to Dulwich College, and has since become something of a legend in the school – a source of huge aspiration for the other pupils. The head told us: 'Nothing can come close to the feeling you get when a child from the Patmore Estate in south London tells you that they are going to Dulwich College and will study to become a heart surgeon.'

Remarks: Set amidst the Patmore and the Savona estates in Battersea, dwarfed by the numerous regeneration projects in the area (most notably Battersea Power Station and Nine Elms construction, which is right next door) and tucked away at the end of a residential street, this small one form primary school could be easily overlooked. Indeed we almost walked past it, which would've been a shame, as this wholly unpretentious school is quite a hidden gem.

The small, but stunningly immaculate and colourful garden which acts as a centrepiece for the school offers pupils the opportunity to sit and read or reflect

Over the past four years, standards of attainment achieved by the school have been among the highest in the country, and its progress measures puts it in the top five per cent of schools. This year alone the school received two ministerial congratulations: for the phonics results (100 per cent) and for being one of the highest achieving schools in the country in terms of attainment and progress.

For any primary school this would be a major achievement, but for a school where the proportion of pupils eligible for free school meals is well above average, and nearly 60 per cent of the intake comes from homes where English is not a first language (32 languages spoken at the school), the sheer ambition cannot be underestimated.

The school's motto, 'The best we can be', is not a useless platitude, but something that they really aspire to for every child. As the head told us, 'We teach our children dignity and respect and teach them to come to school ready to learn'. No time is wasted in helping and encouraging children who speak other languages at home to begin to speak standard English; 'language is our bedrock because of where the different parents come from.' In reception, children are 'spellbound during phonics sessions by the teacher's funny hat, the silly songs they sing to keep them all on task and by the praise they are constantly given for their hard work. Phonics lessons are consequently a joy, and filled with giggling, gleeful responses' – Ofsted.

Teaching generally very impressive and children we saw were well behaved and enthralled in what they were being taught. Innovative use of teaching staff to create small, focused teaching groups in years 5 and 6 has been highly successful, and means that no pupil is left behind, and all are able enjoy high levels of challenge in English and maths. Each class has one teacher and one designated teaching assistant, in order to free up one of them to give individual help to any struggling pupils. 'It's important to spend time with a pupil if they don't get it, before they become disengaged.' Fairly high turnover of staff because of promotion elsewhere. 'Being a one form entry, it is hard to promote staff at St George's, but as we're diligent with our funding, we never have a shortfall.'

Those with special educational needs progress exceptionally well because the assessment and understanding of their needs is finely tuned. Former head said: 'I find it difficult to believe that when I started here, apparently 72 per cent of pupils had special needs. Now there are 12 per cent. I believe too often children are labelled as special needs if they are underachieving.'

The school's motto, 'The best we can be', is not a useless platitude, but something that they really aspire to for every child

Statistics and academia aside, the first thing that struck us on entering the school was how very serene it was. Nobody spoke in loud voices and staff almost glided to their various destinations – we could virtually hear a pin drop outside the classrooms we visited. Evidently, much thought has been given into making this school a calm, inviting and safe haven for pupils – the antithesis to many of their lives. The small, but stunningly immaculate and colourful garden which acts as a centrepiece for the school ('there are around 15 goldfinches in the gardens and we grow our own rhubarb and strawberries') offers pupils the opportunity to sit and read or reflect – and the dinner hall has been designed to overlook these gardens. This is all part of the Calm School Code ethos, which everyone is expected to adhere to.

The second thing that struck us (as we too glided from classroom to classroom on account of the very shiny floors) was how immaculate the classrooms were and how pupils demonstrated such pride in all aspects of their schooling, from their beautifully laminated workbooks (with some exceptional examples of joined up handwriting from the lower year groups), to their pristinely turned out selves in their smart navy uniforms with tied back or braided hair. As one parent said, 'The school is pretty strict on uniform, but that is because they don't want anyone to stick out.'

Very little wall space seems to be taken up by specific topic work but instead by an assortment of learning aids – phonics, maths, famous quotes, charts etc. One wall was virtually made up of aspirational charts. Pupils can belong to the 144 Club (children need to know all their times tables up to 12 and recall them quickly), the 20-20 Club for years 1, 2 and 3 etc etc. Perhaps the most prestigious of all of these is the Superstar award. It is the responsibility of each class team to encourage as many children as possible to become Superstars. All classrooms must have the 'HAPPY' chart (an acronym for homework, attitude, punctuality, participation, yourself)) on display and must demonstrate all aspects of HAPPY to receive their badge. Teachers are responsible for talking to parents about how they can support with any of these areas. At the end of each term the children who have been awarded their Superstar badge receive a reward. Autumn term – Christmas movie at the local cinema. Spring term – party and disco. Summer term – trip to Chessington.

Aspiration seeps through the very foundations of this school, from the extremely well stocked and well looked after library to weekly maths assemblies (where certificates are awarded to pupils who have completed maths challenges) – through to enrichment days at local independent schools such as Newton Prep, where years 4 and 5 get to use the facilities and are taught art, music, sport, science etc by specialist teachers. Some lucky pupils have enjoyed a trip to nearby Chelsea Football Club where strong links have been forged, whilst others sat in amongst the musicians of the Orchestra Vitae. One parent told us: 'Credit to the leadership team at this school for encouraging our children so much that they want to achieve, and then achieve more.'

Breakfast club on offer from 8.15am and after-school care offered until 6pm. A wide range of after-school clubs including dance, cooking, zumba, football, karate, tennis, choir and gardening. Participation in sporting competitions including athletics, cricket, golf, netball and basketball, and swimming lessons offered from year 4.

This is a proactive school in every conceivable way – no opportunity is left untapped. Instead of being bah humbug about the extensive building work in the area, the school has seized the opportunity to work with the architects, designers and builders on the Nine Elms Regeneration Project – and even managed to secure a substantial donation from its developers for a brand new all-weather sports pitch and art classroom.

If this wasn't enough, the school has set up a programme of motivational speakers for the older children and thus far the likes of Baroness Scotland, Sir William Atkinson and broadcaster Julie Etchingham have all come to speak at St George's. The head says: 'We want our pupils to have ambition and aspiration and this programme really helps them to think about careers and life choices.' Generous donations and sponsorship have also provided many rich opportunities for the pupils, including seaside trips (many pupils never having been to the seaside), theatre trips and funding for the new school uniform.

Unspoilt and wonderfully refreshing, the pupils we spoke to talked of becoming chartered accountants, vets, footballers and comedians. What came through were spirited, happy children with big personalities and a real sense of ambition. One particular pupil who was touchingly wise beyond his years, just seemingly so grateful for being at this school: 'I just wish there was a St George's secondary school for us to go to.'

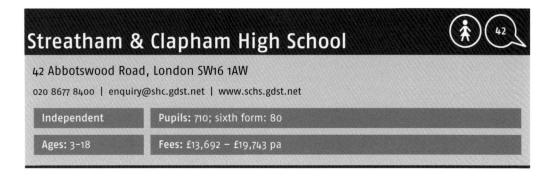

Streatham & Clapham High School

42 Abbotswood Road, London SW16 1AW

020 8677 8400 | enquiry@shc.gdst.net | www.schs.gdst.net

Independent	Pupils: 710; sixth form: 80
Ages: 3–18	Fees: £13,692 – £19,743 pa

Head master: Since 2012, Dr Millan Sachania MA (Cantab) MPhil PhD (40s). Former comprehensive student who gained a double first and a doctorate in musicology at Cambridge and then stayed on as a music tutor for five years before acquiring a PGCE at Kingston University. After stints as head of music at a girls' school in Windsor and deputy head at Immanuel College in Bushey, was delighted to accept this post. 'Are you married?' we asked. 'Yes, to my piano'.

Parents praise his 'phenomenal attention to detail'. One told us he was 'not an obvious choice, but perfect', while another reckoned 'we are lucky to have him'. Other parental comments include 'definitely an individual', 'quirky', 'incomparable' and 'probably just what we needed but not everyone's cup of tea'. The girls seem to love him – 'even though he uses words we've never heard before'. Has a 'rescued' Bechstein grand piano in his study, which they are definitely allowed to tinker on.

Dr Sachania is amazed by the energy of both the school and the girls, which he feels derives from their cultural diversity. Impressed with their intelligence and really wants them to broaden their horizons and achieve beyond their potential 'across the width of endeavour'. Says he has an holistic approach and doesn't believe that pupils should obsess about being competitive with each other. He wants each girl to find her own forte and achieve her own personal best.

Has shortened lessons – 'shorter equals sharper and if necessary lessons can become double'. The sixth form, which is in a separate building, now has its own popular café area while a small lecture theatre is used for a variety of activities, from musical recitals to the once-a-week head master's lecture period.

Head of prep since 2015, Thomas Mylne (40s), previously deputy head of the Gatehouse School in east London. BA from the University of Brighton and PGCE from the Institute of Education; he has also taught at an east London primary school and been deputy head (curriculum) at Wimbledon High Junior School. Interests include cinema, travel, music and cycling; he is married (his wife works in publishing) with two daughters.

Academic matters: Junior girls happy, relaxed and proud to show us their work and talk about what they were doing. Good learning support. All children assessed on arrival at junior school, targets set each term and parents involved early if problems arise. Head meets all teachers once a term to ascertain that children have reached the expected levels.

'The school has really pulled its socks up' – that's the view of one parent we talked to. It offers a broad curriculum covering all the core subjects, and a wide variety of co-curricular activities to ensure pupils can learn and discover in depth. In 2019, 38 per cent A*/A at A level (66 per cent A*/B), and 72 per cent 9-7 at I/GCSE.

Setting in maths, sciences, modern languages and, occasionally, English. Class sizes are maximum of 26, many groups in the sixth form in single figures. All staff friendly and enthusiastic – average age early 40s. About a quarter have been at the school for more than 10 years. A selection of 12 non-core GCSE subjects on offer plus ancient Greek and astronomy. Head sees each year 11 girl individually with her parents to discuss A level choices.

One of the first things the head did was to introduce Kinza, a compulsory enrichment programme offering a range of over 30 topics which the girls study one afternoon each week in the Michaelmas and Lent terms. Staff run courses in subjects they don't teach (including forensic science, beekeeping and Arabic) and mixed age groups work together. Head says the course is 'emblematic of my educational philosophy', aiming to create 'civilised human beings equipped with a philosophy for living'.

Bubbly and enthusiastic head of learning support in school three-and-a-half days each week. School has inclusive policy, as long as girl passes entrance test. Some children have individual teaching assistants who produce strategies to help them deal with problems. Otherwise school provides help in small groups for 20 minutes once a fortnight from year 7 to year 9, and before school, after school or at lunchtime for years 10 and 11. One-to-one help has to be resourced externally.

Games, options, the arts: Surprising to find a school in a leafy London suburb with its own sports grounds and an enormous, all singing, all dancing sports hall, plus a dance studio and fitness centre. Plenty of cups to indicate sporting success. Football, hockey, tennis, athletics and lots of indoor sports. National gymnastic champions recently and notable successes in acrobatics, fencing, tennis and netball. The only criticisms from parents are that the school 'needs to offer more for C teams to improve their skills' and 'the sports department needs better organisation and more staff'. Needless to say, this is being addressed. One mother told us: 'The school is truly inclusive – my non-sporty child loves sport'.

Music strong (as you would expect with a musically talented head master), with lessons compulsory up to GCSE. Several choirs, orchestras and ensembles. Roomful of keyboards specifically for compositions. Parents say art facilities are 'brilliant' and we were impressed too. Large art room, smaller one specifically for the sixth form and separate pottery room with its own kiln. Drama also right up to standard; new creative arts building under construction. When we visited the whole school was involved in A Midsummer Night's Dream, with non-performers making costumes and painting scenery.

DofE taken pretty seriously – girls go trekking in Morocco's Atlas Mountains and have reached base camp of Everest.

Background and atmosphere: School was founded as Brixton Hill High School for Girls in 1887 and was one of the earliest GDST schools. It later became Streatham Hill High School, housed in the building now occupied by the junior school; senior school moved into current premises, previously occupied by Battersea Grammar School, in 1993. Now a spacious, well-equipped school, with recent additions of sixth form floor (popular sixth form café), stunning new dining hall and wildflower meadow roof at Abbotswood Road. The four-and-a-half acres of

Art room with terrific views over London 'Whenever we do art, we know we're going to do something really messy. It's such fun'

ground they stand in are miraculous in this busy area of London.

Junior school's unattractive building (school reports major refurbishments, including a new, 'very attractive oriel window') belies exceptionally light, large classrooms and happy atmosphere inside. Enormous sports hall, where girls can play hockey, and excellent outdoor area with adventure playground and enough space for rounders and tennis, guarantee plenty of fun, games and team training.

We were shown round by enthusiastic, confident girls who led us from the well-equipped nursery (with own outdoor play area) to busy reception classes and virtually every corner of the school. 'Do you want to see the loos?' they chirped. Huge library contains vast range of books and specific reading lists for each year. We also spotted shoes created out of recycled material and models of school areas (our guides proudly pointed out their own creations). Light art room with terrific views over London – 'whenever we do art, we know we're going to do something really messy', said our guides. 'It's such fun'. Science room was locked (health and safety) but they showed us well-equipped computer room and music room. Interactive white boards and computers in all classrooms.

Pupils' general feeling is that this is a happy, focused school. Parents say the support given to pupils is second to none and are adamant that it's 'not a hothouse'. Comments included 'there's no excessive pressure', 'they are allowed to be individuals and gain confidence', 'they mix across the year groups and get to know each other better that way'. One told us: 'At parents' evenings, they really do seem to know and understand our two very different daughters'. Another, with an exceptionally bright daughter, said that the way classes are divided, sometimes by ability, sometimes mixed, works a treat. 'My daughter is never bored', she said. 'The expectations of each girl are relevant to the goals she has been set'.

Pastoral care, well-being and discipline: Deputy head mistress is in overall charge of pastoral care and has a system for identifying problems early. Parents say communication is exceptional – emails are answered immediately and problems dealt with sympathetically. A parent told us of 'some unpleasantness...handled and dealt with properly and quickly'. Another talked about 'problematic disorder' in a particular class, which was 'completely sorted out by the head of department within a week'.

House system ensures girls work together as teams across year groups. Each form has a representative on the school council, alongside a form captain, so ample chances to raise problems. PHSCE programme deals with topics such as relationships, moral issues and citizenship in a sensitive and informed way. Sixth form mentor teams are invaluable – girls often prefer to talk to them rather than a member of staff.

Junior school parents told us: 'Communications are very good. All the staff are positive and professional.' The only thing they felt could be improved was sport. There's always something.

Pupils and parents: Mainly from the surrounding areas of south London and from variety of backgrounds – moneyed professional classes and entrepreneurs to local shopkeepers. Typical GDST range of ethnic and racial diversity.

Around 85 per cent arrive from the junior school. Parents of girls from state primaries said they liked the smaller size classes. Ex-pupils include June Whitfield, Angela Carter, broadcasters Maryam and Nazanine Moshiri, soprano Elizabeth Llewellyn and V&A curator Susannah Brown.

Entrance: Children can join co-ed nursery at 3 or reception at 4 via informal assessments. Further intake at 7+ via tests in maths, English and verbal reasoning. Written report from previous school also needed at this stage.

Eleven plus and 13+ places by interview and maths and English tests, plus science at 13+. Those coming up from the junior school have to pass a test in year 5 and also sit the 11+ exam. At 16+ minimum of six GCSEs required, with 9-7 grades in A level subjects, letter from previous head and interview with head master and sixth form head.

Exit: Around 90 per cent from the prep to the senior school subject to assessments. Some leave at 16 for local comps, sixth form colleges or boarding but around 60 per cent – and rising – stay on. Around same proportion usually head for Russell Group universities. One to Oxbridge in 2019, and one medic.

Money matters: Typical GDST school fees, so more reasonable than elsewhere. Several non-means-tested academic scholarships available and number of means-tested, subject based bursaries at 11+ and 16+. All curriculum-related non-residential trips included in fees.

Remarks: Streatham & Clapham High is on the up. Take one energetic head master, add a good handful of enthusiasm, pep up the curriculum, add ambition and belief, introduce Kinza, tune a grand piano and – eureka – numbers rise. It would certainly appear that something is working. There is now a consistent waiting list for places and numbers staying on for A levels have rocketed from 36 per cent to over 60 per cent. As one parent told us, 'The head master is having an amazing effect'.

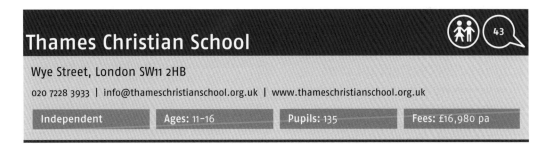

Thames Christian School

Wye Street, London SW11 2HB

020 7228 3933 | info@thameschristianschool.org.uk | www.thameschristianschool.org.uk

| Independent | Ages: 11–16 | Pupils: 135 | Fees: £16,980 pa |

Head: Since 2006, Dr Stephen Holsgrove PhD (50s); first class honours degree in civil engineering and a PhD in numerical analysis from Kingston University. Having worked in the IT sector for 20 years, he set up Thames Christian College in September 2000. His wife, Catherine, is registrar at the school.

Softly spoken, sincere but also something of a visionary, determined to shape a school in line with his beliefs, Dr Holsgrove's personal experience of school failing him up to the age of 16 has shaped his passion for educating children, and often helping

them to find their way to opportunities they might otherwise have missed. Parents are grateful for Dr Holsgrove's dedication, indeed he laughs at our enquiry as to what he does outside of school. They say: 'He is very hands on and interacts well with the students.' 'Dedicated, approachable and passionate about education.' 'Caring and thoughtful, and his kindness follows down through the school.' 'Committed to getting the best out of every child whilst recognising possible challenges.'

On his horizon is the delivery of a brand new school building in 2020, part of a massive local regeneration project. As he shows us the plans we sense he can hardly wait. Innovatively designed, with multiple levels, courtyard spaces and improved location opposite the entrance to Clapham Junction, it will give him a new challenge with expanded pupil numbers – three classes in every year group, not two – and a sixth form.

Academic matters: Founded as a mixed ability school in contrast to the many independent seniors in south London; the ability profile is nonetheless slightly above the national average. GCSE results vary from year to year depending on the cohort. In 2019, 23 per cent 9-7 grades. Most pupils take nine GCSEs, some six, some 11. Most pupils take nine GCSEs, some six, some 11.

We were impressed with the description of how the history teacher uses colour-coding in teaching how to structure an essay, which once grasped is transformative. Strongest performers right now: history, French, Spanish, music and art. Single sciences allow greater depth which suits many. More than the standard fare: additional maths and business studies too. No Mandarin, but can take native language GCSEs. One mother was delighted to find her son's potential for languages spotted, nurtured and quickly proving itself. Mathematicians take part in national competitions and those at the top of their game have benefited from masterclasses at King's College London School of Mathematics. Scientists get out and about too, taking part in the Royal Societies' Olympiads and challenges. Not simply an academic focus, but aims to produce good citizens who will contribute positively to society.

The school's SEN provision is recognised by CReSTeD: all staff have in-house training on dyslexia friendly practices and some staff have higher level SEN qualifications

---

With an average of 14 in each class, classrooms are roomy, with windows high up or obscured by blinds ensuring focused learning in every class we visited. Trolleys of Chromebooks are wheeled in as needed. Several teachers struck us as young but very assured. The head is a supporter of Schools Direct – where teachers learn on the job rather than at university – saying that it enables the school to gain access to the brightest young teachers, he gets their commitment and finds them 'very capable'. Following Dr Holsgrove's lead, what really makes the staff stand out is their real world experience, chosen as role models – the computer science teacher is a former parent here with 20 years' industry experience: 'so geeky, the kids love him', says the head. The long-standing DT teacher whom we saw in action is an acclaimed designer and artist with public commissions to his name.

Seven members of staff have been at the school for more than 10 years and a further nine more than five years. Said a parent: 'I think the teaching staff are very diligent, inspiring and pupil focused.' More than one parent commented that they were 'astounded' at parents' evenings by the level of understanding of their child teachers showed. They judged the amount of homework just right and said that holidays are holidays, with no burdensome projects.

Currently 30 per cent of pupils have identified special educational needs. Each pupil has personalised learning targets in each subject. Some benefit from additional one-to-one or help from a learning support assistant. The school's provision is recognised by CReSTeD, all staff have received in-house training on dyslexia-friendly practices and some staff have higher level SEN qualifications. There is also support for children with speech and language difficulties.

Inside the classrooms we observe a number of supportive methodologies in action: some children have hand-outs on coloured paper, there is a minimum of copying from the board, key words are underlined and all teachers use sans serif fonts for clarity. Seamless communication between staff: SEN colleagues have access via Google Drive to the detail of lessons so that they can be on the same page when discussing any problems with pupils. Just a few with EAL needs, who benefit from the same in-class and one-to-one support. A mother described her son as thriving: 'We put this down to the teachers taking the time to get to know the students and also to their teaching strategies'. Despite this level of support we are told that the majority of dyslexics here would be classed as mild to moderate. Some who migrate here were overlooked as the pace intensified in the early years at other local schools.

Games, options, the arts: The aim is for pupils to find sports they will love sufficiently to continue as adults and it's not lightweight: each week there's a two hourly morning session plus up to two full sporting afternoons. Those with an interest set up their own clubs. No sports on-site, but the high standard of local facilities and coaches bought in makes it a great experience: we're talking football pitches, athletics track, Astroturf, two sports halls, a gym and mirrored dance studio with a sprung floor. Pupils play matches and tournaments regionally and nationally. Successes in athletics. Several parents with daughters believe more should be done to encourage girls' participation in fixtures.

The head enthuses about the importance of creating something, getting beyond the blank page as a skill for life and instilling self-belief

Cross-country and volleyball draw the most, with hockey dominating netball. Thames footballers are champions. For the Americans, baseball as well as rounders.

Art is a highlight, most achieving 9-7, with wonderful drawing skills on show. Graphic communication is taught too at GCSE with great success – we saw an advertising campaign project for TfL which could have easily been mistaken for the labours of an ad agency. Pupils use Macs and the latest software. The head enthuses about the importance of creating something, getting beyond the blank page as a skill for life and instilling self-belief. Facilities include a kiln and laser cutter.

Music teacher formerly of the Tiffin Girls' School, and 20 pupils learn instruments up to grade 7. Variously termed 'the play' or 'an extravaganza' by parents, there is an annual whole school production and a medium sized rehearsal space. Recently: Smokey Joe's Café, a musical theatrical revue showcasing 39 pop standards at the Clapham Grand, with coaching from a professional singer and the school's musical theatre teacher. Concerts throughout the year. Pupils can take LAMDA exams.

Clubs sensibly take place on Friday afternoons. Sporting and creative choices include: life drawing, poetry, orchestra ensemble and 'Jesus & donuts', in other words the Christian Union. Homework club runs every day. Pupils regularly foray around London, with recent trips venues including both Tates, Greenwich Royal Observatory, the British Library, the Dickens Museum, the Globe Theatre and Southwark Cathedral. Meaningful and significant charity work and fundraising. Pupils have the opportunity to go on an annual trip to rural Tanzania to work with the charity, Go MAD. They help build goat sheds and water tanks to provide clean water for villagers. Enterprise is encouraged. Year 10 pupils recently took part in a competition to create a pop-up bookshop project. Biannual careers fair.

Background and atmosphere: The least auspicious entrance of any London school we have visited. A single storey box of a building, formerly a library and community centre, overshadowed by blocks of flats on every side, with few external windows and zero outside space. We left our car perched outside the front door expecting the wrath of a traffic warden at the least. However, once inside the doors, the warm welcome from staff and calm atmosphere of lessons underway began to soothe and enthuse us, and we left with a spring in our step, inspired.

Despite the name, whilst many teachers, parents and pupils have a Christian faith, the school simply reflects Christian values. Starting just 12 pupils, it has now grown to a still petite 135. Parents single out the school's small size as a positive feature. The school proudly notes the next steps taken by its leavers, including PhDs, excellent A level results and awards such as that won by a pupil for his project making a replica anglepoise lamp at Central St Martins. A mother told us: 'My daughter looks forward to going to school and during a long break tends to miss both teachers and students. The children are inspired by past students who have gone on to be great achievers.' 'Every child is noticed and encouraged,' said a parent, and another explained how children are encouraged to 'step up', and how 'the size and structure enables it to be not too exhausting and not too noisy'. All of this tells of a sense of camaraderie and community which we're sure will survive and thrive even as the school expands again.

Pastoral care, well-being and discipline: Parents report that pupils are friendly across year groups and cannot praise pastoral care enough: 'pastoral care is excellent'; 'terrific – excellent communication and ethos of kindness throughout the school' and 'teachers are also very alert to students who are appear to be are disconnected or withdrawn'.

The school believes that emotional intelligence can be taught, and it is modelled by the teachers: 'we are what we do'. The deputy head, who leads on pastoral care, exudes calm thoughtfulness and says that pupils 'feel they can come and talk to us'. The school lives and breathes the fact that every pupil is different, and will help each child think through how to approach and take responsibility for their lives. There is less of a focus on punishment than on understanding the consequences of their choices. Children are rewarded for good behaviour with a points scheme, building towards fair trade chocolate bars. There is a clear code of practice on anti-bullying. Bullying is not unheard of, but parents note that incidents are swiftly and effectively dealt with. There is a school counsellor.

Pupils and parents: Parents describe their peers as friendly. Pupils broadly reflect professional families in the cosmopolitan, multi-ethnic communities of modern London, but a far broader range of family incomes here than elsewhere, with few earning over £100k. Some 25 per cent are non-British, with the largest groups from the USA, France and New Zealand.

Entrance: Applications are in the autumn prior to the year of entry, with two applications per place currently. Entry is via an interview with a senior member of staff and a written test in English comprehension, writing and maths, but the head says: 'We don't turn away children because they can't do tests'. Adjustments for children with SEN. Sometimes a child might be taken on with an agreement to repeat year 7. No places for anyone with behavioural issues; looking for enthusiastic and dedicated learners.

Children enter from state primaries such as Belleville and Honeywell and mainstream or special preps such as Dolphin School, Hill House, Hurlingham, The Roche and The Dominie. The largest concentration of parents is in Wandsworth Town, Earlsfield, Southfields, Battersea and Clapham South, but also stretches to Dulwich, Streatham and north of the river.

Exit: To a mix of state and independent destinations after GCSEs including Ashcroft Academy, Graveney, Wallington Grammar, Harris Westminster and Grey Coat Hospital. As a creative school it's not a surprise to see a regular handful of leavers heading for the BRIT School.

Money matters: Good value fees with all extras included. Bursaries may be on offer for new entrants and also for families who have fallen into difficulties whilst at the school. Most families asked to contribute at least 50 per cent of fees, but some financial hardship bursaries available for 90 per cent of fees. Around five scholarships available per year on entry at year 7 worth up to 20 per cent of fees with no means-testing.

Remarks: If you are far-sighted enough to make it past the unpromising front door, this school offers the prize of meeting diverse learning needs brilliantly. With a new school building on the horizon, we suspect it will soon be more widely known.

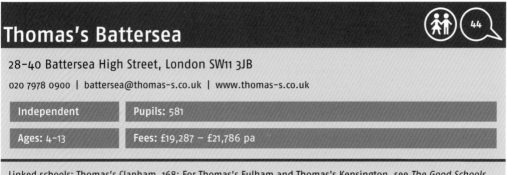

Thomas's Battersea

28-40 Battersea High Street, London SW11 3JB

020 7978 0900 | battersea@thomas-s.co.uk | www.thomas-s.co.uk

Independent	Pupils: 581
Ages: 4-13	Fees: £19,287 – £21,786 pa

Linked schools: Thomas's Clapham, 168; For Thomas's Fulham and Thomas's Kensington, see *The Good Schools Guide London North*

Headmaster: Since 2017, Simon O' Malley (50s); MA English lang and lit from Aberdeen, followed by a PGCE in English with drama and games coaching at Westminster College, Oxford. Previously positions have taken him in and out of London and across the world: most recently at Wellesley House, Broadstairs where he was head for 12 years; initially The Banda School in Kenya, where he went for two years and returned after seven having met and married his wife Katy – they have always worked together; she is resident art teacher.

As impeccably immaculate as his school: we omitted to ask Mr O'Malley how he felt about his inclusion in Tatler's list of hottest headmasters. To our mind, a keen Roger Sterling, the silver-haired ad man of Mad Men, he credits his selection for this most sought after of jobs to his empathy with the cultural values of the school and perhaps his own sound-bitey vision for a school in perpetual growth mode – Better Never Stops. Sporty, he runs

to and from school, has recently completed his first London marathon and enjoys golf and cricket. He has two grown up children.

Despite his taking over from the much-loved Ben Thomas, parents are on board and full of praise: 'He is approachable, intelligent and cares, a lot'. 'He seems to have time for everyone... one morning he will be at a music recital, the same afternoon at an away cricket match.' 'Very inspirational. I really feel he loves what he is doing.' Children smile his way and he congratulates achievement as we go.

Entrance: Sixty-three reception places. To avoid registration lists closing within weeks of birth the lists are now open between a child's first and second birthdays. Classes are selected with a balanced mix of births throughout the year and gender. A strong sibling policy reduces places for newcomers significantly. Children are invited to spend up to an hour taking part in small group activities observed by staff:

they're looking for confidence to undertake tasks, follow simple instructions, language and social skills. The odd occasional place may arise higher up the school. There is a formal assessment during the Lent term for 11+ entrants, when 20 to 25 places become available. There are a few high value bursaries for pupils joining the school at a higher age.

Exit: A mix of London day schools and out of town notables with many opting for co-education. Over the past five years children have consistently gained places at St Paul's School, Eton College, Harrow, Wellington College, Westminster School, Marlborough College, Frances Holland, Dulwich College, Bryanston School, Downe House and many more, with a healthy number of scholarships across disciplines.

Remarks: A new enquiry-based curriculum is in the pipeline for the whole school aiming to set children up well for a lifetime as learners, whilst still meeting the ultimate hoopla of tests and scholarships. The theme of the week at the time of our visit was 'perseverance' and a mother reported as if on cue: 'My daughter is happy to make mistakes, learn from them and try again. She is not afraid to fail, because she is being taught that mistakes are a positive way to learn.'

Every subject is under an impressively rigorous continual review. A major focus is developing a new curriculum for the upper years as the landscape for 11+ and CE exits changes. Spanish joins the mix from year 7 with Mandarin for younger years. French remains, with advanced classes for the many native speakers. Outdoor learning – not forest school, but adventure based – has proved a big hit with pupils and parents. As befits these digital natives the head is keen to stress the school's seamless integration of technology into every subject, whether it be use of 3D printing, programming drones, digital photography or iPads in years 4 and 7, giving children the discernment to use them well.

Maximum class size is 22 or 21 in reception. Classrooms are light, bright and spacious, more often than not full of hubbub and excitement on the day of our visit. Huge windows capture views of the city or towards the inner courtyard and sedum roof of the attractive dining hall. The older part of the school – tiled walls and concrete stairs – has been repurposed for the creative arts, housing a pottery studio as well as large art room. Fabulous drama space with theatrical make-up closets. Large media suite and brilliantly child-friendly libraries with modular seating providing well-used reading nooks.

Given the locale and the scrabble for places, we were encouraged to hear from a parent: 'it doesn't feel like a hothouse' and 'for the junior years very little homework at all apart from reading a book'. More intense higher up: 'Our 13 year old might

have one and a half hours of homework and music practice of 30-45 minutes a night, and this may be after extra school activities.'

Around a third of the 110 teachers have been at the school for more than 10 years, but lots of youthful (mostly female) faces. A mother of two with experience all through the school reported: 'Some of the staff are exceptional; I am very happy with the teaching.'

Spectacular drama full of West End wow: unsurprising once you know the Thomas's schools have their own technical dept staffed by industry professionals

Two full-time SEN staff in a dedicated large space with innovative pods, plus visiting specialists. Sixty children currently identified with SEN – more dyspraxia than dyslexia. A mother of a child with various undiagnosed learning differences on arrival told us: 'The school is incredibly supportive with revision help and timetabling for my son.' Her son added: 'Without Thomas's I would be nowhere'.

An increasingly co-ed focus for sports provision. On the ground this means things like boys'and girls' cricket teams with any player eligible for the 1st XIs. Other main sports for boys are football, rugby and athletics, for girls netball and hockey, with everyone taking part in gymnastics and athletics. The odd Olympian dropping in. Also on offer: tennis, table-tennis league, golf, karate and fencing clubs. A thriving list of trad and on trend clubs – pottery, yoga, coding and girls' football.

A 'particularly strong' music dept hosts over 400 individual lessons a week. Choristers perform at the Cadogan Hall and Albert Hall. Ensembles of every kind: ukulele, rock, jazz and brass.

Spectacular drama full of West End wow: unsurprising once you know the Thomas's schools have their own technical dept staffed by industry professionals. This doesn't stop pupils behind the scenes applying stage make-up, creating posters, prop making. Ambitious productions of Macbeth, Cole Porter's Anything Goes, Disney's Mulan,and Beowulf for year 5 complete with huge monster puppets. An amazed parent commented: 'our shy-by-nature son now wants to be the lead in school plays'. Dance is an important part of the school too.

The zingy lime green used on everything from doors to walls in the new building helps, but the fizz definitely comes from within. 'Vibrant and bustling' are the descriptors we encounter most often from parents. 'Warm, sociable, fun, confident kids, kind, professional and highly organised,' another parent thought apt.

The Thomas's school motto, 'be kind', is written in stone, literally, above the door and the school leads the way with its pastoral care. A father reported: 'an overwhelming sense that they have this square and centre in everything they do.' A mother: 'very caring and very open...a teacher would call me directly just to say that my daughter was sad or upset about a certain thing so I could speak to her at home.'

Social and environmental responsibility is much in evidence, from this year's charitable support of a local community boxing club voted for by pupils, to an enormous pile of bags of clothing heading to good homes. A lovely art installation in a corridor features papier-mâché sea creatures entwined with single use plastics, and children go litter picking along the Thames. A stunning installation above a stairwell called A Shared Future, of suspended clothes found on a Greek beach belonging to refugees, has made political and social issues real for everyone here. A mother told us: 'the focus is on making the child a good person, not just an academic one'.

Rules are clear. The behaviour policy states a precise 6:1 ratio of positive to negative comments from teacher to pupil. Stars are so old hat: children receive 'golden unicorns' for notable behaviour or work. 'Reflection time' is a sanction for misbehaviour. An early adopter of mindfulness, pupils or parents may make use of the school counsellor. An extremely well thought through well-being policy aims to ensure no mental health issues go unnoticed and staff are well-informed on everything from FGM to radicalisation. As a parent confirmed: 'Thomas's keeps up and is always thinking ahead on how best to prepare the children for the world we live in today.'

Pupils travel from as far as Wimbledon and Barnes, Bayswater and Kennington. More than half are local. Large numbers of French and Italian but also Mandarin, Russian and Swedish speakers. Twenty-seven children receive some level of EAL support. Whilst many pupils are inevitably from extremely wealthy families, one mother shared: 'We live in a less privileged part of town and commute half an hour to the school. We have always felt 100 per cent accepted.' This note continues with others describing parents as 'friendly and non-pretentious' and 'within the school walls we're all equal.' One pupil in particular has brought global attention: Prince George. On a practical level this means extra security measures evident from the front door. Visitors have their phones placed in a locker. Parents, however, are simply issued with security passes, no-one has to sign a non-disclosure agreement and new parents and pupils are simply spoken to openly about expectations.

Thomas's Clapham

Broomwood Road, London SW11 6JZ

020 7326 9300 | clapham@thomas-s.co.uk | www.thomas-s.co.uk

Independent	Pupils: 650
Ages: 4-13	Fees: £18,024 - £20,376 pa

Linked school: Thomas's Battersea, 166; for Thomas's Kensington and Thomas's Fulham, see *The Good Schools Guide London North*

Headmaster: Since 2012, Philip Ward BEd (50s). One of the first heads appointed to the Thomas's group of London schools from outside of the Thomas family dynasty, in person Mr Ward is the very image of Hugh Bonneville as the Earl of Grantham. Perhaps it's his winning charm as head of the Clapham family, bonhomie, liberal sprinklings of the word 'chap', not to mention the labrador behind his desk. Any similarity ends there, however, as we found him to be a highly astute, strategically minded leader. Very persuasive; anyone wishing to challenge his point of view could need some determination not to be swept along with him.

Educated at Reigate Grammar School, he read history and PE at Exeter University, thence straight to Uppingham where he became director of PE and chair of the games committee, ascending through the ranks finally to headship of Feltonfleet prep in Surrey.

As he talks he often refers to 'we': part of a husband and wife teaching double act. His wife Sue now teaches year 5 here. The move seems something of a surprise but they are enjoying being in

Parental praise for the teaching: 'Our children have enjoyed a multitude of inspirational teachers who go the extra mile'

London, able to nip into town for an evening. It also went down well with their two grown up children. Milly and Monty, the chocolate labs, come to school every day and have been known to get lucky with the odd cupcake or two not meant for them. They like to get out to the Surrey Hills at the weekends for long walks if they can. During the week, there are a lot of late nights and missed dog walks.

We were impressed by Mr Ward's delightful manner with the children as we went around the school. He knew the name of every child we met. One parent told us, 'The children love him' – we could see why.

Having taught at a senior school, he knows what's in store for children later in terms of pressure, and for now wants them to have fun, a childhood.

Entrance: No registration at birth for those born on or after 1 September 2018 (2023 entry). Instead, registration opens on 1 September three years before entry. Contact the registrar to make an expression of interest and receive a reminder before the lists open. Pupils are selected at an informal assessment day at 3+, most recently seeing some 200 children for 80-ish places. And with no 7+ entrance, this is pretty much it.

This is a neighbourhood school in the main: children arrive from more than 35 different local nurseries. Those at the Thomas's kindergarten in Battersea are no longer guaranteed an assessment. Strong sibling priority, but no promises. Sibling discounts for up to four children. They look for children who will 'have a go' and are genuinely keen as well as sociable and co-operative within a group.

Very occasionally places available higher up the school. Fifteen to 20 Thomas's Fulham pupils move over to Clapham at 11+, their transition now given much greater care and consideration.

New-style show-rounds every few weeks, for groups of six or eight prospective parents to meet the head and see the school – more intimate than previous hall talks, very deliberately sending out a new, more personal and welcoming message from the off.

Exit: The word from parents and pupils is that they have 'absolute confidence' in the school enabling them to reach their guided first choice. Around 20 leave at the end of year 6, 65 at the end of year 8, with some 65 per cent off to board in some shape or form to many different schools. Recent popular London destinations include Alleyn's, Dulwich College, Emanuel and King's Wimbledon; boarders off to Epsom College, Woldingham, Wellington College and Brighton College.

Remarks: The school opened in 1993, and is housed in a huge four-storey Victorian red-brick, typical of many London schools of the time, this one formerly a girls' grammar school in the centre of prime, residential Clapham. Inside, shining maroon tiled corridors, very London tube like, multiply the children's voices at every change of lessons – it's reassuringly loud and exuberant. Reception classes are housed in groovy-looking pods with an in and out space – fun, but quite compact, and perhaps a bit warm in summer – with so much vibrant work hanging from the ceilings, it's like being inside a mobile. Other classrooms 'significantly revitalised'.

The dining room needs some reinvention, currently high windows and too small, so that pupils eat in shifts. The food seemed no better than 'school dinner-ish' to our eyes, and it was Friday, but plenty of fried food as well as more healthy options. Playground recently rejuvenated with the Dragon's Den wooden playground based on Middle Earth complete with Hobbit Hole, Shelob's Web and Rivendell's Castle – plenty of places to hide, climb and burn off energy.

Specialist teaching introduced gradually up the school. Year 6 splits between those going for 11+ and 13+, with former getting much special preparation with past papers. Latter get exam technique and revision strategies in year 8, with a creative post-exam programme of extension subjects. The staff is a stable one, with 15 teachers having been at the school for more than 10 years. In his bid to make the school less autocratic, head introduced a new senior leadership team. Small changes have included greatly reduced homework and a less intimidating approach to school exams. Curriculum being revamped to include thematic inquiry based learning; year 5s upwards use one-to-one iPads to add a creative element.

Parental praise for the teaching: 'Our children have enjoyed a multitude of inspirational teachers who go the extra mile'. 'Very supportive and nurturing whilst at the same time instilling the need for self-discipline and effort.' 'Apart from the French department, which needs a serious overhaul, the standard of teaching is superb. They manage to engage the children with original and inspiring teaching whilst also ensuring that the essential rote-learning/repetition aspects are in place.'

New director of computing and much investment in hardware. French is taught from day one by a native French speaker, but there is work to do for the new head of modern languages, who is expected to 'revitalise the department': indeed, a new approach emphasises international awareness alongside language learning. Latin from year 5, Mandarin now taught in year 4, Spanish a possibility in future.

Around 10 per cent of children have SEN, mainly dyslexia. Emphasis on differentiated learning and in-class support, but some withdrawal for one-to-one lessons. Strong learning support team assists some 150 pupils with a spread of learning differences, including a more able group. Refreshing for a London prep to be so proud of its efforts in this regard.

We were wowed by the group of sculptures children had made by wrapping themselves in foil, inspired by Kader Attia

Great art facilities in a modern, light and bright separate block and an experienced newish head of art (formerly from Feltonfleet) is sensitively designing projects for each year group. Exciting to see a whole row of potter's wheels, and we were wowed by the impressive group of sculptures children had made by wrapping themselves in foil, inspired by Kader Attia's Ghost installation. Cookery a new addition. A film-maker in residence, a former head of art, is no doubt ensuring every moment is captured for the sharpening marketing act, as well as helping children to record and present multi-media projects across the curriculum. New DT specialist.

Sports fixtures list expanded with the aim of enabling everyone to play for a team. New sports ground on the edge of Wimbledon Common with pavilion and changing rooms. For the high achievers some glamorous tours such as South Africa too. Girls play netball, hockey, rounders and athletics. One parent told us: 'The head of sport gets the most amazing results out of the children, training and praising in just the right measure, and always there with a cuddle if they hurt themselves. The kids would throw themselves under a bus for her. The girls hold their own very well against schools with a far bigger pool of pupils and better facilities and the trophy cabinet is weighed down with the evidence of that.'

Boys play football, rugby and cricket. In part to keep the boys beyond 11, the head has beefed things up. We saw two current and former professional rugby players coaching the boys at the cricket nets, using an iPad to compare each boy's batting with that of a famous player. Further thoughts are hockey for the boys and lacrosse for the girls. Weekly swimming off site for years 1 to 4. Ballet part of the curriculum from reception – cue a class of tinies performing to parents and their iPhones on our visit. Mostly girls latterly; the boys who continue are often talented.

Performing arts are an outstanding feature – highlights have included a performance at the Albert Hall in celebration of childhood. A parent commented: 'There seems to be something on every week! It is quite astounding that children are so confident and unfazed by the opportunities to perform, either in sport or on the stage.'

Some 350 children have individual music lessons, currently beginner level to grade 8. A wide range of groups and ensembles, and frequent recitals, soirées and concerts. Those with gifted voices may be invited to sing in the chapel choir, whilst 'new voices' and senior choir provide opportunities for all to perform.

More than 60 before- and after-school clubs include fencing, debating, golf, computer coding, newspaper publishing, running and Airfix modelling (run by the head).

Special days for everything, with plenty of outside expertise brought in to deliver workshops. 'Make a difference day' caught our eyes, with children heading off in mini task forces to spend time in genuinely helpful projects across the community, such as making decorations for their local hospice, visiting a Christian Aid centre and sending cards to sick children. Pupils seem to get out and about, get stuck in and see things for themselves. Woodland Adventure on Wimbledon Common is 'by far the most popular day of term'.

Strong focus on PSHE. A new Inspiring Living course is a philosophy of the school as well as a taught subject. A key component is a new focus on mindfulness (including new landscaped tranquil, green Mindfulness Place), and Mr Ward is at the forefront of the curve. 'We're going to do mindfulness together… more thinking time, more time for reflection,' he says with enthusiasm. We applaud him, but wonder how he will stop his mind spinning with ideas and objectives during his allotted four minutes.

Head and team have set out to reinvent school's pastoral care systems. The head has been known to drop external meetings and return from conferences to pick up immediately on anything that arises. A parent confirmed: 'They take issues such as bullying seriously and take measures to address it instantly.' Parents describe the atmosphere as 'Very caring, and competitive in the right way, ie set out to win, but it doesn't matter if you don't, as long as you try your best'; 'Positive, determined yet caring and fun' and 'nurturing'.

The head says, 'Every child wants a bit of metal on their shirt' and so there are now myriad opportunities to lead and take responsibility: as well as the usual heads of houses and games there are prefects for subjects or for eco and charities, even flag captains.

Parents are not first time buyers in the main: many boarding school educated, and an impressive bunch of achievers. One parent described them as 'vocal! Very involved in all levels of school life.'

South West

Kingston-upon-Thames
Merton
Richmond-upon-Thames
Sutton

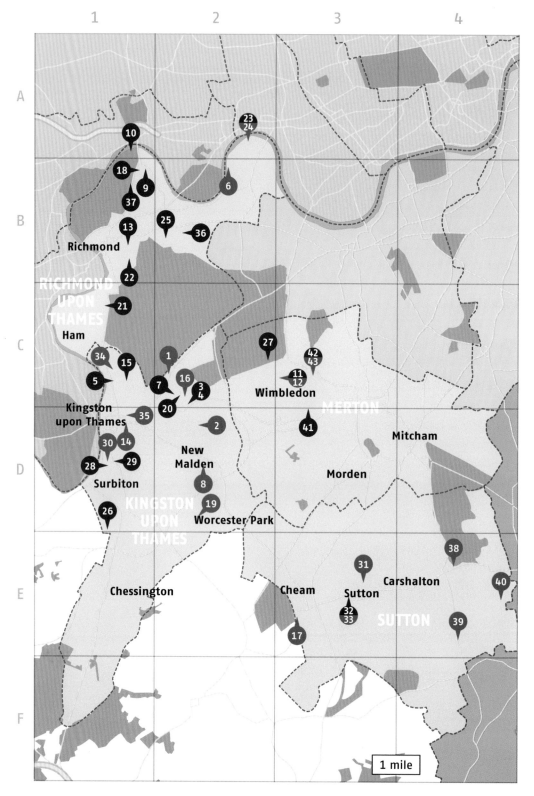

1 mile

SOUTH WEST

South West London and its state schools

Kingston-upon-Thames

With its historic Thames-side setting, well-heeled residents and home-grown celebrities (sightings of best-selling children's author Jacqueline Wilson, who grew up here, are excitedly reported) and almost the lowest levels of deprivation in the country, Kingston's image is against it when it comes to education handouts, to the natural frustration of head teachers. Just 6.3 per cent of Kingston's secondary school pupils qualify for free school meals – the lowest of any local authority in London. It matters: there's a 25 per cent gap in GCSE results between disadvantaged pupils in Kingston (and neighbouring Richmond) and their better off peers. Even so, educationally this royal borough still has masses going for it. Over 80 per cent of primary and secondary school pupils in Kingston attend a good or outstanding school.

As elsewhere, Kingston has been busily adding more school places. In April 2019, five out of six reception age pupils were offered places at their first choice school. Two much-needed new schools, The Kingston Academy (11-18) (rated 'outstanding') and Kingston Community School (a primary, moving to permanent premises in Norbiton in 2020) have helped ease the pressure, as has the decision to make St Paul's (formerly an outstanding junior school, now rated 'good') and its feeder school, Alexandra Infants, into all-through primaries.

Also resolved is the long-standing gripe from residents that many of the places in Kingston's two surviving grammars, the Tiffin School qv (boys) and Tiffin Girls' School qv (fabulous results year in, year out) were going to families living the other side of London. Locals have been mollified by changing entrance criteria that give priority to those living (fairly) locally (but read the admissions policies carefully as they aren't identical).

For the vast majority who fail to secure a Tiffin place, other non-selective secondaries are available, turning in results that range from respectable to exceptional. There's also widespread buddying up – Coombe Girls qv (very successful) with Coombe Boys (getting there). Hollyfield, formerly more down than up, is in a multi-academy trust with Grey Court School – an outstanding National Teaching School in neighbouring Richmond. Girls at the Holy Cross School qv (not to be confused with nearby independent girls' prep of same name) and boys at Richard Challoner qv (fab SEN provision – recently extended) have long-standing and successful sixth form partnership – and consistently good exam results.

At primary level there are plenty of equally desirable schools. Coombe Hill Junior School qv together with Fern Hill qv – both rated 'outstanding' – could, arguably, be joined by 10 or so other high performers.

Faith schools are almost all brilliant. While most prioritise the godly, one – St Luke's – has broken ranks to ditch church attendance as an entry requirement (to mixed media reception). St Andrew's and St Mark's CofE Junior School are outstanding, Christ Church CofE Primary in Surbiton currently down a notch to good, though notable for 'lovely' head and hard working staff, in reassuringly early and staying late at night. If only parents would stop children running through residents' gardens, according to one disgruntled local, it would be practically perfect.

Of the Catholic schools, St Agatha's near Richmond Park is popular with Norbiton's arty-crafty set and rated 'good', as is Corpus Christi Catholic Primary School, though St Joseph's, despite a similarly positive inspection, is less favoured by the chattering classes.

In Kingston's further reaches, less pricy housing meets decent education. Tolworth Junior School (rated good) once renowned for 'tough parents and tough children,' according to local, wears gritty location with deserved pride, with the percentage of year 6 pupils meeting the expected standard in reading, writing and maths back to average in 2018 after a dip the previous year.

Merton

Over 90 per cent of Merton's primary schools and all its mainstream secondaries are rated good or outstanding – no mean feat given recent increases in school places. (The local parent partnership – renamed Merton SEND IAS – based at a local primary school and serving the entire borough, remains steadfastly tiny.)

Despite the territory, parents at state schools 'aren't arrogant – arrogance tends to go private,' reckoned local. A few are boomerang returners – left for dream life in rural(ish) Surrey, struggled with the daily commute and moved back to enjoy local charms, headed by Wimbledon Common's 1,200 acres, used by riders, walkers and picnickers. There's also considerable disparity between different areas. Merton is home to pretty Wimbledon Village and, of course, the annual tennis fest, where even the catering staff are rigged out in designer sportswear, but also takes in Morden and Mitcham where levels of affluence are rather lower.

Noah's Ark like, schools here come in pairs, Catholicism your best option. First class attendance at local churches the result.

At senior level, Ursuline (girls) in particular is 'excellent,' says local, while pointing out that though tip top for those who want to learn, 'you can shrink away if you don't.' Unofficially looks to Wimbledon High qv as natural competitor when it comes to exam results (with over 80 per cent achieving at least five good GCSEs including English and maths in 2018, few nearby state schools provide much of a challenge). Co-ed sixth form, twinned with Wimbledon College, the boys' equivalent, has seen effective pooling of resources. As with any Catholic school, entrance, eye of needle etc, is depending on faith, with rumours of entrants being quizzed not just on church attendance but even subject of Sunday sermon. Occasional difficulties – 'had bad press when rivalry with another school resulted in the occasional fight,' but bar inevitable ups and downs of different year group temperaments, it's all plain sailing. 'Had an amazing time there,' says former pupil.

Not the end of the road if you don't make it there. Ricards Lodge (girls) and Rutlish (boys) are also popular choices, with a successful joint sixth form (with 39 questions to complete, 16+ admissions form should count towards an A level all on its own).

Work in progress at St Mark's Academy (90 of 180 places allocated to practising Christians) is well underway, with results and attendance both getting a bit of much needed oomph. Two Harris Academies, Merton and Morden (both outstanding and with more pupils on FSM than average) do well for pupil progress. A third, Harris Wimbledon, opened in September 2018 in temporary premises, with a planned move to a permanent home in 2020.

To the south west (located by a less than scenic A3 roundabout infested junction), there's Raynes Park High School. Not previously an Ofsted darling, it's gone from requiring improvement to a 'good' rating, helped by peer support from other, stronger schools. Locals also praise help for pupils with high functioning ASD, though performance felt by some to be marred by chunk of pupils whose thirst for learning is somewhat modest. Exam results teeter within the margins of respectability – 45 per cent of pupils getting 5+ in both English and maths GCSE in 2018 – though percentage with SEN and on free school meals are both higher than the national norm. Justifies view, feel locals, that as more on the ball pupils feed through, their motivation and ambition will rub off.

Most of official attention in recent years has focused on primaries which have 'really pushed themselves on,' thinks local, with a widespread raising of standards. Dundonald – currently expanding to two form entry – boasts generally strong results (better in reading and maths than writing) and is predictably big on appeal to middle class professionals, traditional family model much in evidence with working father who is 'something in the City' (admittedly could be Paris or Frankfurt post-Brexit) but possibly, given slightly lower property prices here (relative, we know, in this area) with a slightly less expensive BMW, Audi or Discovery to go with it.

Parents are a hands on lot at Garfield (rated good), with PTA organised events ranging from movie nights to discos.

Many of primaries are scenic as well as successful. Popular Bishop Gilpin has its own fields while Wimbledon Chase Primary (a Good Schools Guide old-timer) is 'stunning' says local (results good as well) thanks to own, beautiful grounds of former manor house, fields front and back and 'masses' of green space. While not the smallest of schools, it isn't the largest, either. 'They've got a good team there who have done a great job,' thinks local.

Plenty of primary appeal elsewhere: Merton Park, St Matthew's CofE, Holy Trinity CofE, Hatfeild (sic), Pelham and Cranmer all well-regarded (though always worth checking that latest results bear out any purplish inspection prose, particularly when inspectors haven't called round for a while). Hollymount also a huge favourite with parents – 'Regarded as the best because of its location,' (in plushville Wimbledon, though has expanded to two-form entry). Excellent results justify local view.

Richmond-upon-Thames
Straddling both sides of the Thames, Richmond's borough limits can confuse even locals (just as well they don't go in for

drumming strangers out of town: they'd probably never leave).

It's made more confusing by cross-borough collaboration. The story so far – Richmond and Kingston pool services for learning support. The coalition works magnificently – so well that the partnership is hived off into Achieving for Children – a not-for-profit social enterprise which would plough any money made back into its services if it made any – which it doesn't (in fact, quite the reverse). This is not on any account to be confused with a separate arrangement made with Wandsworth Council to run Richmond Council's so-called back office functions. All clear? We hope so.

Educational backdrop is largely scenic. South of the river and west of Putney lies Barnes, lined with leafy roads, riverfront mansion flats and low terraced Edwardian and Victorian houses. Old reservoirs, once the source of most of London's drinking water supply, now make up London Wetland Centre and the rather secret but public Leg O' Mutton reservoir near the Hammersmith Bridge – along the route of The Boat Race. Barn Elms – historically discreet site for duels as a means of dispute resolution – is now a vast sports centre, while local shops line the high street, ending at the village duck pond.

Richmond town centre, south west from Barnes, boasts a bustling high street, steep hills with protected views over London that dip down to the river, large houses and extensive gardens behind old brick walls. From leafy to nearly rural, home to Kew Gardens and the 2,000-acre former royal hunting grounds of Richmond Park, it's still just a quick tube, train or bus ride to the centre of London.

The Richmond comprehensives, with the notable exception of Waldegrave on the north bank of the Thames, had until recently been no better than they should be and, in many parents' eyes, rather worse, given excellence of primary school performance that should give pupils a substantial head start. Not that you'd get them admitting their doubts openly. Indeed, more militant members of liberal-leaning book clubs have been known to cold-shoulder those who give up on the state system post 11, though some are to be found hiding behind pillars at independent establishment open days a few years later...

Now, most have perked up no end, thanks in part to strategic partnerships between top performers and needier establishments. South of the river Grey Court School has been transformed over the past five years. There is, however, still some work to do – with two of of Richmond's 11 mainstream secondaries – Teddington and Twickenham Schools – in need of improvement, as of last year.

Primary schools throughout the borough, meanwhile, continue to be oversubscribed (no surprises there), stories of place-less reception children an annual headline grabber in local press. Meanwhile, living as close as you can to the desired school (dustbin in playground ideal if it has own postcode) has never been a better idea. So is downloading a copy of the council's admissions policy and reading it till your eyes bleed to make sense of the myriad of admissions criteria. Worth the effort, however, given that all but two of Richmond's primary schools are rated good or outstanding, while in 2018, the borough's year 6 pupils achieved some of the best KS2 Sats results in the country.

Downsides headed by danger of low-flying helicopter parents (as well as flight path noise). If not ubiquitous, they're definitely a feature of Richmond's school gate life, with Vineyard, says one local, 'operating like an independent school because of its location and the kind of parents it attracts.' Reasonably typical, making East Sheen something of a rarity with 'a less stolidly middle class feel,' says insider. Inevitable loss of intimacy as schools expand is other issue – parents report quietly conscientious middle rankers sinking without trace (in part explains roaring business being done by local preps).

Top primaries south of the river (all currently rated 'outstanding') include St Elizabeth's Catholic Primary School (weeny and wonderful); Sheen Mount Primary School (cracking results and – an area feature – highly motivated parents, with all that suggests), and The Queen's School, Kew (all-round excellence – some pupils go on to independents including The Lady Eleanor Holles, Hampton School and the like). And did we mention the motivated parents?

Plenty of other stars in the firmament, too, from older favourites, including St Mary Magdalen's Catholic School, to more recent additions like Marshgate, which similarly pushes the pace with action-packed days that verge on frenetic, says local.

Sutton

What it lacks in character, Sutton makes up for in academic desirability – and popularity. It's added thousands of primary and secondary school places as well as a brand new secondary school – another Harris Academy (Sutton branch), moved to brand new premises in 2019 after its first year 7 intake started off, as so often, in temporary premises.

Its grammar schools remain its brightest beacon of academic success, all highly selective and producing top class results. Even this microclimate has its own best of the best, however, with a bit of jostling for top position. With GGCE and A levels results as good as these, it can all feel literally, rather (well, very) academic. The bottom line is that if your child gets a place here and enjoys the cut and thrust of the academic pace, they should do very well indeed.

If your child doesn't make the cut (and with that weight of numbers, many very bright children won't) but is a) a girl and b) Catholic, St Philomena's Catholic High School for Girls is a more than acceptable alternative with 59 per cent of pupils getting 5+ in both English and maths GCSE in 2018. Heavily oversubscribed in year 7 (too many Catholic applicants, let alone other faiths), it does offer more hope post-16, when a number of non-Catholics are admitted.

Pick of the also-rans is probably Glenthorne High School (rated outstanding, with well above average pupil progress). Bad old days when known, says local, for 'louder, rowdier, fighting teens,' now firmly consigned to the past. Instead, it's an arts specialist, offering up to 24 performing arts places, candidates completing an online form and attending a competitive workshop.

There's lots of goodness in the area at primary level too, with all but two schools rated good or outstanding. Westbourne Primary School has been rated outstanding and substantially improved inside and out, with netball and tennis court, two football pitches, as well as outdoor adventure playground for younger pupils. Slight deficit on leafiness of surroundings (close to busy A 217 and Tesco), lower property prices the upside.

No shortage of other ultra-desirables, from Nonsuch Primary to St Mary's RC Junior School where 'God is at centre of everything we do' they say – and they're not joking. Baptismal certificate required with application; even looked after children and those with EHCPs have to be Catholic, or living with one. St Elphege's RC Catholic School (motto: 'With God all things are possible,' – with the exception, possibly, of a school place) and St Cecilia's RC Primary both outstanding and similarly stringent.

Definitely a case of 'O, come all ye faithful' in CofE schools, too, with All Saints Benhilton CofE Primary (rated good) allocating most of reception to 'faithful and regular worshippers' (you'll need to take a pew twice a month for two years).

Of the non-religious, Avenue Primary (in desirable South Sutton/Belmont) achieves generally terrific results – though progress dipped slightly in 2018. Honourable mentions also for Cheam Park Farm Primary Academy, Manor Park Primary Academy (both 'outstanding'), Robin Hood Junior and Stanley Park Junior (both 'good').

Cheam Common Junior Academy had dropped from outstanding to inadequate in just five years. The appointment of new governors and a helping hand from more successful neighbours has paid off; it's now back to 'good.'

When even Sutton schools outside the mainstream do well – Limes College, a unit for excluded pupils, is rated 'outstanding' – it's good to know that it's not just the well-behaved high flyers who can soar.

Canbury School

Kingston Hill, Kingston, Surrey KT2 7LN

020 8549 8622 | reception@canburyschool.co.uk | www.canburyschool.co.uk

| Independent | Pupils: 53; sixth form: 7 |
| Ages: 11–19 | Fees: £17,061 – £18,576 pa |

Headmistress: Since 2014, Louise Clancy BEd. Spent 11 years as deputy head of Greenacre School for Girls, Surrey. Has taught at some challenging comprehensives. Teaches GCSE art and design. Described by one parent as 'down to earth. She just loves the children.' Another said, 'Her office is in the middle of the school and she hears and see exactly what is going on. The children like the fact that she is accessible and often pop into her office for a chat. She's easy to talk to but everyone respects her.' Married to a retired policeman. Two grown up daughters; one works in theatre and one in commerce. Now a doting grandmother. Enjoys baking and cooking, which she finds therapeutic, and is a dab hand at portrait painting. Loves travelling, with a soft spot for Cyprus.

Relishes being head here. 'I wanted to be a head of a small school where I could know each child's name. I just fell in love with Canbury,' she says. Ambitious for her school. Very keen to improve the teaching and learning on offer – wants it to go from good to outstanding on her watch. Parents feel she has turned the school around and believe she is determined to transform it further still.

Academic matters: A mainstream co-ed independent school that is able to support pupils of all academic abilities, especially those with SEN. 'We have a reputation for working with teenagers who have needs but are not special needs teenagers. This makes us different,' explains head. Pupils generally take a maximum of nine GCSEs. Due to size of school, results vary greatly from year to year, depending upon cohort. At time of going to press school had not released 2019 results but in 2018, 73 per cent 9-4 in maths and English; seven per cent of grades were 9-7. Science and creative subjects particularly strong.

'We are an independent school. We just do everything on a smaller scale.' School is good at targeting the differing needs of the individual pupils. Everything is done with the intention of making the curriculum as accessible to each pupil as possible. 'We personalise and adapt the curriculum, where we can. We teach to their strengths and we are continually reviewing the students' needs,' says head. Science lessons, for example, are practical-heavy as most pupils are kinaesthetic learners. School offers Spanish as it is considered more accessible than French. For those who struggle with foreign languages, there is also the option of taking a BTec qualification in travel and tourism. 'We don't want their confidence to plummet, so we offer an alternative where we can.'

One parent commented, 'The school is incredibly accommodating. They teach foundation and higher-level GCSEs at the same time, which must be a challenge'. Another parent said at times her son felt some lessons could be better, but overall most teaching was good. 'Spanish is excellent and maths clinic was a blessing. It meant my son could go over trickier topics again, often on an individual basis, which he found really helpful.' Maths is taught in mixed ability classes for first three years, then set thereafter.

Head explains, 'We do have a range of students with quite different needs. Some have no special needs at all but like being in a smaller school. They have looked at bigger schools and felt they were not for them'. Pupils have a variety of difficulties including slow processing, OCD, dyslexia, dyspraxia, autistic spectrum disorder and cerebral palsy. Others have health issues including transplant patients who need a gentler environment where they will not get knocked about in the corridors. Students with high anxiety and school refusers also come here to be nurtured. School does not take on children with behavioural problems. 'Our pupils are happy, and I won't take on new students who will disrupt our existing students. We do not accept children who are violent, and nor do we take children with complex needs as we are too small. No intimate care offered. We only take pupils if we feel we can meet their needs,' states head matter-of-factly. She explains, 'We have able children who can't always get it down on paper. They just need extra support and they do well academically here.'

Many pupils arrive in a vulnerable state with shattered confidence, for a variety of reasons. Head describes how 'some arrive broken and we make them whole again. When they leave, they are fully functioning, productive members of society.' Pupils are very accepting of each other's needs.

Sixth form opened in September 2018, offering a bespoke curriculum.

Games, options, the arts: Plenty of sport offered, with five hours a week in key stage 3 and three hours in key stage 4. Weekly swimming lessons for first couple of years. Kayaking on the Thames and rock climbing also on offer for the more adventurous. Swimming galas, cross-country championships and sports days aplenty. Highly competitive house sport. School also regularly participates in borough events and some pupils perform at national level. Mixed teams, often made up of boys and girls from different year groups. Where possible, Richmond Park used for games lessons as well as school's own playground, with a wonderfully bouncy surface.

Strong performing arts programme that mixes creativity with technology. Christmas entertainment is mostly student-led, where the teachers provide a skeleton of the production and pupils are expected to do everything else. Head convinced one of the many advantages of being a small school is that all pupils can take on a leading role. 'Everyone here gets the chance to be the star of the show!' she smiles.

Stunning artwork throughout school, including a huge mural of the headmistress. One girl proudly showed us her immaculate portfolio, bursting with striking images and thoughtful write-up. Photography popular and school has own kiln. Students from nearby Kingston University come into Canbury to collaborate on projects with pupils.

Pupils were rehearsing enthusiastically for school concert on the day we visited, and parents feel the 'singing is beautiful at Canbury'. Head comments, 'We have extraordinary pupils doing extraordinary things.'

Clubs to suit all tastes including doodling, Minecraft, karate, yoga and nail varnish art (which acts as an informal communication club). Duke of Edinburgh award offered to silver level.

School ensures all pupils get chance to go on annual overseas trip. 'No child is denied the experiences on offer.'

Background and atmosphere: Founded in 1982 by John Wyatt and housed in a large Edwardian villa on Kingston Hill. When founding headmaster retired in 1997, an educational charitable trust was set up, with a board of governors.

Maximum class size is 13. Currently many more boys than girls but ratio fluctuates. One parent admitted that 'at times, the small size of the school has been frustrating for my son. He would have liked a larger group from which to make friends. It can be limiting.' Up to two adults per classroom. Speech and language and occupational therapists come in regularly, as does a counsellor.

Buildings a little frayed around edges but massive ground floor refurbishment planned to include new reception and school hall, flooring and lighting. Rooms are mostly multi-functional. Facilities include a fully kitted-out science lab, ICT room overflowing with Apple Macs and a stairlift. Study Support Suite, housed in the attic, is an oasis of calm where pupils are supported on a one-to-one basis and in small groups. No school kitchen due to lack of space.

School is hot on discipline and British values are upheld. One pupil who had shaved his head was made to stay at home until his hair had grown back

Pupils seem unconcerned by lack of space. On the day we visited, pupils were happily playing at break time in the playground with balls flying in all directions. Much laughter and ready smiles in the corridor. Children seemed genuinely delighted to be here. On spotting the head, pupils bounded up to her and could not wait to share with her how they had found their GCSE exams that morning.

Pastoral care, well-being and discipline: A supportive and caring environment. One parent told us, 'My son had missed a lot of school and had had a terrible time before he came here. He has blossomed at Canbury. He has done everything he should do at school, and more. They certainly know how to get the best out of the kids.'

School is hot on discipline and British values are upheld. Manners are important here. Uniform reintroduced by current head. Mobiles banned apart from at break times and lunch. Once a pupil caught with a cigarette was sent home immediately. Another who had shaved his head was made to stay at home until his hair had grown back. No tolerance for inappropriate use of internet. 'If behaviour is good, they learn,' believes head. The pupils we met were polite and friendly and clearly felt at ease with their teachers. Hands-on head who is quick to tell pupils to smarten up if shirts are hanging out or ties are at half-mast. When pupils need to cool off, members of staff take them for a walk in Richmond Park to clear their heads. 'We don't mollycoddle them,' says head. 'We treat them like all the other teenagers in the country but when they fall, we catch them.'

School is keen to praise its pupils at every opportunity. They are given responsibility with a prefect team headed by head boy and head girl. Success is recognised through house points and badges on school blazers. Headmistress's letter is the ultimate reward. Achievements are celebrated in assembly and prize-giving.

Pupils and parents: Most come from within a 10 mile radius, in particular from Barnes, Putney, Wandsworth, Kingston and Hampton as well as central London, but becoming increasingly local. A sprinkling from overseas. Head says parents are highly supportive and raise huge sums for the school. Current parents are teachers, barristers, solicitors, politicians as well as some media folk.

Parents generally feel they are kept in the loop via weekly newsletter, though one mother complained that parents were not informed early enough about a teacher leaving. Talks regularly put on for parents, including how to cope with teenage anxiety.

Entrance: Non-selective. Pupils come here from a wide number of feeder schools including Parsons Green Prep, Hurlingham School, Finton House and the Lycée. Main point of entry is year 7, though pupils accepted mid-year if there is space.

Prospective pupils join in classes for the day where teachers set 'a number of tasks to establish the student's current level of ability in a variety of subjects'. Online diagnostic assessments also demonstrate the way pupils learn and their potential. Behaviour and interaction with other students are also important in deciding whether school can offer the pupil a place. Sometimes further assessment days are needed before a decision can be made.

Most special needs are identified prior to pupils arriving here but further assessments are carried out in year 7 and extra support is then put in place. Head is frank with parents from the off and personally shows all families around. She wants parents to be aware of what school can and cannot provide.

We have a reputation for working with teenagers who have needs but are not special needs teenagers. This makes us different

Exit: Roughly 80 per cent continue their education at sixth form, with others going on to apprenticeships, and a significant number progress to university. Pupils' destinations have included Blossom House, Carshalton Boys', Coombe Sixth Form, Esher College, More House in Frensham, MPW, Richmond College, Waldegrave and St John's Leatherhead; and they can now stay on in the new sixth form. One parent felt the head has a good knowledge of suitable schools for her son and was supportive in helping find the right place for him. School tries hard to help pupils find relevant work experience and one pupil we spoke to was bubbling over with enthusiasm about her placement in a local primary school.

Money matters: Small number of bursaries up to a maximum of one-third reduction of fees available, to both current and prospective pupils.

Remarks: Parents speak of transformed lives, one saying: 'It has literally been a life saver for my son. They believed in him from the start. I can't speak highly enough of the school.' Another parent enthused, 'Canbury has allowed my son to be the man he should be.' Head says, 'We are the best kept secret in south west London, but the message is getting out. We're being talked about. We really are a school like no other.' School motto sums up school perfectly: 'Unique. Happy. Inclusive.' A remarkable place.

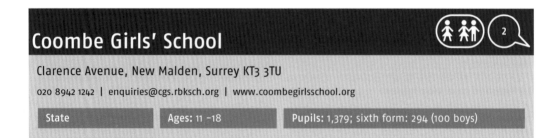

Coombe Girls' School

Clarence Avenue, New Malden, Surrey KT3 3TU

020 8942 1242 | enquiries@cgs.rbksch.org | www.coombegirlsschool.org

| State | Ages: 11 –18 | Pupils: 1,379; sixth form: 294 (100 boys) |

Executive headteachers: Since 2011, Deborah Walls (40s). As executive principal of Coombe Secondary Schools Academy Trust, also has oversight of Coombe Boys' and Knollmead, formerly a failing primary school but now undoubtedly destined for far greater things. Her second time here – after teaching posts at Wallington High School for Girls and Langley Park, did stint in 1996 as head of languages, before being promoted to assistant head, moving back to Wallington as deputy head in 2003 and then closing in on Coombe again when was appointed in same role at boys' school. 'When you've worked [here] it becomes a part of you,' she says. 'It's more than just a job, it's part of your life.'

Discerning readers will also have clocked career focus on single sex schools which, yes, reflects Mrs Walls' strong belief that they're an educational essential. Means chance to find out who you are in safe environment, she believes. 'You can be yourself and let your individuality come out.'

Not that she wants anyone closed off from 'big world of opportunities,' as she puts it. Even before mixed sixth form, many co-curricular activities such as public speaking and ski trip are co-ed, while whole year groups of boys and girls have annual timetabled session themed according to age and interests – year 7s enjoy rocket making, year 8s self-awareness, while in years 9 and 10 there's more formal focus on options and higher education. It's diamond model light, the perfect scenario, thinks Mrs Walls. 'Gives the best of every world.'

Her family's talent for languages (grand-mother, a teacher and languages expert, was a particular inspiration) meant career and special-ism never in doubt, particularly when coupled with precocious ability to see flaws in the system (sussed, aged 11, the drawbacks of teaching languages in English). Enjoys travel, though helping own chil-dren achieve happiness and success are about as close as she comes to a hobby as, unsurprisingly, not much in the way of spare time pursuits.

Still manages to fit in some teaching but thor-oughly enjoys organisational side of the role. Just as well as calls on time come thick and fast, from recent appointment as governor of King's College Wimbledon to beaming in advice to struggling schools, helped by colleagues. As Coombe is a national teaching school, also involved in growing new crops of teachers and bringing returners back into the fold. So many other requests to partici-pate in kudos – and time – heavy research projects roll in that these days, writes risk analysis before making decision. No point spreading resources too thin, she says. 'We sit back and look at it from every angle first.'

While clearly a first class operator, also warm with great sense of humour but above all with burn-ing desire to do her best for the girls, something that appears to permeate school consciousness. 'You may not hear much about her but know she has our interests at heart,' said one. They're also impressively confident in speaking their minds. When we asked year 9 pupil in her presence if she was enjoying producing complex-looking design for tote bag, we got a matter-of-fact 'no.' Sensitive to colleagues' needs, too. During tour, expertly bypassed trainee teacher in danger of losing the thread when confronted unexpectedly by head, assistant head and energetic note-taker.

Goals? With lots still to do, we're not sensing any appetite for a move elsewhere (though must be plenty who'd leap at the chance to recruit her). Parents value her strengths – 'Good combination of organisation, professionalism and approachabil-ity,' said one – and take her other commitments in their stride. While naturally delighted that appointment of new head at boys' school (former assistant head at Coombe Girls') now means Mrs Walls is here more often, parents have boundless confidence in school management's ability to cope when she's called away.

'Ideal person to lead the federation into its next stage of development,' was commendation from predecessor here. Professional and warm, she's sup-portive of other women attempting to get to the top and involved in local initiative for women lead-ers. We suspect that seeing her at work and clearly getting so much from demanding job is probably just as effective when it comes to inspiring future generations of girls.

Mrs Walls believes single sex schools are a chance to find out who you are in safe environment. 'You can be yourself and let your individuality come out'

Joined as executive head in September 2019 by Andy Platt, who had been headteacher since September 2017 and was previously deputy head.

Headteacher: Since September 2019 is Emily Barnes, previously director of sixth form.

Academic matters: School 'honoured' that it remains hugely oversubscribed – and not hard to see why parents would be bonkers to bust a gut securing place anywhere else if successful here. If daughter has tried out (unsuccessfully) for nearby grammars – and many have – don't worry, stress parents. The bright flourish here, some reckon more so than they would have done in the febrile atmosphere of ultra-selective alternatives where it can take full marks just to get noticed. In 2019, 30 per cent of A levels graded A*/A and 52 per cent at A*/B. At GCSE in 2019, 40 per cent 9-7.

Success founded on strong relationships between staff and pupils – confidence boosting a speciality. 'School has really built her up,' said parent of previously shy daughter. Staff feel well supported and, like parents and pupils, given regu-lar slots where can raise difficulties and issues and know will be listened to. Asked if they ever go home, they laugh (but don't actually confirm that they do). Official school day, which runs 8.40am to 3.30pm with five 60-minute lessons, often extends into evening and weekend activities. School also unleavable in career terms, with 27 members of staff (average age 39) into their second decade or more. Newcomers or long-stayers, all exude palpable warmth down to smiley trio on duty to greet latecomers who run velvet glove rather than gauntlet, while row of clocks set to other time zones tells you how tardy you'd be in Buenos Aires.

Plenty of little touches – teacher (male) baking cake for GCSE geography pupils: 'Oh, Sir!' they shout, celebration breakfasts for good results, librarians who take no chances – up to year 8 'we read to girls and they read to us' – and offer full set of daily papers: The Times to tabloids. Above all it's a sense that girls are known and that teachers 'are rooting for them,' said mother.

Curriculum planned to nth degree – each subject served in parent handbook filleted into component parts with garnish of thoughtful enrichment activities, many of a useful nature (times tables tests for maths), others winningly desirable (geography trip to Paris for all year 7s). Some classes are set (maths in years 7 and 8 plus English in year 9), others in mixed ability groups (technology and languages), while science sometimes is and sometimes isn't, flexible approach dictated by range of each year group's ability and changing schemes of work.

Though there's extra stretch for gifted and talented, achievements in all their diversity are celebrated. Nitpickers might point to percentage of low achievers making expected progress in maths – currently it's just 32 per cent according to Dept for Education data. But given latest in series of letters from government, praising results, and stunningly high Progress 8 figures – numbers passing toughest GCSEs – any nits picked would be of microscopic dimensions.

For disadvantaged pupils (around a fifth) mostly a pretty positive picture, with half securing five or more GCSEs including maths and English. Low-ish numbers of pupils with SEN (currently 25, seven with EHC plan), all supported in timetabled hours, with everything from teaching in lessons to room 41 – a dedicated haven for those struggling with sensory or emotional overload in or out of lessons. It's a rare pupil they can't cater for, SEN working closely with staff providing weekly briefing on needs and support. Similar system for EAL pupils including buddy system and catch up or slower paced lessons, though not needed by vast, linguistically competent majority.

Inevitably, families not above supplementing with tutors if pace of lessons leaves children behind. No criticism, says one, just normal for the area. 'A universal problem.' School feels shouldn't be necessary and points to numerous initiatives – tracking

and lots of it, blips quickly picked up with extra catch up and revision sessions for anyone in danger of falling behind. 'Try to get the absolute best out of them,' thought parent and school reckoned to listen to parents and respond quickly, complaints limited particularly now anxiety over turnover of science teachers has slowed, department has no vacancies and (impressively) biologists, chemists and physicists are all teaching own subjects.

Confidence boosting a speciality. 'School has really built her up,' said parent of previously shy daughter

Post 16, there's a split screen approach, more academic subjects here, vocational at boys' school and 35 courses in total. Otherwise beamish Ofsted report had reined in lumens slightly – attendance and results were felt to be below par, some of brightest lured away by excellent fare on offer at outstanding local sixth form colleges.

School has responded by upping budget for careers and uni preparation and bringing in dashing new subjects including A level classics (follows success of Latin GCSE, taught out of hours with support from King's College School) plus government & politics and economics, each new addition somehow woven into the timetable by staff specialist (swears more fun than other hobbies – cryptic crosswords and fiendish sudoku).

Smaller but significant perks such as sixth form snack exclusives (panini, jacket potatoes and sausage rolls) and relaxed uniform code (we admired one girl's dazzling blue Doc Martens, just seen under sombre trousers and conventional shirt) have no doubt played part in improving results and pupil retention.

Games, options, the arts: In addition to all the curriculum must-haves, many wonderful-to-haves such as active Duke of Edinburgh. All this despite limited resources, felt to tail off only slightly in sixth form (dance would be popular addition to the menu, thought several pupils). Plenty lower down the school, though, with year 7s working on cross-curricular project, themed to 'my journey' which culminates in presentation to parents, as well as covering off everything from cultural diversity to healthy lifestyles, touch-typing and research skills.

It's all approached with dash and enthusiasm, visible also in enthusiastic art and DT, dresses cascading ruffles and crank handle wooden toys on display, walls brightened by everything from lavish, Rubens-style picture of woman's torso to accomplished year 9 self-portraits in chalks. Performing arts, felt by parents to have been a notch below par, now on the up again with revitalised productions, some at Rose Theatre in nearby Kingston, courtesy of new, dynamic head of music (peak beard, creative tie) and vibrant drama department.

Sports appropriately energetic, facilities – own grounds as well as impressively large sports hall – felt to give it the edge in comparison with many other more space-challenged secondaries nearby. Houses compete to speed run a mile round the grounds in aid of Sports Relief and teams frequently successful in outside events, year 7 football team achieving silver in borough event, trampolining a particular strength, one former pupil going on to become county coach.

Parents complimentary about achievements though wish lists would include extra coaching, funds permitting. 'It's not a level playing field,' said one with feeling, if not literal accuracy.

Background and atmosphere: Set in heart of New Malden, between lush Kingston Hill mansions and more workaday housing and on same compact site since foundation in 1955 as Coombe County Secondary School.

Original uniform, mustered for diamond anniversary celebrations, a smart affair, including woolly scarf and squashy felt hat. Though both have gone, other nostalgic touches remain, including original wooden bars in gym, space now repurposed as dance studio and occasional exam room.

Site is spotless, courtesy of maintenance team whose devotion extends to post-break litter-picking sessions. Plenty of greenery – year 7s have own grassy area and even the cut-down playing field, which could so easily be sea of mud, is a well-tended space, while small hedges, something of a planting favourite, brighten up odds and ends of space no end.

Plenty of greenery – year 7s have own grassy area and even the cut-down playing field, which could so easily be sea of mud, is a well-tended space

---

Niceness extends to other areas. Floral scent wafts from newer, far bigger sports hall. Particularly fragrant staff? 'Just what the cleaners use,' says teacher. And despite one parental comment that catering had suffered slight decline, range and quality looked impressive, all meals cooked from scratch by team in at 6.00am to add dainty finishing touches, no toasted sandwich minus its upmarket cardboard envelope or St Valentine's Day cake

lacking an icing heart. And all served with sugar-free drinks and low prices (roast and a pud for £2).

Sixth form centre a building of two halves, one for quiet study (plenty of 'shushing' from supervising teacher if it isn't), common room on the other. Appears girl-heavy but boys magically appear at break time (just follow the sound of the football).

Rebuild of this and other less than gorgeous areas (flaking paint is pointed out by teacher with a certain relish) would be top of Mrs Walls' wish list. Pristine additions – geography recently rehomed while staff also have a posh room for best – show what can be achieved.

Pastoral care, well-being and discipline: New pupils eased in with visits to feeder primaries and summer school at end of year 6, including trips to London Zoo – website is big on reassurance, with relaxed pupils sharing tips. First day 'one of the best and scariest, felt was going to die but at the same time really excited.'

New or not, school makes no bones about expectations. With so much going on, likes pupils to get the full benefit of school life and stresses importance of punctuality, with sliding scale of detentions from 10 minutes with tutor after school for one offence to a one hour Friday session for five late arrivals – plus parent meeting. Request for term time absence unlikely to be considered, let alone granted, for anyone whose attendance drops below 98 per cent.

All other breaches (arriving in mufti, failing to stow outdoor coats in lockers, long, fake or varnished nails, using phones during school day) sanctions are strict and explicit, exclusion for 'defiance' the non-negotiable norm for persistent offenders followed by 'formal reintegration [where] your daughter's future will be discussed.' One to avoid, though, stresses school, it's only tiny minority who fail to obey the rules. Just as well, as there's now greater formality (compulsory blazers for all).

Plenty of support for families (we hope that 'talk to your teen' advice on website, containing conversation-igniting gems such as 'That looks interesting, what are you doing?' is as popular as it deserves to be). Parents accept need for rules with slight sigh (decision to ban popular black leather lace up trainer derivative caused a bit of angst), girls similarly philosophical, hitching up skirts again as soon as doorstep length inspection completed.

Teachers approachable and reassuring – 'Ones you click with are a comfort, especially at exam time,' said sixth former – and tough issues addressed head on, from mental health issues and grooming to bullying (including advice on how to cope if child is bully rather than victim...). School has at least one eye fixed firmly on friendship issues, pupils so effectively mixed and matched on arrival that pretty much guaranteed you'll leave with different mates from the ones you arrived with. Pragmatic approach of 'getting everyone to sit down and talk it over rather than screaming at each other,' said pupil, generally felt to be key to resolving majority of difficulties. Special resource provision unit for hearing impaired children (new in 2018) increasing student numbers.

Pupils and parents: By far best known former pupil is children's Jacqueline Wilson (now with a new building named after her); also Olympic athlete Anne Packer. Alumni association, only recently set up, promises to bring many more successful former pupils – plenty of creative and City types – back into the fold.

Regardless of background, packed with conscientious, hard-working sorts and notable for strong sense of community – tragic pupil death led to whole school rag week, everyone contributing, most popular event penalty shootout, sixth form boys doused with water if failed to save goals. 'What could be better?' said girl.

Entrance: From over 900 applicants, takes 210 in year 7, popularity inevitably resulting in a 'Honey, I shrunk the catchment area' issue (under two km in first round of offers), to school a source of mixed pride over popularity and sadness that so many who want to come here can't. Arrive from numerous primaries headed by Burlington Junior School, Christ Church C of E, Coombe Hill Junior School and King's Oak Primary.

Post-16, there's second chance at a place here, seven GCSEs with 6s or better in chosen A level subjects required. More places for girls – 210, compared with 100 boys – and priority for existing pupils, 40 per cent going to external candidates, who'll be vetted for academic potential and attitude to learning.

Exit: 'Aspire' programme offers Oxbridge taster events (with input from King's College School) and STEM-related courses, designed to ensure pupils get the rundown on full range of top careers and courses and don't settle for second best. In 2019, a quarter to Russell Group, one Oxbridge place and one medic. London unis – UCL, King's College and Queen Mary – regularly feature as most popular destinations, others to Bristol, Cardiff, Exeter, Leeds, Nottingham. Recent spread of subjects also includes law and modern languages.

Money matters: Asks for annual payment of £120 per family – voluntary, some families contributing more.

Remarks: Fabulous education, staff who can't tear themselves away and delighted parents. What's not to like? 'A pure comprehensive which is very rare and does what it does really well,' said mother. 'I wouldn't consider anywhere else because my daughter is so happy.'

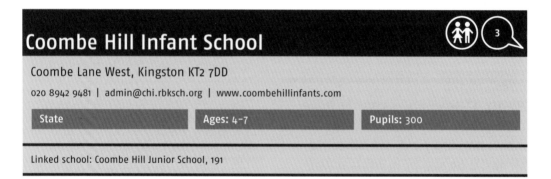

Coombe Hill Infant School

Coombe Lane West, Kingston KT2 7DD

020 8942 9481 | admin@chi.rbksch.org | www.coombehillinfants.com

State	Ages: 4–7	Pupils: 300

Linked school: Coombe Hill Junior School, 191

Headteacher: Since 2013, Janet Berry. SENCo and senior assistant head for three years prior to taking over the headship. Has been at the school for 13 years, starting part time when her children were pupils and progressing through the ranks as they got older.

Entrance: Much sought-after local school. The closer you live the better, although it may still prove difficult to get in. More than 550 first choice applications for 90 places; over half go to siblings.

Admission policy strictly adhered to – medical or social needs get priority. Occasional bulge years add an extra class.

Exit: Almost without fail to the junior school next door. One or two to local independent schools, of which there are plenty.

Remarks: From the moment you walk into it, through the art gallery entrance, you realise that this is a lively school bursting with happy,

Plenty of room to run, climb and explore. Children certainly make the most of it

interested children. A vast ethnic mix – about 60 per cent need some EAL support, mainly in class except in extreme cases. No attached nursery, so some children arrive speaking no English at all while others speak two or three different languages. The resulting mix is 'demanding but fascinating to work with.' All classes – five or more of up to 30 children in each age group – mixed ability. One full time teacher for each, plus a teacher's aide for at least half of the day and other extra staff who help wherever needed. All are highly trained and experienced, often current or ex-parents. 'The school has a really family feel,' we were told.

Fantastic semi open-plan layout, all on one floor, loads of natural light. Corridors of well-equipped classrooms, all with interactive whiteboards, computers and educational displays. Children's creations abound. Pupils enjoy themselves, eagerly joining in all activities. When we visited all of them were absorbed, participating and learning, and eager to show us what they were doing. Three excited year 2 pupils were delighted to take us round their school and point out their favourite places and activities.

Fantastic IT suite, good lending library with videos, games, reading and maths schemes. Great art on display everywhere.

One of the special things about this school (and the junior school next door) is the massive amount of outdoor space. Plenty of room to run, climb and explore. Children certainly make the most of it – log cabin for special projects and areas for planting and learning. Imaginations soar. Pupils have the use of a heated swimming pool (in the junior school's section of the shared open land) in the summer term. Each class has weekly sessions, weather permitting.

Mix of nationalities means cultural activities from all over. Most festivals are celebrated and any excuse for dressing up is grabbed. Knowledge of the world is part of the learning process – every child and every country is important. Music and art are an essential part of the school day.

Lots of after-school clubs that change termly. Sport, drama, music, art, computers and other themes – all good fun, all for a minimum charge.

This is a popular school and houses in the area are very sought after. They are very lucky, too, to have active, involved parents who raise a fortune and provide funds for the school's continuing excellence.

Coombe Hill Junior School

Coombe Lane West, Kingston KT2 7DD

020 8949 1743 | admin@chj.rbksch.org | www.coombehillj.kingston.sch.uk

State | **Ages: 7–11** | **Pupils: 420**

Linked school: Coombe Hill Infant School, 190

Head of junior school: Since 2014, Mark Clutterbuck, previously deputy principal at Chessington Community College.

Entrance: Some 99 per cent of junior school entrants automatically from the infant school. Others all local, round the corner.

Exit: Majority of to local state schools, impressive number to the highly selective Kingston state grammars Tiffin Boys and Girls, more to Coombe Girls and Boys, others all over. With the improvement that has taken place in the current local state schools, very few pupils now move into the private system.

Remarks: A brilliant, buzzing, exciting state school more than ever holding its own against the many local private sector schools. Very much an upmarket area; the pupils are a huge ethnic mix from a variety of backgrounds, with parents who help, encourage and enjoy the multinational involvement.

We were taken round by some senior pupils eager to show us everything that was going on. We didn't miss a nook or a cranny and were suitably impressed. Everywhere was clean, bright and full of happy, thoroughly involved children. Classrooms overflowing with interesting displays. Technology everywhere. Parents told us 'excellent teaching', 'fantastic, exuberant teachers', 'great facilities' and 'really like the way they make learning fun and incorporate different subjects in one lesson'. We were delighted to see a good number of male teachers, two of whom are heads of year. Classrooms a bit squashed but that didn't appear to matter; flexibility is the name of the game. All mixed ability but the brightest separated into four groups for maths and literacy. We were told, 'the teaching is something special, a real collaboration between teacher and pupil, teacher and teacher, and pupil and pupil, they all help each other'. 'No cramming, the education is broad and full, they are taught to debate and to question and to discover for themselves'.

No cramming, the education is broad and full, they are taught to debate and to question and to discover for themselves

Lots of music, singing and playing different instruments. Private lessons available for those who want to learn a particular instrument. Everyone learns the recorder in year 4. Our guides proudly showed us the range available for them to try. Great art on display in the atrium and, when we were there, models of Andersen shelters – 'very difficult to make!' For a state primary, the sport is exceptional. A brand new games area provides for cricket, netball, basketball, football, rugby and other sports, some of which they play competitively against other schools. Not enough, some parents think, but it is a privilege not there for all primary school children, so they are lucky. And they have their own heated swimming pool – two sessions a week for each class. Added to that PE and dance form an important part of the curriculum.

Our guides led us proudly round their extensive grounds. Every class has an outdoor learning day once a year. As well as the usual play areas, there are wildlife areas, including a pond and a 'hotel' for insects, a vegetable garden – 'some we eat, some we sell' – and, really exciting, a pen for chickens whose eggs, of course, also get eaten.

Sympathetic SENCo who seems to really care for the children, making sure no needy child slips through the net. Several groups, run by learning support teachers, take pupils out of class where necessary, but never during a core subject. Non-stop records kept and a provision map for every child in the school. Those with behavioural problems get one-to-one support but they do try to make sure that they are given enough individual space. SENCo works closely with both the behavioural team and the class teachers, trying to tackle problems before they go too far. Says it's important to try and pre-empt difficult situations before they get out of hand. 'I really love my job'. Parents say, 'Children respected and nurtured. Bad behaviour not tolerated'. 'Quick to deal with problems'.

A large variety of after-school clubs which are extremely popular and introduce children to new skills and ideas. An hour a day, all taught by their regular teachers with a minimal charge to cover materials.

Mix of nationalities means cultural activities from all over. Most festivals are celebrated and any excuse for dressing up is grabbed. Knowledge of the world is part of the learning process – every child and every country is important. Music and art are an essential part of the school day. Parents rave about every aspect, haven't got a single criticism. Only worry, will they be able to maintain this high achievement level?

All in all, a tip-top school that has managed and absorbed the necessary expansion over the last few years and the broad ethnic diversity that is Greater London today.

Fern Hill Primary School

Richmond Road, Kingston, Surrey KT2 5PE

020 8247 0300 | office@fernhill.rbksch.org | www.fernhill.kingston.sch.uk

| State | Ages: 3–11 | Pupils: 700 |

Headteacher: Since 2015, Adam Scott, previously deputy head, who has been at the school for over 15 years.

Entrance: Very popular, very oversubscribed, move very close. Usual local authority admissions criteria apply, which essentially means siblings and distance. Obviously catchment varies, but always tight – anecdotally an 800m radius most recently. Due to population bulge, Kingston has had a problem with reception place numbers and the school is expanding. Worth staying on the waiting list as there is a trickle of mobility in the area and odd spaces do come up.

Exit: Be aware that although packed with good primaries, north Kingston is short of secondary school places – though the new Kingston Academy should ease matters, and some leavers are moving on there. Many pupils progress to Grey Court in Ham, which is actually in the neighbouring borough of Richmond. Others feed elsewhere into the Kingston and Richmond secondary systems. Handfuls to the much sought after places at very nearby selective Tiffin grammar schools (NB almost everyone in north Kingston uses private tutoring to try and get to these schools). Some plunge into the private pool (some always planned to), including Kingston Grammar (co-ed), Hampton (boys) and Surbiton High (girls).

Remarks: A top-notch school – regularly vies with neighbouring Latchmere for unofficial 'best in borough' award. Sets high standards, has high expectations and unsurprisingly attracts high numbers of the white middle classes who abound in this area. A real community school – just be aware that the community is north Kingston, swarming with young professionals hell-bent on achieving a first class state education for their brood. After the white middle classes, largest ethnic group is Asian. School says not all is leafy and lovely in Kingston and there is some social housing around, but this accounts for a minority of the cohort.

Ofsted rates Fern Hill as 'outstanding and providing an excellent all-round education', praising pupils' achievements both academically and in terms of their personal development.

Academic standards are good – generally around half the year group achieves above expected levels in maths and science Sats. School acknowledges that many of its pupils enter the school with above average skills but, even so, these results are sparkling and seemingly achieved without too much pressure placed on the children – 'The parents are probably pushier than the school', commented one mother.

There's a distinct private school feel to the place – and not just because the children are beautifully turned out in smart uniform. Everything is orderly and fairly calm, but not sterile, children all appear engaged and on-task, overall a quite traditional feel to things. Children sit in groups around tables, but for year 6 move to rows to support the sense that year 6 is a special year and to ready them for their more formal secondary schools. Lots of praise for teaching staff – stable and nice mix of youth and experience, few men (but including deputy head with high parental approval rating). When staff do leave it is rarely to work at another local school. Teaching assistants everywhere (more assistants than teachers) some class-based, others working with individual children, more senior TAs leading activities such as PSHE, ICT etc.

There's a distinct private school feel to the place and not just because the children are beautifully turned out in smart uniform. Everything is orderly and fairly calm

School packs it all in via a tight timetable and has made real efforts to introduce more creative ways of learning, for example using drama to help pupils empathise with historical characters. Lots of cross-curriculum and project work helps to free up the day – eg non-fiction literacy as part of history, writing for a purpose. Teachers add breadth to the national curriculum diktats introducing supplementary topics of their choice. 'We are always looking at the curriculum and trying to find links'. 'Obviously some subjects need to be directly taught, but in other areas we can pull things together to make things less prosaic and more interesting for the children'. Homework manageable, about half an hour a week for years 3 and 4, rising to half an hour a day by year 6. School adamant that young children need a life and to have time to do other things outside school. 'Homework is not a central part of the school'. Tutoring for entrance to the Tiffin schools is huge in this area and school is reasonably relaxed about it but admits to some concern for any child who is hauled around to take lots of different entry exams.

Specialist French teacher; all pupils learn from nursery with every class having a short French lesson each week, with some language and vocabulary incorporated into the children's learning during the rest of the week. Several other teachers are confident French speakers and the long term aim is for all teachers to be able to teach French to their own classes. Also a specialist music teacher now comes in two days a week which, together with links to Kingston Music (and Arts) Service, has seen some improvements in this area – previously a little weak for this school. There is now a school choir and orchestra in which a few parents play too. Around 45 pupils learn an instrument and each year 3 has an opportunity to learn strings.

Gold award for art, kite mark for PE – school takes this side of the curriculum just as seriously as the academic work.

The school has a special needs/inclusion coordinator with a team of teaching assistants and a dedicated resource, the Rainbow Room. Some 60 odd pupils are on the SEN register. These children are taught with their class as much as possible, with one-to-one or small group sessions used to support this as necessary. EAL support is available but, although some 180 pupils have English as a second language, their English is usually good. Flexible ability grouping within each class, and there is plenty of room to take small groups out for focused teaching as necessary. School has had a good reputation for picking up any problems or learning difficulties early – some parental concern over whether staff will be able to maintain this focus as school expands.

School is very keen on good manners, politeness and respect. Overall pupil behaviour and attitude is great – for the most part these children are on-side and eager to learn. They abide by 'golden rules', the breaking of which results in the loss of 'golden minutes' from playtimes. (But other times they gain – we passed children returning from the playground after a five-minute, mid-lesson 'brain break'.) All the children understand the school's focus on the 6Rs – resourcefulness, resilience, reflection, responsibility, reasoning and respect – promoted around the place by Winnie the Pooh and his friends. 'We are generally very lucky that our children are well-behaved. But there are some little pickles that we need to manage, as well as looking out for the quiet ones so that they don't disappear'.

Plenty of trips and visitors – everything from theatre groups to fire engines and animals. 'There's nothing boring,' said one pupil. 'We're always doing something fun'

School environment enjoys all the advantages that come with having been purpose-built (coincidentally in response to a shortfall in school places back in 1994) including wide doors and corridors and specialist toilet facilities for disabled children. Use of space is very good throughout. Classrooms are all a reasonable size, lots of outdoor activities for the tinies and separate playgrounds for nursery, infants and juniors (though again playground space at a premium as school size increases). Full-time social skills assistant on hand to encourage play and mediate where necessary. External facilities also include an environmental area and inner courtyard with amphitheatre feature.

A lot goes on here and it is all written up, drawn, photographed, modelled, reviewed or rewarded in pen, pencil, paint, clay, crayon – you name it and it's probably up on a wall somewhere

Newish buildings include a sports hall, small hall and music room on the back of the school, together with alterations to the existing hall to make seven new classrooms, an art room, new special needs room and additional multi-purpose small group rooms. The field at the back of the school is landscaped to include an all-weather surface, new football pitch and other playtime activities. Part of the school has become two-storey.

Great displays are all around; a lot goes on here and it is all written up, drawn, photographed, modelled, reviewed or rewarded in pen, pencil, paint, clay, crayon – you name it and it's probably up on a wall somewhere. It's not an especially tidy place, but nor is it sloppy – it's just a reflection of a busy school life.

Strong and competitive house system, busy school council with some powers and facilities all help promote positive peer groups. (Recent pupil decision was to swap the older girls' and boys' loos as it was felt that the boys would benefit from having an open window in their facilities. Pupil power in action.) Lots of after-school clubs, till 4.30pm. No other on site before or after-school care facilities, but the school does have a close association with the nearby YMCA Hawker Centre which provides breakfast and teatime clubs and will take and collect the children to and from school.

Parents feel involved, lots help and home/school communication is good. Colonised by the middle classes who are willing (and encouraged) to get fully involved in school life, the PTA is, as you would imagine, very active and well-supported. 'It's a very special place,' said a parent, 'and we all want to do our bit'. It's a secure, happy place with lots going on. Plenty of trips and visitors – everything from theatre groups to fire engines and animals. 'There's nothing boring,' said one dream pupil. 'We're always doing something fun'.

To our question, 'Any notable former pupils?' school answers positively, 'Not yet' – but you come away feeling that there certainly will be in 20 years' time. You would be delighted to have this state offering on your doorstep – which is indeed where it will need to be for your child to attend.

The Harrodian School

Lonsdale Road, London SW13 9QN

020 8748 6117 | admin@harrodian.com | www.harrodian.com

Independent	Pupils: 1,015; sixth form: 170
Ages: 4–18	Fees: £15,600 – £23,961 pa

Headmaster: Since 1999, James Hooke BSc PGCE (geographer). Educated at nearby Hampton Grammar, followed by Leeds University. Began his career in the City but swiftly changed to teaching abroad at St John's School, Buenos Aires. From 1994 deputy head at The Harrodian, working alongside legendary Peter Thomson, becoming head five years later. Youthful in appearance, he finds seeing young people progress under his watch extremely satisfying and is sad to see them go. This is a head who regularly takes lunch duties, checking queue hoppers, happily chatting with pupils over meals. He moves about the school with calm, purposeful authority, and is, above all, accessible and approachable.

One parent observed, 'Although there have been changes as the school has grown in size, the ethos remains the same at the heart of it, and that emanates from the head.' What is impressive is that in a school of some 1,000 pupils, the head really knows them, taking pleasure in acknowledging their interests and achievements. Parents agree: 'Mr Hooke knows them all as personalities. He stands outside, on the pavement, or on the side of the pitch. Pupils feel connected and valued. He often praises them for things they do outside school and manages to be at everything'. Committed to the ongoing success of the school, he moves effortlessly from leading pre-prep assemblies, to a sixth form planning meeting, to selecting future pupils ('increasingly difficult as demand has grown,' he comments), to evening engagements such as a prefects' dinner in the City. For relaxation, this energetic man can be found on the ski slopes with the school trip or playing golf alongside pupils and parents. When we visited, he was about to participate in a weekend Surrey cycling event.

Mr Hooke has put in place a dynamic, experienced team of senior staff and looks after them, inspiring loyalty. Among them is the calm, capable head of pre-prep, Lucy Horan, who has been in place since 2004. Her previous experience was in the state sector – Our Lady of Victories in Putney and deputy head at the Oratory in Chelsea. Jenny O'Neill became head of lower prep in 2015, herself mother of three Harrodians, so 'I really know the school and Harrodian style first-hand,' and is determined to create 'an even stronger sense of team and community in the prep school'.

Sixth form thrives under stewardship of business-like David Behan, ex-City banker and Oxford geographer, who was appointed as head of economics, and who collaborates with senior colleagues to ensure university application guidance and careers advice is given and changes carefully engineered as new-style A levels work their way through.

Academic matters: 'This school caters for individuals and allows children to be themselves,' was the observation of more than one parent. A broad curriculum caters for different tastes. 'All take single sciences at GCSE', explained the head, 'to ensure they keep their options open'. Streaming in English, maths and languages. Bilingual pupils are expected to study two different languages and all benefit from being taught by wholly native speakers, as we observed. Latin and religious studies survive. No design technology but graphic design, photography, media and 3D design offered. Unnecessary pressure is avoided but pupils are made aware of the need to apply themselves in GCSEs since the AS has disappeared and these grades help to secure future university places. Pupils spoke of the Aspirational Universities Club which they had found helpful.

The cream, well-proportioned building is beautifully pristine with its sweeping lawn and manicured neat lines

Standards continue to rise as entrance becomes more selective. An impressive 80 per cent A*-B at A level (52 per cent A*/A) in 2019 and 71 per cent 9-7 at GCSE. Nevertheless, Mr Behan stresses, 'there is room for the individual for whom three Cs could be a real achievement'. The school is not setting out to be all about examination results, but nowadays there are plenty of high achievements to celebrate.

The number of pupils with SEN (notably dyslexia, dyspraxia and dyscalculia) is small, with one or two per form, catered for both within class and with individual support from the experienced learning support department run by highly praised SENCo. Dedicated staff work alongside one another with individuals in a light, spacious, well-resourced room at the top of the building which, in days gone by, was the headmaster's geography classroom. Typically, a parent praised the provision and how her daughter wanted to go to sessions and had noticed the difference since she had received targeted support. In addition specialist one-to-one EAL tuition is provided for the few that need it.

Quite amazingly, for its location, there are 25 acres of playing fields, as well as two all-weather pitches, netball, basketball and tennis courts

ICT is well provided for with interactive whiteboards and dedicated spacious rooms although we did not see younger pupils with iPads or sets of laptops, and the staff commented that the emphasis remains on teacher/pupil oral interaction.

Games, options, the arts: Highly-qualified sports coaches use the latest recording equipment to improve players' techniques and PE A level is available. Smart dance studio accommodates dance, fencing and gym. Amazingly, for its location, there are 25 acres of playing fields, as well as two all-weather pitches, netball, basketball and tennis courts. On and off-site activities for sixth formers include gym and weight training, swimming, spinning, aerobics, body pump and pilates, as well as rowing. Sport is compulsory throughout, with three or four lessons per week out of 30 for sport/ PE. The emphasis is on participating, enjoyment and representing the school, with the Harrodian regularly hosting tournaments, swimming galas and athletic meets. When we visited the U18 rugby had been almost unbeaten in a highly successful season, with U16 footballers reaching last year's ISFA final. The Ski Academy offers bespoke training in the UK and France for the squad which competes in the English School Ski Championships. The annual golf tournament is very popular and pupils appreciate the wide choices, and sixth formers enjoy a sports afternoon each Wednesday. Attractive heated pool in colonnaded courtyard is open from April to October. The vast array of fixture lists is impressive, catering for a range of abilities, although a few parents we spoke to did not find the amount of sport lived up to their expectations. But one parent explained her son was 'offered a place at Winchester and declined as he wished to remain at the Harrodian and play for the A football team'.

'Superb music,' was parental consensus, with compulsory lessons up to year 9 with music and music technology available at GCSE and A level. Over half the pupils receive individual tuition across a full range of instruments and singing from beginner to grade 8. We encountered one prep boy on his way to ukulele and a girl awaiting her grade 4 singing exam during our visit, outside the school's auditorium with its raked seating. All are involved in annual carol concerts at St Paul's Church, Hammersmith. Pupils enjoy annual Battle of the Bands, an X factor style competition for year 4 upwards. Harrodian rockers compete to participate in the Isle of Wight festival. A sixth former spoke enthusiastically of a choir trip to Athens, whilst younger pupils chatted to us animatedly about many other choir opportunities including cadets (boys), stilettos (girls), training choir, senior choice, chamber choir and the Sixteen. 'All are encouraged to perform in assemblies and so grow in confidence and anyone can audition for parts in productions,' parents informed us.

Artists are very well catered for. We watched seniors skilfully painting in oils and acrylics in one of the many attractive art rooms and admired fine displays. As one might expect in a school promoting creativity, diverse courses are on offer, leading to university places to read history of art and art and design. In response to a design and photography challenge, pupils were invited to create a First World War inspired design to stay in one of the senior courtyard buildings until the end of the centenary. Display cabinets in an entrance hall bulged with highly imaginative shoes created for a house art competition. Drama also flourishes and is very popular. Pupils perform at the Edinburgh Fringe and we met one talented individual who had completed her extended project qualification on set design. The school encourages public speaking and debating, which helps pupils to grow in confidence and puts the young at ease when conversing with visitors like us.

Background and atmosphere: In 1993 pioneering Sir Alford and Lady Houstoun-Boswall bought the then country club for Harrods employees with its 25 acres and sporting facilities, to realise their vision for a co-educational preparatory school where children could thrive in a civilised environment without unnecessary pressure. The school has grown from the original 65 pupils and 12 staff to nearly 1,000 pupils and an established sixth form.

The cream, well-proportioned building is beautifully pristine with its sweeping lawn and manicured neat lines. We saw discreet scaffolding camouflaging the latest sixth form building to provide further facilities. Gardens are immaculately maintained, courtyards, olive and magnolias tastefully placed. One could almost imagine oneself in the country, looking out at the 25 acres of playing fields with pitches galore and, across the road, separated by stylish railings, the magnificent view of the river Thames. The exterior is matched by the interior with its sweeping staircases, vast entrance hall and spacious, well-lit rooms.

Pupils and parents comment on 'the warm, friendly atmosphere which marks this school out'. There is an outstanding sense of a vibrant community and this comes from the top. Both exterior and interior promote civilised values, all magically removed from the traffic, noise and hurly burly of Hammersmith Broadway. No wonder some pupils do not see any need to move to board in the country. The institutional aspects of school have been skilfully replaced by synchronised clocks, so no bells, but carpeting and great attention to decoration.

The pre-prep is self-contained in bright, airy accommodation and a paved courtyard. The conservatory provides space for listening to readers and small group work opening onto Astroturf for all the year round play. The attractive French-style garden, complete with water feature, provides a tranquil setting. The prep school is cleverly arranged so that, although senior pupils work in rooms alongside, younger pupils are not intimidated. In fact the natural mixing of age groups is a pleasure to behold. Prefects organise year 4s to obtain sponsors for a charity Easter egg hunt, and science week takes place throughout the school, from a workshop in the hall to Cancer Research teachers in the senior laboratories setting challenges. The coffee shop is another splendid touch, welcoming parents and visitors in the mornings and providing a convivial space for sixth formers, as well as the many comfortable three piece suites we spotted about the place. Lunches are served in a spacious dining room. Some parents and a few pupils we spoke to criticised the quality of the food. 'Too much pasta,' voiced several. The sausage and mash was very popular when we visited. The libraries are an additional bonus, lined with books and with librarians to hand. We were pleased to note the acquisition of reading desks with lamps straight from the old British Library Reading Room, where seniors were studiously in silence. Again the community spirit prevails with annual events such as dads' reading morning for year 4 to 7 and the annual year 4 Night in the Library event.

Pastoral care, well-being and discipline: Pupils of all ages commented on 'the kind teachers' and 'the welcoming atmosphere'. Bullying they did not see as a problem because 'everyone is so kind to one another'. 'It's amazing – everywhere you go there is someone to talk to,' said one year 8 boy. Much has been put in place to promote this caring community including mentoring scheme. Senior school students are selected and trained to provide one-to-one mentoring of younger pupils who they meet with regularly. They also run inductions for newcomers. There is a student leadership programme which gives year 11 and sixth formers the opportunity to develop and apply for roles as subject sports or community leaders.

The school has introduced mindfulness and life coaching for staff and students. A school counsellor is available for drop in sessions for year 7 upwards on a self-referral system whilst younger pupils require consent from a parent. There are timetabled citizenship lessons for year 9 and circle time for younger pupils. A student council meets regularly.

A healthy balance of gender and age among staff reflects the school community and many desire to return. We encountered one ex-Harrodian gap student and another ex-family member appointed to the staff. A young teacher's mother had worked at The Harrodian and Mr Hooke's own children attended the school.

The house system, alongside swimming galas and sports events, sees a flourishing array of staff and pupils zealously throwing themselves into planning and meetings. Pupils appreciate the house bake off, pumpkin carving competition, drama, music and house quizzes. Parents like the fact that 'Kids organise assemblies and ensure all children perform in front of one another'.

Mixing of age groups is a pleasure to behold. Prefects organise year 4s to obtain sponsors for a charity Easter egg hunt, and science week takes place throughout the school

Pupils were very clear about the range of punishments leading to detentions and their fairness. No uniform except in the pre-prep but there is a clear dress code carefully explained in the parent handbook, and implemented. Parents commented: 'Some might say The Harrodian is an easy, relaxed school where anything goes, but it is no laissez faire country club. Far from it: there is zero tolerance for drugs or bullying. The school acts on bullying swiftly and effectively when it does occur.' A few parents suggested there could be more effort and consistency over pupils' awareness of others and politeness when moving around the school. However, parents feel they can see a member of staff promptly if they have a concern, and approach the head informally, which they would not attempt at a more traditional school. The PTA chair explained 'the school has no out of bounds areas, which means pupils can be happy, and feel free to express themselves rather than intimidated'

Pupils and parents: Notable former pupils include actors Will Poulter, Robert Pattinson, George MacKay and Tom Sturridge and musician Will Heard. Parents increasingly include entrepreneurs, those involved in advertising and public relations alongside professional families and international businesspeople. There is a real sense of continuity, the PTA chair having been there since the school's foundation. Parents value the fact all of their children can spend their whole schooldays here.

Entrance: The catchment area includes Barnes, Mortlake, Putney, Sheen and Richmond, as one might expect, as well as stretching towards Ealing, Holland Park and Chelsea, with a few older pupils travelling from as far as Wandsworth or Battersea by train. Main admission points are at 4+, 8+,11+,13+ and 16+, with occasional places at other times. Non-selective reception places by informal assessment and date of registration. Siblings are given priority but not guaranteed a place. Admission to the prep and above involves exam and interview. There are a few places at 8+ for children from the Merlin School in Putney.

At 11+ there is a diverse range of applicants for some 25-28 places (exam and interview). At 13+, common entrance or school's assessment plus interview.

Sixth form entry requires six or more grade 6s at GCSE, at least 4s in English and mathematics, plus 9-7s in chosen A level subjects. Standards less stringent for internal applicants as external applicants sit mathematics and English examinations, plus interviews in prospective A level subjects (six

or seven external places) and current school reference. As head remarks, '16+ applicants include those who have had enough of boarding, along with girls, in particular, who wish to escape from single sex London day schools'. Increasing numbers staying on after GCSE with new sixth form facilities.

Exit: A decreasing few at CE to trad boarding schools (Eton, Harrow, Charterhouse, Marlborough, Wellington etc) and single sex London day schools (St Paul's Girls', King's College School etc); in 2019, five junior school pupils were awarded academic scholarships by the senior school. Majority stay on for GCSEs now with just a few going elsewhere eg to boarding or tutorial colleges. University destinations varied, ditto subjects, though economics and business currently very popular. Around three-quarters to UK universities (Bristol, Bath and Leeds all popular). In 2019, one to Oxbridge and 13 to study in US, Canada and Europe.

Money matters: Fees are in line with local schools. Limited bursaries are reserved for the unexpected crisis. Limited academic awards for internal candidates at 13+ and 16+.

Remarks: Head emphasises 'The Harrodian is not an international school with high turnover of pupils: rather, pupils reflect London's exciting, vibrant international community'. In this civilised setting, a diverse, cosmopolitan community happily thrives. One parent of four commented, 'The school believes that if a child enjoys where they are, they are more willing to learn', and that has proven to be the case for her family. 'The school understands that every child is good at one thing and if you harness that, then there is a positive outlook'. Current parents believe it 'would not be the right choice for pushy parents or those who shy from informality and creativity'.

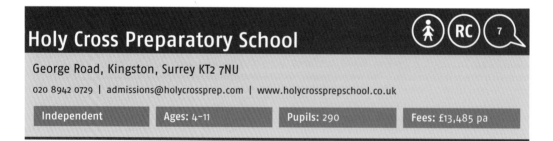

Holy Cross Preparatory School

George Road, Kingston, Surrey KT2 7NU

020 8942 0729 | admissions@holycrossprep.com | www.holycrossprepschool.co.uk

| Independent | Ages: 4-11 | Pupils: 290 | Fees: £13,485 pa |

Headteacher: Since 2011, Sarah Hair BEd (40s). Joined the school in 2004; 'knows the school inside out,' say parents. She has spent time as a class teacher, maths and English coordinator at a previous school then director of learning at Holy

Cross. Passionate about education and IT; she was one of the first teachers in the 80s to have a computer in her classroom. Teaches year 5 computing: amongst her many interests in new technologies is how IT can be used to support education today and in the future.

Married with three teenagers, one son and two daughters, she comes from a family of educationalists, a tradition she is keen to continue. Parents say she has a lively approach to school life and learning and they all appreciate her bright and cheerful personality.

Entrance: Non-selective at 4+; priority to siblings and Roman Catholics, although the school welcomes all faiths. Prospective pupils attend an introductory morning. Admissions staff are friendly and helpful, occasional places do arise and a waiting list is kept for interested families.

Exit: Girls move on to a wide variety of senior schools with Kingston Grammar, LEH, Surbiton High and Wimbledon High often popular. A few to boarding schools including Woldingham, St Mary's Ascot and Epsom College. Other popular options are the local grammar schools such Tiffin School and Nonsuch. Consistently high number of scholarships every year.

Remarks: Whilst Holy Cross is not overly selective it achieves excellent results for all pupils. Well planned and thoughtful curriculum ensures high standards, so giving pupils the chance to cherry pick when it comes to choosing a secondary school. Reasoning is part of the curriculum from year 3. Maximum class size is 22 and all classes have fully trained, high-level assistant teachers. Fantastic grounding in maths, English and computing, say parents. Specially structured English scheme used across the age groups, with a big emphasis on developing good essay writing techniques mixed with lots of speaking and listening tasks. This starts early, with even the youngest members developing the confidence to be able to stand up and address their classmates on a number of topics and share any special skills they may have.

There are small teaching rooms for pupils needing individual support from the SENCo, and EAL is available as required. All specialist subjects are cross curricular, helping to keep learning relevant and to encourage creativity. Well-resourced art and design rooms where pupils can engage with all types of media, much of which is elegantly displayed around the school. Impressive collections of pottery; the girls also benefit from having DT days, enabling them to plan, design and complete their projects as a whole. Science room full of active little girls in their goggles, with interesting experiments taking place and a specially designed area for baking and cookery clubs. There is also a prayer room full of creative prayers written by the girls where they can go to quietly retreat and reflect.

The old coach house is now the computing suite where pupils build websites and learn coding and programming skills. Recently the girls have been experimenting with 'green screen' techniques.

Music is a serious subject with a full-time teacher coordinating and 10 visiting teachers. Early years classes learn recorder, then in year 3 everyone learns a brass instrument. Pupils are taught to read and compose their own music, and many go on to do exceptionally well, joining national youth orchestras and choirs.

Set in eight acres of beautiful, leafy grounds. Pupils benefit from plenty of outdoor space to explore and enjoy, including a two all-weather sports pitches, fantastic pavilion (opened June 2019), two tennis/ netball courts, sports hall and theatre.

The facilities are also used by other schools, for community activities and charity events. Pupils are keen participants in Surrey schools sports tournaments. Younger children have their own outdoor classroom and garden where they grow vegetables, harvest them and then learn how to turn them into soup.

Unique setting for a school bordering London: eight glorious acres of well-tended grounds with views out to Epsom Downs, situated in a historical estate

Lovely Victorian buildings nestle comfortably next to modern additions; the recent multi-function halls are cleverly built into the hillside so as not to lose any of the gardens. Unique setting for a school bordering London: eight glorious acres of well-tended grounds with views out to Epsom Downs, situated in a historical estate that once belonged to the crown and is now part of the pricey Coombe Estate. The house was once occupied by John Galsworthy, author of the Forsyte Saga; in 1971 the sisters of Holy Cross purchased the buildings for a school. Still retains many original features including beautiful stained-glass windows and a wood panelled library.

Warmth and the quality of relationships remain at the heart of the school and the well-established pastoral care system. Sister Ursula, the last remaining nun, has had a long influence on the school, teaching pottery and running the Welcome Room where children come for cocoa and a chat. The school council gives the girls a voice in the day-to-day running of the school and discuss all-important issues including new play equipment and lunch menus. Girls are elected as officers, with each class providing two representatives; all very democratic. The school also runs a house system where year 6 girls are elected as captains to lead their houses in earning house points. They also choose charities to raise funds for and support each year. The Eco Council are active in promoting environmental issues and help the school, teachers, pupils and parents to reduce their carbon foot print and develop sustainable projects.

Parents are unanimous about the positive effects of the school's pastoral ethos. One parent told of the kindness shown to her daughter when she first arrived, making the transition to a new school so comfortable. Wednesdays are homework free to ensure that girls have time to visit friends and pursue outside interests.

A school that shines for its holistic, inclusive and caring approach mixed with academic rigour. Continues to be a fine example of 21st century education, and provides a wonderful start in life.

The Holy Cross School

25 Sandal Road, New Malden, Surrey KT3 5AR

020 8395 4225 | hxs@holycross.kingston.sch.uk | www.holycross.kingston.sch.uk

| State | Ages: 11–18 | Pupils: 941; sixth form: 200 (federated with Richard Challoner) |

Headteacher: Since 2001, Tom Gibson BSc Dip Ed MEd NPQH (40s). Could be government poster star for rejuvenating benefits of headship – radiates fulfilment and energy, though also a possible fringe benefit of lifelong interest in sport. While original career plans as pro after studying PE at Loughborough came to nought (dawning realisation that wasn't going to happen, he says, hit him 'later than my friends'), teaching career, fortunately for pupils in his care, proved thoroughly acceptable alternative. Pretty much inescapable, given that computer has invariably said 'yes' to the idea. 'Whenever I do psychometric tests, always come out as a teacher or social worker,' he says, though without any discernable regrets.

Has viewed education from every angle, as a parent (four children through university, wife an early years specialist), teacher (in variety of co-ed special residential as well as single sex mainstream schools) and an inspector (of 30 or so schools when was seconded to Ofsted eight years into headship). Message he took home (and presumably back to school again) from assorted experiences was that even in struggling schools there's 'always something that's fantastic.' Here, fantastic is the norm, thanks in part to determination to ensure that staff creativity is unfettered by micro management. If teachers are professionals, he says, shouldn't require 'somebody on top of you telling you how to do your job.' Staff are definitely accountable – but must be allowed autonomy to do the job.

As a result, he's reassuring but often background presence to parents, strong, visible and approachable senior management team – 'the people you go to,' felt one mother – mopping up most day-to-day issues. Very definitely hands-on when required, however. When GSG visited, had just come off phone to LA to arrange help for vulnerable pupil. He also (somehow) packs in a spot of teaching, including RS, as well as supporting some year 11 girls on reduced timetable.

Regularly sits in on other lessons, marvelling at other teachers' talents and happy to be outshone. 'Am I the best teacher? No, because that's not what I'm doing every day, and we've got some fantastic people here.'

Takes governmental caprice in his stride. 'Here long enough to adhere to political landscape without being blown off course.' Funding is one current concern (dominates meetings with other heads), recruitment another, though train and promote your own policy does wonders for retention rates (last big outside appointment was over five years ago).

'Teaching's a lovely job but we all need to feel we're progressing,' he says. 'The challenge is to ensure you can reward teachers financially and keep their interest up.' Seems to work, with many teachers there till retirement, though some younger staff are lured away by out of London quality of life – and lower property prices.

Praises his 'bright, skilled, sophisticated' admin team of action-packed enablers. Wish list is their command (collaboratively speaking), funding nosed out, ways and means found to overcome officialdom (recently built sports hall's pitched roof, for example, makes it multipurpose and thus LA-compliant).

Lower sets are tiny and get some of the best teachers, thought parents. 'Tend to do better in bottom set than in other schools,' observed one

Job, though not entirely stress free – 'Of course there are times you worry' – remains endlessly fulfilling. 'Privileged that people trust their daughters to us,' he says – and goal is to repay trust by finding ways for every girl to succeed.

Academic matters: Won't disappoint, offering high-achieving home from home that should satisfy even those robbed of grammar school place – and all on their doorstep. Results just what you'd hope for. Progress made between years 7-11 puts school in top five per cent nationally, GCSE results consistently good, congratulatory letters from top politicians par for the course. In 2019, 90 per cent got 9-5 in both English and maths with 42 per cent at 9-7. At A level in 2018, 31 per cent A*-A grades. Impressive 33 subjects in total (34 counting 'other') offered post-16, including creative writing, human biology and media. Plenty of BTecs, too (from health to performing arts in year 11 and early years, hospitality, IT and science in the sixth form).

But also proud to care, with an overt stress on welcome for girls from all shades of the ability spectrum, something that doesn't always seem to be the case in results-hungry establishments elsewhere. School shines when it comes to learning support. 'Brilliant,' thought parent with dyslexic daughter. 'Help has been amazing.' Safe haven, staffed by SEN team, is open before and after school as well as during the day, with easy chairs, games and jigsaws among measures designed to bring temporary relief to pupils sometimes overwhelmed by lives.

And though there's inevitable worry over performance of disadvantaged pupils (about 10 per cent of school numbers), support is extensive, ranging from financial (uniform to term time and holiday activities) to academic (extra teachers recruited to provide one-to-one support). Mr Gibson is 'just as excited to have child who struggled at primary as someone at top of the class,' and backs it up with quality resources. Lower sets are tiny and get some of brightest and best teachers, thought parents. 'Tend to do better in bottom set than in other schools,' thought one.

Formidable efforts go into working out who goes where, with CATs baseline testing in June for September's year 7 intake, classes ordered according to the results – parents sometimes slightly miffed in the process, but generally mollified by subsequent extensive reshuffling as lights start to emerge from bushels.

Most able take 11 GCSEs including triple science, substantial numbers achieving government's EBacc measurement. Impressive as with just four core subjects (RS, maths, English and science), high take up of options (including geography and history) is down to quality of teaching (even notoriously snide 'rate my teachers' website bursts with praise and stars).

Dynamic history team – 'phenomenal and inspiring' among the many five-star reviews. Head of department is 'brilliant – daughter loves it,' said parent (who, like others, found it hard to name anything she wasn't delighted with) – and mentors colleagues in need of turbocharged pupil-whispering skills.

Maths also strong through the school and set from year 7, English following in year 8. Sciences well-resourced (as you'd hope – this is school's official specialist area), biology and chemistry particularly so with five teachers apiece. Now pushing boat out for physics with recruitment of additional teachers. From also-ran girls' science subject, sixth form take up now moving into double figures (12 in current year 12), despite rival lure of psychology, currently single biggest A level subject.

Just-opened future technology learning room features banks of i-gorgeousness as well as natural daytime lighting, sizzling green chairs as well as licence to doodle (flip up tables double as whiteboards) and join clubs in electronics – leading to extra GCSE – and robotics. And if message about brilliance of science and technology careers for girls isn't clear, shortly to arrive 3D printer, next gizmo on the wish list, should be able to spell it out in a choice of colours and materials.

Overt stress on welcoming girls from all shades of the ability spectrum, something that doesn't always seem to be the case in results-hungry establishments elsewhere

Well-established sixth form partnership with Richard Challoner (also Catholic, high achieving but with boys and co-ed sixth form) adds greater range of subjects (popular) and extra travel time between the sites (less so). 'You've got to get to know boys some time,' thought one pupil – it's just the five-minute minibus journey that's off-putting. 'Effort...' groaned sixth former, who like the others, much preferred the Richard Challoner pupils to come to them, avoiding 15-minute walk under A3 if minibus is full.

Holy Cross Preparatory School

Games, options, the arts: If he could, Mr Gibson would get girls to trade online introspection for more sport. Though smaller size means slightly fewer games specialists than at larger schools (have three rather than five elsewhere), determination and creativity fills in plenty of gaps, from pupil self-starters organising 7.30am fitness sessions to PE-hating group sensibly offered civilised alternative of a walk in nearby Richmond Park.

Provides ballgirls for Wimbledon, PE at GCSE and A level, and pupils see themselves as a sporty bunch, egged on by enthusiastic staff and helped by attractive sports hall which avoids box-like appearance common to so many of its kind, though most games are played in Kingsmeadow, just a few minutes' drive away. Apart from a few more matches for the keen, parents praised expectations ('high') and teams ('strong'), particularly netball (regular fixtures against girls' schools in the area, including independents such as Surbiton High) and handball (recent Kingston and London champions), cricket and trampolining.

Trips many and varied (year 7 camping, year 9 battlefields, sports and language trips, including French exchange) to suit every subject and pocket – trip to Thailand no jaunt for the entitled, requiring pupils to fundraise before working with disadvantaged children there.

Performing arts similarly no Sunday stroll in the park (with or without George). We saw year 7s performing confidently against tension-creating (and intentional) background dissonance, good preparation for rigours of Sondheim's Into the Woods, next on the to-do list (whole school production every two years).

Held together by boundlessly energetic teacher – has to be as 'only one we've got,' said one girl – who organises range of events, from rock and pop festival to musical tour of Kingston town centre – and felt to be talent spotter par excellence. 'Helps you find your inner music,' said year 11 pupil and, having discovered it, channels it into choirs, bands and – for the very keen – music GCSE and performing arts BTec.

Art, taught in enticingly cluttered studio heaving with work, 3D flower springing out from painted background; rhinoceros depicted with surprising lightness of touch a thought-provoking treat for viewer. Popular at GCSE, taken by about third of year 11 pupils, with 10 or so carrying through to A level where can specialise in textiles, art and design and – increasingly popular – photography (a must-do, thought teacher, for anyone planning glittering career as celebrity vlogger).

Background and atmosphere: Smallest girls' senior school in the area, 'though may not feel like it compared with primaries,' says Mr Gibson, with 900 plus pupils rather than the several thousand elsewhere.

Fancifully minded might see school façade, original building protectively flanked by two more modern wings, as embodiment of nurturing qualities that have endured since foundation in 1931 by The Sisters of The Holy Cross. Contemporary black and white photograph shows original five pupils and a rocking horse posing together in eloquent depiction of family atmosphere. Love, respect and living life to full all qualities school espouses today – though without drowning in cosiness, stresses Mr Gibson.

Religious dimension ever present – a cross formed from coloured glass blocks in sixth form centre contrasts with older stained glass in entrance hall – and never apologetically. Catholicism remains defining part of school life, with RS taken at GCSE by all, and compulsory part of sixth form education. Annual retreats offered to pupils and extensive support for Catholic charities including day centre for the homeless in London and orphanage in Thailand.

Homely atmosphere assisted by compact site, tucked into residential road close to centre of New Malden. School does best with existing material, small courtyards squeezed in between buildings – one with long, curved, bright blue benches for break time conviviality – though some more spartan areas remain: dining hall's main decoration is rows of lockers lining the walls.

Religious dimension ever present. Catholicism remains defining part of school life, with RS taken at GCSE by all, and compulsory part of sixth form education

Upstairs, there's the promise of far better things to come. In addition to serving decent coffee and chocolate muffins (a not very well kept secret from rest of school), sixth form centre is riot of colourful brilliance, with neon sign and psychedelic, curvy sofa in eye-bending electric blue and purple.

Uniform, however, is big on homeliness. School's approach is that 'smart uniform means smart brains,' said approving mother. Only issue has been over sixth form blouses – plain only originally allowed, parents unhappy. Happy ending with rules now relaxed and (subtle) patterns allowed to all-round relief. 'A minefield,' says Mr Gibson, with feeling.

No changes planned elsewhere. Years 7 to 11 wear non-negotiable long, green kilt. Not loved, but pupils get used to them and though expensive, made from parent-pleasing quality fabric that lasts. Even better, they're impossible to roll up ('Hurrah,' thought several mothers), which could be factor in several other local schools' decisions to opt for something similar. Summer skirt an improvement for some, owing to paler pattern that makes them 'less visible,' thought one pupil. But though uniform is instantly recognisable, not a taunting hazard – pupils travel without fear on local buses.

Similar approval for school's strict beauty products policy. It's absent from younger faces (at least, those we saw) and limited to natural look among seniors ('no lipstick, eye liner or cat eyes,' said one). Sixth formers, in default business attire, free to apply ad libere though sense of restraint appeared to rule.

Pastoral care, well-being and discipline: School that doesn't stint on detail – new head girl's name already on honours board early in autumn term. 'Treat every individual in holistic way,' said parent. 'It's not just about the academic progress, you get sense that they really do care.'

Settling in process for new year 7s starts with visits to primary schools in summer term of final year and carries on into first term, starting two days earlier than rest of school with just sixth form for company and let out early for lunch in first fortnight. Initial swaddling, including 'non-stop' enquiries about how things are going from teachers who know girls' names 'instantly', can feel a bit excessive, think pupils – but parents are delighted. 'A bit old fashioned – you could feel you're mothered to death but it's a good fault to have,' said one.

If message about brilliance of science and technology careers for girls isn't clear, shortly to arrive 3D printer, next gizmo on the wish list, should be able to spell it out in a choice of colours and materials

Pupil complaints and comments passed up the chain via Student Leadership Team – 'Have a lot of responsibility' – and mood is protective, controlled and gently aspirational. Bullying not common, thought pupils. And if it happened 'school would deal with it,' said one with confidence. Awareness of consequences felt to be undoubtedly helpful in putting off anyone contemplating unkindness – with notable turn of speed when parents need to get in touch. 'You can pick up the phone and talk to the people you want to talk to straight away,' thought one mother.

'Some parents say you can't be caring and high achieving,' says Mr Gibson. 'I say you need to be caring to achieve.' Succeeds, even when faced with challenging behaviour, in keeping girls in school. Appointment of inclusion manager and area where distressed can be supported without affecting education of others helps keep exclusion levels 'minute'.

Mental health problems, many linked to plummeting self worth, a growing problem, not helped by 'enormous amounts of aspiration,' says Mr Gibson. 'Expectation that everything's going to be A* weighs down on people.' School does its bit and more, with mental health-themed assemblies, training for pupil ambassadors and emphasis on coping skills for all to deal with anxiety, as well as more informal support (one parent praised cups of tea and chats available on tap).

Still 'probably not enough,' thought head, whose one (mild) bugbear is tendency for school to be seen by outsiders as sum of nurturing qualities. May be 'sweet, caring and academic' (Mr G recounts qualities with air of one who's heard them many times before), but there's no absence of challenge – or innovation to meet it.

Pupils and parents: Religion the unifying element in school population that spans cultures, ethnicity and lifestyles, with around a fifth speaking English as an additional language and seven per cent receiving free school meals. Area covered extends from Hampton Court round to Chessington, Worcester Park and into South West London fringes (Morden, Mitcham and Wandsworth) as well as Kingston and Richmond, affluence rubbing shoulders with deprivation. Supportive PSA brings everyone together, while girls' friendships span the range. 'Daughter made such a huge variety of friends, from Roehampton council estates to [luxury homes] in North Kingston.'

Entrance: Securing one of the heavily oversubscribed 150 year 7 places a doddle as long as you meet the criteria (Catholic trumps all, with priority, after looked after Catholic children, given to regular – ideally weekly – and priest-endorsed attendance at mass) and remember to fill out the right forms (supplementary information as well as standard common application). One member of staff thought non-Catholics might stand slightly better chance applying for in-year place, but we'd suspect slightly forlorn hope in a school which attracts applicants from almost 50 different feeder schools.

Additional 15 sixth form places on offer for non-locals (but still Catholic). Not unknown for families to move nearer to boost chances of success.

'When you've found the right school, fight tooth and nail to get in,' says Mr Gibson, sensibly tempering this with need to check admissions criteria to work out whether tooth and nail sac-rifice, however extensive, will be sufficient to do the trick.

School big on empathy – will call parents pronto if there's waiting list movement. 'When place came up, the admissions head phoned straight away, said parent. 'Said they knew how anxious we had been. They really care.'

Exit: Up to a third leave after GCSEs. Year 13 leavers head off in every direction – majority to

university including one or two to Oxbridge or to study medicine most years; a few are now opting for apprenticeships. Small but steady reverse flow of old girls returning as staff members.

Remarks: School notable for happiness, sense of security and combination of talent boosting and strong moral purpose. 'Seven years ago, didn't want to come here. Seven years on, don't want to leave,' said current head girl. After just a few hours there, nor did we.

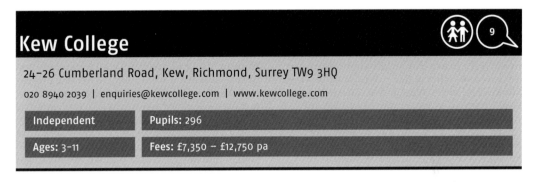

Kew College

24–26 Cumberland Road, Kew, Richmond, Surrey TW9 3HQ

020 8940 2039 | enquiries@kewcollege.com | www.kewcollege.com

Independent	Pupils: 296
Ages: 3-11	Fees: £7,350 – £12,750 pa

Headmistress: Since 2013, Marianne Austin (60s). Read geography at Durham and then spent two years at Sheffield doing an MA in town planning before becoming a chartered accountant, working at the (then) Coopers and Lybrand. Initially fired to teach when her daughter began nursery here, she arrived at Kew College in 2002 and has never looked back. ('I love the school and believe completely in what we're trying to do.') Has taught in years 2, 4 and 6, became deputy head in 2010 and three years later took over the reins. Mrs Austin exudes calm-ness and warmth, and a determination to support and empower all constituencies including her staff, whose professionalism and commitment evidently help to inspire her own. 'We obviously want the children to feel secure and happy,' she says, 'not least because we want to foster a culture which allows them to take risks. And that's a life skill for which the need will never go away.' Loves travel and skiing and spending time with her husband and daughter and with her family in Ireland.

Entrance: Children can start in the nursery aged 3 – there are two classes, one in the morning and one in the afternoon. Get their names down as early as possible – any time from birth. There's no exam-ination or interview, though prospective parents are required, as a condition of entry, to attend an open morning to get a feel for the place. Priority is given to siblings, and to the sons and daughters of ex-pupils. Mrs Austin says this does not occasion resentment 'because it's transparent'. Clear belief

that, so long as parents are invested, this is a school in which almost any child can thrive. 'My daughter came from the state sector,' said one parent. 'There are no airs and graces here, but terrific values.'

Exit: Everyone leaves at 11, many to the big hit-ters in West London, usually with good number of scholarships. Mostly day – boarding very seldom on the radar. In 2019, largest numbers of offers from Ibstock Place, Kingston Grammar, Notting Hill and Ealing and Latymer Upper. Plenty of scholarships and exhibitions offered. Also conditional 13+ places at Eton, and Epsom College.

Remarks: Warm-hearted and effervescent learn-ing environment. Staff are guided by the national curriculum, but teaching and learning go way beyond. In the nursery and kindergarten years, a clear emphasis on social skills and physical literacy, but of also being gently led into reading, writing and elementary maths. By the time children move into the infant house in years 1 and 2, ICT and sci-ence have become more fully integrated, and the children are becoming exposed to more specialist subject teaching. French (emphasis on lots of lovely sounds) actually begins in nursery, and 'under-standing the world' introduces younger children to what will later become science.

Reading is huge here. Right from the start read-ing at home is encouraged. From year 1, a 10 minute spell of nightly homework is also expected and, by gentle incremental steps, this is increased as children get older. A very industrious feel to the place, but none of the anxiety of a hothouse. 'They help children to extend their ambition in every way,' said one parent, 'but without getting het up.' Particular praise for thorough marking – 'lots of red and green ink, full of attainable target-setting and constructive comments,' said parent. Learning support is sensitively managed, with a SENCo and assistant 'The specific needs of children change,' says the head. 'Sometimes it's just a bit of anxiety'. Other issues, such as dyslexia, need longer-term support. But all children, however much or little help they receive, are fully integrated into the life of the school. Occasionally there are those with more significant needs, and every attempt is made to support them.

The school is housed in two big Victorian houses – classic west London stuff. 'We've been lucky,' says head. 'The original buildings were gifted to us by our founder' – something which has allowed the fees to remain at a relatively modest level compared to some. Now a third big building just alongside is home to year 5 and 6 pupils and to the art department. A further consequence is the rehousing of the library – 'right at the heart of the school, as it should be', says Mrs Austin.

Although the present site is on the edge of being cramped – packed lunches on site are essential – there's no sense of crowding. Timetables have been carefully worked to minimise bodies having to jostle, and classrooms comfortably accommodate classes of never more than 20 children. There's no sense of claustrophobia – rather of light, of bustling creativity and of calm good relationships. At the back, just across the school playground is the Octagon – a purpose built block dating from about 2000 which houses younger pupils.

A very industrious feel to the place, but not the anxiety of a hothouse. 'They help children to extend their ambition in every way,' said one parent, 'but without getting het up'

Masses of sport – football, rugby, netball and athletics especially, and plenty of swimming – with plenty of fixtures with other schools. 'It's lovely to win,' says the head, 'which, fortunately, they often do. Sometimes, of course, they don't – and that's education.' There aren't any rolling acres here, so there's a coach ride for everyone on a Tuesday and Thursday afternoon to sports grounds only five minutes away.

The school also hums with music (the Young Voices choir was practising when we arrived – a very joyful sound). A wind band, a strings group, a young voices choir, jazz band, and lots of beat and drumming, and masses of music technology. There's a special art day every couple of years with visits from the specialists at the V&A. Clubs, in and after school, have that same determined outreach – not only those with a digital and IT base, of course, but masses of dance and even one for Lego.

'It's lovely to win,' says the head, 'which, fortunately, they often do. Sometimes, of course, they don't – and that's education'

Pastoral care is taken very seriously. Every Monday, the head meets with staff and their first item of business is identifying pupils who present concerns. The school has identified a range of structures best calculated to serve the children's interests – a house system, of course (excellent for games) but also heads of year who liaise closely with form teachers to ensure a full and up-to-date flow of information and insight. Lots of outings, of course, and older children might take longer school trips – year 5 were at Hooke Court in Dorset during our visit. The school is evidently proud of its traditions as well as of its routines – Founder's Day each spring is a major jamboree, and allows pupils to come together with teachers and other friends of the school.

The policy of teachers of other years visiting all parts of the school frequently helps accustom young children to faces which might otherwise be unfamiliar. Before moving to a new class, there are 'transition' days to help acclimatise, and that extends to opportunities for parents to hear the reflections of parents with older children who've already made the journey. It's easy to spot the confidence which flows between the different constituencies here. The recessional at the end of each day eloquently combines pupil safety with a gentle exercise in toujours la politesse.

The wholeheartedness of the children (very apparent) is suggestive – they seem to have imbibed a confidence and optimism from other pupils and teachers and also, no doubt about it, from their families. This is a school in which the parents' investment – emotional, social and financial – reflects a deep commitment to education in the fullest sense. Parents are big fundraisers for the school (the school minibus and a massive investment in the library are recent examples). Mrs Austin is emphatic that the exchange of confidence and goodwill adds immeasurably to the potential of the school. 'Children all feel part of the bigger picture,' said one parent. 'I don't know quite how they do it, but it's exceptional. They think beyond themselves, and it spills over into everything.'

Kew Green Preparatory School

Layton House, Ferry Lane, Kew Green, Richmond TW9 3AF

020 8948 5999 | secretary@kgps.co.uk | www.kgps.co.uk

Independent	Ages: 4–11	Pupils: 280	Fees: £18,360 pa

Head: Since 2004, Jem Peck BSc (geography) PGCE (science) (both from Kingston University). Taught at St John's, Kingston for nine years, then moved out of education altogether for six years into the corporate world, where he focused on event production, marketing, PR and team-building. Gaining this wider perspective has been 'incredibly helpful' to his current role, he says, 'particularly for recruitment and driving the creative feel of the school.'

A very visible presence throughout the school, he teaches English and reasoning to year 6 and is often in and out of the classrooms. Enthusiastic yet calm, he gets down to the kids' level when talking to them. 'Unlike many heads in the private sector, he praises the children directly rather than turning his back on them to tell the parent,' one parent added. He has a door that's always open (except for the very occasional sensitive meeting) to his office – which, by the way, is both the most stylish and child-friendly we've ever seen for a head teacher, complete with sink-in sofa and swivel armchairs, matching navy furniture, open fire and more toys than many home playrooms have. 'Children know they can pop in whenever they want and they very often do, whether it's to have a jam on my guitar, discuss ideas to improve the school or just instead of going outside to play,' he says. During our visit, even kids that had recently left the school popped their heads in with big smiles. Does it interrupt his day? 'That is my day!' he laughs. 'Paperwork can be left.'

Parents, whom he greets every morning, tell us they also feel welcome to pop in any time. 'There's no need to email first – if you have a concern, you can talk to him, or indeed any of the other staff, that very day,' says one, although another told us, 'You can find yourself being pushed in a direction you don't necessarily want to go when you talk to him. For instance, he's good at persuading you that things you think are important are actually not.'

When not in school, you'll usually find him at sister schools Ravenscourt Park (primary) and Kew House (senior). He lives in Surbiton, has a teenage son and is a keen musician.

Entrance: Entrance is non-selective, with applications accepted on a first-come-first-served basis. This means you'll need to get in quick, particularly as this heavily oversubscribed school (which has some 90-160 applications for every 40 places in reception) accepts registrations from birth. Eighteen months before children are due to start, the school gives the parents a call to check they're happy to continue their journey. An informal taster day helps the children settle in and every year group has two classes of 20, with an equal gender split where possible. Occasional places (mainly when pupils leave because their families relocate) become available higher up the school, for which the school asks to see a report from the current school.

Exit: Most popular by far Kew House. Then Ibstock Place followed by eg St John's Leatherhead and Hampton.

Remarks: The story goes that Maria and Ted Gardener, owners of Ravenscourt Park Prep School (which was becoming increasingly oversubscribed) were walking along the Thames towpath in Kew, when they spotted a tall Georgian style building that they immediately fell in love with. 'Mrs Gardener was so keen to see more of it that she got on his shoulders to look over the wall,' says the head. A year later, in 2004, the school opened there.

Overlooking the River Thames at the back, the location of this school is made all the more impressive by its neighbour – Kew Gardens

Overlooking the River Thames at the back and Kew Green at the front, the location of this school is made all the more impressive by its neighbours – Kew Gardens – where pupils often drop by with teachers as part of their learning. By no means the largest of facilities, you won't get the likes of science labs or food tech areas here, but pupils get full use of these and other amenities at Kew House, the school's sister senior school.

In the basement is the staff room and the school hall, which doubles up as the dining room (and where the very popular food is made from scratch on site); the ground floor is home to the headteacher's office and admin rooms, as well as some classrooms; and the upper two floors house more classrooms (all well-resourced) and private study rooms, including for music lessons. All are spotless, welcoming and colourful, with masses of original artwork (not just paintings, but sculptures and textiles) adorning the walls and shelves, whilst the atmosphere is buzzy, both during and between classes. The single-storey building at the front of the school – again homely and packed with artwork – is the early years centre, whilst three innovative wooden, glass-fronted pods are used for music lessons and small group work for SEN. The playground at the back consists of a double tennis court and a smaller lower level, but fun-packed, outside play area.

The ethos, which aims to be the same as its two sister schools, is all about increasing self-esteem, encouraging children to be confident to ask questions and make mistakes without feeling intimidated – all with the overall aim of enabling them to flourish, not just as learners, but people. 'This is a school that's all about celebrating attitude and effort, not just what is actually achieved,' raved one parent. Parents like that the raison d'être is not getting bums on seats in the premiership senior schools, despite the fact that they do get many kids in there. 'The school gets that not every child is destined to wind up at the likes of St Paul's, whilst still managing to pave the way for the ones who are bright enough to get in without any need for extra tutoring,' said one.

The school's ethos is all about increasing self-esteem, encouraging children to be confident to ask questions and make mistakes without feeling intimidated

Lessons are based on the national curriculum, but with added enrichment. Setting from year 3 in maths and English, although head says 'it's a flexible feast,' and there are subject specialist teachers for art, music, PE and French. French from reception upwards, with Spanish, German and Italian part of the 50 extracurricular clubs on offer per week. Other clubs include sports such as judo, modelling, cooking, digital photography, computer programming, touch typing, writing, film club, children's newspaper, just to name a few. Whilst many of these finish at 4.30pm, the school is open from as long as 8am-6pm for an extra fee (includes tea). Plenty of trips, including residentials.

There's extra (mainly classroom or small group based) provision for those requiring learning support (14 SEN when we visited, two of whom had EHC plans), particularly dyslexia, dyspraxia and autistic spectrum, via the progress centre, which is run by the school SENCo and three other staff members involved on a part-time basis. Specialist help, including speech and language therapy and OT, is brought in. 'If I could change anything, it would be making this a bigger department, with help put in place quicker, but what's amazing about this school and SEN is that issues are never brushed under the carpet or stigmatised, which has been my experience at other schools,' said one parent.

Weekly drama classes for all year groups, with plenty of chances to perform. Film-making is valued, especially in year 6. Meanwhile, the range of art opportunities is more akin to a secondary school, including fine art, pottery, ceramics, textiles, screen painting, Photoshop and more – with more than enough facilities to support it. Pupils' work has been exhibited at the likes of the National Gallery, Hampton Court Palace and Saatchi Gallery – testament to the artistic talent here.

Around two-thirds (190 when we visited) of pupils learn a musical instrument during the school day. 'You name an instrument and we'll teach it if a pupil wants to learn,' says the head. There are two choirs (upper and lower schools), a chamber choir (for which pupils audition), an orchestra and ensembles for guitar, strings and brass. Plus music assemblies. When we visited, year 4s were practising a song they'd written (lyrics and music) ready to perform later that week with a full orchestra.

Sports-wise, only tennis and netball takes place on the school grounds, while rugby, football, cricket, hockey, rounders and athletics are played on the green opposite. Other local facilities enable students to participate in gymnastics, dance, swimming, cross-country, fitness lessons, athletics and traditional team sports, for which there are specialist coaches. Years 3-6 take part in competitive fixtures with other local schools and the school hosts netball, football and rugby festivals.

Pastoral care is strong, helped by the high staff-to-pupil ratio and small class sizes, plus the fact that children are regularly reminded who they can talk to about any concerns. Discipline isn't a word you'll hear much as behaviour is excellent. The last half-hour of lesson time on a Friday is dedicated to 'reflection time,' which allows teachers to reflect on individual or group successes and resolve any

---

'Around two-thirds learn a musical instrument. You name an instrument and we'll teach it if a pupil wants to learn,' says head

conflicts or concerns so that children don't have to carry them over the weekend.

The majority of children live within a three-mile radius – mainly Kew, Chiswick, Richmond, Barnes and Hammersmith. Families are a broad mix of professions including media types, lawyers, bankers and quite a few celebs. Parents are encouraged to get involved in school life, often giving presentations on careers and interests, and there's a lively PA.

Probably not a school for go-getting parents that want their offspring to get top grades in everything, no matter what. Not that it lacks academic rigour, with some impressive pupil destinations proving that the school caters for the very bright. A school for introverts and extroverts alike, we found the atmosphere to be caring, spirited and creative.

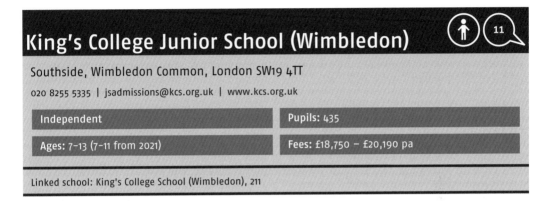

King's College Junior School (Wimbledon)

Southside, Wimbledon Common, London SW19 4TT

020 8255 5335 | jsadmissions@kcs.org.uk | www.kcs.org.uk

Independent	Pupils: 435
Ages: 7–13 (7–11 from 2021)	Fees: £18,750 – £20,190 pa

Linked school: King's College School (Wimbledon), 211

Headmaster: Since 2006, Dr Gerard Silverlock (60s). A senior history teacher who moved to prep schools after distinguished spells at Salesian College Farnborough, Millfield and Lord Wandsworth College. Took up headship of Aberdour Prep in 2002, then headhunted four years later for KCJS, where he's been ever since. No plans to move on or retire – enjoys the job too much. Married to Victoria, a modern languages teacher. They have two sons, both of whom went to KCJS, and two daughters.

Impresses at once as a kindly, scholarly man of sense, and this was universally confirmed by parents queueing up to give praise. 'An excellent head and visible presence'; 'Knows each boy and his parents by name'; 'Charismatic and extremely popular'; 'Clearly loves teaching the boys'; 'The school is very lucky to have him.'

Entrance: Competitive, and getting more so all the time – one mother regretted that 'given the struggle for places at London schools, more and more super bright boys are applying to KCJS and travelling from further afield, making it unattainable for some of those who are more local.' Head confirmed that parents come from as far afield as Esher, Oxshott and Cobham in one direction and Notting Hill and Chiswick in the other.

Around 250 apply for 54 places at 7+. English, maths and reasoning tests and all candidates are interviewed. A further 14 places at 8+, then – currently – six more at 9+ and another six at 10+. From 2021, however, there will be no 10+ entry and there

will be 12 places at 9+. There is no longer any entry at 11+: boys wishing to join the school at this stage now apply to the senior school, which took its first year 7 cohort in 2016. School looks for 'boys who are bright, intellectually curious, nice young men – not perfect, but able to manage themselves.'

The school maintains a local pre-prep, Wimbledon Common Prep (Squirrels). 'It's not a secret that we own it,' Dr Silverlock observed, 'but we've never badged it, and it isn't selective so it can't be an exclusive feeder to us.' Boys apply from an ever-widening range of pre-preps and primary schools.

Financial assistance has largely gone, transferred across to senior school bursaries.

Exit: Almost all to the senior school via the King's transfer exam in year 8, many with scholarships. Boys have to get 65 per cent in their final set of exams, which are set and marked in the senior school. But the average mark the boys achieve in these exams is 80 per cent, so, in the head's words, 'they're not intended to trip anyone up.' Occasionally boys opt for other day schools, recently Westminster and St Paul's, or boarding school instead: destinations have included Eton, Winchester, Harrow, Sevenoaks, The Oratory and King's Canterbury. From 2021, boys will move up to the senior school at 11 without taking an exam.

Remarks: Completely integrated into the senior school, sharing the same superb campus and facilities, but with a uniform and identity that's very much its own. Rushmere, where the year 3 and year 4 boys are taught in classes of 18, is a lovely old Georgian building, made up of beautifully ordered classrooms and a lunch hall especially for the younger ones. Priory is home to the boys in years 5-8, and has some impressive spaces: we really liked the library, with its 17,000 books, full time librarian and silent, respectful hush. Excellent programme of visiting authors has included Jeremy Strong and David Walliams. State of the art music school and concert hall opened in 2018 and brand new sports complex with six-lane, 25m pool, in autumn 2019. 'The boys are lucky to enjoy such surroundings in a London school,' wrote a grateful parent.

Academic excellence is intrinsic to the school's ethos, and KCJS is home to some very high achievers, but every parent we spoke to praised the school's ability to educate and encourage the whole child. 'The teachers know how to get the best out of individuals'; 'Teaching is first class, and my son had handwriting support for a few terms, which helped him'; 'The school tries to encourage downtime as well'; 'Lessons are pitched just right for boys to pique their interest and curiosity and encourage further learning.' We were shown round by three very bright, articulate and charming young men, all of whom emphatically agreed. 'The teachers are always there to help you!' 'They're really supportive. It's not don't, it's always do!' Successful policy of no hands-up in lessons, introduced to encourage boys to be better listeners, and boys aren't always told the grade for their work (although it goes into the mark book), so that they'll read the teacher's comments more carefully.

Boys aren't always told the grade for their work (although it goes into the mark book), so that they'll read the teacher's comments more carefully

SENCo has an open door policy, with boys able to come in any time and ask for help – although it's a rather different role at this school compared with most, because there are hardly any children here with learning difficulties. 'To be blunt, they wouldn't do well enough on the entrance exam,' as head put it. Some boys with dyspraxia, some on the autistic spectrum. But school puts a strong emphasis on them being able to cope with the day's challenges, so this isn't the place for those needing more than a mild level of support. Pupils are most likely to seek assistance with organising their time, or with specific revision tasks.

'The boys are lucky to enjoy such surroundings in a London school,' wrote a grateful parent

Sport, once seen as elitist by some parents, is now proudly inclusive and the school is committed to a Sport For All approach. Lots on offer: football, rugby, athletics, cricket, plus many more. 'All boys are encouraged in sport and play in matches whatever their ability – there is no stigma to being in the F or G team,' according to one mother. Fabulous programme of music, with many wonderful opportunities for boys to take part: six choirs, two orchestras and a plethora of ensembles covering everything from classical to Brazilian drumming. More than 400 boys learn musical instruments, and there are regular concerts, both formal and informal. Drama flourishing, and parents praised the 'hugely dedicated drama teacher' who always finds a part for everyone ('she's useless at auditioning because she can't say no,' observed the head, affectionately). Extremely broad and appealing programme of clubs and activities, everything from cookery to Warhammer. 'We have been constantly amazed over the years at the huge staff commitment to clubs and events,' wrote a parent. Another added, 'The only complaint here is that there is not enough time to enjoy all that is on offer.'

Who wouldn't like it here? 'Only those who might struggle with the work,' suggested our really delightful tour guides. Discipline was described as 'fair and firm', and parents showed themselves satisfied with the pastoral care by having no complaints to make about it. We were impressed by the friendly relations between older and younger boys and the lively and cheerful atmosphere, and the words that came up the most in parent feedback were 'kind' 'fun' 'happy' and 'outstanding'.

Overwhelming majority of pupils come from affluent, professional backgrounds, but it's very much a multinational school: 60 per cent of the boys have one or more parents who aren't British. A third speak more than one language at home, and across the school cohort 29 different languages are spoken. The result, as the head proudly observes, is a school that is very outward-looking. In addition to the plethora of foreign trips you'd expect, there are regular exchanges to schools in Japan and India, where the boys stay with local families, and the school is an active fundraiser for the Obera Schools charity in Kenya.

As one parent put it, 'Despite the focus on success, the boys all seem happy. Four years in, we could not be more pleased with our choice of prep school for our son.' A superb environment for bright, motivated boys.

King's College School (Wimbledon)

Southside, London SW19 4TT

020 8255 5300 | admissions@kcs.org.uk | www.kcs.org.uk

Independent	Pupils: 971; sixth form: 401 (101 girls)
Ages: 11–18	Fees: £20,190 – £22,335 pa

Linked school: King's College Junior School (Wimbledon), 209

Headmaster: Since 2008, Andrew Halls MA (50s), previously head of Magdalen College School, Oxford, prior to which he was deputy at Trinity in Croydon and head of English at Bristol Grammar School. His father was head of a grammar school, but he himself came up through the comprehensive school route, something which has very much shaped him as an educator – 'I've always been keen to reduce the dislocation between the state and the independent sector.' Read English at Cambridge, where he achieved a double first, and went straight into teaching because he loved his subject and was (and still is) fascinated by education. Married to Veronique, a French teacher, with two grown up daughters. Interests include reading, theatre, running – and anything to do with schools. Regularly writes for the Sunday Times, and his opinions are sought by many other quality papers.

Arrived at KCS to find 'a really lovely school' but wanted to strengthen its position in London, feeling that it was occasionally overlooked. It is not overlooked now. It was never exactly a slouch, but parents agree that the focus on academic achievement has been extended under Mr Halls's leadership, and with it the school's profile – which is now stellar. Commonly bracketed in parents' minds these days with London's top selectives eg St Paul's, City of London, Westminster – no mean feat for a school out in the burbs.

Parents clearly appreciate all he has done for the school – 99 per cent of them described the school as well led in a recent survey – and value the open culture he's created, with one describing KCS 'a very healthy institution'. There was praise for his regular appearances on the touchline at Saturday sports fixtures and his 'frequent, informative and carefully prepared' communications. 'The head is doing a great job in leading the school, and is held in very high regard by the students, mainly due to his friendly nature in mixing and in speaking to so many of them, especially at lunch times.'

Academic matters: Between 2008 and 2013 this was an IB-only school, and the general consensus was that you couldn't be taught the programme better anywhere in the UK. Results continue to be extremely impressive: in 2019 pupils averaged 40 points out of 45. A levels reintroduced in 2013, and in 2019, 79 per cent A*/A. At GCSE – which here are mostly IGCSEs – 95 per cent of grades were A*-A/9-7 in 2019.

Handsome building faces a secluded part of Wimbledon Common – a lovely location for a school

Curriculum is both deep and broad, allowing students to grow intellectually in every direction. English department breathed erudition, with truly inspiring quotations on display from Jane Austen, Milton and de Montaigne. Languages offered include French – compulsory until the sixth form – Spanish, Italian, German, Russian and Mandarin Chinese. At GCSE almost everyone takes further maths and triple science, the latter taught in a splendid new science block that devotes a floor to each science. Specialist sixth form lab allows for a more relaxed intellectual atmosphere, and experiments can be left in place. 'The science department is fantastic – one of the best, a real strength!' enthused a sixth former. Parents praised the 'exceptional' teaching. 'One member of staff in particular has gone way beyond his duty to encourage, inspire and give confidence to our son,' reported a satisfied father. 'KCS is a wonderful school where the teachers are very dedicated to each and every pupil,' wrote another. The articulate, poised and likeable students we spoke to confirmed that the school did not encourage a results culture – 'People bounce off each other, because they ask interesting questions. The teachers encourage it as much as they can, because so much teaching here is based around discussion.' 'The teachers always go beyond the syllabus,' were typical comments. Superb facilities for just about every subject. We loved the large, modern library, with its separate areas for 'silent' and 'quiet' study – then found that it was about to be redeveloped to give students even more space.

School has an excellent SEN policy which ticks all the boxes, and the Learning Enrichment department, as it's called here, offers support to the few students with mild learning needs who make it through the school gates. But this was one area where parents did express disquiet, claiming that their children had been viewed as a problem the school wasn't interested in solving, and hadn't received the help they'd needed. EAL support is reportedly strong. The school is in the process of appointing a new head of learning enrichment.

Games, options, the arts: 'Amazing! There's so much to say – where do I start?' cried one sixth former, when asked about the drama. Regular productions include big musicals such as West Side Story and Shakespeare's The Winter's Tale, staged in the main theatre, and more intimate and experimental works in the drama studio. The school also has a long track record of taking productions to the Edinburgh Festival Fringe. The sixth form drama scholars run a club for younger students, and the annual house play festival involves around 150 pupils each year.

Is the school competitive, we asked? Much smiling at this, before a personable lad answered, 'There's a nice amount of competitiveness. We're all trying to push ourselves'

Music is outstanding but inclusive, with orchestras and ensembles to cater for every level from jazz to chamber music, and a particularly strong choral tradition. Plenty of opportunities for pianists, too – concertos, concerts, masterclasses. New music block (including a concert hall seating 200) opened in 2018 and will up the ante still further. Visual art is of a very high standard, with some gratifyingly edgy and imaginative work on display – not least the female nude that seems to be obligatory fare in these schools full of clever boys.

Sport is extremely strong, with notable successes scored not only in staples such as rugby, cricket, football, athletics, hockey and netball, but in many more niche areas – fencing, fives, badminton, rowing, sailing, to name but a few. Loads on offer, and everyone encouraged to take part. Extensive playing fields at the rear of the school and a further 20 acres three miles away, and new sports complex and swimming pool (currently in

what our guides described as the 'green tin can building') due for completion in 2019. Lively and varied programme of clubs and activities: debating, creative, writing, Greek, art drop in – no need for anyone to be bored.

Perhaps the jewel in the crown, however, are the Co-Curricular Fridays, which all pupils named as one of the highlights of their week. Every Friday afternoon around 350 students go to various 'stations' (the school is partnered with 27 state primary, secondary and special schools) to help out: hearing children read, teaching, generally helping out. Students can also opt to join the CCF – very popular here – or work on arts projects. The result is a school which, said one student, 'is genuinely a community-based school,' adding, 'I'm not just saying this because it sounds good – it really is.'

Background and atmosphere: Founded in 1829 as a junior branch of King's College London and originally housed in their basement. Moved to Wimbledon in 1897 in order to expand and compete with other London day schools that were relocating to the suburbs in quest of fresh air and playing fields. Junior school opened on the same site in 1912. Girls admitted to the sixth form in 2010, and the first year 7 cohort started at the senior school in 2016. Still retains ties with its illustrious forebear in the Strand, not least in the school colours.

Handsome Victorian red-brick building faces a secluded and tranquil part of Wimbledon Common – a lovely location for a school. The site is much bigger than at first appears, encompassing both modern and original styles in a pleasing architectural polyglot that charmingly reflects the KCS ethos of scholarship and innovation. Beautiful old Great Hall with organ and all the fittings rubs shoulders with wind turbines and solar panels, and attractive internationally-flavoured sculpture points the way to the much-loved multi-use games area. Even when full of noise and excitement, as the latter was when we visited, the school exudes civilised and cogitative calm. The fabulous sixth form centre, spacious and equipped with its own reading room and fair trade café, made us feel envious of all the confident, courteous young people relaxing therein.

Pastoral care, well-being and discipline: Those who join at 11 stay in the same form with the same tutor for the first two years. At 13, all boys are allocated a house, where they're under the care of a form teacher who registers them and a tutor who acts as their 'moral guardian'. Tutor groups, consisting of 12 students of different ages, meet twice weekly. Tutor system was described as 'excellent' by a father, who added 'it gives us a ready outlet if things occur which we need to discuss

---

Students confirmed that the school does not encourage a results culture – people bounce off each other because they ask interesting questions. Teachers encourage it as much as they can, because so much teaching here is based on discussion

confidentially.' 'The tutors really fight for you!' affirmed one student.

The deputy head introduced an initiative called Kindness at King's, and it genuinely seems to have worked. Parents speak of 'a great sense of camaraderie among students,' commenting 'the pupils are truly nice kids', and time and again emphasised how happy their children were at the school. Pupils concur. 'One thing that's very present in the school is pastoral support,' said a sixth former, while a lower school boy exclaimed, 'Older students talk to you; you're not just a little boy on the side!' A slight feeling from the year 7s we met – the first such cohort to join the senior school – that they would like more interaction with the older boys, but this was qualified with 'When there's a year 8 it'll be better.'

Was it competitive, we asked? Much smiling at this, before a personable lad answered, 'There's what I would call a nice amount of competitiveness. We're all trying to push ourselves.' A sixth form girl added, 'The competition here is healthy. We arrive with the attitude that we want to be challenged.' All the girls praised the inclusivity of the sixth form and denied the school was in any way boysy – 'It really doesn't feel like that.' One said she'd applied to KCS because 'my sister raved about it – she looked forward to every single day.'

Discipline described by head as 'quite traditional and firm'. Pupils would be expelled for drugs, theft, systematic bullying, etc, although head was unable to remember the last time he'd had to do this. Students adamant that any bullying was 'quickly eliminated with quite a lot of severity.'

Pupils and parents: Pupils mostly from affluent backgrounds, some of them extremely so, but all of them from homes that greatly value education, and, according to head, where at least one parent has been to a very good university. 'The children are highly motivated, but they don't think cash is king, and their parents don't want them to live in a bubble.' Good ethnic diversity, and plenty of international families. Notable Old King's include Charles Dickens Jnr, Robert Graves, Alfred de Rothschild, Dante Gabriel Rossetti, Buster Mottram and Roy Plomley.

Entrance: Head is proud of having introduced year 7 entry point for the senior school – entirely justifiably, we think. The junior school still goes up to 13 but from 2021, junior boys will all move seamlessly up to the senior school at 11+ with no entrance exam required). Currently, 44 11+ places are now available in the senior school, and at least half of these are filled by boys from state primary schools. Some 350 applied for the first intake in 2016, a figure which is increasing year on year. At 13+, currently 80 boys come up from the junior school and join the lower school cohort, together with around 35 boys from other London preps. Hardly any space for boys at 16+, but 50 girls join at that point, some from local independents such as Wimbledon High or grammars such as Tiffin or Nonsuch, some from much further away – a recent sixth form girl came from Essex on a 100 per cent bursary, and is now doing well at Harvard.

At all stages the school is looking for applicants who share the love of learning here – 'We want students who have a willingness to enjoy what we teach, academic ability and humanity.' A sixth former told us cheerfully and without any conscious irony that 'the school is very good at selecting those who'll survive – I mean, enjoy and thrive here.'

Exit: Hardly any leave at 16+ – literally one or two. At 18+, a really glittering set of destinations. For the past five years some 25 per cent to Oxbridge (43 in 2019, plus 15 medics), the rest to Imperial, Durham, Bristol, and similar. Growing numbers to North American universities (11 in 2019). Subjects chosen include English, history, languages, mathematics, sciences, economics and engineering – not that many lawyers, interestingly, because one imagines there must be a fair few among the parents.

Money matters: Not one of our cheaper schools, but up to 100 per cent bursary assistance at 11+, 13+ and 16+ for those who need it. Bursaries are rigorously means-tested, and the families visited at home. Scholarships offered at the same entry points for academic achievement, music and sport, with art and drama added for the older age groups, but these are mainly honorific and carry only a small financial value eg £1,500 reduction in the fees.

Remarks: Intellectually exhilarating yet principled, this is selective education at its very best. For those able to take advantage of what it has to offer, a real golden ticket.

King's House School

68 King's Road, Richmond, Surrey TW10 6ES

020 8940 1878 | schooloffice@kingshouseschool.org | www.kingshouseschool.org

| Independent | Pupils: 420 |
| Ages: 3–13 | Fees: £7,380 – £17,550 pa |

Headmaster: Since 2011, Mark Turner BA PGCE NPQH (40s). Studied French and Spanish at Bristol before training at Sandhurst with six years in the army. After leaving, taught at Merchant Taylors' before joining Durston House, Ealing where he was deputy head for nine years. Married with four children, two of whom are at the school. Feels he is lucky to head such a good, friendly, and mainly local school. Says it has a strong sense of community and provides a broad education. Parents like the fact that he teaches French to year 4, thereby getting to know the senior boys, and say he's 'very approachable' and 'a classic boys' prep school headmaster'. Feel that he has made the school gentler. One of his aims is to unite the three sections of the school: at the moment they feel like separate entities. To that end, he spends more time in the junior section than his predecessor, which can't be a bad thing.

Entrance: From the term they turn 3, boys and girls at nursery level. Then reception, boys only, September after 4th birthday. No testing, places offered a year before entry in order of registration. Siblings take priority. A few more places at 7+ and 8+ subject to passing entrance test. Occasionally places occur at other times, each individually assessed. Mainly families from surrounding areas including Roehampton, Kingston and Barnes. Buses run from Chiswick and Putney.

Exit: A handful at 11+, trying to beat the rush, but the school does not give this much support. About two-thirds to boys' only London day schools at 13+ with Hampton, St Paul's and King's College Wimbledon all high on the list. Big range of boarding schools, with Epsom College, Charterhouse, Eton, Millfield and Winchester the recent favourites. Several scholarships, both music and academic, most years.

Remarks: On three sites in leafy Richmond. Seems a happy, hard-working school. We were taken round by two delightful, polite and enthusiastic senior boys under the eagle eye of the school's marketing manager – we were certainly given the spiel.

Large nursery building on two floors. Huge, bright rooms with different areas for learning and play. Plenty of constructive fun to be had by eager under-4s, both boys and girls. Parents love it – one even said 'flawless'. Two outdoor playgrounds, one for physical play, one for creative/imaginative play. They think of everything these days. Send your children here and your sons get automatic entry to the junior school. Your daughters? They seem mainly to head off to the Old Vicarage.

The junior school – reception to year 3 – is just across the road from the senior. Two reception classrooms on the ground floor have their own outdoor play areas where all is still reasonably relaxed. It may only be the beginning of learning but they are definitely being prepared for the next stage; homework starts straight away. Writing practice first, then, when they are ready, reading. Only 10 minutes at a time but it's still homework for 4 year olds.

The rest of this rather rambling house contains two year 1 classes and three each for years 2 and 3. Average class size about 20. All have a classroom assistant as well as a fully trained teacher. It is at this point that the serious learning begins. More work, less play. Classrooms are not enormous but they are bright and buzzing. All the boys appeared happy and attentive. Space is at a premium, the library fills in a corridor and a piano lesson seemed to be going on in a passageway. The IT room contained a lot of slightly restless boys learning computer basics. But, no worry, there is plenty of room for burning energy outside in the big playground which, cleverly, has a partially covered area. Parents full of praise for Mr Gower, head of juniors, who they say is extremely approachable and quick to answer emails. He's usually there to welcome boys in the morning. Also, we were told, all children love Nurse Jo who cures all their woes.

In year 4 they move across to the senior school where they can take advantage of some bang up-to-date facilities, of which our guides were rightly proud, and the real pressure goes on. Initially all classes are mixed ability and, apart from those subjects needing special equipment, are classroom based. In year 5 they begin to build up towards the common entrance syllabus and are setted in English and maths. Two science labs; DT and art rooms; two computer rooms including a suite of Macs for composing and design; a music room; a theatre where, our young guides boasted, amazing productions are put on; and a well-equipped music room. Parents say 'music used to be one of their weaknesses but is now one of their greatest strengths'. These are lucky boys.

Rugby, football and cricket all played competitively, there are 25 rugby, 34 football and 20 cricket teams. Wow! And they have silverware to prove their prowess

There's plenty of outdoor playing space as well, for organised and free play, that area having been completely revamped recently. Parents say it's a 'shame there's not wider extracurricular'; 'there could be more broader based after school clubs'. We got the feeling that the emphasis is mainly on the curriculum, with the pressure to succeed being the be all and end all. A 21st century London problem? Or just a lack of understanding that there is more to life than passing exams? The head comments: 'We believe the breadth and balance of our curriculum is a strength and is far from being too focused on the academic. We also feel that while some schools reduce art, DT, drama and ICT to carousel lessons, we still give them regular lesson time up to year 8.'

We didn't see the 35 acre sports ground as it is a coach ride away in Chiswick, but we have seen a DVD and it looks pretty impressive. Senior boys go there twice a week and junior boys once. Rugby, football and cricket all played competitively – 25 rugby, 34 football and 20 cricket teams. Wow! And they have silverware to prove their prowess (including Prep Schools Rugby Nationals U13 winners). Tennis, swimming and athletics also figure. Astroturf area within the senior school grounds and a well-equipped gymnasium ensure plenty of PE.

Inevitably, in a non-selective school, there is a wide variation in ability but, parents tell us, lots of help in the junior school who are 'quick to pick up struggling children and help them so they don't get left behind'. Continual monitoring; boys needing specific help are given it free of charge – 'we give them the building blocks' – being taken out of class for an hour at a time. Free, individualised education programmes provided.

Strict code of behaviour both in and out of the classroom, weekly PHSE sessions and a pupil teacher ratio of approximately 12:1 ensure that the majority of problems are caught quickly. House and tutor systems also provide continuous monitoring. Parents say, 'communication lines excellent and emails responded to quickly'; 'quick to pick up on problems and good at keeping on top of them'.

Communication certainly seems to be a great strength; no parent could say they are not kept fully up to date. From the headmaster's termly letter to the weekly school newsletters, everything is covered. Information on matches, charities and school trips, contributions from teachers, prizes and praises – it's all there. An active and busy school.

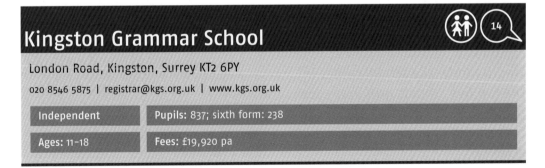

Kingston Grammar School

London Road, Kingston, Surrey KT2 6PY

020 8546 5875 | registrar@kgs.org.uk | www.kgs.org.uk

| Independent | Pupils: 837; sixth form: 238 |
| Ages: 11–18 | Fees: £19,920 pa |

Head master: Since 2014, Stephen Lehec, previously head of Aylesbury Grammar School. He joined Aylesbury as deputy head from Maidstone Grammar in 2006, becoming head in 2008. He has a history and English degree from Southampton and a PGCE from Oxford. Softly spoken (for a head) and personable, he works from an office so lush that it wouldn't look out of place in an interiors magazine or, at any rate, a Heal's ad. Not that he spends all his time there, with pupils telling us he's 'so much more hands-on than the last head.' Teaches year 7 history (and was trying to find time to start teaching sixth formers too when we visited) and meets regularly with pupils across all years. 'I never want to be the kind of head to say, "Remind me who you are,"' he explains.

Meanwhile, staff praise his collaborative leadership style and his reshaping of the executive team that encourages more sharing and avoids anyone being able to say, 'That isn't my job.' Parents describe him as 'available', 'pragmatic' and 'open to suggestions'. 'There's no element of "Leave us to it, we know best",' one told us. Refuses to over-push academia at the expense of developing the whole child.

Lives locally with his wife and two daughters and is a keen football, cricket and tennis player, having coached teams up to county level – although the school itself remains his biggest passion. 'If you asked my wife what's my biggest interest outside of work, she'd say "work",' he laughs.

Academic matters: Strong results across the board – in 2019, 65 per cent A*/A grades and 84 per cent A*/B at A level/Pre-U; 87 per cent 9-7 grades at I/GCSE – although maths is the clear stand-out subject here. A whopping four maths choices alone at A level. 'We support people who want a bit of maths to supplement their qualifications right up to those wanting to study it at Cambridge,' says the head. For both GCSE and A level, other popular subjects include English lit, sciences (where there's a good gender split) and history, and the school also offers IGCSEs in maths, English, languages, and sciences. 'We're big on the facilitating subjects here,' explains the head, 'although lots of A level students also add on the likes of theatre studies, PE or politics.' Pre-U in economics and 70-80 per cent take up of EPQ – often with pupils revisiting areas they gave up for GCSE, such as Italian. Some pupils yearn for cookery, although they do get the opportunity to cook at home and bring in the fruits of their labour for assessment and tasting.

> *Traditionally, the school comes in the top five schools nationally for hockey and is amongst one of the best co-ed schools for rowing in the country*

Language department – an uplifting environment, with bunting made from European flags hanging from the ceilings – currently musters 15 languages, with year 7 pupils choosing two options from French, German, Spanish and Italian, plus Latin. In addition, there are options to do taster courses in everything from Mandarin to Danish and Russian to Polish. By year 9, pupils can pick up other languages more formally, with all students studying at least one language for GCSE and many studying more. Greek taught in collaboration with Tiffin boys. IT very much embedded into learning, with plenty of IT breakout areas across the subjects, many in full use when we visited. A little setting in maths and PE from year 7, 'but it's more tiering than setting,' says the head.

A new timetable system of longer, 50-minute lessons, has gone down well and the teaching staff are widely praised by pupils for providing interesting lessons and extra help when required, including extension classes and one-to-one tutoring. Not that the pupils are expected to give up oodles of their time. 'Far from it, teachers are really understanding that we have busy lives,' one told us. 'There's no sense of underachievement or failure if pupils don't get top marks,' said one parent. 'The ethos is more about encouraging and enthusing pupils,' said another. Lots of professional development opportunities to help attract and retain the best teaching staff.

Learning support department helps those on the dys strata, mostly mild, a few moderate. Learner profile compiled for all children seen by educational psychologist or specialist teacher – school a great believer in constant monitoring and tracking to ensure progress. Lots of laptop users and open to those with aural/visual impairment – 'so long as they can cope with the site.' One parent, with a child who unexpectedly became partially sighted, told us the school has been 'magnificent.' 'It was bolt from the blue for us and for them when she got this curious genetic condition, but they quickly assessed what they'd need to do to support her and to ensure she didn't stand out.'

Games, options, the arts: Hockey, rowing and, most recently, cricket, are the three strongest sports here. The school has also boosted netball and football, once considered the poor relations. Good gender split (the school's best cricketers were female when we visited), with netball the only sport played only by one gender and even that is being redressed, with the school considering using handball as way of getting more boys into it. Other sports – of which there are 25 options by sixth form – range from spinning classes to sailing. Plenty of sporting accolades, with 20 international level girls and boys at the school, and five currently playing at international level. Traditionally, the school comes in the top five schools nationally for hockey and amongst one of the best co-ed schools for rowing in the country – particularly good for a co-ed school, where they only have half the potential numbers of single sex schools. Around 80 per cent take up among pupils for Saturday and after-school sports.

Music a source of huge pride and joy. Three orchestras, four choirs, along with plenty of quartets and quintets from guitar to saxophone

The unfortunately-named Cage (two onsite courts with soft surfaces) is well-loved by pupils, along with the school gym. And although some sport takes place on the Fairfield – a field across the road from the main site, which is also used by Tiffin and maintained by the Royal Borough of Kingston – most of it happens off-site at Ditton Field, a 22-acre facility a bus ride away. Other sporting venues used by the school include St Mary's University and Hampton Court for Real (Royal) Tennis. A few grumbles from parents that there isn't more sport on site, although they quickly catch themselves sounding spoilt – this is London, after all.

Music a source of huge pride and joy, although it's seen by some, including the head, to have historically spread itself too thin, with too big a range of functions, so watch out for some more honed evening performances in the future. Three orchestras (beginners, junior and senior), four choirs (first year, juniors, seniors and chamber – which had recently sang at the Vatican when we visited), along with plenty of quartets and quintets from guitar to saxophone. Excellent facilities and around 250 private music lessons a week, many of which take place in the colourful contemporary pods, located in a school courtyard. 'Music tech is amazing,' added one student. 'You get to actually produce music from the word go.'

Exceptional performing arts centre produces some very polished performances (they used proper airline seats on stage and filmed 500 minutes of scenes around London that were used for background for one recent performance). But then again, professional staff come from a theatre background and there are regular visiting actors (Samantha Bond's daughter Molly Hanson, a former KGS school captain herself, when we visited) helping with everything from LAMDA exams to drama school applications. 'My son has really found his feet, thanks to the drama here – his confidence has grown immeasurably,' one parent told us.

Art and DT also excellent – masses of workshop/studio space, and we drooled over brilliantly conceived and executed works of art, both 3D and paintings, much of which you'd pay good money to hang on your walls. Professional quality furniture made by GCSE class, perspex clocks and clever ceramics make you want to get your hands gummy.

Co-curricular opportunities – which range from knitting to foreign language film club and from philosophy to debating club – fill a 40-page booklet, with many parents saying this is what gives Kingston the edge. Most pupils do at least one a day, with one telling us, 'I set up a new club myself – the economics society.' School usually open from 7am, with last staff leaving as late as 10pm.

Masses of trips, with the school taking full advantage of all the theatres, galleries and cultural events the capital has to offer, along with national residential trips and international residentials to the likes of Iceland (geography), Rome (choir) and Gibraltar (netball) just in one half term, and many others such as South Africa (hockey), Sri Lanka (cricket), China (cultural exchange), Utah (skiing), New York (art and drama) every year or two. Plenty of languages exchanges every year. A hardship support fund seeks to assist those in need.

Background and atmosphere: Whatever you do, don't put the school's postcode in your satnav (which takes you to the back of the school, where there's no entrance) and even when you do find the front, be warned there's no parking on site (although, thankfully, there are good public transport links). But despite the metropolitan location that's a nightmare to get to, inside the school you quickly forget you're in the midst of Kingston's tarmac tangle, thanks to the relaxed, welcoming and buzzy environment.

The original building is an attractive, well-kept, old-fashioned looking grammar school, while newer, modern buildings provide plenty of bright, airy spaces to learn, with particularly impressive science labs. Good café for sixth form, with TV, stereo system, drinks and snacks (and always someone playing chess, apparently). Space isn't lavish here, by any means, though what they've got has been used wisely and it is less cramped than some of its central London peers. The next big project being planned is a multi-million three or four storey building to include new changing rooms, space for engineering and art studios, bigger dining facilities (currently quite tight), additional library space and galleries with a real wow-factor – with the school hoping to build by around 2020.

Pupils – who wear white shirts and grey uniforms in years 7 to 11 (business dress in the sixth form) – look cheerful, both in lessons and during breaks, when they spill out into the various outside areas, including Fairfield during summertime. Strong student voice, with recently reformed school forum changing the likes of the lunch queuing system through to mobile phone rules. Renewed catering means take-up among year 9s (when, traditionally, pupils have moved to packed lunches) is now 95 per cent and is still popular in the sixth form when students are allowed out of school for lunch if they wish. Good home/school

IT links. Fabulous sixth form development offices – a one-stop shop for exams officer, careers advice, head of sixth form and more.

Pastoral care, well-being and discipline: 'It's ridiculously caring here,' says the head – a bold claim by anyone's standards, but pupils and parents concur. Good system of heads of year, form tutors and heads of house – 'they get to know you really well' – along with a robust buddy, prefect, mentoring and house system that encourage friendship across the years, and plenty of positions of leadership among pupils, including older ones mentoring younger ones. 'I always say that, "If we don't catch you in the wash, we'll get you in the rinse," because it really is the case that if anything is bothering anyone, we have enough systems in place both to notice and to help,' says the head. Bullying and stress minimal. 'They're quick to pick up problems and keep parents in touch. It's in the culture of the place,' said one parent.

Bullying and stress appear to be minimal. 'They're quick to pick up problems and keep parents in touch. It's in the culture of the place,' said one parent

Discipline scarcely an issue here, with non-verbal and verbal warnings, misconduct marks, summons to head of year and occasional after-school detentions generally all that's needed – although head has excluded pupils for a day or two occasionally, for the likes of foul language and misuse of mobile phones. 'We need to show we won't tolerate these things on the rare occasions they do happen,' he says.

Pupils and parents: Mostly from a three mile radius (although increasingly from Clapham and central London), so at least they probably know how to navigate Kingston's surreal road system. That said, over 95 per cent of pupils come by bus, train, bike or walk. From over 150 primaries – some 60 per cent from state schools. Parents are a mixture of the predictably wealthy types and those who bend over backwards to afford it. School encourages plenty of parental involvement and there's a thriving PA. We found the pupils quietly ambitious, grounded and confident.

Notable former pupils include Edward Gibbon (The Roman Empire one), RC Sherriff (of Journey's End fame) Michael Frayn, Jonathan Kenworthy, James Cracknell, Andy Sturgeon (imaginatively roped in to help with the reshaping of the school's landscape), 2012 Olympic gold medal rower Sophie Hosking, a founder of Not On The High Street Sophie Cornish, and Hotel Chocolat's Peter Harris, as well as Ian Fortune, who was awarded the Distinguished Flying Cross (RAF version of the VC).

Entrance: The main entry points are 11+ and 16+ with some spaces available for 13+ entry. There's also an option to sit a 10+ deferred entry examination in year 5 to secure a place in year 7 (for which over 200 sit the test for around 20 places offered). More or less equal number of boys and girls. Interview seen as important – the school looks for potential, not just academic achievement, and it also helps weed out the overly tutored. Even at interview stage, the school is blind to whether the pupil goes to a state or private school. 'Unless, that is, they turn up in their straw boater, which some do,' says the head, smiling. Around 1,000 sit the 11+ test, with 360 interviewed, from which up to 250 places are offered for the 125 or so places they could fill. 'We're well aware people have more than one iron in the fire,' says the head, with lots of parents deliberating over issues such as, 'Do I go for Tiffin, which is free, or Kingston Grammar for its reputation?' School works closely with the feeder schools – especially at 13+, so as to not to encourage unrealistic applications. For external 16+, entry involves sitting exams in the A level subjects opted for, followed by interviews. Some 20-30 external offers are made every year.

At year 7, five forms of 20-25 pupils, dropping to an average of 16-18 in GCSE groups and to single figures for A level groups. 'I'm not convinced smaller class sizes necessarily affect outcomes, because good teaching should work in any size class, but it does mean we get to know the pupils better,' says head.

Exit: Around 80 per cent stay on into sixth form, for which pupils need a 9-6 grade average in their GCSEs including grade 7s in their chosen or related subjects and 8 in maths. Post A levels, 98 per cent go to university, 10-15 per cent after a gap year, with over 70 per cent going to Russell Group universities and an annual sprinkling to Oxbridge – 10 in 2019. 'We actually get quite a few pupils turning Oxbridge places down, for example to go to Royal Veterinary College or Imperial to study medicine,' says head (two medics in 2019). Top destinations include Nottingham, Bristol, Birmingham, Exeter, Manchester, London, Warwick, Durham, Southampton, Leeds – and a few to art and drama colleges. Biggest range of courses you could imagine, with maths, science, history and humanities among the most popular.

Money matters: Scholarships typically worth 10 to 50 per cent of fees available at all entry points and awarded on results of tests for academic scholarships and application and assessment for art, drama, sport and music. Bursaries worth up to 100 per cent of fees also at all entry points and means-tested – with the school aiming to fill 5-10 per cent of places a year this way. Worth a serious look if you are local, clever and strapped.

Remarks: There's no shortage of good schools in this area, all with their particular highlights, but this stands out for being relaxed and friendly, with an underlying buzz that seems to get pupils

willingly and happily doing their best. 'There's a kind of intimacy about it that makes it the kind of school you wish you'd been to,' said one parent, whilst every single pupil and parent we spoke to, bar none, raved about the fact that the school really understands each child and what makes them tick. We found the extracurricular offering also stands out. Indeed, the ethos is all about developing the whole person, not just getting them through academic exams. A school that really lives up to its motto, Work Well and Be Happy, this is a place that sets young people up for a fantastic future.

Latchmere School

Latchmere Road, Kingston, Surrey KT2 5TT

020 8546 7181 | office@latchmereschool.org | www.latchmereschool.org

State	Ages: 3–11	Pupils: 944

Headteacher: Since 2008, Julie Ritchie CertEd BPhilEd MSI SIP (Special) (late 50s). Hails from a proud Grimsby fishing family, but weighed anchor at an early age and headed for education instead. Previously at St Matthew's CofE Primary School, and shortlisted for head of the year award. Before that, developed an expertise in special needs at Dysart special school in Surbiton, as well as inspecting schools for Ofsted. Most recently, oversaw the extension of Latchmere School to sponsor academy status, mentoring a school in nearby Twickenham with the Latchmere magic.

'I'm very systems driven, very organised,' she tells us, and clearly they work: one of the largest primary schools in the country and within the top 10 per cent academically. The coverted Outstanding stamp from Ofsted has recently been downgraded to a mere Good and she's on a mission to recover it. 'We go out from Latchmere to win, not to come second,' she explains, with reference to the sports matches, but we had no doubt it applied to wider fields too.

She doesn't teach a class but 'does the gate' each morning at the infant side of the school, so becomes familiar with all the new arrivals. 'It speaks volumes,' said one mum; 'she's accessible'. In her office she has a crib sheet of the children's photos; 'I practise and make sure I do know them all,' she confides. Children round the school all know her and give her a cheery response.

Previously married, with two grown up children, she radiates efficiency and quality, with not a hint that she has been at her desk since 6.30am.

'Mrs Ritchie has high standards,' we heard from one parent, another added, 'I wouldn't mess with the headmistress'. We liked that she communicated clearly, without resort to statistics or education-babble. Her vision is to take the school attainment to above its target, 'but we don't want to grow beyond our expertise'. We had no doubt she would win that match too.

Entrance: Via the Kingston upon Thames admissions system, oversubscribed for the 120 reception places, with waiting lists for in-year applications too. Catchment area varies each year, but is never beyond one kilometre. Wide range of ethnic groups make up 50 per cent of the intake, as well as MOD children (five per cent) from local barracks. We heard the queue at open day was like Harrod's sale.

Exit: The head sees all parents in year 5 about secondary choices. 'We talk not just about academic ability but about taking your child to extra things, including rugby or swimming – that's where the scholarships sit'. Most move on to The Kingston Academy or Grey Court School, with a few to Tiffin Girls and Boys. Leavers also scoop a handful of scholarships each year at independents, including Kingston Grammar, Hampton School, King's Wimbledon.

Remarks: A high achieving school, by national and local standards, despite its four form entry. The national curriculum is enhanced by creative subjects: drama, music, art, history, geography, French and computing. The school has recently abolished sets in maths, yet continues to exceed the national average. One mum said, 'my son knows that he's strong at maths, they celebrate it, but equally they don't overdo it'. For literacy, we noticed that while reception and year 1 children were getting started with a reading scheme and elementary spellings, year 6 were flying with Radical Writing and Kandinsky.

'Our SEN is super,' boasts the head, not only for the select 14 who make up the Topaz resource base for diagnosed ASD children, who integrate with the mainstream classes. In addition there is an adapted suite on the upper floor for the 10 per cent with other conditions, from mild literacy problems to more specific needs. We heard from one parent, 'My son has OT in the attic every day for movement breaks; his TA accompanies him. I am overwhelmed by the support'.

Staff (50 per cent men) include a range of ages. Some newly-qualifieds emerge each year from the School Direct programme that Latchmere leads. 'We attract young people who want a really good career in education,' remarked the head. A parent commented, 'I find a lot of the teachers go above and beyond the line of duty'. Staff are organised into middle and senior leaders, some are trained in therapies, in addition there are visiting speech and language and occupational therapists; the school also employs an educational psychologist. 'My son has developed such a relationship with his teachers. That's the sign of a good teacher and a good school,' avowed one mum.

'We go out from Latchmere to win, not to come second,' the head explains, with reference to the sports matches, but we had no doubt it applied to wider fields too

Sport is robust, as demonstrated by the gold-level kitemark for games. PE has a strong presence within the curriculum in the form of football, rugby, hockey, netball and cricket, as well as swimming for years 1 to 5 with specialist swimming teacher, Mr Pool. This is matched by a wealth of extracurricular clubs after school. Thirteen teams play in local leagues, as a cabinet full of silverware testifies, with B and C teams in some sports.

Art hits you in the face, quite literally, as you walk round the exuberantly decorated school, with pendulous stars in the year 2 corridor and a wonderful tissue jungle in the nursery. The school hosts three choirs and an orchestra, with individual instrument tuition available through

Art hits you in the face, quite literally, with pendulous stars in the year 2 corridor and a wonderful tissue jungle in the nursery

the Kingston Music Service. Each class performs at their own assembly, and parents are invited. 'They were allowed to make up the script themselves,' one mum told us; 'it was really whacky and fun'.

A cloud of billowy cherry blossom hovers over the playground, giving the place a newly-washed look, appropriate to the neat Tudor estate which it serves, north of Kingston town centre. Founded in 1936, Latchmere school grew over several decades as twin infant and junior schools, before reunification in 2007 which enabled greater use of the large grounds, including shared playgrounds and a modern block at the rear. The front overlooks Latchmere recreation ground, a popular open space for locals jogging, dog-walking and perambulating with buggies.

At one end of the long corridor which connects infant and junior schools, we found the colourful nursery, where tiny children were enjoying the dolls house-style sheds or delving in water tables in their own secure outdoor area, overseen by a generous number of nursery nurses. Classrooms for reception and key stage 1 children lead off a long corridor splashed with cornflower blue doors and charming floor to ceiling photos of students at work and play. Older children's classrooms are reached beyond the well-stocked Jacqueline Wilson (alumna) library, while year 6s mount the stairs in a separate block to their own multi-coloured lockers. The junior hall with a large Olympic mural is used for drama, PE and three lunch sittings, with familiar favourites on the menu like macaroni cheese and arctic roll.

Outside two playgrounds brim with children on climbing equipment, shooting hoops or playing ping-pong, during staggered breaks, to avoid overcrowding. 'The playground can get very noisy,' commented a mum. In addition there is an impressive suite of Apple computers, a food tech kitchen and the pièce de résistance, a summer swimming pool, in what appears to be a giant polytunnel.

Despite its size, the site did not feel crowded, but there are systems for children with anxiety or well-being issues, such as the worry box set up by pastoral care. Discipline is also dealt with methodically, through positive behaviour management. 'We have consequences, but we don't get very far with them,' the head explained. 'Every school has bullying. We do deal with it straight away; we work to build up resilience, and to resolve it.' One parent

King's College School (Wimbledon)

commented, 'Sometimes I think it wouldn't be a bad thing to address these things before they crop up.' Another remarked, 'The children are impeccably behaved; if there's a issue it is all dealt with quite quickly'. Parents were pleased with the swift responses to their enquiries by email, or face to face at the school gate. 'It's an incredible system – a well-oiled machine,' enthused one mum.

Animated children buzz about in their blue uniforms, most of which is available to buy at chain stores. Parents are equally engaged in PTA tasks, welcoming new parents and organising a social calendar with a disco, comedy night and fundraisers. 'Parents are very generous,' we heard. 'They switch the PTA round every two to three years for an injection of new ideas'. Class reps email weekly and the office issues a newsletter. We heard parents comprise 'a rich mix', and that the school 'normalises any differences'. Commuters can drop children off early for breakfast club, while one mum of a younger child added, 'there are not many working mums in my child's class'.

A successful school with all the advantages that a large population can bring, while the highly organised structure nurtures individuals, too. An experienced head referees with high expectations and brings out the best in her team. Final result: well-rounded students and happy parents. A clear winner.

Marymount International School

George Road, Kingston, Surrey KT2 7PE

020 8949 0571 | admissions@marymountlondon.com | www.marymountlondon.com

| Independent | Pupils: 260; boarders: 55 full, 14 weekly; sixth form: 90 |
| Ages: 11–18 | Fees: Day £24,985; Boarding £40,515 – £42,305 pa |

Headmistress: Since September 2017, Meg Frazier, previously head of upper school at the Stone Ridge School of the Sacred Heart for girls, Washington DC (one of 147 Sacred Heart schools in 30 countries). History degree from Dartmouth College, has over 25 years of teaching and admin experience in the Washington area in the Jesuit and Sacred Heart networks of US and international schools, plus worked with international boarders at Georgetown Prep in Maryland. Describes herself as an avid gardener and reader, a rusty golfer and a life-long sailor who enjoys cooking and travel. She and her husband have three children, one daughter studying in London and two sons, both seniors in US colleges.

Academic matters: Marymount is a Catholic secondary girls school offering the IB middle years programme (MYP) and IB to an international community. The first (1979) girls' school in the UK to take up the IB in Britain, Marymount's grade 6-10 curriculum is built on solid institutional foundations. In 2019 pupils scored an average of 36 points, with 25 per cent earning 40+ and 30 per cent awarded bilingual diplomas.

No resting on laurels; they've been reviewing the MYP to align it with IGCSE content, ensuring all topics are covered in the MYP context by end of grade 9. School wants parents to be assured of MYP rigour: the priority is to be learning-driven, not taught to the test. Range of IB subjects and results is excellent. Lots of sciences, 'and we do lots of field trips', say the girls. The school is offering a relatively new IB course, environmental systems and societies, which satisfies either the IB science or IB humanities requirement. 'My sister likes geography and science so it's perfect for her.' Marymount's MYP covers the broad spectrum of disciplines, with the interesting addition of philosophy to introduce the girls to 'the language of philosophy' before they embark on theory of knowledge at diploma level. Fab Lab (fabrication laboratory) full of computer controlled tools that can make 'almost anything' is used to teach computer programming, coding, robotics and design, and aiming to stimulating creativity across the arts and sciences. As would be expected, religious education is also a key part of the MYP.

School prides itself on the wide range of languages offered. Extra mother tongue support in German and French in grades 6-8 dependent on enrolment. Parents warn that languages are sometimes subject to demand and in a small school it's not always possible to satisfy all requests for second language. It seems that there are mixed messages here and prospective parents are advised to discuss this at the early stages to clarify. The school does its best to support girls in working out alternative options – as one pupil explained, 'a friend who speaks Thai is taking IB Thai mother tongue; she's self-taught with the help of a tutor'.

The school is wireless throughout; iPads now in grades 6-9 and move up the grades as pupils progress; girls were excited to show off the first new Mac TVs, and there are more to come. The library has undergone a complete refurbishment – it has 9,000 volumes and membership of London Library enhances the collection.

Classes never more than 16 and many, particularly at diploma level, only four to six, fewer still for languages. Some classrooms are designed with small seminar-style groups in mind.

The teaching faculty is an international bunch, average age 40s. Pupil-teacher ratio is six to one and all staff seem to know most of the girls, affirming parent comments about supportive and nurturing environment with a caring individualised approach. Low turnover and enough long-termers to provide a cohesive core. Plenty of support staff and school nurse on site.

Mild/moderate learning difficulties and other issues managed collaboratively by the learning resource coordinator, teachers, parents and students themselves. Lots of individualised support throughout the school and the girls themselves were quick to talk about peer tutoring offered during free periods or after school.

Zumbathon, a fundraising activity involving the whole community beeping and bopping, swinging and swaying to music, was highly popular and yielded no casualties

The enrichment programme for able students has about 40 on the register. These students are invited to apply to programmes sponsored by Ivy Leagues (Stanford, Yale, Princeton, Johns Hopkins) and top tier UK universities. Additional provision includes extracurricular activities as well as resources which are made available to students for independent study and wider reading.

Games, options, the arts: Mix of competitive and non-competitive sporting activities available for all grades on and off site. If the school does not offer a particular sport they will help connect with local teams. Marymount is part of the International School Sports Association and they have produced an impressive record of results in soccer, badminton and tennis at championship tournaments hosted by member schools in different parts of Europe.

One pupil training with the Chelsea Ladies' development squad and several play with the Richmond Volleyball Club. When girls were asked why they chose Marymount, one replied that she came for the sport and when you hear that one of their football trainers is with Chelsea, no prizes for guessing which team Marymount girls support.

Musicians have plenty of opportunities to play in ensembles and chamber groups. About 20 per cent take private instrumental or singing lessons; school boasts a 100 per cent pass rate in grade exams. Entry to the choir is by audition and choristers participate in school concerts and annual tours to European cities, performing in major churches and cathedrals. Teachers encourage girls to perform in local festivals and competitions.

Drama is inclusive and the entire community builds up to a major production each year. Keen thespians can participate in ISTA (International School Theatre Association) festivals and when we visited girls were buzzing about their weekend ISTA trip to Stratford upon Avon. LAMDA examinations offered. Visual arts seem focused on painting and photography – the girls tell us that the art teacher is an inspiring photographer. Framed art by generations of pupils displayed throughout the school. Fab Lab includes a range of 3D printers, laser cutters and other digitally driven tools.

Consensus is that the most fun of all is the 'international day', when everyone shares their culture and cuisine. 'The Japanese do the best, and the [boarding] girls are already planning even though it's still months away'. Zumbathon – a fundraising activity involving the whole community beeping and bopping, swinging and swaying to music – was also highly popular and yielded no casualties.

As a Catholic IB school, community service involves everyone at Marymount. Middle schoolers do environmental projects that include cleaning along the bank of the Thames. Older girls volunteer in local activities including soup kitchens and schools and further afield join other RHSM students in projects working with children in places such as Zambia. All students take part in the spiritual life of the school and attend an annual retreat. Girls of all faiths come to Marymount and this provides opportunities for students to learn about other beliefs and traditions; care is taken to ensure that everyone feels comfortable at mass and prayer. We visited on a Hindu feast day and the girls said they had started the day with a Hindu prayer; Muslim girls wear their headscarves with confidence.

Boarding: Almost one third of the pupils board and there are four halls, each with its own duo of houseparents. Boarding rooms (some bunk beds) have recently been refurbished and facilities are clean and pretty tidy. Boarding areas are kept locked during the school day unless a girl has a reason to be back in her room. Oldest boarders have the spacious shared bedrooms above and the remaining nuns living in a wing just off their hall. Sisters no longer teach but are very much part of the fabric of the school, occasionally eating or sharing cocoa and study evenings with the girls.

'The teddy bear topiary sold me,' said one father. 'How can you not love a school that has teddy bear topiary?'

The school's proximity to Heathrow is an attraction for boarding parents; the girls say that the school's proximity to London is the attraction for them. The lure of London aside, boarders enjoy theatre and music trips as well as days out to the seaside (Brighton) and theme parks such as Longleat. There's plenty going on inside school too, including dance and music workshops and opportunities to explore and develop one's faith. Worth mentioning here that the school also takes weekly boarders from local (ie London) families and it is sometimes possible to arrange short-term boarding for day girls whose parents travel.

Clear procedures allow boarders off-campus freedoms to visit friends and family while ensuring their safety. One guardian who has long looked after boarders during half-term breaks told us that some older girls feel the school is too strict. She helps them, and their far-off parents who hear the grumbles, appreciate that the school is being cautious and not unreasonable. Two exclusions in the last few years of boarders who, after several warnings, broke the rules about leaving campus.

Background and atmosphere: Established in Kingston in 1955 by 10 nuns from the Religious of the Sacred Heart of Mary (RSHM), sent by the Eastern American Province. Mid-19th century French founder of RSHM aspired to provide charity for all classes through schools, homes and orphanages that worked interactively across socioeconomic barriers. Schools opened in France, Ireland, Portugal, England, the US and later Latin America and the rest of the world. The first sisters who came to Kingston started a 'year abroad' programme for US university women, then a school offering the US secondary school curriculum. Early 70s saw the arrival of Sister Anne Marie Hill, a determined Irish mover-and-shaker, well known in international education circles and now executive director of the network of schools. She introduced the IB, making the school more relevant to its growing international student body and reflecting RSHM's original ethos. During the noughties

Marymount had a series of heads as RSHM grappled with transition to lay leadership and during that time the board of governors was created.

School works closely with the other Marymount partners under Sister Anne Marie's guidance, meeting every six to eight weeks to discuss areas such as strategic planning and communication. Increasingly involvement with the international network of RSHM schools – 19 worldwide – is now bringing more opportunities to the pupils.

The school is based in an affluent part of Surrey occupying a large Edwardian house plus various more recent additions connected by walkways. Elegant grounds with lawns, manicured flowerbeds and sculpted hedges. 'The teddy bear topiary sold me', said one dad, 'How can you not love a school that has teddy bear topiary?' (We presume he had already consulted the GSG about minor details such as teaching and pastoral care.) Main house, with original wood panelling and stained glass, is head office and reception. The nuns are loved by the girls and parents appreciate their presence. Small school chapel is used by boarders and local community alike.

Modern blocks house multi-purpose classrooms, the newly refurbished library and university and careers counselling rooms. Another block has the gym (floor replaced recently), music rooms and auditorium for assemblies, all-school mass, drama. Yet another has more dorms, new dining hall with a 'chef's theatre' – and, school tells us, much improved food from new catering company – classrooms, infirmary, student lounges. A new quasi-Scandinavian wooden structure houses more small tutorial rooms just right for the many language classes and designed with IB language examination conditions in mind. Most of the buildings surround the garden and have big windows that bring the outdoors in and give a refreshing sense of space and light.

The girls are reflective about the realities of being in a single-sex environment. They feel they are able to focus more on learning, but would like to find a partner boys' school

Pastoral care, well-being and discipline: Spiritual values underpin the ethos of Marymount, rooted in the mission of the RSHM, 'that all may have life'. These values are made explicit on the website: even the most casual browser will see them on every page, running alongside photos. School welcomes girls from all faiths but we think it might not be a comfortable environment for the girl who has none. Plenty of support available at the school: academic, social, emotional and personal; more expertise called upon if necessary.

Spiritual values of the Religious of the Sacred Heart of Mary underpin the ethos of Marymount and are made explicit on the website. The school welcomes girls from all faiths but we think it might not be a comfortable environment for the girl who has none

Parents' Association hosts a welcome back family barbecue during the first weekend of the school year when boarding parents are there dropping off daughters so they are able to meet day families. One parent said the school went out of its way, allowing their daughter to board temporarily so she could start at the beginning of the year, before the family transfer to London took place. Another described how the teachers made an effort to encourage her daughter to join the orchestra for a big performance, even though her late arrival meant she had missed several rehearsals.

Pupils and parents: Marymount girls are internationally diverse, cheerful, articulate, academically motivated, quietly confident and as a bunch, quite enchanting. More aspirational than ambitious, they love their school and really enjoy having peers from all over the world. They look out for each other, especially new ones, and although one day girl said she wished there were more ways to get closer to the boarders everyone, including day parents, feels that the day girls and boarders are pretty integrated.

The girls are reflective about the realities of being in a single-sex environment. They feel they are able to focus more on learning, but they would like to find a partner boys' school and the student council has made some moves in this direction. Trouble is that 'all the boys' (schools) seem to be taken', but they have not given up. 'When adolescent girls become interested in boys, it can be frustrating to see how much they measure themselves against the approval of the boys in the group. Without that distraction they can develop as intellectually rigorous learners; they are their own people.'

The families that choose the school value the ethos of school, its Catholicism and internationalism, but are equally attracted to the IB. There are 40 nationalities in the school, British representing just over half. Other significant groups are German, Spanish, Japanese, Chinese, US, Australian, Korean and Italian. The numbers within these groups are balanced very carefully to facilitate integration. The school bus service extends into London to Sloane Square and more routes are under consideration.

Parents' Association organises events including outings for parents which are appreciated by newly-arrived expats.

Entrance: Local families are urged to attend one of the open days. Inbound expats on 'look-see' trips to London may book appointments. Girls' admissions based on availability and a review of school reports and teacher references plus interview. English language fluency is required with exceptions made for younger students for whom English is a second language. Most classes have waiting lists so best to apply a year in advance, though there is some turnover so you could be lucky.

Day girls come from most SW London postcodes including Richmond, Wimbledon, Putney, Chelsea, South Kensington.

Exit: Most head to university and the chart we saw on the college counsellor's wall listing every 12th grader's destinations confirms that they are applying to many countries. Counsellor stays in close contact with parents, especially boarder parents, about each girl's plan and the process they must follow depending on the country of their destination. PSAT and SATS also offered.

In 2019, offers from destinations as varied as Sheffield University, SOAS, Maastricht University, McGill University, Canada, Gettysburg College, USA, IE University, Spain and Ecole Hôtelière de Lausanne, Switzerland.

Money matters: School has no endowment so financial stability is maintained by tuition and fundraising initiatives. 'Being an international school and in the current economic climate, we need to be sure we are guarded and forward looking – we can't rest on our laurels.' The PA also fundraises for activities that support the school and pupils.

Scholarships (academic, art, music, drama, sport, community service) for grade 6 and 8 students. Some offered for grades 10, 11 and 12. Some financial aid available for means-tested students. About 20 per cent of the pupils benefit from this.

Remarks: Successfully serves a niche market of internationally-minded families seeking a girls' school with a Catholic ethos. In the words of one parent, 'We've been over-the-top-happy. The school provides excellent support and people from all over the world fit in and are welcome there.'

Nonsuch High School for Girls

17

Ewell Road, Cheam, Sutton, Surrey SM3 8AB

020 8394 1308 | office@nonsuch.sutton.sch.uk | www.nonsuchschool.org

| State | Ages: 11–18 | Pupils: 1,320; sixth form: 370 |

Headteacher: Since 2016, Amy Cavilla BA (40s), following what school terms 'interim leadership structure' after the abrupt departure of predecessor.

Educated at Godolphin & Latymer, MFL degree at Leeds, previously taught at Tiffin Girls (there for 12 years). Comes with fully formed love of girls-only education and sympathy with the ideals of grammar schools. Smart, chic (sporting dashing asymmetrical hem to meet parents), she has two school age daughters. Impressive at open days, combining nice, motherly way with young visitors with hands on reassurance for nervy parents. 'Personally showed a group of parents around which doesn't usually happen,' said one. 'Have only heard good things about her,' agreed another.

Brings promise of a steadier hand at the tiller (reinforced by federation with Wallington High School for Girls). School has been getting through its heads faster than is healthy (anything but 'strong and stable'). But with results and added value rising again (not that they've ever been exactly bad), things are on the up.

Just as well. While grammar school parents tend not to mince their words, those at this school have been dishing them up whole, plain and unvarnished (even if polysyllabic). We've heard of one child not taking up a place in year 7 and some off the record grumbling by some members of staff (it's not always been the happiest place to work, some feel).

But that was then. Now there's Ms Cavilla, exuding air of calm control, staff rallying behind her and a new sense of optimism. She appears to be winning pupils over in small incremental steps. 'She's lovely,' said one. 'There's been a general improvement [since she came].' 'The school is neater,' we were told.

Academic matters: Results excellent. In 2019, 83 per cent of GCSEs were 9-7. At A level, 55 per cent of grades were A*/A and 79 per cent A*/B. Cynics might exercise 'so what' muscle but head – rightly – stresses government Progress 8 score. Between end of primary school and year 11, school adds three-quarters of grade to each girl's GCSE results. It's impressive, putting school in top two per cent

nationally, no mean feat given that it's recruiting the best of raw talent in any case and is up against other super-duper selective establishments.

Current government comparison table – based on progress – puts it two places above Tiffin; no other similar school within 75 miles does it better. 'Can't fault it for the grades,' said parent. Ofsted rating of good (reaffirmed January 2017) no doubt frustrating – biggest question mark is over exceptionally able sixth formers, felt not to be sufficiently challenged. Where they get it really right, results are amazing – school accounts for a tenth of all GCSE and A level classical Greek entries nationally. Also praise for improved value added in A level physics, chemistry, biology and mathematics.

The head appears to be winning pupils over in small incremental steps. 'There's been a general improvement since she came'

Currently economics, geography and English literature felt to lag behind and school needs to deliver more of the good stuff – additional top grades at A level 'should be even higher given starting points,' says Ofsted. No doubt something head will have in her sights for the future. In the meantime, parents stress school's focus on preparation and results. 'They're fantastic, pushing and pushing and monitoring the children, and obviously want them to obtain A*s and As all the way through,' said one.

Not big on SEN, with 'zero per cent' of pupils in receipt of an EHCP and low numbers generally, despite detailed policy. Where learning needs exist (and it's generally in their milder forms), we were told by one parent that girls' drive to succeed can mask difficulties so effectively that their SEN may not be identified while they're here.

The other bugbear (confusingly also the elephant in the room) is how much success is down to tutoring – up to three-quarters of all pupils, according to one parent, some having extra tuition five days a week. Ms Cavilla is not keen and says so. 'Vehemently put out that they don't want extra tutors but want them to have trust on the teachers – I thought that was very positive,' said one. Chances of making a difference are another question altogether.

Most girls take 10 or 10.5 GCSEs (RS short course) then study three A levels – though a substantial chunk, often the Oxbridge hopefuls, opt for four or more (one sixth former was studying maths, further maths, physics, chemistry and economics).

Though no prizes for guessing the big hitter subjects (maths has own corridor; science has two and 11 labs), school is also working hard to convey horses for courses message with girls encouraged to do subjects that appeal. Inspiring teaching very often does the rest: girls who take drama as a fourth A level subject, originally intending to drop it at the end of their first sixth form year, very often carry it through.

Impressively, niche subjects, axed elsewhere, are still on the books here, even when classes are diminutive – two for A level computing, for example. GCSE options (20 to choose from) include Latin, product design and modern foreign languages (girls can opt for triple science or triple languages). Highlight is astronomy. Impressive telescope ensures close examination of the stars they're reaching for and inspiration, we assume, for planet based house names.

Pupils praise the number of trips (previously few and far between, say parents, now impressive for languages and history), quality of the homework ('fun and exciting,' said year 7) and the teaching, gentle at the start but moving to a more dynamic, questioning approach further up the school. While pupils have their likes and dislikes, most staff felt to be hitting the spot. 'She's been thrilled with her teachers – she was whooping when she got her timetable,' said sixth form parent.

Corridors feature hard-hitting questions – asking pupils to consider evidence base for treating HIV with garlic, for example, as well as displays of the 'Did you know?' variety (marking birth of famous scientists, for example). Plus the occasional glimpse into behind the scenes conversations – like the open letter from year 11 pupils thanking staff for 'doing the demanding (and probably underpaid) job of looking after us all day.'

Of the stand out subjects, history department much name-checked for 'passionate' staff team who encourage creativity. Papier-mâché hill fort is one of many enjoyable displays, while a drawing of Mona Lisa and cardboard Renaissance rooftop structures, created by year 7 pupils, form scene setting introduction to the 15th century. We can't speak for Leonardo da Vinci but they certainly impressed us.

Learning enjoyment is helped by free choice – no GCSE option blocks, no need to sacrifice a favourite subject. Pick what you want and the school will (somehow) make it work. Similar richness at A level, with extra support for those aspiring to Oxbridge or med school. But stress that it's not all about the results. 'Teachers say that exams are important but not the most important thing you'll ever do,' said pupil.

Impressive telescope ensures close examination of the stars they're reaching for and inspiration, we assume, for planet based house names

Teachers clearly happy – 'I don't count the hours, I love it here,' says one. Long stayers (up to two decades or more) are common and there are few vacancies even in the trickier subjects with, for example, all sciences taught by a full complement of specialists.

Games, options, the arts: Academics could so easily reign. But even though skiing is described 'an educational trip' to prospective parents, head is pushing benefits of being well-rounded rather than merely single minded. And though additional push is sometimes needed – school insisting that pupils leave the building in summer to ensure that the keen 'don't just sit in the library and work' – plenty of fun to be had.

No shortage of things to do once enticed out of the classroom, with normal big sports block including not just the usual cavernous hall but also dedicated classroom that confers useful prestige to GCSE and A level sports and PE studies classes can sometimes be viewed as a slightly dusty subject).

In addition to highly successful land-based sport (recent National Schools Championships finalists for badminton, borough winners in rounders, London netball champions, plus football, hockey, athletics, volleyball) – school has access to taa-daa quality swimming pool, built and managed by private firm (open to the public at evenings and weekends, though girls and paying customers have own entrances). Shame it lacks raked seating (means no galas and it's positively crying out for bunting and some noisy cheering), though 'we're not complaining,' says teacher. Lots of individual successes (archery and judo among them) and impressive creativity elsewhere – recent gym and dance display themed to 'A night at the movies' featured everything from Mission Impossible to Mary Poppins.

Activities, many after school and at lunchtime, include work with local community (get togethers for senior citizens with pupil-organised entertainment and cake); clubs (gardening visibly translates into quality shrubbery round the pond); sports tours and events. Mega highlight is 'ball girling' (school's description) for Queen's Club Aegon Championships. 'We arrived [...] saw each other in the beautiful kit for the first time [...] set off at 7:30am and sang songs all the way,' says newsletter account. DofE bronze, silver and gold (now back after gap caused by staffing issues and increasingly popular – mass recruitment in year 9 with 170 currently signed up) plus CCF offer plentiful heavy duty yomping (including popular overnight camping trip sustained by army issue rations).

Sparkling new library combines popular fiction with seating in eye-popping hues – lime, turquoise and navy (reduces chances of falling into a gentle doze)

Drama and music both busy and varied with many choirs and bands and 300 or so pupils learning an instrument (lots of violinists) in school, some reaching diploma level. Visual arts impressively accomplished and popular, judging by pupils' high levels of enthusiasm, quality work dotted around the school. Art room with high ceilings and wide windows spills over with colour and interest, from year 7 drawings of portraits of backs of heads (pigtails so detailed that every hair appears to have been accounted for) to attractive wire sculptures.

Background and atmosphere: While no opportunity to reinforce girls' stature and potential is missed (recent production – Blue Stockings – focused on first Oxbridge women students....) there does seem to be an inordinate amount of baking. We'd hope that boys' grammars also pride themselves on exquisite looking cakes topped with mathematical symbol as part of Pi week – but have our doubts.

Cake making aside, school, founded 1938, has stuck consistently to its principles of aspirational education for girls, aiming for 'excellence in all aspects of its work,' says website. Since 2015, federated with Wallington High School for Girls through Nonsuch and Wallington Education Trust (making the featureless acronym NWET). Jane Burton (previously headteacher of Wallington Girls) is the CEO, though all schools have 'own headteacher and unique identity,' says Ms Cavilla. Pooled resources add extra clout to eg careers advice and Oxbridge preparation.

Site is next to (and originally part of) Nonsuch Park, once home to eponymous palace, long gone, built by Henry VIII and intended to be so dazzling that none such could compare – hence the name. No-nonsense layout (arranged round one very pretty quad – complete with beautiful, plant fringed little pond and one rather more workaday one) has been recently enhanced with two new buildings beloved by everyone bar art team (blocks out good chunk of natural light). One is home to performing arts. The other houses vast, smart sixth form centre; heads of department, behind glass, like supervisors in very upmarket zoo, overlook the café and work and play areas (lots of cosy corners – as well as joltingly lime green chairs). There are new science labs too. Sparkling new and well-resourced library suffers from slight textbook overload – pupils arrive as keen readers though GCSE word load 'sucks some of the fun out it,' admitted one older pupil. Combines popular fiction (reassuringly well-thumbed Jacqueline Wilsons) with seating in (more) eye-popping hues – lime, turquoise and navy (reduces chances of falling into a gentle doze).

Pastoral care, well-being and discipline: It's not always felt like the happiest place, and arriving with plenty of natural resilience remains a definite advantage, say parents. 'There wasn't a lot of encouragement or praise,' said parent whose child bailed out after GCSEs. Disquieting rumours of bullying also persist. However, school is clearly doing its best to introduce more underpinning in the form of resilience and conflict resolution training. The current head is felt to be making effective changes, and visible kindness of staff (one searching out pupil to tell her that missing item had been found) seems to suggest that prevailing wind is now more temperate than previous Arctic blast.

Happiness may not always be top of mind (cover page of sixth form prospectus is the only one to feature photograph of jolly, shiny, folder-wielding girls – the remaining 50 are text only). But 'if they're not happy, they won't thrive,' says member of the pastoral care team. House system is initially form-based to ensure instant bonding and competition with hotly contested sports and music (including annual Battle of the Bands). Loyalties tend to 'diminish up the years,' said older pupil, and are shaken up altogether with new classes in year 10. End of year winning teams scores reckoned in the thousands in year 7 and hundreds by year 10.

As elsewhere, other underlying worry is of pupils driving themselves too hard, also identified by Ofsted as needing extra attention. Balance is inevitably a hard one to strike. Even year 7 pupils stress that organisation 'is up to you' – teachers won't issue reminders so essential to 'write things down and tick off subjects' – and there's an assumed ability to cope. You will be guided (diagnostic board in chemistry corridor lists symptoms to help pupils work out when they need support) but not led.

Regular assemblies (year and school) 'generally convey a moral message', LGBT society is flourishing, while head has introduced peer mentoring in addition to the many academic clinics designed to unravel knots (of understanding, organisation or just worry). Nurturing now unmissably big, and includes pastoral care team (with own room) and pupil mentors. School has removed obvious stress points – recently doing away with homework over the summer holidays for younger year groups (persuading parents not to fill in the gaps themselves is, we'd suspect, an ongoing battle).

Pupils and parents: Car driving parents don't do much for community relations, blocking neighbouring streets and taking a devil may care approach to three point turns. 'Park across drives and refuse to move,' said enraged local. Similar cavalier attitude to parking in the turning space at the school, said insider. 'School has given up and just lets them do it.'

While chutzpah may be a unifying factor, there's diversity in every other direction including alumni – best known are cyclist Jo Rowsell, singer Katie Melua, journalist Christina Lamb and historian Suzannah Lipscomb.

School takes from 100 feeders, catchment is wide and new pupils will often arrive knowing no one. School makes much of support for less affluent families – around six per cent – who qualify for pupil premium and, impressively, make more progress than pupils overall; major expenditure is in study support. For those who can afford it, creative PTA has neatly combined pain of regular contributions to swell coffers with a raffle – donate £5 a month for potential prize of £500 – and also organises regular events.

Entrance: Realistically, need to be comfortably within top 10 per cent of ability range. 'Otherwise may not be happy,' says head, who also emphasises manageable commute, so that trade off for gaining a place isn't death of social life. She urges perusal of bus and train routes in advance: 'Girls should be able to travel here easily'. Would that put parents off? We very much doubt it.

Candidates sit qualifying selection test (register between May and August, conglomerate test with other local grammars) and if successful, take second test (shared with Wallington) in maths and English in autumn term (other schools operate different second tier tests). Possible to sit abroad if current school confirms that will take place under exam conditions.

Normally around 40 external pupils join the sixth form. Need average score of 49 based on best eight GCSE/IGCSE subjects.

Exit: Depending on who you talk to, numbers leaving post-16 have been higher than you'd expect, with Glyn's co-ed sixth form proving particularly popular.

Impressive range of higher education destinations, though not university fixated – one student recently offered hotly contested Sky Sports apprenticeship. Normally good numbers to Oxbridge (11 in 2019) and to study medicine, dentistry and veterinary science (22 in 2019).

Remarks: In the past, we had the sense of a school that felt a little inward looking, reflected in beautiful but tiny canvases on display, minutely examining window frames or ironwork railings. With school illuminated by radiance of academic success, let's hope that Ms Cavilla can continue adding a much-needed dollop of warmth to the picture.

The Queen's CofE Primary School

Cumberland Road, Kew, Richmond, Surrey TW9 3HJ

020 8940 3580 | info@queens.richmond.sch.uk | www.queens.richmond.sch.uk

State   **Ages: 4–11**   **Pupils: 417**

Co-head teachers: Since September 2019 Voulla Demetriou, previously deputy head, and Jenny Stroud, previously assistant head.

Entrance: Two-form entry, so 60 reception places each year. Usual admissions criteria: looked after children, medical needs, siblings. Thereafter, at least one parent must be a 'committed and regular worshipper' at one of the three Kew Anglican churches (St Anne's, St Philip & All Saints', St Luke's); after that, it's down to proximity. Rather convoluted – if in doubt, contact the school office.

School is oversubscribed, but not dishearteningly so. Also worth applying further up, as much of the Kew community is professional and mobile, and occasional places do become available.

Exit: As you'd expect in this locality, a high number of private and grammar school places every year: Latymer Upper, Hampton, Lady Eleanor Holles, Tiffin, Kingston. Popular non-selective state school destinations include Christ's, Waldegrave, Sir Richard Reynolds and Richmond Park Academy. As with other state primaries, school doesn't prepare for 11 plus, and parents report that a fair degree of private tutoring goes on in the upper year groups. The children, however, were inclined to attribute their success to the school. 'It's really, really helped me get into the school I'm into,' said one engaging year 6 lad, who could have passed for Benedict Cumberbatch in his young days.

Remarks: Queen's is sited a stone's-throw from Kew village, which inevitably accounts for some of the school's character. As far as we could tell, this was a London-accent-free zone, and all the pupils we met were chirpy, well-spoken, well-mannered and quite delightful. We suspect that there isn't huge social diversity, and we saw very little cultural diversity as we looked round the lunch time crowds. (School says that it has above the national average number of pupils from ethnic minority groups.) But that said, the school works tirelessly to give the best school experience possible to its students, and clearly succeeds. Parents were incredibly warm in their praise, with the school's kind and friendly ethos mentioned again and again: 'A very positive culture of caring'; 'My two children love it there, they go happily every day'; 'The outstanding thing has been the care from all the staff'; 'The great strengths of the school are the atmosphere and the teachers, who are of a high quality and very dedicated'; 'A very friendly, inclusive environment'; 'Gentle and positive'; 'All the staff care about every child'. The children unanimously confirmed this. 'Is it friendly here?' we asked as we moved about the school, and group after group gave us an instant and emphatic 'Yes!'

The Anglican faith is central to the school's ethos, and plays a greater part here than we've seen in any other CofE primary school. Fathers Nigel and Peter from St Anne's and St Luke's take assemblies every week, there's a Passion Play every year complete with crucifixion scene, and attendance at church services is regular and frequent: when we visited, for instance, the whole school had just returned from Ascension Day service. Even competitions can be devotional in nature, with the winning entries in the Easter Crosses competition making a colourful display on the school's website. But there was nothing dour about any of it, and the children impressed us with their cheerful and confident benevolence towards life, the universe and everything. There was also a happy awareness of other faiths, and visits to a synagogue and a mosque had been followed up with some lovely work.

The standard of writing and maths that we saw was very high, and Queen's academic record is sterling: most children here achieve well above the national average, with a number of them successfully taking the level 6 tests (a pass at level 6 is expected of the average 14-year-old). Robust systems of monitoring are in place to make sure that children's performance is being tracked. One parent criticised the 'large and ill-defined projects' set for homework and felt that the school didn't do enough to push the children to do as well as they possibly could; whilst another, conversely, felt that the school put too much emphasis on getting the children to perform 'excessively' well in their Sats. The majority, however, said they were contented with the academic provision. 'Very good academic results achieved without extra pressure on the students', and 'an excellent academic environment' were typical comments. There are bang-up-to-date interactive whiteboards in every classroom, an attractive library and excellent, well-thumbed resources. Much recent working on bringing SEN provision up to scratch, and we liked what we saw of this area.

Despite its small size, the school fields two orchestras and two choirs, and a wide variety of instrumental lessons are offered. 'The concerts are brilliant!' enthused one parent

Popular breakfast and after-school clubs are welcomed by working parents, and there's a lively programme of extracurricular activities, with music being a particular strength. Despite its small size, the school fields two orchestras and two choirs, and a wide variety of instrumental lessons are offered. 'The concerts are brilliant!' enthused one parent. 'Every time you go into school your hear children singing or playing music!' Views on the sports provision were a little cooler, with many parents and pupils (boys in particular) wishing there were more, but everyone agreed that it was getting better, with a large new Astroturf, and there was much praise for a recent cricket tournament. The school insists that the amount of sport at Queen's has 'dramatically increased' over the past year, and two swimming trophies in the heads' office bore testimony to sports being 'one of our vision priorities.'

Queen's is the only school in the country to change its name according to the gender of the reigning monarch – it was The King's School until 1953 – and is held in warm regard locally. A recent alumni evening was well attended and produced some misty-eyed comments in the visitors' book. But there's no question of things standing still. These are clearly exciting times for a school that has much to be proud of.

Richard Challoner School

Manor Drive North, New Malden, Surrey KT3 5PE

020 8330 5947 | rcb@challoner.kingston.sch.uk | www.richardchalloner.com

State　　　Ages: 11–18　　　Pupils: 1,017; sixth form: (federated with Holy Cross): 236 (25 girls)

Head: Since 2015, Sean Maher BA (40s). Previously deputy head, rising through the ranks after being offered first post here four weeks into teacher training in 2001. Leadership skills amply demonstrated during secondment to Catholic secondary in Kent, transforming it in just under 18 months from 'requires improvement' to 'good' by upping expectations, improving discipline and putting classroom walls back in. 'Anyone could have done it,' he says modestly. Award of Kent Headteacher of the Year suggests anyone probably couldn't.

A local boy, combined studies at Emanuel and St Mary's Twickenham (studying English and history) with helping out in family bakery in Raynes Park (nothing like removing freshly baked loaves at end of night shift for sense of fulfilment, he says).

Little ruffles his feathers bar increasing amount of time spent on plugging growing holes in funding – every minute not spent helping pupils is a minute wasted. Tidiness also a major preoccupation, all senior teachers issued with own litter pickers. As badges of office go, not glitzy (sadly, there's no short but moving presentation ceremony either) but important, sending unambiguous message about standards and expectations.

While convention matters – uniform code for sixth formers specifying 'conservative' haircuts unlikely to change – Mr Maher also promotes the 'right sort' of Jesuitical rebelliousness – standing up against the prevailing wisdom rather than 'pointless' defiance. 'Boys need to be able to articulate their views – and unfortunately in society there is so much they need to stand against at the moment,' he says.

Devout, kind and focused on the pupils, he's a popular choice. 'Has best interests of everyone at heart,' says mother. No surprise that would-be staff will be asked if they really love children. 'Can tell straight away if they're really very awkward with the question.'

Impressive without being intimidating – 'Serious,' thought junior pupil – though older ones appreciate deadpan humour that's not far beneath the surface – and recently sang to whole school in assembly to demonstrate virtues of risk taking. 'He's down with the kids,' reckoned senior pupil – though Mr Maher isn't convinced.

Above all, a force to be reckoned with. His son, starting at the school soon, plans to 'come and have a cuddle if he gets into trouble,' says Mr Maher. 'I said, "Son, if that's what you think, you've underestimated me".' We suspect that's unlikely to be the case for very long.

Academic matters: 'You won't see one child not engaged with their learning,' says head. Naturally we put this to the test during tour – and he's right. From year 7 French class on a virtual shopping trip – 'Un grand sac de Doritos Chilli 'eatwave s'il vous plaît' – to year 8 boys' thoughts on constructing a balanced argument in English – 'Always talk through problems; don't keep it in,' there's minimal fidgeting or disengagement.

Even class of year 10 maths pupils, all blazer-clad and diligently working through mind-expanding algebra in boiling hot classroom, and year 11 pupils who have gone straight from first GCSE (RS) to revision session (physics), are impressively focused if a tad goggle-eyed – there's no study leave here, just a collapsed timetable to keep everyone on task.

All contributes to cracking results. In 2019, 70 per cent of pupils achieved 9-5 in GCSE maths and English, 28 per cent of grades at 9-7; 23 per cent of A levels awarded A*/A and 52 per pent A*-B. Success down to inspired teaching delivered with dedication and plenty of innovation. Younger pupils now have own iPads (top years who have missed out as not here long enough to pay them off are philosophical about greater good) and even insets, last one involving staff treasure hunt, sound fun.

Teaching team is bursting with young talent, with plenty of senior teachers barely in 30s and now heads-in-waiting, some former pupils who were taught by 50 or so veterans who've been here for a decade or more. Old or novice, sense of pride in their work visible in corridor after corridor crammed with pristine displays – we particularly liked the Poetree, with poems nestled among painted branches and the swathes of playing cards in the maths corridor, each with probability problem.

Energy courses through the place – head is a strong believer in keeping boys busy and the pace is correspondingly brisk. Despite DT's demotion from core subject to option in line with government requirements, most boys still take 10 GCSEs, down from 11 (slimmed down to six for some SEN pupils). Reduction a possible relief given one former pupil's comment about ease of overdosing on arts or sport activities 'and then realising you've got an exam in a month...'

Most subjects are set from year 7 with two innovative transition classes in core subjects helping first years who hadn't hit Sats targets bridge gap between primary and senior school. 'Some present with big challenges,' says teacher, who's using colour-coded activities (red for independent learning, yellow for group work) to 'teach boys to learn.'

Everyone gets together for other subjects including DT (freeflow rooms, 3D printer and fab projects including programmable robotic cars). Well-resourced food technology, hospitality and catering a big hit with year 10 pupils, particularly top set types who find relaxation in creation of immaculate macaroons, sushi and crostini.

The head is impressive without being intimidating – and recently sang to the whole school in assembly to demonstrate the virtues of risk taking

Range continues at sixth form level with 28 A levels and five BTecs, some high demand subjects (maths, history, geography and psychology currently top list of favourites) offered both here and at partner girls' school, Holy Cross, others split between the two – timetable immensely complex to sort but currently working well, minibus plying between the two sites 'and easy to catch as long as you organise yourself,' said pupil. No plans for combined sixth form – with almost 500 pupils across two schools, semi-detached existence works better.

Generously proportioned and resourced learning resource centre, open on Saturday mornings and in holidays, provides a shelter for anyone having a rough time. Determined librarian's mission is to ensure that everyone reads – books must be carried at all times – while staff post current title on their classroom doors – maths teacher was deep in Candide; head tucking into The Jesuit Guide to Almost Everything, a recent gift from a colleague.

High expectations extend to SEN pupils – 76 pupils in much-admired ASD unit which takes LA-referred pupils (all with EHC plan) plus 12 in years 7-11 with social, emotional and mental health needs who get imaginative support – life skills programme recently boosted with acquisition of aquarium and (very popular) pet guinea pig. Focus is on inclusion with help from 26 learning support assistants. 'The philosophy is very much "we want you in the classroom",' says Mr Maher.

Current SEN team praised by a parent for 'exemplary knowledge of needs' and commitment to pupils. 'Chilled out, calm and very good at working out what students' individual needs are,' thought dyslexic pupil – extends to letting sixth formers taking three rather than two years to complete courses. 'If you can't do it one way, you can do it another,' supportive teacher tells parents. Building on expertise with new MLD unit for 16-19 year olds.

First class communication helps hold the whole thing together. 'Every teacher knows what's going on,' said parent. There's plenty of support, from timetabled revision classes to informal chats over coffee, particularly relished by sixth formers. 'Get on so well, wasn't that teacher and pupil divide,' said recent leaver. And humour is always on tap. 'Aah, isn't he lovely,' says wording under pic of puppy outside science lab. 'He's a guide dog for the blind and if you don't wear safety spectacles, you might need one...'.

Games, options, the arts: Not the right place for staff in search of quiet life and 4pm finish, warns school. With many charity-linked events – rough sleep event in school grounds raised over £7,000 – extracurricular programme spilling over into weekends and evenings, trips (rugby tour of South Africa) and clubs including art, video and media as well as vibrant house system with 40 events – house music competitions demand original composition as well as normal solo and group acts, rewarding extra commitment with bonus points – not surprising that potential staff recruits are asked what can bring to the party.

Best to arrive at interview with at least one extra talent and be prepared to offer it freely (there's no extra pay). 'Do it because of the impact it has on the children,' says Mr Maher. Recent sports award event a case in point, with staff (and some partners) organizing sit down evening meal for 180 winners and their teachers, reflecting considerable achievements.

Head is delighted with considerable sporting achievements, particularly in football where teams regularly reach final eight or better at national and district level, though would love to see rugby doing even better especially given permanent underdog status against largesse of independent school resourcing.

Pupils, bar desire for a swimming pool – likely to remain on wish list for foreseeable future – had few complaints and instead were eloquent about the way that whatever their interest, school's encouragement had helped them discover it – and find themselves. 'If it hadn't been for here, wouldn't be playing at county level,' said sixth former.

Arts equally popular, teaching highly rated, dynamic music teacher leading erudite GCSE discussion on monophony, performing arts BTec recently added to the mix.

Impressive facilities include imaginatively revamped St Bede's building include airy first floor multi-purpose hall, while bright dance studio (head's ambition is to give it official standing on the curriculum) is good enough to be hired out to private firm who no doubt relish its up to the mark light wood finish and mirrored wall as much as the pupils.

There's big performance space (large theatre) and gem of a drama studio, once the gym – its transformation into flexible, well curated black-ceilinged space with roll on, roll off seating, a professional lighting rig and teeny but impressive sound and lighting box yet another brainchild of previous head, who also managed to carve out funding and space from a corridor for tiny recording studio which is, courtesy of acoustic tiles, very nearly soundproof. Together provide worthwhile settings for ambitious plays and musicals that range from Shakespeare to home grown, one production each year touring in Hungary. 'A massive inspiration,' said past pupil.

Sunny art room, rather empty on day of visit, contrasted with sombre but highly accomplished monochrome tableaux on display, screaming mouths skewered with 3D spears. 'It's linked to fear and inability to express yourself,' said jolly teacher. Not a problem that afflicts many of the pupils here, judging by popular debating society propositions that range from pros and cons of immigration ('fiery,' says diplomatic member of staff) to 'Is feminism still relevant?' (Yes).

Background and atmosphere: Catholicism at its best though you don't have to share Mr Maher's beliefs to get the most from it. Chapel is of modest dimensions, though removable partition ensures

that the growing numbers attending weekly mass (chaplain is parish priest and a school governor) can be catered for though 'knows his boys – never takes more than 20 minutes,' says the head.

Success celebrated whenever it crops up. Basketball star blushingly praised for efforts is told by Mr Maher that he will make a fuss in assembly

Tangible manifestations of faith are numerous but not relentless – our favourite was Eric Gill-like Madonna and child in entrance to new block – an alternative design for school's foundation, finally realised on 50th anniversary, marked by bussing whole school to Westminster Cathedral on double-deckers for a special ceremony.

Once undersubscribed and so rough that 'story was you had to nail salt and pepper pots to the table,' says staff member, school has changed mark-edly though perceptions, particularly among the smarter Wimbledon Village set, have been a bit slower to catch up.

Their loss. The immediate surroundings may not be SW19-friendly, but even the most aesthetically sniffy will enjoy beautiful greenery of the ancient Hogsmill River that runs beside playing fields, as well as astonishing transformation of school itself. With curved roofs, plenty of wood-cladding and even mellow(ish) brickwork school presents unified face to the world, avoiding normal piecemeal additions so often derived on a one thing after another basis. Even the little details like repainting all the external window frames grey make a huge difference.

Inside, many of the long corridors running length of main teaching blocks have been transformed with glass panels, smart blinds and bright white paint. Outside there's a 3G pitch (superior artificial surface that can take conventional football boots) and athletics track – pupils allowed on grass only in late summer, mingling – happily enough – on the tarmac for rest of year.

It's masterpiece of nifty financial footwork by previous head ('genius in finding and stretching money – turned school from 1950s dilapidation to one fit for 21st century,' says head). No wonder even backroom bean counters are jolly – a rare sight indeed.

Even yet-to-be-transformed areas with Crittall windows, grey-flecked lino and thick brown tiled windowsills are so well-maintained that have a rather desirable vintage look, though once head's money-charming skills are fully realised (and there's no chance they won't be), will doubtless get the necessary upgrades.

Pupil areas have been given similar TLC, with sixth form combined social and study area and bistro a particularly desirable perk. Though occasionally used for special events, normally out of bounds for lower school pupils who can only yearn over passing trolleys packed with seniors-only fizzy drinks (as can buy up the road, no point in not offering) as well as bacon, sausage and croissants for break (all cooked in-house). Chips (girls) and southern fried chicken 'n' cheese baguette (boys) the top 16+ faves though, judging by prodigious quantities of food enthusiastically put away by lower school pupils and numerous lunchtime choices (including pasta, paninis and a veggie option) nobody appears to be suffering.

Pastoral care, well-being and discipline: 'It's like a family business,' says Mr Maher who (though not by way of proof) reports boys in lessons occasionally addressing him as 'mum'. Literally so, as many teachers don't just come in singles but often in pairs and occasionally in sets. We ran out of the times we were introduced to one teacher and told that partner or a sibling (they even do a nice line in twins) also worked here.

Winner in what would be cracking Top Trumps game is the Maher clan. Mrs M senior works in the café (and unfortunately wasn't in on day of visit as we were dying to have critique of son's leadership style), Mrs M junior, his wife, is a chemistry teacher, brother taught geography here and son is a potential pupil.

As in best run families, school discipline is achieved effectively with minimum of fuss, down to 'passive supervision' – staff always there but presence is low-key, issues often resolved through informal chats with favourite teacher.

Librarian's mission is to ensure that everyone reads, including staff – maths teacher was deep in Candide; head tucking into The Jesuit Guide to Almost Everything

Head speeds departing pupils on their way at end of day (no doubt fitting in a final litter check) while other staff patrol local shops. Even former pupils don't escape (one 30-something pillar of community told off for poor parking, reported distinctly gleeful wife).

'Very calm here,' said recent leaver, who felt that while would always be some naughty boys ('Don't let them tell you there aren't' – they didn't)

response would be speedy and compassionate. Having witnessed the barely discernible fall-out from just one incident – pupil briefly and calmly removed from classroom after melt-down – we can only agree. Response to inevitable unkindness is similarly 'fantastic,' said parent.

'If you focus on the small things, you very rarely get to the big things, so we focus on the small things unrelentingly, shirt tails, top buttons, sensible hair cuts,' says Mr Maher. Rules are strictly enforced with sensible concessions. 'I abhor locked rooms,' he says – and they aren't, well-stocked fitness suite (like dance suite rented out after hours) the only exception – a health and safety rather than trust issue.

There's authorised queue-jumping for autistic pupils otherwise overwhelmed by lunchtime noise, younger boys using the outside entrance, year 11s, swelled by privilege of age, allowed to arrive via the hall, biometrics guaranteeing speed service for all.

Deliberate litter dropping was, unsurprisingly, taken very seriously, punishment – donning high vis jacket and doing a whole-school clear up – very definitely matching the crime.

Above all, success celebrated where and whenever it crops up. Basketball star blushingly praised for efforts is told by Mr M that 'will make a fuss in assembly,' while there's tea and cakes with the head for frequent 'above and beyond' award winners ('go to Waitrose the night before and clear the shelves,' he says) successes recorded on honours board (updatable paper rather than carved on wood). Senior teachers dispense the beverages, boys serve the food. 'A nice touch,' said parent. 'Do praise effort.'

Pupils and parents: Most illustrious former pupil is probably Spiderman actor Tom Holland. Others into professions (law) or sport – including Britain's first wheelchair referee.

Family feel is pervasive, with 16 or so girls joining modestly co-ed sixth form (plus 30 or so who come over from Holy Cross) instantly slotting in, praised by head for sparkiness and openness to change. Can be harder for routine-loving boys joining in year 12, thought school insider – nobody's fault, just down to intensity of bonds formed in earlier years.

Entrance: With hefty oversubscription and around four applicants for each of 150 year 7 places, essential to be realistic. 'Effectively if you're not a practising Catholic and you're not in one of our feeder schools [Corpus Christi, Our Lady Immaculate, Sacred Heart, New Malden, St Agatha's, St Cecilia's, St Clement's and St Joseph's, Kingston], it's going to be very hard,' says Mr Maher.

Strength of faith matters (weekly church attendance is one of entrance criteria). Then it's down to home address (living in two local deaneries helps) and distance to school gates.

Post 16, minimum of 10 external candidates accepted including small numbers of girls, permanent members of the school's own sixth form. All faith criteria as before, most courses requiring grade 6 or better in related GCSE.

Exit: About a third leave after GCSEs. Majority of year 13 leavers move on to higher education with many gaining places at Russell Group universities.

Birmingham, Warwick, Nottingham, Portsmouth and Kent all popular destinations. Often several to Oxbridge (none in 2019). Just under a fifth carry on in further education and programmes, remainder opting for apprenticeships including Civil Service fast track and BBC broadcast engineering.

Remarks: Faith-inspired, purposeful leadership and energetic teaching deliver first rate education that's big on family feel and hot on detail. Inveterate litterbugs might struggle.

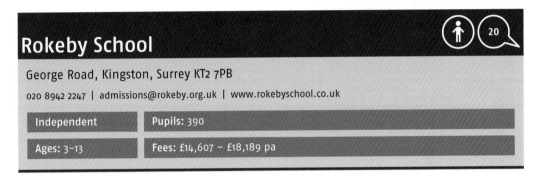

Rokeby School

George Road, Kingston, Surrey KT2 7PB

020 8942 2247 | admissions@rokeby.org.uk | www.rokebyschool.co.uk

Independent	Pupils: 390
Ages: 3–13	Fees: £14,607 – £18,189 pa

Headmaster: Since 2007, Jason Peck BHEd NPQH. Joined school in 1996 as a year 4 and science teacher, becoming deputy head in 2004. Has seen one son through the school and has one still there – 'it means I see things from both sides,' he says.

Initially keen to train as a vet, only to realise during work experience that he was thoroughly squeamish. Absence of James Herriot moments led him instead to a spell travelling and running own business, arriving at Kingston University in mid-20s better versed in ways of world, he feels, than some younger out of the egg fellow students. First and only previous post was in tough middle school in Merton.

Personable, open and with a good sense of humour, he operates from his tucked-away corner office, which boys told us they visit strictly 'by appointment only,' although they did say they see plenty of him during the school day, with year 5s getting an extra dose as he teaches them science ('It helps me to really get to know the boys, which in turn helps with finding the right senior school'). Dresses up for World Book Day and charity days. 'He's nice,' was the most we could get out of the boys, although parents (especially of boys in the lower school) were more loquacious. 'The ethos of Mr Peck, which is totally child centric, cascades through the whole school to all members of staff,' said one, while a star-struck mother gushed, 'Without wanting to sound like a ridiculous schoolgirl, I'm totally in awe of him – he's so human and real, constantly developing and

growing the school.' One parent felt that higher up the school Mr Peck was less visible and his vision for the school less clear, but school points out that he attends everything, helps out with the morning drop off system, defines his vision and direction for the school at the annual speech day and provides updates in termly newsletters.

Any spare time, he says, is spent writing his first novel. 'Well, someone's got to fill JK Rowling's shoes,' he laughs.

Entrance: Catchment tends towards Wimbledon and Putney more than Kingston and up into Teddington/Richmond, although that's starting to change. Many parents live practically on the doorstep, lapping up the added convenience of next door Holy Cross, a similarly high-performing prep for the sisters.

Parents perceive the school as becoming increasingly selective, but school insists that 'while there is a level of selection, it's very low key.' So-called discovery morning that takes place in autumn term the year before entry into reception is, according to the school, 'an opportunity for a two-sided discussion to work out if we are the right place for their son, definitely not a pure assessment. You can't test at 2 – just not possible.' A few leave at end of year 2 to go either to King's College Junior or St Paul's Juniors, with those at the top of knee-deep waiting lists soon filling the spaces.

Exit: Every year group heads off to between 12-18 schools, with most popular destinations recently including King's, St Paul's, Hampton and Epsom College, with a one or two most years to Eton, Charterhouse, Cranleigh, St John's and Whitgift. Every year, one or two boys leave earlier because they are not keeping up academically – 'we are very transparent, so if we have concerns whether a boy can thrive here, we let them know as early as year 1,' says head.

Remarks: Sandwiched between two other similarly grand-homes-turned-schools, Rokeby is reached via private roads with barrier-only entry (for which school issues passes to non-residents). As with so many schools, the reception area, reached by the original front door, gives a flavour of what's in store – in this case, a homely, friendly vibe and impeccable manners.

As with so many schools, the reception area gives a flavour of what's in store – in this case, a homely, friendly vibe and impeccable manners

---

The original solid Victorian building, with its (in places warren-like) carpeted corridors and classrooms of varying sizes, is home to year 4s upwards ('the point at which the level of work starts to really ramp up,' said one boy), with younger ones taught in newer (2013) purpose-built lower school, complete with gorgeous performing arts theatre where we saw littl'uns practising for their nativity play. Head admits the school could do with a couple of extra classrooms ('not because we are short on them, but for greater flexibility') and a new hall in the main building which, we clocked, can surely not have changed since the 1980s. But overall, facilities are excellent, including huge touchscreen boards, three whizzy science labs ('there are lots of practicals,' say boys), assorted music rooms (tuneful solos from windows – standard here is high) and fabulous corridor and classroom displays (some of them floor to ceiling) among the highlights. Cosy upper school library has brightly coloured chairs, well stocked shelves and a cheery librarian, but the rows of desks all facing forwards have the disappointing effect of making it feel like yet another classroom. Outside space is limited but maximised, with various beautifully-equipped playgrounds, courts, smallish Astroturf and year 8 common room (a log cabin).

Parents told us Rokeby is 'not right for families who want to take a more relaxed approach for their son's education'. 'It's no hothouse, but you do need to be able to keep up with the academic rigour,' elaborated one. Most schools we visit brag about personalised learning, but Rokeby aims to take it to the next level, assessing and monitoring to the hilt, taking into account every boy's strengths, interests and individual needs when devising their learning plans. 'It's not just about the teachers' awareness of different learner types – auditory, visual and kinaesthetic etc; we hone in at a much more micro level,' claims school. 'Very quickly, the school observed our son's talents and interests and has sought to develop them with stretching classroom work but also opportunities outside of school, such as a history discovery day at a senior school,' confirmed one parent.

Lots of staff enthusiasm, including much-admired DT teacher (all kicks off with ball mazes in year 3, progressing to robot wars and even design-led working speakers in year 8), charismatic drama specialist ('we do loads of the backstage stuff like lighting too,' said one boy) and history teacher ('who actually brings the past to life'). Latin a bit of a Marmite subject – 'it dominates compared to history and English,' groaned one boy. Two form entry up until year 2, then pupils are split into three forms for year 3. Art and sports, drama and music taught by specialist subjects from the off, DT specialist from year 3 then all from year 5. Setting in maths and English from year 5 (the year 'when everything is about maths and English,' admits school) and in French and science from year 6. French is taught from year 2 and Mandarin from year 3.

SEN department has one full-time and two part-time staff members who 'mainly guide teachers how to support boys to manage in their lessons, rather than taking them out of the classroom'. Parents generally satisfied ('any learning support needs are picked up very quickly with an array of specialists at hand to help the boys navigate through,' said one) although another told us her son struggled with a teacher 'who seemed to think [his SEN] was his lack of attitude and effort,' but head of year subsequently 'put in place a whole support system for him which worked brilliantly.' On the welfare side, boys can see the ELSA (emotional literacy support assistant), which helps them with things like anxiety (but they can't self-refer), and there's also mindfulness on the menu for most boys, plus a counsellor who's called in when needed. Boys describe it as a 'caring' school. Bullying at a minimum, they say, 'because there is so much work in place to prevent it.' No suspensions for two years.

Short, sharp shocks, aka tiered detention system, manage any poor behaviour but boys told us you can get through the whole school without one if you play your cards right. Lots of recognition and rewards – not just verbal praise, but

Boys describe it as a caring school. Bullying at a minimum, they say, 'because there is so much work in place to prevent it'

certificates, awards etc. Manners so flawless that Rokeby boys are renowned for their politeness – but the boys we met from the upper school seemed so focused on their etiquette and saying the right thing that at times we felt we wondered if we were getting a rather wooden version of their real selves. Even standing with arms straight, hands gripping over each other, seems to be a uniform stance here. The moments they let their guard down, however, were a joy – earnest boys, but with added playfulness and candour.

Sport a major feature of school life, with a similar level of tracking that you'd expect in academic teaching. Plenty of success in cricket, football and rugby (main sports), with athletics on the rise. County and national success at skiing, county success at cross-country. School recently introduced a more able sports programme to develop their elite. Boys said they'd like more PE – 'by the time you've changed clothing, there doesn't feel much time left,' said one. But plenty of extracurricular opportunities, from karate to tennis, with other clubs covering everything from LAMDA and debating.

Boys are encouraged not to do too many at lunchtimes, however, 'because they need a break.' Trips galore – both days out such as Latin to Bath and residentials abroad eg annual football tour to Holland.

Music boasts the usual school orchestra and various ensembles, with superb choirs – junior, senior, chamber and training, including an emphasis on making sure boys whose voices are breaking don't bail out of singing too soon. Lovely art studio, with boys' favourite projects including African sunsets (lower school) and Animal Farm trophy heads (year 8s).

Families – a socially active bunch – range from 'the extremely wealthy' to dual income families who give their all to afford the fees – although breakfast club (from 7.30am) and homework club (until 5.45pm) surprisingly undersubscribed. Though school has its own transport, including minibuses and coach, the school's biggest challenge remains transport. 'Parents know they have to get stuck on a busy road at 8am if they drive here,' says head.

Could so easily be swamped by pressure and riven with nerves. And that's just the parents. But while results give it undeniable cachet as a prep whose top leavers continue to have the entrée to some of south west London's most sought after senior schools, this school is about so much more than getting hard results. We found the boys engaged with everything the school has to offer, and extremely proud of it.

The Russell Primary School

Petersham Road, Richmond, Surrey TW10 7AH

020 8940 1446 | info@russell.richmond.sch.uk | www.russell.richmond.sch.uk

| State | Ages: 3-11 | Pupils: 264 |

Headteacher: Since 2011, Samantha Leir, previously deputy at the school. Her first teaching job was at Russell in 1994. From there she went to work for the local authority as a lead literacy teacher. Returned to Russell as deputy in 2003. 'She's always been a huge part of the school,' said one parent.

Two sons who both attend schools in Surrey. Grew up in Wales, the only girl with four brothers, so rugby is a big part of her life. Supports the Ospreys (Swansea). Her sons and husband also play rugby. She enjoys reading, cooking and swimming.

Entrance: Currently one form entry. For nursery places apply direct to nursery and for school through local authority.

Exit: Most go on to Grey Court in Ham, a couple to local grammars (Tiffin Girls' and Tiffin School), a handful to independent or church schools (Christ's, The Green School, Gumley), or to Waldegrave School for Girls if they live in Twickenham.

Remarks: Originally two schools (Petersham and Orchard Junior) built in the 1950s, they joined together to form the Russell School in 1980. Set in four acres of grounds and new buildings recently completed; now 'deep in the process of designing play spaces and landscaping'. Hot school dinners are cooked fresh on the premises.

Now shares a site and expertise with Strathmore special school, though the schools are run separately.

There are gifted and talented groups for maths and writing. A Battle of the Books competition is available for gifted readers in year 2 and year 4.

Music is important here. A specialist music teacher is at the school for half of the week. She is also responsible for the school choir and orchestra. Children can learn recorder, flute, guitar, violin and even the harp. There are trips to the Royal Festival Hall and each year the school takes part in the O2 Young Voices competition. 'My son was so proud to be representing the school at the O2 centre,' explained one parent.

Drama is also strong, and as well as a big Christmas production and a year 6 performance (last year it was based around the theme of Pompeii), there is a talent show for the whole school.

The new-ish deputy head leads sport at the school. Lunchtime and after-school clubs include gymnastics, athletics, basketball, football, netball, judo and golf, as well as chess, Spanish and art. A private company (Fit for Sport) runs a breakfast club from 7.45am to 8.30am, and after-school care from 3.15pm to 6.00pm, both at extra cost.

'Since Mrs Leir took over we feel much more welcome at the school,' said one parent

Parents are drawn from across the social spectrum. Some children live in the huge mansions on Petersham Road while others are drawn from the council estate over towards Ham. The PTA organises social events and parents are encouraged to come into school for special assemblies. 'Since Mrs Leir took over we feel much more welcome at the school,' said one parent.

It feels like a village school and it's amazing to have such space on the outskirts of London. If you can turn a blind eye to the state of the grounds you'll feel very smug that your children have a place here.

St Elizabeth's Catholic Primary School

Queen's Road, Richmond, Surrey TW10 6HN

020 8940 3015 | info@st-elizabeths.richmond.sch.uk | www.st-elizabeths.richmond.sch.uk

| State | Ages: 3–11 | Pupils: 298 |

Headteacher: Since 2014, Jane Hines BA (40s), after 10 years as deputy head and six as a class teacher here. Before that was based in Bristol, where had completed a classics degree before moving into teaching. Loved the subject but, coming from a family of dedicated, fulfilled teachers, no other career exerted the same pull. News of appointment greeted with delight by parents, who already knew her as voice of kindly calm authority and (correctly) anticipated more of the same. 'Very calm and quiet, a real listener – have never seen her anything other than totally serene,' said parent.

But it's not just about maintaining the status quo. Mrs Hines is as dynamic (supported by strong leadership team) as they come. 'Very receptive to ideas,' said approving parent (we suspect she gets to do a lot of listening). In a short space of time, has brought in specialist teachers (a rarity in any cash-strapped school), transformed the site and ensured everyone buys into the process.

Happy and united staff – revitalizing mix of long stayers and recent arrivals – are with her all the way, recruitment pinpoint sharp (though very high standards mean that a few don't make it past probationary period). 'Want this to be a place where staff can innovate and try things out,' says Mrs Hines. Remains 'the best job in the world,' she says. If she has one (small) regret, it's that she isn't currently doing more teaching. Though won't take on a full time commitment as 'Tend to be called away for meetings,' she does plan to teach one or two lessons a week. 'Important to have that connection with the children.'

Entrance: Despite priority for demonstrably committed Catholic families from four local parishes, there's hope if you're not. A bulge class, added every three years, greatly improves changes of success for applicants from other religions (Eastern Orthodox followed by other branches of Christianity) or even none. 'We welcome applications from everybody,' stresses Mrs Hines.

Exit: Top Catholic senior schools for most. Vast majority to highly rated newcomer, Sir Richard Reynolds, others to Gunnersbury, Sacred Heart Convent, Cardinal Vaughan and The London Oratory School. Some girls to Waldegrave and handful of pupils each year to independents such as Putney High and Hampton (use of tutors not unknown).

Remarks: Even in high-achieving Richmond, St Elizabeth's would be having a bad year if its leavers didn't exceed borough averages. Nearly all year 6 pupils achieve at least level 4s in reading, writing and maths. While not, of course, the only reason parents choose the school, knowledge that in addition to a loving, Catholic ethos in cosy, small-scale environment, child is going to end up with a first class education does wonders for peace of mind.

Cynics might wonder whether given the location – lush lower slopes of Richmond Hill – and motivated parents, school simply can't go wrong. But success is never a given. Even here, there's considerable variation in family backgrounds. Over half the pupils now speak at least one other language, some arriving with very limited English, initially lured into the language by talking about their interests.

Success for all comes about through focus on the individual. 'Don't rely on any one tool,' says Mrs Hines. Throughout, rewards are based on how hard you try, not how clever you are. 'Teachers don't just care about our marks – they care that we're happy,' says year 6 pupil. Staff in complete agreement. 'Tests do not lead our judgement,' stresses senior teacher.

Writers' wall, changed every half term, features stories that are a personal best for their authors, not just the same old top talents. 'It's the pupils we're proudest of,' says teacher. Similar spirit – rewarding effort rather than straight brain power – prevails elsewhere. When all the children who had represented the school in sport were asked to stand up in assembly, 'was almost everyone,' reports a parent. 'Not always the same sporty kids doing stuff.'

For older children there's a big push on community involvement as role models for reception pupils. Year 6 chaplains develop entire assemblies for them from scratch – prayers, story and activity, while play leaders teach them to take turns at break. 'Look after them as though their own brothers and sisters,' said mother. 'It's a lovely thing for them to appreciate everybody.' Fun, agreed year 6 pupil – 'though they can be a bit wriggly.'

It all helps towards gaining coveted Governor's Awards – mini D of E scheme with desirable badges awarded for service, skills and growing independence – vast list ranges from leading a school club

to locating 20 countries of the world and cooking a healthy meal. Everyone – with support from school – gets bronze, extra keen go for silver and gold.

Less than secret ingredient in success is teaching staff, most women (the perennial issue of the missing men in primary school teaching) who are 'unbelievable,' said a parent. 'Exhausted at the end of term but they're still smiling.' Add dedication – 'All work well beyond their hours,' said mother – and with happy, united team working to high standards, most parents had a virtually blank wishlist. A few start with initial reservations about how the many teachers with own children here balance dual roles – but not for long. 'It adds to their commitment – and if someone goes out socially with teacher who is a friend, would always put their professional hat on,' said one parent.

Polished lunchtime rehearsal of Bugsy Malone under way when we visited, impressive dance movements accompanied by talented young saxophonist

Even staff job shares are a model of effective communications, full-time TAs – one per year group in reception to year 2 – who stay with the class all week providing valuable sense of continuity. 'Don't know how they coordinate it but they don't miss a thing,' says parent. Skill, love of teaching and ability to construct active, exciting lessons undoubtedly help, though the basics are never forgotten, evening sessions for parents – starting with maths – showing how building blocks are put in place between reception and year 6. Must be working as while literacy is popular – 'Can let your imagination go wild with stories,' said year 6 pupil – most children rated maths as top subject. 'Fun learning new things – teachers help you through hard questions but don't tell you the answer.' Whatever the subject, clearly enjoy themselves, from year 2 pupils' pictures themed to 'Sky in the pie,' to a bit of creative headscratching as year 3s produced self-portraits for their reports, instantly switching from productive conversation to joining in with teacher's song, marking end of the lesson.

While those needing a bit of extra support or stretch will have separate group sessions, school doesn't go in for setting – not good for confidence. Instead, success is down to differentiation – highly effective because all children are known inside out to every teacher: no unknown unknowns here. Learning needs taken in school's stride – won't turn anyone away and if can't support a pupil themselves (and with excellent training for TAs that includes support for dyslexia and speech and language development, there's plenty they can) will look outside, often involving Richmond's highly rated Achieving for Children team. On day of visit, upbeat play therapist had just finished a session in the school's bright, cheerful library, a comforting space to work through difficulties. 'Can let go of their feelings here.'

School food was only aspect of life that some parents felt could do with some (minor) tweaking. Constantly under review, says school, with pupils pre-ordering so last in the queue don't miss out on best sellers (pizza a favourite), everything cooked from fresh and a salad bar recently added. Staff vote with their cutlery sets (around half have school lunches) and Mrs Hines and deputy both (other commitments permitting) eat with the children every day, 'which shows how good it is,' they point out. On day of visit, absence of mess and cleared plates suggested was going down a treat with the pupils too.

With academics ticking over nicely, the most welcome development (mentioned by every parent we spoke to) has been loan of specialist teachers (music, sports and – coming soon – French) from St Richard Reynolds. Provides non-teaching time cover for other staff, a bit of smart planning that keeps costs down.

Parents are pinching themselves in disbelief over speed of change, with weekly class music lessons for all coupled with accomplished school productions – polished lunchtime rehearsal of Bugsy Malone under way when we visited, impressive dance movements accompanied by talented young saxophonist, reception diners, knives and forks poised between plate and mouth, a gratifyingly awestruck audience. With new instruments to try, samba drums a popular addition, and excitement of having some of work recorded, difference is tangible. 'I notice a big change in their enthusiasm,' says parent of previously less than keen child who now arrives home singing new songs.

Whizzy head of sport has revitalized what was previously slightly low key area, at school four days a week, in first thing and often on days off as well, and spending every waking hour dreaming up new and exciting things to do, report parents. Includes setting up swimming squad and running extra sessions to help prepare for matches. 'Lives and breathes sport and has a passion that's spreading through the school,' says Mrs Hines. Now has suitably aspirational space with Astroturf courts on junior playground – and school can host fixtures at home rather than borrowing space from Christ's, neighbourly C of E secondary school just down the road.

All happens on a compact site where 'every spit of space is used,' says staff member. Cleverly done, corridors minimal, monoblocks of colour creating sense of calm so stimulation comes from the teaching rather than the paintwork (riots of colour very much last year's pedagogy...). It's especially notable in bright, pristine reception classrooms, slightly separate from rest of school, opening onto cheerful, well designed freeflow playground, natural wood fence and climbing frame a nod to Richmond Park which runs just the other side of the back fence.

Energy carries straight on into myriad activities before and after school – and at lunchtime, with even reception having a go (though wouldn't do more than one a week). 'Tons and tons,' said mother, including big band, breakfast club, cookery, art, Lego club and DT. Parents, too, are immersed in life of the school, commitment extending well beyond fairs and cake sales to arranging for external speakers to come in and give talks.

'School has a lovely feel to it,' said parent, 'and Mrs Hines has taken it on and beyond where it was before. Our children there are so lucky.'

St Paul's Juniors

Lonsdale Road, London SW13 9JT

020 8748 3461 | spjschoolsec@stpaulsschool.org.uk | www.stpaulsschool.org.uk

| Independent | Ages: 7–13 | Pupils: 490 | Fees: £20,712 pa |

Linked school: St Paul's School, 243

Headmistress: Since 2016, Maxine Shaw (late 40s). Warm and calmly informal, Mrs Shaw strikes a very reassuring presence in one of the most highly powered prep schools in the country. She has plenty of experience as well, having been head of a pre-prep for one of the Harpur Trust schools in Bedford and, more recently, at a prep in Limpsfield. 'I've enjoyed them all,' she says, 'and this is as good as it gets'.

First female head of the school and winning much praise for calm management and coherent values, although one or two mutterings that emphasis on good manners and considerate behaviour might compromise academic edge. 'I'm with her every time', said one admiring parent, 'but you can never please everyone.'

Three children, the eldest at university. 'Between school and family,' she says good-naturedly, 'I find my time is pretty well taken-up.'

Entrance: Inevitably, a very oversubscribed school. The main entry points are 7+ where 54 boys are admitted (from around 350 applicants) and 8+ when another 18 boys join (around 260 applicants). They sit tests in English, maths and reasoning. No past papers. Those who don't make the cut at 7+ are able to reapply at 8+ and feedback is given to parents following the 7+ exams to help them decide whether to try again. Another tranche of boys, usually those who have been at state primary schools, arrive at 11+ (over 400 applicants for 36 places). They take the ISEB online pre-test at St Paul's and, if successful, are invited back to sit written examinations in English and maths. There is also a short interview.

Exit: Virtually all to St Paul's, with any leavers generally due to family relocation.

Remarks: A school in which almost anything seems possible. Head suggests that a child here is a bit like 'an octopus on zip wire – two legs are needed at all points to take proper care of academic matters – but that still leaves a further six'. She evidently identifies the school as both an originator and a facilitator of opportunity of all kinds. It is a broad and generous vision and, given the preoccupations of some of the parental constituency, even a bold one. But all the resources, moral and material, seem to be here and, the more it is fulfilled, the more children of all kinds will flourish here.

This isn't an archetypical prep school: it began life in West Kensington in 1881 and then relocated, along with St Paul's, to its present site in Barnes in 1968. Physically and psychically, it's part of St Paul's, one of the great senior schools in the UK, something which provokes looking outwards. The site is enormous but, thanks to the massive redevelopment of recent years, there is aesthetic style and beauty around the place. Also lots of green spaces, including a new forest school area for use by the youngest two years, part of school's enhanced outdoor curriculum, and – just a stone's throw away – the Thames.

That bigness, and the historical hinterland, both impact on the atmosphere. 'There's a lot of laughter,' says the head, 'and much of it in the classroom'. She says this with understandable

approval: academic and wider learning here is something approached in the context of sociability and confidence. Both traits were reflected in all the children we met.

Very determined efforts by the school to widen access. There are several 100 per cent bursaries but, as the head ruefully acknowledges, 'sometimes that isn't enough'. Resources are needed to ensure that all pupils are equally able to access the full range of provision – trips which cost extra and so forth. 'We do our best on that,' says head, 'but it's not only about money. It's about giving confidence and reassurance in subtler ways than cash. And, well, we do our best there too.'

Head suggests that a child here is a bit like 'an octopus on zip wire – two legs are needed to take proper care of academic matters – but that still leaves a further six'

Brimming confidence and high aspiration can breed complacency, and the school tries hard to subvert this. 'We talk a good deal with the children about privilege and responsibility,' says the head – but she also acknowledges that example is the most important part of education. She smiles at the memory of old-style philanthropy in many schools (collecting food for harvest festivals and so forth). 'Now our pupils don't just deliver food to food banks,' she says, 'they stack shelves'. The school council selects a charity, to which fundraising efforts will then be directed. Likewise, when pupils visit The Fish Centre, a local project for the elderly, they don't just perform, but mix. 'A lot of board games,' says the head fondly. There are links with local schools for shared sport, and plans are afoot to extend this outreach in the context of music.

School buses run by St Paul's senior school, as well as some organised by junior parents. Typically two parents' evenings annually for each age group: one focused on pastoral matters, and one reporting on academic progress. Three or four mini-reports with effort and attainment grades are sent home each year, and there is one detailed full report. St Paul's parents are typically not short of ambition and drive, as well as many being affluent. Head finds them 'hugely supportive' and 'usefully involved'. Clear sense that the present head relishes and respects the milieu from which most of her pupils come, but – in looking for best practice – may not necessarily confine herself to it.

The great singularity of the school is that it doesn't do common entrance because virtually everyone goes off to St Paul's senior: 'Gaining admission to the senior school is not a given,' reminds the head, 'they have to perform.' St Paul's is one of the great academic schools in the UK and is determined to keep it that way.

Still, Mrs Shaw is not weeping crocodile tears about not being constrained by CE. She doesn't use the word 'shackled' but one senses this is what she and some of her prep school head colleagues feel. 'It's an examination which still makes a big play around rote learning,' she says. 'Of course there's a place for that, but not too much, and not too often. Our pupils are given the chance to fashion skills of synthesis and analysis,' she says, 'and I know which I prefer.'

Some 55 teaching staff in the school – of whom all are professionally qualified and plenty of high-flyers. Many are long-established: the longest-serving teacher, at the school for 30+ years, is retiring shortly. Men and women share equally in positions of responsibility, and there is plenty of young blood as well. Head evidently relishes the mixture of youth and experience: 'I know every academic school says this, but we really don't function as a hothouse – there's none of this business of having accelerated pupils two years ahead of their peers. We want children to enjoy the present moment.'

SEN provision relatively low key, as one might expect of a highly selective school, but there is a teacher is on site four days a week and kept busy, mainly helping those with dyslexia and dyspraxia.

Youngest pupils, aged 7 or 8, are taught mainly by their own form tutors, but gradually gravitate to specialist teachers. Form tutors are the adult axis of young pupils' lives at school, although a buddy system makes for an easy interaction between older and younger boys. Aged 9, boys are mixed into new forms which will take them through to the end of their key stage 2 education, although the curriculum is a good deal broader – engineering, classical civilisation and Latin all playing a part. At 11, boys embark on their key stage 3 education – with ancient Greek now part of the mix for all upper thirds (year 8).

As one might expect, lots of the very best. The combination of overwhelmingly bright and confident pupils translates well into life beyond the classroom. Occasionally, a few pupils may need to take a coach to playing fields in Barnes, but only if the school pitches are waterlogged: the school shares in all the superb facilities of St Paul's senior.

The main sporting focus is rugby in autumn, football in spring and cricket in summer. Teams are very successful in the strongest sporting circuits in the London area. There's also masses of choice, especially as the boys get older – tennis and swimming squads in every year group and, later on, rugby 7s, athletics and cross-country, and also

badminton, water polo and fencing. Two afternoons of games each week for most pupils: top talent inevitably is carefully nurtured, but the school firmly adheres to a sport for all philosophy and with over 200 rugby, 150 football and 140 cricket fixtures each year, the proof is there that competitive sport is open to all. 'The breadth,' said a father, 'is awesome. When I think back to my own days at prep school, I don't know whether to laugh or cry. My son, and every son, really does have the chance to be, and to find, himself.'

Clubs galore. One recent addition, launched at the initiative of a pupil, is a magic club which performed for an audience of prep school heads

For all the gung-ho and joyousness of mainstream team sports, the school is perfectly well aware that, for many pupils, there is no special merit in continuing them indefinitely. A multi-sports programme is offered to pupils in their last year at school: head says this 'is widely appreciated and actually brings some boys much more into sport.'

Music is equally high-powered. The super-talented have all the opportunity to develop individual prowess, but there are orchestras (two full ones) and ensembles in abundance. Recent musicals – Scrooge and Oliver! – were notable as much as anything else for drawing off the whole range of age and experience within the school. Junior choir fields some 80 boys who sing at morning services, carol services and school concerts, and there is a junior recital choir of 30 boys which sings at special functions and outside concerts.

Tremendous art and drama, with big lunch time clubs in both. Big (and regularly-changing) displays of pupils' work are all around the school. As well as timetabled lessons, boys can also take part in cross-curricular drama workshops, provided by London's first-rate Theatre in Education groups. Plenty of theatre visits to the nearby the Orange Tree in Richmond and the Lyric in Hammersmith as well as the West End. After-school drama includes a technical theatre club – perfect for those who love learning about light, sound and set design. Four large scale productions annually, with frequent extras added in. Drama productions include Ivan the Fool, Arabian Nights, The Emperor's New Suit, The Witches and Around the World in 80 Days. Also an annual talent show.

Clubs galore: bridge, chess, classics, coding, cookery – the list is endless. Pupil choice is a big feature of the lunch time clubs. 'The boys choose their own,' the head explains, 'and we take big steps to ensure the choices really reflect their own interests rather than those of teachers or parents. It's enormously empowering.' One recent addition, launched at the initiative of a pupil enthusiast, has been magic club which performed ('with great panache') before an audience of prep school heads.

Also many trips, some in term time which are included in the school fees: outdoor adventure and teambuilding camps, and a week-long residential field trip in the Lake District. Holiday destinations can be more exotic: recent ones include NASA's Kennedy Space Center in Florida, Silicon Valley, volcanoes and geysers in Iceland, and cricket in Barbados.

There's a pastoral team led by the deputy head who works closely with the heads of year, each liaising with form tutors, who are the first point of contact for parents. One deft touch is that each form room houses a 'pupil welfare box', allowing pupils an effective and private way of raising a concern. All pupils belong to one of four houses, encouraging contact across forms and year. There is also a cross-year buddy system, especially aimed to give reassurance to younger pupils when they first arrive at the school.

Busyness – that curse of early 21st children of ambitious parents – seems carefully managed here. Head perceives less stress than at many other schools, 'but also more support'. She is particularly struck by the effectiveness of pastoral care, which she ascribes partly to deft systems, but also to the time invested. 'There is a weekly meeting of pastoral leaders,' she says, 'which considers, minutely, any pupil causing concern. Look: it's a school, and sometimes there are worries. But we aren't sitting on our hands.'

All pupils have their own iPads for use in all subjects, but experienced IT staff and strong firewalls ensure that this is a safe and wholly constructive addition to young learners. Not many disciplinary anxieties – 'what little emerges is typically the product of overexcitement and inexperience,' says the head. 'The children tend to have a good framework of reference. If, exceptionally, they find they are in a detention, they usually understand why they are there.' There have been no recent exclusions. One parent admitted to having been 'frankly uneasy' about taking up the place her son was offered. 'I feared hothousing and macho competitiveness,' she said, 'and I couldn't have been more wrong. There is great intelligence and humanity.'

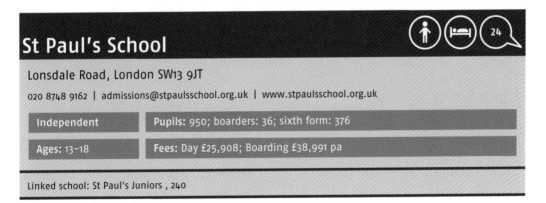

St Paul's School

Lonsdale Road, London SW13 9JT

020 8748 9162 | admissions@stpaulsschool.org.uk | www.stpaulsschool.org.uk

| Independent | Pupils: 950; boarders: 36; sixth form: 376 |
| Ages: 13–18 | Fees: Day £25,908; Boarding £38,991 pa |

Linked school: St Paul's Juniors , 240

High Master: Since 2011, Professor Mark Bailey (50s). Career has included both academia and education: former head of The Grammar School at Leeds, he has also been a fellow at Cambridge and at All Souls, and professor of late medieval history at the University of East Anglia, with whom he continues to be involved. Found time to be a rugby international (1984 to 1990) and is now president of the Cambridge University Rugby Club. A thoroughly engaging, astute, relaxed and kindly man, the complete reverse of what one might expect of the high master of such a venerable institution as St Paul's. We meet many head teachers who are fonder of their school than of the pupils in it. Professor Bailey, extremely clever himself, still cherishes the

achievements of others. A people-person through and through, who likes 'reading, walking and the wines of the Rhone Valley'. Talks with a refreshing lack of jargon. Married to an HR consultant, and with a teenage son and daughter.

Self-imposed mandate on coming to St Paul's was 'Not to meddle with what this school does outstandingly well; leadership of exceptional institutions is as much about stewardship as change.' That said, he is skilfully overseeing a vast programme of refurbishment that is transforming the 1960s site into a school for the 21st century, and steering both school and students towards greater meritocracy and social responsibility.

Marymount London

Stepping down in August 2020 to return to his chair in later medieval history at the University of East Anglia. His successor will be Sally-Anne Huang MA MSc PGCE, the first female high master in the school's 500+ year history and currently head of JAGS. Has also headed Kent College, Pembury. Educated at Lady Margaret Hall, Oxford where she read classics and English. PGCE from King's College, London. Taught English and classics at Sevenoaks, where she was also housemistress. Sixth form housemistress at Roedean before becoming deputy head, a post she held for four years. 'A breath of much needed fresh air!' commented a JAGS parent.

Two teenage sons. Interested in children's literature and is particularly keen on Marcus Sedgwick's novels. Loves theatre of all kinds, especially immersive theatre and frequently heads to nearby Globe. In the holidays, she is at her happiest walking her beloved dogs in Wales. Though brought up outside Manchester, she 'wants to be Welsh' and is an avid Welsh rugby supporter.

Academic matters: The St Paul's recipe for academic stardom remains the same: cream off the very brightest, recruit the very best, light the blue touch paper and stand clear. The resulting sparks illuminate the sky. As one boy put it, 'The real pleasure about being here is going off-piste academically.' Another said, 'The quality of the teaching is beyond compare. It really pushes you further.' Parents agree. 'The teachers are brilliant at their subjects'; 'They're highly skilled at imparting their knowledge'; 'The teaching is simply superb'. A recent inspection report summed it up: 'The effectiveness of questioning in lessons, both from pupils and teachers, is outstanding.'

Broad and challenging curriculum includes ancient history, engineering and technology, and an excellent range of languages, Italian, Russian and Greek among them. Exam success is seen as a by-product of the boys' broader intellectual development; in 2019, 80 per cent of A levels/Pre-Us were A*/A or equivalent; percentage of A*-A/9-7 at I/GCSE always in the high 90s. Amazing science building offers 18 laboratories, but such is the subject's popularity that, according to staff, 'space is still tight'. Beautiful library, silent and inviting, and facilities everywhere are excellent, although we were amused to see far fewer interactive whiteboards in the classrooms than we'd seen in a state primary school the week before. Interactivity here is still verbal and cerebral perhaps, rather than fibre-optical. Huzza! But we applauded the really intelligent decision to install air-conditioning in all teaching rooms, ensuring that minds stay alert in the muggiest of weather. (How many times have we seen pupils wilting in the heat of south-facing temporary classrooms?) Specialist support is given to those few students identified as having special needs, but this isn't the place for anything more than mild cases.

There are no plans to introduce the IB, which the high master describes as 'enforced breadth'. Various subjects eg modern languages and philosophy and theology now Pre-U. A levels now nearly all linear; boys take three or four (five if they take two maths) and can add EPQ.

You can feel the thinking going on here. Academically, a very special place.

Games, options, the arts: Superb facilities include six rugby pitches, six football pitches, five cricket pitches, swimming pool, courts for rackets, squash and fives, and its own boathouse stuffed with sophisticated rowing craft. The students wax lyrical about the sport on offer here – 'Sport for me has been the highlight here'; 'There is so much!'; 'It's a big part of my life at St Paul's'; 'Most of my friends have been the ones I play sport with' – and we saw dozens of boys throwing themselves about the playing fields in organised and impromptu games of just about everything.

> *The St Paul's recipe for academic stardom remains the same: cream off the very brightest, recruit the very best, light the blue touch paper and stand clear*

Music and drama are both extremely strong; concerts are held in the world-class Wathen Hall, and new Samuel Pepys Theatre was recently opened. Art is taught in a magnificent suite of rooms, and the engineering and technology room is surely every young boy's dream. Clubs cater for every taste, although oddly enough we didn't see any, despite having arrived at lunchtime; even the four lads we finally came across in the 3D art room turned out to be revising their French ('I don't know why they're doing it here,' mused the art teacher). But the student-produced magazines we read were testament to the vibrancy of this community of thinkers: page after page of exceptionally mature, sparkily written articles on cinema, sport, current events, modern architecture; a real treasure trove of ideas.

Boarding: St Paul's is a day school – one of only two to be included in the Clarendon Commission's 'nine great public schools of England' – but it does have a very small community of boarders as well, a quarter of them from overseas, who seem to exist to justify the superb round-the-clock catering which all the boys, day and boarding alike, can access if they need to. Boarding facilities have been recently upgraded, and the boarding provision was praised in a recent ISI report. Study bedrooms, common room and TV room, music practice rooms and computer suite. At least two hours' prep a night followed by supervised activities eg music or sport keep boys busy during the week. Many boarders go home at weekends, often after Saturday morning sports matches.

Background and atmosphere: Founded in 1509 by Dean John Colet, and moved four times before arriving in 1968 at its present riverside home in leafy (and very wealthy) suburbia. A £77 million ongoing redevelopment has transformed much of the site. Visitors now are presented with an exceptionally elegant, blond, modern school campus; an architectural version of the Paulines we met, really, and with the same air of informality and purpose.

Having survived the Great Plague, the Fire of London, the Civil War and the 20th century, St Paul's can afford to relax and enjoy its own success. 'Academic rigour and loose ties' was how one parent described St Paul's today, and this was echoed by the high master: 'It has the feel of an über-grammar school. It's more like a university than any other school I've known.'

It's cool to be clever here, and so, inevitably, there is peer pressure to do well. This is mostly positive, say boys and parents, and drives everyone on, although one parent added, 'If you were at the bottom of the class, SPS would be a horrible place.' But high master denies this emphatically: 'More time than ever has been put into teaching underachieving boys and providing better support.' And another parent observed, 'The bottom of this particular pile still represents an extremely high level of achievement.' We saw boys working with good humoured focus for an eccentric and witty geographer who was padding around in Muppet-motif socks, interspersing teaching points with cheerful insults which the boys lapped up and batted back, in time-honoured boys' school way. (But there was a detailed scheme of work on the board that accorded with modern practice, demonstrating that old and new styles of education can be blended successfully.)

Indeed, SPS remains an extremely masculine community, where the testosterone coming out of the circuit gym knocks you over at 20 paces; and perhaps this shows most in the school's being unaware of just how masculine it is. The surmaster insisted that there was much 'mutuality' between the boys' school and the girls' school, but this was flatly contradicted by the Paulines we spoke to, and by one mother who felt that the school could do much more in this regard. We were ourselves surprised to find a large-scale female nude looking breastily down on us as we ascended the art department stairs, and more surprised to find another one as we went down a different way. There were

> 'It has the feel of an übergrammar school. It's more like a university than any other school I've known,' says the high master

no male nudes on display, and we couldn't help wondering why, out of all the subject matter that might have been on show, the school had chosen these particular canvasses. Although at time of our visit there were 'no plans whatsoever to admit girls at any stage of the school; no parents, boys or staff have ever suggested it' (high master), school has recently, and publicly, opened discussions on whether to do just that at sixth form – we'll watch with interest to see how things progress (and whether the Rubens-y stairwell goes gender-neutral). But the Paulines we met were very personable young men, and the same mother who wanted more contact with SPGS also affirmed, 'Paulines are lovely, decent boys, really articulate, fun, clever and very nice.'

Pastoral care, well-being and discipline: Vertical tutoring system, ie mixing the ages of form groups so that younger and older boys are together. The concept is simple: boys will listen to their peers sooner than their parents, so utilise the more experienced boys for pastoral care and to lead extracurricular activities. It's been in place for over 10 years, and is clearly popular. As one parent commented, 'From the moment they arrive, the 13 year olds meet boys in every other year and get a sense of what they might do.' Tutors stay with the boys throughout their time at the school, and, says school, often become family friends – the advisability of which the school may be reviewing. The nature of this hand-picked community means that bad behaviour is rare: 'There's an intuitive understanding of where the boundaries are,' says high master. 'I've never seen any evidence of bullying here,' was a typical student comment, and surmaster concurs: 'We have very, very few boys that would do what could be called bullying more than once, and if they do, we apply school sanctions quickly.'

Pupils and parents: One of the most expensive day schools in the UK, and compared with similar institutions, financial support for poorer families is small but increasing – see Money Matters. The result is a community which is highly diverse religiously and culturally, but not socially. Parents mostly ambitious and successful professionals with sons to match, hard-working and free-thinking. Old boys list reads like a Who's Who of Influential Britons: a sample includes John Milton, Samuel

Pepys, Field Marshal Montgomery, Isaiah Berlin, Oliver Sacks, George Osborne, Rory Kinnear – and Nicholas Parsons.

Entrance: State educated parents who are starry-eyed for their children but don't know the entrance procedure should start reading it now. SPS takes about 180 13-year-old boys each year, but it's impossible to go there directly from a state school. The 13+ candidates apply either from St Paul's Juniors, whose 80-90 boys nearly all go on to the senior school, or from any other prep school – usually those in the London area. St Paul's Juniors has its own admission procedures at 7+, 8+ and 11+; see our separate entry, and don't leave it any later than September of your child's year 6 (be grateful: it used to be year 5). Prospective Paulines sit an online common entrance pre-test at their prep school, on the strength of which about 350 are invited for interview. The school then makes conditional offers: boys have to get at least 70 per cent at common entrance. Entry from 2021 onwards will not depend on passing the CE but on 'continued good conduct and academic progress at their existing prep school, including an unreserved reference of support from their school in year 8.' The school is looking for 'intellectual curiosity and embracing of

novelty'. About 20 more boys also join in the sixth form, which at SPS is called the Eighth. Currently consulting on taking girls into the sixth form.

Exit: Notably slow in releasing its sixth form leavers' destinations ('many pupils take a GAP year and apply to university after taking their A levels'), latest numbers we have are for 2018: 53 Oxbridge places, the rest to Bristol, Durham, Imperial, Edinburgh, UCL and other top universities. An increasing number obtained places at US universities such as Harvard, Yale and Princeton. Most popular courses: economics, engineering, geography, history and medicine.

Money matters: Scholarships are honorifics only – £60 pa and a silver fish in memory of John Colet. However, a more generous means-tested bursary scheme now on offer with support for families with an income of up to £120k(!) subject to doing well in the entrance tests. Some remission for families who send three or more children to the school.

Remarks: For very bright, confident, motivated boys who like to think for themselves, St Paul's provides a truly unrivalled education. A unique start in life.

Sheen Mount Primary School

West Temple Sheen, London SW14 7RT

020 8876 8394 | info@sheenmount.richmond.sch.uk | www.sheenmount.richmond.sch.uk

| State | Ages: 4–11 | Pupils: 600 |

Headteacher: Since 2009, Ian Hutchings BSc PGCE NPQH (40s), married with two daughters. A boy from Bournemouth, he studied geography at St Mary's, Twickenham followed up with a PGCE and then launched straight into the world of primary education, where he has happily remained. He is very much at his ease here, having arrived as deputy head and then landing the top job. Coming across as a serious and dedicated man, an outsider might find his sense of humour more apparent on paper than in conversation. However, although dry, it is certainly there and his knowledge of and confidence in the school comes across in spades, whatever the medium.

He works very closely with his deputy, Maria O'Brien, and although they face opposite directions in the small shared office, they are definitely heading along the same path when it comes to

running the school. Their agreement on aims and implementation is obviously built on mutual trust, particularly necessary at the moment as IH is also helping out at a school in another borough. This is an unsurprising decision as his belief in state primary education is deep-seated and his energy is immediately noticeable. Computing is what makes his eyes light up and he manages to fit a teaching slot into his schedule, saying, 'I love to see the children working with IT ... I learn so much from them.'

Entrance: You may need to live within spitting distance of the school as the catchment area is tiny, normally less than 500m. There is now three form entry at reception but the demand is such that you probably need to live within walking distance of the school, although they do take in the odd Richmond refugee. The increased intake has not resulted in more room for new arrivals as the larger number of siblings take up the extra places. Places further up the school are as rare as hens' teeth and usually only occur when a family moves from the area.

Exit: Slightly fewer takers than previously for the independent secondary sector, now down from 60 per cent to 50 per cent, partly due to the usual villains of less cash and the ever rising bar of the top London public schools ('10 years ago most of our children could get into any school;). However it could also be down to IH's enthusiasm for the local state schools, Grey Court in Ham, Christ's in Richmond and, in particular, Richmond Park Academy, which has a new head and is 'definitely on the up' as well as being just down the road. IH does not allow his enthusiasm for the state sector to stop him from maintaining close contact with a very wide range of independents and children end up in schools all over London (up to 20 different destinations in any one year), but always with a contingent heading to Hampton, Ibstock and Kingston Grammar.

Remarks: Walking down the path, on a grey winter's day, past a slightly tatty banner advertising Activity Camps, our hearts immediately lifted on spying a customised pink scooter with an equally pink pony's head attached. This is a friendly, outwardly relaxed encampment in a tidy, prosperous-looking corner of west London, which also contains a shiny gastropub and an architecturally undistinguished church. Parents move here specifically because of the school and some have known wailing friends to move out when their children have failed to get a coveted place. The functional buildings, including a new separate reception block with its own fenced off space, sit comfortably on their generous corner site and there is plenty of room for letting off steam outside. The expansion two years ago, 'a brilliant piece of juggling, despite the building chaos,' according to one parent, has allowed for a more logical arrangement of year groups as well as a cheerful room, housing a full-time inclusion leader for those in need of extra help or simply a bit of TLC.

IH says that he 'inherited a very well run school with tried and tested methods' but there's been no complacency on his part, and the systems that he has introduced, in particular the Learning Book (of which more shortly), ensure that every child's progress is constantly monitored. From the word go when a child is accepted, visits, play sessions and trial days take place, followed by a huge amount of time and attention to detail spent in composing the three teception classes, a task that would make a cabinet reshuffle seem a piece of cake.

When we visited, a reception class of rabbits (the others are dormice or squirrels) were busily stuffing small, shiny objects into tennis balls and were only too happy to discuss their methodology whilst others were counting pencils, the concentration visible. The nature theme for classes ends at year 2, somewhat of a relief for the head – 'I don't think I could cope with 19 animals' – but the children keep in the same carefully constructed forms all the way up the school.

Parents move here specifically because of the school and some have known wailing friends to move out when their children have failed to get a coveted place

At the start of year 1 the Learning Book, in which they do all their written work apart from maths, provides the framework for progress and also ticks the green box, eliminating paper wastage. Explained by IH, who modestly said he'd nicked the idea, as being a way of easily keeping an eye not only on marked work but also on handwriting improvement and that bane of most small children's lives, 'tidiness'.

In every classroom all the way up the school the hands (and in one case a crutch) shot up for the chance to be chosen to present their book to the head. The waving crutch – 'careful you don't bash anyone' – and the small girl, bright red with excitement ('don't forget to breathe, you might explode') were dealt with by a real pro, who appears to walk the narrow line between commanding respect and showing humorous, detached affection with the ease of a tightrope artist. 'His lightness of touch is amazing,' was one parental quote. Parents talk about their children thriving beyond expectation due to the 'brilliant', teachers with children coming home bursting to tell their mothers that 'guess what, he's going to give us free extra help in lunch time' or 'maths is not really like a lesson, it's such fun'. Regular feedback like this makes it hardly surprising that the Sats scores are consistently above the borough and national average.

Sheen Mount doesn't just say that it is a fully inclusive school but practices what it preaches, judging by the beaming faces of the children with special needs, ranging from mild dyslexia to Down's Syndrome. 'All children are treated exactly the same,' said the mother of a SEN child and thoughtful touches like a special session at the Christmas grotto and extra swimming help provide real reassurance. The staff also practise their well-honed integrating skills on a number of, technically, EAL children who have spent the first part of their lives abroad, although it's often not too serious a problem as many have had their Ps and Qs polished by the English half of a dual nationality marriage.

A fairly new, dedicated head of PE has made a 'tremendous difference' and after-school clubs for football, goalkeeping and badminton are all popular, although they may not be quite as keen as the mums' football team who recently came back from a tournament clasping medals, one sporty mum describing it as a 'world cup winning moment'. Top of the pops in internal clubs at the moment are Coding, 'taken by me,' said a grinning IH, and choir, both of which require parents to be at the keyboard the moment the opportunity goes live to sign up. External providers stretch the options offering Mandarin, Technokids, dance and a Kids' Guide to Money and Finance, maybe useful when suggesting to your parent what to do with the money saved by sending you to Sheen Mount. No dedicated art room but school plays and masses of additional music (40 per cent of children learn an instrument or singing) provided by Richmond Music Trust.

Away from the classroom, happy faces in the dining room (sausages and mash top choice for both children and teachers) and a minimal number of packed lunches show that a major effort to up the standard of the food has paid off despite the additional problems of providing for a challenging number of allergies. Considerable thought is taken over much anticipated trips, outings and a year 3 sleepover – 'it was magical – are all pronounced a big hit by parents.

IH does also spend serious brain-time on communication, possibly as an excuse to indulge his love of IT. It has definitely paid off because there is a really clear website and a weekly newsletter which has won plaudits from several parents. They all agreed that he was both visible and easily approachable if you wanted to talk and that if you couldn't see him, Mrs O'Brien was always there to listen. It's busy two way traffic here because this is a very hands-on school as far as parents are concerned, finding lots of money for extras but also mucking in with everything from swimming coaching to building the Christmas grotto.

There could be an argument that it is relatively easy to run a state primary sitting on the edge of Richmond Park, where the parents take such an active interest and raise bundles of cash, but it would be unfair to take anything away from this shining example of a junior school, brimful of eager small faces soaking up their lessons.

Shrewsbury House School

107 Ditton Road, Surbiton, Surrey KT6 6RL

020 8399 3066 | office@shstrust.net | www.shrewsburyhouse.net

| Independent | Ages: 7-13 | Pupils: 340 | Fees: £19,335 pa |

Headmaster: Since 2010, Kevin Doble BA (law and political sciences), PGCE (40s). Educated at St John's College, Johannesburg and has a postgrad degree in management. Previously second master and acting head at Edge Grove prep and before that head of English at Newlands School and Vinehall prep. This is his first experience of a day school, although he likens it to 'a boarding school with no beds' because of the breadth of opportunities on offer.

Eloquent, witty, driven and evidently relishes the vitality of the school day. Boys treat him like a celebrity – 'he's amazing,' 'inspiring,' 'kind,' 'really funny,' 'a great listener' and 'the best storyteller' were among the accolades we heard; 'not at all stuck up like the last headmaster I had,' added one. And with no prompting, these boys reeled off at least one anecdote to back up each claim – one told us about his ghost stories that have them spellbound;

another about his stimulating lessons (he teaches year 5 English). 'He has the well-being of every single boy at the heart of everything he does – that's his starting point, and everything else follows,' said one parent, with others calling him 'passionate,' 'dedicated' and – for one mother – 'a big pull for why we chose the school.' Referring to the pupils 'these little guys,' this is not a head you'll ever see give an answer of 'because we say so' – although pupils did tell us they'd like to see the school council have more meetings and more say overall.

At the gates morning and night and out on the touchline as often as possible. 'You don't have to attend the same drama performance on both evenings,' joked staff with him recently. When he can be lured inside, he directs operations from his large but homely office that's packed with books, art, sports memorabilia, and big, comfy leather sofas.

A guest umpire for school and county hockey, he lists his recreations as sport, drama, children's literature, opera, painting and drawing. Keen traveller, enjoys going out for meals and generally 'recharging' during weekends and holidays.

Entrance: At 7, there are 62 places available, with around four applications for each one. Currently receiving requests to register children at birth. Most come from pre-preps, including its own Shrewsbury House Pre-Prep and The Rowans Pre-Prep (now part of the Shrewsbury House Trust), Wimbledon Common Prep, Park Hill, Lion House School and The Merlin. Around 10 per cent (down from 25 per cent a few years ago) come from the state system. Used to be a very local school, but catchment area has doubled in recent years, with 70 per cent of pupils now bussed in from over five miles away – many from Putney and Fulham.

'We say to parents that if you think this is the sort of culture you'd like for your son, and we think he will be able to thrive here and access the curriculum and wider opportunities, then it's almost certainly the right school.' But you won't get away completely scot-free on the assessment front – while registration is on a first-come-first-served basis, all offers are conditional and dependent on a one-day test ('to check our culture really is right,' insists head) in the autumn before anticipated entry. Those who apply too late for a conditional place are put on the waiting list and may be moved onto the 'headmaster's list' (about eight places are kept back for this) for an assessment, but again it doesn't guarantee a place. The school should be your first choice (current school heads are consulted). Occasional places available higher up the school. Some bursaries available

Exit: Very few leave at 11; most stay until 13, when they progress to some 15 senior schools, including King's College School (Wimbledon), St Paul's, St John's (Leatherhead), Westminster, Hampton School, Epsom College, Wellington, Charterhouse, Tonbridge and The Royal Grammar School (Guildford). A few go to Eton and Harrow. Parents say the head is 'very knowledgeable' when he discusses future schools for their sons, starting in year 5. 'He knows each boy and each school incredibly well, so he makes finding the right school a breeze – it's impressive,' said one parent. 'He won't sell you a fake ticket – he will absolutely tell you which school is right, having done all the leg work himself,' confirmed another.

School tracks boys after they leave – 'we want to know exactly what happens to them, even where they go to university, and what they study, as well as what clubs and societies they join, as it tells us a huge amount about the notion of engagement,' says head.

Remarks: Located on a quiet road in an upmarket residential area of Surbiton, the school is one of the UK's oldest preps, having celebrated its 150th anniversary in 2015. Based around a Victorian house, but with additional purpose-built classrooms and impressive facilities all on a six-acre site (including a huge all-weather pitch and a further seven acres at Almshouse Lane), they've recently had the green light for a further £15m of building works to include new dining hall and performance centre, among other things.

All the extracurricular you could shake a stick at including rifle-shooting, judo, fencing, model making (Spitfires) and Nerf wars and (most popular of all) cookery

It's all home to a first-class prep, where academic rigour is balanced by an equally strong offering in arts and sport. But parents must be as committed as their sons. 'It's not a drop-off-and-get-on-with-it kind of school – you're expected to be at all the matches, attend the events and talk to the school at length about the next school, as well as encouraging your son to take up every possible opportunity and work extremely hard,' one parent told us. Add to the academic and extensive extracurricular offering a packed sporting programme, rehearsals, performances, charity initiatives, competitions and trips and you'll get the picture – these are busy boys and devoted parents.

Intellectually, boys need to be above average to cope here, despite the school taking a range of abilities, say parents. Homework is 30 minutes to one hour plus per night, right from the beginning. But – surprisingly, perhaps – the boys take it all in their stride.

A broad-based, eclectic curriculum is delivered by a talented teaching team. We saw plenty of lively lessons in practice, albeit a few yawns too. A French lesson, taught by a native speaker, with boys vying for an opportunity to speak, is typical. Similarly, lots of fun and experiments in science. Some great subject-specific classrooms, including one of the best history rooms we've seen – a modern museum with the teacher's own collection of helmets and weapons secured to the wall. Library also impressive – welcoming and cosy, with over 6,000 books, and lots of magazines and newspapers on display. 'We love it,' our guide said, telling us all about the reading buddy scheme.

Average class size is around 16, with an eight-to-one pupil-teacher ratio overall, with classes getting smaller as boys move up the school and into sets (setting in English and maths from year 4, French from year 5). Streaming from year 6, with up to a third of boys showing the most aptitude studying the same syllabus but at a faster pace (and setting still in place for the remaining two-thirds). Scholarship streaming from year 7, which can include the additional language of ancient Greek. Everyone studies Latin from year 5.

Less than 10 per cent of boys have a learning difficulty, with classroom-based help the only provision on offer. 'If a boy needs help outside the classroom, this isn't the school for them as we don't want them to miss out on the broader curriculum,' says head.

The school has an outstanding local reputation for sport – for many parents, this is their deciding factor. Main sports are football, rugby, cricket and hockey, with other activities including basketball, tennis, shooting, rowing (for the senior boys) and chess. And while many of the boys participate at regional or national level, the school gives equal weight to 'not quite there yet,' with boys regularly changing teams during their time here. 'Everyone gets top-notch coaching – with friendships formed across every team,' said one parent. This, coupled with the huge pride the boys have in representing their school, undoubtedly gives them the edge – they have a 70 per cent win rate across the board.

Music another stand-out subject, with the majority of boys taking instrumental or singing lessons, and there are 25 different musical groups (many open to all), with jazz and brass band especially popular. As with sport, 'boys are encouraged to beat out eight bars on the drum even if they've only had three lessons,' said one parent. Meanwhile, an annual summer soirée gives the top performers a chance to shine. Light-filled art studio is a hub of creativity, as is DT, with both regularly used in a cross-curricular way rather than mere add-ons. Drama not as good as it could be, say parents, but with a performing arts centre in the pipeline, there is optimism. LAMDA on offer and all boys do English Speaking Board exams. All the extracurricular you could shake a stick at – including rifle-shooting, judo, fencing, model making (Spitfires) and Nerf wars and (most popular of all) cookery. Post-common entrance exams, boys also have a go at sewing, ironing and first aid.

Not exactly strict, but clear expectations around behaviour – pupils write the school's code of conduct. Kindness features at the top, which boys told us 'keeps bullying to a minimum' (and is dealt with 'that very day' when it does happen, say pupils). Manners noteworthy, with no boy getting away with slacking, slouching or scruffiness. Pastorally outstanding, say parents, with one boy telling us, 'I've lived in three different countries and this is the school I settled in quickest – by a long shot.' Diversity is celebrated, say pupils – 'we are like one big family, really.'

A high achieving, purposeful all-round school, which is more inclusive than a first glance might suggest. A prep, in the truest sense of the word, where boys thrive by being a big fish in a small pond. But it's not for the faint-hearted.

The Study Preparatory School

Wilberforce House, Camp Road, London SW19 4UN

020 8947 6969 | admissions@thestudyprep.co.uk | www.thestudyprep.co.uk

Independent | Ages: 4–11 | Pupils: 320 | Fees: £14,175 pa

Headmistress: Since 2011, Susan Pepper MA PGCE NPQH (50s). Attended Godolphin & Latymer, then read modern history at Somerville College, Oxford. Did a brief spell as trainee manager for Nationwide, but quickly realised education was her métier. After finishing her PGCE, she taught history at Seaford Head School and St Paul's Girls', then moved to Francis Holland Sloane Square as head of history. It was clearly a happy move, because she stayed for another 20 years, becoming in turn head of sixth form and deputy head.

Made the crossover to primary years education when the headship at The Study Prep came up, and loves everything about it. The feeling is mutual. 'Very good, very thorough, so straightforward,' say parents. 'An excellent headmistress, very approachable'; 'She's done amazing things for the school'; 'Her door is always open and she has always given her time and advice when we needed it'; 'Always interested in the girls' achievements both in and out of school'; 'Her focus is the girls, and she really does know them.'

Runs the debating club, and remains an inspirational history teacher – 'My daughter loved her lessons and history is still her favourite subject.' Married to a draughtsman, with one grown up son.

Interests include horses – 'The love of my life!' – and reading. A self-confessed crossword puzzle fanatic.

Entrance: At 4+, automatic sibling entry, thereafter by ballot. Around 120 apply for up to 48 places. School is completely non-selective at this stage, and doesn't ask to meet any of the applicants. 'We never know who we're going to get,' observed the head of the pre-prep, proudly. 'We're genuinely all-round.' Applicants for any occasional places that might arise for years 1 and 2 are given an informal taster day while the teachers observe them.

Usually a handful of places at end of year 2, and school assesses for these: papers in maths, English and reasoning, plus informal interview. Same procedure for any available places in the upper year groups, although school doesn't usually admit into years 5 and 6.

Bursaries available from year 3.

Exit: At 7+, a handful of leavers because of selective 7+ entrance point at neighbouring schools. School doesn't prepare children for this, but doesn't block it either.

At 11+ to a whole range of impressive schools. Most popular destination by far in 2019 was Wimbledon High School, followed by St John's Leatherhead, Surbiton High School and Kingston Grammar School. Occasional St Paul's Girls' successes. A very small number each year to board at eg Roedean, Benenden, St Mary's Ascot, but not many – parents here are generally in favour of the day school ethos.

Extracurricular provision seen as one of the great strengths of the school. 'My daughter would participate in everything if she could, and she pretty much manages to!'

Remarks: The school is spread across two sites, both of them exquisite. In the heart of Wimbledon Village, years 4, 5 and 6 are in Spencer House, purpose built as a school back in 1905 when the original head, Miss Sidford, felt the need of something bigger than her own front room for her burgeoning student roll. Ten minutes' walk away, Wilberforce House, acquired in 1992, is home to the first four year groups, and occupies a truly magical position on Wimbledon Common's west side. Around 60 per cent of the intake is from SW19, giving The Study the feeling of a village school, although plenty come from further away – Wandsworth, Putney, Southfields, Raynes Park,

even Fulham. After school care now offered until 6.30pm, to huge relief of working parents.

Classrooms are immaculate, well-equipped and inviting, with interactive whiteboards and all the fixings. Charmingly old-fashioned wooden desks with lift-up lids for the older girls ('The girls adore them!'). Small but newly revamped libraries, dotted with children sprawling luxuriously on scatter cushions, attest to the importance of books here. Specialist ICT teacher has bank of laptops and tablets at her disposal in addition to work stations in every classroom. Delightfully refurbished outdoor play areas. Exciting plans for Wilberforce House site prove that school isn't content to stand still.

Maths and English setted from year 3, an approach which parents welcome, saying it has enabled their daughters to be appropriately stretched and challenged. It certainly seems successful, judging from the high quality of the work we saw. Lessons are lively but focused, and the girls remain impeccably well-behaved. There are at least two members of staff for each class, a teacher and an assistant, ensuring that pupils get the attention they need.

For geography, history, science, etc the school recently adopted what it calls the Creative Curriculum, whereby all the subjects are taught under the umbrella of a particular theme each term. Thus the year 1 pupils had just finished beautiful portfolios on Out of Africa, for which the work included designing a ladder to help a visiting toy monkey down from the top shelf in the classroom, while the year 3s worked on some delightful Creative Recycling projects after the mysterious appearance of Stig's Dump in the school garden.

We were struck by how creative the teachers were, never mind the students – colourful and intriguing lessons seem to pour joyfully out of every classroom and wonderful displays are everywhere. 'We got letters in hieroglyphs when we were doing ancient Egyptians and we decoded them!' remembered one child fondly, and 'They make the lessons such fun!' was a comment we heard from every girl we spoke to. Excellent facilities for science, and school has increased the amount of practical work the girls do. 'Previously there was a very strong concentration on biology and it was all too facts-based. Now it's much more practical and hands-on.' French taught from reception – we listened to some year 4 girls chirrup away in delightful French accents. Spanish taught from year 6.

Homework kept to manageable levels for the younger ones, with about half an hour per night being standard. Big hike from year 3 to year 4, however, and again from year 4 to year 5, and a few parents told us they thought it could be excessive, particularly once the 11+ exams were over – 'The girls could be given a bit more time to relax,' was a typical and rueful comment. Others wished that there could be less poster and project based homework, with one adding that hours spent on this had impacted her daughter's enjoyment of certain subjects. A year 6 child told us, however, 'I don't mind all the homework, because you have to prepare for senior school.'

Full-time SENCo plus team of part-timers oversees provision for those with additional needs, mostly dyslexia and dyspraxia. Because girls are accepted unseen into reception, school occasionally has to work with parents to find an alternative school for children with more than moderate needs that can't be supported adequately here.

Extracurricular provision seen as one of the great strengths of the school. 'My daughter would participate in everything if she could, and she pretty much manages to!' wrote one mother. Wide-ranging sports provision includes netball, cricket, hockey, offered at school's own sports grounds at Beverley Meads, plus swimming at Wimbledon baths. 'I've been struck by how many more sporting opportunities my daughter has had at The Study than she will have at the senior schools we looked round!' commented a parent, sadly.

Drama and music both 'outstanding', according to parents, taught by specialists with 'limitless energy'. Girls can learn virtually any instrument and eagerly participate in choirs, orchestra, jazz, etc. 'I credit the school with discovering and nurturing our daughter's love for music,' was one parent's verdict. Regular productions are ambitious and hugely popular, ranging from The Wizard Of Oz to Macbeth, and LAMDA offered from year 4. An astonishing array of clubs encompasses fencing, yoga, horse & pony, chess, street dance, martial arts, music theory, touch-typing – the older the girls, the bigger the choice. Unending succession of trips – the Polka Theatre, British Museum and Hastings were some of the most recent when we visited. We thought the visual arts really exceptional. Under the guidance of remarkably expert, knowledgable teaching, pupils here produce work that is sophisticated and imaginative.

'I have nothing but good things to say about the pastoral care at The Study,' wrote a mother, and every parent said the same. A different value is taught each month – respect, kindness, generosity, resilience, etc – and the older girls all take part in peer mentoring the younger ones. 'It's great fun!' said a year 6 pupil, 'and sometimes it's easier to talk to another pupil than a teacher when something's bothering you.' Much praise for the EQ Prep, a programme whereby counselling and support for both children and staff are embedded into the running of the school. The result seems to be a particularly happy community. The girls are chatty, lively, courteous to others and contented. 'We don't have many arguments, but the teachers sort things out really well if we do.' 'Everyone is really friendly here, and everyone makes you feel welcome.' We were also impressed at how, despite hailing from what has to be one of the most affluent areas in London, the girls didn't seem remotely materialistic: told to choose a treat for coming top in a recent house competition, they asked if they could sit on chairs during assembly. The widely-praised head of Spencer House attributes much of this to the school's non-selective ethos. 'You get the range of abilities and talents and passions, and the girls learn to support each other.'

Classrooms are immaculate, well-equipped and inviting, with interactive whiteboards and all the fixings. Charmingly old-fashioned wooden desks with lift-up lids for the older girls ('The girls adore them!')

The flip side of being such a kind and happy place is that staff can get out of practice in dealing with issues on the rare occasions when they do arise. Whispers reached us regarding a year group with some over-dominant personalities who, a number of parents claimed, hadn't been satisfactorily dealt with. There was also a perception that the school could be firmer with strong-willed parents who try to push their own child's interests ahead of everyone else's. ('Should be stronger with these parents, although they are very scary!' was how one mother put it.) School surprised and disappointed to learn of these comments, and responded: 'The school has robust policies and procedures for dealing with any pastoral issues that arise and the staff are well trained and experienced in implementing them.' And we must add that, despite these wrinkles, everyone who contacted us was unanimous in recommending the school, including the ones who had the above-mentioned concerns. 'Our daughter has been extremely happy at The Study and is sad to be leaving.' 'She has really loved her time there, and wishes that there was a Study Senior!'

We really liked this school, with its joyfully creative and caring workforce, and thought it conclusive proof that all-girls education from an early age can be simply brilliant. The children here struck us as articulate, loved, personable, relaxed, comfortable with themselves and others, and above all, completely and superlatively themselves. And that, surely, is what real girl power is all about

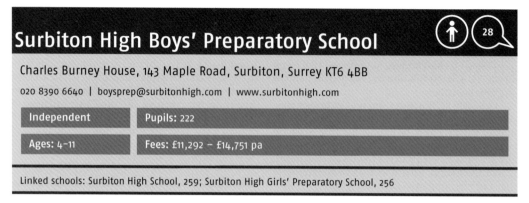

Surbiton High Boys' Preparatory School

Charles Burney House, 143 Maple Road, Surbiton, Surrey KT6 4BB

020 8390 6640 | boysprep@surbitonhigh.com | www.surbitonhigh.com

Independent	Pupils: 222
Ages: 4–11	Fees: £11,292 – £14,751 pa

Linked schools: Surbiton High School, 259; Surbiton High Girls' Preparatory School, 256

Headteacher: Since 2015, Sally Ralph BEd. Masses of experience at all levels. Started off at Feltonfleet School in 1984, moved to Rowan Girls' in 1988 and was then head of St David's School in Ashford, Surrey before starting here in 2009, working across the girls' and boys' preps in acting and deputy head roles before being appointed to current role.

Calm in the face of challenges. Just as well, when faced with task of transforming elderly, listed office block into second building for younger pupils and turning car park into a playground. It's worked a treat.

She's felt to be nice and supportive by parents. 'Really liked her approach – she was really welcoming,' said one. Relishes her job. 'I enjoy working with children, love seeing those sparks and how intuitive they are.' Wasn't in search of senior roles ('I don't think anyone goes into teaching for leadership') but happy to grasp the nettle when the opportunities came up, helped by United Learning, parent organisation, which runs umpteen courses to develop skills.

Her expertise, like the prep's, is in teaching boys and recognising and celebrating their differences. Boys, she says, are sensitive creatures so good teaching is about their well-being, managing their distraction, encouraging collaboration and helping them to become resilient. Has cultivated excellent relationships with senior schools. 'She does a fantastic job of liaising with them through the transition process and building strong links,' says staff member.

Best bit of the job is being out and about, talking to the boys – staff sit with them at lunch. Favourite photograph shows her at a school event in the rain, 'boys huddled round me, like mother penguin.'

Clemmie Stewart, head of the girls' prep, is strategic head of both schools to provide consistency.

Entrance: Up to 32 pupils in two reception classes via informal assessment – numbers have doubled over past few years. And enquiries for places are

showing similarly gratifying rise there can still be occasional places in other years, so always worth asking. Year 6 pupils act as buddies for new boys – notably proud of their chicks' achievements during the year.

Exit: Currently most popular destinations are Claremont Fan Court School, Halliford School, Kingston Grammar School and Ewell Castle School. One or two to Hampton School, King's College School, Royal Grammar School and Epsom College. All take 11+ and go to mix of schools ('Discussion between the 11+ and 13+ would be my specialist subject on Mastermind,' says head). Each year 6 pupil is allocated a senior teacher who works on interview skills.

Remarks: Acquisition of a second building and substantial investment in the first has silenced complaints of slight neglect compared to investment in the senior and prep girls' schools that make up the Surbiton High School triumvirate. From September 2019, two forms all the way from reception to year 6 (used to be one).

Reception to year 3 are housed in former office block backing on to senior girls' quad, with partially roofed (and consequently slightly echoey) playground – reception use mezzanine area above – that shows no trace of first life as a car park, now successfully reclaimed with grass (fake), trees (real) and adequate space for ropes to swing and break time football, though one pitch has a single goal and many disputed results. 'Good for negotiation skills,' says teacher.

Seniors – years 4 to 6 – occupy original premises: pretty villa in the next road, walking the two minutes to senior school dining hall for lunch each day (neither boys' building has own kitchen). Playgrounds 'work nicely,' say pupils. Small front area (for older boys) notable for gorgeous flower arrangement (courtesy of gardening parent), bigger back section flora free, instead planted with open fronted locker stores ('push bags to the back if raining very hard,' say boys). All under review, in consultation with school council (which has also requested cricket nets at the front. 'Quite impossible,' say tour guides, gravely).

Scarcely needed anyway, what with the extensive pitches, fields and courts, shared by seniors and prep schools, just 10 minutes away in Hinchley Wood (also use Esher Cricket Club). Like senior school, boys' prep is big on gymnastics (compete at national and regional level) and not bad elsewhere (with School Gamesmark Gold Award to prove it). Recent sports tours to Paris and Madrid (rugby and football) with chance to 'visit a stadium' (woo hoo).

Facilities, while inevitably lacking the purpose-built polish of the girls' prep, are extensive, with bright and airy classrooms – only current disappointment is older boys' library with piano at one end of the room and fewer books than might be expected at the other. 'Bring in books from home,' said tour guide, though we're assured that reinforcement volumes (lots) are on the way. (School is investing £20,000, which should pay for several sets of collected works...)

Education is impressively thorough and achieves a good balance between '"I can't do this," or "It's too easy",' said pupil. Similarly, sports for all programme (just won an award from the TES) ensures that participation is matched with enthusiasm and skill levels.

Average class size is 17 (max 22) – small at the start, slightly larger by year 6. Teacher to pupil ratio ranges from between one to eight (reception) and one to 16 by year 6 (though lots of smaller group work with specialist teachers in maths and English). Some tutoring inevitable though parents felt that less here than in other establishments. One parent, who had her sons assessed, was told not to bother as school was preparing them really well. 'Very reassuring.'

Education is impressively thorough and achieves a good balance between 'I can't do this' and 'it's too easy', we were told

Around 25 pupils with EAL requirements – range of support includes one-to-one and differentiated curriculum. About 20 pupils have learning needs, mostly mild, majority dyslexia focused but not exclusively – support includes group and one-to-one support, study skills and handwriting club. Some issues with poor behaviour resulting in parental unhappiness. Majority of boys, however, 'are there because they want to learn,' said parent.

Par for the course in any school that – like this one – has praiseworthy desire to be genuinely inclusive (something that other establishments could learn from). Currently has pupil with an EHCP and is seeing more with severe anxiety. Whole-school focus on well-being includes staff sitting with boys at lunchtime to tease out any problems and encourage them to talk – it's the time when they're at their most relaxed and open.

Playground with grass (fake), trees (real) and break time football, though one pitch has a single goal and many disputed results. 'Good for negotiation skills,' says teacher

With SEN, takes things one year at a time, talks frequently to parents, and – should school not be the right place – supports transition elsewhere. 'The school is trying to balance everyone's needs and is in a difficult position,' said parent. School stresses that assessment process is now more robust to ensure that is confident about being able to support pupils with behavioural issues.

Favourite subjects include maths (one brainbox took GCSE maths in year 4 – and achieved an 8) and sport (mentioned by many pupils of all ages), though art also got a mention. 'Can get lost in my mind.'

In reception (where one door was disguised as a doubledecker bus – 'Your journey begins here', the other as a train) pupils were mastering the number one, some timing how long it took to knock down a skittle, others measuring assorted items that might, or might not be longer than a metre.

Year 2 pupils, meanwhile, were (literally) separating fact from fiction by working out what sort of books might feature, say, a glossary, while year 3s examined coin designs with impressive levels of attention. Over in the senior building, year 5 pupils were tackling A Christmas Carol with diligence if not wild enthusiasm. What did they think of it so far? 'A complicated book...' said pupil, cautiously. Effective differentiation, rather than setting, is the rule here – year 4 maths class was choosing from bronze, silver or gold problems from the board.

Pace is brisk, in class and out. Annual production is split between years 4 and 6, other years watch (and have informal concert). In year 3, all pupils learn violin or cello and a brass instrument in year 4 (but not simultaneously) and a quarter have individual lessons. Range of choirs and ensembles, beginners to budding music scholars and annual production – includes The Lion King.

Clubs include academically focused – Latin and entrance exam preparation among them (prepare for 10+ as well as 11+) as well as eg chamber choir, ensembles. Requires commitment – one of our guides was regularly in school for 7.45am. Some held jointly with prep girls – welcomed, as long as reasonable mix. 'I was on my own thinking "where are my friends?"' said senior boy.

Achievements matter but attitude gets almost as much attention. Individual and team sports stars are recognised for manners and sportsmanship, not just results. 'It's about camaraderie, support and respecting everyone,' said senior pupil.

Best teachers, say pupils, are kind and fair. 'Give us fun things to do,' felt one. 'Give us good opportunities and hardly ever shout,' thought another. 'If misbehaving, given warnings first.' (Verbal warnings disappear from the system after a week, written warnings remain on school record.) Very rare for pupils to be asked to leave – would only happen if all other options exhausted; one during current head's tenure so far.

Our junior guides were courteous and solemnly conscious of their role (highly effective recruitment tool, say parents), springing to hold door open when test fire alarm sounded, one wagging a disapproving finger at waving friend. Senior pupils ditto – as well as loyal. 'Timetable must have slipped out,' said guide, when we clock fact that no pupils are learning clarinet, saxophone or recorder this year.

Many boys' blazers twinkle with badges, including choir and platinum star – one for every 100 house points. (Girls' prep pupils were ever so slightly sniffy about this – 'have fewer but value them more,' said one.) One tour guide had collected the full set and was wondering whether was worth going round a second time. Another – once equally decorated – had lost the lot in the wash.

Noise, as top years move between classes ('to prepare us for senior school,' said year 5 pupil) inevitably 'a bit stompey-ish going up the stairs' but bearable.

Parents choose the school because, said one, 'we wanted our boys to be boys.' Having seen the thorough, thoughtful approach to education on offer here and the delightful pupils it produces, hard to disagree.

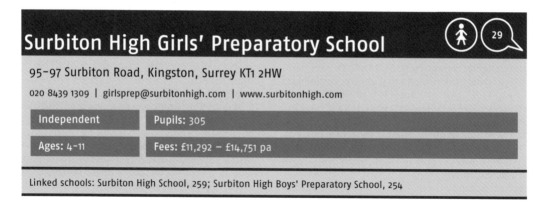

Surbiton High Girls' Preparatory School

29

95–97 Surbiton Road, Kingston, Surrey KT1 2HW

020 8439 1309 | girlsprep@surbitonhigh.com | www.surbitonhigh.com

Independent	Pupils: 305
Ages: 4–11	Fees: £11,292 – £14,751 pa

Linked schools: Surbiton High School, 259; Surbiton High Boys' Preparatory School, 254

Head: Since 2015, Clemmie Stewart BA, 30s. Joined school in 2014 as director of teaching and learning. Before that, four exhilarating years first as a class teacher, then behavioural and inclusion lead at state school, part of new team recruited to bring it out of special measures after 'one of worst Ofsteds ever.' A 'huge learning curve,' she says. Yes indeed, especially given contrast with previous NQT role as year 5 class teacher with added housemistress and games duties at lovely but not terribly gritty Farleigh Prep.

Why do it? 'Confidence-boosting – challenging expectations and getting staff on board.' Return to the independent sector down to lure of enjoyably challenging job coupling autonomy with breadth of responsibilities.

The drive she's brought was definitely needed. In the past prep was known as nice but not especially demanding, making the jump to seniors quite a push (in marked contrast to top quality outside candidates prepped to the eyeballs).

'There was always the guarantee of a place in the senior school but not a sense of desire for girls to do brilliantly,' says the head. Now, there's a rigorous curriculum, and robust assessments designed to 'understand the academic make up of the girls … how they think, what makes them tick and wobble – then we design the curriculum round that.' Get it right and girls aren't just prepped to get through the 11+ but 'ready to spring out at the future and grab it.'

Could all have been so different had this former music scholar at Twyford not realised that only teaching would do and switched to English as degree subject. Now enjoys music vicariously – hard not to warm to a head so proud of pupils' achievements that invited the chamber choir to sing at her wedding (photograph has pride of place in her office). 'Was magic to have them there and meant all my friends and family could see how wonderful our girls are.' School can cater for a wide range of characters, she says. 'All have something special about them and it's our job to find it.'

Wants pupils to feel they've 'won' at something at least once a day, academic or otherwise. Likes to get a regular teaching fix – currently achieved by providing cover for other staff as needed. Takes English and humanities in her stride – maths more of a challenge.

Not prescriptive. Felt to be a good listener – to staff as well as pupils. Has made social action projects more than a charity special but part of life of the school. Wanted, she says, to 'burst the Surrey bubble in a gentle, informational and educational way,' though without making pupils 'feel guilty for being here.' Links with local homeless group have led to invitations to one former rough sleeper addressing the girls and staying in touch, to the benefit of all.

Pupils say she's 'kind', 'nice', 'encouraging.' 'Never strict – always happy with what you're doing.'

Has a relaxed, kindly manner with them, even handing over her own watch to our guides when they weren't too sure of the tour timings. Her own sound exhausting, involving a 6.00am start from home in Hampshire, home again (on a meetings-free day) for 8pm. But no, it's all good. 'Works for me because I do my best thinking [on the way],' she says, also pointing out the lovely long holidays. In any case, 'it's such an energising school and the girls are such a joy that it doesn't feel like coming to work.'

Sentiment presumably shared by everyone else – 100 per cent of staff feel 'empowered to work' according to survey by parent organisation United Learning (anon, we're assuming, so no arm twisting behind the bike sheds).

She's a wow with parents. 'Children adore her, she's so welcoming, knows everyone's name when going into the playground, pretty much there every day,' said one. 'She's just really nurturing, young, very successful, that's really important to the girls. Feel she's a lovely role model for the girls.'

Entrance: Up to 32 pupils in reception via informal assessment mornings, with occasional places in other year groups. As with the boys' prep, most pupils come from within a three-mile radius. No scholarships or mean-tested bursaries though it's an area that might just be revisited – head is keen. Lots of attention paid to outreach – team visits every nursery school sending a pupil here, Easter egg hunts and singalongs for prospective pupils helping ensure that school is familiar and favourite place to be well before they start here.

Exit: No girl in theory denied a place at senior school. 'There are 48 girls in year 6 and 48 seats at the High School,' says the head. In the event, around 80 per cent of pupils now go on to senior school, taking the entrance exam but for setting purposes only. In 2019 awarded 15 scholarships. The odd leaver to Guildford High, St George's College, Tiffin Girls, Sir William Perkins and Waldergrave. Inevitably there's some tutoring. Head not delighted. If parents must do it, keep it to mastering a specific challenge but can end up being 'self perpetuating', she says.

Remarks: Girls' prep is housed in pleasantly undemanding red-brick building on a compact site a minute's walk from the senior school buildings. It's had a sizeable makeover – and it shows. Rooms, from science labs to classrooms, are large and well equipped, reception a colourful, happy home for pupils, quietly engaged in end of day activities like adding glitter to glued letters, and creating smartboard pictures of fireworks.

Unsurprising that what captivates parents (on top of growing academics) is the quality of the visual and performing arts. 'Looked round the art department and thought, "This is unbelievable",' said a mother.

As in the boys' prep, all pupils learn violin or cello in year 3, a brass instrument year 4 and put on an annual musical, Mary Poppins for the girls while the boys got Lion King. (We'd love to see a swap next time round.)

Hard not to warm to a head so proud of pupils' achievements that she invited the chamber choir to sing at her wedding (photograph has pride of place in her office)

Main outside space is at magnificent Hinchley Wood, 10 minutes away, with elegant sufficiency of spaces and facilities for sport – and there's plenty on offer: netball and hockey in autumn (down to D teams but no worries – 'just means the people ... need a bit more support,' explains kindly year 6 website author), athletics, rounders and tennis in spring and summer, cricket and football recently added. Recent successes include top spot for U12 skiers at English Schools' National Finals (also strong at gymnastics) and in hockey and football – website notable for celebratory rather than triumphalist style. Have also won TES award for Sporting

Choice for All – with 80 clubs offering sessions in a range of sports to 3,500 pupils aged 4-18.

On the premises, there's a main playground, grassy (artificial) and with trees (one recently removed – 'we kept tripping over the roots,' said pupil) and mature hedge (real) while the tinies have their own, secure home, with notices on sheds spelling out what's on offer (though 'lots of spiders', apparently the chief feature of retired reading hut, didn't achieve official recognition).

Girl tour guides – two in year 6, one in year 2 – were delightful. Year 2 pupil tended to wander slightly off message, lingering by the playdough in reception ('I want to touch it') and making the most of the empty, colourful library (funded by parents, designed by teachers, in-your-face decor something the head is gradually coming to terms with) by trying out the cosy reading nook in a cushioned hollow between the stands of books.

If environment has had a makeover, academics have been enhanced even more. Parents praise teachers. Went into the job loving it and it shows. English and maths are reckoned to be particularly strong, with senior staff coming over to strengthen links. 'Teachers really stand out ... willing to take on parents' concerns and do a little bit extra to ensure that they are confident and understand what they need to understand,' said mother.

Homework manageable – extensions allowed for valid reasons. Just as well given other commitments – doing four or five clubs a week is not uncommon

Probably quite a lot extra required given that standards have shot up since Ms Stewart's appointment, with add ons including extra homework and one-to-one help. So successful that we heard from staff that senior school science has now had to up the content – juniors so far ahead that close to year 9 work when starting year 7.

Supported by excellent TAs, 'always personable, smiling and engaged with parents – so you have lots of friendly faces to approach if you've got a problem,' said parent. 'Brilliant.' Work imaginative with lots of forays into new vocab – like year 6's description of Frankenstein's 'glint of evil and demise.'

Where efforts can be inspired by connected curriculum, they are (though only where it slots in naturally) – though our admiration of year 2 African landscape pictures (acacia trees silhouetted against purple and red sunsets) and sand poems by older pupils turned out to be serendipitous rather than synchronised. There's much focus on learning values (which pupils and teachers, know by heart), year 4s pictured as caped crusaders, describing super strengths to work on ('giddiness' one of the more unlikely, but most fun).

Homework manageable – extensions allowed as long as valid reasons given. Just as well given other commitments – four or five clubs a week in school (and several others out of it) common, cookery one of the most popular, some with prep boys as well. One pupil felt more joint activities would be useful. 'We have to meet boys so if we did more we would get to know them as people.'

Favourite subjects include maths, computing, science, art and sport. Lots of exciting lessons going on – year 2s enjoying Skype conversation with wildlife conservationist. Teachers are 'funny'. Few quibbles, though one pupil did feel that as so many lessons were about following instructions 'one by one by one', would 'like to do more brainstorming.'

Average class size is 17 (max 24) – small at the start, slightly larger by year 6. Teacher to pupil ratio ranges from between one to eight (reception) and one to 16 by year 6 (though lots of smaller group work with specialist teachers in maths and English). Familiarisation with the senior school (sensible given its potentially daunting size) starts with a week in year 5 combining lessons and basic navigation. 'It's not just the academics, it's the transition and allowing the girls to feel safe,' said parent.

Support is gladly given to the 20+ pupils with EAL requirements (one-to-one and differentiated curriculum on offer). Similarly willing to accommodate the 50 or so with SEN. Most disabilities are dyslexia based but can also accommodate ASD, ADHD/ADD, visual and hearing impairment and physical disability. We liked thoughtful touches which included coloured – not white – walls next to smartboards, to reduce the glare for dyslexic pupils.

Pastoral care clearly done very well, described by one parent as 'outstanding'. Some pupils had experienced those tricky friend to frenemy issues. One, initially reluctant for parents to talk to school, in case it made things worse, agreed it had helped. 'Teachers sorted it out very well.' Year 6s are paired with a reception buddy and new pupils in other years get a friend to who looks out for them 'if anyone's being mean.'

Buddy bench by entrance: many girls we spoke to had used it – successfully – if didn't have break time pals. Pupils who are particularly good at caring, empathy, patience and respect are rewarded in assembly with leaf that's added to values tree – from bare branched to mass of greenery by the end of the year, and there are more formal sessions touching on mental health issues in top two years.

Though most will progress to the senior school, will be rare occasions where things don't always work out. Inevitably, says head, 'things will emerge that make us wonder if [it's] the right place.' Could include severe anxiety, needs requiring substantial one-to-one support. If family wishes girl to stay on, will do their best to support. Otherwise, will help parents find places elsewhere.

Rising standards coupled with automatic entrance to senior school are big selling points for prospective parents, who tend to be vocal locals, often working full time to pay the fees, with some high net worth families from the leafy uplands of ultra-salubrious areas like Kingston Hill. Diversity of families is, says head, greater here than at many other independents in the area. 'Children are

mixed in every sense, some parents are fine, others have sacrificed everything for them to come here. It feels very normal.'

'We'd drive through, see all the girls and think "that's a proper school",' said a father. 'Couldn't quite believe it when she was accepted. It's been really good fun for us as well. I'm quite jealous of my daughter.'

'Wasn't the most academic school ... so went into reception as figured that if school was going to pull its socks up, it had time to do it before my child was in the firing line,' said parent. Worth waiting for, with school now producing smart, successful and vocal pupils. 'Once, my daughter wouldn't say boo to a goose but now you can't shut her up – she'll stand in front of the class and talk,' said parent.

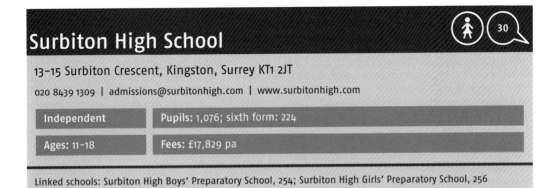

Surbiton High School

13–15 Surbiton Crescent, Kingston, Surrey KT1 2JT

020 8439 1309 | admissions@surbitonhigh.com | www.surbitonhigh.com

Independent	Pupils: 1,076; sixth form: 224
Ages: 11–18	Fees: £17,829 pa

Linked schools: Surbiton High Boys' Preparatory School, 254; Surbiton High Girls' Preparatory School, 256

Principal: Since January 2018, Rebecca Glover BEd, NPQH. 50s. Previously head for four years at Hull Collegiate School (also part of United Learning). Before that, was assistant and then deputy head of Tadcaster Grammar School, preceded by director of sixth form at Roundwood Park School in Herts. Originally a PE specialist – first post was as head of games at Hymers College in Hull, followed by head of PE at the Broxbourne School.

This is her first post in an all girls senior school and she's a convert. The volume is lower, not down to subliminal messages from the patriarchy, she thinks, just the inevitable tendency of boys to 'go out and do rough and tumble fighting and shout at their friends across the corridor. Girls just don't,' she says.

One former pupil felt that predominance of 'good girls' could make it harder for more outgoing characters to fit in. Not at all, says Mrs Glover. 'We have the ability to find the best in every girl, so if they are dramatic, artistic or musical we hone in on what their talents are.' Pupils we spoke to agreed. 'People aren't looked down on for being loud,' thought one.

Mrs Glover is unlikely to be proverbial new broom, felt parents. 'No plans for broad, sweeping changes. What she wants to do is tinker with things to get that extra one per cent so we get better and better.'

Pupils who have had the chance to get to know her (normally towards top of the school) praise her interest in their plans. 'Very friendly.' Those who haven't would like to. 'Obviously she's so new but I hope she gets to know us a bit more,' said one senior pupil. She's very visible at the younger end of the school, teaching year 7 geography and around out of hours.

While not 'a slave to the step count', she runs by the Thames at 6am most mornings. Sees parents along the way but is usually a dot on the horizon before they've finished their double take. She also competes in half and full marathons and has even introduced walking meetings with the two prep school heads. (Staff, asked how they'd characterise her, said they'd put on running shoes and race round the school.)

Stresses that success of the pupils isn't just about results (good though they are) but added value (nearly a whole GCSE per pupil). She's also focusing (with prep heads) on increasing community involvement, recently recruiting a member of staff to work on everything from supporting homeless charities to offering lectures. 'It's not about leasing the facilities but for people to experience things that they can't elsewhere.' Parents generally supportive as long as efforts aren't diluted. 'I think we want the focus to be here in the school,' said one.

Felt to be settling in and 'making a difference to process and communication,' said parent, 'A watcher and waiter whose style is yet to be fully unveiled.' Two children, one attending the school.

Academic matters: If you want the staff to bristle (they're super loyal here), mention school's former status as the runner's up prize – home for those who don't quite make one of the nearby super selectives. Felt to be far less the case now. 'Certainly driving the standards up,' said a parent. School laments league table construction. 'Parents don't understand how they work.' Points out that with their big pupil numbers and wide intake, bare percentages don't give a sense of how individual child will do. 'If you have a top achieving daughter and they're here, they will do exceptionally well.'

In 2019, 60 per cent A*/A, 90 per cent at A*/B at A level; 70 per cent 9-7 at GCSE.

School's description of qualities of successful pupils sound guaranteed to make them so rounded they could bounce into school each day. They will be 'ambitious for themselves, focused, definitely happy pupils with a willingness to try things they haven't tried before, take risks and learn skills for tomorrow.'

Substantial effort is put into getting them there – school was praised for finding potential role models who could help with work experience or advice on how to follow in footsteps. 'Totally inspired by meeting credible woman engineer,' said parent. 'School goes a step further to give them that exposure to traditionally male-oriented careers.'

STEM subjects (studied at A level by about 40 per cent of pupils) consistently head the tribute list – with teachers who are 'fantastic, phenomenal,' said parent. 'So good. [They] help you if you didn't understand and give up their own time,' said senior pupil. Physics (like other sciences, taught separately all the way from year 7), notable for 'hilarious, amazing' teacher. Maths ditto. The best staff command respect, tempered with humour and an ability to translate the toughest concepts in a way that 'simples it down' (as good a description as we've encountered).

Plenty of interesting add ons elsewhere, like restoration of Victorian casts from Athens marbles by classics students, gently mouldering away in ICT suite, about to go on show to an admiring public.

It's all delivered by teachers, average age of 41, many long stayers (55 plus have completed 10 years or over). Class sizes average 24 (smaller in GCSE and A level years). Teacher-pupil ratio around one to 13. Plenty of varied and imaginative teaching styles, says school, though classes we saw featured teachers out front, directing operations, girls impressively focused but cheerful, even in A level biology class covering respiration – 'possibly the hardest lesson,' said teacher.

The disorganised have been helped by a new app where all homework is uploaded by the staff – though textbooks are still available

For around 50 pupils with EAL, offer one-to-one support and differentiated lessons (all based on individual assessment). Support mild learning needs – majority SpLD related though also ASD, ADHD and ADD, visual, hearing impairment and physical disability – around 170 pupils currently supported.

Currently provide – but not limited to – one-to-one, group support, study skills and handwriting club. Nothing school won't consider as long as child can keep up academically and is happy. 'Will go to nth degree to make this work,' says the head. On the rare occasions it doesn't will involve parents at every stage.

Incentives include popular reading challenge (rewards include sweets and book vouchers) to encourage lifelong love of books (though plenty of keen pupils who probably don't need much incentivising).

Disorganised have been helped by new app where all homework is uploaded by the staff – though textbooks are still available. 'I use online in the classroom and paper textbook at home,' said pupil. Also run 'consolidation weeks' during major events (like fashion week), an opportunity to catch up on work left undone 'or anything they didn't understand.'

Perhaps inevitably, academic success brings extra baggage in the form of tutors who are, says parent, employed by 'a lot' of families to help children pass the entrance exams. 'Will be hard on that child as they may struggle without more tutoring,' thought a mother. Head stresses that tutoring shouldn't be needed, particularly given staff willingness to offer extra support (catch up sessions run before and after school and at lunchtime). 'We're here for them – that's part and parcel of what we are as a school.' Parental anxiety, however, goes beyond any rational concern.

Games, options, the arts: All the add ons you'd expect, including popular DofE at all levels (currently 170 takers), and a few more you probably wouldn't. Best event – by far, thought girls – is the annual fashion show, theme announced November, happens March. Themes range from film genres to 'fear of being normal.' 'Many people's highlight,' said pupil.

In addition to a composer and writer in residence (if Armistice centenary poem read in assembly by year 9 pupil laureate to anything to go by, quality is extremely high), there's also an entrepreneur in residence who's passed round the year groups, sparking ideas for doing interesting things with money. (Strict limit on cake sales as rather too popular.) Every pound raised gets a house point, with enough keen as mustard types 'to carry the waverers,' said pupil. The highlight is Enterprise Day which celebrates world-changing innovations including year 8's bookmark with camera to enlarge the words.

Year 10s partner other local schools to explore crowdfunding. All part of creative agenda, recently recognised by TES award, designed to boost the imagination as well as raising squillions (well, thousands, anyway) for good causes. Good works include fundraising for Kilimanjaro Young Girls in Need with fundraising and visits – teachers about to visit to share expertise.

Sport once better than academics. Now, however, 'they've improved the academic quality but allowed the sporting girls to shine,' said parent. While it remains a big part of life here, sixth formers can choose eg spinning class, boxercise and yoga – 'good to relieve tension,' said one, and pupils reckoned you're 'not looked down on' if it's not your thing. Even the J and K netball teams get occasional matches if not a full calendar. Inclusion recognised by recent TES award. 'Testament to our approach,' says school.

Carrots include de luxe trips: Barbados for netball, Argentina for hockey – with added bonus of life lessons in 'learning to handle ... money' – and, a first, Porto (football). Lots of high quality wins in all these areas and others. Sports successes range from hockey to rowing as well as skiing and gymnastics. Parents praise quality of teaching – 'exceptional,' said one, while numbers representing school at national/GB level are currently round the 30 mark. OG Chemmy Alcott's achievements continue (surprisingly, says school) to cast a long shadow. 'Foundations of the ski team have come from her success,' said mother. Olympic level gymnastics have also (literally) taken off – though landed successfully again.

Only niggle is amount of parental involvement required. One mother felt that many of those playing in top teams at school would also be involved in outside clubs – commitment required isn't something every girl has time, or desire, to do. 'What you want is to give everybody the opportunity to try and to play at least at a social level. I think they're doing that with netball and hockey. With other sports, they're not,' said one.

A lot of sport (not skiing) takes place a couple of miles down the road in Hinchley Wood where vast acreage of playing fields on site extends to woodland and a hill (site for popular annual dads' and kids' camping fest and is an antidote to the urban siting of the schools).

Performance standards have shot up in recent years to concert pitch – staging production of Wind in the Willows in New Wimbledon Theatre to accommodate audiences. Have 30 visiting music teachers, 380 weekly instrumental lessons (rotating so miss something different each week) and 25 different co-curricular activities, from choirs (two a capella) to music theory support groups.

Background and atmosphere: Founded 1884 by the Church Schools Company (now United Learning), the first school in what would subsequently grow into an educational behemoth, with 70 state academies and 12 independent schools.

If this were a Monopoly board, this chunk of Surbiton would all be in school colours of green and silver. Senior girls' school growth mainly linear, though former Assembly Rooms (venue for assemblies, concerts and lunches – older girls encouraged, though not compelled, to bring their own) are on the other side of the heavily calmed road (20mph zone).

There's an entrepreneur in residence, sparking ideas for doing interesting things with money. (Strict limit on cake sales as rather too popular)

Architecture ranges from bland (and soon to be revamped) sixth form block to pleasant main building, where most of the lessons take place. It's smart and tidy, accessorised with assorted proofs of school achievements including an impressive trophy cabinet and glossy photographs of school life.

The layout is generally a doddle (helped by hotel-style numbering), bar a couple of classrooms accessed by own staircase – older pupils step in to redirect baffled year 7s at the start of every school year. Attractive courtyard with two fountains at the back and the venue for some productions also enjoys the sounds of cheerful play from younger prep boys' playground.

Antidote to overwhelming tidiness, as so often, is provided by art department, with excellent natural light (can see Hampton Court from its big windows), entrance marked by stack of canvases, works pleasingly varied. 'No house style,' points out member of staff – though there is – literally – one: a cardboard house like a stage set, each room peopled by different characters. Potters have own kiln, photographers a mezzanine floor and own dark room.

Radiates sense of being happy in its own skin, pupils ditto, helped by easy care and smart uniform. Apart from school's insistence on a blazer in the sixth form ('am sure 95 per cent would prefer not to wear one but it's not a battle we're going to take on,' said one), feel they've got off lightly compared with friends in other schools handicapped (sartorially and possibly literally) by ankle-length skirts.

Pastoral care, well-being and discipline: School carefully tempers rise in expectations with impressively thought through approach to mental illness. 'To say it doesn't happen is naïve,' says the head. 'It definitely is an issue in lots of schools and we're no different to any other highly academic girls' school.'

While one parent felt that pastoral care here is 'a little tougher than in the prep schools' (strict drugs and drinks policy – but no unscheduled departures under Mrs Glover's watch so far), staff are impressively aware of pressure on pupils and make it their business to get to know as many as possible, even creating a bespoke app to memorise names and faces – there's even a league table.

School has opened a well-being centre and makes seeking help easy. Pupils can self-refer to school counsellor (one of team of three), for example, whose office is tucked away so suitably anon, concerns taken further only if it's a safeguarding issue. 'Ninety per cent of the time it's just that the girls need someone to talk to,' says head. 'We are very good at referring girls before it becomes critical.'

School also ensures that teachers don't crumble under the pressure themselves. From a no email day every term to staff yoga, staff make well-being something 'we do for yourself and try to instil in others.' Even the staffroom chocolate drawer can remain (almost) untouched. 'Sometimes just opening it and walking past is enough,' says saintly teacher.

May not have all the answers, but doing best to be responsive, think parents. Bullying won't ever disappear but – even if it takes time – there will be someone to go to. 'A couple of members of staff were really lovely and really helped me out,' said pupil. 'From then on, I felt there was always someone I could talk to.'

> On our visit, we saw a row of static bikes, goal to ride 4,500 miles: distance to the Tanzanian school they're fundraising for

Pupils and parents: A nice place to be a parent, with strong friendships formed early, sometimes lifelong. Girls ditto. 'End up with a very close community [who] go on holidays together,' said parent. Social media, including WhatsApp used to organise socials including annual ball, auction and Christmas Fair.

Perception from one parent was that extensive smartening up has done wonders for marketing clout. 'Attracts a better calibre of student and brought up the profile of parents.'

Smartness doesn't however extend to elaborate pre-school cosmetic preparations. 'I'd say the time I get ready in has become less and less,' said pupil. 'Now I have maximum sleep ... you're not having to impress everyone.' Parents agreed. 'I'm lucky if mine brush their teeth,' said one. 'You don't have that handbag culture here,' confirms a teacher. 'There's no show of wealth and I don't think they appreciate showiness.'

Energy on status and appearance thus saved appears to be usefully redirected – on day of visit, queues were forming by a row of static bikes, goal to ride 4,500 miles: distance to the Tanzanian school they're fundraising for.

Generally felt to attract down to earth families, so un-precious that may (we were told) even play down their wonderfully talented offspring rather than big them up.

Most UK born with English as a first language – small number of international students (mostly Asian). Former pupils cover the range from politicians (Nicky Morgan MP and Baroness Liz Sugg) to skier Chemmy Alcott and Radio 1 DJ Mollie King.

A roughly equal split between working and stay at home mothers, a few ladies who lunch types, many others having to think hard before parting with thick end of £1,500 a month out of taxed income. 'Have to be very convinced you're doing the right thing.'

Entrance: Average intake for year 7 is 144, via maths and English tests. Takes from 45 or so feeders from state and private sector alongside own prep. Too many to list but range from Bishop Gilpin CofE, Coombe Hill and Esher Church School (all state) to Holy Cross Prep, Hurlingham School and Kew College – every area, in fact, served by extensive school bus route (10-mile radius). Once registered, can sign up for 'Who am I?' sessions so registered pupils can have a taste of life at the senior school (don't say what happens if still unclear). About eight join in the sixth form.

Exit: Have consistently lost around 20 per cent post GCSEs – most to co-eds or local colleges, but more are staying on. Eight to Oxbridge in 2019.

Money matters: Means-tested bursaries for year 7 and sixth form entry, including help for existing pupils who couldn't stay on post-16 without financial help. Will also provide emergency financial support (for bereavement or 'emergency situations.').

Scholarships, worth 20 per cent, cover the usual suspects (academics, music, sport) and also drama, art and photography.

Remarks: Large, successful but easily underestimated, school has moved slowly but surely from back up option to first choice. One notch down on the pressure and several up on the support makes it increasingly the smart choice for ambitious, busy and down-to-earth families.

Sutton Grammar School

Manor Lane, Sutton, Surrey SM1 4AS

020 8642 3821 | office@suttongrammar.sutton.sch.uk | www.suttongrammar.sutton.sch.uk

State	Ages: 11–18	Pupils: 950; sixth form: 290 (17 girls)

Headmaster: Since September 2019, Ben Cloves, a mathematician and previously deputy head at Wallington High. Married to Jo; two sons.

Academic matters: Highly selective and usually in the top 10 per cent of the highest achieving schools. Needless to say, it delivers mostly excellent results: in 2019, 83 per cent of exams were graded 9-7 at GCSE; 51 per cent A*/A at A level (80 per cent A*/B).

The secret to their success, it seems, are the teachers. 'Nobody lets you fall behind'; 'teachers regularly give up lunchtimes to help you' etc, say pupils. 'There's real enthusiasm for their subject – you see them getting really excited about it, even when they've worked there for years, and that really rubs off.' 'They don't necessarily stay on curriculum if we're really interested in a particular area – I love that.' Good mix of male and female, including in senior roles, most of them long serving; 'We only change one or two staff a year,' says school. Parents like the fact that they can email form tutors.

All three sciences and maths extremely strong. Plenty of large and light (though not all state-of-the-art) labs, greenhouse on the roof and pupils breed trout and salmon to release into the River Wandle. Seemingly infinite science-related project clubs and pupils regularly win the likes of UK Engineer of the Year and Intech science awards; one boy was listed as one of Time magazine's 30 most influential teenagers in the world for his science inventions, about which he's even done a TED talk. Sixth formers help to teach science in primary schools, while some local schools visit Sutton Grammar to experience working in a lab. Early work experience is arranged in hospitals for those considering careers in medicine.

School is big on curricular (and extracurricular) breadth, so no need to fret about arts and humanities being shoved aside. 'The way we see it, everyone does everything for three years, then everyone specialises a little, but still keeping it nice and wide within their 11 GCSEs – or 12 if they're doing extra maths.' 'I think it's what makes this school stand out from the grammars in the area,' one boy told us. Upshot is that all boys must do at least one 'doing, making or acting' GCSE such as PE or drama, plus all take RE, a humanity and a language. No classics, modern languages only – boys choose from French or German from year 7, then can add a second (including Spanish) from year 8. Setting in maths from year 9, with a bottom set for English in years 10 and 11 for those who need extra support. Homework built up incrementally, 'so there's never a time when you feel they're suddenly starting to pile it on,' said one pupil. Plenty of help with UCAS and careers, with all pupils seeing a dedicated careers advisor at least once in year 10 and again in year 12.

Citizenship taught from year 7 to 11 ('which means we can teach areas like democracy and politics, including radicalisation, not as a bolt-on but as integral') and enterprise from year 9 to 11 ('There's no point in our students doing these amazing inventions if they don't have the skills to sell them').

Commitment to breadth continues into sixth form, with options from the 23-strong A level menu including DT, drama, PE, photography and business studies and, impressively, there's a promise from the head not to cancel subjects that only get three or so takers. Most popular in terms of numbers are (you guessed it) maths and sciences, but history, geography and economics are also considered worthy pickings among pupils. Rigorous computer science skills are taught up to year 9, leading to good numbers choosing it at GCSE and A level – 'Some of our strongest maths students love the problem-solving aspect.'

SENCo oversees SEN provision throughout the school for those on statements, SpLDs, sensory impairments or high functioning ASD. When we visited, the school had more EHCPs (eight) than two of the local comprehensives ('and certainly more than the other local state grammars'), which has meant no shortage of effort is put in to support students with additional needs – but neither the school nor parents claim it's perfect. 'We don't always deliver the goods, but we have a deserved reputation for caring'; pupils have to be able to cope and enjoy the fast moving and competitive environment. 'The provision has sometimes been excellent, other times not so good, but I'm not sure it would have been better anywhere else,' said one parent.

Games, options, the arts: If you're after lush green fields, plentiful courts and vast pitches, you'll be disappointed – 'It's always a bit of a worry on open evenings when you see some parents shocked at our tight little site'. But nobody really minds once they realise the students head off to a 27-acre sports ground 15 minutes away in Cheam for an afternoon of games every week. 'It's great, albeit a bit dated,' said one student about the grounds shared by old boys and Surrey football clubs; and back on the school site there's an onsite sports hall with gymnasium plus largish heated open-air swimming pool (admittedly not looking its best during our winter visit).

Probably not a school for the highly competitive who are dead set on thrashing other schools at everything on the sports field, but inclusivity is the name of the game here, with most boys are guaranteed to play in the A/B teams at some stage. And parents and pupils alike appreciate the way 'PE staff put so much effort in to finding activities students will really enjoy, whether that's badminton or table tennis.' Football is top sport in winter and athletics has replaced cricket's number one spot in summer. Cross-country (through local woods), basketball and gymnastics (in sports hall) also popular. Well established CCF (run with Nonsuch High) and DofE programmes.

Some imaginative art on display around the school, with option to take it at GCSE and A level.

But it's not just art for art's sake – this school is a fine example of helping to transform STEM into STEAM by increasingly combining art and design with science, technology, engineering and maths, which those in industry claim is essential to meet economic needs in the 21st century. 'Product design is particularly popular,' one boy told us.

Sciences extremely strong. One boy listed as one of Time magazine's 30 most influential teenagers in the world for his inventions, about which he's even done a TED talk

Chamber groups, orchestras and choirs engage in a range of musical pursuits, including a cappella singing. Tuition on any instrument of a boy's choice can be arranged, with the four practice rooms all in full use all the time. 'I wouldn't say it's a massively musical school, the kind where you hear music as you walk about, but the opportunities are definitely there if you want them,' says one pupil. 'I did not expect my son to be so musical and yet he wound up doing music at A level,' a parent told us.

Music and drama departments team up with Sutton High School for biannual musical production. Both schools and parents pull together to produce fabulous productions. Drama on the curriculum: a reasonable number of boys go on to take GCSE and A level theatre studies. LAMDA courses and exams on offer too. The old gym has been converted into one of two drama studios.

The push on extracurricular (as well as the canteen being open for breakfast) means things start to get busy most mornings from around 7.45am, with the last students heading off around 6pm; club list is huge with everything from board games to Young Enterprise club and from electronics to Rubik's cube club, plus all the usual range of sports. During the summer term there is an annual activities week. Trips include foreign travel (some students came up with the idea of a charity-focused trip to Malawi the year before we visited, which they persuaded staff to run – 'it was the best 15 days ever,' one pupil told us), adventure sports camps and a year 9 visit to the First World War battlefields. Some older pupils try their hand at teaching in local primary schools.

Background and atmosphere: Opened as Sutton County Grammar in 1899, charging fees of two pounds and 10 shillings per term. More or less everything you could want is on the compact site, with an eclectic mix of old and new buildings neatly surrounding the central tarmacked playground

Nonsuch High School for Girls

area. Latest additions include a two-storey maths block, sixth form centre, bigger dining room and extra science lab. 'The facilities have improved a lot over the last 20 years,' says school, although some boys feel it's a shame there aren't more outdoor areas. Light-filled library with dedicated librarians doubles up (as do many areas of the school) as private study areas for sixth formers, although shame not to see more books on the shelves.

Since 2017, sixth-form co-ed. 'We're a boys' school and that isn't going to change, but we took the decision to take in girls principally because of funding issues and because being a little bit bigger helps all subjects to be more sustainable.' The girls appear confident and everyone agrees they've 'helped sharpen things up.' 'And it's not as if the school is a stranger to girls – we've always had them around for CCF and they have historically been able to come and do single subjects as members of another school.'

> 'You're not just a result on a spreadsheet,' one boy told us. Counsellor available one day a week, although some pupils we spoke to were not aware of this

Students from year 10 upwards are allowed to go off site during their breaks and lunch hour, 'though many stay as the food is so much better than it used to be,' a pupil told us. Sandwich bar in the playground (known as the Snack Shack) helps to relieve the lunchtime crush. Stylish but small canteen serves hot meals. Everything runs like clockwork in this traditional, focused grammar school and pupils have a strong sense of pride in it.

Pastoral care, well-being and discipline: Fifth house recently added to existing four; besides the usual inter-house competitions, this system – along with year group tutors – forms the structural base for pupil welfare ie older pupils given responsibility to look after younger ones in same house. 'You feel the school really cares about you – you're not just a result on a spreadsheet,' one boy told us. Counsellor available one day a week, although some pupils we spoke to were not aware of this.

Pupils are taught to respect others and take responsibility for all aspects of the school and themselves. Everyone is expected to follow a strict but fair code on behaviour, hair and uniform. Faculty-run lunchtime detentions for more minor misdemeanours like forgetting homework ('some departments are much more lenient than others,' say pupils); Wednesday detention under deputy

head with letter home to parents for more serious stuff like regular smaller offences or bigger ones such as swearing – 'but most never get one,' pupils told us. No permanent exclusions in recent years; around 10 temporary ones at most in any one year for anything from theft to violence.

'It's virtually non-existent,' says school re bullying; boys told us it does happen occasionally, 'but it's usually short lived and the usual things that people get bullied for in school – like being keen on studying – aren't picked on here,' said one.

Parents' information evenings and discussion groups run on a wide range of topics, often led by outside speakers. Parents are canvassed on subjects they'd like to know more about each term and pupils are welcome to attend too if they wish.

Pupils and parents: Parents mostly professionals from a wide mix of backgrounds – wealthy Surrey and south Londoners through to those from less affluent areas. Good transport links a boon for those further away. Around 60 per cent Asian (a lot more than the proportion in the local community, says school) now entering from year 7; the remaining 40 per cent dominated by white British and scatterings of other cultures including Korean and Afro-Caribbean. Communications between school office and parents could be better, we were told – 'We get emails from the office and there are always mistakes, so you often get another three before the information is actually correct,' said one parent.

Boys are well-behaved, motivated and (with some exceptions of some surprisingly tongue-tied year 7s and 8s that we met) articulate. At least half come in expecting to become doctors (which may come from the parents or the boys, 'but because we keep the boys on multiple tracks for longer than other schools, and push the extracurricular so hard, they are easily able to change their pathway if they choose to').

The Suttonians have a very active old boys' network and a large number of them remain involved with the school. Famous alumni include Brian Paddick, Christopher Bigsby, David Bellamy and David Farrar.

Entrance: Places are highly sought after. Nearly 3,000 boys take the Sutton-wide selective eligibility test, which covers the five local grammar schools and involves English and maths multiple-choice questions. Register by mid-August. Around 1,000 get through to phase two, an exam set by the school with more open-ended questions, also in English and maths. Seventy-five of the places go to the highest scorers within a set postcode that 'doesn't go far beyond the Sutton boundary'; the other 65 are chosen purely on scores. PTA runs mock test days for around 2,000 children each year wanting to prepare for them. At 16+ around 40 competitive entry places are available for both girls and boys into the sixth form – successful applicants will need around three 9-8s and three 7s at GCSE.

Exit: Almost all to university, although the occasional pupil takes up a specialist apprenticeship in the workplace – 'we very much encourage this if it's right for the pupil'. Ten to Oxbridge in 2019, 12 medics, two dentists and one vet. Others to a range of top universities, with London colleges, Southampton, Exeter, Bristol and Warwick all popular. Three to university abroad in 2019. Engineering currently the most dominant subject; law also becoming more popular.

Money matters: School asks parents to support the school financially – up to £50 a month, with around 80 per cent taking it up, 'although some pay more like a fiver a month. The money flows in because

parents value the breadth of what we offer'. PTA raises around £80,000 each year for the benefit of pupils and for school developments.

Remarks: It's made clear to these bright boys (and now girls in sixth form) right from the off that the sky's the limit to what they can achieve, with some fantastic opportunities that reach well beyond the curriculum to ensure no potential in any area is missed. But what most impressed us was the way this all seems to happen in the most unassuming, down-to-earth way and without undue pressure. There's a smaller school vibe here, which has all the benefits of wraparound pastoral care, but it works hard to produce independent, mature thinkers. For many pupils – those who thrive on hard work and embrace intellectual experiences – it is a springboard to a very bright future.

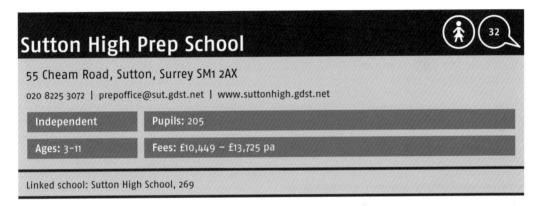

Sutton High Prep School

55 Cheam Road, Sutton, Surrey SM1 2AX

020 8225 3072 | prepoffice@sut.gdst.net | www.suttonhigh.gdst.net

Independent	Pupils: 205
Ages: 3–11	Fees: £10,449 – £13,725 pa

Linked school: Sutton High School, 269

Head of junior school: Since 2015, Anne Musgrove BA QTS (40s). With a BA in education studies from the University of Warwick, she has over 20 years' experience of teaching in both the independent and maintained sectors including a number of years in Australia. Formerly deputy head (academic) and acting head at Putney High Junior School, she joined Sutton High Prep School as deputy head in 2014 before promotion to head.

Gentle, smiley and softly-spoken, but don't be fooled – she is a strong leader with a single-minded passion for the school, 'working crazy hours' (as one parent puts it) to ensure the school continues on the accelerated academic journey she has set it on. 'The school had pockets of excellence, but I felt we needed to rewrite the curriculum to get better scope and sequence overall. So we got in an educational consultant and have joined up the dots between subjects,' she says. Parents say the result is a 'more focused school academically, but without being the hot-house that many preps are around here.'

Girls clearly adore her, feeling able to pop into her cosy office (complete with beanbags – purple, as most things are in this school – for pupils to sit on) to discuss anything from friendship issues to a certificate they've gained outside school. 'She's super-kind,' one told us, beaming. Parents are impressed too. 'She's superb – I'm a massive fan,' is a typical comment. 'She knows all the girls by name and sometimes when I go to collect my daughter, I'll see her chatting to her in the playground, which is just wonderful.' 'She's totally engaged, as well as really listening to everything you say as a parent. In fact, she regularly asks parents for input,' says another.

Lives near Bushy Park, where she continues to pursue her interest in art and art history by visiting galleries and museums in the UK and overseas.

Entrance: Girls can join the nursery from the half term before their third birthday onwards and move on to reception at 4+. Younger children attend an informal play session – 'get ready for Sutton High

Prep School day' – before being offered a place; from 6+ girls sit assessment tests, run by the head. 'Because girls come from a range of different school experiences, it's their potential that we're looking for and we test them both verbally and non-verbally, as well as talking to them about their interests,' says the head, who adds that girls need to be able to adapt to a fast-paced curriculum, with different specialist teachers for subjects including French, PE and music – 'which, let's face it, doesn't suit all children.' For entry into other years (not unusual) phone the school to enquire about occasional places.

Exit: At 11+ around 60 per cent of the girls move to the senior school. Remainder mostly go to co-eds or local grammar schools – the latter being Sutton High's hottest competition. Girls making good progress are given a guaranteed place in the senior school in year 5; those who are not suited to moving up there will already have been advised (via an ongoing conversation) to give them plenty of time to find an alternative.

Remarks: Set in the leafy suburb of Sutton – where more parents pay out on junior schools than senior ones (the good local grammars are free, after all) – this traditional school has long offered a broad and balanced curriculum, backed up with strong pastoral care. The difference under the current headship has been shifting up a gear academically, with a rejigged curriculum and girls' progress now tracked in minute detail.

Dedicated music teacher links her subject with the rest of the curriculum ('We're currently doing songs with year 5 on recycling and the Tudors,' she told us)

Nursery and reception have their own purpose-built building – an environment where they largely develop their own learning, with a focus on instilling basic literacy and numeracy skills through structured play while also developing independence and confidence. Moving up the school – where girls are taught in the main prep school building – English, maths and core skills become the focal points, peppered with plenty of music, drama and sport alongside traditional subjects. Setting for maths and English from year 4. French from nursery; Spanish from year 3, and Latin from year 6. Homework of around 30 minutes a day from year 3, moving up to around an hour for year 6. Subject specialists for PE, music and languages – and from year 6, DT, art, Latin and science. ICT embedded into learning, with all year 4 and 5 girls getting their own iPads.

Parents praise the way teachers (who include a few old girls and just one man when we visited) really get to know the pupils – 'which means they can really adapt to each girl's learning style,' as one parent puts it. 'I now know, for example, that my daughter is an auditory learner and how she best learns. The level of detail – which I know involves lots of behind-the-scenes meetings about every girl – is amazing.' Other parents compliment the way teachers develop a love of learning and natural curiosity in their young charges.

Parents are less impressed, however, with class sizes, which – although can be as small as 12 – have been known to exceed 25. 'I know they have more teaching staff to cater for larger classes but still, this number isn't so different from state schools,' says one.

School has a good reputation for identifying SEN (around seven per cent when we visited), with a part-time SEN co-ordinator who is entirely classroom-based. 'That is our philosophy – ensuring that SEN isn't seen as something separate to everyday learning,' says head – although we were concerned to hear from one parent who decided not to disclose her daughter's SEN, albeit very mild, to the school at all for fear of her child being 'stigmatised by other children.' Another parent told us, 'I'm not convinced this is the best school for someone with a behavioural issue like ADHD.'

Physically, the school is tidy and well-maintained, with additions to the original two-storey Victorian building over the years. Notable facilities include a well-stocked library and impressive science lab. Colourful (although with an over-use of pinks and purples that borders on sickly) corridors lined with children's art, poetry and other achievements. Neat, amiable, highly confident and self-assured girls from a wide ethnic mix appear happy and involved in their work.

Plenty of curriculum-enhancing day trips, including the Globe Theatre, Kensington Palace, Hampton Court and – on the day we visited – Brighton beach for year 1s who were waiting excitedly in their pirate costumes. Residential trips start gently in year 4 with a two-day trip away, moving up to four days for year 5 and a week at PGL for year 6.

Drama is incorporated into the English curriculum and taught by class teachers. Dedicated music teacher works extremely hard and successfully, also linking with the curriculum ('For instance, we're currently doing songs with year 5 on recycling and the Tudors,' she told us), as well as producing two big concerts each year and regular musical assemblies. All pupils learn keyboard and recorder in class; individual tuition is available on any other instrument. Art offers equally wide-ranging

Discipline, is more carrot than stick, with a lot of emphasis on golden rules for the younger ones and right track for older girls

opportunities, including everything for textiles to mosaics and sculptures to acrylic painting.

Sport is big, with a wide range of fixtures (one week of play followed by one week to review and consolidate), and plenty to get everyone else interested too. 'The PE teacher repeatedly encourages my daughter to put herself forward for things like a lifeguard course – they're not just there for the naturally sporty,' says one parent. The 25m indoor pool, large refurbished gym and modern dance studio are all shared with the senior school, while the prep school children have three of their own hard courts and a small field as well.

Building on the pastoral care that comes as a natural result of teachers knowing the girls well, there's also a play buddies system, plus plenty of leadership roles. 'With my daughter, they put in so many little touches to help build her confidence,' gushes one parent.

As for discipline, it's more carrot than stick, with a lot of emphasis on 'golden rules' for the younger ones and 'right track' for older girls, which encourages them to do everything from being punctual to striving to do their best. And while there are 'consequences', they're all pretty gentle – reminders, warnings, time out and (worst case scenario) meeting with parents. 'If girls misbehave,

there's generally a reason and it's our job to get to the bottom of that,' explains head. Occasional bullying is nipped in the bud.

High expectations around uniform staying neat (purple again). Food is excellent, with lots of choice – 'the best of all the schools I've worked in,' says head and we can concur it's very tasty.

A whopping 60 extracurricular clubs on offer include everything from gardening to chess and debating to street dance. And working parents will delight in Tops and Tails, the on-site wraparound care facility from 7.30am-6.30pm down in the senior school, in addition to breakfast and homework clubs available at a reasonable hourly rate.

Parents hail from as far as Wimbledon, Southfields and Epsom, along with lots of local families, many of whom work in the City or run their own businesses. School's proximity to Sutton station means some take the train, dropping their offspring on the way to work, while others use the minibus or drive (with the usual niggles around parking – although head says you can easily park a few minutes' away and walk). No PTA, but they do have the Sutton High School Association (basically the same thing, but where the school takes over the logistics part of events like Burns Night celebrations and summer parties).

In summary, this is a small, pastorally-strong and evolving school with tailored learning and an increasingly academic focus that, thanks to the impressive wraparound care, may be particularly suited to working parents. 'This is a rare South London school that is ambitious and gets good results, but that is not pressured. It's one of the main reasons we moved to the area,' says one parent.

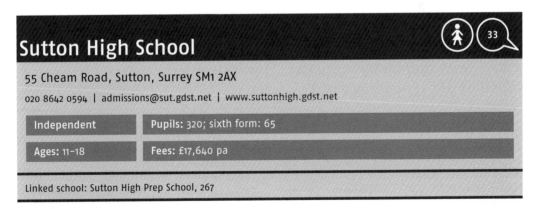

Sutton High School

55 Cheam Road, Sutton, Surrey SM1 2AX

020 8642 0594 | admissions@sut.gdst.net | www.suttonhigh.gdst.net

Independent	Pupils: 320; sixth form: 65
Ages: 11-18	Fees: £17,640 pa

Linked school: Sutton High Prep School, 267

Headmistress: Since 2012, Katharine Crouch BSc NPQH (50s). Biology degree from Leicester. Joined Sutton High School in 2003 and has held many roles including head of biology, head of pastoral and deputy head. Before that she worked at South Hampstead High and Tiffin Girls' School. Still teaches biology and PSHE when she can. 'Having a teaching role is important in keeping me rooted in what we are all here for,' she says. Girls say, 'It means we see her not just as a figurehead, but someone who really gets the day-to-day education bit.'

A jolly, convivial and candid woman who gives a warts-and-all version of school life ('Our Victorian buildings with character can present some challenges for teaching'; 'Our PTA was not a thriving place' etc), she makes a refreshing change from the rose-coloured-spectacled heads we so often see. And while lots of parents have little to do with her ('There's just no need when things tick along as smoothly as they do here,' said one parent), those that have had cause to see her describe her as 'approachable', 'forward-looking' and 'very on the ball.' 'She has a very loyal team of staff around her – that says a lot in itself,' said one. Possibly off the back of more general complaints we heard from parents that 'communications from the school have traditionally been poor,' she now invites parents to regular coffee mornings to offer input on issues like plans to refurbish the school hall.

Leaving in December 2019. She will be succeeded by Mrs Bethany Dawson who has been deputy head of Sutton High since 2017.

Academic matters: While not as strong as some schools in the borough, there are solid results across the board in academics and the arts. In 2019, 67 per cent 9-7 at GCSE and 36 per cent A*/A at A level (77 per cent A*/B). At GCSE, best results in maths, biology, Latin, drama and DT, while at A level, maths, science, geography, art and DT are among those with the biggest wins. Setting in English, maths and science from year 7. Girls choose two foreign languages out of German, French and Spanish – first choice is guaranteed, although second is not. Latin also available from year 8.

Girls and parents praise teachers for 'going well beyond the call of duty' – with staff always available, including out of hours by email

Girls and parents alike praise teachers for 'going well beyond the call of duty' – with staff always available, including out of hours by email and running subject clinics where necessary. 'The lessons are very interactive too, with a good mixture of PowerPoint, games and debates,' one girl told us. No complaints about homework, which builds up from one hour a night max from year 7. 'You notice the difference in year 10,' pointed out one girl.

Specialist teacher for SEN, who (although not an educational psychologist) is qualified to test for dyslexia, among other things – 'great for those who are borderline SEN,' said one parent. One girl statemented when we visited, with around 10 per cent mild to moderate SEN. Most help is within the classroom setting, says head, with some one-to-ones also available. 'I've been impressed – they've helped my daughter enormously with her dyslexia,' a parent told us.

Enrichment programme for years 7 and 8 on Wednesday afternoons in second half of summer term. Girls work on a topic such as languages (options include Urdu, Greek or Mandarin), music (girls learn guitar, percussion or handbells), STEM (girls design and build their own model) or sport (fencing, trampolining options). Meanwhile, sixth formers' enrichment programme involves a mixture of speakers (on issues ranging from mental health to living with HIV), work experience and visits to places including parliament and a university library (to learn research skills). Good, practical help is also available as part of this, with all sixth formers taught about budgeting and money management, for example. Girls praise the careers advice, with careers office handily located in the library and biannual careers fair, which invites representatives from many companies into the school to pitch career paths and ideas to the girls.

Sixth formers also undertake the Extended Project Qualification to help prepare them for university – a fair whack of extra work alongside A levels, but generally considered a good thing to do. Friday afternoons are set aside for community service and fundraising activities.

Games, options, the arts: Stand-out sports facilities include large refurbished gym, modern dance studio and 25m indoor pool – all shared with junior school and open to pupils and their families at weekends and in the holidays. Plenty of tennis/netball courts also dotted around the grounds, although girls have to be taken by minibus to nearby Purley Leisure Centre for hockey and to David Weir Leisure Centre for athletics and annual sports day. Winter core sports are netball and hockey; and in summer, girls focus on tennis, rounders and athletics. For gym and swimming (both hugely popular), there are extracurricular clubs run by coaches and sporty girls compete in plenty of house and in local competitions (doing particularly well in county athletics and cross-country championships). But while the school reassured us sport is not just for the elite ('You're not made to feel irrelevant if you're not a really high achiever,' echoed one girl), a disappointingly high proportion of parents seem to dismiss their daughters as 'unsporty – so I couldn't really comment on sports provision.' At sixth form, sports offering expands to include the likes of bouldering, ultimate frisbee and badminton. Assortment of sports tours organised regularly to all parts of the globe.

The arts fare well across the school, particularly music, with dedicated music teachers, lots of practice rooms and music technology suite. Choirs include chamber (audition only), year 7/8 choir and mixed choir. Fine groups of young instrumentalists play in a range of ensembles and tuition can be arranged for any instrument. Consequently, there are some dynamic and well-thought-of orchestras. School hall recently transformed into performing arts space with raked seating and professional quality sound and lighting; drama is a popular GSCE and there's always some A level take-up. No whole school production, but plenty of single and joint year ones, plus joint drama productions (and music concerts) with the boys of Sutton Grammar.

Full range of art and design offered up to A level, with options including painting, pottery, textiles, and resistant materials – with lots of wow-factor examples (reassuringly current) displayed throughout the school, some on vast canvases, although perhaps not as avant-garde as we've seen at some schools. Light and airy art rooms to work in, including one dedicated to textiles and a separate sixth form art room 'so the girls at this level have their own space to focus on larger pieces of work,' explains head.

Before- and after-school clubs offer further opportunities for sports and music, plus some less predictable offerings such as robotics, Christmas crafts and a creative STEM club (where you make everything from bathbombs to ice cream). Most teachers run drop-in clinics to provide extra support for individuals and extension work. Residential trips a huge strength, with recent examples including year 8 trip to Dorset (annual), Iceland (geography) Geneva (science), Florence (art), Berlin (history), plus two annual ski trips and even (drum roll, please) Galapagos Islands every four years – just to name a few.

Background and atmosphere: Founded in 1884 with just a handful of pupils. Over the years, as pupil numbers have grown, neighbouring buildings have been purchased alongside a rolling building programme to keep pace with modern demands. Latest additions include the dance studio and extension to dining room ('It was a bit embarrassing before – not now!' says head – and we can vouch for the fact that it serves excellent food, with the fish pie we were served easily of dinner party standard). George's Café upstairs also available for more casual dining experiences for year 10s upwards (and all girls during break times). Sixth form centre is notable, with lovely modern spaces for work and play (including the fabulous top floor, appropriately named room The View with colourful couch and oodles of computers for focused work). Library is a decent size, including quiet and less quiet working areas – and to the girls' delight, not just books but DVDs to borrow too. 'You get them for three weeks, if you want,' a girl told us excitedly.

'My daughter has been happy and confident right from joining because of the way they have treated her, and the result has been that she's done really well academically'

In the midst of all the buildings (which feature the junior school on one side of the school and seniors on the other), well-maintained gardens and sports areas create a cloistered look, while inside the school is light and airy with neat noticeboards displaying useful information and some outstanding schoolwork. Busy pupils move round the site in an orderly way – but with a good sense of fun too. Girls have a good local reputation and the school is always interested in setting up community links, the most well-known being their work and artistic pursuits with Sutton Grammar.

Pastoral care, well-being and discipline: You'll be hard pushed to find a parent that doesn't reference the pastoral offering as the key strength of the school. 'Girls don't feel under pressure to be a certain way or certain type here and they're very supportive of each other,' said one. 'My daughter has been happy and confident right from joining aged 11 because of the way they have treated her, and the result has been that she's done really well academically,' said another – and that, really, sums up the philosophy of this school. 'We don't frown on competitiveness – for instance, we love our house competitions – but it doesn't seem to turn edgy,' says head, who says they very rarely come across classic problems such as eating disorders and self-harm. Approachable teachers, visiting counsellor (whom teachers are not afraid to refer girls to even for minor things), school nurse and clued-up head all help, believe parents and girls. 'I had one friend with some problems and the school got her back on track so quickly.' Also to the school's credit, all new entrants are allocated a buddy and form tutors and heads of year monitor academic progress, personal welfare and development with military precision. 'Leadership opportunities for the girls are in abundance,' added a parent – and student council helps compile the code of conduct in partnership with staff, giving everybody a chance to have their say. 'I like the way the school encourages girls to have a wide circle of friends. The attitude of "I've got my friends already, thanks," is wildly discouraged,' added another parent.

Detentions are the main sanction for misdemeanours ranging from late homework and messy uniform to inappropriate language, with a tiered system of short lunchtime detention, after school detention and (the most shameful) head's detention on a Friday afternoon. But most girls go through the school without one and head says bad behaviour 'just isn't an issue here,' with only one temporary exclusion in the last year. The school is even pretty relaxed about smartphones, with girls allowed them in lessons with permission – for example to take photos of the whiteboard instead of copying it all down, plus using the device for research where appropriate. Bullying rare. 'Girls can be bitches in any all-girls school – or any school, for that matter – but they seem to nip anything nasty in the bud here,' said one parent.

Pupils and parents: Good mix, socially and ethnically; lots of local business families and City types. Others travel from the edges of south west London and various parts of Surrey. School is conveniently located close to Sutton station so attracts a wide catchment, while school minibus services are available from Wimbledon, Southfields, Tadworth and Worcester Park. The Sutton High School Association (replacing the PTA that was going nowhere fast) means the parents get out of all the tedious logistical side of social and fundraising events, and just get to enjoy the fun bit. Old girls (reunions arranged twice a year) include Dora Black (Lady Russell), Susan Howatch, novelist, and Rt Hon Ruth Kelly, former Labour party politician.

Entrance: Around three applications for every place at year 7. Entrance by 11+ examination in maths,

English and online maths, verbal and non-verbal reasoning tests plus an interview with a senior member of staff. At 16+ (when around 10 new girls join) entrance test consists of general papers, verbal reasoning and interview with the head of sixth form. At least eight GCSEs, grade 7 or above in subjects chosen for A level.

Exit: Around 25-30 per cent leave at 16+, mostly to co-ed or grammar school sixth forms. 'The biggest reason given for girls leaving after GCSE is financial,' says the head. At 18+ more or less everybody goes to a wide variety of mostly top universities or art colleges, with currently popular choices including Leeds, Southampton, Exeter, Nottingham, Sheffield and the London unis. Science, maths and medicine courses for about half. Others to study history, languages and art, one gaining place on BBC Broadcast Engineering sponsored degree and apprenticeship. One to Oxbridge and one medic in 2019.

Money matters: Academic scholarships at 11+ and 16+ based on top performance in entrance or public exams. Other small scholarships awarded for art, music, drama and PE. Means-tested GDST bursaries are also available for up to 100 per cent fees.

Remarks: A small, friendly school suited to those who want a single sex education where girls don't get lost in a crowd. Pastorally, it is outstanding, with the school firm in its belief that if you ensure girls are happy and ready to learn then they will shine academically – which does indeed prove to be the case here.

The Tiffin Girls' School

Richmond Road, Kingston, Surrey KT2 5PL

020 8546 0773 | contact@tiffingirls.org | www.tiffingirls.org

State	Ages: 11–18	Pupils: 1,161; sixth form: 321

Head teacher: Since January 2016, Ian Keary BA NPQH, 40s. Previously head of school at highly rated Glyn, part of a multi academy trust in nearby Ewell, for three years, which he joined as deputy head in 2012. Reported to the overall executive head, the ideal way of developing leadership skills. Before that, eight years at Tiffin School (the boys' grammar, just down the road), four as assistant head.

Sporty (degree was in sports studies and English, gets vicarious fix these days as the father of two games and rowing mad sons), he's also warm, soft spoken and – as this reviewer can testify – generous with this time. He's proving a hit with parents and pupils, a tribute given that his appointment marks a definite change for school that's been used to heads of a different ilk – 'school-marmish,' as one mother put it.

Hands on, and how. Appears regularly in lessons, talks to pupils and even serves in the canteen. 'Doesn't want to seem too managerial,' said pupil. Teaches two IT lessons a week. Impressive given demands of the job and, he says, a good way of staying in touch with pupils and alleviating the admin-heavy side of his role (predictably puts in the hours wading through paperwork, much of it linked to applying for more money to improve the needier parts of the building).

Pastoral side appears to be big focus, feel parents – 'he really seems to care and that's true of a lot of the teachers as well,' thought one. His newsletters, balancing all aspects of school life, give a good insight into his leadership style. 'Everything gets equal mention,' said a parent who – like pupils – praised his unstinting attendance (close to 100 per cent) at school events. 'At every concert ... he's been there, get the impression that he supports everything round the school.' Also a good speaker, which plays well with highly articulate parents who put a premium on a nicely turned sentence.

He's thoroughly enjoying the job. Tolerant of new ideas if purpose and benefits are clearly presented by pupils (they will be); one of recent highlights was a tent in the foyer for rag week. That said, no plans for drastic changes – though office's previously pink walls are now white (similarly coloured chairs are on the wish list, pending spare cash).

He sees himself as a champion for young women – and a feminist. The goal is to ensure that pupils achieve don't just achieve academically (almost a given) but cope with setbacks, too. Ultimately it's 'about the passion and support that the staff show toward the girls ... and giving them the belief that they can go out and make a difference in the world.' Given the number of activities they manage here – 'You'll start thinking they're my senior leadership team,' jokes Mr Keary (well, we think he was joking) – he's ensuring they get off to a wonderful start.

Academic matters: Let's not beat about the bush – fabulous results are the alpha and omega here and the reason school is so wildly oversubscribed. They're so used to success here that anything below a 5 doesn't actually appear on their results info (for GCSEs). Even 6s are relatively rare. Not that this is exactly headline grabbing news given that it's pretty much the same story year in, year out. In 2019, GCSE results were 94 per cent 9-7, ditto (or very close) in previous years. At A level, 91 per cent of grades were A*-B and 73 per cent A*/A. Eleven GCSEs the norm – seven compulsory (including three sciences and a foreign language); three options from impressive list that includes Latin, DT and drama. Most start with four A levels and

drop one at the end of year 12, plus EPQ – some do extras out of school.

While competitive entrance exam guarantees fabulous brainpower, school's strength, say parents, is making sure teaching quality does more than merely take it for granted. Even Ofsted (which hasn't dropped in since 2009 – is this a record?) says that 'achievement is outstanding because the ... majority of pupils make the maximum progress possible...' Well spotted.

The place to develop your feminist agenda, thought one parent, approvingly. 'School is very good at getting 16-year-olds to be political and vocal'

We saw lessons whose total silence reflected the sustained concentration demanded by the task. No fidgeting, just immersion so total that visitors can tiptoe in and out again, pretty much unnoticed. In happy contrast, wonderfully lively year 7 French class practising letter sounds at high volume (and with authentic sounding) Gallic intonation could be heard a corridor away.

Some inevitable variation in teaching quality, reckoned pupils, but teachers 'all have passion for subject' and don't stint when it comes to offering extra support. Curriculum, too, has been rejigged – where possible – around big, ambitious themes that give context and perspective from the lower school up. You don't just study Frankenstein but take in the whole gothic movement while you're about it, while Grapes of Wrath forms part of the larger canvas of the great American novel – an approach that doesn't solemnly add enrichment to the syllabus but makes it an integral part. Analytical skills, too, are developed early. Year 8 pupils, for example, complete mini EPQ using null hypothesis model (a concept that this reviewer, unlike the pupils, had to go home and look up). Topics – eg impact of Pakistani culture on London and Londoners and impact of ethical issues on British shoppers – impressively analysed.

While girls excel in every area, STEM subjects are particularly big. There's nothing they don't do, from Arkwright scholarships (win a steady number) to UCL lectures, with 13 labs of different vintages catering for demand – physics, in particular, a growth subject seen as stepping stone to engineering-related courses.

Some parents felt school should help more with extra preparation and mock interviews required for high pressure entrance exams. School disagrees. 'We will provide opportunities but we're not going to do it for you,' says head. It's all there for the taking, confirm pupils, if you have the gumption to ask for it. One successful med school applicant had worked with teachers and other pupils to hone interview technique. 'Wouldn't have succeeded without it.'

Only area of weakness identified by historic inspection was inconsistencies in prose writing, now a focus for teaching, reading encouraged with a welcoming library/LRC re-sited in former atrium overlooking playing field, fiction section as big as factual titles.

Let's not beat about the bush – fabulous results are the alpha and omega here and the reason school is so wildly oversubscribed

Given admissions process, geared to selecting those able to cope with fast-paced, whole class teaching (teacher to pupil ratio is 16.5), unsurprising that relatively few pupils – currently just seven – have identified SEN. Mostly specific learning difficulties (mild), one with high functioning autism, none with an EHCP. EAL figures, in contrast look high at over 35 per cent but in practice only a small number need support. 'Many pupils are two to three generations in, so it's not so much of an issue.'

Only downside was the reports of tutoring, not just for the entrance exams (rife) but throughout school careers, including rumoured Saturday classes that cover the school curriculum a week in advance. Perhaps inevitable? – 'Will be the girls who never go out at university and work all the time,' thought one mother. 'Parental prerogative,' says Mr Keary, with resignation.

Inevitably, you don't come to a school like this without sky high expectations – shared by teachers, rightly ambitious for their pupils – 'daughter feels that would be letting the school down if didn't get the top grades'. Encouraging, though, that school and pupils are aware and honest about the pressures – and sense and sensibility prevail wherever possible. Recently, did away with year 7 end of year exams and pupils were clear on advice to avoid working all hours – though can be their own worst enemies.

'All very well saying to very conscientious girls only spend 40 minutes [on homework], but she will spend two hours,' said one parent. 'Difference with boys is if boys do badly in a test it was a rubbish test, if girls do badly, they think it's them. It's this sense of them always having to do very well and creates a cycle,' said mother.

Trips help leaven the intensity of the learning experience, helping staff and girls see each other in more relaxed mode: 'let their hair down – good for everyone,' said parent. School is budget conscious (if can get there by public transport, they will) now notifying parents of costs further in advance. One parent felt trips had been slightly thin on the ground. Plentiful now, counters school, from year 9 battlefields trip to year 11 geographers off to Swanage.

Also enjoyed are shared activities with the boys' school, including the Tuesday programme, aimed at thinking beyond the normal timetable. 'More would be great,' thought parent.

Staff clearly like it here – unusually there were no vacancies, teaching or otherwise, on the website. Only role on offer was that of governor – unpaid, still attracting many suitable applicants.

Games, options, the arts: The place to develop your feminist agenda, thought one parent, approvingly, particularly at sixth form level. 'School is very good at getting 16-year-olds to be political and vocal.' Debating here is flourishing, girls triumphing against some famous names and developing confidence and polish along the way.

All the big ticket activities like Duke of Edinburgh (bronze to gold medal) are on offer as well as clubs, some delightfully niche, set up by the girls – crochet, Scrabble and ukulele orchestra currently feature.

Girls do nothing by halves, from the cakes (featuring emojis and books) baked to celebrate the school's birthday, to year 9s' mini Young Enterprise scheme, importing and selling phone holders – making a cool £400 or so along the way. Also enter masses of competitions and events, from the arty (Kulturefest) to the digital (like Little Big Challenge, all about adding connectivity to everyday life). Pupils tend to sail through to the finals and very often win.

Sports – highly competitive (as you'd expect) with what parent describes as concentrated 'win, win, win,' approach – yield some good results, particularly at borough and county level. 'Girls who do it, do very well,' said parent. More encouragement for borderline enthusiasts would be good, felt another, echoed by some sixth formers who can drop all sport in their final year.

Art is sensational – GCSE works looks like A level, A level looks like degree show; we want it all. Much is on huge canvases – 'acts of bravery,' points out Mr K. Music, however, currently getting most parental applause, dynamic head of department felt to be taking performance of all sorts to new heights. Popular subject, with two GCSE classes, Pre-U rather than A level for sixth form, normally two to three going on to study at university, while many girls learn instruments – 200 individual lessons a week. The comments – 'Out of this world,' 'breathtaking,' 'of an incredible standard' – could have filled the entire review. Highlights many and various – from the ensembles to the recent 'very funny' production of Alice – with music written by pupil.

Background and atmosphere: All too easy to assume that fun has to be levered into the curriculum – a bolt on to the serious business of getting those results. Anything but. Painted towers of flower pots outside and mouthwatering display of knitted, ceramic and papier-mâché cakes in the foyer (theme: indulgence) are pointer for scope, variety and general excitement of life here.

Within minutes of arriving, we'd seen a catwalk rehearsal (pupils preparing to model their creations) and been treated to an astonishing and moving drama club improvisation themed to Frankenstein's monster with inarticulate howls (non-verbal unreasoning?) as well as laughter and tears. And this was just the lunchtime slot. School's well-named head of creativity (a smiling blur in the distance) must work round the clock.

Parents – and pupils – stressed time and time again that jollity is part and parcel of daily life. Take school birthday party celebration where everyone '… goes a bit bonkers, cheering and singing,' says mother. 'They seem to be allowed to have fun and be a bit silly and that's really important.'

Within minutes of arriving, we'd seen a catwalk rehearsal (pupils modelling their own creations) and an astonishing drama club Frankenstein–themed improvisation

It all happens on a stunning site, substantially rebuilt after fire, started by building workers (not in school hours, fortunately). End result was creation of light, airy new wing, with a new building for drama and DT under construction.

The older side, too, is improving: sixth form centre with three areas – socialising, work plus light chat, and silent study (complete with immaculate kitchen – 'we tidied it specially' – for hot drinks and microwaveable treats).

Bar slightly overgrown bits (moss sculptures in small back quad agreed to be past their best), site is well managed, girls very respectful of surroundings, bags neatly stowed, dining hall impressively clean at the end of busy lunchtime session – tribute to recently revamped menu.

Pastoral care, well-being and discipline: 'School will say make sure you get an early night and eat properly – it's obvious, but at least they're trying,' said pupil. Similarly, mega award ceremonies reward more than academic success. 'My daughter didn't get a single prize – but said it's not an issue because people know they're getting the prizes for effort.'

It's necessary, given mindset of these conscientious girls where, said one parent, 'Fragility of their self-confidence is an issue' – never more so on A level results day when tiny number miss out on the grades and university place. 'We want them to get into clearing as soon as possible,' says Mr Keary. Instant identification and removal for tea and sympathy on top of current system ('see member of staff' online flag when pupil first logs on to get results) would be on at least one parent's wish list.

Impressively, have ditched year 7 exams. Other initiatives include timetabled pastoral hour each week, flourishing pupil-run LGBT society, mental health ambassadors and promotion of role models from every culture. Sixth formers we spoke to, passionate about importance of every pupil feeling happy within own skin, praised school's willingness to implement their ideas – latest, administered by full time pastoral care specialist, is stress bucket, full, on day of visit, of hundreds of tightly folded notes, each an anonymous worry all the better for being jettisoned.

House system felt to be focus for good-hearted but intense competition (one of the head girls, officially neutral, had 'accidentally cheered for old house…'). Brings everyone together – sixth formers very conscious of visibility to younger pupils.

Strenuous efforts by the school see impressive turn of speed when issues need resolving. 'Something occurred on social media, contacted school early one morning, within 20 minutes had call from tutor … it was instant, so if you raise questions with them, they take it very seriously.'

Pupils and parents: Slight polarisation between socialite parents and those who take a back seat – paths usually set at the start of school life. The keen (via form reps) arrange year group meetings, meals out. 'It is sociable if you want it to be.'

We heard varying views on how well pupils got on – perhaps unsurprising in a large school. There were a couple of grumbles about monocultural friendship groups but most were frankly baffled by the idea. 'The girls mingle completely,' said one mother. 'Ethnic backgrounds don't make any difference.'

School keen to balance 'celebrity' and professional achievements of alumnae, who cover surprisingly large range. Creative element includes author Lynne Truss and writer Jan Etherington. Plenty of more conventional high flyers, from Grace Capel, human rights barrister, to award winning obstetrician Caroline Knight. Any other old girls cordially encouraged to contact alumnae organisation.

Entrance: At year 7, two-stage entry process, girls sitting maths and English tests in October, top scorers invited back for stage two in November. Priority for those qualifying for pupil premium funding who live within designated area made up of 44 postal districts (they now get a 10 per cent allowance in selection tests) – though postal districts can change (several have been removed) – so do check the admissions criteria regularly. 'If you live outside the catchment area, don't expect to get a place here,' says school.

For sixth form, minimum entry is eight GCSEs, four at grade 7 or better and four at grade 6 or better. Almost no places at any other point.

Exit: Single figures post-GCSE do not make it into sixth form, a few choose to study elsewhere (mostly to co-eds). In 2019, 30 Oxbridge places and 34 medics, plus four to study dentistry.

Money matters: Discretionary sixth form bursary fund – three types of funding depending on need. Paid monthly to recipients and designed to fund textbooks, trips, specialist equipment for specific subjects, travel to school. Additional direct bursaries available from the government for students classified as vulnerable – for example, living in care.

Remarks: Expect to be challenged, encouraged and inspired – but not spoon-fed. Robust of mind will have a ball. Asked why she came here, one year 7 pupil told us that she hadn't been certain at first as though friend had told her it was a nice school 'she didn't support her answer.' Fortunately an open evening provided all the evidence she needed.

Tiffin School

Queen Elizabeth Road, Kingston, Surrey KT2 6RL

020 8546 4638 | admissions@tiffin.kingston.sch.uk | www.tiffinschool.co.uk

State | Ages: 11–18 | Pupils: 1,260; sixth form: 393 (including girls)

Headteacher: Since 2015, Michael Gascoigne BA, 40s. Knows the school inside out – joined as history teacher after completing PGCE (Institute of Education) and training in some tough schools (think recreational chair-throwing). Subsequently became head of history here (1999), head of sixth form (2004) and deputy head (2009) – each promotion fortuitously happening just when was debating looking elsewhere (no coincidence, we suspect).

First generation in family to go to university, bursary to independent school firing career ambitions, though initially directed at policing or law. All changed when he took a temporary teaching post and thoroughly enjoyed it.

Humane, as articulate as his pupils (and that's a big compliment), he's a thoroughly likeable man who understands how boys tick and values his staff (he ensured teachers' room got much needed refurb ahead of other deserving projects).

It's no cinch. Constant pressure on budgets (spends a lot of time fundraising), and dealing with problems out of his control are the main downsides – as (occasionally) are the hours he puts in. Arrives at 7am and leaves whenever ('wife would say it's

not early enough'). We'd suspect it's often close to 12 hour day, plus Saturday mornings.

All so far outweighed by the good parts, headed by relish for challenges ahead. 'No virtue in standing still,' he says – putting it into action with three million pound building programme and forging ahead with plans to ensure school becomes an ever more influential local presence through outreach and collaboration. 'A lovely guy, approachable, reassuring,' was one parent's verdict. Combines insider knowledge with at least one eye on future developments. 'No shoe-filler,' thought parent. 'Has his own ideas and agenda.'

Academic matters: Rich balance of subjects from year 7 based on fortnightly timetable. Slightly more English in first year, separate sciences from year 8 but, impressively, keep up art and music as well. Latin for all, also religion and philosophy and fortnightly session on 21st century life. Everyone takes separate sciences, one language and (unusually for non-religious school) religion and philosophy at GCSE plus three options ranging from humanities to Latin and Greek, PE, dance (a rarity anywhere, let alone in maintained sector) and DT.

Sixth form choice of around 20 A level subjects – including those rarities, Latin and Greek (maths, sciences and economics consistently popular), plus games session and non-examined enrichment course (with Tiffin Girls).

Class sizes (average of 30 to end of year 9 dropping to 24 in GCSE years and 16 in the sixth form) no barrier to exceptional results. In 2019, 75 per cent of GCSEs graded 9-7; 59 per cent A*/A at A level (84 per cent A*-B).

And not a question of taking the best, shoving on to academic conveyor belt and letting them off again at the other end (though with the prizes coming thick and fast, from Arkwright Scholarships to 99 boys gaining gold certificates in Junior Maths Olympiad or the Junior Kangaroo and year 13s winning the Student Investor Challenge – top out of 10,000 teams – they probably could). Progress 8, new government assessment tool, puts school in top five per cent for the value it adds between year 6 and year 11 – so complacency certainly isn't the order of the day.

Staff stability helps (20 on the books for at least 10 years – average age of teachers is 40 and 44 for all staff) – though recruitment as problematic here as anywhere else in London – property prices mean 'move out in droves'. Magic ingredient is school itself. 'There's an attachment that grows on you,' says Mr Gascoigne. Some churn is healthy – 'don't want all staff to be here for years and years' – but with most teachers leaving for senior posts elsewhere, controllable, so new staff can learn in an experienced department.

Ability to suck up facts may be profound (it certainly impressed us) but these boys don't tolerate dull teaching. 'It is not good enough to sit at the front and feed them facts'

Subjects generally organised by corridor (and door colour – though with pea green for geography, dark green for physics and something between the two for biology, it pays to mug up on pantones). Doesn't take long to work out where you are, say pupils and in any case, there are plenty of clues, like the helmet ('Norman,' said tour guide, authoritatively) in history office and pickled lobster-like creature ('a crayfish – has flatter and wider tail') outside the science rooms, though guide voiced slight disapproval at location – 'out of place, should be biology when this is clearly chemistry.'

School catches boys in magic few years between arriving packed with enthusiasm and ideas and losing it to adolescent cynicism, says head. One boy arrived in sixth form with a fascination for fungi. 'Not the usual thing but we knew he'd love it here.' Helps to be proactive about trying new things, we were told by pupil, though come as you are and you'll be accepted. 'Here it's cool to care about knowledge,' agreed school insider. Certainly true of tour guides, thrilled to be here, erudite and delightfully tickled by oddities of school life – the mystery bricked up door 'to nowhere', the religion and philosophy office – 'strangely placed as the classroom is downstairs.'

Perhaps unsurprisingly, few pupils have statement of SEN – just 0.2 per cent, a tenth of the national average. That said, school caters for range of learning needs – though at 31, numbers are still low – ranging from hearing and sight problems to specific learning needs and Asperger's. Support comes via TA plus part-time additional needs literacy specialist who helps boys with dyslexia or organisational issues.

To teachers with the right approach (and parents struggled to find any without), they're a dream audience. Homework is 'about right,' thought pupil – neither excessive nor inflicted with a heavy hand. Instead, teachers will guide rather than lead, mention for example that there's a test coming up and leave the boys to make the connection.

Ability to suck up facts may be profound (it certainly impressed us) but these boys don't tolerate dull teaching. 'It might sound naughty,' said one (it doesn't, honest), 'but if I'm sitting in physics being lectured on the forces acting on a ball falling from the sky, I'm likely to be less interested than if I'm looking at a cross section of a cell' (they build their own from plaster of Paris and plasticine and they're awe-inspiring). Head agrees. 'It is not good enough to sit at the front and feed them facts. You need to know your subject, and to encourage them always to ask questions – that's how they learn.'

Games, options, the arts: Breathtaking. Just one issue of fortnightly head's newsletter (essential reading if you want a cross section of day-to-day life here) included the latest school trips (GCSE and A level art students to Venice, year 9 classics to Bath, year 7 to London Zoo), sporting success (cross-country) and performing arts, with 'particularly active' dancers doing their stuff at half time during the Four Nations rugby final at Olympic Park and working with the Royal Ballet and Ballet Rambert. Year 8s learn capoeira, a couldn't-be-better fusion of dance and martial arts. Pirouettes have never before packed such a punch.

Sign up for the choir and pupils could end up performing with world class orchestras – Mahler's third with the LSO, Stravinsky with the LPO and Tannhaüser at the Royal Opera House in just the last few months, plus choir tours all over the place, as well as appearing on the Blankety Blank

Christmas special hosted by David Walliams. They're not blasé, though can be tiring. 'Came back from Royal Opera House and fell asleep in my uniform,' said one veteran.

There's something to impress wherever your eye, or ear, falls, from art (surreal paper scissors and screwdrivers, mounted on clock mechanisms and ticking away the hours – message, if there is one, too deep for this reviewer), to rugby – 16 teams – almost a quarter of all pupils, who regularly give independent sides a drubbing – and rowing. Saunter through nearby Canbury Gardens of a Saturday and you'll often see boats waiting to be launched and some of the 100 boys involved warming up with a few laps by the bandstand – one of the few state schools to offer it at all, let alone on this scale.

Other sports – cricket (main summer sport), basketball, badminton, tennis, cross-country and athletics – are also available and to equally high standards.

Timetable helps, with music, drama and dance allocated six periods between them in year 7 – more if you add on games – and equal to science or maths. Means school 'can grab you early,' said parent, who'd seen son suddenly (and unexpectedly) blossom into a talented singer. 'Everyone's got something different to them,' said one.

Sometimes spark a new idea (one year 8 boy, initially reluctant to try dance, had already reached post-GCSE level; another had done 15 nights on stage at the Royal Opera House). But it's not just the conventional who flourish. 'If they want to learn the sitar or electric guitar or bongo drums then teachers let them,' said parent. 'The point is that they realise that the pleasure out of music is performance.' Top singers may end up as choral scholars but first year string players, scratchily delivering first orchestral performance, will get equal levels of applause.

'We encourage participation way beyond the lessons – school is not just about simply collecting the certificates,' says the head – and pupils praise resulting diversity. Trips are vital part of the process – and not just educationally. 'Playing pool in the evening changes things, you see boys in a different light,' says the head. And while missing lessons does create practical issues, school's view is that benefits outweigh need to catch up later.

In a day that stretches well beyond either end of official hours (dance rehearsals starting at 6.30am were the earliest we discovered – though choir, drama and sport require similar commitment) boys' ability to manage all their interests and academic work on top can be a worry to parents. Some, naturally organised, learn self-management early. But even the borderline chaotic somehow get through. 'My chronically disorganised son coped because he really wanted to do it,' said parent.

'Trips are vital and not just educationally. Playing pool in the evening changes things, you see boys in a different light,' says head

Background and atmosphere: Three cheers for Thomas and John Tiffin, brothers and wealthy Kingston brewers who between them left £150 in the 1630s to invest in the education of deserving boys. Canny investment in land by executor did their memories proud, though it wasn't until the late 19th century that eponymous school was finally opened (original site now home to local primary). They moved to current location in 1929, acquiring 30 acres of playing fields in Thames Ditton in 1948 (now owned by the old boys to kybosh any thoughts by rapacious governments of cashing it in for housing). Became voluntary aided, converted to academy in 2010 and are currently keeping close eye on opportunities created by potential expansion of grammar schools.

We don't doubt that J and T Tiffin would be chuffed with what their legacy has achieved. Behind the public persona of the horribly packed and inevitably anonymous open days is a warm, friendly school that's hard to leave. Many don't – or not for long. In quick succession we met retired deputy head, now back as a governor and unofficial archivist (school can trace every old boy since 1880) and former pupil, now a PE teacher here. 'Feels like home,' he said. 'I've even used my house key to try to get into the sports hall.'

Warmth extends to the admin team who keep cool while staying on top of copious amounts of lost property, from Tupperware packed with spectacles to the many missing bags – 'boys pick up the nearest one if worried about being late.' Jumpers ditto.

Pupils notice and respond. Helpful, caring teachers are 'best thing about the school,' said one, who had successfully mounted campaign to get a school corn snake (sadly on study leave – or serpentine equivalent – on day of visit). 'Wasn't dismissed as a silly idea.' Head finally gave blessing – once proper care plan had been presented and agreed.

From head's formal garden with sundial and homely bird feeders (lovingly tended by gardening parent) to cricket pitch, and MUGA surface which ...'is a pitch,' says head (amid in the swirl of jargon about multi-surfaces, G4s and suchlike, all you really need to know), site is greener and bigger than partial views from the three streets (and modern flats) that frame it would suggest. (Art rooms, appropriately, provide best panoramic view.)

Definitely has its architectural moments, from historic – attractive 18th century listed building housing classrooms, uniform shop and IT (marked by dainty china figurines) – to last century (1990s art and DT block). There's also cutting edge modernity in attractive two storey circular learning resource centre, bookcases radiating out from central desk and complete with spiral staircase inside (sixth form only) and sedum roof (outside).

Its twin has now emerged home to a stunning new dining hall, with five new classrooms and an IT suite up top, replacing the previous incarnation housed in a vintage Portakabin. Food is more than a match for the new surroundings: sweet and sour chicken and pasta with basilico sauce among the highlights.

Outside, careful design with smaller footprint will add more playground space and greater streetside appeal with glassed windows even offering reflections of the 14th century Lovekyn Chapel, the oldest building in town (though they don't own it – rather to their relief given the costs of upkeep). Means more streetside appeal for this distinctly average patch of Kingston – so a public benefit.

Though money is invariably tight (and tighter here than many assume), careful juggling ensures it goes where most needed. Yes, a few tatty staircases could do with a paint job but the displays are bang up-to-date, performance spaces are many and varied and even the gothic-windowed, red-curtained old style school hall also has thoroughly modern lighting rig. While Macs reign supreme in IT, spick and span food technology room stays well up to temperature and DT, still offered to A level (one of the only local schools to do so) remains beautifully dovetailed, nobody's complaining.

Pastoral care, well-being and discipline: School can't take on all the weight of world's anxieties, says Mr Gascoigne. Pressure to succeed – 'not unique to selective schools,' he points out – that flows down from management to teachers and pupils isn't helpful but can be overemphasised – and certainly the pupils we saw seemed notably uncrushed and extremely cheerful.

He sees social media demanding instant response, impossible to switch off, as a greater contributor to anxiety. School works with mental health worker who's in school for a day and a half each week and includes drop in system. 'We can't solve every mental health problem but can do best to help,' he says.

Merits for good work, contributions to lessons, attitude and helpful acts (in that order) more sparingly awarded after year 7. Lead to certificates, presented in assembly. Best of the lot is head's certificate (platinum) though it doesn't come along often. Dark face of the coin, demerits, treated with caution by teachers.

While will always be the odd behavioural issue and very occasional exclusion (for normal offences), it doesn't happen often. Most other difficulties (occasional missing laptop key) are caused by overdoing the joie de vivre that's inevitable consequence of considerable freedom. IT rooms, with prefect supervision, open at break, for example. 'Boys are not yet the finished product – will make mistakes, do things they shouldn't do. We're ultimately training them for independence and maturity in the real world,' says Mr Gascoigne.

Merits for good work and helpful acts lead to certificates, presented in assembly. Best of the lot is head's certificate (platinum) though it doesn't come along often

There's much talk here of levels of happiness. Competition kicks in early – brilliant for bonding. Houses have recently increased from six to eight with rise in pupil numbers – one year 8 pupil, who'd moved as a result, initially very torn, though now wearing new tie with great pride – though form competitions, starting early in year 7, are also hard-fought. 'We sung [sic] our hearts and souls out,' writes first year pupil in newsletter of inter-form singing competition held within weeks of joining the school.

Pupils and parents: You find generations of local families who have come here, as well as fair share of celebrities, more tending towards performing arts and sport than straight brainbox, Nobel-winning fame as you might possibly expect.

Big hitters (literally in some cases) include sportsmen Alex Stewart (cricket) and Rob Henderson (rugby) as well as artist John Bratby and Jonny Lee Miller, an ex-husband of Angelina Jolie (probably happier being noted for starring role in Elementary). School is mounting major drive to round up alumni (especially the successful City types) and encourage them to do their bit for support.

Many current families need no urging. Joining the PTA is a good way to get in the swim and there are also subject-specific spin off groups fundraising for rugby, rowing and – probably the busiest of the lot – music. Each has own little community – 'Have got a whole load of new friends,' said one mother.

Main ethnic groups are white British, Indian and Asian. Area isn't immune from deprivation and school argues good case for looking beyond official government tally of disadvantaged pupils based on free school meals. If assessed based on other measures – postcodes, social class and levels of education (significant number of parents didn't go to uni, for example) – school's intake broader than it appears. Keen to broaden mix still further, in line with government thinking – possibly through changes to admissions policy. Definitely a case of watch this space.

Entrance: Entrance day could be a tourist attraction all on its own, Kingston streets packed with small boys and their parents queuing to get in. Same crowds turn up in Sutton and even Slough to try their luck at selective schools there, says head, so not as daunting as it looks.

Admissions now favour locals after considerable legal to-ing and fro-ing overturned previous cross-London (and further) free for all. Now there's an inner priority area of within 10km of the school and an outer priority area extending 14km to Kingston, Wimbledon, Thames Ditton, Surbiton, Richmond, Hounslow. Better all round, says head, shorter journey times ensuring that more can enjoy the before- and after-school activities.

Also more places – now 180 year 7 places (was 120 just a few years ago) allocated in two-stage admissions process, each consisting of English and maths assessments, weighted so as not to disadvantage younger candidates, with some priority for those on pupil premium. Some occasional places in other years – new candidates only: those sitting but unsuccessful at 11+ can only try again

for sixth form, when need (as do existing pupils) minimum five 7s and three 6s at GCSE with 9-7s in three desired A level subjects. Around a third of sixth form, now including girls, are new.

'Didn't think I'd get in,' said pupil remembering the agonising wait after merry round of entrance exams. One family was poised to accept independent school place, knowing that fees would be a struggle. 'Would have been the unluckiest boy in the school. Here, feel like the luckiest.'

Exit: Vast majority to Russell Group and regular large contingent to Oxbridge (22 in 2019, plus 17 to medical school).

Money matters: Asks for voluntary donation – if possible £520 a year per child, to some a chunky sum. Understood that won't be affordable for everyone – pay what you can. Over the years, it's funded goodies including new labs and cricket nets – and there's also (discreet) help with uniform costs and school trips for those in need.

Remarks: Engage, inspire, excel, is the motto. It's more like a check list than an exhortation. Delivers 'well rounded, well read, normal human beings,' said a parent. 'It's an independent education provided by the state and we are very fortunate.'

Tower House Preparatory School

188 Sheen Lane, London SW14 8LF

020 8876 3323 | admissions@thsboys.org.uk | www.thsboys.org.uk

Independent	Pupils: 190
Ages: 4-13	Fees: £13,548 – £15,357 pa

Headmaster: Since 2009, Greg Evans BSc MA PGCE. Was director of studies at Sussex House for five years and at Kings House Richmond for nine years before that. Early 50s. Genuinely loves his job and lives for the school. 'I always put the boys first. I keep their interests front and centre when making any decisions,' he explains. Wife is Icelandic, and they regularly escape to their place in Reykjavík. Teenage son and daughter. Self-confessed sports nut. Recently taken up spinning at the gym in an attempt to stay fit. Currently enjoying the challenge of learning the trumpet for first time. 'I am not an empire-builder, but I like to think I have improved

the place.' Boys adore him; parents hold him in high esteem. An exceptionally dedicated head.

Entrance: Non-selective. First 18 to register are guaranteed a place. Siblings very rarely turned down – 'there would have to be something spectacularly wrong, as family is at the core of what we do.' Places generally fill up three years in advance with bulging waiting lists, so sensible to put names down as soon as possible. Not unknown for parents to check out the school before their son is born. Occasional places further up the school are snapped up quickly. 'We could probably almost double in size tomorrow, but we wouldn't be the same school.

People come to us for a reason. We are the only single-sex, single-form boys' prep school in south west London and we are not giving up that niche on my watch!' states head.

Exit: St Paul's, Hampton, Reeds School and Epsom College currently the most popular destinations, with others off in ones to eg Harrow, Millfield, Eton, Sherborne and Wellington. Head states, 'From a recent cohort of 20, I am very proud that boys went to 15 different schools. We make sure that the boys go to a school that is suitable for them. I tell parents very plainly to their faces that if I think they are trying to send their son to a school where they are going to be unhappy, that this will effectively be a mental scar on them all the way into adulthood.' Parents feel head knows their sons inside out and that he offers well-informed advice. Robust numbers of art, music, drama and sports scholarships. Vast majority stays through until 13; only a handful has left at 11 in the last few years.

Remarks: School is located on a residential street in East Sheen, on the edge of Richmond Park. No rolling acres but school is creative with space it does have. The façade is not beautiful, though the new build for reception pupils is a great improvement on the Victorian privies that it has replaced.

Warm, happy, family feel to the school, but it is nevertheless ambitious. One form entry with 18 in reception, roughly 20 per class thereafter. One mother commented that its small size was one of its selling points: 'Boys all know each other well and that gives them confidence.'

Junior and senior sections on same site, with plenty of interaction between the two. Older boys hear younger ones read and help them out at lunchtime. A healthy amount of hero worship goes on. Junior school considered to be gentle by parents, a place where little boys can be little boys. Every Friday morning reception boys head for the forest school where they build dens, climb trees and jump in muddy puddles. Some parents we spoke to felt that the transition from one part of the school to the other was hard: 'It's a big leap to go from such a nurturing junior school to a full-speed London prep at the end of year 3, but this has to happen at some stage.'

Emphasis on impeccable manners: boys are expected to shake their teacher's hand and look them in the eye as they say goodbye at the end of each day. Head wants them to look back on their prep school with a sense of pride. 'We send well rounded, polite but humble young men on to their next schools.'

House system is at the centre of the school. Boys are apparently more scared of getting a rocket from their head of house than the headmaster. 'They don't want to let the side down. We're a small

school and it is very apparent if you stick your head above the parapet. We have a sense of collective responsibility here'. Community spirit is important. Pupils play music at local care homes, clear the river bank of weeds and regularly raise money for charity.

Head beams when he talks about the drama here: 'I have the most gifted head of drama in the country. Boys will crawl over broken glass for him'

No academic scholarship class 'as it would be divisive and that goes against everything that we stand for.' If a child is sitting a scholarship, then teachers put on supplementary lessons as necessary. Though uncommon here, head believes that tutoring is a mistake: 'If your son needs to be tutored to the hilt to squeeze into a school then you're doing him a disservice and you are setting him up for a fall in the future'. Head aims to deliver a bespoke education, 'a Harley Street approach'.

Most able boys are well stretched, with setting in some subjects from year 3 onwards. According to one mother, the top set for Latin in year 8 certainly gallops along at a fair crack. One parent commented that 'if your son is clever, he will do very well at Tower House. The average boy finds it a little harder.' Another disagreed and felt that, given its non-selective intake, the school caters successfully for all abilities.

Reading is taken seriously and a reading wall records numbers of books read by each boy during the term. For the group of pupils who reads the most, a huge bag of sweets awaits. Library is enticing: jam-packed with adventure books and offset by jazzy mood lighting.

Currently 35 have some sort of mild special educational need, usually dyslexia. Small group booster sessions offered; 10 per cent receive individual support from full-time SENCo. Rare for a boy to need support throughout his time here.

Very successful on sports front. The envy of every other prep school in London with its access to the Bank of England's beautifully manicured sports grounds, just a stone's throw away. Excellent sports tuition from a host of specialist coaches. Head smiles, 'We've moved away from the enthusiastic history teacher coaching the first XI!' School is particularly strong at cricket, reflected in its eagerly-anticipated biennial sports tour to Barbados. All senior boys included, irrespective of sporting prowess. All boys from years 3 to 8 make a team of some sort. One father stated that 'Tower

House can hold its own with the great names in the prep school landscape.'

'Art in every form is stretched and pushed here and it constantly amazes me. If you are creative you should come to us,' states head. Inspirational art teacher is supported by two talented artists in residence. Fantastic DT – boys keen to get out the saws, vices and hammers at every opportunity. Music is thriving too and 80 per cent learns an instrument. There is something for everyone on the music front including numerous choirs and ensembles.

Drama deservedly gets the headlines. Head beams when he talks about the drama here: 'I have the most gifted head of drama in the country. Boys will crawl over broken glass for him. He has ambitions for the boys which many other people wouldn't even consider. We see how far we can push it'. To date, Tower House is the only school, prep or senior, that has produced a full-length feature film which premiered in the West End. Head explains, 'We don't try to replicate that every year, though, as it would take over and we'd get a reputation for being a bunch of luvvies!' Head sees drama productions as being great team-building exercises as everyone can contribute, from the uber-confident thespian who delivers impassioned speeches to the lower-key boys who would rather focus on props or lighting. The current record is 91 boys involved in one performance. Here, as elsewhere, school lives by its motto of 'an opportunity for every boy'. Starry ex-pupils include comedian Jack Whitehall and actor Robert Pattinson.

Pastoral care is a priority. School has ring-fenced well-being and resilience sessions every half term. Boys are encouraged to de-stress regularly, whether through yoga classes, practising meditation or running before school in Richmond Park. 'We aim to give the boys the toolkit by which they can face the pressures of modern life'. Head has noticed outside pressures on the boys are increasing, not only academically but also on the co-curricular front, such as selection for sports teams and musical ensembles. 'Parents sometimes over-expect,' he laments.

Current clubs include debating, chess, touch-typing, sewing and maths games. One parent we spoke to felt that the clubs on offer could be more ambitious and less sport-centric.

School aims to make fees as all-inclusive as possible, so parents do not have to keep reaching for the cheque book throughout the term. Unlike many schools, learning support lessons, clubs and residential trips are not seen as extras. Full and part funded means-tested bursaries available from year 3.

Mostly professional families. Both parents tend to work. Excellent communication between school and home. Parents give talks to boys about their careers, in a variety of fields including medicine, law and journalism. Cosmopolitan mix, including significant numbers of Scandinavians and Spaniards at present. Head has introduced a grandparents' day and thinks it is important to involve them in their grandchildren's education, particularly as so many of them foot the fees.

A remarkably inclusive school that feels like a traditional boarding prep. One mother commented that 'it does what it says on the tin. It prepares them very well for senior school'. Another parent went further: 'The headmaster and his staff have one single objective – that of educating boys to the highest possible standard, whilst nurturing extracurricular talent, instilling courtesy and the highest moral values.' Undoubtedly, Tower House is thriving.

Unicorn School (Richmond)

37

238 Kew Road, Richmond, Surrey TW9 3JX

020 8948 3926 | registrar@unicornschool.org.uk | www.unicornschool.org.uk

Independent	Pupils: 173
Ages: 3–11	Fees: £7,170 – £13,170 pa

Headmaster: Since 2013, Kit Thompson BA (Oxford Brookes), PGCE (Roehampton) (late 40s), previously deputy head (academic) of Twyford in Hampshire where his wife teaches part-time. Initially a banker, he chose teaching early in his marriage becoming an NQT at The Unicorn, staying three years with English specialism. 'What attracted me back to the Unicorn was the school's distinctive ethos, a parent-owned family school and broad curriculum with its emphasis on creativity, laughter and learning.'

Commuting from Winchester, with a family Wimbledon bolthole when necessary, he enjoys the balance in his life. Three teenage daughters keep him busy and he relaxes by playing tennis, golf, or taking long walks with the family labrador. Holidays in Cornwall rather than exotic destinations and he has been known to accompany the biennial school ski trip.

Mr Thompson enjoys guiding the school forward, taking the articulate, highly-involved parents – some of them Old Unicorns – and grandparents with him, and has no immediate thoughts of moving on. Proud of the excellent inspection findings in his third year, he has made changes quietly but purposefully. The head's office has relocated from the top floor to beside reception and front door, making him very accessible; appreciated by staff and pupils alike.

Unchanged is his commitment to the school's ethos, which all newcomers, staff and parents, must buy into. Opening the front door at 8.20am, he enjoys welcoming all and seeing, as we witnessed, 'pupils smiling, relaxed but not disrespectful', just as they are when he takes lessons, break duties or assemblies. He knows the entire school community by name, as he told us. 'A great strength is the size of the school and the constant conversations.'

Entrance: Into nursery in September after child's third birthday with places offered from 18 months prior to entry, so parents say 'you almost have to put your name down at birth'. Siblings and children of past pupils are given priority. Arrival in other years involves assessment in English and, in juniors, maths. Single form entry throughout with maximum of 22. Slight movement at 7+ for variety of reasons, including relocation and occasional misfit between pupil and school. Up to 100 per cent means-tested bursaries available. One parent described how welcoming the school is, praising helpful office staff, and how 'teachers interviewed my child's bunny and Mr Thompson interviewed my daughter on a seesaw which completely put her at ease'.

Exit: Most popular recent destinations Harrodian, Ibstock Place, Kew House, Kingston Grammar and St James Boys, and most head for London day schools. Some off boarding at eg Charterhouse, Downe House and Tudor Hall, others to state schools eg Grey Court, Tiffin Boys and Girls and the West London Free School. Head liaises with local schools and is an inspector with boarding and day experience. He believes, 'Everyone's got to trust. I hope and expect parents to trust us.' With the help of deputy and assistant head he offers guidance over future school choices with a range of options and parents feel supported throughout: 'He steps in when necessary.'

Remarks: Founded in 1970 by parents seeking an alternative to what they judged to be education without creative spark, The Unicorn is a registered charity and a limited company by guarantee with parents members whilst their children attend the school. Governors are board directors and since Mr Thompson's arrival, there are two co-chairs, one parent and one non-parent. Housed in an attractive, double fronted Victorian villa, the school benefits from being opposite Kew Gardens, close to Richmond Park. Games take place in Chiswick at Dukes Meadow and the University of Westminster playing fields, with swimming nearby at Pools on the Park.

'Teachers interviewed my child's bunny and the head interviewed my daughter on a seesaw which completely put her at ease'

Originally considered bohemian, not so now, the school has retained its special ethos – as current Old Unicorn parents we spoke to emphasised – of providing a child-centred education. 'A wonderful place to learn, creative and allowing for children's individuality'. Most pupils are local: from Kew, Richmond, East Sheen, Chiswick, Barnes, Twickenham, St Margaret's and Ham with some within walking distance. There is a healthy mix of Europeans and a steady flow from the Far East.

The curriculum includes specialist taught science, computing, music, creative arts, French and PE. Time is set aside every day for reflection and developing thinking skills: Brain Time in years 3 and 4, philosophy lessons for years 5 and 6. Classes divided into groups of 11 for many specialist subjects, maximising facilities and excellent staff:pupil ratio. Parents explained, 'They gently ease the pupils towards 11+, putting the right focus on 11+ preparation without narrowing the curriculum'.

No formal EAL lessons, instead pupils are catered for in the classroom. School has identified about 25 pupils as having special educational needs but does not claim to cater for severe learning difficulties. One parent we spoke to with an older child identified on the autistic spectrum thought the school lacked experience dealing with this, but praised the head, 'who has bent over backwards to help', and the head of learning support, who has ensured staff have been given further training. Additional learning support is provided in pairs or small groups with some one-to-one expertly coordinated by well qualified staff. Parents pay for these lessons but they are subsidised by the school. Individuals are given differentiated work,

and reading books are chosen with librarian's guidance. Touch typing is offered after school.

Every Thursday afternoon year 3s upwards enjoy 12 or so extremely popular extracurricular clubs, mostly covered by fees with contributions for the priciest. Compulsory debating one term for year 5s, good preparation for interviews, and parents are actively involved. Some ferry pupils to Ham for riding, Slough for sailing, others lead cookery or gardening clubs. We saw enthusiastic potters, artists creating marbled eggs, others learning fencing. After-school clubs include La Jolie Ronde French, chess, karate, modern dance, musical theatre, choir, music theory and swimming, and end at 4.45pm. Juniors attend residential trips in Surrey, Cornwall and Cumbria.

This is not a manicured, purpose-built environment but a well-maintained, stimulating, setting with happy children engaged in learning, as we witnessed in a year 4 group mathematics session on problem-solving using an interactive board. Age groups are mixed: older pupils listen to younger pupils reading; year 6s travel with nursery pupils to swimming. Staff often team teach so there is plenty of communication about the children. Underpinning this is assessment data which includes emotional as well as academic information and signals to staff if a pupil is anxious or needs intervention promptly. Pupils describe their teachers as 'friendly and fair' and parents agree, 'they really know your child'. Inspectors judged teaching to be 'excellent, challenging pupils and fostering interest'. Parents of older pupils explained how their children were always busy, extended with differentiated work, including different text books, and setting in English and mathematics. Recent use of puzzles and riddles and reasoning for all has gone down well as school prepares for entrance examination shift. Many praised 'a bespoke education'. Parents seeking loads of formal testing, drilling and grading might well find this approach disconcerting.

Pupils are encouraged to be confident, as we saw in a polished year 4 assembly on Romans and Celts involving drama and music, revealing pupils' considerable knowledge of the topic. 'My child was a real ankle clinger when he arrived, and now he has become a public speaking competition winner and happily played his saxophone in front of hundreds of Cubs'. Weekly drama leads to school productions such as year 5's Macbeth and year 6's The Rocky Monster Show.

Elected school council representatives and head boy and head girl change termly. A house system has recently been introduced. Pupils like the competition and encouragement to gain house points. Staff ensure individual's strengths are recognised. As one parent applauded, 'it could be a certificate for being a smiley person or helpful in the playground, or for knowing all the dates of the kings and queens of England'. The assembly hall rainbow mural displays unicorns on distinct colour-coded paths (as each class is a rainbow colour, beginning with red and concluding with ultraviolet), for demonstrating the 14 Unicorn virtues. Recently behaviour has been a focus, with teachers and volunteers paying attention to the consistent application of the school's code of conduct.

The broad curriculum and creativity are fundamental. Musicians perform regularly. The Unicorn Singers have won competitions including gold in the junior vocal ensemble at the Richmond Festival, and reached the national finals of youth festivals. Three-quarters of the pupils learn an instrument.

Many praised 'a bespoke education'. Parents seeking loads of formal testing, drilling and grading might well find this approach disconcerting

Separated from the main building by the large playground is a coach house with spacious ground floor provision for early years, with walled garden and mud kitchen. We climbed the narrow staircase to a newly established spacious, light, well-equipped art room with its two specialist teachers. We admired a year 5 collage inspired by Holbein's Two French Ambassadors, part of their work on the Tudors. Witty and carefully executed, the left-hand figure sported the photographed head of Mr Thompson, and the right that of his deputy. Observant pupils had accurately reproduced the entrance hall's Victorian tiles, as well as the head's brown shoes and deputy's striking trainers. There is a kiln but no DT room, although puppets and models are made in organised workshops. Recently all classes drew on the theme of Kew Gardens, collaborating with animation artists to produce a short film. Unsurprisingly, the school has been awarded a gold Artsmark.

Kitchen on site: hot food was the only thing pupils suggested could be improved about their school, although parents seem happy with the menus.

Space is at a premium. The playground is made good use of with an Astroturf netball/football/running around area in one half and exciting play equipment in the other. This might deter parents who prefer more on-site games areas for their sporty offspring. Fixtures in netball, hockey, rounders and cricket for girls; football, hockey and cricket for boys. Recent successes in swimming, hockey, football and netball tournaments.

Involving parents throughout, The Unicorn is a welcoming, community, 'not a finishing school for primary pupils,' explained one parent, comparing it with other local schools. All agree 'it combines being nurturing with achieving high academic standards and creatively developing individual's strengths'. Parents who prefer to be distanced from school or whose primary focus is academic success with regular testing and regimentation may not find the ethos suits. 'Children are happy, not pushed in a certain direction', say parents, whilst articulate, relaxed pupils are full of praise for their teachers and school.

Wallington County Grammar School

Croydon Road, Wallington, Surrey SM6 7PH

020 8647 2235 | enquiries@wcgs.org.uk | www.wcgs-sutton.co.uk

State	Ages: 11–18	Pupils: 1,096; sixth form: 349 (57 girls)

Head of school: Since 2016, Jamie Bean BA (30s). First degree in history and ancient history from the University of Nottingham. Unusually, he has worked his way up the school since joining in 2004 as teacher of history and classics, touching every step on the ladder from year leader to deputy on the way – pointing out there isn't a job in the senior leadership team he didn't try for size during colleagues' maternity leaves. He teaches a year 9 history class and a year 10 classics class, on which an appreciative parent commented: 'He teaches our son classics with tremendous verve and enthusiasm.' Having attained the ultimate accolade from Ofsted – 'outstanding' in all categories – in the school's 90th year, there is now space for him to focus on core values and his aim to make the school more outward facing, developing students' aspirations beyond top grades and necessarily a career in the professions.

Very tall and bearded, he lives in Tooting and cycles to school every day. During downtime he combines his love of photography and travel, bringing back inspiration for students. He doesn't remain aloof, within reason, doing an assembly on his own wedding last year. We find him to be refreshing, passionate about this school but unamused when we wonder whether his name has been a cross to bear in the teaching profession: 'no-one remembers Mr Bean,' he says dismissively to this not exactly ancient editor.

Parents tell us he is 'enthusiastic with a genuine love for the school. Always challenging the boys to strive for 100 per cent in all they do.' A mother added: 'My son says that he takes the pupils' opinions into account.'

Academic matters: In 2019, 45 per cent A*/A at A level; when we enquire as to where next with performance, does the school aspire to further leap up the league tables to bite at the ankles of the some of the south London independent big hitters, Mr Bean says firmly: 'we don't judge ourselves by A*/As,' focusing more on value added – the school is in the top one per cent nationally, which given the already highly selective intake is impressive.

Pupils choose three or four A levels. Classics, art and design, philosophy, government and politics are added to the standard fare. A very strong showing in maths and further maths for top grades. Also performing well are economics, geography, history and Spanish. Relatively high numbers gaining less than a C in A level computer science since its introduction. Small numbers of linguists, after the popularity of French and Spanish lower down the school, and artists hugely outnumbered by scientists.

Sixth formers go off syllabus every Wednesday afternoon, allowing them to take up a sport, follow humanities programmes or attend popular guest lectures. Speakers have included a criminologist, members of government and leaders in companies such as Google.

In 2019, 71 per cent 9-7 at GCSE. Most opt for single sciences with plenty to celebrate results-wise. Plenty of science going on beyond the classroom too. One year 12 student followed in the footsteps of other WCGS boys in achieving the highest possible award in the Cambridge chemistry challenge in a field of 7,000. Year 12s also took part in a biology Olympiad and Imperial summer school to explore life sciences.

Two popular DT choices, unusually – electronic products and resistant materials, with new, state of the art labs. Drama included for creative performance types, plus business studies. Healthy numbers taking PE too. It's a surprise to see catering and hospitality on the curriculum, rarely encountered elsewhere, inspiring the odd chef and a food tech lab on the horizon. All other points of the compass straightforwardly academic. RS is compulsory. Almost everyone adds further maths to maths and does brilliantly with it.

Class sizes in some years compare well with the independents, averaging 25, a few up to 30. At A level the average is 18 and the largest 26. A 'deep thinking challenge' in every lesson stretches the most able and post marking students write their own 'purple pen response' as a further reflection on their work.

'Quite young, full of energy and ideas,' says the head of his staff. Twenty have been at the school for 10 years or more. Mr Bean says they are the reason pupils are passionate about their subjects, they know the students well, 'there's a lot of compassion and respect'. Confirmed by a pupil: 'they care a lot about each person, you're not just another potential A*.'

A parent added: 'The teaching is tailored towards identifying weaknesses and then looking to strengthen and improve those areas.' 'He finds the lessons interesting, engaging and challenging. He is encouraged to think deeply and to further research his subjects. He even finds the homework interesting!' said an amazed father.

Sixth formers go off syllabus every Wednesday afternoon, allowing them to take up a sport, follow humanities programmes or attend popular guest lectures

There is 90 minutes of homework a day from year 7. As ever, some parents report this is as minimal and others a burden. One mother felt that it's tough on her year 9 son, who comes home has a brief snack and works on homework until 9pm most nights and then holiday homework too. Another pointed out: 'Students seem to be tested frequently and have a much greater workload than my younger son who attends a non-selective state school. There is, however, a much publicised support network throughout the school to help students who might need it.'

Sixth formers make use of large private study areas equipped with banks of computers for silent private study and make do with a corner of the dining room for break out moments, as they don't have a common room.

Some 70 students with varying identified needs including ASD, dyslexia and dyspraxia. Each student with SEN has a personalised IEP that is delivered in lessons. There's a dedicated SENCo and a learning support assistant. Mr Bean intends to 'increase opportunities and support for those who are struggling'.

A large proportion of boys, 45 per cent, has English as an additional language but none are in the early stages. There are reading and writing workshops in years 7 and 8 to ensure that all students have a solid foundation in English before starting their GCSEs.

Games, options, the arts: 'There's an opportunity every single day to do something off syllabus,' says the head, but the school is aiming to expand what they're doing with world class enrichment opportunities via an extended lunch time.

All students from years 7 to 11 have an hour and a half of games per week. Not compulsory in the sixth form. Biggest numbers playing rugby, some recently on tour to Canada – now sixth form girls too are fielding teams – then cricket and football, and pupils tell us that basketball is popular. We hear from parents that even those who have not played rugby at primary school can make it to the A team. A big table tennis contingent and plenty of outdoor tables in the playground. Two rugby pitches on site, a cricket square and an Astroturf cricket strip, plus nets. High praise from parents for the teaching ability and dedication of the sports teachers and coaches.

Seems rather quiet on the musical front, although the head tells us it's growing, and certainly there is a busy musical calendar and house music competitions, plus a new music block. Less than 100 studying instrumental grades. Jazz and wind bands for all year groups and choirs in key stages. A delighted parent told us of her son's confidence being nurtured as he became engaged with the artistic life of the school: 'He is of a more introverted nature but still felt he could take part in two drama events.'

Good numbers doing DofE: 80 gaining bronze this year. Possibly the most famous work experience placement of recent times was a WGCS boy at Southern Rail – you may have heard him making headlines with his initiative when given the chance to man their Twitter feed during the much-loathed strikes. Sixth formers set up and run societies for the whole school. Rather a highbrow list, many with an academic focus, running until 5pm and all free of charge: notably film theory club, football discussion society and computational thinking society.

Background and atmosphere: The school was first founded in 1927, initially fee-paying, then became a grammar school in 1944. Plenty of keeping calm and carrying on during WW2 when bombs struck the building. In 1996 a new science block was opened by Sir Chris Woodhead, old boy.

From the moment we step inside, the building seems rather institutional; everything is durable – glittery concrete stairs, no frills. Classrooms are large, looking out onto wide corridors. Admittedly the day of our visit is bitterly cold and we need to hop between buildings on our tour, but there's not much charm in evidence and the most litter in and out that we've ever seen, not to mention abandoned bags in corridors and in the playground, as if someone suddenly shouted 'fire!' an hour earlier.

Absolutely not related to a lack of pride in their school, though, according to parents. The head suggests there is a family feel amongst staff and students, an example of this being the mandatory year 7 assault course, where the whole school turns out to cheer them on.

Pastoral care, well-being and discipline: Boys could be nervous on arrival in year 7, but this is taken care of with events prior to the school year as well as an extensive four day induction. 'Supportive' was the word most commonly used by parents to describe not only the pastoral care but the ethos of the school as a whole.

'We're building well-rounded individuals… the last thing we want to do is build well-behaved robots,' says Mr Bean. 'The high level of pastoral care is one of the school's greatest assets,' said a father. 'The older children are actively encouraged to act as role models for the younger boys and support them in house events.' Another shared: 'The relationship between staff and students is great, with no barriers or "them and us" mentality.' Not entirely spotless with regards to bullying: we did encounter one parent who had cause to speak to the school, but staff were swift to deal with concerns.

Plenty of traditions such as houses, privilege stripy ties and house competitions with cups donated by old Wally boys. Meanwhile, current hot topics regarding mental health and gender are very much on the head's radar and his approach is collaborative, inviting the school community to consider assumptions, for instance that boys and girls have different uniform rules in the sixth form, to find a way forward.

Pupils and parents: Most come from Croydon and Sutton but such is the draw of this school that bright sparks may commute long distances equipped with determination, railcards and parental enthusiasm for excellent free schooling.

It's not easy to see each other out of school, but they do. Some sixth formers drive in. As befits south London, it's a richly diverse community: most boys were born in the UK, but other countries of origin with significant numbers include India, Pakistan, Nigeria and Germany.

Supportive was the word most commonly used by parents to describe both the pastoral care and the ethos of the school as a whole

A mother relayed of her son: 'He absolutely loves the school. He feels that all his friends are a really good bunch of boys and are a good influence'. The sixth formers we meet are sincere, articulate and exclusively positive about their experiences, one about to head to his Oxbridge interview the following week. They feel the school isn't cliquey and advise getting involved.

Girls first joined the school sixth form in 2000. The girls we met felt welcomed by the boys from day one. Invited to accessorise with their own drawn-on moustaches for 'Movember', there's a determination to include. Perhaps in need of a domain of their own, however, they proudly show us their loos with positive mantras on the mirrors.

You'll need to make space in your digital life for another WhatsApp group – Wallington parents seem more connected to their peers than is often the case. Parents spilled the beans on their peers, surprising us with their enthusiasm: 'Generally, very supportive and hands on,' thought a father. 'Genuinely lovely,' said another.

Entrance: Eleven plus tests take place in September, but register ahead in year 5. The school PTA lays on familiarisation tests, now big business, stretching over 10 days of nervous prospects. Papers consist of maths and English multiple choice based on the primary curriculum – no verbal or non-verbal reasoning. The competition is fierce, with seven applicants for every place, although since the Ofsted inspection the school anticipates even more of a crush. Gaining a pass mark in the 11+ enables one to list WGCS as a preference on the local authority application form, though not necessarily a place. Students with SEN may qualify for extra time or rest breaks. Up to 15 places for boys on free school meals and 15 for those in specific local postcodes, then children of staff working for the Folio Education Trust.

No longer has 13+ entry. For year 12 entry all external applicants (including girls) are asked to complete an application form from GCSE results day onwards. Three applicants for every place.

Exit: Two to Oxbridge and 14 medics and dentists in 2019. Meanwhile very many other highly desirable destinations are solidly impressive with serious subject choices the norm. Healthy numbers of medics. Between 50 and 60 per cent to Russell

Group universities. This might be higher except for a group heading off on gap years. Strong clusters to Birmingham, Nottingham and Durham. Economics, engineering, chemical engineering, biomedical sciences and chemistry in chunky numbers, but there's also space for philosophers, the odd ancient historian and a few architects.

Remarks: Don't expect frills for free. Places are fiercely contested at this south London grammar school for a reason – excellent teaching in a supportive atmosphere that sees the bright (everyone) go far. The young leadership know exactly what they're about and have the respect of the pupils.

Wallington High School for Girls

Woodcote Road, Wallington, Surrey SM6 0PH

020 8647 2380 | info@wallingtongirls.org.uk | www.wallingtongirls.sutton.sch.uk

State | Ages: 11–18 | Pupils: 1,500; sixth form: 450

Headteacher: Since 2016, Richard Booth BSc. A former grammar school student, he gained a degree in economics from Hull and travelled extensively, living in Australia for a spell, before returning to Hull to train as a teacher. This is his first headship, having been deputy head at Townley Grammar School and assistant head at St Olave's Grammar School. He has two daughters, both now at secondary school.

Outwardly relaxed (and lacking the bone-crushing handshake that's customary among male grammar heads), but surprisingly reserved – not a single titbit offered about interests or passions. 'He doesn't give away much about himself, which is a shame because you want to see the man behind the headteacher,' one parent told us, while others said they felt 'unqualified' to comment on him because they 'don't know anything about him.' Among those closer to the school's inner circle, however, there's a strong feeling that he's 'quietly transformational.' 'He's absolutely brilliant and has made a real effort to put the girls at the heart of every piece of decision making, from bringing in sports they are interested in to ensuring not one girl slips through the net,' said one parent. Pupils told us he strikes a 'good balance between friendly and formal' and they all consider it 'a great honour' when he teaches them (currently year 13 economics). Particular praise for his 'heavy involvement in extracurricular'; currently running girls' rugby. The rest of the time, he says, 'I try to get out of my office whenever I can, but probably not as much as I should.'

Buck stops with previous Wallington head, Jane Burton, who is now CEO of the Girls' Learning Trust, which includes Nonsuch High and, more recently, Carshalton High, alongside Wallington. The schools share a team of trustees, but retain own

governing bodies, and although there was initial parental anxiety, that's all water under the bridge now. 'Bottom line is they're happy that the three schools still have their individual freedoms when it comes to vision and ethos,' explains head, who adds that the advantages of the trust were 'always a hard sell because they mainly exist behind the scenes – cost savings, sharing best practice and high-level teacher training, among them.'

Academic matters: As you'd expect, results terrific. In 2019, 82 per cent 9-7 at GCSE and 70 per cent A*-B and 44 per cent A*/A at A level. But while it's easy to see these results as the inevitable consequence of admissions process – clever in, clever out – head gets most animated when talking about the school's 'value added' scores, particularly how the most disadvantaged students now achieve in line with, or better than, other students (10 per cent are on pupil premium). Progress levels in sixth form particularly strong; 'There's been a real focus in the last few years to improve teaching and learning at this level, challenging and stretching the most able while still supporting those at the bottom,' says head.

School insists it's no exam factory, with any pressure coming from the girls themselves or their (often very aspirational) parents – 'we are certainly not a school constantly telling girls to do better than last year,' says head. Pupils concur – 'The school does everything it can to stop it, but you do see some girls getting stressed around exam times, especially those from quite pushy backgrounds,' said one.

Eleven GCSEs the norm, with all girls expected to take separate sciences, RS, a humanity (geography more popular than history) and one language (girls choose two in year 7 from French, German

289

and Spanish, with school doing its best to accommodate preferences – roughly equal numbers for all three by GCSE). Strongest GCSE results found in maths, RS and English language, while the most popular of the non-core subjects are psychology and business studies (subjects are surprisingly wide-ranging here and also include GCSE rarities such as photography). At A level, a whopping 29 subjects are available, including media studies and DT four different ways. Maths, languages, biology, politics, philosophy and geography get the best results, while the A levels attracting the biggest numbers include maths, biology, chemistry, physics and psychology. All take at least three A levels and most do an EPQ, usually with great success. All credit to the school for encouraging them to get used to the format in year 10 when they have the option of doing the higher project – 'we are big on encouraging independent learning and enjoying learning for its own sake right from the off,' says head.

We'd heard the school was strong on music vocals but hadn't expected to hear year 11s singing (beautifully) in the corridor before their music lesson had even begun

Setting only in maths from year 7. Otherwise, girls are taught in one of seven houses in years 7, 8 and 9; and although they are still registered in their house groups in years 10 and 11, they are mixed up into new teaching groups for some subjects, 'partly to build up resilience to change.'

SEN not prevalent (32 girls when we visited – mainly dyslexia, dyspraxia and dyscalculia), but parents are pleased with the support provided. 'My daughter has dyslexia and the school has made a huge effort in the classroom to ensure she keeps up and she's triumphed brilliantly as a result,' said one. Relatively small turnover of staff, according to school, although some parents 'disappointed with the number of supply teachers my daughter has had.' Permanent staff, however, praised for being 'very committed' and 'really caring about both their subjects and the girls themselves.' 'The teachers are really good at making sure you keep up – they don't let the brightest girls answer all the questions in class,' one pupil told us. 'You can go to them at break time, lunchtime or after school and know they'll give up their own time for you,' voiced another.' Disappointing to see many closed classroom doors during teaching time, though, and almost exclusive use of chalk and talk style teaching (with the exception of sciences, where we

saw practicals galore), but girls assured us many of their lessons are interactive – 'sometimes, nearly the whole lesson is taken up with debate.' Five school days a year given over to enrichment, which include subject specific trips to the likes of Royal Observatory, Maritime Museum and London Zoo (residentials also on offer, such as geography field trips, while overseas trips include annual ski trip and netball tour to Barbados).

Games, options, the arts: Parents with girls in the A teams certainly have no complaints; 'the opportunities are vast and they really support them,' said one. Those with girls in a B (or lower) teams, however, aren't all so gleeful – 'they don't get anything like the same opportunities and I think that needs to be addressed,' said one. Fear not if your daughter isn't sporty at all – 'we're about finding your own passions, whatever they may be,' insists head, although no girls gets off the hook for the obligatory two hours of sports/PE lessons a week ('whatever the weather,' added one pupil, shuddering at the thought). Core sports are netball, football, rounders, cricket and athletics, the latter being the brightest shining star – 'we have been the borough champions for six years in a row – I remind pupils that's more times than Brazil has won the World Cup,' smiles the head. Dance and gym also prevalent in winter. Mammoth field, all-weather pitches (no Astroturf as yet, though four tennis and netball courts have been added to existing two) joined by magnificent sports hall, a yodeller's paradise, and mirrored dance studio.

Art (available at GCSE and A level) is strong, with manifestation of excellent quality displayed throughout the school, but why oh why lose all the natural light by pulling down huge dark blinds? As for drama (also available at GCSE and A level), the mere mention of it invites gush and fervour among pupils, who were itching to tell us all about recent performances including Sister Act, Hairspray and 39 Steps, and show off their new (second) drama studio, where they get involved in everything from directing to lighting. 'If you can't sing, though, it kind of rules you out from these big musicals – I'd like to see more house plays,' one parent told us.

Creativity also a feature of tech block – a real treasure trove of ideas, with fab A level creations including terrific lamp complete with fronds of LEDs and mood lighting, while younger girls were busy designing innovative underground spaces that would give the likes of London Underground a run for its money. No wonder so many become inspired, with around 10 students going on to study engineering related courses at university. Spreads the joy with lots of outreach to local primaries and enters many competitions like the Faraday Challenge.

We'd heard the school was strong on music vocals (recent finalist on TV The Voice is former school pupil) with five choirs, but hadn't expected to hear tens of year 11s singing (beautifully) in the corridor before their music lesson had even begun. Glee and 60-strong gospel choir both audition only (latter mostly seniors), junior and senior versions open to all. School orchestra and ensembles aplenty, plus impressively full looking timetables for peripatetic teachers. But pupils said they 'wish music lessons were as good as extracurricular music.'

Common sense approach to timing of the school day with earlier start and finish (8.25am to 2.50pm) and prompt close on Friday afternoons; packed programme of after-school clubs (all the predictable sports ones through to more unusual likes of yarn bombing) mainly Mondays to Thursdays only, ensuring that everyone (including hard-pressed teachers) can start weekends promptly and with clean conscience.

Background and atmosphere: Founded just over 125 years ago in 1888. About six minutes by bus from Wallington station, it's a fairly easy trek compared with boys' equivalents and presents unthreatening face to the world with mellow coloured brickwork, although the size is deceptive from the front.

Most recent additions include new snazzy library (open all hours – or a fair few of them), new science labs, spacious sixth form common room (a mass of tables and purple chairs – impressive number of sixth formers actually working at them, not just chatting) and new silent-study area for sixth formers. Next on the facilities wishlist is expanding the canteen (a real bugbear of students – 'you can queue all lunchtime and never reach the front'; a pity, they say, as 'the food is actually pretty good'). Most of the rest of the school is a maze of warren-like corridors, brightened wherever possible with rows of pictures, and classrooms of varying sizes and with varying degrees of natural light.

Pastoral care, well-being and discipline: In addition to form tutor and head of year, those with problems have access to counsellor and ELSA (emotional literacy support assistant). 'And we do have problems – no more so than other schools, I'd guess, but there's no point in denying it,' reported one pupil candidly. But rather than ringing alarm bells, we admired the honesty, which seems to run through the veins of this school and which, according to the girls, helps keep discussions open and honest around everything from bullying to self-harm to eating disorders. Masses of posters, assemblies and PCHE lessons are devoted to mental health, along with Sharing is Caring campaign, which encourages girls who are worried about a friend to tell someone. Bullying, say girls, is mercifully rare and 'tends to mean friendships turning sour rather than anyone being purposefully targeted.'

'Not exactly strict – more firm but fair,' say pupils. 'And you always get warnings.' For most, that's enough to prevent the rule bending happening a second time – although a behaviour points system is in place, with anything from forgetting homework to talking in class potentially landing you in the (centralised) bad books and, eventually, in detention ('but these are rare and mostly for lates,' say pupils). Two temporary exclusions within the last two years; no permanent ones.

No-nonsense, down-to-earth, warm and bright. And thats just the parents. For pupils, add to this list hard-working, eager to learn and considerate

Pupils allowed to bring phones in and encouraged to use them for research in some lessons, as well as being allowed them for personal use in the 'phone zones' clearly marked throughout the school. 'Mobile technology isn't going to go away, so I see it as our job to educate them how to use it responsibly,' says head, who says it's caused very few problems.

Pupils and parents: No-nonsense, down-to-earth, lacking affectation, warm and bright. And that's just the parents. For pupils, add to this list hard-working, eager to learn and considerate. 'And they're all so different – one of my daughters is geeky, another sporty; everyone can fit in here,' reckoned mum. Everyone speaks their mind here too – no gushing for gushing's sake.

Around 80 per cent ethnic minorities, 'mostly Indian, after which there's quite large numbers of Tamil and black African students,' says head. No cliques, though – in fact the school is known for embracing cultural diversity (and won an award for it, too) with gusto, with events including cultural evenings with performances celebrating differences.

Entrance: Following early September deadline for applications, anything north of 2,500 hopefuls sit the SET test (the same test for all five grammars in Sutton) either here or at Nonsuch. The 900-1,000 who get through are then invited to sit the second stage test at Nonsuch and the 800 who survive this hear in sufficient time to include either this school or Nonsuch (or both) on CAF (common application form). But with only 210 year 7 places to fill at each school, many go away empty handed when formal offers are made in March.

Those who jump through both hoops successfully hail mainly from Sutton, with many from Croydon (rarely from the other side of Croydon, though), all across the borough into Surrey and a few as far into London as Tooting (nearly half the places are allocated to highest scorers, irrespective of where they live). 'Many girls the only ones from their primary school year and the most we'll see from any one primary school is five or six,' says head.

Cleverness, though essential, doesn't have to be extreme, is message. 'Girls who come achieving above expectations in Sats would be of similar ability to pupils at the school,' says head, although he admits most are tutored to death regardless.

Exit: Loses around 5-10 per cent after GCSEs – either for more vocational courses or to go to co-ed

schools. In 2019, five to Oxbridge and 25 medics, one dentist and one vet. Over half of the remainder to Russell Group. Top destinations include Bristol, Birmingham, Southampton, St George's and Nottingham. Most popular courses are science, engineering, maths and economics.

Remarks: School speaks of warm, friendly and purposeful atmosphere. Yada, yada, we'd normally retort – another bland statement. But from the moment you walk in, this school has a sense of authenticity, enthusiasm and amiability that gives an impression of genuinely living its mission statement. And when parents or pupils criticise, it feels constructive never bitter, with a view to making a school they love even better. Though equally desirable, not all grammars are the same. We loved this one.

Wilson's School

Mollison Drive, Wallington, Surrey SM6 9JW

020 8773 2931 | office@wilsonsschool.sutton.sch.uk | www.wilsons.school

| State | Ages: 11–18 | Pupils: 1,220; sixth form: 295 |

Head: Since 2014, Nathan Cole BA PGCE (30s), previously deputy head. Read history at Nottingham and was a postgrad at Cambridge. Began his teaching career at Saffron Walden County High and joined Wilson's in 2006, rising through the ranks to become deputy head in 2010. 'The school is in my blood. I love the bones of the place,' he says.

Born and bred in Yorkshire (where he was the first person in his family to go to university), his boyish looks and exuberance mean you could be forgiven for fleetingly mistaking him for one of the pupils. But rest assured your slip-up will be momentary – he is known for his authoritative strength of character and exacting standards. And it is this, combined with his sparky wit and playful banter, which has won him such great respect among the students. 'This school was great before he came along, but it's pretty much faultless now.' 'He's strict, but always fair and never stuffy.' Parents similarly gushing. 'A more committed, approachable and efficient headteacher you will not find.' 'He makes the boys feel they own the successes of this school, not him – and that generosity of spirit ripples through the whole school.'

The kind of head who is as at ease doing lunch duty as teaching PSHE to year 7s as tutoring sixth formers (all of which he does), he says, 'How can I put this? I'm not your stereotypical six foot two

silver-haired grammar school head and I do not sit in an ivory tower.'

Lives a nine-minute (yes, it's that precise) drive away in Purley; he is a keen musician, 'fair-weather tennis player' and an expert on the history of Italian fascism. 'If I get the chance, I also enjoy eating in decent restaurants, although mostly it's the school canteen for me.'

Academic matters: One of a handful of grammars in the area, all high achieving, this one stands out for getting even better results than the others, as well as its supportive, 'we're-all-in-this-together' ethos, and as such makes for a friendly environment in which the innately clever child can thrive.

Boys achieve startlingly good results – in 2019, 90 per cent 9-7 grades at GCSE. Ten-and-a-half GCSEs are the norm – eight core, including separate sciences, while the half refers to the short RE course. Strongest results in maths (so many finish with 9/8s that it's practically de rigueur), English and languages, while the most popular non-core subjects include business, history and geography (also more musicians than the norm). Setting from year 9 in maths, sciences, English and all languages except Latin. But with the bottom sets still getting 9-8s, there's no real stigma about being in lower ones – and regular assessments ensure plenty of movement across sets. 'All that testing is quite a shock at first, but it's a good way of making you realise that natural talent alone doesn't cut it here – you need to work really hard too,' one boy told us. Homework heavy in year 7, drops in year 8, then picks up pace again in year 9, according to the boys. Languages start with French or German in year 7, with some boys picking up Spanish in year 9.

In sixth form, boys select four A levels from a modest menu of traditional subjects (not a whiff of photography, business studies, psychology etc), plus either a formal extended project qualification (EPQ) or an internally assessed project. Maths, daddy of the big hitter subjects here, is taken by all but a handful of sixth formers, with exceptional results, although surprisingly few (around 10) boys take it at degree (with most using it for degrees such as engineering or economics). Other particularly well-liked A levels include sciences and economics. Overall, 94 per cent A*-B (73 per cent A*/A) at A level in 2019.

Notable repartee between boys and teachers, while also respectful on both sides. 'The teachers are so into their subjects here,' one boy enthused. 'We came out of a maths lesson the other day, only to find that half-an-hour later the teacher emailed us excitedly about something she'd worked out that was relevant to the lesson.'

You could hear a pin drop in the corridors – despite the open doors of the classrooms – when we visited, with straight-backed, silent and captivated boys hanging onto every word of the animated teachers. 'Not all lessons are like this – they can be very interactive, especially the further you move up the school,' one of our tour guides assured us. Lots of extra help on offer, with regular review discussions and valued catch-up clubs in just about every subject, introduced originally for GCSE pupils but now, by popular demand, run from year 7 – often by a combined effort of sixth form and subject staff. Support also for those with learning difficulties, with some Asperger's and dyslexia cropping up now and then (seven statemented when we visited), although more than one boy told us, 'I don't know anyone with SEN,' with one adding, 'it isn't really a school for people educational problems.' Head, however, says, 'I think this is a good thing – that boys are not labelled as SEN.'

Games, options, the arts: Sport excels here, although it doesn't tend to be a deciding factor for parents. 'We'd choose this school every time even if they didn't own a tennis ball between them,' said one. Great outside facilities, certainly by south London standards (including 13 Astroturf courts and sizable fields – no time wasted on coaches here). Good range of sports, including less predictable offerings such as table tennis, rugby (a growth area) and climbing. Fixtures every weekend, in which the school does particularly well in football, cricket and badminton. And for the less or non sporty? 'We have some F teams,' said one boy. 'If you like football, but you don't excel at it, nobody cares,' said another. 'And if you don't like sports at all, that's also fine – people would just accept you might prefer, say, music or drama.' And with chess considered a sport here (hundreds play and succeed on the national stage), it's probably not something you're likely to hear anyway. Regular sports tours, mostly within Europe, with the odd exotic opportunity thrown in, such as cricket in Barbados. Some Olympic hopefuls in badminton.

Many clubs are student-led, with students setting up everything from Rubik's cube to knitting clubs – 'to say some boys are quirky would be an understatement,' comments head

Signs of artistic talent abound, with some inspired pieces on display in the snazzy exhibition area. But it's DT that really gets the artistic juices going here, not least because it's valued on 'serious' academic courses such as chemical engineering. Unusually, life drawing classes are taken from GCSE up (and very good the results are, too).

Music, meanwhile, is superb, with every year 7 boy learning an instrument with a peripatetic teacher. Upshot is a 150-piece wind band debuting at Christmas – with many boys developing a love of music they may not otherwise have had, plus lively membership among the various school orchestras and ensembles. 'Music has gone through an extraordinary transformation and the wonderful thing about it is that it's not just about producing excellent musicians, but seeing the boys stamp their feet with glee at the end of the concert because of their teamwork – and seeing the orchestra exploding in size,' one parent said. Choirs also popular, with an excellent barbershop including recent performances of Haydn's Nelson Mass and Mozart's Requiem.

You only have to mention the word 'drama' and boys' eyes light up, with everything from drama soirées to junior and senior productions providing opportunities not just in acting but in lighting, sound production, costume and set design etc (plus opportunities for keen musicians too). 'I stage managed our recent production of Midsummer Night's Dream and it was the best show I've ever been involved in,' said one student – one of many who took pains to tell us that no play is staid here, each given a modern twist. 'You should have seen us doing the set design – we even found an old unwanted bath chucked in a skip that we wound up using in the play.'

Extracurricular life is buzzing, with boys (especially in lower years) reeling off lists of all they do – not just in sports (although they dominate), but philosophy, chess, rocket clubs etc. Many are student-led, with past students having set up everything from Rubik's cube club to knitting club – 'to say some of the boys are quirky here would be an understatement,' says the head. Tip-top CCF (now one of the largest in the country in conjunction with a local girls' school – the military camouflage outfits were out in force when we visited) and DofE to gold award also on offer.

Background and atmosphere: Many grammars give the impression of being a throwback to the 1950s. This one doesn't – 'deliberately,' says school. Founded in the 17th century in Camberwell and, with the exception of a 38-year closure in the 19th century after a financial scandal, going strong ever since and celebrated its 400th anniversary in 2015. In 1975, lured by the space and local council's pro-grammar stance, it moved to its current premises, once part of Croydon Airport, and commemorated in nearby street names like Dakota Close and Hurricane Road.

While it's no looker from the outside – with square brown buildings set uncompromisingly in a large, plain playing field – the interiors aren't half bad. Corridors might be on the pre-loved side, but the classrooms, full of lovingly tended displays, more than make up for it. Science labs, too, slightly dishevelled from the outside, are a hive of well-resourced activity within.

Motto is 'Non sibi sed omnibus' (not for oneself but for all) and boys, parents and staff wax lyrical about how it underpins every aspect of school life

No shortage of impressive large scale areas, either, including the traditional main hall – recently refurbished and a large sports hall and gym. But there are also more intimate and surprisingly luscious touches. The south canteen – as distinct from north canteen – (they don't go a bundle on fancy names; library has resolutely not morphed into a learning resource centre, for example) has cutting edge lighting, un-school-like black and orange walls and doubles as an attractive additional concert venue. Years 7-8 now have own new lower school with dining hall and classrooms, and there's also a mobile eatery for boys who want

to wolf down something to eat then get onto the playing fields. Sixth form common room given a recent facelift.

Pupils whizz purposefully round the site, without so much as a skew-whiff tie in sight (instant black mark if they did).

Pastoral care, well-being and discipline: Motto is 'Non sibi sed omnibus' (not for oneself but for all) and boys, parents and staff wax lyrical about how it underpins every aspect of school life. 'Boys are so positive about each other's achievements – and so encouraging of each other even if they're not the best at something,' one parent told us. Approachable form tutors are first point of contact for pupils and parents, who stay with the same group for two to three years – 'very easy to talk to if you have any concern at all,' said a parent. Unusually, each form has two tutors throughout years 7-11, with pupils in years 9-11 registered and tutored in small groups of 15. First class transition arrangements, with year 7s taking precedence in the lunch queue during their first term.

As with any highly academic school, anxiety can be a problem. 'But they're good at pinpointing early onset symptoms and treating them quickly,' said one parent whose son became anxious – and there's a reassuring amount of talk among boys and staff (including head) around mental health awareness. Ditto with bullying, which boys say is 'extremely rare.' On-site counselling is available one day a week, plus occasional peer mentoring offered – and there's also a school nurse. 'One of the most important things for me is that boys feel able to be open about their feelings,' says head.

This is a strict school and they make no bones about what constitutes unacceptable behaviour, with the tiered detention system used widely ('You get more in the lower years so you learn your lessons early,' said one boy). But there's some wiggle room, with a warning system when it comes to things like late homework, for example, and even the penalty is a starter detention lasting 10 minutes. With plenty of chances to step back from the brink – and all school rules backed up with logical reasoning – pupils considered the system a fair one. No permanent exclusions in recent history, but a handful of temporary ones most years.

Mobile phones allowed only if they're switched off and locked away (and no photographic equipment allowed on phones for years 7/8), although some teachers may give permission to use them in some lessons – for instance for a dictionary in German lesson. Rules relaxed in the sixth form centre.

Pupils and parents: Pupils are an utter delight. Courteous, chatty and good-humoured (and – joy of joys – not entitled; 'I can't bear entitlement,' says head), they have an almost evangelical desire to

Corridors might be on the rather pre-loved side, but the classrooms, full of lovingly tended displays, more than make up for it

draw you into their world and tell you about every aspect of the school. Families encompass every major culture and religion and, currently, speak 40 languages between them – a source of great pride for the school. As to parental involvement, there's a PA, which raises significant sums of money through its social events – 'but there's no pressure to get involved if it's not for you,' said a parent.

Alumni include actor Michael Caine, fashion designer John Galliano, opera singer Mark Stone, mountaineer Paul Deegan and aviator Sir Alan Cobham.

Entrance: Ignore the horror headlines of 10 applicants per place – the reality is more like four to one, with boys coming from around 75 feeder schools and no set catchment area ('although few travel more than 10/15 minutes to get here'). By law, there's no advantage in having a brother here (much to head's disappointment).

Two-stage entrance process, which you have to register for by mid-August. First, the selective eligibility test – the same for all Sutton schools, which involves English and maths multiple choice questions. 'All pretty average stuff,' says head. Those who are successful then invited to a second-stage (and notoriously harder – 'but not ridiculously hard') test, specific to the school, involving English and maths open-ended questions. 'There's no verbal or non-verbal reasoning because we know this is the

bit you can coach children to succeed in.' For the same reason, doesn't make past papers available.

Total of 180 places offered in March to highest placed candidates and where there's a tie break, Sutton children have preference with distance to school the final deciding factor. None of the boys who get a place is told his mark, says head. 'I don't want boys to say, "I was in position X." I want them to come in seeing themselves as equals. Even the staff don't know the mark.'

No automatic entry into sixth form, with offers based on six 7s and individual criteria for subjects studied. Around 10-20 new boys join at this stage, most with at least six 9-8s.

Exit: Around 10 boys leave post-GCSE – for all the usual reasons such as relocation, wanting to join a co-ed or study a course this school doesn't offer (plus the odd one that doesn't meet the sixth form entrance criteria). As for the rest, it's top subjects and top universities (85 per cent Russell Group) in the main. In 2019, 14 to Oxbridge. Surrey, Nottingham, Imperial and Warwick among other popular destinations. Common subjects include medicine (13 in 2019), economics, dentistry and engineering – plus history and geography, albeit in smaller numbers. Head keen that boys don't feel forced own one single route, however – 'we had a boy doing a one-year apprenticeship at Jaguar, for example, which led to him doing his degree on the job.'

Remarks: Bright, clever and funny, and that's just the staff. Hard not to warm to a school where all the students do so well and with such grace. Boys here are hugely generous about other people's successes and learn to fly high without feeling they need to step over anyone else on the way – a valuable life lesson, if ever we saw one. Meanwhile, a wicked sense of humour ensures it remains a Pollyanna-free zone. A great place for boys who are effortlessly clever.

Wimbledon Chase Primary School

Merton Hall Road, London SW19 3QB

020 8542 1413 | wcps@wimbledonchase.merton.sch.uk | www.wimbledonchaseschool.co.uk

| State | Ages: 3-11 | Pupils: 750 |

Head: Since September 2019, Jill Augustin, prevously head of Handsworth Primary School. She has a PGCE and a masters in education from the Open University. She has been interim executive head at three primary schools in challenging inner-city areas of London as well as heading schools in London and Essex. She supported the school as an independent consultant for several months before taking on the headteacher role.

Entrance: At 3+ to the nursery and 4+ into reception. Now expanded to three-form entry. Non-selective; applications must be made through Merton Council, usual admissions criteria. For occasional places in older age groups contact school or the council.

Exit: At 11+ majority to Ricards Lodge, Rutlish, Raynes Park, Ursuline or Wimbledon College. Others to Sutton Grammar, Nonsuch, Tiffin and Whitgift.

Remarks: Continues its long-held reputation for being one of Wimbledon's favourite choices for primary education. Very well thought of all round; academic expectations and achievements are high. Pupils are set by ability in maths from year 4. Stunning Starts, Marvellous Middles and Fabulous Finishes are how staff capture the children's imaginations and talents through the creative curriculum. Pupils are taught via many different media: lessons can include acting, music, dancing, art, design and technology. History and geography topics come alive through a variety of exciting activities. Everyone feels the positive impact and thrill of the creative curriculum; most notably these exciting projects have helped the children develop their writing skills. The arts make up an important part of the curriculum; full-time music teacher and specialist teachers for choir and orchestra also run brass groups, recorder club, drumming club and boomwackers percussion group. Teachers from Merton Music Foundation visit the school every day to give individual instrumental lessons. Musical evenings, assemblies, plays and concerts provide plenty of occasions for everybody to show off their performing skills.

Sizeable premises for a primary school. Playing fields, cricket pitch, tennis courts, a lovely wildlife area and gardens provide numerous outdoor and sporting opportunities

Sizeable premises for a primary school, originally built as the girls' County Grammar in 1924. Playing fields, cricket pitch, tennis courts, a lovely wildlife area and gardens provide numerous outdoor and sporting opportunities. The children grow fruit, vegetables and flowers and are taught about which plants will attract particular birds and insects. Nursery and reception classes have their own specially-designed playgrounds attached to their classrooms, with new wing added to create space for expanded intake. Now space for 730 pupils. Stylishly-designed new building to accommodate classrooms, cookery room, specialist music rooms, an additional ICT suite, gymnasium and after-school care rooms. Some parents felt that the expansion and building would be disruptive for pupils, but now all appear to be in agreement that despite the odd hitch, the new space and facilities are an advantage for all.

The school is fully wheelchair accessible and has a 16 place unit for children with speech, language and communication needs

Over 35 native languages are spoken by pupils; effective EAL programme; consequently nearly everyone does very well in Sats. Inclusion manager coordinates SEN, with two specialist teachers and a team of teaching assistants; also a visiting speech and language therapist and a play therapist. The school is fully wheelchair accessible and has a 16 place unit for children with speech, language and communication needs. Pupils attending the unit join with the main school in the afternoons for the creative curriculum, sports and music activities.

Exceptional range of clubs and activities. Friday film club run by a parent in conjunction with the British Film Institute has produced some successful young film critics. Far-reaching pastoral care; older pupils can train as peer mediators and playground buddies; any child feeling unhappy or needing to talk to an adult can post a note in the worry box. Parent support adviser is available to any parent who might wish to discuss their concerns. The Wrap Around Centre enables the school to offer a breakfast club, full-time nursery places and after-school care.

Parents are very much partners at Wimbledon Chase, assisting with hearing children read, clubs, general maintenance and the upkeep of the extensive grounds. Fundraising is also high on the strong PTA's agenda; dedicated parents' room, the nerve centre for meetings and a relaxing cuppa. Always keen to involve the wider community and improve their skills base: non-parent volunteers are welcome; a local volunteer has taken on responsibility for maintaining the wildlife garden.

An exceptional and innovative school and community with pupils, parents and staff all apparently delighted to play a part. Enthusiastic children bounce into school each morning eager to know what the day holds in store.

Wimbledon High Junior School

Mansel Road, Wimbledon, London SW19 4AB

020 8971 0902 | info.juniors@wim.gdst.net | www.wimbledonhigh.gdst.net

Independent	Ages: 4–11	Pupils: 325	Fees: £15,339 pa

Linked school: Wimbledon High School, 298

Head: Since September 2019, Claire Boyd, previously head of Sydenham High Junior, and before that head of lower school and on the senior leadership team of Ravenscourt Park Prep, so considerable experience teaching every level of junior education. She has a politics degree from Royal Holloway College and a PGCE from Roehampton. She lives locally and enjoys taking full advantage of the rich cultural life of the city as well as taking long walks on Wimbledon Common and practising yoga regularly.

Entrance: Selective at 4+. Testing in November prior to entry. Specially designed, supposedly relaxing, activities in a nursery school environment. 'We're looking for potential, not what they already know.' If successful, a follow-up in January. More places available at 7+ when assessment covers English, maths and verbal reasoning, together with an interview that includes reading. Occasional places higher up. No sibling priority. Intake mainly from local Wimbledon and surrounds.

Exit: Most girls (around 90 per cent) move on to the senior school but take note, this is not guaranteed. Tests in year 4 identify those who may not make the grade and parents are pre-warned that their daughter 'could be better off in a senior school with a slightly slower pace'. This can also apply to less able siblings. All the rest offered senior places, some with academic or music scholarships.

Occasional moves to pastures new, often with a scholarship, recent destinations including St Paul's Girls' and Kingston Grammar. Some head for local grammars.

Remarks: A top school – a brilliant kick-off into the world of single-sex private education. Creative curriculum, ensures breadth and motivation, a desire to learn and discover. Based on literacy, tying in maths and linking in all other subjects in many different ways. School says: 'Phenomenal! It really works.'

Our guides – happy, vivacious year 6s – obviously loved their school and were quick to show us everything that was going on. A library on every floor – 'we're at the top and ours is the best!' (Well,

it did contain a large display of cups.) All children, from the youngest to the oldest, looked thoroughly involved in what they were doing and were keen to explain their activities to us. They grow up as they (literally) go up the school building.

We saw the youngest, at ground level, sitting on the floor or clustered round tables, listening to stories, gathered in small discussion groups, immersed in what they were doing: learning to learn. Easy access for outside play.

Upstairs, larger classes for the older children – average 24. Two years to each floor. Still a generally relaxed feeling of informality, outdoor clothes falling from their pegs in the corridors. Jolly-looking classrooms with plenty on the walls. Every child looked interested in what they were doing. Specialist labs for the older pupils. High tech equipment used but not excessively. IPads recently introduced into Y3 but school says not totally wedded to them yet. Homework for years 4, 5 and 6 periodically done online.

Regular PE in the gym and weekly swimming in the pool: amazing facilities for a smallish school

Nowhere is there a feeling of pressure, but these girls are definitely high achievers. Parents say: 'Girls are supported but not mollycoddled'; 'develop confidence as they go through'; 'well prepared for move to senior school'.

All children screened for SEN on entry and again in Y2. Approximately five per cent need extra help. Constant watch kept by the learning support coordinator who works with teachers to ensure all SEN pupils are accommodated in lesson plans – typically for barriers to learning such as dyslexia and dyspraxia. Progress tracked and peripatetic one-on-one help provided where needed. EAL not a problem despite the number of bilingual children in the school. Specialist coordinator/mentor for the gifted and talented.

Fantastic music, vocal and instrumental, a particular feature of the whole school. Plenty of opportunity to start early. Specialise in different instruments each year – percussion, recorder, keyboard, brass. Events, concerts, performances and regular musical shows. GDST Young Choir of the Year finalists recently; have sung at Queen Elizabeth Hall and the Royal Albert Hall. Musicals, concerts and plays put on in the ultra modern Rutherford Centre, which is much enjoyed by juniors and seniors alike.

Regular PE sessions in the gym and weekly swimming in the pool: amazing facilities for a relatively small school. Other sports played down the road on the site of the original All England Lawn Tennis Club. 'We set out to go there at a walk,' said a teacher, 'but after a while, we start to jog and then run there.'

What a pleasant surprise to find such a happy and purposeful school hidden away in a busy London suburb. On the whole the girls, and their parents, appear to appreciate it.

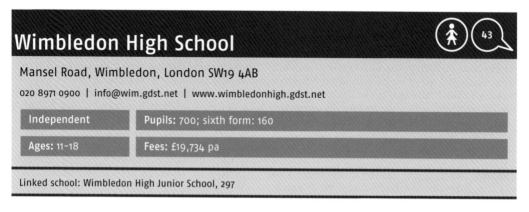

Wimbledon High School

Mansel Road, Wimbledon, London SW19 4AB

020 8971 0900 | info@wim.gdst.net | www.wimbledonhigh.gdst.net

Independent	Pupils: 700; sixth form: 160
Ages: 11–18	Fees: £19,734 pa

Linked school: Wimbledon High Junior School, 297

Headmistress: Since 2014, Jane Lunnon BA (Bristol) (40s). A North London Collegiate School alumna, read English at university and, after an initial career in marketing, decided she'd prefer to teach. Immediately found a job at Wellington College where 12 years saw her progressing to head of English and assistant director of studies. Then to Priors Field as head of sixth form and, later, deputy head. Returned to Wellington in 2010 as senior deputy to Anthony Seldon, who, she says, taught her to 'be ambitious in your aims'. She played a key role in the leadership team, working to increase the profile of girls in the school. Thence to Wimbledon High. She and her husband, who is still at Wellington, have two teenage children and live on the college premises.

Wedded to girls-only education, Jane Lunnon is determined that 'academic excellence is underpinned by outstanding pastoral care within an engaging curriculum and equally stimulating co-curriculum'. She believes in the need to develop the girls' confidence and self-belief, combatting what she refers to as the 'intensity of self-effacement in women'. Says it's a real privilege to run a school so full of magic and alchemy with very bright girls and outstanding results. Believes in model leadership and that the girls should have 'the capacity to be secure and go out into the world with confidence'. Enthusiastic and talks non-stop – apparently very popular with parents. Warmly

supported by the GDST, Jane Lunnon has exciting plans for development. What has been done already during her short tenure is mind-boggling.

One of only the GSG's second set of identical twin heads: her sister, Jenny Brown, took over as head of St Albans High in 2014 and is the new head of City of London School for Girls.

Academic matters: Without doubt an academic school. Testing starts at entrance level in the seniors and progression from the junior school is not automatic. Classes are bigger than many – up to 28 – but decrease when setting starts in year 9, averaging 22 for GCSE classes and fewer for A levels.

Senior school curriculum is broad and demanding. The 'gentle' years, before GCSE, introduce them to the joy of learning. They are encouraged to explore and challenge. Excellent support for all the core subjects but there is some feeling that optional subjects are assessed less frequently which, given that the girls are encouraged to cover a wide range, seems, to some, unfair. But, then, it depends on your feelings about assessment.. Some parents feel that they would like to see their daughters' course work assessments more often – 'it would be good to be more involved'.

Many GCSE subjects on offer and the last few years have seen a considerable shift to IGCSEs. Outstanding results. In 2019, 91 per cent A*-A/9-7 grades at GCSE and 71 per cent at A level (89 per cent A*/B). A double-edged sword this – some very bright girls are then tempted away by top schools with mixed sixth forms. However, there is also a steady stream coming in to the sixth from other schools, including some from the state system and rumour has it that some of the girls who leave WHS are not – as so often – completely happy with their moves.

Games, options, the arts: Not, historically, the sportiest of schools but that is changing. A fantastic swimming pool and large sports hall in the grounds, alongside great games facilities 10 minutes' walk away on the site of the old All England Lawn Tennis and Croquet Club. Parents say, 'it's a pity they don't swim regularly once a week'; nonetheless, they are rightly proud of their swimmers: national, county and regional prize winners; their hockey and netball teams who tour internationally every second year; their cricketers; and, recently, of their star rowers, one of whom came fourth in the National Junior Sculling Head. Skiing, taekwondo and fencing have also produced winners and there is an equestrian team waiting in the wings, an annual tennis tour to Portugal and a netball tour to Spain. So – a great range of sporting opportunities. Of course, they are also proud to ballgirl at the Wimbledon Tennis Championships every year. We met some of the Y7 sports enthusiasts and were impressed, not only with their achievements but also their confidence and ability to talk about them.

Very strong in music and drama. Fantastic music, vocal and instrumental, a particular feature of the whole school. Plenty of opportunity to start early. Musicals, concerts and plays put on in the ultra modern Rutherford Centre, which is much enjoyed by juniors and seniors alike. Some 80 per cent of senior school have individual music tuition and all of Y7 are members of the drama club. We were lucky enough to walk in on the senior chamber choir practising for a concert in St John's, Smith Square and, at the end of our visit, to hear some 'jamming' which included exceptional piano playing. Impressive. Several girls reach grade 8 in their choice of instrument and some work for diplomas, both classical and jazz. One Y13 girl was crowned GDST Musician of the Year recently.

Our guides proudly showed us the Rutherford Centre, a great facility for all the performing arts. Plays, musicals, plenty of dramatic opportunities for everyone – on and off stage. Sixth form drama students are now regulars at the Edinburgh Festival.

Clubs galore; the list is endless and imaginative: from art to biomedicine, debating to the Duke of Edinburgh, scribbling to engineering and many more. Also several trips and expeditions (including senior and junior World Challenges) organised

each term, home and abroad. A busy, buzzy school where idling is not encouraged and plenty of time is given to co-curricular activities.

Background and atmosphere: This GDST school had its 135th birthday in 2015 and was top of the league table that year. A somewhat unexciting entrance to the building belies the buzz that you get as you walk round it. Stone staircases lead to bright corridors, windows onto the happy, busy atmosphere that emanates from both classrooms and laboratories. Girls look relaxed and involved. Rooms subject based. Teachers and parents, as well as students, can have coding lessons in the ultra-modern computer room. We gather a complete overhaul of the building – Project Ex Humilibus – has started, complete with a lift with new STEAM facilities, new hall and sixth form centre top of the list.

Sixth form currently has its own house with relaxing and study areas, common room and café. The girls are allowed to wear their own clothes from the Easter of Y11 onwards, and 'have fun playing ridiculous games'. Relationships with teachers are easy and they are absolutely not spoon-fed. They say the lack of boys 'doesn't fuss us. In fact, it's probably less hassle'.

Pastoral care, well-being and discipline: All are screened on joining the senior school, whether they are juniors coming up or new entrants. Any anomalies are picked up and monitored and parents immediately involved. The school is very aware that capable and high achieving children can often mask their need for support and that the crunch point is at the beginning of Y10. All problems, however mild, are taken extremely seriously and teachers are constantly on the look out for signs of eating disorders etc. 'Learning to learn' lessons are wisely given in year 7.

Relationships with teachers are easy and girls are absolutely not spoon-fed. They say the lack of boys doesn't fuss us. In fact, it's probably less hassle

---

G&T children are offered weekly enrichment afternoons in years 11, 12 and 13. The school is active in the London Challenge that enables talented girls from neighbouring (but less privileged) schools to participate in particular projects.

House system encourages a good mixing of age groups and, parents believe, increases confidence and crosses all boundaries. Masses of fundraising, either for the school or for special concerns and charities. Parents say: 'helps them learn about money'. Girls clearly look after and care for each other.

Pupils and parents: Not yummy mummies, more parents keen to get the best education possible for their daughters. Often both working. No school transport, so either live within walking distance (about half), or on a good public transport route. Some 20 per cent speak a language other than English at home. All keen to give their children a good, well-grounded education. A school that encourages individuals, so anyone could fit in. The majority have a good sense of community; a thriving Parents' Association.

Our tour guides were some very chatty year 9s whose fervour and ability to talk matched their head's. This school produces bright, open minded, self-motivated girls

Notable former pupils include: K M Peyton (author of Flambards series), Professor Lynn Reid (first woman to achieve rank of professor of experimental pathology in UK), Professor Marilyn Butler (first female rector of Exeter College), Michelle Paver (author of Chronicles of Ancient Darkness), Margaret Rutherford (actress) and Eboni Beckford Chambers (played netball for England).

Entrance: Selective at 11+: tests in VR and NVR for all candidates. Second stage for those who reach required standard is creative assessment day with group activities to assess problem solving and teamwork skills. An interview with the head may follow. Offers made at beginning of February.

At 16+: a taster day in May alongside girls in own Y10. In November, tests in verbal reasoning alongside up to four 20-30 minute written papers in the subjects they want to study at A level. Those wishing to study art, music or drama interviewed by head of department. All candidates interviewed by head and director of sixth form and take part in a short group discussion on a current media issue.

Exit: A few at leave at 16+. Of the remainder, together with those who join from other schools, a good handful to Oxbridge (14 in 2019) or London and the rest mainly to other Russell Group universities. Seven medics in 2019. According to parents, the advice and guidance they are given about courses to follow and choice of university is second to none. Nearly all get to where they want to go.

Money matters: Academic and music scholarships on offer in Y7 – parents are disappointed that there are none for drama but there is a new sports scholarship. Many more offered at sixth form level in a wider range of subjects – academic, art, drama, music, sport. Perhaps this would be a good time to reward long stayers, who have been at the school all their lives, rather than mainly to tempt new entrants?

Remarks: Quite a school. It's extraordinary what has been packed into a relatively small space in the middle of a busy London suburb. First of all we were startled by a head who exudes enthusiasm and finds sitting silently impossible (though she does listen, too, and answers questions); secondly, we were taken round the school by some very chatty Y9ers whose fervour and ability to talk matched their head's. This school produces bright, open minded, self-motivated girls. Jane Lunnon has some major improvements organised. An excellent school for girls who want to open their minds, cooperate and grab what is on offer.

South East

Bexley
Bromley
Croydon
Greenwich
Lewisham

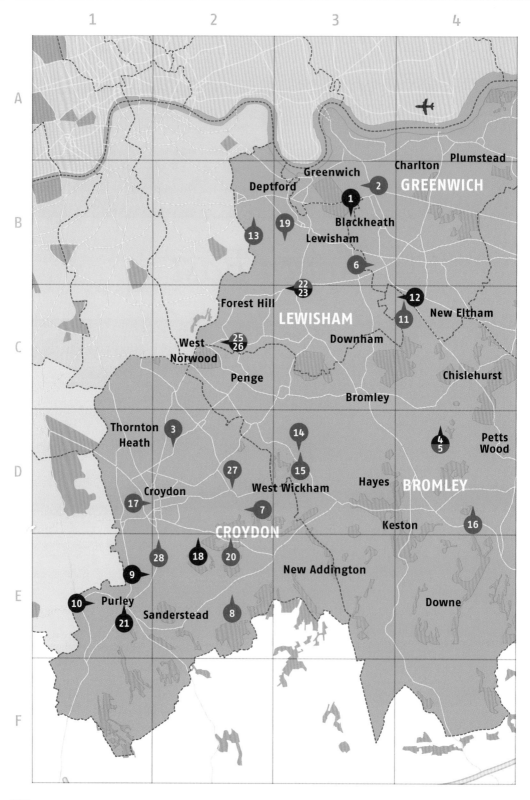

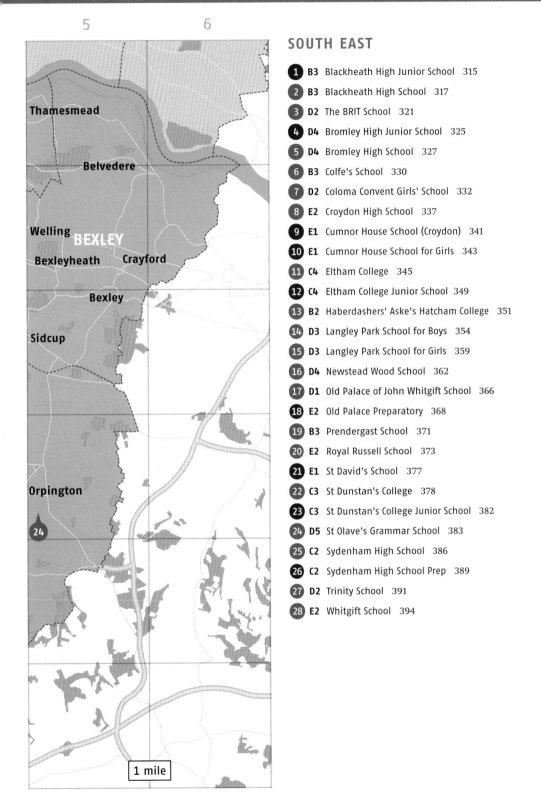

5   **6**

Thamesmead

Belvedere

Welling

BEXLEY

Bexleyheath   Crayford

Bexley

Sidcup

Orpington

24

1 mile

South East London and its state schools

Bexley

On the edge of open countryside but only 12 miles from central London and still within sight of the towers of Canary Wharf, Bexley was extensively developed between the two World Wars. An amalgamation of suburbs around the older Erith and Bexleyheath, with the A2 Rochester Way streaming through en route to Kent and with golf courses and grammars, it hardly feels like London at all.

There are no fewer than four grammars to 'choose' from: Bexley is the current favourite with seven applicants for every place, with Chislehurst and Sidcup close behind. However, in performance terms at GCSE it's single sex all the way with Townley (girls) and Beth's (boys) leading the borough. Children no longer automatically sit the test for these schools; candidates must opt-in online to take it, and only the highest performers will be guaranteed a grammar school place. Bexley is a specialist language college – all pupils take two – with a further specialism in science and maths. Beth's has an international dimension and is a hub school for Mandarin. Townley specialises in performing and visual arts, plus maths and computing.

Despite the catchments expanding slightly in the past year, moving here for grammar entry alone would seem quite high stakes as, to our minds, good state plan B options are thin on the ground. It has been noted that many of those pupils who achieve well at 11 are not achieving at a similar level a few years later, but so much is changing. More grammar school forms of entry at year 7 would assist, and Beth's has recently added one. Bexley's catchment remains the tightest at 2.3 miles but there is a little more air to breathe at Chislehurst and Sidcup where last year you might have lived 5.1 miles from the doorstep. Meanwhile, there is always further afield: many Bexley children also sit the Kent Test aiming for the north west Kent grammars of Dartford and Wilmington.

Grammars aside, Catholic families have the option of St Catherine's for girls and St Colomba's for boys; the latter seems to have shed its poor image but results are extremely underwhelming. Non-church-goers might consider Harris Academy Falconwood, favoured by Ofsted and which does well in terms of progress and GCSE grades. A new all-through (3-18) contender is Haberdashers' Aske's Crayford Academy: the school teaches seniors in single sex groups, has proved a hit with families and is performing well. Worth a visit are Hurstmere boys' school in Sidcup and Leigh Technology Academy, Dartford, notable both for innovative teaching and its eco building design – the college structure may make its size less daunting. Bexleyheath Academy's unfathomable popularity must surely start to wane since it is failing to deliver results and parents say 'run a mile'. Whichever option you favour, be prepared to dance the fandango through myriad admission criteria, banding tests and supplementary forms pertinent to each type of school.

There are not as many enticing primaries here as in neighbouring boroughs, perhaps why (together with Brexit) in contrast to many London boroughs 90 per cent received their first choice of schools last year. The stars of performance, rating and location rarely fall into alignment, so proximity to the various commuter stations may also come into play and open day visits are essential.

Those of Catholic faith are well placed. Notable faith schools are St Paulinus CofE, St Stephen's Catholic, St Thomas More Catholic, St John Fisher Catholic, Old Bexley CofE, St Fidelis Catholic and St Augustine's CofE. The cluster of Bedonwell, Belmont, Barnehurst and Bursted Wood to the north-west of Bexleyheath are the most popular. Tiny Barrington near the station is massively oversubscribed. Full marks to Westbrooke school in Welling, which has gone from bottom of the class to 'outstanding' in all categories, and popular Barnehurst, now four years old and 'outstanding' from the get-go, is performing brilliantly. Upton joins them this year, to the credit of an exceptional new head. Disappointment for parents at Jubilee and Peareswood, where standards have slipped and the schools now regraded as 'requires improvement'. Uptake remains cautious at Bexley's first free foray, the Hope Community School in Sidcup, but headed up by a former staff member from Birkbeck Primary, for the pioneering it has to be worth a look. As the name suggests, Lime Wood, the new free primary school in Erith, has an ecological outlook.

Bromley

One of the greenest boroughs, Bromley includes part of the Kent Downs and was home to Enid Blyton and WG Grace in its heyday. For some, Bromley is 'London without the horrible bits', while urbanites may feel it threatens the twin perils of both village and suburb. Bromley is made for commuting – fast, short journeys into central London one way and the M25 on the doorstep.

Undoubted star of the secondary show and in 2017 a major source of newspaper headlines, is St Olave's grammar for boys qv in Orpington. It regularly features in the top 10 UK state schools, sent a staggering 26 to Oxbridge and 33 to medical school in 2017 and has a co-ed sixth form. Competition for places at roughly eight to one could be worse, and the catchment area is huge, extending to Southwark and Lambeth. Parents threatened legal action when their children were asked to leave after failing to get three Bs in year 12 exams, resulting in the school's head resigning at the end of the year. The assistant head has now taken over the headship.

Otherwise it's academies as far as the eye can see – compared with other boroughs one is almost spoilt for decent choices. Newstead Wood for girls qv in Orpington is selective, has recently increased its intake and performs excellently. Alternatively, the Langley Park qv schools in Beckenham, one for each sex – the boys' school with a stunning new building, enviable sports coaching and a co-ed sixth form – are often cited as reasons for moving to the area. Well-thought-of back-ups might be Bullers Wood (girls, but takes boys in the sixth form) and the new Bullers Wood School for boys, a free school focusing on the EBacc that opened its doors (albeit in temporary accommodation) in September 2018.

Superlatives abound as Ofsted tries to do justice to 'outstanding' Hayes School, which now has one of the smaller catchments. Darrick Wood is newly 'outstanding' and Harris Girls' Academy Bromley does particularly well by the less advantaged, or there's Harris Academy Bromley, where inspectors last year were left scratching their heads for suggestions of improvements.

A budding doctor in the house? In 2020, the 10 storey SHaW Futures Academy will be built near to Bromley South station, will specialise in science, health and well-being and is supported by King's College Hospital Trust and Canterbury Christ Church university.

For those looking to begin their children's schooling here tempted by a large number of excellent schools, gaining a desired place is nonetheless challenging: parents advise us it is unusual to be in the catchment for more than one of the popular primaries, nail-biting when some such as Perry Hall are oversubscribed to the tune of seven to one and catchments are teeny-tiny. Applications at Valley, Clare House, Alexandra, Darrick Wood and Highfield are not far behind, so perhaps take a look at strong academic performers such as Crofton, now with a 180 pupil intake, Downe and Oaklands. Help is at hand with several new primaries. Parents have swiftly jumped on board the two new Harris primaries, one at Kent House, the other at Shortlands – the group knows what it is doing and both schools have been graded Ofsted 'outstanding' in their initial inspections. In the south, La Fontaine Academy is a French/English school with three reception classes since 2018 – the newly refurbished building has been a long time coming but is slated for 2019. Sure to create something of an increasing stampede on its new site in September 2018, the Langley Park primary specialising in maths will provide a way into the senior schools.

Church-going families get a good deal here since church schools, despite their often excellent results and ratings, are not attracting such fierce competition for places. St Peter and St Paul Catholic, St George's Bickley CofE, St Mary's Catholic, Chislehurst CofE, St Mark's CofE, St Vincent's Catholic, Holy Innocents Catholic, St James' RC and St Joseph's Catholic all do well.

Croydon

With Elle magazine recently suggesting a brave rebrand of the borough as 'Cro-do' on the advent of the trendy Boxpark and the highly anticipated Westfield (now a step closer following Sadiq Khan's green light), will Croydon's unfashionable status finally be at end?

Croydon's state secondary school scene remains less than eye-catching: last year's GCSE results in key subjects were below the national average. A few manage to stand taller. Harris Academies dominate in terms of popularity. Crystal Palace is the top performer by a mile and consequently oversubscribed to the tune of 10 to one. How long before they're tempted to take more through the front door? There are two more in Norwood and Purley, and for budding dotcom entrepreneurs there's a new Harris Invictus free school with a specialism in e-business, a dynamic female head and top marks from Ofsted from the first. Admissions arrangements for these academies are highly complex in their attempts to be equitable, so read the small print early. Woodcote High and Riddlesdown Collegiate, newly 'outstanding' for all but sixth form provision, are worth more than a glance. Orchard Park High is the new name for Edenham High since converting to academy status and John Ruskin Sixth Form is busy implementing a three year improvement plan following Ofsted's publication of its shortcomings. Croydon is also home to the famous BRIT school qv for 14 to 19 year olds – the only free performing arts and technology school in the country, with much to sing and dance about.

West Croydon's Coloma Convent qv is one of a kind, frequently cited as the top girls' comprehensive in the country. It is worth noting that stellar local independents Whitgift qv, Trinity qv and Old Palace qv offer unusually generous bursaries, making these three possible alternatives to state schools, for those willing to compete. Also popular is Archbishop Tennison's co-ed CofE High School. Sutton's Wallington Grammar is in discussions to open both a sporty 11 to 18 co-ed comprehensive free school here and possibly the first of Theresa May's new grammar schools in the shape of a 1,000 place 'annex'.

The picture for a while has been so-so primaries – despite moving up the national league table of boroughs significantly – with more primaries inspected last year seeming to remain 'good' rather than achieve the ultimate gold star, and those that 'require improvement' reaching double digits. Beaumont Primary near Purley heads this year's Sats, has a newly minted Ofsted 'outstanding' in all categories but a puny single form of entry. Oasis Academy Byron, similarly acclaimed, is a better bet with a catchment area of over a mile. Around Sanderstead are Ridgeway (Kate Moss's alma mater), Atwood, Gresham, Howard, Park Hill and Fairchildes to the west, all sought after. Halt the horses: Beckmead near

West Wickham may have gained Ofsted's approval and its head an OBE but Sats seem seriously awry. Further north places are in high demand at White Horse Manor, Elmwood, Gonville and buzzy West Thornton. Quite a few additional forms added across the borough: Chipstead Valley, where applications soared by 60 per cent since its 'outstanding' rating, has gained one and seen the catchment relax. The new Chestnut Park with its three form entry tempts more pioneers each year.

With so many chasing places it's worth seeking schools that are somewhat overlooked, despite their good results: perhaps Oasis Shirley Park Primary, Heaver's Farm or New Valley. At some point the baby bulge should be catered for as academy openings show no signs of slowing down. Harris Primary Academy Purley Way, new in 2016, is open for takers from far and wide. However, Paxton Academy Thornton Heath, which opened with an innovative vision in 2014 before becoming known by locals as 'Portakabin Academy' due to a struggle to find a permanent home, has officially lost its way due to poor leadership.

Notable faith schools include St Cyprian's Greek Orthodox, St Chad's and Regina Coeli, with Ofsted best including Coulsdon CofE, St James the Great RC, St Thomas Becket, St Mary's Catholic Infants and St John's CofE. Parish Church Infant's, always a favourite, has a new name: Minster Nursery and Infant school. The new Krishna Avanti primary offers vegetarian meals, yoga and '21st century spirituality'.

Greenwich

Centre of the universe for the past 200 years, the Royal Borough of Greenwich has the classic splendours of parkland, Sir Christopher Wren's naval college, and views of the river and the City at its heart. The east – Woolwich, Plumstead and Eltham – is more affordable than Blackheath to the west, and the area increasingly attracts young families who have outgrown Docklands flats. Commuters may choose from ferry, cable-car, or train and North Greenwich is only one stop to Canary Wharf on the Jubilee line.

When even the estate agents admit that state school choices are known to be poor, there really is a problem. For now tumbleweed blows through the top of the performance tables, scores are decidedly average, leading many families to opt for south London's independents or try for neighbouring grammars. Greenwich Free School, based in a former nurses' home backing onto Woolwich Common and founded by the former head of education, has put the embarrassment of its initial Ofsted grade behind it and is now beginning to fulfil its expected academic promise. Good for early risers, the school day starts at 7.50am. It will offer a sixth form starting in 2019.

Despite rather lacklustre GCSE results in 2017, Woolwich Polytechnic School for boys in Thamesmead is worth exploring: it was the first school in the country to go beyond 'outstanding' and win the Exceptional Schools Award from Ofsted. An eight form entry sister school for girls opened for year 7s in September 2018. Other options might include the Harris Academy, which has some distinguished leaders and scores well amongst similar schools. It's extremely slim pickings: schools we might have put forward in previous years are simply failing to shine academically. Capitalising on the borough's many bilingual families, the new International Academy of Greenwich has opened its doors in Lee with a high calibre head, formerly of Westminster Academy, and will apply to offer the IB middle years programme, though a permanent site is still a way off in 2021. Royal Greenwich UTC was short-lived and is now a free school sponsored by a host of universities and Transport for London.

Catholic girls are in luck, however – St Ursula's gets great results, offers Japanese and exceptional extracurricular opportunities. St Thomas More is co-ed, performs well too and has seen almost £1m invested in new sports facilities. St Paul's Academy, Abbey Wood enjoys a new building, does well by Black African pupils in particular and is seen as 'good' with 'outstanding' behaviour.

In previous years, Greenwich primaries offered a rather exhilarating ride: they seemed to plummet up and down in favour, but more recently those that were 'good' have stayed that way with a few newly 'outstanding' such as Cherry Orchard, Millennium, Deansfield and Foxfield. The borough has done particularly well by higher ability and early years pupils. St Peter's Catholic primary is the latest to reach the top. Oversubscription is rife for the chosen few, with tiny catchments – several schools have recently expanded over two sites. Extremely popular is the excellent Brooklands in Blackheath, followed by the two Invicta schools, Horn Park, Halstow, Cardwell and Millennium. Further to the north Timbercroft and Windrush are out-shining a fair many and something of a steal. Unusually, applications for James Wolfe School measure distance from home to the doors of not the school but Greenwich Town Hall.

Faith school chart-toppers include Our Lady of Grace, St Mary's Catholic, St Patrick's Catholic, St Peter's Catholic, St Thomas More and Eltham CofE.

Lewisham

Lewisham is undoubtedly 'inner city' with regards to crime headlines, but for those attracted to the environs of Blackheath or Dulwich but wanting more for their money, Telegraph Hill, Crofton Park, Ladywell, Hither Green and Brockley offer period properties and increasing numbers of lattes. The East London or 'ginger line' overground direct to fashionable Shoreditch and the City has invigorated Forest Hill and Honor Oak Park, to name but two.

The borough has invested to the tune of £300m in the past decade in refurbishing or rebuilding its schools, so there is plenty of kerb appeal, but secondary schooling in Lewisham languishes near the bottom of London league tables for GCSE performance. Brighter news is that some of the better performing schools are rapidly expanding. The popular Prendergast School qv for girls (co-ed sixth form) has specialisms in languages, music, mathematics and computing and leads the way in terms of academic performance. It started a reception intake in September 2014, en route to becoming an all-through destination. Within the same federation is Prendergast Vale, a co-ed 3-18 school in central Lewisham.

Haberdashers' Aske's Hatcham College qv, 3-18, in New Cross is one of the most oversubscribed state schools in London, with applications standing at 11 to one – GCSE outcomes are better than national averages, for sure, but none too dazzling. It specialises in music and ICT but is known for strengths across arts, mathematics and science. The expansion news here is the recent opening of Hatcham Temple Grove Free School primary with the curriculum taught immersively in both English and German. Clipping at its heels is Students of Sydenham School, not be confused with the independent Sydenham High, which has recently moved into its new £26m building, providing STEM spaces and a new library. Some Lewisham parents with sporty children are tempted by Sedgehill, one of the few with decent sized playing fields despite a lot of work to be done academically. Forest Hill School for boys is failing to inspire and now faces intense scrutiny. An eye-catching major build project in the borough is the smart new building for Brent Knoll School on Perry Rise, Forest Hill for children with complex educational needs.

Due to the huge jump in birth rates since the turn of the millennium, bulge classes have been all the rage in Lewisham primaries such as Horniman, Edmund Waller and Elfrida and have led to permanent expansion at John Ball and Holbeach without seeming to take much pressure off the oversubscription numbers. Luckily there are plenty of nicely performing primaries, so those free to choose may want to aim for a 60 intake at least. With over 400 applicants last year, chances of gaining a place at Brindishe Green, Lee or Manor, Beecroft, John Ball, Fairlawn or Horniman are slim. Perhaps include in preferences: Childeric, Rushey Green (complete with green roof and open air grass amphitheatre), Coopers Lane, Tidemill and Gordonbrock, all doing well by children. Set to be deluged are Downderry, Holy Cross Catholic and Kilmorie, having raised the bar to 'outstanding'.

Strong contenders for Catholic families include: St Mary Magdalen's, St Joseph's Catholic, Our Lady and St Philip Neri, St Saviour's Catholic and St Winifred's RC. For Church of England followers and non-believers scrambling for 'open' places there are: St Stephen's CofE, All Saints CofE, St Margaret's Lee, St Michael's, St John Baptist and St Bartholomew's.

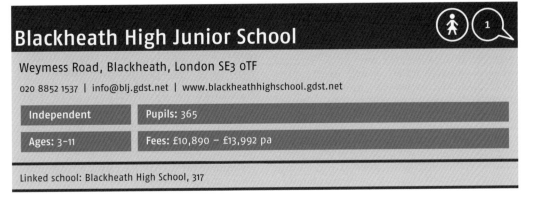

Blackheath High Junior School

Weymess Road, Blackheath, London SE3 oTF

020 8852 1537 | info@blj.gdst.net | www.blackheathhighschool.gdst.net

Independent	Pupils: 365
Ages: 3–11	Fees: £10,890 – £13,992 pa

Linked school: Blackheath High School, 317

Head of juniors: Since 2012, Sarah Skevington (early 50s), LLB Sheffield PGCE, formerly head of the school's early years dept. She practised as a solicitor specialising in family law then retrained as a teacher. She has taught throughout the EYFS and key stages 1 and 2 at local state primaries including Brindishe Lee – 'outstanding' in every category – and Invicta, which she found both challenging and inspirational.

She went to school in Greenwich, at St Ursula's and has raised her family here. Her three grown-up children attended a co-ed school, but since teaching at a GDST school she really appreciates 'what single sex can do for girls', and as a working mother has 'sympathy for working parents'. In her spare time she likes walking in Greenwich Park and lots of trips to the cinema and theatre.

Mrs Skevington is calm, quietly spoken and welcoming. Her office is the home of Florence the labradoodle, who on the day of our visit had flopped silently beneath her desk, offering a tantalising glimpse of a grey furry foot. Children delight in walking Florence. A parent commented: 'Mrs Skevington is wonderful. She has grown into the role since taking it over and we are very happy with the direction the school is taking under her leadership. She is very good with the girls who really like her.' Another, 'She is professional, personable, level-headed, I could go on...'

She pays tribute to her incredibly hard-working staff, saying this is very much a Blackheath community school, 'it's culturally diverse and all the better for it'.

Entrance: By interview with parents and child. Whilst the child plays, the head is looking for parents who 'understand our offer', in other words are not super-pushy or those who might baulk at no formal homework in reception.

Now has two full-time nursery classes.

Exit: Most (some 60 per cent) move up to the senior school. If the head considers that it isn't the best

place, will discuss with parents at an early point. Remainder mainly to day independents eg City of London Girls, Alleyns, JAGS and local grammars in Kent and Bexley, eg Townley and Newstead Woods. Others occasionally off to board.

Remarks: The junior school building is the original first GDST building. Inside is a beautiful Victorian school hall, brought up to date with the insertion of coloured panels into the large lantern skylight. On the sunny day of our visit the hall was full of bright colours, while children below practised their circus skills. A grand, double stone staircase sweeps down from the entrance to the classrooms on the ground floor. The walls feature quotes from inspiring women of our times: Maya Angelou, Anita Roddick and Deborah Meaden.

Classrooms are large, bright and airy, with one teacher and one teaching assistant in every class of 16 in nursery and around 48 girls in every other year group. Classes vary between excited exuberance at year 1 to quietly attentive year 5s. The library, recently rescued from an ill-judged make-over, has had its wonderful parquet flooring revealed, with new freewheeling bookcases in spring colours. Some girls are library prefects and make book recommendations. Playground in full swing at lunchtime was quite a sight, with girls busily making the most of all the different levels: there is climbing equipment, space to run around on hard surfaces, a sandpit in a separate area for the nursery, a maths hut, sensible sun canopy provided by the PTA, and even a small forest school, which the head admits is more concept than actual woodland.

Asked for an example of good teaching, the head cites lessons where year 5s designed an app, then linked up (virtually) with the nursery children, who tried out the app, giving instant feedback. 'Simple stuff done well,' says the head. She observed the head of English teaching girls about persuasive writing styles, saying the girls were hanging onto her every word, and later tried out their new skills writing to ask her to do away with homework.

A parent agreed her daughter is taught 'without feeling she is under pressure. Subjects are taught in an engaging, fun way which increases her enthusiasm to learn and do well.' Another liked the fact that 'the teachers use innovative ways to get concepts across – for example using a "money week" to make the concept of money and savings so much more exciting, and asking parents who work in the financial services sector to come into class'. The French teacher is the best of both worlds, a native French speaker, trained as a teacher in England. Currently there are iPads in group sets, but the school is working towards one for every pupil.

The junior school has 72 girls on the SEND register with needs such as mild speech and language difficulties, dyslexia, dyspraxia and other mild learning difficulties. Needs are catered for within the classroom through differentiation and TA support as well as small group and one-to-one withdrawal. The head says that dyslexia is on the rise. One parent who was appreciative of the school's support nonetheless found the part-time SENCo to be 'extremely stretched'.

Sport is set to have a change of pace with the appointment of another specialist PE teacher. To date, not the sportiest. Head and parents wish the school playing field was closer – it is a bus-ride away. To allow girls as long as possible on the field they have recently introduced a club prior to PE, so that parents drop girls off at the field. Dance is offered as part of the curriculum. Swimming is at the local pool.

The library, recently rescued from an ill-judged make-over, has had its wonderful parquet flooring revealed, with new freewheeling bookcases in spring colours

Music flourishes under the 'talented and energetic' head of music: there are 150 music lessons currently timetabled each week for instrumental or vocal lessons – from beginner to grade 6. From the youngest performers in year 1 through to year 6, every year group entertains parents at an annual tea-time concert, and the juniors recently joined the seniors for a beautiful performance of Noyes Fludde at the Royal Naval College. Year 2 girls can have a generous 10 lessons for free on a new stringed instrument to really test whether they like it. The chamber choir is award-winning – four times in a row at the Beckenham Festival.

A Stone Age workshop stopped just short of making fire in the school hall with two twigs, and seemed to be delivered by an actual cave man

Girls recently displayed clay busts made in DT at Ranger's House owned by English Heritage in the good company of European masterpieces. We enjoyed the display of a recent holiday project where girls chose any piece of art to recreate photographically at home, with staff joining in too: super renditions of The Girl with A Pearl Earring, Frida Kahlo self-portraits, and our favourite: Mrs Skevington, the school caretaker and Florence posed as Mr and Mrs Andrews by Gainsborough.

A Stone Age workshop stopped just short of making fire in the school hall with two twigs, and seemed to be delivered by an actual cave man. The school makes the most of London, with girls popping out to explore the Cutty Sark, the front row at Wimbledon and further afield. Boasts over 50 clubs and must be one of the few junior schools with own radio station. A GDST alumna, Rachel Joyce, author of The Unlikely Pilgrimage of Harold Fry, adjudicated the annual poetry competition. 'They really do a wonderful job of including all the girls in class plays, assemblies, nativity plays,' said a parent. The hall is large with retractable raked seating so that everyone and their iPad can get a good view.

The co-curricular and extracurricular programme not universally popular with more than one parent who wished for more focus on academics. One said, 'I am not convinced the school is capturing the academic potential of all the children', and another, 'may not be a bad thing to ramp up the academics a notch.' The head says children are learning a great deal through structured play and that they don't drop everything for Sats, but nonetheless girls gain a plethora of level 5s, including girls who are more than mildly dyslexic and some level 6s, with girls exiting at 11 'ready for anywhere'.

Transitions are managed thoughtfully. Year 5s feel much more grown-up with the provision of lockers in their classrooms, as they begin to move around to specialist teachers. Year 6 pupils are made to feel special with a prize-giving and lunch with their parents before they head off to senior schools.

We agree with a parent who said, 'The school is friendly and welcoming – it feels like a family.' And everyone, but everyone, agreed on fabulous pastoral care, with one saying: '[It] is exemplary – the main reason we chose the school above others. Not only do the staff look out for the girls, they are encouraged to look after each other, and the buddy group system works well to encourage that. My daughter is thrilled that she can call some of the big girls her friends'.

Parents say the happy pupils we saw at lunchtime cannot wait to get to school in the morning. They might be described as 'bright and sparky, polite and well mannered, kind and empathetic.

It's not for kids who want to be pushed, graded or constantly winning.' And as for self-portraits, a parent obliged: 'A nice mixture from different backgrounds and cultures who all want their daughters to enjoy learning.' One parent with a talent for slogan writing summed it up: 'Childhood is not a race and at BHH they enjoy the journey.'

Blackheath High School

27 Vanbrugh Park, London SE3 7AG

020 8853 2929 | info@bla.gdst.net | www.blackheathhighschool.gdst.net

| Independent | Pupils: 364; sixth form: 68 |
| Ages: 11–18 | Fees: £17,139 pa |

Linked school: Blackheath High Junior School, 315

Headteacher: Since 2014, Carol Chandler-Thompson BA (in history) and PGCE, both from Exeter (early 40s), formerly head of the Girls' School, North London Collegiate, Jeju, in the Republic of Korea. Prior to setting up NLCS in South Korea, she spent seven years as head of history and politics at NLCS. Before that, teacher of history and head of PSHE at Haberdashers' Aske's School for Girls, Elstree.

The move to Korea enabled her to continue to be part of NLCS with the remit of setting up a school from scratch. She was drawn to the GDST for its 'girls first' philosophy but also the sense of community where 'older girls don't feel too superior to talk to the younger ones'.

Youthful, open, highly articulate and full of energy for the transformations in hand, she lives in Woolwich with her partner, Emma, and although barely having time for sport these days (though something of a triathlete), she enjoys the downhill run home from Greenwich towards the river when possible, and being back in vibrant London after the monoculture of Korea. Having said that, she misses Asia and we met her just prior to a holiday in Sri Lanka.

It's never easy following a longstanding head – her predecessor, Mrs Laws, was head of Blackheath High for 14 years – but girls and parents alike quickly took to Mrs C-T. A parent said, 'She is approachable, energetic, personable and committed and will clearly blend her own ideas and purpose to good effect within the school as her influence evolves. She very quickly secured a place of affection and respect amongst the girls

and staff.' A pupil: 'She's refreshing; different in such a good way'.

The ISI's verdict on the sixth form, 'good and sometimes excellent', is a somewhat lukewarm tribute amongst a sea of 'excellents' for all other aspects of the school. As well as reinvigorating staff and teaching, she is bringing her experiences from NLCS's highly successful sixth form. And whilst she's very happy for the school to be known for the strength of its pastoral care, she has focused on moving that reputation to highlight academics. Having heard her talk about her involvement in this year's 11+ selection process, we've rarely heard of such care and attention given to spotting potential beyond mere performance on the day.

Also on the agenda is raising the profile of sport. Never known as a sporty school – amusingly illustrated by girls in the playground sitting chatting either side of the nets on the table tennis tables – the head has appointed a new director of sport.

She aims to ensure no ceilings are put on the girls. 'Girls are stretched and pushed here but they don't succeed through the failure of others; it's about challenging themselves'. Whatever girls want to do, whether it's apply to Oxbridge or become a professional singer, the school will absolutely support them. The word 'aspiration' crops up a lot, and parents say, 'She was very quick to pick up areas which needed improvement and is addressing them eg widening the girls' aspirations... she is very thoughtful and passionate to further advance the school.'

Academic matters: In 2019, 67 per cent 9-7 at GCSE and 29 per cent A*/A (60 per cent A*-B) at A level; results don't dominate league tables or the GDST leader board, but the head says it's about value-added.

No surprises curriculum-wise. GCSE science starts in year 9. Excitingly, as befits the Greenwich location, a handful of the top physicists are invited to study astronomy GCSE, alongside similarly selected state school pupils. Most lessons taught in mixed ability groups apart from maths, set from year 7. Computing, not ICT, thankfully. School, and the whole GDST, is keen on STEM subjects and a recent look to the future event allowed girls to have their eyes opened by an engineer, a dentist and a computer programmer. Art and design flourishes and is as popular as the single sciences. Plenty of keen actors: drama is a likely choice.

Proud to be one of the first schools to offer Mandarin. All pupils take Latin from year 7 plus a choice of modern foreign languages from French, German, Spanish and Mandarin. Some leeway for girls with SpLDs. Carefully structured language trips and exchanges, gaining in adventurousness as girls go up the school, taking in Paris, Trier in Germany, Castellón in Spain. 'Exchange trips with a school in Germany from year 8 onwards fostered her interest in and ability with the language, as did the encouragement to do work experience in Germany in year 12,' said an approving parent.

Things get more varied at A level with the addition of economics/business, further maths, music technology, textiles, theatre studies, politics and psychology. Highest grades recently in art and design and English literature. Biology, chemistry, business and economics rather bring up the rear and none of the mathematicians reach the tip of the top.

A parent said, 'Every subject area has had at least one teacher who has been inspiring and is completely trusted by the girls'. Our guides went further, telling us how much they appreciated the excellent standard of teaching; they could only think of one instance when a maternity cover teacher had not been up to scratch, but they felt it was quickly dealt with, and convinced us they wouldn't hesitate to raise this with the head of year. Another parent said, 'As a result of the excellent and inspirational teaching, she has developed a passion for the subjects which she intends to study at university.'

Co-curricular flourishes: eco week saw year 6, from the junior school, and year 13 geographers working together to experience what life is like for slum dwellers. During the recent election, the politics society organised mock elections with some pretty impressive drop-in guests, including all of the local party candidates. The newly introduced Wollstonecraft Programme, far more vibrant and modern than it sounds, offers girls from years 7 to 11 a non-examined choice of courses including the creation of Girls' Hour for broadcast (think R4 Woman's Hour), creating and marketing apps, global perspectives and introduction to film analysis.

The school makes the very most of its situation in Greenwich, recently putting on a stunning production of Britten's Noyes Fludde at the Old Royal Naval College

The clunkily titled Matrix of Knowledge course in year 11, subtitled A History of Western Civilisation in 23$\frac{1}{2}$ Lessons, prepares girls for entry into the sixth form and Russell Group applications – it develops critical thinking, research and debating skills and culminates in explorations of the riches of London such as The Wellcome Collection and Sir John Soane's Museum. Theory of Knowledge takes this further in the sixth form. And whilst the school isn't considering IB, other elements from this such as the extended project are in place. Originality is the order of the day: one girl even grew her own skirt. A parent added: 'The school offers an excellent series of TED lectures'. The librarian said she's just had her book budget increased and girls say the selection is well-chosen and they can also request anything they want.

Plenty of praise for the school's career preparation. Girls are encouraged to start thinking of their aptitudes and possible options for their future from around year 9. There are trips to inspire. Girls in years 9 and 10 were given a behind the scenes tour of Microsoft by interns, who had each fought off 60 others – let's hope they are being paid. Sixth formers make use of online help from Unifrog. A parent told us: 'My daughter received excellent advice, encouragement and support from the careers teacher regarding a work placement in year 11, and an opportunity in year 12 to shadow an undergraduate at a Russell Group university.' Another, 'The quality of the guidance and the fact that it is offered early ensures that the girls can build a very strong application, when the time comes, for places in further education.'

The head speaks warmly of the SENCo, currently studying for a masters, who initiated the 'pupil passport', where each girl records what works for them and their particular learning style in the classroom. The senior school has 56 students with a form of SEN, including dyslexia, dyscalculia and dyspraxia, and currently one child with a statement/EHC plan. Girls receive in-class and out-of-class support, which incorporates differentiation or small group or one-to-one support, depending on need. The head has also appointed a separate EAL co-ordinator.

Games, options, the arts: Despite its location close to the edge of Blackheath and more or less alongside Greenwich Park, the school's five acre sports field with a pavilion and an all-weather pitch is a short bus-ride away. This offering boosted by the recent addition of fitness suite and outdoor games court. Winter sports are netball, hockey and cross-country. Summer sports are rounders, athletics and tennis. Girls benefit from the wider GDST network for competitions as well as local tournaments. Girls try fencing, trampolining, gymnastics, table tennis, football and dance. The annual Iron House race sees 40 athletes from across the school, including staff, showing their stamina in Greenwich Park, including the gruelling near-vertical climb to the top. It's a breeding ground for competitive runners.

Girls with a love of the wider outdoors enjoy D of E – everyone does bronze, with just a hard-core few making it to gold. Also on offer is an international three week World Challenge – previous trips have been to Namibia, recently to Peru. The cost is steep but girls raise the money themselves, rather than digging into the bank of mum and dad. There are also taster sessions in canoeing, sailing and horse-riding, and girls get a chance to go on PGL adventures to challenge any fear of heights and brave the English weather.

The school makes the very most of its situation in Greenwich, recently putting on a stunning production, Noyes Fludde, at the Old Royal Naval College. The head of music, a former professional drummer, has shaken things up. There are over 200 music lessons a week and extracurricular is chock full of music: orchestra, chamber choirs, samba band, rock band, ukulele orchestra, glee club and a number of percussion ensembles. There are biannual international music tours, and many pupils study at junior conservatoires. Everyone arriving in year 7 can take part in a taster scheme where they have the opportunity to learn an instrument free of charge.

There are clubs timetabled for each year group from Viking and Anglo-Saxon club in year 7 to Iron Woman, self-defence, debating club, crochet collective – who meet in the outdoor classroom – and an F1 club. Any sixth former can start a society.

The theatre is a purpose-built performance space on campus, but pupils also put on plays at Greenwich Theatre. A parent enthused, 'The drama was outstanding...always thoroughly engaging and bursting with energy and enthusiasm.' A competitive audition recently resulted in the world premiere of creepy Coraline: an ambitious adaptation scripted by the drama teacher. Plenty of rehearsal spaces and professional equipment.

High quality art is displayed around the school. We were lucky enough to see the GCSE and A level examination pieces, including dresses one might covet, much in demand for the end of school ball. The art teacher welcomes all into the studio, even if just to do their homework in inspiring surroundings.

Background and atmosphere: The first purpose-built GDST school, opened in 1880, it maintains the tradition of a thorough academic education for girls for highly competitive fees. The school is situated on one of Blackheath's fine Georgian streets, although now very busy with traffic. A tall, red-brick building with stone dressings, with the somewhat odd addition of a 1960s church, currently used as a dance studio. Recent additions include a new library and resources centre, specialist teaching environments for art, design and technology and music; a new mac suite and apple technology in all classrooms and expansive exhibition and gallery spaces. A brand new sixth form centre aims to inspire a mature atmosphere to bridge the transition to university.

Parents enthuse about the school's warm atmosphere, saying: 'By the time my daughter reached the GCSE years, the teachers knew her as an individual rather than as a number'; 'very positive atmosphere, friendly, supportive, collaborative'; 'everyone is enthusiastic about learning and has an open mind to new ideas incorporating very well the different cultural backgrounds the girls are coming from.'

New girls take part in a summer school, more for fun than anything else, with cake–making and a picnic in the park, making sure no-one gets lost on day one

Old girls include talents in all areas, particularly the media, perhaps most notably: Mary Quant, Baroness Jay of Paddington, Labour politician, Helen Lederer, comedian, and Katie Stewart, cookery writer.

Pastoral care, well-being and discipline: The head has split the roles of deputy into academic deputy and pastoral deputy, and there is a new part-time school counsellor. Pupils who volunteer are given training in peer mentoring by Childline. Mentors are assigned a year group and available at lunchtime, before and after school. One we spoke to clearly enjoyed it.

Parents praise the emotional support given to the girls: 'The teachers frequently remind the girls of the importance of finding time for rest and relaxation in their busy schedule to safeguard their well-being in what will be a very challenging world.'

The head girl team takes the pressure off one individual and shares around the privilege. They clearly feel listened to and that this is their school. They've initiated eating with the lower school girls once a week, like kindly big sisters. The transition to year 7 is thoughtfully handled – new girls take part in a summer school, more for fun than anything else, with cake-making and a picnic in Greenwich Park, making sure no-one gets lost on day one.

Even the fabric of the school has a new pastoral focus to support the good work going on among staff and pupils; there's a wellbeing sedum roof where girls can relax. It sits above an architecturally designed courtyard with its own 'mini Louvre' at the heart of the school. There's even a 'pod' contemplation space for meditation and idea generation.

Pupils and parents: Pupils come from a diverse range of backgrounds. Nearly one third are bilingual.

The clunkily titled Matrix of Knowledge course in year 11 prepares girls for the sixth form, developing critical thinking, research and debating skills and culminates in explorations of the riches of London such as The Wellcome Collection

Who is this school for? Parents say: 'girls who do not fit into a stereotype but have their own thoughts and opinions'. The sixth formers we met seemed confident, sincere, happy and very mature: a delight. Without boys to impress, there were none of the false eyelashes or make-up we've seen at co-eds recently. Girls between lessons were exuberant, loud, even.

A mother with two daughters at the school enthused: 'My children are ready for anything; they have been prepared step by step from juniors onwards to become increasingly independent. They are totally trustworthy and sensible. They can cope with minor emergencies and they look after one another. They support one another emotionally and practically.'

The PTA is active and seem a relatively down to earth lot, organising car boot sales with bacon butties.

Parents feel in touch with the school. They receive grade cards or full reports twice a term with detailed information about a girl's progress, as well as strategies and suggestions for improvement. School days are long, cue a sigh of relief from working parents: pupils can arrive at 7.30am and stay until 6pm. There are also minibus routes ferrying girls from all across Greenwich, Rotherhithe and Lewisham.

Entrance: There are 60 places at the 11+ stage and most recently there were around 190 applications. No guaranteed place for junior school pupils, but all year 6 girls take the entrance exam in maths, English and non-verbal reasoning. Senior staff interviews all candidates. Best performing girls attend an academic scholarship interview with the head. Any SEN students with an ed psych report are granted extra time. The school has introduced a 13+ entry point with scholarships available for exceptional external candidates. Most girls fairly local but a few from as far away as Dartford and Chislehurst in Kent and Leyton, East London.

Into the sixth form, there are 60 places available, currently undersubscribed. The girls we met described lots of their peers being attracted elsewhere simply to try something new – and by 'boys'. You'll need a good range of GCSE results with 9-7s in the subjects that you wish to study, plus an excellent school reference.

Exit: Subjects from anthropology at Bristol and Aberdeen to zoology at Leeds. Between a third and a half leave post-GCSE. Around half of sixth formers to Russell Group destinations eg Warwick. One to Oxbridge and three medics in 2019. Few linguists. It's a very arty list of leavers, heading off for art foundations, even a famous shoe design course, but balanced with plenty of scientists, medics, a medical geneticist and dentist. These girls have found their passions and are not afraid to specialise.

Money matters: Scholarships and bursaries for girls entering years 7 and year 12 only. Scholarships based on entrance test results to a maximum value of 50 per cent of fees. In addition, scholarships are awarded for art, music and sport at 11+. A bursary of up to 100 per cent takes into account means, plus academic merit. There are a variety of sixth form scholarships including four provided by HSBC.

Remarks: The girls may not be super sporty, but they certainly seem super happy, comfortable in their own skin and a great recommendation for the school. One to watch under the dynamic head with academic ambition and transformative building works.

The BRIT School

60 The Crescent, Croydon, Surrey CR0 2HN

020 8665 5242 | info@brit.croydon.sch.uk | www.brit.croydon.sch.uk

State	Ages: 14–19	Pupils: 1,346 (831 girls, 515 boys); sixth form: 961

Principal: Since 2012, Stuart Worden BA MA GTP (50s). Previously school's director of theatre, though involvement stretches back, one way or another, almost to its foundation in 1991. Before that, was all over the place (literally, not metaphorically – he's highly organised) as, like so many of school's staff, has combined education, education, education with production, production, production. Though past isn't yet mythologised, may yet happen, given that when whistles through key moments of his career, 'the years change each time,' says affable minder.

First act of our (possibly world exclusive) version opens in Chichester, where the 'first and only' theatrical type in his family (brother, also in education, got there by more conventional means), he was taken on regular trips to the theatre – 'virtually at the end of my road' – by 'lovely' mother. Was hooked, particularly by the language, leading to writing/producer roles with everyone from the National Theatre to the Royal Exchange Manchester, Playwrights' Co-operative and Working Title Films.

Teaching cropped up early on, too, with FE/HE posts on the film writing MA course at Sheffield University in 1990 as well as a spell as drama teacher at Lansdowne College in Kensington, reprised during two years at the Chichester College of Technology in 1991-1993.

May not look like conventional head (he's creative industries smart, down to intelligent glasses) but is meticulous when it comes to rock solid efficiency of school administration. His ethos is creativity within a framework, from the details (photographic ID for visitors, lessons that run to time or he'll want to know why) to the big things – buildings, new and refurbished, that are no architectural folly but really work.

Wants students to leave not just with creative potential on the way to being realised but equipped with hard-headed entrepreneurial nous to back it up (there's praise in literature for a student's massive online following).

His long term involvement in community arts – helped create Steam Industry, a theatre for all initiative – has also led to blossoming of school's outreach programme which is increasingly varied and demanding, though also, he stresses, 'purposeful and long term.' Virtuous circle, too, as those seeking to make career in the area can opt for community arts practice UAL qualification – developed by school and so far unique in the UK.

Pupils work with hospice patients, asylum seekers and rape victims and also act as talented big brothers and sisters to pupils in new, much-needed primary that Mr Worden helped get off the ground – projects naturally including a home-grown musical. BRIT Kids, for local 8-15 year olds, includes free community performances and classes, themed day for tinies, too.

He attracts huge praise from staff. 'He's professional, a good leader, very polite, expects high standards and is very positive,' thought one, speaking for everyone else.

Pupils, too, like his friendly, hands-on approach. 'When I needed help with recording for radio, he was like, "give me a minute and I'll do it",' said one. As a result, takes a while for everyone to work out who he is, particularly those whose previous experiences with authority figures were of a bruising nature. 'He doesn't give out a principal vibe,' said year 11 pupil who had only recently clocked who he was.

Head stresses importance of being 'nice and kind. Creativity and the arts need you to be open and willing to share your skill with others'

Older pupils, though, had no problems with identification. 'Love the way he comes round, sits with us and chats,' said sixth former. 'Not like any principal I've met,' reckoned another. 'He makes an effort to talk.'

Perk of job is 'daily' feedback about pupil success (during GSG visit, it was smash hit involvement in London Fashion Week). As to qualities required by prospective students, he's 'not sure' where talent features in the equation or passion, either, come to that. Instead, stresses importance of being 'nice and kind. Creativity and the arts need you to be open and then you should be willing to share your skill with others. I think that's a special quality.'

Is regularly asked whether school might extend to cover wider age range or sprout satellite versions in the regions. Likely to remain a one-off, he thinks, an 'extraordinary' place that does far more than equip pupils for careers. 'Parallel with that is the sense that the school goes to so many people and uses the arts to enrich their lives.'

Academic matters: Wouldn't be hard to see school as a giant performing arts centre with added classrooms. Not that 'straight' academic teachers would thank you for the description, or principal, come to that. ('Not a Fame Academy' a recurring leitmotif in literature). Staff are either traditional types who 'come here because they think it's the right school to teach at and want to be part of what we're doing here' or creative industry professionals who want to teach 'in a place that specialises in what I'm skilled at,' thought principal. No passengers: choreographers, film makers, playwrights, composers all welcomed but need to commit to training: on the job GTP programme is particularly popular.

Academic staples are bunched together, with sociology, humanities, science and musical theatre in East Wing (actually the main building of Old Grammar school – pay attention at the back). While inevitable focus on performance can make it seem as if you're never more than two minutes from a rehearsal, rooms are well-soundproofed to avoid stardust leakage into classes.

Staff work hard to harness pupils' energy, GCSE groups enjoying animated discussions on causes of youth crime in lively sociology lessons, maths teacher moving us along from fidgety class, distracted by visitor. 'This is a creative enterprise,' says young, happy-looking teacher. Once here, it's a hard place to leave. Teachers, like pupils, praised 'inspirational' atmosphere – latest arrivals include new head of costumes, fresh from EastEnders – and warmth that 'sucks you in'. Though no coloured hair (something of a pupil speciality, though 'they get over it after the first year'), they span the gamut from blouse and skirt to finest beard, bomber jacket 'n' red trainers combo.

Star quality tends to reside in BTec/UAL results. Full-on approach makes results extra impressive. In years 10 and 11, pupils take BTec level 2 diplomas (counting as four GCSEs) as well as following well-equipped and solidly taught GCSE classes in core subjects – some streamed, if ability range demands it, subjects broadly EBacc-themed. Given intake at year 10 – nerve-wracking standing start for any teacher – results are spectacularly good when it comes to performance-related topics such as dance and drama, and pretty respectable in the must-do areas, too. In 2019, 40 per cent 9-7 grades at GCSE (including BTecs); 48 per cent got 9-5 in both maths and English.

Inevitably, still greater pressure for sixth form, with UAL level 3 extended diploma, equivalent to three A levels (choice of broadcast and digital communication, community arts practice, dance, interactive media, music, musical theatre, technical theatre, theatre and visual arts and design) the starting point with rich rewards. In 2019, 48 per cent gained distinction, the highest possible grade. In the same year, 41 per cent A*-B and 14 per cent A*/A at A level.

Results are spectacularly good when it comes to performance-related topics such as dance and drama, and pretty respectable in the must-do areas, too

Welcome flexibility allows teachers to devote whole days to some post-16 UAL modules. 'Means you really get to learn,' thought one, approvingly. Course options can lead to slight difficulties: not everyone, for example, is drawn to the sewing that's currently a must-do part of the visual arts and design and technical theatre arts courses – though discussions are currently under way on possibility of evolving a stitching-light option.

For those needing extra help – there's screening for all during May induction day – terrific SEN is a huge strength, generously accommodated, including cosy, cushioned area and Smartboard-equipped classroom – 'keeps sense of routine' – where struggling pupils (SpLD biggest need, also some ASD and ADHD) get parallel lessons at slower speed, multisensory approaches added 'until it works'. Most staff 'very supportive and recognise that approach builds self-esteem'. Doubters (and there are a small number) are won over by success stories, including pupil who went from U to A* in English GCSE.

Whatever the choice, it's a full-on commitment, eminently do-able for the already organised, efficiency step-change required for those who aren't, and a tough old regime for all which can come as shock to anyone expecting straight drudge for drama swap.

'Same as any old school but one where there's less time for academic subjects,' thought slightly jaded year 11 boy. Even with sensible timetable structuring separating academic and performing arts days, extra workload means 'you need to push yourself and get ready to learn.'

Games, options, the arts: Stuffed with opportunities for performance and just about everything that goes with it, arts naturally the main drain on space, from eight music rooms, all soundproofed (plus innumerable additional rooms for individual lessons – drums, vocal, keyboard, bass all popular) to two theatres – one, Obi (as in benefactor Sir Maurice Oberstein rather than Kenobi) complete with two-storey barn doors to make scenery shifts from adjoining scenic workshop easy peasy.

Textiles/costume design space in main building a pleasure to experience, too, recently remade with retractable door splitting teaching space, allowing GCSE students to spark off older pupils.

Hands-on stuff rules, however. Literally so in case of portable appliance test, pupils shinning impressively up ladders to check the lights. 'Need to understand what's dangerous,' said teacher (and a useful all-purpose teenage rule, too).

With students billed by specialism (dancer x and musician y) in school literature and so much going on, can sometimes be hard to know where lessons end and the extracurricular begins. Even college awards nights become performances, most recent complete with Great Gatsby staging and X Factor style audience votes (which would brighten up more conventional speech days elsewhere no end).

Driving everything is all-round enthusiasm, fuelled by wide range of sixth form specialisms and staff contacts – brilliant, of course – with some interactive media students, for example, getting chance to work with Aardman studios.

Sixth former taking BTec in technical theatre had had a ball working on Tim Burton-inspired costumes for Hamlyn, put on in local theatre and one of 40 productions through the year ranging from Artaud and Brook to Brecht, Caryl Churchill and much in the way of full-blown Shakespeare, many others with words and scores written by the staff and/or pupils.

Traditional educational add ons far from absent, however. Duke of Edinburgh runs as conventional course (though Jack Petchey awards – imaginatively awarded for academic rather than community service excellence in years 10 and 11 – do not). Sport isn't neglected either. School has own Olympian to its name, and while council has hung on to school's (small) sports field, necessitating relocation of sports day (and other fixtures) to nearby Norwood Lakes, the keen have school gym – somewhat battered but serviceable – for basketball (popular girls' team, which meets on Mondays, 'vicious', thought year 13 boys, admiringly).

Background and atmosphere: Patriotic acronym is down to British Record Industry Trust – great and good still feature on governors' list – whose funding and influence led to school's foundation in 1991 (after Mrs Thatcher, fearing creation of home for resting thesps, had been won round – or so the legend goes).

They're hugely proud of what they've created, says principal, and with good reason. Despite growth of vocational training colleges covering the 14-19 age range, school remains a one-off, the only free (prospectus uses capitals to emphasis) performing arts and technology school in the country, state funded but outside LA control.

Set within easy walk from Selhurst Station – not likely to become new Hoxton any time soon – school, though not an obvious looker from the outside, is full of thought, care and taste when it comes to the interiors. Inevitable tired corners mainly in vintage old school building (site originally housed Selhurst Grammar), one of three of varying styles and vintage. Newest, light and bright, is very plush indeed though smart rooms and corridors largely rule throughout the site, with plenty of tarting up (paint 'n' porthole doors even in otherwise non-refurbished areas, for example).

Feel is urban grit, rather than Surrey Downs (even feels like a long way to leafy South Croydon) with undeniable pressure on space. No pupil common rooms, for example (one year 11 girl had asked teacher to keep an eye on possessions during the day – gladly done, too) – immaculate carpeting in many corridors provides comfortable sitting space for the needy (speckly stone finish remains in original school building) with one student sitting by banked lockers busily sorting out vast pile of music.

Academic year is unusual – five eight-week terms, interspersed with fortnight breaks. Officially this 'supports delivery of the curriculum and ensures students return refreshed'

Little in the way of school jargon, bar slightly confusing names. (Blue Block, though lovely, isn't blue.) Main (and alias-free) building, built new for school's opening, has been substantially refreshed. Features include internal windows opening out on to corridors (principal's office too, at his request, providing a window on to the world), walls liberally decorated with high quality art (everything from Aboriginal-motifs to Banksy lookalike and delicate Japanese figures disporting themselves against parchment backdrop).

Academic year, too, is unusual with five eight-week terms, interspersed with fortnight breaks. Officially 'best supports delivery of the curriculum and ensures students return refreshed', though according to one teacher, production demands mean 'you'll often find students coming in over the holidays'.

With the exception of occasional overt whackiness – bins spray painted in wild array of colours following theatre teacher's guerrilla decoration initiative over the summer holidays – what dominates is sense of all-through professionalism.

And while absence of uniform, bells (and whistles, at least off stage) may not tend towards the norm, expectations certainly do, with teachers unlikely to indulge in too much time-drift as 'students will tell you when break is,' reckoned one.

Pastoral care, well-being and discipline: It's a busy old day; lights up 7am, not dimmed until 12 hours later. Though 'no-one will be here all that time,' says principal, some will operate in unconventional hours – drama and dance students, for example, warming up in the early hours before auditions or classes, studios booked up way in advance so pupils can edit their films.

Outstanding attendance, particularly at sixth form level, testament to commitment but also in stark contrast, in some cases, to pupils' unhappy educational experiences elsewhere. Several talked about feeling 'like outsiders' in other schools. Here, blend of rigour and tolerance seems to suit everyone. 'I felt I'd found people like me,' reckoned one sixth former.

'We think it's a good place to be looked after,' says principal, who is particularly proud of large scale speed meet and greet induction where grizzled year 11 veterans help newly arrived year 10s to settle in.

Body image can (predictably) be an issue, countered by strong message highlighting the glory of the individual, school stressing its more unconventional successes such as Adele to ensure that identikit size nothings aren't touted as the only aspiration worth pursuing.

On-site counsellors, presence discreetly advertised to students via form tutors, provide additional back up, while healthy eating (just about the only niggle otherwise superlative inspection report could find) is now a major school focus, with year 10 science pupils reporting on savoury snack fat content to year 13 dancers, canteen staff challenging pupils 'in a friendly way' if appear to be opting for unhealthy/minimalistic lunch (those on free school meals compelled to have healthy meal, though 'it's not about being a dictator but guiding and supporting,' thought staff member).

Staff enforce gentle discipline – students in library, verging on slight chattiness in quiet zone, were instantly quelled by (silent) entrance of smiley but no-nonsense librarians. Creativity within a framework something of a necessity, especially with school jam-packed, recent BTec additions adding another 200 to sixth form so 'as much as can take without bursting,' says school.

May be a timetable but there's 'no "you will do this number of hours" – it's their school,' says

Blend of rigour and tolerance seems to suit everyone. 'I felt I'd found people like me,' reckoned one sixth former

principal. Adds up to atmosphere that engenders sense of independence combined with professionalism – a lesson for the future, as with sixth form pupils given permission to leave lesson to conduct library research, but with return time and teacher expectations clearly outlined.

Pupil voice is heard loud and clear, too, in everything from 'almost daily' cake sales to fundraising for forthcoming productions to active student council which recently voted to ban environment-unfriendly disposable cups at lunchtime, 'commit to bringing in refillable bottles'. No wonder giant painted portrait of the blessed Jamie on wall of bigger canteen dispenses saint-like smile like a South American folk hero by way of inspiration.

Pupils and parents: Education should be accomplished without removing innocence along the way, thinks the principal. 'Friends assume it's going to be like Fame, but it's really down to earth,' felt sixth former, though performers in particular exhibit healthy dose of chutzpah and aren't backwards in coming forwards, adding in a couple of pirouettes and a solo on the way in. We enjoyed early morning dancing huddles outside (professional-looking gurning, too, in one case) – and tales of close harmony rivalry in the canteen.

Though unified by drive – 'at an ordinary school she'd be the leader of the pack, here, she's in a class with 30 of them,' reckoned mother of aspiring dancer – school community otherwise diverse. Families range from chimney sweeps to the loaded, many drawn from immediate area, which is 'socially complicated,' says principal, characterised by side-by-side pockets of affluence and deprivation – eligibility for free school meals is above the national average, and school also runs 'BRIT loves Selhurst' campaign, offering free tickets to locals.

Entrance: Not for everyone. One talented singer-songwriter had opted instead for Guildford ACM. 'They advertise it as once you go there, 75 per cent of your future career is done, but I know it's hard work.' Some find the place for themselves – press coverage is pretty much non-stop. One girl, now in sixth form, paid first visit to keep friend company and ended up the one with the place.

A minority very local (15 per cent from Croydon), though vast majority (75 per cent) from South London, remaining 10 per cent, selected on raw talent, not postcode, can come from anywhere in UK. (School stresses desire to avoid impossibly long journeys, somewhat spoiling effect with X-Factor winner Leona Lewis, quoted as describing two-hour round trip as 'so worth it'.)

Oversubscribed all the way through, less so for those entering in year 10, massively for sixth form. For 14 year olds seeking place in year 10, process less daunting, though useful to muster clear ideas on what pupils would gain from coming here.

Technical courses based on portfolios followed by workshops the norm. Inevitably stressful for would-be performers. 'She got recalled, she cried, she stuffed up in her first audition and thought "that's it" – but got in,' said parent who felt school wasn't looking for fully formed talent (there are rumours of already successful child stars being turned away) but 'something in kids that they can bring out – they don't necessarily want someone who's completely polished and finished and looking for it as a way into the next big thing'. A fair comment, thought school. 'It's about unlocking potential rather than a finished product.'

Exit: In a handful of cases, some year 11 pupils may not make the sixth form, most after discovering that love for performing arts has worn off. 'Might get to age 16 and think, I don't want to be a dancer – I want to do something else with my life,' says principal. 'They might just change and that's a good thing.'

At least 70 per cent, usually more, do carry on into sixth form, and almost everyone, even those who leave post-16, go on to further and higher education elsewhere – most recent extreme example swapping bright lights for animal husbandry.

Principal stresses proof that employability issues amongst the young can be triumphantly overcome. According to school survey, 70 per cent of past pupils end up working in creative industries. A few are household names but this is definitely not yardstick of measurement. All, says principal firmly, are superstars even if not household names because 'are the best box office manager or record label executive.'

School's well-designed vocational courses, with an eye and a half on the future, help speed the process along. Community-related courses, for example, lead to a virtuous circle, helping local bodies and in the process raising future trained community facilitators – a growing area for well-regarded HE courses such as Royal Central School of Speech and Drama's applied theatre and education BA degree. Others end up at RADA, Rose Bruford, Drama Centre, East 15, Bristol Old Vic, Guildhall and LAMDA, or head off to university – Leeds, York, Sheffield and Birmingham among them. Occasional one to Oxbridge.

Once through, you'll find their words, music, performance, directorial and backstage talents just about everywhere you look, from fashion shows to musicals, national theatre to community arts, in the UK and internationally.

Remarks: Vocational dazzler with some academic bright lights as well. An educational showstopper, and one you definitely won't want to walk out of half way through, which tempers sprinklings of stardust with lashings of nuts and bolts reality checks. That's what they say. We secretly think it's like collecting every school's coolest kids and putting them in one place. If we could set this review to music, we probably would.

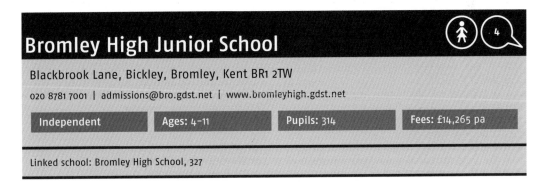

Bromley High Junior School

Blackbrook Lane, Bickley, Bromley, Kent BR1 2TW

020 8781 7001 | admissions@bro.gdst.net | www.bromleyhigh.gdst.net

| Independent | Ages: 4–11 | Pupils: 314 | Fees: £14,265 pa |

Linked school: Bromley High School, 327

Head of junior school: Since 2012, Claire Dickerson BA (Anglia Ruskin University). Since arriving at the school 14 years ago, she has seen the school from all angles: beginning as a year 4 class teacher before moving to reception and then taking on the headship, at a particularly exciting time as the school moved to its own version of a creative curriculum.

We found her to be focused, warm, open and an accomplished wearer of heels. Parents tell us: 'She is very approachable and we feel that we can have access to her whenever we need it'; another said, 'Our daughter was thrilled on her first day when Ms Dickerson was able to remember all their names and she takes a personal interest in each and every child.' Her outside interests are skiing, swimming and theatre. She lives locally and has two grown up children in their 20s.

Entrance: There are two forms of 20 pupils at 4+ and an additional eight girls join at 7+. The 4+ assessments are in the January prior to entry and 7+ assessments are held in the November of year 2. Most recently there were 80 applications at 4+ and 20 for the year 3 places. Thereafter a waiting list for occasional vacancies.

Exit: Around 70 per cent move on to the senior school, with about a quarter off to local grammar schools. The school is very clear that it is not a prep school and girls will not be prepared for external testing, leaving them free to explore a broad curriculum throughout years 5 and 6.

Remarks: The new curriculum has freed the teaching from Sats: instead the focus is the creative and cross-curricular, which the head feels has inspired the staff and 'sparked' the girls. Reception girls might be sculpting a mermaid, but they are learning about building 3D shapes and developing their research skills by investigating appropriate sea companions. Parents seem highly delighted with the imaginative approach to learning; one told us: 'The teaching throughout has been fantastic, varied, and full of different learning opportunities such as visitors and trips that have enhanced the curriculum'. One aim is to give each child the confidence to put forward their own ideas. Year 6 girls describe having 'talk partners' which change every three weeks, where they pair up to discuss topics, and that those who have finished their work will buddy up with a girl who might be stuck.

On polar fun day a real-life explorer shared tales of blubber and frostbite. Pupils dug up the grounds searching for archaeological artefacts on Roman day. We have seen plenty of Tudor houses built from cereal boxes and straw as part of the history curriculum, but never heard of them being set on fire to no doubt replicate the Great Fire. This seems to sum up the staff's ability to take things to the next level here.

The counterbalance to this is a careful teaching of the core subjects of reading, writing and maths. Maths is nearly always taught separately from the cross-curricular work. Handwriting is all joined up for most by the end of reception. A new system has been introduced for comprehensive academic tracking which, coupled with close home/school links, ensures that if a child does have a blip it can be talked about and supported. Homework escalates gradually, starting with some over the weekend in reception. There is a computing suite and years 5 and 6 each have an iPad which remains at school.

Literature is often at the heart of themes; World Book Day decorations adorn each classroom door, the library is well-stocked, houses are named after authors and the girls had recently enjoyed a visit from children's Laureate, Chris Riddell.

The choir's weekend trip took them to Belgium where they enjoyed a visit to a chocolate factory and also sang at the Menin Gate memorial at Ypres

Girls like to come to the library at lunch times if they're in the middle of a particularly good book. Languages are taught to give girls a flavour of what they might go on to study: French throughout, then Spanish in year 3, German in year 4, Latin in year 5 and double French in year 6 culminating in a five day trip to France. Girls say they are ready for it, as they've 'been practising' with shorter trips such as the choir's weekend trip to Belgium where they visited a chocolate factory and also sang at the Menin Gate memorial at Ypres.

Girls benefit from being able to share all of the sports facilities of the senior school, such as the indoor pool, and are the current GDST gymnastics champions. They seem to try everything and are playing an increasing fixture list, including a few against boys' schools. A recent win against a local independent boys' school was particularly important says the head, not so much for the win, 'but knowing they can compete as equals'.

The music wing contains practice rooms and a high ceilinged performance space. Lots of individual musical tuition and girls learn the recorder in year 3. Wind and string ensembles and the chance to play with senior girls in the orchestra. The junior school is the reigning Bromley Festival schools' choir champion in its age group. A year 5 girl is currently playing Matilda in the West End. There are whole school drama productions twice a year. This summer it's the Mikado.

A tempting array of weekly clubs. Some sporting and musical, but also ballroom dancing, nature garden, chess club, circus skills, 'hot off the press' and our favourite: guinea-pig club.

The junior school building is tucked behind the senior school and a major redevelopment will be finished in 2020. Plain, brick-built, functional, some of the classes and the library have nice views across the tennis and netball courts to the woods of Jubilee Park. Plenty of playground space, mainly tarmac but the year groups are carefully divided: the reception children have a large weatherproof canopy and a pirate ship; there is a fake grass Teletubby hill for the slightly older girls and plenty of space to run around for the Hawthorns, years 3 to 6. Making use of the grounds, the school has also adopted elements of the forest school outdoor learning.

The atmosphere is orderly but relaxed with children exuberant in PE and busy at playtime. Classrooms are large and utilitarian with meticulous displays. Girls were particularly neat in their uniforms of traditional summer dresses and grey wool blazers on the day of our visit. A parent: 'Every facet of the school seems to run like clockwork'. Confidence is most often mentioned by parents, with one telling us, 'Our youngest daughter is a completely different child since starting Bromley High. She has grown in confidence and has really thrived'.

Working parents may be delighted with the breakfast club, which runs from 7.30am. Additional fees for this and the after-school club. Had better hope that trains run on time, as late pick up fees are steep.

A large proportion of girls for whom English is an additional language, reflecting bilingual families. Just a few with a SEN. A part-time SENCo leads a team of eight teaching assistants who offer additional classroom support to any child needing a little more individual attention. One-on-one support is available where needed. Parents seem unanimous in the trust they place in the head and her staff and the 'nurturing' pastoral care to be found here.

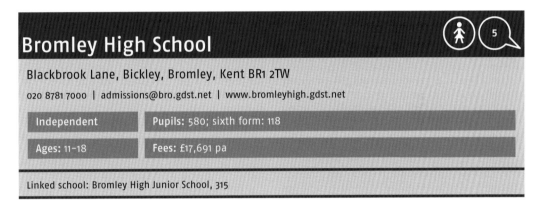

Bromley High School

Blackbrook Lane, Bickley, Bromley, Kent BR1 2TW

020 8781 7000 | admissions@bro.gdst.net | www.bromleyhigh.gdst.net

Independent	Pupils: 580; sixth form: 118
Ages: 11–18	Fees: £17,691 pa

Linked school: Bromley High Junior School, 315

Headmistress: Since 2014, Angela Drew BA PGCE MBA (50s). She studied English literature in Durham and then spent a year working with mentally disabled adults before entering teaching. She is an ISI inspector. Previously deputy head (academic) of Epsom College. She was head of English and drama at The Mary Erskine School in Edinburgh and has taught at George Watson's, Whitgift and Prior Park College. She teaches AS thinking skills from Y10. Friendly and open, she wears her headship lightly. A hope and ambition for the girls is that they will not just be prepared for the modern world but lead it.

After the departure of her relatively short-lived predecessor, Mrs Drew's initial year must have been spent on something of a caffeine high as she hosted 30 coffee mornings with groups of parents. 'She is passionate and proud of the girls, supportive and comes to so many events during school time and outside school hours. I believe she promotes the importance of an all-rounder with particular focus on the academics,' said a mother. Another: 'I think the headteacher has come into a well-established and successful school and she has made her mark. She has shaken up the PE department and this has improved. She has employed extremely

good teachers and bought in different teaching methods'.

Married with a grown up son and daughter, Mrs Drew enjoys reading and theatre and is a committed Evertonian. She lives nearby in rural Kent.

Academic matters: There has been a great curriculum shake-up in recent years, with most recent results not reflecting the wider choice of subjects available to GCSE students. As well as the expected core curriculum girls could choose dance, photography, classical civilisation, economics or additional maths. The sixth form offering adds in psychology, government and politics, business studies, plus a Pre-U in theology and philosophy. In 2019, 67 per cent 9-7 at GCSE; 52 per cent A*/A at A level.

In the sixth form classes do not exceed 14 pupils, some tuition groups are just a handful, and girls seem unfettered to pursue their own interests. Indeed this seems to be a strength of the school. Subjects don't have to be chosen with any timetabling restrictions and our sixth form guides described being encouraged to find their passions, no matter how slowly these emerge, whilst teachers offer guidance with a weather eye to careers and UCAS applications. Mrs Drew: 'We're very focused on where they're going, but they are free as to how they get there'. Triple science, literature and maths are the core (and the mathematicians really shine). For two consecutive years, upper sixth girls have gained the Salter's Award for the second highest chemistry A level mark in the UK.

The school isn't considering the IB but elements such as the extended project are on offer. Up to 16, few stray far from the more academic subjects: most take nine or 10, including several IGCSEs. Plenty of modern linguists, but curriculum changes have provoked a huge resurgence in classics – 39 girls were studying Latin in year 10 when we visited. When we queried whether Mandarin is on the horizon, Mrs Drew says she is 'tempted'. DT, but no food technology: a swing too far from gender stereotyping? Having seen the girls' impressive rainforest cakes in the geography bake off, perhaps there is little left to teach.

More than 20 teaching staff have been with the school for over 10 years. The school's latest ISI report declares teaching to be 'exceptional'. Praise for the teaching from parents ranges from the extremely appreciative to slight wistfulness from a couple who have come up from the all-singing-and-dancing junior school. A typically balanced report: 'There are some teachers who clearly go above and beyond to be approachable and encouraging and these members of staff are well liked and respected by the girls.' The head appointed a new academic deputy, a former head of science at St Paul's Girls', who has encouraged independent learning and 'risky' lessons. Mrs Drew has also introduced external workshops led by graduates to cultivate good study habits for both pupils and parents.

GCSE artists took a study tour of Vermeer's Amsterdam; meanwhile year 11 biologists extracted the DNA from strawberries and the historians put Hitler on trial

Trips, masterclasses and competitions inspire free thinking beyond exercise books. Year 12s were recently boggled by a speech recognition lecture by a leading light at Google; sixth formers secured tickets to see Simon Russell-Beale perform their set text at the National Theatre; whilst GCSE artists took a study tour of Vermeer's Amsterdam; meanwhile year 11 biologists extracted the DNA from strawberries and the historians put Hitler on trial. Terry Waite was soon to take part in a cross-curricular 'brain day', discussing how he survived captivity.

The curriculum has switched from ICT to computer science, a new computer lab has been

unveiled and GCSE and A level students joined 20,000 classrooms worldwide in two weeks of 'an hour of code'. Science labs are well-equipped and gradually being modernised. Meanwhile, girls have been proud winners of two Arkwright engineering scholarships. Serious contenders in the national Maths Challenges. Year 10s also recently won gold in the national Biology Challenge. A parent told us that the girls have so many public speaking opportunities it becomes 'second nature'. Those year 10s seem to be on fire, having also qualified for recent Oxford finals of the international youth debating championship.

Maths is set immediately on entry; science is set in year 9 and English from year 10. As always, parental thoughts on the amount of homework down to the individual child's stamina: some think it's a lot, particularly in the exam years, whilst some 'could actually do with a bit more' lower down the school. Holiday homework 'keeps things ticking over'.

Only a tiny number of girls receiving one-to-one support for identified learning differences as support is provided in lessons. Most girls with SEN have dyslexia but a few have dyspraxia or are high functioning ASD. No additional fees for learning support. Those capable of working up to three years beyond their chronological age are offered extension opportunities within the curriculum and via clubs, competitions and collaborations across the GDST, maths masterclasses and a STEM day.

Everyone does work experience in year 11 after GCSEs. The head recently took a group of year 10s – anyone who wanted to come – to meet an old girl at Cambridge. Teachers are said to be 'plugged in' to additional opportunities such as CV boosting competitions to enter. The GDST alumni network of 75,000 is invaluable for arranging work experience. Café Scientifique is a drop-in lecture series where girls are exposed to parents and old girls with inspiring careers and life experiences. And those prepping for Oxbridge have the benefit of the whole network of schools to form a cohort.

Games, options, the arts: Sport is compulsory for all girls up until the end of lower sixth. Upping the ante – bringing the fixture list and ambition in line with the 25 acres and facilities – was one of the head's first priorities. She recruited a new director of sport, previously head of netball at Alleyn's, and a male hockey coach. The U16A hockey team was Kent county champion. Someone is keeping score as they tell us the hockey teams have played 123 fixtures in the last year celebrating over 300 goals. The Olympic size Astroturf is now floodlit. Girls compete in netball, athletics, swimming, cross-country, rounders and are accomplished gymnasts. Increasing numbers getting to go on the bus, as the school fields A-D netball and rounders teams. Sixth formers are thrilled with the new gym, like

Mrs Drew's nonplussed response to our enquiry about exclusions suggested that discipline is not something she has to worry about

a mini health club, for use with a buddy at lunch times or after school. Year 10s give zumba and aerobics a go. The school's indoor pool can also be used by girls' families one evening a week and Saturday mornings. Girls able to brave the British weather enjoy the bronze and silver Duke of Edinburgh challenges, compulsory in year 10, with a couple completing gold before reaching university.

More artists than musicians in terms of academic study, but a very musical (and all-Steinway) school. Music theory is taught to years 7-9. We met a lone A level student, studying music tech. The majority of girls learn a musical instrument or have vocal tuition. Last year the senior school music tour was to Prague. One parent suggested there would be more take up of instrumental lessons if girls did not miss important lesson time. Some 24 peripatetic music staff teach to grade 8 on 16 different instruments and over 60 per cent played their way to a merit or distinction last year. There is regular success at Bromley and Beckenham Music Festival and girls have performed at Southwark Cathedral, the Royal Festival Hall and enjoyed tours to Spain and Normandy with choirs and ensembles.

Each year sees dance and drama productions with students performing, singing, playing in orchestra, and lighting, choreographing and undertaking backstage skills. One has a starring role in EastEnders.

High quality art is displayed around the school. We squinted through the door at the appealing art studio with mezzanine level as exams were in progress. Several pupils have exhibited at the Turner Contemporary Gallery. The DT facilities are extensive and enthusiastically used with the usual laser cutter but also a 3D printer.

Lunch time is deliberately long. Clubs range from the cosy such as 'knit and natter' and card games, the sporty – rugby, horse-riding or squad training – to the stimulating: robotics, DT divas and TED talks club. Musicians might try jazz, percussion or chamber strings. We were assured girls do not spend their lunch hours cutting up cadavers but were intrigued to note the forensics club. Sixth formers are equally engaged running their own discussion group, most recently on the death penalty.

Background and atmosphere: The school opened in 1883, aiming to provide education for girls on a par with that of their brothers, and the first entrants

described it as a bit like being in the army: there are photos of girls doing PE wearing ties. Originally in a Victorian building, the school relocated to its present site in 1981. The wooden honours boards line one of the modern corridors, their name in gold being something the girls still aspire to today.

The campus is spacious and green but with few mature trees to take the edge off the already plain buildings. A Parents' Association's recent purchase was sturdy wooden parasols to provide much-needed shade. Views come into their own from the upper floors – a science teacher jokingly referring to his lab as the penthouse. There is the large Crompton library – Richmal Crompton, the author of Just William, taught at the school – open until 5.30pm every day to facilitate homework. Sixth formers have their own large, light common room where they can eat their lunch, hang out on sofas and study in free periods. The dining hall is newly decorated in a zingy lime with lots of fruit and salad in evidence.

The grey and burgundy uniform here is particularly smart, with blazers on when not in lessons. The fashion seems to be for patent loafers with knee socks. Girls assured us that there isn't an 'it' bag culture. Sixth formers look smart and ready for anything in 'business attire', mostly jackets with skirts but they are free to express some individuality.

Girls burst out of lessons onto the wide carpeted corridors seeming relaxed. Asked to describe the school, a parent said, 'I feel there is pressure for the girls to succeed but above that I feel they push each girl individually to get the best out of them'; another, 'I feel the school is quite competitive – but very caring as most teachers know each girl individually and care for their welfare.' One of our guides said fondly of her time here since the age of 4: 'it's a really nice bubble'.

Pastoral care, well-being and discipline: Everyone we spoke to praised the school's pastoral care. 'I think the school provides excellent pastoral care. Teachers are involved and approachable and seem to work together,' said one. Parents universally expressed confidence in the school's ability to take care of any issues of bullying and felt that their daughters would be able to raise it. The school has one of the most thorough positive mental health policies we have seen, with a particular awareness of eating disorders, depression and self-harm as very live potential issues for students. There is a part-time student counsellor and 'big sister, little sister' pairs senior with younger girls.

Rules seem low key. Girls are allowed to wear 'discreet' make-up from year 9, earlier than many. Mobile phones to be kept in lockers away from lessons. From Mrs Drew's nonplussed response to our enquiry about any exclusions we gather that discipline is not something she has to worry about. Girls are engaging seriously with the current new wave of feminism and issues such as university rape culture. They have recently set up a LGBT club.

Pupils and parents: Although parents describe the school as 'mixed', it is not as culturally diverse as more central London schools with just over 10 per cent of girls speaking another language at home. Mainly white British with a mix of other ethnicities including Chinese, German, Portuguese and Hindi. The majority of girls come from the local area of Orpington, Bromley, Beckenham and Dulwich via a direct train route, but a proportion of girls also travel in from rural Kent.

The commutes of working parents are well-supported with both a free breakfast club from 7.30am and a homework club after school until 5.30pm.

Entrance: Over 70 per cent of the junior school girls transfer to the senior school, the majority without an 11+ assessment, although some choose to sit the test. Places for outsiders are offered via testing in the January prior to entry in verbal and non-verbal reasoning and creative writing plus a short mathematics extension paper. We are told that competition is stiffening as pressure for places increases. Pupils with identified SEN are given 25 per cent more time.

Pupils join from a range of independent prep schools and state primaries including Breaside Prep,

Blackheath Prep, Merton Court, St Christopher's, The Hall, Rosemead Prep, Oakfield Prep and St Olave's Prep. External applicants to the sixth form subject to GCSE entry requirements, school reference and interview.

Exit: Some 30 per cent leave at 16 to enter mainly co-ed sixth forms. Around half of A level leavers to Russell Group universities with LSE, UCL, Exeter, Bristol, Sheffield, Warwick, Bath and Nottingham amongst the favourite destinations; One to Oxbridge in 2019, three medics/dentists.

Money matters: Bursaries and scholarships in penny numbers for girls entering at year 7 and the lower sixth only, including honorary scholarships and minor awards for artists' materials and music lessons. Academic scholarships based on entrance test results. Bursaries are available on entry to the senior school and offer up to full fees for the academically gifted who could not otherwise afford to attend. Parents should expect their finances to be scrutinised in detail on application and each year thereafter. Some sixth form scholarships for which candidates must prepare a written application.

Remarks: A selective school, offering a wonderful range of opportunities to widen horizons and develop new interests. Suits academically able girls with lots of drive.

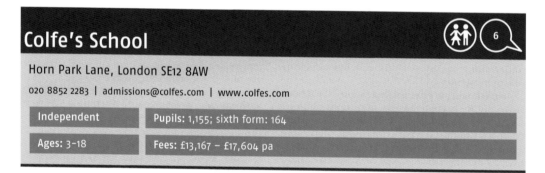

Colfe's School

Horn Park Lane, London SE12 8AW

020 8852 2283 | admissions@colfes.com | www.colfes.com

Independent	Pupils: 1,155; sixth form: 164
Ages: 3-18	Fees: £13,167 – £17,604 pa

Headmaster: Since 2005, Richard Russell (50s), previously deputy warden of Forest School. Educated in Ireland and went on to read classics at Cambridge. He started his career as a Latin teacher; teaching initially attracted him as it would allow him to pursue his interest in archaeology and attend digs during the long summer holidays. Knows everybody and what they're up to, teaches Latin to year 7. He spent 15 years at Sevenoaks coordinating the IB programme; however, he has never thought it particularly suitable for Colfe's and is a great fan of A levels. A professional and pleasant person, say parents, easy to get on with and ambitious for his

pupils. He lives in Blackheath with his wife, who works in the City. Nowadays holiday times see them heading for their house in Sicily, where they make their own olive oil.

Head of junior school: Since 2016, Catriona Macleod MSc. Worked at several London prep schools, becoming head of science and then deputy head at Streatham & Clapham junior school, head of juniors at Dunottar School, then head of junior school at Knightsbridge School. Has recently worked in a senior role at a free school in Hertfordshire.

Head of pre-prep: Since 2013 is Sarah Redman (50s) BEd. Mrs Redman was deputy head of the nursery and pre-prep school for some years before becoming head teacher. Parents comment on her warmth and friendliness, 'exactly the sort of person you can entrust your small child to'. Married to a fellow teacher, who is head of a local state primary, with three grown-up children, one of whom is an actress. She enjoys gardening, theatre, arts and crafts, the influence of which can be spotted around the pre-prep.

Academic matters: Well-planned academic curriculum in the junior school runs alongside inspirational sport and arts options. Six-year-olds upwards learn French and Spanish in alternating years. Mixed ability classes of around 18; each child is monitored regularly to check progress. Lively pupils perform well in both national and house competitions; particularly successful teams for maths and chess. 'A very caring school, where the teachers recognise every child as an individual.'

In 2019, 52 per cent 9-7 at GCSE, with particularly strong showing in maths. At A level, 50 per cent A*-A and 83 per cent A*-B. Maths, English and the sciences are popular closely followed by economics and history. Most take nine or 10 GCSEs including a language, choice of German, French, Spanish or Latin. Whole school aim is to make classes active and stimulating; everything is in place for high flyers who might be heading for Oxbridge but also for those who might need to go more gently. Setting for maths, sciences and languages. History and maths departments are particularly strong performers; provision for accelerated learning groups for additional maths qualifications. Sixth formers can take Extended Project Qualification. Students with mild specific learning difficulties are supported by specialist staff. The library is a well-used resource, with full-time librarian who also doubles up as head of careers, open until 6pm, during Easter holidays and to students on study leave. Outstanding advice and guidance on selecting courses and universities. The school recently ran a conference to introduce the option of going to university in the Netherlands.

Games, options, the arts: Arts and sports are strong all round, structured to suit all tastes and talents. 'Sport for all' policy means there is something for everyone, be it dance or being a member of one of the successful rugby teams. On-site facilities including a gym and 25m swimming pool, which hosts swimming galas, kayaking, water polo and lifesaving courses for year 10s. Additional large playing fields at Leathersellers' sports grounds a few minutes away by minibus on the Sidcup Road. Former Surrey and Kent opening batsman coaches cricket, and athletes often selected to represent Greenwich

in the London School Championships. More or less everything on offer on the sporting front for juniors too, with lots of house competitions. Junior girls' netball team have been national prep school champions. CCF with its unique Army Air Corps unit popular, as is DofE, with many progressing to gold award.

Outstanding guidance on selecting courses and universities. The school recently ran a conference to introduce the option of going to university in the Netherlands

Large art department includes printmaking equipment, a kiln for ceramics and a dark room. Parents comment on the energetic drama department; pupils encouraged to write and produce their own plays. LAMDA classes, stage management and technical theatre skills all on offer; impressive variety and number of productions. Up-to-date music rooms and individual soundproof practice studios; swing bands, orchestras, and choirs galore. Huge range of clubs and societies to join: particularly popular are maths, chess and debating along with many inter-house competitions, quizzes, drama, sports and concerts. Regular outings, theatre visits and trips abroad; sixth formers visit the Gambia annually to help build and maintain a school. Good participation in the arts, but relatively small numbers go on to take these subjects at A level, drama and media studies taking the lead over art, design and music.

Art is incorporated into much of the junior school curriculum and classrooms are bursting with interesting displays, models and sculptures. Specialist art teacher organises a big end of year exhibition. Musical education starts early with recorder in year 1 and ukulele in year 2. With around 80 per cent taking instrumental lessons, the school boasts choirs, orchestras, chamber groups, rock band and specialist brass programme. Creative drama, regular plays and lots of opportunities for performers in musical and dramatic assemblies. Dance workshops are popular and include everything and anything from flamenco to African dancing.

Background and atmosphere: Founded in 1652, to educate 'the poor boys of Blackheath' by the Rev Abraham Colfe of Lewisham. Later the school was left in the trust of the Leathersellers' Company, whose livery members make up a majority of today's governing body. Leathersellers have recently pledged an additional £1 million in bursaries. Was a state boys' grammar school for some years before opting to go independent in the 1970s rather than become a comprehensive school. Went fully co-ed in 1999. Strong links with six state schools, five local, one in the Gambia.

Corridors adorned with pupils' work and achievements; atmosphere is positive and busy with smartly dressed, friendly pupils and helpful staff. Bleak, utilitarian brick buildings softened by shrubs and trees; new Stewart building houses sixth form centre and Roebuck café.

Junior school in green and tranquil setting on the edge of the main school; new buildings mean the school can now accommodate three classes across the age groups.

Pastoral care, well-being and discipline: Pastoral care continues to be excellent and very much part of the school's ethos. Well-established house system in senior school; everyone attends regular house tutor meetings; years 8-11 are in vertical age groups, sixth formers and year 7s in separate groups. There are lots of opportunities for leadership and mentoring within the house system to help pupils develop maturity, gain confidence and a range of life skills. Frequent house activities and competitions ensure everybody is involved in the school community. School nurse and independent counsellor. Parents say home-school links are encouraged and the head of pastoral care is always available to speak with them. One commented that pastoral staff have done well in creating a supportive and caring atmosphere. Pupils seem thoughtful and considerate to others, older pupils particularly good at mentoring younger ones. 'A very caring school, where the teachers recognise every child as an individual.'

Pupils and parents: Mainly professional types from Blackheath, Lewisham, Lee and more recently other areas accessible via train links. Head is keen

to recruit from as varied a pool as possible, so a lot of effort is made to encourage children from state primaries as well as independents to apply. Big old boys' and girls' society runs a number of activities and fundraising events. Everyone is invited to the annual service in memory of the founder Rev Colfe. A good all-rounder school producing an interesting range of pupils going into many different careers. Alumni list reflects the school's diverse range: Eric Ambler, author, Lord Vaizey, economist, Kenneth Grayson, first professor of theology at Bristol University, to name but a few; also actors, musicians, politicians and sportspeople.

Entrance: Most join juniors at 3+ or 4+ via information observation morning. Year 3 no longer a main point of entry; assessment for occasional places further up the school. At 11+ interview, reference from current school and exams in maths and English. Sixth formers are offered places on the basis of an interview, reference and predicted GCSE grades.

Exit: At 11+ about 80-90 per cent move into the senior school; a few opt for local state grammars. Around 10-20 per cent leaves at 16+ for sixth form colleges. At 18+ to huge a range of different universities (majority Russell Group), including two to USA in 2019.

Money matters: At 11+ and 16+ scholarships and means-tested bursaries are available for drama, art, sports, music and academics. Around 20 to 30 per cent of pupils receive some form of fee subsidy.

Remarks: Pleasant, relaxed atmosphere. Provides a high standard of education without being overly competitive. Its focus on individual successes and promoting a balanced approach to life and learning is not to be underestimated in today's hectic world.

Coloma Convent Girls' School

Upper Shirley Road, Croydon, Surrey CR9 5AS

020 8654 6228 | webadmin@coloma.croydon.sch.uk | www.coloma.croydon.sch.uk

| State | Ages: 11–18 | Pupils: 1,057; sixth form: 269 |

Headteacher: Since September 2019, Sue Collins, previously deputy head. She joined the school in 2004, becoming head of sixth form, assistant head and then deputy head in 2015. A Coloma sixth former herself, she studied maths at Liverpool and

a PGCE at Roehampton Institute. Began her teaching career at Cardinal Newman Catholic School in Hove, moving on to a range of schools including Northampton School for Boys, Riddlesdown Collegiate and Croydon High School. She has also taught adult education evening classes, been a supply teacher at the International School in Amsterdam and completed a masters in education from the OU and a diploma in Catholic leadership from St Mary's University.

In her spare time, she enjoys music, theatre, gardening, walking and 'occasional, tentative cycling'.

Academic matters: Consistently one of top comprehensives in the country for results and progress, achieved through blend of top teaching, forensic (and largely behind the scenes) analysis and, school's secret ingredient, exceptional choice for pupils. Everyone, high achiever or otherwise, can opt for subjects that they enjoy and thus will excel at. 'I've got way too many favourite lessons,' enthused year 10 pupil.

GCSEs for all in English language and literature plus maths, science, RS, a language and humanity. But it's the options list that's a thing of beauty – offered within the timetable where possible (art and design, business and communication and DT) and as twilight club if not (PE and Spanish) with music featuring on both lists to ensure enthusiasts don't miss out because of a subject clash.

In 2019, 71 per cent got 9-5 in both English and maths GCSE, 40 per cent of grades at 9-7. Immediate benefits obvious, breadth enabling vast majority to gain at least one grade 7. 'Even weakest can be strong in some subjects,' says school. Pupils agree. 'Made me realise that I could push myself and my capabilities here,' said one.

At A level, with 61 per cent of grades at A*/B (27 per cent A*-A) in 2019, more of the same, with girls listing their dream subject combination (30 to choose from) and school (assuming large enough group to make finances and logistics work), making it happen – timetabling a marvel of ingenuity. Many complete four A levels and a handful do five, everyone taking PE, PSHE and religious studies on top. Firm emphasis on facilitating subjects with several nods to wider range of interests including health and social care and DT. No BTecs – money the major factor, though in ideal world, would offer both. No IB either – current system felt to offer breadth and to spare, grateful medics recently coming back to extol joys of leavening sciences with arts or a language.

Minimal setting and none in year 7 – avoids any sense of being programmed for failure. 'Spend the first year sussing out where they need to develop,' said parent. Class sizes sound big – maximum of 30 for first three years, 24 in years 10 and 11 and 14 in the sixth form (17.5 pupil to teacher ratio overall) but often far smaller, stresses school.

No resting on laurels. Even quiz former pupils on what could be improved – uni-standard referencing techniques, for example, recently added to sixth form curriculum. Strong staff team of just under 80 includes half a dozen or so former pupils influenced by strong desire to 'return the favour', as a parent put it, devotion to duty likely to be stand-out quality in application letters. Morale is high with happy blend of newcomers and long termers (23 have been here for decade or more), school a pioneer of in-service training and keen to welcome in new ideas.

Calm, low-pressure atmosphere. 'Some of daughter's friends at other schools are always stressing', thought parent, 'here they prepare them gently'

Organisation is straightforward. Teachers teach, senior management manage, helped by data crunched anyway you want it, courtesy of resident expert. No decline too small to pinpoint or too difficult to reverse. Masses of lesson observations, positive reviews – what worked well, what could have worked even better, deliberate avoidance of corporate blame game and focus on collaboration emphasised by titles – team leaders rather than heads of department.

Girls, similarly, encouraged to put in the effort – long-ish school day can end at 5.00pm or later – but never to feel that 'school is continuously holding them to account'. Take learning needs in their stride (just over 100 pupils with SEN, five statemented and 110 with EAL requirements), working with primary schools to ensure smooth transition and offering range of support that includes one-to-one and in-class help.

Results in calm, low-pressure atmosphere though 'plenty of organised noise,' says teacher. Trust in the school required – difficulties may not be raised until parents' evening, and one mother felt more feedback during the year would be useful. Overall, approach felt to be on the button. 'Some of daughter's friends at other schools are always stressing,' thought parent. 'Here, they prepare them gently.'

Games, options, the arts: 'Gives the children all the opportunities,' said parent. Every day jam-packed with total fulfilment for arty, active or both – helped by flourishing parents' association that's stumped up for new laser cutter for DT department (works wonders on wood) and refurbishment of two grand pianos (the two aren't connected). Community the focus for fundraising, 100-strong charity committee choosing different cause each year as well as supporting linked school in Uganda. Runs special charities week featuring talent show and daily cake

Prendergast School

sales (carrot a dominant and healthy ingredient, stresses school) but not allowed to spill into vital learning time.

Pupils are expected to make the most of activities – school stresses impact on outcomes – and most stick to termly pledge to try something new, 70 sixth formers, for example, turning up for optional netball club. Those who don't tend to change their minds pronto – 'got a bit boring when everybody was leaving for a choir competition or a match and I was just sitting there,' said one.

Annual visit to Lourdes can be life-changing. And nobody minds if it's the budget rather than the de luxe version...

Trips, likewise, ranging from French and German exchange trips to netball tours (South African recently), hone practical and socialising skills, while annual visit to Lourdes can be life-changing. And so what if it's budget rather than de luxe version? Twenty-five hour coach journey for year 9 Austrian ski trip was 'nearly the best part,' said pupil. Even year 7s pack in Disneyland excursion, teachers still smiling at midnight, despite coach's cargo of 'grumpy girls burned out with far too many sweets,' said parent.

While parents rate every area as 'exceptional', music is perhaps most exceptional of the lot, recently acquired specialist music status merely official acknowledgement of the fact. Think not just big but bumper-sized, with eight choral groups and 500-strong main choir (all year 7 pupils expected to sign up for practical demonstration of virtues of cooperation, regardless of singing ability). Also two orchestras, numerous bands including – amazingly – a six-strong harp ensemble and over 300 individual weekly music lessons (French horn, bassoon – even double bass to grade 8). While already run 40 events each year (schedule is described with heartfelt sincerity as 'hectic' – audition-only St Cecilia Singers' triumph in national choral competition one of many successes), 'to do' list constantly being extended, multi-school youth music festival latest to be added.

Just as busy and successful on other fronts. Out of school hours, high-energy clubs range from CCF (run with Royal Russell, local independent school) to DofE, though plenty of others – including chess and prayer clubs – of a more cerebral nature.

Sports also described as 'exceptional', say parents (no surprise there), from range (orienteering, kickboxing and handball all on the menu) to successes. Recent Croydon champions for cross-country, indoor cricket, table tennis, often moving on to success at county, regional level and sometimes national level. Lacrosse particularly noteworthy. School one of few (possibly only one) in state sector to offer it, yet regularly trounces independents like Brighton College.

Teamed with generous facilities (two gyms, all weather floodlit sports pitches, field and track in extensive grounds). If three 50-minute sessions for first two years (two in year 9 and one in years 10-12) aren't enough, umpteen ways of filling any spare gaps, like early morning fitness sessions for those who don't get their kicks (penalty or otherwise) from team sports. 'Stuff happens at lunchtime, before school, after school and at the weekend, I don't know how teachers have a family life, to be honest,' said parent.

Background and atmosphere: Everything derives from living the motto, 'labore est vocare', which is known and understood by all, each lesson starting with a prayer. Parents approve. 'It's a good grounding to think of others and have a bit of reflection, whatever your spiritual beliefs are,' thought one.

Upholds values of educationalist The Very Reverend Canon Van Crombrugghe, who founded the Congregation of the Daughters of Mary and Joseph in native Belgium in 1817 in premises owned by Count of Santa Coloma. Convent opened 1869 in Croydon, school followed two months later (with just one pupil), moving to current home (with rather more) in 1965. Links with order still close, sister ('young in spirit and delightful in every way') running repository. Josephite brothers, meanwhile, went on to found St George's College in Weybridge, relationship as cordial as distance between the schools will allow. Initially independent, school joined maintained sector as grammar, becoming a comprehensive in the 1970s and merging with sister school, St Anne's, which survived flying bombs (commemorated by touching stained glass panel in chapel entrance) but couldn't withstand vicissitudes of shifting educational policy.

'Stuff happens at lunchtime, before school, after school and at the weekend, I don't know how teachers have a family life, to be honest,' said parent

Site is neat, tidy (beautifully clipped shrubbery lines attractive paths), survival of original Victorian buildings (coach house particularly pretty) and inevitable Portakabin presence offset by tactical use of trees. Giant specimen is framed dead centre, to magnificent effect, by picture window in vast, airy performing arts hall, one of many improvements and new builds that keep coming, courtesy of non-stop grant applications and budget-finessing. Others include an all-weather pitch, sixth form centre, after-school users radiating industry under its curved roof, as well as 50th anniversary Jubilee Building, home of 'brilliant' art and boasting eccentric but charming turret.

Some economising elsewhere, low tech computers lovingly maintained rather than cutting edge, lunches paid for with real money and non-flushing loos or wobbly chair legs logged by pupils and staff on paper slips. With funding for just one technician and small but dedicated maintenance team, staff and pupils expected to treat this like home from home only better (slightly exasperated note in staff loos impresses need to keep the bowls clean...).

Girls as spick and span as the premises, non-negotiable school uniform policy including compulsory white socks or tights for juniors (helps make them more visible to motorists). No makeup or body spray or 'unnatural hair colourings' and letters home stress importance of retaining modesty, even on home clothes day. Goes down well with parents. 'Not appropriate to be flashing your cleavage when you're 15 and going on public transport,' said one.

Pastoral care, well-being and discipline: Structure ensures continuity, with form tutors normally unchanged through to GCSEs. Each year 7 and 8 form group also gets two sixth form prefects to help with settling in process. School stresses importance of self-motivation and personal responsibility, parents expected to ensure daughters' punctuality, arrange dentist appointments outside school hours and to avoid term time absences (requests need to be made at least a month in advance).

The 50th anniversary Jubilee Building, home of 'brilliant' art, also boasts an eccentric but charming turret

Sanctions and rewards as clearly worked out as you'd expect, commendations awarded for effort and attainment and teachers encouraged to 'catch pupils being good in order to find opportunities for praise and rewards.' Misconducts awarded for everything from using mobile phones in lessons (they're also banned on school trips) to failure to sign homework diaries. Escalation of reports; exclusion for most serious offences – though a vanishing

rarity, with a strong emphasis on forgiveness. 'We all make mistakes and need to move on,' says school.

Girls as spick and span as the premises; school uniform policy includes compulsory white socks or tights for juniors (makes them more visible to motorists)

Friendship issues usually resolved, though long-term bullies would be asked to leave if didn't change their ways (and with serious incidents kept on file for six years, strong incentive for them to do so). Clearly works – almost unheard of for pupils to be asked to leave. Little details all taken care of, down to staff escorts out of school and on to local buses – 'don't have to do it but helps keep the girls safe'. 'Really lovely,' said parent, while bus drivers comment on courteous behaviour (witnessed first hand when they stopped this reviewer leaving vital bag behind).

And sensitive support extends also to parents who report that if family crisis strikes, will be contacted by dedicated pastoral head to see how they're coping and offer a sympathetic ear.

Pupils and parents: Bright, motivated pupils will do well – rebels or late sleepers may find it harder, though 'wrong sort of rebellion is tamed,' reckons member of staff. Important, stress parents, to be realistic about school's expectations. 'Have to be in at 8.10am and factor in your journey – if that's difficult for you then this is not the school for you,' said one.

Depth of religion, too, needs to be thought through. 'Can't lag it,' stresses mother. While sex education is offered according to government guidelines, you're left in no doubt as to school's stance, say parents (marriage first). School delights in happy integration of pupils who span range of backgrounds and circumstances and develop streetwise (but sensible) nonchalance, heading off to shops or homes in Bromley, Coulsdon and Crystal Palace on public transport. More affluent learn to appreciate good fortune along the way. Daughter 'realises what she has is pretty damn good,' said parent. Locals connected with the school – one in eight of women in Croydon, it estimates – feel the same way. 'I do as much as I can to support them,' said one former pupil.

Tend to live long and prosper – one recently made it to ripe old age of 107 and like pupils, have plenty of opportunities to be involved, from joining choir directed by retired head of music to helping organise events – usually plenty of volunteers and warm welcome for all. 'Can turn up and go to anything on your own – not cliquey at all,' said parent.

Entrance: Five form entry – total of 150 in year 7. Applications from families from other faiths (number 7 on admissions criteria) or none (number 8) in theory welcome, but vanishingly unlikely to translate into offer of a place given 700 applications each year and 450 or so Catholic families ahead of you in the queue, though school never takes popularity for granted. 'We welcome everybody.'

Early and whole-hearted commitment to Catholicism is required and attendance at mass, baptismal age and first communion will all need verification. Ever-shrinking home to school distance the tie breaker.

Around 30 per cent of sixth form from other schools, when faith criteria no longer apply. Minimum six GCSE passes at 4+ for mixed course (BTec/A level), increasing to eight grade 6/7s for four A levels. Need to be on your toes as school barely advertises the fact – prefers those already in the know.

Exit: Loses around 40 post GCSE to co-ed sixth forms, mostly those taking vocational subjects and a few with longest journey time opting for an easier commute. Over 90 per cent of leavers either to university or art foundation courses, 40 per cent Russell Group. All sciences well represented though wide range also includes English, psychology and law. Two medics in 2019.

Large variety of universities include Surrey, Sussex, KCL, Leeds, City, Warwick and Exeter. Four to Oxbridge in 2019; one to US. Lead up to applications process predictably thorough with own, qualified careers advisor (a rarity), highly detailed website content and early planning – pupils in year 8 play interactive games that match interest with possible careerss.

Money matters: Some funding for residential trips for parents on benefits.

Remarks: Awe-inspiring in every direction, bulging with extras despite limited funding. 'The school is like a clock tower: you need to make all the cogs work together,' said pupil. Swimming pool would do wonders for the mechanism. Caring hedge fund managers should apply direct to school.

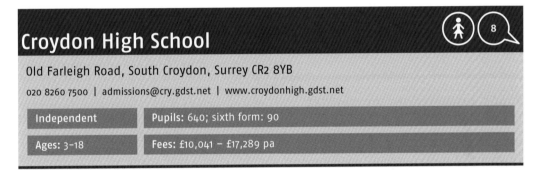

Croydon High School

Old Farleigh Road, South Croydon, Surrey CR2 8YB

020 8260 7500 | admissions@cry.gdst.net | www.croydonhigh.gdst.net

Independent	Pupils: 640; sixth form: 90
Ages: 3–18	Fees: £10,041 – £17,289 pa

Head: Since 2016, Emma Pattison BA (30s). Previously deputy head (academic) at St John's School, Leatherhead, preceded by spells at Guildford High School (four years as head of MFL for juniors and seniors) and Caterham (languages teacher and head of year 8). Experience in co-ed schools hasn't dimmed enthusiasm for single sex education. 'When you can tailor the curriculum for the kinds of things you know girls will enjoy, it's so exciting,' she says.

Though teaching runs in the family (mother and grandmother) it was only after a short spell as a management trainee that Mrs Pattison saw the light and changed careers. Describes first headship as wonderful 'in every way', from school culture ('sensational') to buzzy and engaging pupils – 'had the year 8s in yesterday for tea and cake and just laughed with them for half an hour.'

Staff also a thoughtful bunch, one giving Mrs P something 'to help you spend time with your daughter' (approaching school age). Not, as we'd speculated, a cloning kit but a jar layered with pre-measured cookie ingredients. No doubt a parenting essential given the long hours she puts in. Piano practice (she started her degree in music before switching to languages) is already confined to weekends.

Makes it her business to know what's going on – and it shows. She has a little list based on parent concerns. While the precise contents were undivulged, it seemed identical to ours. High flyers are encouraged to aim for the stars, the keen to get their share of the sunlight. Unloved junior school lunches and moving up day (previously disorganised) have been transformed, while the substantial fee hike between junior and senior schools is being smoothed out. Girls feel she cares what they think, parents are favourably impressed by her know-how. 'Very on the ball,' said one.

Junior head: Since September 2019 is Sarah Raja, previously deputy head. She has a degree in primary education from Canterbury Christ Church and an MSc in education leadership from Leicester; spent seven years at Sutton High as class teacher and KS2 coordinator before joining Croydon in 2015.

Academic matters: Focus, says head, is on selective but bespoke education. High teacher to pupil ratio (one to eight), small class sizes (average 17, maximum around 22 and often fewer, under a handful for A level) and solid support (drop-in or individually tailored in the senior school) all help. One pupil was taking maths, further maths and music plus a science for A level; another philosophy and ethics, drama and politics. GO (girls only) tagline (on careers-linked literature) reinforces the fact that anything is possible.

Numbers of younger teachers are growing. 'There's something of a generational shift,' says school. Maths staff get particular praise. Motivators for joining (and staying) include excellent facilities (labs in particular), though pupils' attitudes are the clincher. 'Can teach, don't have to be a policeman, love practising craft and seeing the penny drop,' said senior maths teacher.

Pupils' attitudes are the clincher. 'Can teach, don't have to be a policeman, love practising craft and seeing the penny drop,' said senior maths teacher

Junior timetable synced with senior school, some specialist teaching from nursery, more added as pupils move up. Ambitious languages – Spanish (years 1, 2 and 3) German (year 4) and French (years 5 and 6) build up to Latin in top year. Also run creative thinking days (focus on problem-solving) and, for older juniors, philosophy.

Junior maths now transformed. New passport (also covers reading and writing) gives juniors (and parents) goals to achieve in their own time with a certificate at the end. 'Not just everyday sums, it's games – fun – such a good way of encouraging the kids to learn more,' said parent.

Pace, never sluggish (individual sciences from year 7, for example), 'kicks up a notch in year 9,' said a parent. Gentle insistence on organisational skills pays dividends, say parents. While there's tolerance

---

Head was delighted that one of brightest and best sixth formers had heart set on agriculture college and a farming career

if homework or a test missed, pupils must be proactive with (credible) explanations – and a lack of engagement is swiftly communicated to parents.

Good range of GCSEs and IGCSEs (constantly under review) includes options like computing and 3D design, spice provided by trips (for computing as well as more conventional subjects).

Most go on to three A levels (business studies a recent addition) plus extended essay, four if have the appetite and ability. Ditto those who prefer to channel spare energy into sport. 'Let them do what they want to do,' says head. Standalone AS subjects, like photography, also on offer. Approach translates into consistently good results. In 2019, 73 per cent of GCSEs grade 9-7. At A level, 48 per cent A*/A grades.

While 2014 inspection report was largely glowing, commented that independent learning didn't always come naturally to the school. Watching year 4 juniors working out how royal barber would go about shaving Henry Vlll (very, very carefully), and year 8s embarking on effortless improv themed to Taming of the Shrew with a complete absence of self-consciousness, it was clear that things had changed. 'Not shy, not cynical – that's a girls' school,' says head. For able seniors, there's the GO-Beyond programme where teachers expand on off-curriculum topics – 'How to develop your very own language,' say, or 'Russia'. The really exceptional (rather than merely gifted) juniors have Altitudo programme, resulting in impressively mature work, such as an imagined (and completely credible) conversation between Decartes and Locke.

The message is that no career is impossible, reinforced by careers in the classroom event for juniors (bring a cryptanalyst to school) to Pathways Mentoring for sixth formers. While doctors and lawyers pop up regularly to enthuse and inspire, head was delighted that one of brightest and best sixth formers had heart set on agriculture college and a farming career. No point pushing Oxbridge when it won't suit, she says. 'Some get there and are miserable because they're not super academic though they are super bright.' Communications are very effective (email, Twitter – one account per department), quick responses at all times. 'Very reassuring and efficient,' said a parent.

School's size and philosophy means no middle ground to get lost in. Head of learning support works across the school and all pupils are automatically assessed for special provision (extra time/movement breaks) in public exams. Most pupils are highly able though support, for the 24 junior and 30 seniors with identified SEN, mild only (specific learning difficulties, autism, ADD/ADHD, sensory processing, visual impairment) is extensive and sensitively handled. Junior pupils, for example, often receive subtle in-class support rather than being singled out for lunchtime sessions. It's 'so girls don't feel self-conscious,' said mother.

Expectations are high, pupils thriving on challenge and with a prodigious work ethic. Homework is chunky but sensibly allocated, online and in planner, so no excuse for forgetting (one parent reckoned lure of the smartphone was significant factor in time management). 'Won't suit those who aren't prepared to work with their children,' stressed mother. Buy in and pupils will do well. 'Results are very good if you follow what they tell you to do,' said another parent.

Games, options, the arts: Keen, committed and talented can be on the go non-stop. 'Could join a zillion clubs,' said parent. Can lead to a few lunchtime clashes, though sensible catering ensures that no one goes hungry. Recent additions like rugby and football join existing lineup – handball to dodgeball, swimming to golf, with space and facilities inside (dance studio, fitness suite, impressive pool with tiny flotation jackets for nursery pupils) and out (netball courts, Astroturf and a new pavilion). Successes include biathlon (national), hockey and tumbling (regional), and swimming, netball and cross-country (local).

It all starts early, from participation in the whole school play (some year 5s share the stage with seniors – enjoyable for all) to free violin or lessons in year 3. It's in addition to the 150 individual lessons a week, from beginner to diploma level, and leads on to bigger things and sometimes huge ones (half a dozen or so double basses are lined up in the senior school music room).

Art, too, evolves from inclusive junior school displays representing every shade of talent to impressive senior school work (like the GCSE picture where painted legs meet fabric trainers with real laces). Even charity work goes way beyond cake sales. The goal is to produce girls, says head, with 'compassionate ambition'. Charities a case in point: pupils select preferred good causes and pitch their case for share of the funding. Results in enduring links with local groups, which include Women's Aid and knife crime reduction. Fundraising highlights included a fashion show, male models courtesy of local boys' school (one tastefully accessorising high end frock with a plaster cast following rugby injury).

One mother's perception is of school having to hold back the keenest and encourage them to keep at least two lunchtimes a week clear. Another

felt a bit of gentle enticement for the less gregarious would be helpful. Head has already zoomed in on concerns. With dance club – raised by several parents – on the way, and more focus on the keen but non-virtuoso sporting and musical element, nobody should feel sidelined.

Background and atmosphere: Founded in 1874 and part of the Girls Day School Trust, school moved to current base in 1966. Boasts 20 hilly, attractive acres in south Croydon (with a natural amphitheatre in the dip), buildings wearing their architectural vintage (red brick and white fascias) with pride.

Uncompromising on the outside but inside one of the most efficient and welcoming schools we've ever come across – and that includes the parents, available just about instantly to extol the delights of this small scale haven for girls, and come to its defence (criticise at your peril). Nothing like the friendly reception – door holding, wonderful behaviour as matter of course – to convert prospective parents. 'Just felt right,' said one, who had instantly succumbed.

Junior block classrooms are generously proportioned suites. Star attraction is the 4D room with touch sensitive floor, soothing sounds and projected images – used to inspire stories (we could have stayed all day). There's one oddity – the weird, claustrophobic staircase (Mrs Pattison prefers 'quirky') leading to year 4. 'The girls love it.' (There is an alternative route.)

Otherwise, school is spacious and easy to navigate. Keep going and you should end up back where you started. Plenty of light, large halls en route. Main (school assemblies); huge and impressive (sport); attractively teamed with green chairs, light wood tables and colourful piles of fresh fruit (dining).

The goal is to produce girls with 'compassionate ambition'. Charities a case in point: pupils select preferred good causes and pitch their case for share of the funding

Refurbishment was underway when we visited, blue carpets replaced with businesslike grey with ivy leaf motif (which garlanded pupils at inaugural prize giving). In among the pristine modern science labs, one old era survivor (wooden benchtops and a faint aroma of long ago experiments) lingers on – for now at least.

Sixth formers' attractive area features small, round tables on one side (two girls working in squashed but companionable silence). On the other, waiting-room style blocks of expectant-looking chairs (it's occasionally co-opted for assemblies) and walls packed with quotes. 'It is never too late to decide what you might have been' (go for it, George Eliot).

Pastoral care, well-being and discipline: Strength of care felt to be exceptionally strong. One pupil cited teacher at another school turning away a pupil in difficulties. 'Said he had too much marking. That couldn't happen here.' Girls encouraged to look after each other (strong buddy scheme in place). 'Will assist so nobody feels all alone,' thought parent. Small size normally an advantage – only downside the small friendship pool. 'Can get tired of the same faces,' said a parent. Posters in junior school extol pupils to 'tell how you feel, tell a teacher, tell a friend' while effective house system (juniors and seniors have their own) has inner layer – smaller group of 15 'families'.

Uncompromising on the outside but inside one of the most efficient and welcoming schools we've seen – and that includes the parents, who extol the school's delights

Staff (particularly in senior school) recognise mental health issues as big (and daunting) responsibility. Teachers with their own daughters there (fair few) felt school's efforts – peer listening, links to Young Minds and close dialogue between parents and staff – all help. 'No school will say it has no problems and would be lying if they did but staff and girls care and are looking out for you,' said one member of staff. Eating disorders – 'heart-wrenching,' says head – supported in whatever way is best, including staged return when pupil is ready.

Pupils and parents: Many current parents work, majority local, others from Caterham, Oxted and Dulwich. 'We are not just a local school,' stresses head. Minibuses are a useful addition to trains and trams – both a slight hike away. Around half from minority ethnic backgrounds – British, European, Pakistani, Indian, African, Caribbean, mixed background, Sri Lankan, Bangladeshi, Japanese, Chinese, Greek, Turkish and Asian – languages (Tamil, Farsi, Swahili among them) equally varied. EAL support provided where needed.

PTA's mission is to forge ever closer links between senior and junior parents. Not everyone is keen. Small element said to feel responsibility ends with setting up of fees on direct debit – but we'd suspect are a small and rapidly dwindling band, given sense of purposeful accomplishment that dominates life here.

Alumni include obstetrician Wendy Savage, novelist and commentator Jill Tweedie and – best known of the lot – much missed cellist Jacqueline du Pré.

Entrance: Main entry points (juniors) are nursery, reception and year 3. In year 7, half the intake is from own juniors, half from over 20 local primaries and preps. Additional places in year 9 and sixth form, steady trickle in other years. Non-refundable registration fee, deposit on acceptance of place. Overseas applications welcomed, Chinese students in particular (accommodation/guardian must be arranged separately). Head impressively addresses them in – we assume – Mandarin on the website, where the final page of international section is also printed upside down (either layout glitch or appeal to Antipodean market).

Assessments at every stage. For nursery, 45 minutes of structured play (informal, can't be prepared for) under watchful eye of the head. Designed to ensure pace won't be a problem and 'don't turn many away,' says school. Five mornings from the off, full time attendance the goal for all.

Proportionately longer assessments further up the school. Reception – an hour in small groups – picture matching and sorting objects, co-operation and good use of spoken language. Seniors tested in maths, English (writing, reading, VR) plus interview and reference (approximate minimum score of 105 in year 7 but often much higher – some siblings may not make it). Limited sample papers – year 7 only available online. At sixth form, external candidates will need minimum of six GCSE passes at grade 6, depending on A level choices.

Academic scholarships (year 7) based on entrance exam performance and interview. No percentages given but think small – it's all about the honour. School's juniors sit exams for awards, otherwise have automatic entry. Also art and design, drama, music (minimum grade 4 in at least one instrument but usually much higher) and sport.

Similar range in years 9 and sixth form, where also offers Jacqueline Du Pré scholarship (music) and – unusually – for year 13, Jenny Park Award (English and the arts). Additional awards in range of subjects.

Exit: Vast majority of juniors expected into year 7. From year 5, focus on how to achieve transition with additional support rather than giving notice to quit.

In 2019, 36 per cent departed post-16 (mostly to local co-eds). Rare for school to ask pupils to leave at the end of year 11 or year 12 – and won't happen without much prior discussion. 'Not about saying you're not welcome but asking if three A levels are the right profile,' says head. Unscheduled departures for other reasons very rare. Sixth form numbers will be boosted as numbers rise through the school – and three form year groups become the norm once more (recession hit hard). In 2019, one to Oxbridge and three into medicine or dentistry.

Money matters: Bursaries, some via GDST for years 7 and 9, two sponsored by HSBC for state school

sixth form candidates, available. May be more help for deserving leavers.

Remarks: 'They're so happy there – and that's all I ever wanted, to have a lovely environment where they didn't feel threatened and teachers are more like their friends,' said junior parent.

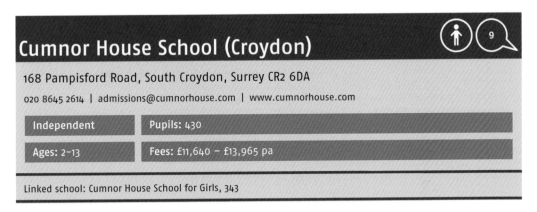

Cumnor House School (Croydon)

168 Pampisford Road, South Croydon, Surrey CR2 6DA

020 8645 2614 | admissions@cumnorhouse.com | www.cumnorhouse.com

Independent	Pupils: 430
Ages: 2–13	Fees: £11,640 – £13,965 pa

Linked school: Cumnor House School for Girls, 343

Headmaster: Since 2017, Daniel Cummings, previously head of the White House school in Balham and the school's fourth head in 18 months. BEd from Exeter; taught in Australian primary schools whilst on a year's travelling; helped to set up the Epsom and Ewell School Sport Partnership; taught at Merton primary schools before being joining the White House in 2013. His wife, Abigail, is also a teacher.

Entrance: Three form intake with 20 boys maximum in a class. Automatic entry from the school's Cumnor House Nursery, which parents told us they found a very attractive feature of the school. Otherwise, boys come in at 4+ for a taster day, which for most is nothing to worry about. Maths and English are checked to ascertain if the child will cope at Cumnor, but not formally assessed. Other entry points at 7+ and 11+. School aims to be as inclusive as possible, and all kinds of families pay the (very competitive) fees to send their boys here.

Exit: Given the school's non-academically-selective admissions process, Cumnor's exit record is truly remarkable. Students can be prepped for either 11+ or 13+ depending on parents' and boys' wishes, which, families affirm, the school is always careful to consult. Those who opt for 11+ are put in a dedicated class. Vast majority to Trinity or Whitgift, with Royal Russell, Caterham and Epsom College next in popularity. Such is the school's success that refugees who come to Cumnor at 11 often pass at

13 with scholarships into schools which turned them down two years previously. 'We've been in the game long enough to know what the senior schools are looking for.' And year on year, the results prove them right (39 scholarship offers in 2019).

Remarks: After years in the schools' reviewing business, we were nonetheless surprised by the fervour with which parents talked to us about Cumnor House. 'It's a lovely, brilliant school. I would recommend it to anyone and everyone!' cried one mother. 'The boys there are lovely young men, and the teachers are amazing, they always want to go the extra mile,' said another. 'It's been a really positive experience for our son,' said a third. 'We couldn't fault it.' 'No negatives, and nothing to regret. It's fantastic!' said a fourth. And this is just a sample.

Whilst they hurled themselves around the playgrounds at breaktime, they were nonetheless well-behaved and considerate

Cumnor House is surely triumphant proof that single sex education from an early age can really work. If a How-I-Hope-My-Son-Will-Turn-Out contest existed, the boys we met here would all be candidates to win. Their manners are astonishingly good. Everywhere we were greeted with courteous smiles and handshakes; in one instance, even with a bow. Whilst they hurled themselves around the playgrounds at break-time, they were nonetheless well-behaved and considerate, both to each other and to us. 'You might want to walk quickly, 'cause it's raining,' urged one of our tour guides with anxious politeness.

Everywhere we saw evidence of lively and careful teaching, and the boys were vociferous about how much they enjoyed lessons. 'History is my favourite, because it's all about old things, and did you know that Henry VIII died because his bottom exploded on the toilet!' cried a year 2 lad enthusiastically. The older boys were more conservative in their praise, but no less warm. 'The teachers are very kind', 'They're inspirational!' 'Lessons are always fun', 'Because of my science teacher, I want to be a scientist,' we were told. Work on the walls was imaginative and of a consistently high standard. Strong SEN team supports boys in need of extra help; the school welcomes all learners, although the school acknowledged that boys with more than moderate learning difficulties would struggle at Cumnor, and we ourselves felt that this wouldn't be the right place for them.

'History is my favourite, because it's all about old things, and did you know that Henry VIII died because his bottom exploded on the toilet!' cried a year 2 lad enthusiastically. Older boys were more conservative in their praise, but no less warm

Parents in search of flashy facilities might initially be nonplussed by Cumnor's honeycomb, let's-patch-on-another-annexe-here school campus. The main site used to be residential, and the impression is still of a large, rambling house full of staircases and inglenooks. Decor-wise, it would be fair to say that it lacks the feminine touch: somehow, despite the displays and children's books lining the walls, there isn't much colour in the place. Desks are endearingly old-fashioned, and occasionally downright scruffy. But honestly, who cares? The classrooms are all well-resourced, there's an excellent ICT suite, the boys radiate contentment and their achievements speak for themselves. And there's nothing scruffy about the sports facilities: the huge sports ground boasts £50k's worth of new cricket nets and a new clubhouse, the sports hall is adequate and the swimming pool block was warm, light and inviting, which may be why the reception teachers were all in the water with their young charges when we visited. Cumnor's swimming is very successful (the swim squad practises from 7am), and the school has won national as well as local competitions. Football, rugby, cricket and athletics are likewise strong, nurtured by a team of very dedicated PE teachers. Old boys include Mark Butcher, Alistair Brown, David Sales, Chris Robshaw and Elliot Daly.

For the non-sportsmen, however, there is plenty of other fare on offer. Music is flourishing, with over half the boys learning at least one musical instrument, and a pleasing variety of bands and ensembles to join. The school's choral singing is particularly impressive: previous fixtures include Salzburg Cathedral and the Barnardo's National Choir Competition (which they won). Drama is also lively, and the school puts on at least two productions a year. There are lots of clubs and societies, and the boys are encouraged to try new things. 'We don't want boys who are in at 8.30am and out at 3.30pm. We want them to take risks. We tell them, if you haven't auditioned for the school play, why not? If you aren't learning an instrument, why not?'

A few years ago Cumnor joined the Cognita schools group, thereby increasing its financial clout in a very competitive locality. The Lodge Schools on the other side of the Purley Way declined and fell during the financial crisis, whereupon Cognita bought up most of the site and asked Cumnor to open a girls' school (see our separate entry) and expand Cumnor House Nursery. Reception boys are also housed on this site in Woodcote Lane, and we wondered if that didn't provoke grumbles from parents dropping off more than one child. But no: the school runs a shuttle service between the two sites, and parents can choose to which one they deliver both sons and daughters, knowing that the school will safely ferry their children to where they need to be. (And this, frankly, is more than can be said for some of the parents; the thoroughfare outside the Pampisford Road site gets very exciting at drop-off time, as local residents will feelingly confirm.)

The Croydon area is multicultural, and one of Cumnor's greatest successes is the way that it takes a highly diverse group of boys – every colour and creed is represented on the school roll – and helps them all become polished and likeable English gentlemen, in the best possible sense of the phrase. It may not be the place for the kind of child who just isn't into school no matter how good it is; incurable mavericks would be exhausted by the ebullient enthusiasm and team spirit here. But make no mistake, this is boys' education at its best.

However, we and no doubt parents hope that the current head will bring stability and have a longer reign than his several recent predecessors.

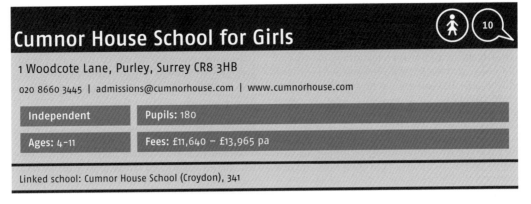

Cumnor House School for Girls

1 Woodcote Lane, Purley, Surrey CR8 3HB

020 8660 3445 | admissions@cumnorhouse.com | www.cumnorhouse.com

Independent	Pupils: 180
Ages: 4–11	Fees: £11,640 – £13,965 pa

Linked school: Cumnor House School (Croydon), 341

Head: Since 2018, Amanda McShane BA PGCE, previously deputy head and head of science at The Old Vicarage School in Richmond-upon-Thames. Music degree; started her career as a year 6 teacher at a Surrey state primary school, becoming head of science and head of music before moving to the independent sector.

Entrance: Families span range of cultures and backgrounds and, increasingly, a greater geographic area. Surrey and South West London (Tooting, Clapham and Streatham) feature increasingly as minibus network (shared with Cumnor House Boys' School) helps to widen the net.

Many pupils move up to reception from one of two co-ed Cumnor House nurseries – both officially affiliated to the boys' school; all nursery pupils automatically offered a place in reception as long as the school can meet their needs. External candidates register (after visiting – there are weekly tours and regular open days) and are accepted on a first come, first served basis. Welcome applications in other year groups when assess ('with a small "a",' says school) over half a day to 'ensure that this is the best school for them and that they will be happy here.'

Scholarships awarded to exceptional current pupils though school didn't want to put a percentage on it (mega honour and glory but low monetary value). Bursaries also for existing pupils if families fall on hard times.

Exit: Nineteen scholarships in 2019 – most academic, some music and sport. Offers from schools ranging from Croydon High, JAGS and Old Palace to Woldingham, Roedean and Wycombe Abbey.

Remarks: Site is approached through chi chi private estate, mini mansions fronted with pavements soused in gravel (man with a brush and pan busily sweeps up the excess). There's been a school on this six-acre, gently hilly site for 100 years (lion on small commemorative lawn marks former pupils killed in WWI). Went into decline after the 2008 crash and was acquired by Cognita in 2010, making it the newish kid on the block in comparison with boys' school.

It's blessed with generous playing fields, a multi-use games area (netball court with go-faster stripes for range of sports) and garden with raised beds (each year group tends its own). Assorted playgrounds are well used, while reception pupils, delightfully rounded up for lessons with clapping games and songs by older 'buddies', mainly stick to their own space, also an outdoor learning area.

Heart of the school buildings is a pretty Victorian villa with preserved period quirks and homely rather than glitzy ambience. Newer buildings off to the sides include an unobtrusive teaching block and sports hall that avoids common distribution ambience with blond wood flooring and red-painted beams.

Under new ownership, has become a highly regarded alternative to the area's other girls' junior schools. Several exist but are mostly linked to senior schools – fine for those sold on the ethos, less so if you fancy a punt at other schools, including the excellent state grammars in the area.

Heart of the school buildings is a pretty Victorian villa with preserved period quirks and homely rather than glitzy ambience

Here, anxious parents are soothed with the balm of reassurance that whatever senior school you have in mind, your child will be carefully prepped for it (three entrance exams generally suggested as the maximum). There are plenty of staff (a mix of ages and experience) on hand to help, a good teacher to pupil ratio (just one to nine full time equivalent) and small class sizes (average mid teens, maximum 20).

Small size means it feels like home, thought one pupil, who had felt diminished by numbers and lack of attention at previous school. 'Here, teachers will pick a girl who is calm and puts her hand up nicely. In my old school, they just picked the noisiest.' Wouldn't work here, with universally wonderful manners, notably 'the ones you see when they don't know you're looking'. We were greeted politely. 'I hope you have a good visit,' said one pupil, gravely. (We did.)

Parents, meanwhile, had nothing but praise for school's calm, confidence-inspiring approach. If pupils' appearance doesn't put their minds at rest (blazer plus natty headgear – beret with a boater in summer) staff know-how generally does the trick, on open days and beyond. 'They gave me a lot of information on exactly what I was looking for,' said a mother. 'Meticulous planning,' say school inspectors – and parents agree.

There's clarity about what's taught and when. Take 11+ preparation. While school stresses that ideally pupils should enjoy free time over the summer holidays – 'they need a respite' – parents can ask for practice papers at the end of year 5. 'You feel looked after,' said one. Sense of security filters down to pupils. 'There's not even one day my daughter's said, "I don't want to go to school",' agreed a parent.

It's a tribute to high quality teaching that sees pupils through all the basics (French currently the only MFL, Latin offered in top two years). There's no setting, teachers versed in excellent differentiation. No room for doubt as to how your daughter is doing, with annual VR/NVR, reasoning, numeracy, reading and spelling tests to monitor progress as well as annual academic exams and informal assessments. Clearly going well in a Lake Woebegone way. 'Nearly everyone got over average,' exulted a pupil of recent exams.

If pupils' appearance doesn't put parents' minds at rest (blazer plus natty headgear – beret, with a boater in summer), staff know-how generally does the trick

Inspectors (in 2014) had noted a few gaps in the recruitment process and governance. School has since upped the ante and every box is now ticked several times over. Pictures of school's safeguarding leads are much in evidence and assemblies stress, and stress again, the need to 'tell a grown up if you're sad' – pupils we met were impressively aware of this.

Looking after people is something everyone here does well, from lunches (cheerful chef, in at 6am to get homemade bread and biscuits on the go), to learning support. A small number of pupils (currently nine) have English as an additional language. Just one has a diagnosed learning need but 10 or so more have some support from class teachers which, say parents, is sensitively handled. Similarly, misbehaviour is quickly dealt with and sanctions sensibly applied (may miss a favourite lesson, for example).

Having the boys' school nearby is a great asset but also – inevitably – a source of comparison (especially as fees are the same for both). Line up the clubs and girls have fewer – one parent pointed out that even if she wanted her daughter to do an after-school activity every day, it wasn't available for her year group. It's also a more ladylike offering (ballet, textiles, swimming, computers, book, gym, pottery, chess, art, drama and Bollywood) compared with boys (current affairs, drama, chess, Italian, classics, Mandarin, Russian, history, Spanish, science debating and computers).

While relative size and different leaving age (boys stay to year 8) accounts for this school's fewer resources (boys have two science labs to girls' one, for example), the feel is a tad unemancipated and appears to extend into timetabled lessons (girls do food tech and science; boys have physics, chemistry and biology from the off). The boys' school also wins on scholarships, regularly scoring far more relative to its size (especially for sport, but academic too).

'Boys are different, girls are different but we would like [girls] to have the opportunities,' said one parent. 'We don't want them to feel left out.'

Girls do have separate sciences, stresses school (a term for each), while clubs are affected by demand. Spanish was tried and only got a handful of takers while Mandarin came and went when teacher moved on. Life skills training for both boys and girls is on the horizon, boys will soon be on their way over to enjoy food technology (they can already sign up for after-school care provision) and girls will have more access to boys' school activities. The goal is 'general parity' between the two schools. Clubs may not be identical but girls won't go short, school says.

Sports widely felt by parents to have been on the underwhelming side here – while the U11A girl netballers had nine fixtures in a recent school year, for example, the U11A boy footballers had 32. Visitors who, like us, noticed an absence of current awards in the cabinet shouldn't be alarmed – they were at the engravers 'to update our achievements,' explains the school.

Girls already do well in swimming galas (it's over to the boys' school to use the 'superb indoor heated swimming pool'). Tag rugby is available as a club, hockey now added to the list (so recently that at least one parent wasn't yet aware of this), all helped by recruitment of a third PE specialist who will ensure that there's more on offer for everyone (currently those not selected for the small number of teams can end up feeling left out).

Performing and visual arts, in contrast, are a star attraction. Girls reckoned there were around four productions a year (some with boys' school). Music is good, with an orchestra and choice of choirs, chamber (selective) and main (which isn't, though you get a separate badge on your blazer for both). Specialist teachers give 90-ish lessons a week, up to grade 5 or so, many of the keenest playing several instruments. As we toured the music room, a group of four year 5 girls was arriving for first band practice, composing the music to go with their own lyrics.

Art consistently gets the top rating, thanks to 'amazing', department (of one) who presides over a room brimming with creative clutter inspiring works ranging from a collection of gold-painted papier-mâché athletes suspended from bicycle wheel to ceramic animals.

Currently a model of decorum, school is a gentle oasis that inspires trust – parents couldn't praise it highly enough. Add a bit more oomph to extracurricular and sporting options to ensure that girls don't feel second best to the boys up the road and it will be practically perfect.

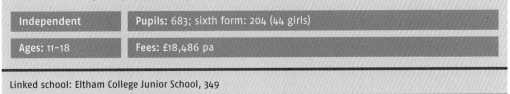

Eltham College

Grove Park Road, London SE9 4QF

020 8857 1455 | registrar@eltham-college.org.uk | www.elthamcollege.london

| Independent | Pupils: 683; sixth form: 204 (44 girls) |
| Ages: 11–18 | Fees: £18,486 pa |

Linked school: Eltham College Junior School, 349

Headmaster: Since 2014, Guy Sanderson MA (Oxon) PGCE (40s). Studied PPE and then modern history at Trinity College, Oxford. Having started out as a stockbroker in the City, he followed this with a stint at the UN High Commission for Refugees in Pakistan and Afghanistan before teaching at a series of academic independents – St Paul's, Whitgift, City of London Boys' School and Reigate Grammar, where he rose to head of sixth form and deputy head.

His office, newly decorated in tasteful grey with fresh flowers and framed photography of the boys in action, is a small sign of his modernising intent and ambition to make the school one of the country's best independent schools. However, it is important to him to be able to do this in his own time in his own way and not to be straitjacketed by targets. The parents we heard from seemed pleased the school is being given something of a shake-up. One confided: 'The head is clearly very driven and personally career oriented. From my perspective this is no bad thing. If he does well it will mean that the school has done well.' And: 'Determined to improve the school's academic standing, modern in his approach... he knows the pupils and is interested in them individually.' 'He is not, however, afraid to say no and stand steadfast by his principles.'

In tune with this dynamic image, Mr Sanderson tweets encouragement to the far-flung corners of Elthamians' daily activities. Boys will find his door open at lunch times and he's delighted to find they drop in to suggest ideas for new clubs or initiatives. Year 7 boys are invited to his office on their birthday for a doughnut. In answer to our question as to whether there should be a head girl as well as head boy, he says that it is simply a case of the best person for the job and in the case of this year that means there is. With a wife who is a FTSE 100 headhunter it's a topic of debate.

Mr Sanderson relocated from rural Sussex with his wife and three children. A keen skier and open water swimmer, for the past two summers he's swum the Bosphorus. The family lives in a house overlooking the playing fields, together with the chickens, but not the pigs, from Sussex.

Academic matters: In 2019, 85 per cent of grades were A*-A/7-9 at I/GCSE; 68 per cent A*/A at A level (93 per cent A*/B). Senior curriculum wise very trad but with a careful eye to future global employment prospects. More academic subjects have been added and the less academic such as sports studies removed. Timetabling isn't completed until each boy's preferences are accommodated.

Everyone does single sciences at IGCSE and the short-course RS. A level additions are economics, psychology, government and politics, pure and further maths, unusually geology (a 30 year tradition) and recently introduced computing. Maths is the most popular A level and taken as an IGCSE. All those from the top sets taking maths early have consistently gained A* and mathematicians throughout the school regularly compete nationally. Years 8 and 9 have been finalists in UKMT for the past three years. There are very strong student numbers in economics: currently the second largest A level cohort. A glittering array of highlights from the science department. The physics department is recognised as a centre of excellence by the Institute of Physics with stellar grades; most recently a chemist was in receipt of the prestigious Roentgenium award; year 10s were also finalists in the Royal Society of Chemistry's challenge in Kent. The school regularly produces Arkwright scholars who go on to study engineering at the country's most desirable destinations. One Eltham geologist scored the highest geology A level mark in the country, losing a mere four marks.

French, German, Mandarin and Spanish are introduced gradually over the first three years with boys choosing a minimum of two. The head has appointed a new head of classics, introduced ancient Greek to complement Latin and says all language appointments will be either Oxbridge graduates and/or native speakers. Italian is available and Russian off timetable. Whilst French holds its own with several studying French alongside their chosen degree subject at university, German is the second most popular language. Of nine recent Mandarin GCSE passes, only one was a native speaker, though A level Mandarin is only available off timetable to native speakers.

Venues for recent music performances include Ronnie Scott's, the Barbican, St John's Smith Square, the Royal Albert Hall and beneath the hull of the Cutty Sark

Class sizes average 22 but with smaller teaching sets in all languages, maths, science and some creative subjects. A quarter of teaching staff have been at the school for over 10 years but the head says this is a changing picture. Keen to develop staff, he devolves leadership, empowering them to run with their own project ideas if it will benefit

Rugby is the school's big thing: England U16 champions for two consecutive years, winner of the U15 Kent 7s and 13 county players

the school. One of our guides said of the teachers: 'They're all passionate about their subjects; lessons are very interactive'. The head tells us of a lesson he witnessed recently where the boys were studying glaciation using edible foodstuffs. Parents are aware of teaching standards being consciously raised. For the most able, there is a head of academic scholarship running a programme of debating, lectures from outside speakers and encouraging boys to prepare and deliver papers to their peers.

There is a full-time learning support teacher. All new pupils are screened on entry for possible difficulties. Around 10 per cent with identified SEN needs, the majority with dyslexia but a few with ADHD, ASD or communication issues. The school says that the majority of cases are quite 'mild' and most support is within lessons. A dyslexic pupil described the school as: 'Nice atmosphere. Positive, helpful teachers'.

Despite the hard-working atmosphere and desire to up the academic ante parents do not feel there is too much pressure – the extracurricular provides relief from academic work, year round rather than annual testing is a relief, with not too much holiday homework and sufficient time left within the year for revision.

Pupils are carefully prepared for university exits, including a new focus on US universities. A pathways programme ensures pupils are en route and prepared for possible careers, making use of the network of Eltham alumni for work experience placements.

Games, options, the arts: No doubt that almost everyone is sporty but that seems to be mostly by dint of encouragement and breadth of opportunity. Rugby is the school's big thing: England U16 champions for two consecutive years, winner of the U15 Kent 7s and 13 county players. Winners of U15 and U16 county cups in hockey and cricket. Players of international standing are in good company, with a couple representing England in fencing, a GB skier and three England internationals and last year's U13 England chess champion. Coaches are often national players but the head stresses to them that they must have an interest in teaching not just the elite but 'the grass roots'.

Plenty of opportunities to try new things such as climbing or sailing. For those with a lighter interest there are clubs and societies for table tennis, basketball and pilates. With regards to having a go, the school aims for all boys to represent the school in an activity. Glad to see the girls as well as boys have a tug-of-war in the annual house competition.

The school is proud of its musicians who achieve exceptionally well academically with the last few years, consistently delivering an Oxbridge place or two. Around 65 per cent of pupils learn an instrument. One parent told us: 'I was particularly touched to see my child play a string instrument in his first term as we are not a particularly musical family.' Choral singing is a high point. Ensembles, choirs and orchestras play across London. Recently parents were treated to performances at Ronnie Scott's, the Barbican, St John's Smith Square, the Royal Albert Hall and beneath the hull of the Cutty Sark.

This is the first school we've visited with its own art gallery. The Gerald Moore Gallery houses school and external exhibitions. The exhibitions assist students to achieve offers from top graphic design, fine art and architecture courses. All the art teachers and technicians are artists and pursue their own practices and an artist-in-residence has a studio within the department.

Drama is on the curriculum for all years 7 to 9 and is available at GCSE and A level. The drama department produces a major musical every year – recently Les Misérables with student-led orchestra. Students also directed, acted, managed and teched a production of Richard III. Those jaunting to Edinburgh for The Fringe were rewarded with 5* reviews in the national press for their performance of Sweeney Todd. Plenty of distinctions in LAMDA exams.

Clubs and societies often seem to be extending in tone but Dixieland band, 'magic: the gathering', slick sticks, run for fun, Fair Trade and Morris dancing caught our eye. Those looking forward to a far-flung expedition may need a head for heights with past destinations including Nepal and Borneo whilst students tackle DofE from bronze to gold.

Background and atmosphere: Originally founded as a boarding school for the sons of missionaries, boys attend chapel twice a week as part of a strong Christian tradition with caring for the community still an important part of the school's ethos. Since moving in 1912 to this elegant 18th century mansion with a columned entrance, surrounded by 70 acres of green fields, it has grown in size, stopped taking boarders and girls have been part of the sixth form since the 1970s (and will soon join the lower school). Despite the increase in size, boys and parents referred approvingly to the school so often as 'small' that we checked the pupil numbers. The atmosphere is peaceful but buzzy indoors and out;

students engrossed in lessons or off to play sports with huge kitbags.

Apart from the elegance of Central Hall, now housing the humanities classrooms in style, with its beautiful wooden boards of Oxbridge scholars and charming sepia photographs of sports teams gone by, the school comprises a collection of blocks in various states of repair. The science block is so delightfully retro we expected to bump into the Enigma Machine at any moment. However the new Turberville Building has extended the sixth form centre out into the playing fields (mirroring the students' imminent transition to university) and also provides new language classrooms, a new mathematics suite of classrooms and a well-being centre. The DT facilities comprise a series of large professional-looking workshops with a laser cutter, 3D printer and a CAD-cam suite. The library is large and well-resourced with books, journals or ebooks, with a separate sixth form area up a spiral staircase.

The science block is so delightfully retro we expected to bump into the Enigma Machine at any moment

The school's most famous alumnus is Eric Liddell, the Olympic athlete who won gold in the 400m at the 1924 Paris Olympics, forever immortalised by Chariots of Fire, hence the namesake sports centre, which provides on-site indoor cricket nets, a 25 metre pool, dance studio and fitness suite. In addition £3.5m is earmarked to further develop the sports facilities including a new pavilion, second Astroturf and 4G rugby pitch.

We asked to meet a few sixth form girls, curious to hear about their experiences. Those joining from girls' schools spoke of wanting to find larger teaching groups for their A level subjects. Whilst all felt slightly nervous on arrival, they don't feel in a minority, as the numbers suggest. They spoke of finding the boys welcoming, the atmosphere competitive academically, offering them different points of view, but less 'cliquey' and more relaxed socially.

Will accept girls into year 7 (and year 3 in the junior school) from 2020, becoming co-educational throughout by 2024.

Pastoral care, well-being and discipline: The school as a whole receives glowing praise for its pastoral care, the front line being form tutors. One mother told us of the care and consideration her son received during a difficult time at home. Co-curricular clubs run pre- and post-school, whilst a breakfast club allows parents to dash for the commute. A careful and detailed anti-bullying policy and zero drug tolerance. Incidents are not unheard of but parents report that they are swiftly dealt with. A fairly strict, disciplined environment with quite a long list of sanctions available to teachers to keep efforts up to scratch academically.

The deputy head is the head of pastoral care. Parents universally praise pastoral care here, one going as far as to describe it as 'exceptional'. This is certainly one of the best resourced pastoral care teams we have encountered: two qualified nurses, a doctor, counsellor and two chaplains. Boys waved to the nurse during our tour. When we quizzed the head as to the school's consideration of the kind of mental health issues variously affecting girls and boys today he was engaged and had recently returned from a conference on the subject.

This is one of the best resourced pastoral care teams we have seen: two qualified nurses, a doctor, counsellor and two chaplains. Boys waved to the nurse during our tour

There is a recently appointed head of transition to ease in year 7s. Form tutors, the pastoral front line, are described as 'accessible and generally very quick to respond to any concerns' and now stay with boys for their lower school and then middle school years. Communication between school and home is felt to be excellent.

We raised the news stories still to be found on a Google search of the school concerning the conduct of two teachers. The incidents were before the current head's time and concerned activities outside of the school but have resulted in a review of safeguarding and DBS checking procedures for staff.

Pupils and parents: The majority of students come from within a five mile radius, taking in Blackheath, Greenwich, the Isle of Dogs and Surrey Quays but also south to Bromley, Chislehurst and Sidcup, Orpington, Farnborough and West Wickham. Far fewer with different languages spoken at home than we see in central London schools. A tiny few international students. Working parents are catered for: pupils could be in school from 8am purchasing breakfast in King George's Hall, whilst the library is open for after-school study until 5.30pm, not to mention myriad activities taking pupils until the end of the day, often with no extra cost. Parents were described to us as including 'multi-millionaires' and the 'down to earth'.

What kind of child would Eltham suit? Parents mention 'all-rounders' and 'bright, motivated, independent children who will rise to a challenge'.

The head says there is no Eltham boy; it will simply appeal to those who want to make the most of opportunities.

Entrance: Academic standards are high and entrance is by selection based on academic merit and on an assessment of the pupil's likely positive contribution to the school. Everyone needs a good reference, and computer adaptive verbal and non-verbal reasoning is now a feature of testing at every stage. The majority of pupils come seamlessly through from the junior school and 40 to 50 external pupils join at 11+, with around five (including girls, from 2020) competing for every place. External candidates take entrance papers in English and maths. Those with SEN needs may be allocated additional time. New 11+ joiners hail mostly from local preps including: The Pointer School, Blackheath Prep, Breaside, Heath House and St Olave's but also Chislehurst C of E Primary. Only a few joining at 13+ but it is an increasingly competitive entry point. Candidates sit papers in English, maths and a modern foreign language or Latin.

External candidates to the sixth form take an exam and if successful are interviewed. In recent years girls have arrived from the local GDST schools and St Ursula's Convent, amongst others. Candidates sit papers in two subjects of their choice. Offers made are subject to a minimum of six 9-7 grades at GCSE including the four subjects of further study.

Exit: Almost all boys stay on to the sixth form. The trend has been for departing pupils to head for Exeter, York, Bristol, Warwick, Durham, Leeds, Southampton, Imperial and Loughborough, so one can be pretty confident of attaining Russell Group aspirations. Five to Oxbridge and seven medics in 2019.

Money matters: A generous number of scholarships on offer at each entry point, which could be for academic ability or music, sport, art and drama (16+ only) – the financial reward varying from the token to the quite substantial. Everyone sitting the entrance test will be considered for academic scholarships, with further requirements for music, art and sports scholars. Fewer than 10 per cent of pupils are in receipt of means-tested bursaries, which could range from a helping hand to 100 per cent of fees.

Remarks: With an energetic head on the case and money being spent in bringing the facilities up to scratch, plus the imminent advent of girls joining the main school, it could be a wonderful place to find a niche and increasingly achieve great things: heading in a more academic direction than of late but still extremely sporty.

Eltham College Junior School

Mottingham Lane, London SE9 4RW

020 8857 3457 | juniors@eltham-college.org.uk | www.elthamcollege.london

| Independent | Ages: 7–11 | Pupils: 227 | Fees: £16,161 pa |

Linked school: Eltham College, 345

Master: Since 2010, Edmund Cavendish (50s) MA (Oxon) PGCE. Studied modern history at Queen's College, Oxford. Deputy head at the senior school for five years. Prior to this, he was head of history and then head of sixth form during 16 years at Ipswich School, following four years at Merchiston Castle School in Edinburgh. This junior school setting was new for Mr Cavendish, but he relishes the enthusiasm of the younger boys and feels his experience of the senior school – he still teaches the Oxbridge historians – is helpful in enabling him to bring the two schools together, very much a focus since the arrival of Mr Sanderson, the head of the senior school. He dips in and out, ensuring he teaches something to each year so that he gets to know each boy. Another focus has been ensuring the stretching of the most able wherever their talents lie – this could be in the shape of elite coaching for the sporting or opening up the senior orchestras to junior musicians.

Parents say he is 'is a great champion of the traditions of the school' and 'I think the work he is doing on mental health is amazing and the implementations made mean a less stressful, more enjoyable schooling'. He lives close to the school, has been married for over 30 years and has two grown-up daughters, one working in Burma, the other for McKinsey, and two dogs that have as prominent billing in the framed photos in his office.

Leaving in July 2020.

Entrance: Capped at 60 across three forms of 20 boys at 7+ entry and then rising to no more than 22 boys in a form for years 4-6. Candidates are assessed in maths and English, including an element of verbal reasoning and reading. Historically chances of getting in have been pretty good but applications are increasing. The same test subjects for entry at 8+, 9+ and 10+. Pupils mainly enter from local preps and pre-preps such as Babington House, Bickley Park, The Pointer School, Breaside and Colfe's. Open mornings in the autumn.

Will accept girls at 7+ in 2020, gradually becoming co-educational throughout.

Exit: Pupils from junior school are not required to sit the 11+ exam for the senior school and all but a dozen head there, often with scholarships. Those leaving do so mostly due to a change in family circumstance eg relocation, plus a few to the local grammar schools. Other initiatives ease the year 7 transition and have built the all-through school feel: boys become familiar with the buildings, facilities and teachers.

Remarks: All of the usual curriculum subjects. As well as French, Mandarin is taught from year 3, which boys describe enthusiastically as 'fun, but hard sometimes'. Boys are set for maths throughout and for English comprehension from year 5. ICT rather than computing at the moment. Terms alternate between DT and art. There is a focus on developing cross-curricular thinking skills via 'philosophy for children' whilst following a growth mindset approach of challenging every boy to believe intelligence isn't fixed but can be developed. Plenty of fun workshops and curricular trips to the London museums and galleries on the school's doorstep as well as short residentials further up the school. No doted-on school pets – the science lab terrapins have been replaced by giant African snails.

The school seems like a family home that can afford to get bashed about a bit without anyone worrying about the soft furnishings

A slightly mixed picture from the few parents we hear from regarding teaching. One satisfied parent: 'I have been nothing but happy with the teaching' and another: 'All subjects are taught to a very high standard'. Whilst for another: 'The junior school could do with the shake-up currently refreshing the senior school'. It seems this is very much on the cards. The boys we meet who strike us as fairly free and easy with their views are whole-hearted in their praise: 'The teachers are very kind; when you are feeling stressed they help you' and 'They want you to get the best marks possible'.

The parents we spoke to welcomed the fact that testing here does not feel intensive throughout. Mr Cavendish elaborates that teachers 'don't over-hype' tests and that a new system of monitoring enables the school to build up a picture of how each child is developing. At the end of each half-term boys receive a grade card with a mark for effort and attainment. In years 3 and 4 boys tell us 'everyone is mad about collecting merits'. By years 5 and 6 it's no longer 'cool' to collect them but boys nonetheless make use of the teachers' comments. A parent reported: 'Homework seems OK: in year 6 it's around 20 minutes each day. There are revision packs during the holidays which aren't compulsory'.

No doubt that almost everyone is sporty but that seems to be mostly by dint of encouragement and breadth of opportunity. The core sports on offer are rugby, football, hockey (on the up, reaching the regional U11 finals) and cricket for two afternoons a week plus a brief gym or swim period. A mother saw the benefit of sports teaching by both male and female coaches. Boys are wowed by the coaches with national team experience. Competitive fixtures and galas, inter-house competitions plus clubs in which to try new things such as judo or basketball. Every effort is made to encourage boys of all abilities to don head-to-toe stripes and play for the school. This year every boy played rugby in at least one match fixture. There are plenty of individual successes too – one boy plays for Kent U11s cricket and three skiers were recently selected for the national training squad. The teaching of fencing must be good: we met one boy who tried fencing for the first time at a school open day and is now GB number two with highly ranked team mates to spar against. Boys also excel in chess competitions and LAMDA exams. One parent summed it up: 'The diversity of activities allows most children to find a niche that they can feel part of'.

Music is a significant part of the curriculum and 85 per cent of pupils have weekly individual lessons, currently up to grade 5 – the high uptake inspired by a project which enables all boys in years 3 and 4 to receive five weeks of free instrumental tuition. There are several choirs and ensembles and an annual music concert. Plenty to aspire to: trebles enjoyed singing alongside the seniors recently at the Barbican with the LSO. Years 3 and 4 perform an annual play or musical, as do years 5 and 6. As on our last visit, however, we hear consistent rumbles about the focus on a talented few: 'the chosen ones reappear very often across activities'.

A school for the sons of Victorian missionaries, with a house named after Dr Livingstone of 'I presume?' fame, the school relocated to its current site in 1912: a Victorian mansion with an uninspired modern wing extension. Inside, this provides for a high-ceilinged art room and a multi-sided hall with floor length windows overlooking the playing fields. The chic grey paint of the senior school makeover is yet to reach the outpost of the master's office but classrooms are being transformed from top to bottom into brighter spaces with the boys' approval. The small library – 'we love David Walliams' – now boasts coloured beanbags popular for hanging out or doodling on wet days. There are separate outside spaces allocated at breaktimes to the younger and older boys. Art displays could be improved in our opinion, but boys are justly proud of a wonderful mosaic of London they helped to design and make to celebrate the school's centenary. It seems like a family home that can afford to get bashed about a bit without anyone worrying about the soft furnishings. The high decibels at break time only add to the atmosphere.

Every effort is made to encourage boys of all abilities to don head-to-toe stripes and play for the school. This year every boy played rugby in at least one match

A mother otherwise very happy with the school did tell us that she believed 'less confident children can sometimes be allowed to hide in the background'. There seems no doubt that it is a competitive place. At the same time, there is no need to conform: we hear that difference is accepted and quirkiness happily embraced – certainly borne out by the boys we met who seemed to listen to each other and respect individual talents. One thing that might unify boys here: we'd describe our tour guides as keen as mustard. Our overwhelming impression was of the boys' enthusiasm for their academic subjects. We raised an eyebrow at the idea of a Latin club at lunchtime, not a bit of it; two relived being caught out in a comprehension test by a tricky piece of grammar as if it was a narrowly missed sporting goal.

The school as a whole receives glowing praise for its pastoral care, the front line being form tutors. One mother told us of the care and consideration her son received during a difficult time at home. In line with national averages there are currently fewer than 20 pupils with any form of SEN, almost all of whom have dyslexia, a couple with ASD. Pupils are supported by individual lesson plans for in-class support and some booster classes. Boys tell us their friends with dyslexia value the support but inevitably don't like feeling different. Some 43 pupils are listed as EAL but most have adequate English, given the entrance requirements. Co-curricular clubs run pre- and post-school, whilst a breakfast club allows parents to dash for the commute. Boys were keen to tell us about their efforts at charity fundraising and seemed modestly unaware of how they'd been chosen for leadership opportunities. Boys talk about 'we' much of the time and clearly feel proud of their school.

Haberdashers' Aske's Hatcham College

Pepys Road, London SE14 5SF

020 7652 9510 | hreception@haaf.org.uk | www.haaf.org.uk

| State | Ages: 3–18 | Pupils: 1,840; sixth form: 356 |

Principal: Since 2018, Alex Williamson, previously headteacher of Rutlish School.

Head of primary phase: Since 2015, Emily Gyimah, previously deputy head at Hatcham Temple Grove. Degree in primary education from Brunel; spent two years as a KS1/KS2 class teacher at Monson primary school and then taught for five years as a KS1 and literacy leader at Hatcham Temple Grove. She was then promoted to Haberdashers' Aske's Federation phonics consultant, a position she held for three successful years before returning to HTG in 2014 as deputy head.

Academic matters: One of the primary phase's unique selling points (the other is its music) is its German immersion programme, which pupils begin in year 1. According to the school, the children are taught for half a day, every day, in German, and staff with ability to speak German are actively recruited. It's had a big impact on the children's academic performance. 'Our phonics results went through the roof, because German is very phonic in the way it's spoken' with 'skilled and fluent German speakers coming up through the school ranks.' This is all excellent stuff, and we were thrilled to have 'Heads, shoulders, knees and toes' sung to us in German by a flaxen-haired child of 6 who could have stepped straight out of Hamlyn. Every primary parent we spoke to, however, told us a different story. 'My son's been doing it for two years now, and he can only tell me the nouns. He doesn't have any better grasp of German than if he'd been taught it in the usual way,' said one parent. Another said: 'It was sold to us as an German immersion programme, that they'd be taught in German every afternoon, but in reality, it's turned out to be a couple of afternoons a week and it's teaching things like colours and days of the week. It isn't immersion.' Even the most enthusiastic of school supporters said: 'I don't really know if they teach the German – just once in a while, maybe.' Quite a mismatch. School please note.

In 2019, 25 per cent A*-A/9-7 at GCSE. At A level: 50 per cent A*-B, 25 per cent A*/A.

Parents are generally satisfied, with most reporting that academic standards are good. 'Homework is prolific,' said one parent, adding, 'but it's mostly well thought through, well explained and supports classwork.' One parent was unhappy, reporting that their very bright child was 'constantly bored during lessons' and that 'the curriculum, especially in science and maths, is very basic, and the teachers, with a few exceptions, are not willing to take pupils beyond it.' The school contests this: 'We have the experience to help G&T children to get on,' and the leavers' destinations are certainly good. And adds: 'We run The Brilliant Club for our academically able students. You join in year 9, and you're assigned a PhD student [from Goldsmith's over the road] and given a task to do.'

Wide range of languages – year 7s get to choose two from German, French, Spanish, Mandarin and Latin, and higher up the school there are opportunities to learn classical Greek. Sixth form courses are 'strongly academic' – no BTecs offered, only A levels; the IB was explored but rejected as not inclusive enough for HAHC students.

Our impression was that the academic performance is very creditable given the non-academically selective intake, and that the school is both enriched and held up to critical scrutiny by a highly articulate parent body who expect the best and give no quarter when they don't get it.

Games, options, the arts: The school has its own sports centre in Nunhead, and students can do cricket, basketball, volleyball, football, netball and rugby (when we visited, the rugby team were about to head off to play another Haberdashers' school in Monmouth). Sport plays an active part in the junior school curriculum, with basketball, athletics, swimming and football on offer and funding awarded for Saturday and after-school provision. School adroitly links this with academic achievement – 'you have to be in the reading group to be in Saturday football.' The Little Leaders Group offers leadership exercises for children who don't get out much at home. Plenty of trips: river walks, London Eye, museums, visits to the theatre, all helped by an active parent body. Good programme of drama, and children are encouraged to do public speaking in assemblies etc.

The primary phase music was uniformly praised. Class music begins in reception, everyone learns recorder in year 3, and in year 4 those who are progressing well – generally around half of the class – are invited to learn violin, cello or clarinet. 'It's the discipline and the dexterity; and it's much easier in year 4 than when you're an older child.' The lessons are free and all children are allowed to carry on in year 5 if they want to, which at least a third of the year group always do. Those who don't want to continue can still be involved with the junior choir, and the Haberdashers' Livery Company and Temple Grove Trust can award bursaries to parents whose children want to learn other musical instruments outside school. Lots of concerts and the choir busks in Lewisham Shopping Centre to raise money for the 999 Club.

The music in the senior school is astonishing. No other word for it. We see many schools which claim to have marvellous music, but they really do have it here. We sat, open-mouthed, through student performances of Soave il Vento from Cosi Fan Tutte (sung in Italian), Mozart's Divertimento No 1 scored for two clarinets and a bassoon, Bartok's Mikrokosmos on the piano – all of it delivered with exquisite taste, sensitivity, musicality and technique. Then, just as we were preparing to move on, the choir started a ravishing rendition of Lotti's Crucifixus and we sat back down again. 'It's like being at a professional concert,' said the vice principal, with pardonable pride.

Unusually for a state school, classical music takes centre stage here, but it's for the many, not the few. Virtually all the children learn at least one instrument, and the lessons are free. The school abounds with orchestras, chamber music and choirs of every kind, and there are jazz bands too. Parents were uniformly delighted with this aspect of the school. We heard comments like 'all the music groups are fantastic'; 'there are concerts all the year round, musicals and even a school opera'; 'the music staff teach with ambition, enthusiasm and humour, and my children love it' and 'HAHC is a vibrant place where you are encouraged to fulfil your artistic potential.' We heard a murmur that rock music doesn't get quite the same

encouragement, and the school admitted that this might be so. But what is on offer is so amazing, that it's hard to grumble. HAHC choirs provide the music for City Hall's annual Remembrance service as well as carols for Southwark Cathedral. The Haberdashers Company regularly asks school to provide chamber ensembles for events. As the vice principal put it: 'A very good part of this school is that the students gain the cultural capital to function beyond it.'

On a different note, the CCF also flourishes at HAHC, attracting some 160 students, and with a Corps of Drums that is, according to a visiting instructor, 'better than Eton's.'

The music in the senior school is astonishing. We sat open-mouthed through student performances delivered with exquisite taste, musicality and technique

HAHC is proud of all aspects of its enrichment programme. The school is 'thronged' with students after lessons finish, says vice principal – but parental feedback we received about it was mixed (music excepted). A common complaint was that it was hard to get information about the various clubs and activities and that a number of initiatives, such as Artsmark and DofE, had unravelled due to poor organisation or lack of assessors. 'All a bit half-hearted,' was how one parent described the netball, and another said that her children felt that 'a huge opportunity is being missed in terms of sport... things just don't get organised.' These concerns were at odds with the school's excellent facilities and range of provision offered. School robustly defended its record on Artsmark ('We've handed out the certificates in assembly') as well as on sport, and says that DofE is now thriving, with a coordinator in place and a plaque awarded by the Duke of Edinburgh recognising the its commitment. The students we spoke to seemed happy.

Everyone agrees that debating is strong. Sixth formers have started a tutoring cooperative, coaching students from lower down the school and getting paid for it too. In general, HAHC students seem to gain confidence and skills from what is an unusually broad and intellectually stimulating extracurricular programme.

Background and atmosphere: One of the Haberdashers' 'family' of schools, both state and independent, and one of three schools in the Haberdashers' Aske's Federation, the others being Knight's Academy in Bromley and Crayford Academy in Bexley.

The primary phase was originally Monson Primary School, which was failing. HAHC took it on in 2008 and turned it around in three years. It is now rated outstanding. The school was being extensively refurbished when in 2010 a builder managed to cause a fire that gutted the place. The primary children and staff camped on various floors before moving into the new building in 2015.

Hatcham itself is divided between three sites. Jerningham Road, built in 1889 as a girls' school, now houses years 7 to 9 and is a very pleasing old Victorian red-brick. The older students study at the Pepys Road site, a rather gruelling 15-minute walk up Telegraph Hill. Minibuses shuttle pupils and staff between the various school buildings, all of which appeared well kept, blending tradition (stained glass, honours boards) with bang-up-to-date innovation and décor; in the parts we were shown, at any rate. School is co-educational, but in years 7 to 11 teaching is in single-sex groups wherever possible.

School-home communication much criticised by parents and we ourselves found this a difficult school to make contact with. (New direct lines for each school may help: until recently, all calls to any of the Federation schools had to be routed through the Haberdashers' Aske's Federation office, a system which parents loathed.) School counters that it has a policy that all emails must be replied to within 48 hours, that its communication is 'pretty good and pretty effective' and that all parents receive a handbook at the start of each year. But acknowledges, 'these days there's a need for real-time information.'

Pastoral care, well-being and discipline: Behaviour at HAHC reflects the school's large and diverse intake, but is perfectly fine, and all pupils we spoke to reported feeling safe here. The uniform is smart and smartly worn.

Many people commented on the school's 'good and healthy' atmosphere. 'The children respect the staff and the staff are interested in the children themselves, what their interests are and what makes them tick,' said one mother. Another wrote: 'The atmosphere is friendly and good pastoral care is provided.' The young people we met were courteous, assured and proud of their school. 'It's very welcoming here; I've made a large group of friends,' said one. 'The music department is great at involving everyone'; 'there's a really nice community feel here and the older and younger students talk to each other' were typical comments. Parents report that SEN provision is much improved and HAHC is the borough's school of choice for wheelchair-using students.

As we walked about the primary phase, this impressed us as a lively, happy and well-behaved community of children. There were a couple of

dissenting voices, including one who claimed that if it hadn't been for the automatic entry to HAHC's hugely-oversubscribed secondary phase she would have moved her child to a different school. The majority of parents, however, told us they were very happy with both the academic standards and the pastoral care. 'My daughter loves it – she wants to go even when she's sick,' said one mother, and others agreed. Comments included: 'The teachers are always helpful'; 'well done to all the teachers keeping standards up during all the moving about'; 'the encouragement and welcome my daughter receives has made her time at the school a pleasure,' and, from a mother without much English, 'I think it's a good school, really, really good.'

Pupils and parents: Reflecting the area, this is a very diverse community both socially and culturally, with about 50 per cent of pupils coming from ethnic minorities. As one member of staff dryly observed, at the end of the school day equal numbers turn either right into the Telegraph Hill conservation area, where a five-bedroom house might go for £1.3m, or left towards New Cross and some of the worst social deprivation in London. A number of professional musicians send their children here for the music provision. The school appears genuinely to integrate all its various members successfully. Ofsted recently wrote: 'The promotion of racial harmony within the college's richly diverse community is exemplary.'

Entrance: Two form entry to primary school. Sixty places in reception, with four more available further up the school. Usual state school admissions criteria apply: looked after children, medical needs, siblings, proximity. Oversubscribed. About 25 children come up from the school's own nursery, but parents should be aware that a place at the nursery does not guarantee a place in reception.

According to Ofsted, 'The promotion of racial harmony within the college's richly diverse community is exemplary'

Senior school massively oversubscribed, with at least 10 applications for every place. Some 64 pupils from primary phase year 6 have automatic entry. Ten per cent of places allocated on musical aptitude – these pupils are selected by aural test. Otherwise, standard local authority criteria apply: looked-after children, siblings, proximity etc. No longer uses banding. 'Admissions is a hot potato for this school,' admitted the vice principal. Appeals by parents are in excess of 100 each year, but be warned – the school's decisions are almost always upheld, 'because we're exceptionally compliant with the rules.'

About 60 to 100 sixth form places available to external students – no admissions tests, but a minimum of six 9-4 grades required at GCSE, the same as for internal students.

Exit: Almost all primary pupils transfer to HAHC secondary phase, to which they have automatic right of entry. After year 11 about half progress to the school's sixth form, the rest to a variety of post-16 provision. Some don't get the grades necessary to move up to year 12 at HAHC and go to other local schools and colleges; a tiny number opt for Dartford Grammar and the IB. Careers officer follows the progress of all leavers, and the school is proud of having had no NEETS (young people not in education, employment or training) for five years.

At 18, about 70 per cent to university, including some 30 per cent to Russell Group. In 2019, three to Oxbridge and four medics. Recent destinations include Manchester, UCL, Imperial College, LSE, Nottingham, Leeds, Sussex, Kent and Bangor. Others into apprenticeships, most recently to Bloomberg and Commerzbank AG.

Money matters: State-funded academy. Parents not asked to pay voluntary contributions, and vice principal looked astonished when we asked if they were. Unusual and generous provision of scholarships to the 10 per cent selected on musical aptitude – the school will partially fund them to train at the Saturday junior departments of the main London music colleges, the Royal Academy of Music, Royal College of Music, Guildhall and Trinity. In addition, instrumental lessons offered at HAHC are free to all students, regardless of ability or level.

Remarks: A large and flourishing comprehensive that's lifted above the crowd by its results and amazing music and attracts many aspirational families into the area. Plan early if you want your child to go.

Langley Park School for Boys

South Eden Park Road, Beckenham, Kent BR3 3BP

020 8639 4700 | office@lpbs.org.uk | www.lpsb.org.uk

| State | Ages: 11–18 | Pupils: 1,710; sixth form: 624 (250 girls) |

Headteacher: Since 2013, Steve Parsons (40s); has BA in history from King's College, MA in school effectiveness and improvement from the Institute of Education and the professional headship qualification, NPQH. He has lived nearby in Beckenham for many years with his wife Ruth, also a senior school headteacher, and could not quite believe the fortuitousness of the top job arising at Langley Park at just the moment he felt ready to take on a headship.

Having come straight from Dunraven School, the highly sought after south London co-educational state secondary in Streatham, where he spent seven years as deputy head, he would seem to be a very good fit. As Dunraven too underwent lengthy transition to new buildings, he is relieved to find himself in Langley Park's stunning new quarters post the spade-work. Prior to Dunraven he was assistant head at Crown Woods College.

Parents told us: 'I find him inspiring and a great leader for the boys' and 'he seems a committed, positive and hardworking head'. We found him to be very approachable, focused, modest, extremely tall and not lacking in courage, not only in taking over from a much-loved predecessor but in resolutely describing himself as a fan of football – more armchair than playing these days – in a school where rugby is the sporting religion.

Academic matters: Good results given the non-selective intake. In 2019, 51 per cent of boys achieved 9-5 at GCSE in both English and maths, with 18 per cent 9-7 grades. English language GCSE is so good the school is in the top five per cent of results nationally. At A level 21 per cent A*/A, 45 per cent A*-B in 2019.

Everyone can find their level, with the seven entry forms at 11+ divided into eight ability-based learning groups at key stage 3, 10 at key stage 4 for English and maths. There is definitely no resting on laurels in sight: the head has ambitions for academic improvement, introducing the new year 7s recently to Dr Carol Dweck's Growth Mindset, inspiring them to believe they can do better and that everyone has the potential for success, a philosophy which will be taken up by the whole school.

He's also aware of the need to future-proof students by teaching flexibility and adaptability to meet a barely imagined future job market.

Curriculum wise, at GCSE there is science at every level – so triple or general science and three art and design choices. Some creative options rarely on offer elsewhere at 16+, such as film studies, media studies, drama and dance, point the way to this being an amazingly artistic school. The idea behind the Langley Baccalaureate, promoted by the school instead of the EBacc, is that pupils are encouraged to retain an arts or creative subject when they're making their exam choices.

Pupils are also advised to study a modern foreign language, but it is not compulsory. German is twice as popular as Spanish and even more popular than French – more by tradition than design. The school has no plans to switch the emphasis at the moment. Special status in maths and computing with links to other schools to offer masterclasses. And the school is one of the few state schools offering engineering.

Apart from English and maths, the three sciences, particularly biology, are the most popular A level choices. There are also higher education oriented subjects on offer such as law, philosophy, psychology, economics, politics and further refined arts subjects – fine art and music technology.

On our visit the staff room was buzzing with a vibrant mix of grey haired and younger teachers including several former pupils. More than 20 per cent have been at the school over 10 years.

Parents see staff as hard-working and committed, enthusing: 'teaching staff are inspirational, very knowledgeable about their subjects and keen to stretch the students', 'the teaching is inclusive and of a high quality,' and 'assessment and feedback is thorough.' There is particular praise for English teaching, and the inspired geography teacher with packed classes who uses angel cake to explain coastal erosion – delicious! Pupils give rave reviews, mentioning teachers plugged into the wider world, bringing the latest research back into the classroom, and nothing being too much trouble.

Several parents we spoke to were in agreement regarding the relative lack of intense pressure and level of homework – very little or no homework during holidays – from lower school to sixth form. Whilst this could be good news for some, one, not alone, said: 'We live in such competitive times and I personally think my boys could be pushed harder'. The head disagrees, believing many feel the pressure on their sons is quite high.

Sixth formers are entrusted with independent study, nine free periods a week, and have several light and airy spaces, plus the café, around the school to work in, only lightly supervised by teachers based in semicircular goldfish bowl-like hubs. Pupils see the advantage of having their teachers close to hand – they always know where to find them when they need help. Students we saw were working diligently and told us, 'If you say to others "I need to work" they respect that'. The library with full-time librarian is open every day until 7pm.

Particular praise for English teaching, and the inspired geography teacher with packed classes who uses angel cake to explain coastal erosion – delicious!

The sixth formers we met impressed us with their drive and focus – they were determined on their university applications, one to Cambridge – and saw the school as doing everything to prepare them for their final exams: 'We work backwards from the final exam from week one'. Parents have confidence in the school's preparation for the next stage. Students speak of help with UCAS forms by a specialist, and joining with pupils from other south London schools in preparation for Oxbridge assessments.

With more than 30 learning support staff – visible in every class we visited assisting pupils – the needs of those with learning differences, particularly those with autism, are exceptionally well catered for here, attracting more than the average numbers to the school. The Sunil Centre, the base for learning support activities, is a discrete part of the school with its own courtyard garden and even magazine. Some 76 pupils are currently offered support and specialist input. Much is done in the classroom through differentiated learning, but the Sunil centre also provides quiet, smaller spaces and a separate exam room.

Four per cent of students have EAL requirements. The second most prevalent home language, after English, is French, followed by Lithuanian.

Games, options, the arts: A very sporty school – seven pupils currently play at national levels in sports from cycling to squash. Almost the only 'old school' features of the modern building are the traditional wooden boards in reception honouring sporting heroes.

A minimum of two hours sport a week is compulsory until the sixth form, and each Saturday one quarter of every year group represents the school in matches. 'We play the best of the best: all the independents', says the sports director of the fixture list. He commands an accomplished coaching staff, including former national league coaches, and 27 of the entire school staff are involved in extracurricular sport too.

Sydenham High School

No football; rugby takes centre stage in every way, not least the newly-seeded pitch in front of both the main school and sports building. On our visit it was still being cosseted behind fences, tantalising our guide who wondered if he'd ever get to play on it. The trophy cabinets bulge with local and national trophies for rugby, hockey, cricket and athletics. In the spirit of inclusivity, parents would like to see more matches for the lower ranked teams. New million pound hockey pitch. The under 16s were recently national champions, the first state school to make it to the top.

The school has held the Artsmark gold award for well over 10 years. The art department flourishes at an exceptionally high standard. Five students were recently chosen to have their work displayed in The Mall galleries at a Royal Society of British Artists exhibition, with two students being honoured as RBA scholars, a first for the school. The department holds an annual summer show where A level final work is hung for friends' and families' enjoyment in a local church. For those wishing to pursue the subject, a former pupil fresh from the cool of Shoreditch had recently returned to inspire budding graphic designers. The sixth form magazine was recently the winner of three national awards.

The 600 seat performance hall, also the home of the Bromley Symphony Orchestra, is rarely out of use. Dance is exhilaratingly popular here. Recent collaborations saw the PE department taking to the stage, whilst pupils provided an inspired interpretation of a WWI love story as part of the school's commemorations. The riches of London's dance scene are mined, such as during a recent trip to see Matthew Bourne's Swan Lake at Sadler's Wells. A level dance is a new option. One parent: 'Our boys are not particularly interested in dance or drama; however, our eldest recently took part in a short dance performance during a show and loved it.'

A busy music department with dedicated practice rooms, large teaching spaces and a technology suite. Around 400 pupils learn an instrument, either during school or through private lessons mostly facilitated through a link with the Bromley Youth Music Trust. A dozen or so have reached the pinnacle of grade 8 and beyond, with some students performing in the National Youth Orchestra, the London Schools Symphony Orchestra and the London Jazz Festival. There are Christmas and summer showcases, an annual music tour and gala concerts.

Several by-invitation lunchtime and after-school music clubs such as wood and string quartets or, for something a bit different, cantabile, or Cuban band.

A society or club for most academic subjects each week plus a few extras such as Jaguar cars, GCSE dance, Christian union and scrum half clinic,

which sounds as if it mends broken noses, but apparently is more about technique.

Enrichment really comes into its own in the sixth form, with everyone taking on a couple of new things as well as their A levels, which can be either a sport or arts subject. Most popular are rugby, football and table tennis, but almost a third of students are trying out Japanese, with others learning Dutch, counselling or taking part in the Duke of Edinburgh Award or a current affairs group, Think Tank. If performing arts is more their thing, students can experiment with dance, taiko drumming, creative composition or world music.

Background and atmosphere: The school has been through a number of metamorphoses in terms of buildings, names and indeed locations since its first incarnation in 1901: at one point a technical college, then a grammar school. Having settled on its current location in Eden Park, Beckenham, it eventually outgrew its buildings, leading to a huge development project to create the site we see today. Pupils moved in during 2012, whilst the old school was entirely demolished.

Appropriately enough, given the sporty nature of the school, on first sight the whole complex appears like a smart new sports centre with ample parking. The red-brick main building with curved roof and exterior walls appears hardly large enough to house over 1,600 pupils, but inside the design functions brilliantly, with large classrooms, mezzanine levels, spacious corridors hardly appearing to be corridors because of light from above and large break-out study areas for sixth formers.

A very sporty school. Almost the only 'old school' features of the modern building are the traditional wooden boards in reception honouring sporting heroes

Each of the lower years has its own small playground. During our visit, seagulls swooped down trying to snatch snacks from the boys – 'time to get the hawks out,' said a passing teacher, not joking, apparently.

Pupils in the lower school wear maroon blazers, graduating to less eye-catching black ones. Then sixth form boys may wear a suit of their choice and girls have recently adopted a jacket of their own choosing – all look very smart.

Perhaps it was our exuberant guides, but as we walked the school we felt palpable excitement and energy amidst hard work. Everyone is agreed on the inclusive ethos of the school. One parent told us,

'The school is competitive but it seems to us that every aspect is valued at the same level. This is great as the boys always seem to be able to feel proud of some achievement: receiving a good grade, being in a team for rugby, being identified for great effort in art, having the opportunity to dance on a stage, working on a science project.'

Works collaboratively with new multi-academy trust formed by Langley Park Girls, Hawes Down junior school and Hawes Down infant school. The Langley Park primary school opened in 2016.

Pastoral care, well-being and discipline: School rules are traditional – no earrings for boys. Pupils need a cycling proficiency certificate to bring a bicycle to school. Respect, calm and litter picking mandatory. Mobile phones are allowed for sixth formers, but must be handed in lower down the school. The head says that exclusion figures are 'very, very low' and that 98 per cent of parents recently surveyed were very happy with the pastoral care and discipline at the school.

During our visit, seagulls swooped down trying to snatch snacks from the boys – 'time to get the hawks out,' said a passing teacher, not joking, apparently

Form tutors are the linchpin of pastoral care. Several parents mentioned talking to staff on behalf of their child, but also reported problems being swiftly dealt with to their satisfaction.

There is deliberately no separate sixth form building, so that the younger years have role models around the school. The appointment of prefects by the head is like a mini job application – those putting themselves forward must each gather four or five recommendations from teachers.

Some thought might be given to the external sixth form candidates, who seem forever after to go by the unfortunate label of 'externals'. Our two tour guides both bore the label resolutely, but thought it unlikely their fellow externals, or indeed girls, would ever be school captain.

Pupils and parents: Parents as well as pupils are proud to belong to the school. We're told 'the term Langley Boy is one that is highly regarded and proudly stated.' One parent explained: 'The school attracts gifted boys and later girls for the sixth form, who work in an educational environment that expects a lot of them. This high expectation draws parents that would normally be looking at independent schools.'

By far the majority of pupils are white British, with other white, black Caribbean and black African larger ethnic groups. The head describes his pupils as: 'confident, hard-working, proud of their school, articulate, supportive and active.'

Who will thrive here? Clearly the sporty, arty and academic, but parents add: a child who is 'well mannered, respectful, takes pride in their school's reputation, is a team player and competitive'; 'this school will allow your child to achieve their academic dreams and to bring out talents they never knew they had.' We'd only add the school seems to support and nurture ambitions and interests wherever they lie.

Communication with parents has been a weak spot and parents still shared a few niggles with us, but the head cites recent surveys of parental satisfaction.

Entrance: There are 220 places annually at 11+. With applications at just under three to one, chances of getting in could be far worse, but you will need to live within one mile of the school. Local estate agents say many move nearby simply for the school, creating something of a squeeze on prices. There are 45 local feeder primaries, including Balgowan, Clare House, Hawes Down, Highfield, Marian Vian, Oaklodge, Pickhurst Junior and Unicorn.

It's far harder to get into the sixth form: most recently 850 candidates fought tooth and nail for 150 places. Girls from Langley Park Girls School next door are subject to the same admission criteria as others.

Exit: Some 80 per cent stay on to the sixth form, with those leaving mostly going on to do vocational qualifications. The same proportion then head to university, very slightly more girls than boys.

Recent destinations include Kent, Portsmouth, Brighton, Sussex and Bournemouth, with 25 per cent of those taking university places heading to Russell Group destinations such as Birmingham and Southampton. Most popular subjects seem to be English, history, law, accountancy, engineering, physics and business with quite a few medically related, plus some budding pharmacists and psychologists.

Remarks: An exceptional example of comprehensive education with a sporting and artistic offer to match many an independent in smart new facilities. Easier to enter at 11+ (boys) than battle into the sixth form with increased competition from all around including girls.

Langley Park School for Girls

Hawksbrook Lane, Beckenham, Kent BR3 3BE

020 8663 4199 | info@lpgs.bromley.sch.uk | www.lpgs.bromley.sch.uk

| State | Ages: 11–18 | Pupils: 1,581; sixth form: 388 (40 boys) |

Headteacher: Since September 2018, Katie Scott, previously head of Portslade Aldridge Community Academy in Brighton. Taught history at Haberdashers' Aske's Hatcham College, head of history at Cator Park School in Beckenham, assistant principal at Haberdashers' Aske's Knights Academy, then vice principal at Sir Robert Woodard Academy before joining Portslade in 2015.

Academic matters: The reason parents send their daughters here. 'It was the academic side that appealed,' said one, who moved house specifically to secure a place. Plenty to shout about, too, with 68 per cent getting 9-5 grades in both English and maths in 2019 and 28 per cent 9-7 grades. Progress 8 impressive. Particularly high percentages in single subject GCSE sciences and fast track languages, both reserved for most able. Students now take fewer GCSEs 'to reflect the increase in rigour' of the new GCSE specifications and allow more teaching time for each, with staff encouraged to include problem-solving and risk-taking into lessons.

Good news continues in sixth form. While new vocational courses are being added to roster that currently includes business, travel, health and social care with aim of broadening appeal (almost the only 'could do better' in otherwise glowing inspection report), the emphasis is unapologetically skewed 'towards the more able students'. Results – 60 per cent A*-B, 20 per cent A*/A grades in 2019.

Success doesn't, however, come at expense of the 200 or so pupils with special needs, many speech and language related (about 20 have statements). Good-sized and centre stage learning support unit, home to two key workers under direction of deputy head with SEN background, is widely appreciated as a whole school safety valve offering help for anyone under pressure.

Add enthusiastic teachers, including one working her socks off to spark discussion on ethics of designer babies amongst slightly somnolent GCSE biology class, and the technology head extolling the wonders of the computer programmed laser saw that cuts anything (Goldfinger would be envious, though less fussed by its ability to add detailed floral motifs) and it sounds like roses all the way.

Well, up to a point, Lord Copper. There's the odd wilting bloom. Success in some small but perfectly formed subjects (GCSE music, growing fast, consistently secures 100 per cent 6s or higher) is balanced by occasional whole-subject wobble (applied science a case in point). And despite GCSE success in languages, one of school specialisms (others are technology and sport), numbers die away post-16, with totals for German, French and Spanish scarcely into double figures (reflection, sadly, of national malaise). It's not for want of trying, what with Mandarin and Latin both available as popular lunchtime and after-school clubs, and the 150 EAL students, many bilingual, able to take community languages as additional GCSE. Currently, advanced linguists who take French GCSE early follow a slightly waffly culture-related programme with some cake-making but little academic bite in year 11. School's plan to move them on to AS level work may help though, judging by less than encouraging results in other schools, it may not.

> '*It was the academic side that appealed,' said one parent, who moved house specifically to secure a place at the school*

Then there's the little matter of boys' school next door which clocks near identical GCSE results to its neighbour – 'girls should do at least six per cent better,' says school – and is also seen as the place to go for sixth form sciences. Resulting mini brain drain especially in chemistry and physics is cause for concern but could soon be reversed with appointment of whizzy new head of science who comes with tried and tested Pied Piper-like A level recruitment skills. Shouldn't be rocket science – sixth formers who ignore hype and stay on for science are glad they did. 'Class sizes are very big in the boys' school – I knew the school and the teachers and the course seems to suit me,' said one.

School wants everyone, including staff, to up their game, crunching primary school data so hard you can almost hear it squeak in effort to identify budding talent from arrival in year 7 and laying down the law with clear minimum academic goals for pupils (with hope, of course, that these will be routinely exceeded). 'Boys are often deluded about their own potential, whereas girls tend to under-estimate themselves.'

Games, options, the arts: Sport highly rated. 'Amazing,' said one pupil. Lots to do and places to do it in – large if slightly sombre sports hall and gym inside and five tennis courts and an all-weather pitch in addition to five acres of green space outside. Old girls include Ellen Gandy, 2012 Olympic 100m butterfly finalist, and with current pupils making literal waves in diving and even water polo, and figuratively in squash, could be first of many.

Favours the competitive (lots of wins for netball and hockey squads in local championships) so 'you need to push yourself,' said parent. Theoretically, however, something for everyone and if the time-tabled sport doesn't do it for you there's probably a club that will, from yoga to fencing. 'They really shine. You name it and they'll have it,' said pupil.

Robust though sport is, tends to be swamped by performing arts, which have pirouetted across website and ousted match results from shared online notice board, replacing them with close-ups of recent and seemingly non-stop round of acclaimed productions. Frequent high-quality, whole-school collaborations between dance, drama and music include large cast versions of Annie and Alice in Wonderland, which have gone down a storm, while with around 300 students learning instruments, there's a decent range of ensembles, too, including 50-strong jazz orchestra which recently toured China.

Highly effective school council gets things done – broken soap dispenser that had languished for weeks in one of the toilets was fixed within days after complaints

Mini BRIT academy feel never stronger than with dance: tap and street offered, but classical ballet a particular strength, masterminded (and frequently choreographed) by three dance teach-ers whose remit covers everything from hit versions of Twilight and Beauty and the Beast to GCSE, A level and, coming soon, BTec courses complete with glamorous overseas revision courses, all appar-ently done without drawing breath. Indeed, a new dance studio was recently opened by Deborah Bull

of King's College London. Motto, unsurprisingly, is 'anyone can dance,' though, as sixth form boys as yet unconvinced, male performers are currently imported from next door.

In addition to 'look at me' events, lots of look-ing after others, with pupils from year 9 onwards lending a hand at local primaries while year 12s, who have Wednesday afternoons free thanks to miracle of timetable coordination, can opt to fill them with voluntary work, often as part of thriving DofE programme, open to all though you'll only get the go ahead if you're doing 'what your pre-dicted grades say you should be,' said one. You can't keep staff away either: science teacher – a 'bundle of energy' – awarded MBE for educational work in community.

Background and atmosphere: In its 90-year his-tory (last 50 on current leafy site), school has had several Time Lord-like incarnations, beginning as a county girls' school, becoming a grammar in 1945, a comprehensive in the 1970s and achieving the full collector's set with academy status in 2011. Connections with the past haven't been sloughed off, however, with original society for old girls (known as Adremians) still going strong. There's also traditional, ultra-smart uniform much cooed over by outsiders, less so by current parents faced with dry-clean-only blue piped blazer and hard-to-press pleated tartan skirt. 'I get granny to iron it,' confessed one.

School design, mid-20th century standard issue, features two-storey main building with sep-arate blocks for drama/sport, science (11 perfectly decent labs), sixth form and technology (newest and nicest of the lot with six well-equipped work-shops), together roughly framing three sides of large and picnic table studded if slightly bleak courtyard (the main R&R outside area until student council secured leave to use 'head's own garden', a green and pleasant space round the corner). Effect is pleasant and unintimidating. New girls get maps and are quickly at home – in some schools you feel satellite tracking and emergency rations wouldn't come amiss.

Everyone now very nice about multi-million pound newly rebuilt boys' school (similar name, no relation). Wasn't always thus. A predecessor head fought plans all the way to Supreme Court and won what turned out to be pyrrhic victory as second application was nodded through shortly afterwards. Bridges now mended, cordial relation-ships re-established and girls offered use of new facilities, notably the hear-every-bat-squeak acous-tically advanced auditorium – 'when boys aren't using it,' says school, without apparent irony. Big brother (though a benevolent one) rules.

Make do and mend philosophy only goes so far, however. An additional floor on top of sixth form

Co-educational, though boys so thin on the ground that spotting them is not unlike a real-life version of Where's Wally?

building (including café and social facilities) has recently opened, likewise a new dance studio, and there is planning permission for new music block.

Surprisingly little sense of overcrowding, and there's even a whole school assembly once a term or thereabouts – though 'if it were all boys, there would be accidents,' says school. (One pupil confessed to eating outside 'even when it's raining' just to get away from it all). Children seem to move in mysterious ways (possibly by converting themselves to compressed data format at busy times, more likely by learning to keep elbows in when using corridors). It's particularly noticeable at break, when what should be a scrum for the food and drink somehow isn't.

Mood is welcoming, helped by delightful, offbeat art displays (ceramic artichokes on sticks, anyone?), partial door 'n' floor refurbishment (light wood/portholes combo gives vaguely Nordic/nautical feel depending on preference), and homely areas including large, book-lined library, well used in and out of school hours, which hosts termly themed parties complete with cakes to keep reading top of mind when 'other things step in,' says librarian, diplomatically.

Pastoral care, well-being and discipline: Four houses; Lambda (yellow), Kappa (blue), Sigma (red), and Gamma (green) – fortunately no Brave New World Epsilon – as much an admin tool as a motivational one, used for imposing a little organisational clarity on eight-form entry. It's two forms to a house (block booking, no arguments) and little sense of feverish competition 'except on sports day,' say girls.

Friendship issues inevitably the biggest problem cited by parents, especially lower down the school. 'They look so grown up,' said worried mother who mentioned daughter's need to apply defensive make-up following pressure to fit in. If there is a problem, overwhelming pupil consensus is that there's always somebody to talk to – 'even the canteen people are friendly,' said one. Staff are often very popular, with tears on departure, though 'a few scare me, and I'm the parent,' said one mother. Relationships improve the further up the school you go. 'Students do have problems with teachers – no school's perfect but mostly they're great and there if you want them,' added another. Discipline, though firm, is considered: if there's out

of character bad behaviour, staff will 'try to find out where you're coming from first,' said year 11 pupil, with exclusion very much a last resort and help provided, wherever possible, in situ.

Officially, form tutors are first point of contact, often staying with same group for several years. Parents praise ease of communication – teachers are listed in pupil planners and there are individual email addresses for all, up to and including head. 'If you expect other members of staff to give out their contact details you should be willing to do the same thing.'

Highly effective school council, a model of its kind, 'lets teachers know what students are thinking, rather than what they assume they are,' said pupil, and gets things done – broken soap dispenser that had languished for weeks in one of the toilets was 'fixed within days' after complaints. It's helped by involvement of sympathetic teacher who 'is on our side but is honest and will say if we're asking for outrageous things.' Youngest girls have as much of a voice as senior pupils and an equal chance of being chosen from full meeting to present ideas to head. 'You even hear what sixth form are doing,' said one.

Pupils and parents: Tight catchment area means many new pupils arrive with others they know. While behaviour is 'fairly standard for teenagers these days; you stop for 10 minutes to let them cross and nobody says thank you,' harrumphs slightly gloomy local, her experience seems exception rather than rule: on morning of our visit no sign of anything other than almost universal good manners. Lots of hands raised in salute to waiting cars as girls (boys, too – a symphony in blue and burgundy respectively) arrived in their hundreds.

In school, too, doors are routinely held open and there's general sense of courtesy towards others (helped, quite possibly, by numbers of teachers in corridors, though a benevolent rather than sentry-like presence).

Parents are necessarily local, many the hardworking exemplars praised by politicians of every hue. As a fair percentage commute to jobs in London, don't necessarily see much of each other, although with quite a few events (first class fireworks display, for example) 'opportunities to socialise are there if you want them,' said one.

Entrance: Large school, tiny catchment area (has shrunk to under a mile before now though normally hovers just over). Means that despite size of intake (240 places in year 7) it's routinely oversubscribed and there's always a waiting list. Pupils come from nine or so local primaries (Oak Lodge, Marian Vian, Highfield Junior, Pickhurst, Unicorn, Balgowan, Clare House, Hawes Down and St Mary's Catholic Primary) though feeders in name only as attendance is no guarantee of place and distance (barring standard priority given to looked after children, siblings and now some staff children) is king. Estate agents testify to school's popularity. Parents vote with their square feet. 'We specifically moved to get a place,' said one (though other more dubious practices aren't unknown either).

Three-quarters stay into sixth form, again oversubscribed (minimum of 10 places available to external candidates, usually more in practice) and, like majority of local schools, co-educational, though boys so thin on the ground (around 20 a year) that spotting them not unlike real life version of Where's Wally? A level places dependent on securing minimum of seven GCSE passes (about 50 turned away at application stage) with minimum grade 6s in four including chosen A level subjects, 9-7s preferred for toughies like chemistry and teacher recommendations for languages. Anyone opting for performing arts will also need to pass audition.

Exit: A third or so who leave post-GCSE stay close, some moving to boys' school next door (with a few, who don't care for the size, moving back) while a very few opt for selective grammars like St Olave's and Newstead Wood or independent schools like Trinity School in neighbouring Croydon. A few head off to larger colleges to study work-related courses, though school keen to slow exodus of less academic – should have 'right to continue here even if not high flyers'.

No compromises when it comes to onwards academic journey. Almost all make it into higher education, nearly all first or second choice universities with Bristol, Leeds, Warwick, Southampton 'all popular,' says head of sixth form, and the most able encouraged to try for Oxbridge. Normally a couple of places each year (three in 2019) and two for medicine. Law, business and administration, biological sciences and creative arts and design (including music and drama) head the list of subject choices, with social services, maths and English not far behind and a light dusting of languages and engineering.

New careers academy 'will provide specific advice and guidance backed up with seminars, careers days, contact with employers and practice at interviews and skills'. School 'has been commended for its outstanding preparation of UCAS applications.'

Remarks: Short on square feet but, remarkably, feels as if has enough breathing space for everyone, helped by honest, intelligent leadership, enthusiastic staff and pupils who seem happy to be here and for the most part do well. A real breath of fresh air.

Newstead Wood School

Avebury Road, Orpington, Kent BR6 9SA

01689 853626 | office@newsteadwood.co.uk | www.newsteadwood.co.uk

| State | Ages: 11–18 | Pupils: 1,082; sixth form: 300 |

Head: Since September 2018, Alan Blount, previously deputy head. A graduate of both Exeter (biology and education) and Canterbury Christ Church (masters in leadership and management in education) universities, he taught science at Oxted School and Carshalton Boys Sports College before joining Newstead Wood in 2014. Despite a girls' grammar being such a different kettle of fish ('friends said, "Seriously, are you sure Newstead is for you?"' he laughs), he was appointed assistant head within a couple of months and headteacher four years later. 'Headship was definitely on my radar, but I didn't think the opportunity would come up here or so soon,' he admits.

Wide-eyed, smiley, bounding with energy and bursting with ideas, he exudes excitement and passion about the school yet manages to avoid clichéd and predictable headteacher boasts and is refreshingly willing to admit where there's room for improvement (facilities, music and sport among them). 'Oh my God, if you could see his assemblies – we actually look forward to them,' said one pupil, with others telling us, 'he puts his enthusiasm into absolutely everything', 'is extremely open to ideas' and 'really wants to connect with the students – you always get a conversation out of him in the corridor'. Parents like him too, calling him 'very hands on' and 'always creating a feel-good factor about the school'. They also praise him for his 'fresh ideas' and 'great weekly newsletter'.

Educated at his local comp, he was the first in his wider family to go to university, having done a gap year in hospitality, including opening a new restaurant in Crawley (cooking is still a passion). 'It was more a case of giving university a go because everyone else was doing it than having a burning desire to teach,' he admits. 'But I absolutely loved it.' Still teaches (science in year 10, as well as to wannabe dentists, vets and medics in sixth form). Describes the students as 'like sponges, they soak up everything – they are amazing. I'm so lucky to be here.'

A keen sportsman and gardener, he grows his own veg and keeps chickens.

Academic matters: There's an ethos of really knuckling down but it's not so much an academic hothouse as the sort of place where if you don't work reasonably hard you're the odd one out. 'My daughter can cope well in a class with intelligent children who are keen to learn and she organises herself well – that's the kind of child this school is best suited to,' reckoned parent. Exam results are consistently impressive – in 2019, 86 per cent 9-7 grades at GCSE. A level results no less creditable: 69 per cent A*-B grades and 42 per cent A*/A grades.

Building learning and thinking skills, including critical reading and referencing, happens from day one; problem solving permeates the curriculum. School places great emphasis on staff and pupils 'co-constructing' the learning experience and on staff leadership and development – they should be critical questioners and facilitate, rather than direct, learning. There's an active school parliament and there are both subject and house captains who feed into decision making and who support fellow learners. Broad setting in maths from year 7. French from year 7, plus choice from either Spanish or German, with all three taken up in year 8. Japanese, Mandarin and Latin also available at GCSE. Teachers generally deemed 'excellent', albeit some 'who aren't up to scratch', according to parents and pupils. Strongest departments considered to be geography, English, classics and languages.

No set pathways at GCSE and no cases of 'computer says no' to timetabling – 'somehow they make it work for you as an individual', said a student. EBacc and triple science available to all, but there's no shame in doing double science (usually up to 18 students a year, generally to make way for another humanity) and the arts, music, drama and PE are valued as much as the harder academic subjects. In sixth form, most do three A levels, although some take four or five – all comes down to results and potential. A level menu largely traditional, although psychology and economics are also available – as well as music and drama if numbers allow (most years). Art popular. EPQ well-taken up.

For those with mild SEN, there's a mix of support both in and outside the classroom, including touch typing on offer. School good at recognising issues too – one parent told of how she spent all her daughter's primary school years trying to find out what was wrong, 'but Newstead spotted exactly what it was within just three months, then put in all the support my daughter needed'. Head says that every year there are more access arrangements for exams eg laptops, extra time, different coloured paper etc.

The head took two students to the House of Lords the week we visited on the back of their attempts to help tackle (with detailed plan and speech) the refugee crisis in Yemen

Exceptional careers guidance (a Lifetime Achievement Award from Investors in Careers sits alongside their Gold Award) not only from careers advisers but teachers themselves, who embed advice into lessons especially further up the school. Beyond Newstead night and workshops from alumnae seen as highlights.

Games, options, the arts: The extracurricular not so much shines as dazzles and the fact that so much of it is student led is a reflection of the extent to which leadership and participation characterises this school. 'You'll be hard pushed to find a sixth former who doesn't voluntarily take on extra responsibilities,' said a parent. Indeed, there are 60+ student societies ranging from debating, politics, the environment, medicine to law, all run by year 12 pupils; and we heard how the head took two students up to the House of Lords the week we visited on the back of their attempts to help tackle (including detailed plan, with speech) the refugee crisis in Yemen.

For others, too, judging by the somewhat overwhelming stream of calendar reminders on the electronic board in reception, there is little excuse to be idle, with masses of after-school and lunchtime activities, as well as positions as sports ambassadors, Arkwright scholars to promote engineering in schools, language teaching in local primary schools, maths and debating competitions, Dragon's Den workshops (school partners with 7billionideas) and charity events. You'll find everything from year 7s sprucing up all lost property stationary and selling it off in pencil cases to raise money for Cancer Research and year 9s crocheting and selling daffodil badges to raise money for Marie Curie. We visited on Japanese Day, with almost every classroom so absorbed in everything from creating ancient Japanese toys to calligraphy that they barely noticed us. Under the banner of 'enrichment', every Wednesday afternoon is put aside for these and other pursuits, with a different focus for each year group including elective options for years 10 upwards where they choose to study additional non-examined options or devote time to volunteering or elite sport.

'Considering it's a highly academic school, I think they do pretty well,' was a typical parental refrain regarding sport, many of whom praise the 'inclusive' element 'which embeds a love of sport'. Students are similarly minded – 'the school is surprisingly not that bad and there are some exceptional athletes, yet they still make you feel included if you're not amazing', said one. Good performances in rounders and cricket, with football on the up and they've just started rugby and rowing (partnership with London Youth Rowing) – and for those less keen on team sports, there's everything from yoga to boxing (with cycling spin room on the wish list for head). But some parents felt more could be made of sport and a few self-proclaimed sporty students told us they do all their sport outside because, as one put it, 'in the end, this is an academically focused school so sport doesn't feel like a priority'.

Music 'used to be good', according to students and parents, a nostalgic glint in their eyes. But we heard how 'it's been left by the wayside a bit since certain key teachers left' and 'needs a pick-me-up'. School orchestra? 'Hmm... I'm not sure if there is one,' said students. Choirs? 'Possibly, for the younger years... I'm not quite sure' etc. The reality is they have Vox CC, gospel choir, folk group and various ensembles plus jazz band and African drumming but lack numbers and impetus they need to excel. But head is by no means oblivious and has plans to capitalise on the many students that play or sing to grades 6, 7 and 8.

Recent spending, explains the head, has had to be on the fundamentals eg roof and windows ('the whole school used to rattle when the wind blew')

Drama is a different story – 'definitely not sidelined', said a parent. It's popular at GCSE (though not A level), with wide take-up for the whole-school plays, and one of the highlights of the year is the performing arts festival in which year 9 classes reduce a musical to 15 minutes. 'They do everything from directing to acting to lighting and even sixth formers delight in remembering their go at it,' we were told.

Judging from the high quality of art displayed throughout the school, there is no shortage of

talent and students rave about the teacher expertise in photography, sculpture, drawing and ceramics, among others. Lovely to see excitable students making their own props for their forthcoming play too. However, one student felt that while it's good that you get a lot of free rein in art classes, 'I sometimes think the nuts and bolts foundation teaching is a bit lacking'.

Background and atmosphere: Set in a quiet residential area, with wonderful views across the playing fields towards the downs, but the school buildings, though quite spacious, are unremarkable and jumbled – the 1950s, when she school was established, not perhaps the best architectural era. Various additions and upgrades over the years but inside, many of the corridors and classrooms look tired and in need of repainting, although the walls are brightened with artwork and some areas have been spruced up. Recent spending, explains the head, has had to be on the fundamentals eg roof and windows ('the whole school used to rattle when the wind blew'). Well-stocked library, with 'amazing' librarian – 'I'm studying dentistry and she's always looking out for relevant articles for me', a student told us.

Atmosphere is collaborative and supportive with a strong emphasis on nobody being left behind, either academically or otherwise – students, for example, are quick to tell school when they see younger students looking lonely, including on public transport (the travel buddy scheme helps prevent this and neatly combines environmental targets to reduce car use with accompanying year 7 pupils on public transport their first few weeks). Food gets a bad press – 'my daughter hates it,' said more than one parent, but new caterers were due to start after our visit (head's background in hospitality no doubt coming in useful).

Pastoral care, well-being and discipline: 'These students are highly driven and put a lot on themselves,' says head. So school is careful ('sometimes too much so,' believe some parents and even some students) to help these youngsters learn how to chill out, with home-work free weeks (usually before holidays – good for staff too as who wants a load of marking during half term?) and they've reduced the 'normal' number of GCSEs to 11 (some were doing 16 before) and A levels from four to three.

And when the pressure does get the better of some students – and it can, they say, albeit with the pressure 'definitely coming from themselves or their families, never the school' – there are a number of options. These include a part-time employed counsellor, trained mental health ambassadors and a student support manager who runs the student support room, a safe space that student can go to if they have a 'I've just got to get out of here now' feeling in a lesson or want somewhere quieter to be. With multiple computers and comfy chairs, it has a cosier feel than a traditional classroom 'and you'll often find the radio on'.

Having had students that identify as boys, school is well-versed in transgender issues, including the use of pronouns, and has two gender neutral loos

Students chat freely about issues like self-harm and eating disorders – some felt 'there's an extreme amount of mental health issues' whereas others mused that 'perhaps it's just we talk about it more'. Understandably, a student suicide a few years ago has left scars; school says it used the experience to 'change a lot'. Having had students that identify as boys, including in younger years, school is well-versed in transgender issues, including use of pronouns and it has two gender neutral loos. Generally a progressive ambience, with students proud of, for example, their LGBT societies.

Communications with parents on the up, much to parents' delight after previous heads (sixth formers we met had had four alone during their time) being 'less public facing'. 'Now we get a friendly face and always a hello – it's a massive change', said one, with all reporting a good response to concerns voiced, whether individual (friendship) or more general.

Bad behaviour practically non-existent, with no permanent exclusions in living memory and only the odd one or two temporary ones a year, if that. Occasional incidents of bullying are addressed, with the girls themselves tending to side with the victim. Informal vertical contact is encouraged through clubs and older pupils acting as mentors, plus the travel buddy scheme.

Pupils and parents: These spirited, articulate and savvy young women (and young men at sixth form) are a joy to spend time with and reflect the same forthrightness, friendliness and zest as their headteacher. 'They might not always remember to hold the door open for you, but that's only because they've got a million things going round their head – they mean to be polite,' he says. In the main, parents are ambitious and go-getting – head has his work cut out managing expectations. Families come from a wide range of socio-economic and ethnic backgrounds (seen as good – 'they're not cocooned in a bubble,' said one parent) but it's not considered an Orpington school ('a shame in many ways,' said another) with most hailing from

several or more miles north and south (fewer from Croydon, for example, even though it's nearer as you have to get three buses door-to-door). Notable former pupils include Olympian and current Commonwealth and European Championship gold medallist Dina Asher-Smith, actress and former model Gemma Chan, former general secretary of the Royal College of Nursing Christine Hancock, clarinettist Emma Johnson, comedian Josie Long and actress and singer Kim Medcalf.

Entrance: Around 1,200 applications for 160 places in year 7. Entrance tests in verbal and non-verbal reasoning in September. Standards high, but the test experience 'more friendly' than for other local schools. Preference to those who live within nine miles, then those on pupil premium, then children of staff. Of those that pass muster, around 60 per cent come from state primaries, the rest from small independent schools. When, very occasionally, places come available further up the school, those on the waiting list are invited to take an age-appropriate test and the highest scorers offered a place. Additional places are available for sixth form entry for those – including boys – with a minimum of eight GCSE grades 9-6.

Exit: Those entering at 11 are expected to stay the course until 18 and only a few leave at 16, mostly to pursue specialist studies, eg performing arts or media studies. Those leaving at 18 overwhelming to university, about 60 per cent to Russell Group – Southampton, London, Warwick, Exeter, Bristol, Nottingham, Durham, Manchester among popular destinations. Humanities and sciences courses dominate current application forms, but there's real breadth across the rest. In 2019, eight to Oxbridge and eight to medical/dentistry school. Degree apprenticeships promoted and increasingly taken up (school offers apprenticeships itself to show they believe in their worth).

Money matters: Dedicated and enthusiastic parent-run Providing Excellence Together (PET) and PA raise up to a staggering £100,000 annually, which funds the artists in residence each year and extra teaching resources. A covenant scheme and continuous fundraising events and activities to support the ongoing developments.

Remarks: Capable and committed girls (and boys at sixth form) do extremely well here. To families that have heard of the school this will probably come as no surprise, but what is less well-known is the really friendly and supportive vibe within which they achieve their soaring success. Not for anyone after whizzy, modern facilities with all the mod cons, but it's all fit for purpose and the students don't even seem to notice.

Old Palace of John Whitgift School

(🧍) (17) 🗨

Old Palace Road, Croydon, Surrey CR0 1AX

020 8688 2027 | admissions@oldpalace.croydon.sch.uk | www.oldpalace.croydon.sch.uk

| Independent | Pupils: 490; sixth form: 80 |
| Ages: 10–18 | Fees: £14,609 – £16,096 pa |

Linked school: Old Palace Preparatory, 368

Headmistress: Since September 2019, Jane Burton, previously CEO of the Girls' Learning Trust (GLT). With an economics degree, she had a career in business before becoming a teacher in her mid 30s. Appointed headteacher of Wallington High School for Girls in 2012, then executive head of Nonsuch and Wallington Education Trust when it was formed in 2015, becoming CEO in 2017 when it was renamed the GLT. Married with a teenage son.

Academic matters: The curriculum in year 7 begins with standard fare with the inclusion of Latin and French or Spanish. By year 10 keen scientists and stargazers may also take up GCSE astronomy, whilst if Latin is going well, why not add in a GCSE in classical Greek? Mandarin is offered as part of a club after school.

In 2019, 76 per cent 9-7 at I/GCSE, with Latin, RS, maths, English and history getting the best results. Ten subjects is the most common, some may opt for fewer if it makes sense for them. French is by far the most popular language taken to GCSE with native speakers able to notch up another.

At A level in the same year, 48 per cent of grades were A*/A, with the mathematicians outstripping all comers in terms of top grades and something new – psychology – proving both popular and engaging with plenty of As. A healthy list of choices including classical Greek, drama and theatre studies and government and politics.

Eighty or so teaching staff. Teachers 'very dedicated, always go the extra mile – they're all running clinics in the lunch hour if a girl wants extra help... but, girls have to do the running and come and ask for that help.'

A year 7 father observed of the teaching he has encountered: 'high standards across all subjects but also accessible introductions to new topics.' Another parent: 'Teaching is of a very high standard. It is clear from the marking by staff that they are diligent and alive to a pupil's abilities. Homework reflects that the pupils are expected

to think laterally and expand their knowledge themselves.'

There are exams twice a year, which girls mostly take in their stride in preparation for GCSEs to come. A year 7 mother sent this message to prospective parents: 'not as intensive as I had been led to believe from the school's reputation.' The 'palace group' is for gifted and talented – offering individual mentoring and encouragement to undertake projects outside of the curriculum. There is a series of lunchtime lectures – recent topics on the art of conducting, what we owe to the Athenians and the ethics of Shakespeare.

Sixth formers are ably prepped for law and medical school applications as well as UCAS, and enrichment offers the university friendly experience of an EPQ, current affairs, financial awareness, science and ethics, food and nutrition and community service.

> *We had to admit to some disappointment on finding little trace of majesty in Queen Elizabeth's bedroom – now a classroom*

Pupils with SEND and EAL needs achieve success in line with their peers when it comes to exams. A parent with a hearing impaired daughter described gratefully how 'every teacher has made accommodations for her to maximise her learning and yet in such a discreet way that she has never felt singled out.'

Games, options, the arts: With the site the very anathema of green space or lush sporting facilities, this is something for prospective parents to take on the chin. The school does have its own 25m swimming pool, the use of Trinity's Astroturf for hockey and girls travel to playing fields by minibuses, a great recent addition to the school. The sporting ethos is inclusive, with the school looking to 'beef it up so that we can play more fixtures'. To that end a new director of sport has been appointed. Currently girls play rounders, hockey and football and take part in cross-country, athletics and dance. Fencing and trampolining have just been introduced. A parent commented: 'My daughter has taken part in lots of swimming competitions and I feel the standard of instruction she has received has been great.' Plenty of excellent sportswomen amongst the pupils – some participants in the London Youth Games, the water polo team took part in the English Schools' championships and contains a national player. Sporting clubs at lunch and after school include tennis, rounders, water-polo, fencing, indoor athletics and swim squad.

'Music is both high quality and inclusive – a real stand out,' a delighted mother enthused, with highly accomplished staff. As one might expect, the choir regularly performs evensong at Croydon Minster as well as the country's finest cathedrals – St Paul's, Winchester and Salisbury and St Mark's Basilica in Venice. Take your seats (and bring warm coats or sneaky hot water bottles for some spaces) to hear regular recitals and concerts from choirs, orchestra, chamber groups, polyphonic choir, brass group, wind and piano chamber music, recorders and a school speciality – the steel pans. Pupils perform at local Beckenham music festival and are involved in productions such as a recent ambitious Tchaikovsky's Eugene Onegin.

Over 120 clubs. Parents talk of girls struggling to fit in all of the clubs, activities, performances and shows they want to be involved with. Hip-hop dance, critical thinking, anatomy club, mindfulness, Italian film, ceramics and more jostle for attention – good to see both an embroidery club and feminist society sharing a timetable.

Background and atmosphere: Who would have thought that the Archbishop of Canterbury summered in Croydon? But for centuries, he did just that when journeying from Lambeth, and occasionally hosted the royal court here in the oldest part of the school, adjacent to ancient Croydon Minster. Later, when the commoners drew too close, the archbishops removed themselves and the building suffered the indignity of becoming a linen printers, bleachers and laundry. By 1899 the Sisters of the Church were given the building by the Duke of Newcastle and founded the school. Archbishop John Whitgift, with the approval of Queen Elizabeth I, built almshouses and a school for the poor here in 1596, which became the charitable Whitgift Foundation now funding the Whitgift and Trinity schools.

One needs a certain amount of determination to reach the school amidst flyovers, terraces,

ring-roads and tramlines: it's an urban mash up that makes stepping inside the school walls a huge relief. Once inside, the grade I listed old palace offers wonderful spaces such as a beautiful chapel and a great hall with the finest hammered ceiling in southern England. We had to admit to some disappointment on finding little trace of majesty in Queen Elizabeth's bedroom – now a classroom. A beautifully crafted modern building in red brick with stone mullions and cloisters provides ample teaching space and labs. Then, over the road there is the technology annexe housing art studio, DT, music rehearsal spaces in a light and bright environment and a large modern dining room where everyone eats together. On the top floors there's a professional dance studio, theatre rehearsal room and a sixth form common room where girls relax.

Over 120 clubs. Hip-hop, critical thinking, anatomy, mindfulness, Italian film, ceramics and more – good to see an embroidery club and feminist society sharing a timetable

A mother described the school's atmosphere as 'caring, and whilst wanting to maximise achievement in every girl, does not do so in a strict competitive environment but a nurturing one that works to each girl's strengths.'

Pastoral care, well-being and discipline: There is a Church of England framework to the school: all Christian festivals are celebrated with no opt out. Lots of praise for the pastoral care: 'excellent pastoral care – both processes and, more importantly, people who genuinely care' being typical. Few seem to have had any encounters with the anti-bullying measures, but one mother told us: 'I have had one occasion to speak to the school about low level bullying and they handled this brilliantly.'

The four pillars or central beliefs of the school – service, courage, emotional intelligence, learning – are delivered through the house system. Girls in sixth form take assemblies – 'it works best when girls hear from their own age group'. The ability of pupils across year groups to work together as a whole is singled out for praise by the ISI. Lots of charity work in evidence in the community and further afield – playing with children in a local hospice and befriending the elderly in a local care home.

Pupils and parents: 'Mixed: an ethnic, racial and faith mix,' says school, 'open-hearted, not angels!' Very definitely a helicopter-free, unpushy parental set.

Entrance: Somewhat awkwardly, the prep school finishes at year 5 with pupils completing year 6 within the senior school (together with some new entrants from outside) and sitting the 11+ alongside external candidates; and although 90 per cent of girls are offered places, they are not guaranteed. It's also a chance to gain scholarships and the head's award, which recognises high performance in either English or maths. A few peel off to grammar schools. External candidates arrive from a wide slew of primaries. Good transport links, motivated parents and an extensive network of school minibuses bring the school within reach of, for instance, Sutton, Wandsworth, Bromley and Herne Hill.

Despite the lengthy list of assessment topics – English, maths, reasoning, social interaction, parental support, general knowledge and creativity (assessed through maybe looking at a piece of art or talking about their work) – the competition for places is only very mild compared with more fashionable London boroughs.

Any child with an ed psych's report is allocated extra time. This is one of the few schools to state openly that they are looking for 'parental support'. We presume exceptions made for self-starters succeeding so far without it.

Exit: An impressive list of university destinations. Over 60 per cent to Russell Group, five medics, one dentist, one to US and one to Oxbridge in 2019. Rather than straightforwardly academic subjects, as is something of an understandable trend these days and also perhaps reflective of a hard-working parental community, choices seem mindful of career directions, with a predominance of –ologies – criminology, psychology, marine biology – or, for instance, modern languages together with business.

Money matters: Around 45 per cent of pupils are assisted by some kind of bursary from the extraordinarily wealthy £5m Whitgift foundation – one of the largest in the UK – providing up to 95 per cent fee remittance. As a guide household income would need to be below £70k to apply. There is also a long list of scholarships and exhibitions (for year 12) which are not means-tested and are offered depending on performance in the entrance tests.

Remarks: A sense of history and her place in it awaits girls at Old Palace. Step inside for a transformative academic education.

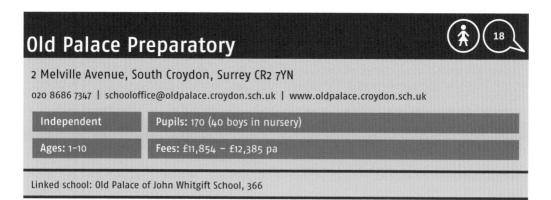

Old Palace Preparatory

2 Melville Avenue, South Croydon, Surrey CR2 7YN

020 8686 7347 | schooloffice@oldpalace.croydon.sch.uk | www.oldpalace.croydon.sch.uk

| Independent | Pupils: 170 (40 boys in nursery) |
| Ages: 1–10 | Fees: £11,854 – £12,385 pa |

Linked school: Old Palace of John Whitgift School, 366

Head of preparatory: Since 2015, Tim Horton MA FRCO, degree in music from Jesus College, Cambridge. Previously at The Hall, Hampstead, but has also taught at Abbots Bromley School and Birkdale School, Sheffield. This is his first headship. He was attracted by the diversity of this community in particular but being part of the charitable Whitgift Foundation was important too – he says: 'it's much easier to teach values if you practise what you preach,' and there is a certain freedom here too: 'you don't have to put all of your focus on the bottom right hand corner of the budget sheet'.

Mr Horton radiates warmth, amiability and impeccable politeness, slipping in and out of teacher mode in classrooms at ease with every child

whom we encountered and name-perfect. His two youngest children, a boy and girl, clearly delight in attending his school, even if it's not always easy to remember when he's in headmaster mode. Hard to believe, but his family also includes two older children, another boy and girl – having teens and toddlers at the same time raised a few eyebrows, but typically he says that it worked surprisingly well.

He felt this school 'had a huge amount to offer but was not outward facing enough.' That's all about to change, with new signage just the beginning. He'd like to collaborate with parents, to increase their sense of ownership of the school and for the school to be 'more actively proud'. With so much space to hand, there is clearly room for expansion. However, Mr Horton says the prep 'is going to grow gradually, otherwise we might lose the character of the school, the family atmosphere.'

Parents told us: 'He is a lovely, personable headmaster, who always takes the time to speak to the parents either at the door in the morning or in a private meeting.' One enthused: 'He has only been at the school for two years but quickly became part of the fabric of the school and I couldn't imagine it without him.' He is seen to have placed a particular emphasis on 'kind behaviour and good manners.'

Head of nursery is Jacqui Hines NNEB (40s), two teenage girls, one a gold medal gymnast. Feisty, fast talking with a supportive, calm deputy – 'I run around like a loon. She's the yin to my yang' – and runs a tight-knit team of 35 full and part-timers. Started as second in command, promoted to current post, three months in. Can't imagine doing anything else. 'Children are so lovely and innocent and speak their mind. Whatever you're pouring into them, you're shaping their lives'.

Entrance: For 4+, assessments are held in the reception classrooms covering language and social skills, maths, physical and creative skills as well as understanding of the world. Parents are also required to attend an interview with the head of the prep or deputy. We've previously described the intake as 'oversubscribed', but with two applicants for each place it's something of a breeze compared with schools even a fraction closer to central London. A fair few newcomers join the prep in other years and are quickly absorbed, with firm friendships quickly established, say pupils.

At 7+, pupils are assessed through written testing as well as an interview with the head. Choral scholarships available at this point. Pupils with any SEN needs will be supported during the assessment process and the possible provision within the school discussed with the head.

Exit: For girls at the nursery, assumption (by parents and school) is that they'll go on into Old Palace reception. Though their passage there isn't automatic (there's an assessment), in practice 'all our girls get places,' says head of nursery. Boys tend to stay in the independent sector, with Cumnor House and Elmhurst the most popular destinations, Park Hill Infants for those going on to state schools.

Year 6 is part of the senior school, on a different site, and everyone moves up automatically. They all take the 11+ there and some 70 per cent stay on for year 7 and above (though this is not guaranteed), many with scholarships, while others move on to local grammar schools.

Remarks: The average classroom size is 18 and maximum is 22. This is an academic school. The aim is

for year 5s to be working a year ahead of expectations, with no need for Sats prep. The most able are stretched in the classroom with extension built into every lesson, and all children have individual targets. No homework in reception, just under two hours per week in years 1 and 2, building to just under three hours by year 5.

The girls throw themselves into everything with gusto. Staff, too, who last Christmas surprised pupils with a performance on steel pans whilst wearing reindeer antlers

An 'excellent mix of child-initiated and adult-led activities,' says the ISI, which notably judged the school's early years foundation stage to be 'outstanding'. Much evidence of fun, hands-on learning and cross-curricular project work higher up. Year 3 built a 'ring of fire': impressive erupting volcano models, including one made of chocolate rice crispies. DT and computing are included. French from reception and a modern foreign languages 'experience' designed to fill a few cultural gaps on the way.

Fourteen staff have been with the school for more than 10 years and are described by the incoming head as as a strong team who pull together. Parents talk in glowing terms: 'The teaching staff are always so supportive of the children. They never say they cannot do something. Instead they encourage and support them to achieve their goals.' A mother with two daughters at the school told us: 'Not only are they technically brilliant, but they have an amazing ability to inspire the girls to learn. Both girls seemed to just 'get' reading, but that was absolutely down to the skill of the teachers and the fantastic teaching assistants. I can't fault them.' Mr Horton's daughter is so enthused she now colours everything purple and green (the school uniform colours).

Quite low profile provision regarding SEN. The learning support co-ordinator is based at the senior school. Any pupils with a SEN, such as dyslexia, have an individual student action plan outlining differentiation needed within the classroom, but no one-to-one support. Those with more complex learning difficulties and an EHCP would have one-to-one (subject to funding). Progress is regularly reviewed. Only one pupil with EAL needs currently. Pupils may attend extra English lessons and are provided with extra work allowing them to catch up with English and key vocabulary in different subjects.

There are plenty of sports fixtures for girls from year 3 upwards, and the ethos is inclusive

– everyone has a chance to compete. There is at least one session of PE per week and older pupils have a sessions of games too. No minibus scrambling, with a large playing field and playgrounds doubling up for tennis and netball right here. Everyone has a swimming lesson each week at the senior school pool. Dance is taught by a specialist. There is a squad and a club for every sport. Not so many glittering sporting achievements; when we asked we were told about the year 3 and 4 borough cross-country championships gold medal.

Music flourishes, with a good range of free taster sessions in year 3 and many learning instruments, excellent facilities (a big, terraced room, piled high with xylophones and five practice rooms dotted round the place) and a decent range of groups, instrumental and vocal, headed by the audition-only junior polyphonic, which performs with seniors in Croydon Minster. We arrive during a rehearsal for the Christmas concert by years 3, 4 and 5. Nothing short of joyful and exuberant. Mr Horton feels it exemplifies the spirit of the school – 'we're not a typical girls' school' – it's quite a robust environment' – which far from being a metaphor for needing to be quite resilient to survive, here seems to mean girls throw themselves into everything with gusto. Modelled by staff, too, who last Christmas surprised pupils with a performance on the steel pans whilst wearing reindeer antlers.

Much evidence of fun, hands–on learning. Year 3 built a 'ring of fire': impressive erupting volcano models, including one made of chocolate rice crispies

Bridge, ballet, orchestra, swim squad, Spanish, rounders and much more all on offer as pre- and post-school clubs.

Now situated within the former Croham Hurst senior school, the buildings are quite a ramshackle collection, some more nondescript than others, connected by covered walkways. Once inside everywhere smells clean, is warm, calm and bright. Classrooms are large with massive picture windows. We encounter children quietly digging in soil for rocks and creatures during a biology lesson and totally engaged in learning how to work out the value of an acute angle by thinking in terms of pizza in maths. A new science lab is intended to give science a bit of a lift within the school and the prep works closely with the senior school with regards to STEM subjects. An attractive library is well stocked with books and used for the accelerated reading programme.

We encounter children in maths totally engaged in learning how to work out the value of an acute angle by thinking in terms of pizza

Does Mr Horton's day finish in time for Homes Under the Hammer, we wonder? He has the developer's eye for potential and a north London teacher's amazement at all of this space – three large halls suitable for indoor sports, rehearsals, assemblies and gymnastics, even spare classrooms which can be set up for break-out activities, such as a jungle complete with soundtrack and lighting for book week. During the holidays he found a two bedroom flat and a set of changing rooms he didn't know existed.

A mother of two told us: 'Both of our children absolutely love the school, and my son is always so thrilled when he asks if it's a pre-school day and we say yes!' Another with children higher up the school said: 'The school is so warm and caring; however, there is a positive undertone of competitiveness. Healthy competition is encouraged in a caring atmosphere.'

Pupils eat in houses. Year 5 girls enjoy the responsibility of mentoring reception children – this begins with an introductory letter over the holidays and is a long term commitment rather than something that fades after the first day. As top dogs, without a year 6, they acquire the trappings of seniority early: all can be prefects and get to sit on benches not the floor during assembly.

The majority of pupils have English as their home language, with a couple of handfuls of overseas nationals, currently from China, India, Mauritius, Nigeria and Taiwan. Almost everyone mentions the diversity of the children and families here in an appreciative way.

Very well set up for working parents (most). Open from 7.30am with a free breakfast club, then an after-school club runs until 6pm. No need to panic during school holidays either, as a third party provides a full-time holiday club for a reasonable fee.

Children can attend the nursery from the age of 1 upwards. Open 51 weeks of the year, with a waiting list (though most are eventually accommodated). For the baby room, early registration essential. 'We get women phoning us the day the baby's born.' Mobility is prerequisite for the toddler room (most start aged 12 to 15 months); freedom from nappies, or close, for kinder room (around 2). Some children do full 7.30am to 6pm days from the start, others attend just a few mornings or afternoons a week.

Rooms are fairly plain and, dare we say, a little uninspiring, but well equipped, huge and full of light with above average staff to child ratios – plenty of glitter and dressing up corners. Those under 3 experience a curriculum focused on developing personal, physical and communication skills. Pre-schoolers aged 3 to 4 are sensitively divided into half yearly age groupings, progressing to the 'transition' class where they are readied for reception with an increasing amount of teacher-led activities and subject-based learning, graduating to pinafores and striped shirts and mixing with older children in the playground.

Prendergast School

Adelaide Avenue, Brockley, London SE4 1LE

020 8690 3710 | admin@prendergast-school.com | www.prendergast-school.com

| State | Ages: 11–18 | Pupils: 827; sixth form: 218 (106 boys) |

Head teacher: Since 2016, Paula Ledger. Read history at Goldsmiths, masters at Kings' College and spent time early in her career briefly in the independent sector and in Japan, before moving into maintained schools, becoming latterly deputy head of one of the Harris academies. Very approachable, and manages to communicate that she is quietly confident.

Having inherited a school which won 'outstanding' in every category in its most recent Ofsted Inspection (that was in 2013), Ms Ledger might be seen as having an easy ride, but she is calmly ambitious for the school. She has a big passion for girls' education in general, and for raising their numeracy in particular – 'hating maths has been such a feature of so many girls' memories of school for so many years,' she says. 'I want us to take our part in changing that.' Wins much praise from parents for safeguarding academic standards and 'for being consistently approachable'.

A mother of school age children, Ms Ledger identifies herself strongly as a parent living in the local area, and is evidently driven by the determination to work on behalf of it.

Academic matters: A level results in 2019 are slightly better than previous year: 18 per cent of grades were either A* or A, and 47 per cent were B or better. A level curriculum is broadly based with the opportunity to take BTecs in a number of cases. At GCSE, 32 per cent of grades were 9-7, with 61 per cent getting 5+ in both maths and English. Prendergast is one of the top 10 per cent non-selective schools for attainment in the country. 'One big plus,' said a parent who has seen several children through the school, 'is the consistency of good results. Pupils and parents have learned to rely upon the school to play its part.' Another parent said her child had never found her feet at primary school, but thrived at Prendergast. 'I think the school freed her up. She's loved the challenge and loved the diversity.'

Games, options, the arts: Very strong arts – textiles especially, and it is telling how prominent these feature in the school's online promotional video.

A huge music profile. 'Any pupil can learn almost any instrument at school', the head insists, 'and many take up the chance'. There are different choirs – a gospel choir and an a capella group among them. Year 7 has a music lesson en masse once every week, which (given the timetable constraints under which all schools labour) says a great deal about the scale of investment in the subject the school believes appropriate. There are music assemblies once a fortnight and plenty of touring for those in choirs and orchestras – one recently to Belgium – as well as an annual array of concerts (one open air), a big one at Christmas as well as an annual Founders' Day Concert.

A musical is performed annually, but there are lots of smaller productions, mainly under the aegis of drama GCSE which has become popular and successful. Plans are afoot to introduce it at A level. 'We place a huge importance on making drama accessible,' says the head. 'One big plus of musicals is the number of people who can be involved on or off stage.'

Games are taken seriously, but the provision is not what you'd get in most independent schools. There's one lesson a week for games lower down the school. Depending on the time of year, offers rugby, netball, football, rounders, cricket and athletics. There are some matches, but a crowded fixture list against other schools is not a big part of the school psyche. 'We have no reluctance to encourage individual sports,' adds the head. With the Olympic velodrome so near, competitive cycling is unsurprisingly popular. The Duke of Edinburgh Award has acquired a significant profile, with some 25-30 pupils each year going for bronze and silver awards, and some achieving gold. Sport melds seamlessly into opportunities for self-expression.

There are lunchtime and after-school clubs every day: music ensembles, gospel choir, rugby, netball, handball, cheerleading and homework clubs – the list goes on. 'My children have just soaked this up,' a parent said. 'The variety proves that the school really values people's differences. Choir for some, games for some. And Star Trek for others.'

Background and atmosphere: Prendergast is just one of a cluster of local schools whose foundation was a result of philanthropy. It enjoys a close relationship with the Leathersellers, a livery company, which continues to invest in the school in a range of ways. Perhaps the most conspicuous of these is support for gap year students to spend months in the school working as mentors. 'They're not teachers,' the head explains, 'but they are fantastic role models, and add greatly to the quality of the experience of school for so many of our children'. The Leathersellers offer scholarships and also help underwrite some of the expense of higher education in some deserving cases, and use their access to the City to help pupils enjoy some of its advantages and glamour. The Sir John Staples Society hosts regular talks – David Blunkett was a recent visitor ('a lovely man, but his dog put his muddy paws on my new shoes,' according to one attender) – and the school is invited each year to the Lord Mayor's Parade. 'These may sound old hat to some,' says the head, 'but to us these occasions can mean the world'.

The Sir John Staples Society hosts regular talks – David Blunkett was a recent visitor ('a lovely man, but his dog put his muddy paws on my new shoes,' according to one pupil)

Pupils look unobtrusively tidy and are happy to be around school. There's a distinct lift in most steps. There's a uniform up to GCSE, but not in sixth form. One father said that his son and daughters ensure that evening meals are never dull. 'They're opinionated and very interested in the world at large, and also the local area. I think we owe the credit for that to the school. It's a big gift they've given.'

Pastoral care, well-being and discipline: We drew a strong sense of confidence from among pupils. They believe they are lucky to be in a school that is high achieving – the concept of 'excellence' and 'outstanding' are very real to them. There is also the sense that the teachers 'really care' – this thought was projected particularly strongly from a group of 13 year old girls, not always an age group which is indulgent. Pupils insist that there is very little unpleasantness among themselves but that, when it does happen, it is acted upon at once. 'That's what the teachers do, and it's what the pupils want.'

Pupils and parents: Annual parents' meetings for each year group with all subject teachers, and a termly report in addition. One parent emphasised how ready teachers are to set up individual meetings with parents if there are difficulties or anxieties which need more immediate attention.

Entrance: Ten per cent of places are for music scholars, via a series of aural tests designed to measure potential, rather than favour pupils who have already learned to sight read, or taken grade exams. The other 90 per cent of places are allocated on the basis of how far applicants live from the school gates.

Exit: Two medics, one Oxbridge in 2019. Others have left to study eg engineering at Imperial. 'Our top flyers include some from challenging backgrounds, including looked-after pupils,' says the head, rightly proud. Strong anecdotal sense that the sixth form is especially talented at creative subjects and languages. The school has exceptional success at getting pupils to art schools (the top ones – Central St Martins, Slade etc). Textiles is very strong and pupils have won several British Fashion Week awards.

Money matters: Support given to some students in the sixth form – 50 bursaries given this year. Three Leathersellers' Federation bursaries awarded each year to students about to go to university, comprising £700 towards each year of study.

Remarks: A remarkable school, doing remarkable work. Among its greatest virtues are its close identification with the local area – in socioeconomic terms, a very mixed area, but not of the kind which usually makes headlines. The school embodies a calm pride in itself. One parent said her daughter had told her after a recent prize giving, 'I'll always be a Prendergast girl.' Her mother added: 'Pretty good, I thought.' So do we.

Royal Russell School

Coombe Lane, Croydon, Surrey CR9 5BX

020 8657 4433 | admissions@royalrussell.co.uk | www.royalrussell.co.uk

| Independent | Pupils: 1,076; boarders: 154 full/weekly (from age 11); sixth form: 222 |
| Ages: 3–18 | Fees: Day £11,661 – £19,311; Boarding £38,169 pa |

Headmaster: Since 2011, Chris Hutchinson BMet. Second headship – first was at Newcastle School for Boys, which he joined in 2007. 'Teaching is in the blood,' he says. Opted for metallurgy degree but decided against engineering career. Worked for family owned and run school in Wales for two years, followed by formal teacher training at Cambridge and posts in top schools, starting with Clifton in 1990 where he met wife Alex – also a scientist. ('Some unfortunate Cliftonites were taught a lot of Hutchinson chemistry and physics.') Left as head of physics, moving to Wellington in 2000 in same role where was also a boarding housemaster.

Had completed full cycle (years 9 to 13) at Newcastle School for Boys when post here came up. Was encouraged to apply and felt instantly at home, compatible ethos of 'getting to know people well, giving them an individual opportunity to shine and supporting, rather than pushing them, on their journey' the clincher. He fits in a bit of energetic teaching and has advanced child recognition skills. 'Knows them – every one,' said staff member in full on Tiny Tim mode. Pupils equally chuffed. 'So, so good – really engages,' said one. 'Makes the effort to get to know you,'

Mrs Hutchinson has secured matching role at Woldingham (minimal rivalry for same pupils – so far, only one has moved between the two schools). Mr Hutchinson's hobbies include singing, gardening, Herefordshire, old Land Rovers and exercising his pets: dog Bosey (who spent considerable part of the interview curled up in his master's chair) and Linus the cat. Reflective, funny and kind, Mr Hutchinson is a major attraction for parents. Staff ditto. 'I took the job because of him,' said one, who praised mastery of details – 'Reports broken locks, picks up the rubbish' (he does, too – only gave up on stray banana skin on walk round because of its advanced stage of decomposition). 'Nothing is too trivial.' On day of visit, had just written 71 congratulatory notes to cast and backstage team of school production.

Headmaster of Royal Russell Junior School: Since September 2019 is John Evans, previously senior deputy head at Haberdashers' Aske's School.

Studied English and education at Cambridge; has taught English at Dulwich Prep London. Married with two children.

Junior and senor school reviews, previously separate are now combined, with blessing of the school. Reinforces sense of togetherness that emanates from the top.

Academic matters: Known as a gentler alternative to more selective schools in the area, though 'we do get the brightest students,' says school. Now positioning itself as 'the family school of choice in south London' (plays better than Croydon, 'a sell too far' for gentrified sunny uplands of Nappy Valley, Wandsworth and Balham).

Entry requirements may not have shifted but winds of change are definitely well above zephyr level, starting with results. In 2019, 44 per cent of A level grades were A*/A (68 per cent A*-B) and 53 per cent of GCSE grades 9-7, while government-issued value added table recently put school right at the top of the country.

Heads have trimmed, rather than hacked, their staff teams, felt by parents to be stronger, if a work in progress. 'You'll hear some rumblings and grumblings in the car park and it's usually about staff,' said one. Thirty, average age close to 40, have completed first decade (one cheery and popular geography teacher on way to notching up ruby anniversary). For seniors, maximum class size is 24, average 18 to year 9, 15 for GCSE years and just eight for sixth form. Junior class average is 17 (parents make feelings known if numbers pass 20 in busy year).

New generation of vibrant staff newcomers love it here. One raved about mentoring ('have grown as a person'). Energy exemplified by new junior school librarian who has created oasis of great charm with imaginative use of lighting – Chinese lanterns, netting studded with fairy lights, even reading by torchlight sessions.

Despite school togetherness, juniors have own staff temperamentally suited to this age group. Combines specialists (music, computing, French, Spanish, sport and science) from nursery upwards with dedicated class teachers. Continuity and security means pupils 'retain their childhood for as long as they can'. 'System works,' agreed parent. 'Always somebody to hear you out and help you.'

In senior school, star subjects include A level biology, as popular with boys as girls. History, though, is the chart-topper, converting the marginally interested into passionately keen. Differentiation is a key part of the process, teachers praised for willingness to explain a topic in limitless different ways until it clicked ('and if that doesn't work, will ask someone else to explain it to you'). While 10 GCSEs is the norm, will adjust if necessary, provide after-school sessions and generally do what it takes. 'Always there to help,' said pupil. Nurturing qualities appreciated by parents – 'you won't get that in some [other] schools,' said one. International pupils similarly feel exceptionally well looked after. Though English isn't mother tongue for around 20 per cent, who can arrive with large gaps in learning, expectation is that all will take GCSEs and A levels. Support is flexible, generally at no extra cost and often yields rapid results. One new international sixth form boarder was delighted to have passed GCSE maths in first term. Junior school support similar, with one pupil attending local centre part time.

Perks for boarders include after-school exploration of fleshpots of Croydon and exclusive access to swish-looking coffee machine

School's reputation for SEN remains undimmed. Currently, two senior students have EHCPs and between 14 to 20 per cent have ILPs. Have coped with 'very' autistic pupil, ADHD, and specific learning difficulties. Support includes additional literacy and numeracy sessions, assigned teachers who work with pupils in and out of lessons, though with just one full time member of staff in the senior school, there's a limit to the numbers they can help.

Parents also praised efforts with very able. 'School invests in children that need more time either because they're slightly behind or ahead – they have different programmes and challenges,' said mother of junior school pupil.

Games, options, the arts: 'All the space a child could need to run, jump and cartwheel,' says junior prospectus, with 110 acres well used by all, from nursery school pupils walking the 1.3 km cross-country circuit (in a morning) to boarders taking it at a rather faster pace 'for fun' (takes all sorts).

Strong house system (juniors have their own) promotes cohesion and competition usually at healthy rather than arms race levels

Bar an all-weather surface that, frustratingly, needs duvet day if there's a hard frost, facilities and options are top notch, including new pavilion (not picturesque but home to host of extras including gym and physio suite), and two swimming pools.

Little, indeed, that isn't offered, to parental (and inspectorial) approval. 'Everything is there so children don't need to spend lots of time away from education by driving to swimming,' said one. Sports successes could go up a notch or two, think some, though limited by smaller pool of talent to draw on, compared with single sex schools. Rugby, notable by absence, heads the parents' wishlist (and likely to remain there), hockey felt to get fair share of resources and then some. Overall, though, 'win more than we lose,' thought a pupil, results pages revealing impressive football success (teams reach semi-finals of London and national contests) but mixed fortunes elsewhere.

Junior school activities range from numerous informal concerts (music is timetabled from nursery) to residential trips from year 3 and over 40 activities (pupils pack in up to five a week), including coding club, swim squad and media club (filming and editing).

Same again for seniors – one year 10 pupil involved in choir, extra sport, Mandarin and popular CCF (night exercises more of a draw than drilling). Model United Nations vast – school hosts annual international conference and gamely lends other local schools placards for their own events.

Bar slight glumness from senior school pupil analysing recent production rather than doing it ('Interesting work?' we asked. 'Not particularly,' was the response) enthusiasm for the arts abounds. No wonder, given trips (West End to New York for thesps) and lavish facilities including auditorium in performing arts centre, the base for regular productions (Importance of being Earnest, Wind in the Willows). Pianists among the 200 or so musicians have new Bechsteins – I live in this practice room,' said one – with concerts in venues including the Royal Albert Hall for those who do make it outside.

Boarding: Most of the full boarders in the senior school stay on for weekends and must attend at least three activities (fireworks and go-karting among them) a term. Other perks include after-school exploration of fleshpots of Croydon and exclusive access to swish-looking coffee machine

in dining hall. Homesickness still strikes but 'keep talking' was advice from one boarder, and will pass. For anything more serious, school has medical centre staffed round the clock.

Girl boarders have one house that backs onto junior school (Queen's – think revenge end of social housing). Boys do better with two (Oxford and Cambridge, now in two wings under one roof), all with day pupils too. Further six houses for day pupils only; flexi-boarding so day pupils can stay on for extra sport or rehearsals. Rooms and bathrooms are generally tidy and pleasant and happy, trusting atmosphere prevails with personal possessions left out, not locked away.

Website features overseas students (Bogdan from Romania and Yizhou from China among others) extolling the virtues of the school in their mother tongues

Though British boarders are substantially outnumbered by Chinese (majority in sixth form) and other nationalities including Russia, Armenia, Bulgaria and Ukraine, school, unlike many others, ensures that everyone mixes in multi-national social groups. Horizons are impressively expanded for all pupils, with boarders enjoying tea with local families. Website features overseas students (Bogdan from Romania and Yizhou from China among others) extolling the virtues of the school in their mother tongues.

Background and atmosphere: Ten minutes by tram from East Croydon, green and pleasant site, complete with own deer herd, offers antidote to crowded London senior schools. Originally a charity, founded by City of London clerks to support a colleague's orphaned children in 1850s. Grew into a school named for its first president, former PM Lord John Russell. Moved from New Cross to Purley in 1866, acquired this site in 1924. Sir Aston Webb – best known for Buckingham Palace façade – responsible for regal design. Added Royal to mark 1953 coronation and in 1961 became co-ed on single site. Upped numbers of fee payers in the 1970s to avoid closure (previous philanthropic desire to educate pupils FOC laudable but ruinous). Since then, has gone from strength to strength.

Buildings mainly very easy on the eye (and being attended to where they're not). Oldest is group of 1850s cottages with octagonal tower. Grander elsewhere including mirror image staircases that face each other across flashier of two quads, joining original building and later additions.

'Top of agenda was to turn this into a single school journey,' say heads. So junior school pupils get to know senior school early, using theatre, chapel and swimming pool and, from year 3 up, have lunch in the blue, vaulted dining hall (featured in TV hit show The Durrells). Plenty of space for traditional library and 'practical' block – DT room filled with sound of merry hammering as year 7s enjoy high volume metal beating. And despite lack of riches, site is smart, ditto pupils in recently revamped uniform that's high on practicality (largely washable) and low on crested shirts.

Similar neatness round the grounds (bar pair of school bags languishing, Hansel and Gretel-like, in undergrowth). Even food ingredients painstakingly handwritten on blackboard. Salad Nicoise contents – 'fish, sulphites and egg' – helps those with allergies. 'Learn how to manage them,' said parent. Thirsty have choice of squash in every conceivable flavor. (Milk, also offered, is 'not that popular,' thought pupils.)

Pastoral care, well-being and discipline: A happy place. 'It's a punishment to keep son off school,' said junior school mother. 'My child absolutely loves it,' agreed another. Teachers supportive if families hit difficult patch. 'Will go above and beyond,' said parent. Pupils similarly complimentary. 'Does take time to settle in but you do feel welcome,' said one. Tutor groups help new pupils settle into school with older senior school pupils providing informal help to younger. Chaplain another source of support, chapel open all day for anytime prayers.

Heart of multi-layered friendship groups is strong house system (juniors have their own) which promotes cohesion and competition – usually at healthy rather than arms race levels. Add forms and streamed subject groups and 'you can have social groups that extend through the school – it takes some getting to grips with,' said parent.

Around one senior school pupil a year withdrawn or asked to leave (normal issues...) but it's sensitively handled, Mr Hutchinson often asking 'headmaster mates' to take a pupil who has lost their way. It's then, he reckons, that you discover just how much of an educator you are. 'They make awful decisions but shouldn't be punished for the rest of their lives.'

Most focus is on rewards for the triers. Even the prefects, who told us they can impose detentions (head says otherwise), never do ('though we might remind everyone that we can,' said one).

Pupils and parents: Slightly more boys, many locals among day pupils (80 per cent from Croydon), rest from south London and into Surrey and Kent borders, lots of diversity, cultural and financial. 'Pretty much all walks of life,' said junior parent. 'And when you're doing reading at night, books aren't just about pink skinned children, which is great.'

Junior and senior parents tend to tread separate paths and organise own events. It's a homogenous mix – cars ranging from second hand to luxury marque, some parents dwelling in marble halls, others scraping school fees together. Wraparound care offered to Increasing numbers of working couples. Not flash, thought parent. 'Have quite a wide breadth of people there, and I think that gives it a nice atmosphere.'

Only mystery is where leavers end up. Not into the limelight, at least so far. 'We have a great many success stories, but nobody famous,' says school.

Entrance: Increasingly popular and currently at capacity in every year group. Undaunting entrance process. 'Very gentle' says school. Junior school entrants arrive the September after third birthday, are observed in small groups (no interview or formal test). 'We're looking to see if on track with development, communications and ability to interact.' More formal assessments further up the school – all joining in years 3 to 6 must be senior school shoe-ins.

Around 90 per cent go on to the senior school, some guaranteed places in years 4 and 5; they sit exams only if want to be considered for awards, often scooping the top scholarships, though there's no favouritism, stresses school.

For senior school, main entry point is year 7. External candidates sit entrance exams in maths, English and VR. Minimum score around 105, average of 111 and 128 minimum for scholarship candidates. Further 20 places in year 9. Varying numbers in year 12 – no entrance exam, with places based on GCSE performance.

Current popularity means school could probably nudge up selectivity a notch – but won't. 'Have niche in market,' says school, 'and we want to preserve it – we've just upped the quality of what we're doing.'

Exit: Loses a few juniors to local grammars and other independents such as Alleyn's and Caterham. Seniors tend to stay on post-GCSE. Many to London unis; others to study eg economics at Loughborough, aerospace engineering at Swansea, fashion and textile design at Southampton. Three to Oxbridge in 2019.

Money matters: No endowment to speak of but prudent management and fundraising keeps things ticking over nicely. Offers scholarships (academic, sport, music and drama) and bursaries of to 100 per cent (income shouldn't exceed £40,000).

Remarks: Think fab site, rising results, unified and inspirational leadership (and the odd deer) and get on that tram.

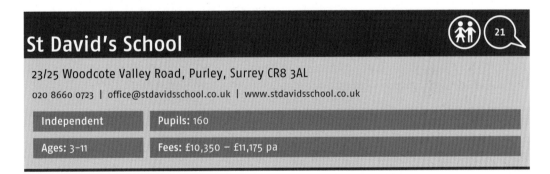

St David's School

23/25 Woodcote Valley Road, Purley, Surrey CR8 3AL

020 8660 0723 | office@stdavidsschool.co.uk | www.stdavidsschool.co.uk

Independent	Pupils: 160
Ages: 3–11	Fees: £10,350 – £11,175 pa

Head: Since 2011, Cressida Mardell (40s) BA PGCE, a classicist. Before joining St David's in 2007 she was a senior teacher at St Christopher's School, Epsom. Parents appreciate her positive approach, hard work and sound judgement, alongside a jolly personality and a good sense of humour. She lives locally and enjoys holidaying in France and walking with her two lively Border collie rescue dogs.

Entrance: Most join the nursery at 3+ (18 places); another four places in reception. Non-selective at this stage; occasional places in year 1 upwards subject to 'satisfactory assessment'.

Exit: Most popular destinations at 11+: Croydon High, Wallington County Grammar, Whitgift, Riddlesdown, Trinity, St Philomena's, Royal Russell, Wilsons, Caterham.

Remarks: Mixed ability school, which skilfully blends academic excellence alongside a good range of musical, creative and sporting opportunities.

Founded in 1912 with just five pupils, by Welsh (hence school's name) sisters Margery and Mary Talfourd Jones. The school has thrived through the decades and today's multicultural clientèle is still proud of its founders' Welsh connections. Pupils join in the Eisteddfod Festival and fly the flag on St David's Day.

Dedicated class teachers run maths and English lessons mostly in the mornings and then teach specialist subjects in the afternoons. There is an ICT room and a room for arts, science and technology; pupils often split for these subjects so class sizes are around 10, optimising opportunities for individual attention and development. French is taught throughout the school and year 6s learn Latin. Specialist teacher visits three days a week to assist children with any special educational needs. Additional support is provided in small groups, one-to-one or in class at no extra charge. ESOL can be arranged.

Very busy music department has a gifted and talented choir, brass ensemble, string ensemble and rhythm group. Most pupils play at least one instrument; older pupils are introduced to filming and music composition with the occasional commission, most recently a jingle for Halfords. Some great achievements on the sporting front; St David's has its own large playing fields a few minutes' walk from the school building complete with new all-purpose facility including Astro football pitch and tennis courts. Gymnastics is particularly strong; the school has won the ISA competition on several occasions. Swimming is another area where pupils excel, with eight children being selected to train as divers at Crystal Palace for the Olympics programme.

The school is proud of its founders' Welsh connections. Pupils join in the Eisteddfod Festival

Parents felt clubs had been rather limited; this is now an expanding area, and the aim is now to offer a much wider choice of activities, after-school and at lunchtimes. Chess team have made it into Champion League finals for primary schools and the maths team recently came third in the Sutton Maths Challenge. After-school care (at extra cost) is provided by the Jancett Nursery Group until 6.30pm.

Refreshingly, St David's has retained its independence and remains a small charity with a non-selective intake, so far avoiding being swept up by one of the large education businesses. Very successful results at 11 into the local grammar and independent schools, especially considering the non-selective intake and inclusive approach. Terrific value for money.

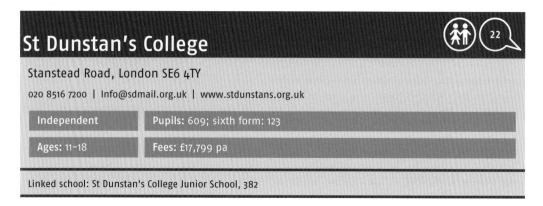

St Dunstan's College

Stanstead Road, London SE6 4TY

020 8516 7200 | Info@sdmail.org.uk | www.stdunstans.org.uk

Independent	Pupils: 609; sixth form: 123
Ages: 11–18	Fees: £17,799 pa

Linked school: St Dunstan's College Junior School, 382

Headmaster: Since 2014, Nicholas Hewlett BSc PGCE (30s): the youngest head we've yet to meet, but youth becomes him. He's still bouncing with excitement after several challenging years in post. After a brief spell in the City, he headed to King's College London to study geography, followed by a PGCE at the Institute of Education. Landing his first teaching job at Dulwich College, within three years he moved to Magdalen College School Oxford as head of geography, becoming housemaster, contingent commander of the CCF and director of the annual arts festival.

We were somewhat startled to hear a wish from a mother to hear him sing until we encountered his CV. Performing as a tenor soloist throughout his 20s, he also sang at one time as a lay clerk for New College Oxford. In 2011, he was part of the team that helped to lead a flagship school on the island of Jeju, South Korea, under the banner of North London Collegiate School. He credits being a part of transition and the brilliant leadership and mentoring at these schools for his confidence to lead the reinvention here.

The aim is to create one college rather than two quite separate schools and invigorate academic ambition, which he likens to 'tightening the plumbing of this incredible, beautiful building' whilst retaining the inclusive, diverse ethos of the school – a cornerstone of which is the introduction of a revitalised extracurricular offer named the Forder Programme, inspired by a pioneering early head who took boys on adventures all over London. Mr Hewlett lives in Croydon where he grew up and his interests include travel, literature, cooking and antique maps such as the beautiful one adorning his office.

We heard nothing but boundless enthusiasm in return from parents: 'He is ambitious for the college and very driven to secure its success, which is laudable. He is not afraid of change and he has conviction'; 'He is approachable, friendly and clearly driven. He also has a wonderfully eloquent turn of phrase.' Our sixth form tour guide appreciated greater transparency, more student voice and one-to-one drop-ins.

Academic matters: In 2019, 35 per cent A*/A and 69 per cent A*-B at A level and 57 per cent 9-7 at GCSE. Mr Hewlett's been on nothing short of a mission, observing lessons, mentoring and training staff with potential, doing significant pruning elsewhere, appointing a deputy head academic with experience of both Westminster school and the state sector, and students have had to raise their game too. Pupils are now innovatively graded on 'learning characteristics' such as 'engagement' or 'organisation' instead of simply the hard to measure 'effort' as well attainment.

On the ground, a student told us of 'an influx of better teachers'. The head says that his team is now in place and it's a matter of embedding. Parents speak of a change of pace: 'We are very happy that our children are aiming higher than before. It certainly isn't too intense.' Another, 'I have been impressed by the energy and enthusiasm displayed by all the teaching staff'. Naturally, there is still work to do. One parent also praised the teaching but said: 'Class discipline is less good, with a high level of ambient noise irritating for the more engaged students.' Whilst a mother said: 'It may benefit from developing a more competitive atmosphere for the more able students.'

The head likes the principles of the IB but also the rigour of A levels, so has decided to drop the IB in favour of the college's own diploma. This will consist of A levels combined with 100 hours of co-curricular and a global perspectives Pre-U short course taken in the first term of year 12.

Everything you'd expect at GCSE in terms of curriculum choices, including Latin, and the languages taught are French and Spanish, German is offered, but no Mandarin. PE for those not wanting to be completely confined to a desk. Beyond the compulsories, Spanish and history are the most popular currently. Barely a handful of Latin students. More artists than musicians. Mathematicians, single scientists and historians perform well. Things get a little more varied at A level with the addition of drama and theatre, economics, and business studies. Most popular sixth form subjects last year were maths, physics, geography and art and design, with the most A* by far for the mathematicians. Plenty of artists, but no drama or music students at this higher level. Teachers are free to choose whichever exam board best suits their cohort. Class sizes are a maximum of 25 until GCSE, then 15 in the sixth form.

All of the parents we spoke to said that they don't feel their children are unduly pressured: 'The school has a policy of not setting homework during the holidays. A project is set for any children who would like to do something, but it is entirely voluntary'.

The school has always had above average numbers of SEN pupils. This continues: 95 students have learning support needs, 70 per cent of these with dyslexia. Learning support is for mild needs only, and only as far as this can be accommodated in class (no one-to-one provided).

The red 'Hogwarts' building is at once impressive and in places shabbily homely. Lots of staircases with wooden handrails – no sliding – and a galleried Great Hall

Some 15 per cent of the senior college are registered with EAL needs. There is an EAL co-ordinator and students are supported in class and through withdrawal. In years 10 and 11 some EAL students can study for the GCSE in English as a second language.

Plenty of trips, workshops, competitions, adventures and fun drop-ins. Actor Adrian Lester gave the drama students four weekly workshops; English students make the most of London theatres, recently feasting on The Curious Incident of the Dog in the Night-time, A View from the Bridge and Othello, and year 12 and 13 mathematicians returned with a slew of medals from the UK Maths Challenge.

Games, options, the arts: It's all here in terms of sports facilities including a swimming pool, cardio gym and weights, with more currently being brought up to scratch at the Jubliee sports ground. Sports are compulsory. The core are rugby, football, hockey, netball, cricket and swimming. Some individual successes: a couple of boys play for their county cricket team. A parent: 'My son throws himself into all sporting activities...it has been an enormous boost to his confidence and self-esteem that his commitment and achievements have been recognised'. In contrast another said: 'The children have felt under-prepared for their matches.' Help is at hand, with a newish director of sport who isn't just focused on the elite or fixture results, but wanting every child to 'reach their physical potential'.

Some 200 students learn an instrument, from grade 1 to diploma level. A sizeable uptake, but by no means the most musical school we've visited. A mother told us: 'The gifted musicians are few in number and there are few opportunities for chamber music or innovative use of the talent pool'. However, plenty to thrill the ears in a rich timetable of recitals and concerts – some in beautiful London churches. The musical head believes the musical life of the school is very good. The St Paul's Symphonia recently joined school musicians in a festival concert.

Behold – towers of jewelled couscous displayed in tagines, the freshest of baby-leaf salads, home-made soups in terracotta bowls, bread baked every morning

Seriously impressive art lines the corridors, particularly the self-portraits. Large, light and popular DT workshops, including a separate space for sixth formers to work on their projects. A 3D printer and laser cutter. Students feel drama has taken a step up and there are 'lots of opportunities' with the appointment of a newish head of drama; there are now three or four productions a year. The lower school recently relished putting on Bugsy Malone complete with splurge guns. A cross-discipline Gothic Evening included everything from gentle electrocution – the science dept – to one teacher reprising Kate Bush's version of Wuthering Heights. The drama studio looks very professional, all black, framed with lighting rigs, complete with sound desk. The inaugural St Dunstan's Arts Festival showcases the school's music, drama, art and dance for the fee-paying public.

The Forder programme provides 100 activities a week, is compulsory and runs every lunch-time, but still with space for a lunch break. Pupils must try something creative, active and as a service. Sixth formers as part of the St Dunstan's diploma must lead, must do something new and must commit for a term. It gives students plenty to write about come university reference time. Sixth formers also gain leadership opportunities taking activities into the junior school.

Debaters find their voice in national and international competitions. We were shown rooms of shiny Apples and Dells – pupils will leave school with the versatility of understanding both. CCF offers army and navy experiences. DofE challenges run up to gold. A selection of fun-looking co-curricular – after-school, before or at lunch times: Mexican art and craft club, French culture club, Amnesty, Hans Woyda, draw and print drop-in, swing dance and fashion appreciation caught our eye – some additional charges for specialist sports classes such as judo.

When we entered the incongruous, modern dining hall, which has a Pringle shaped roof and our guide claimed 'they are the best school lunches in London' we expected hyperbole. Behold – towers of jewelled couscous displayed in tagines, the freshest of baby-leaf salads, home-made soups in terracotta bowls, bread baked every morning to Paul Hollywood standard and eight varieties of seeds in copper buckets.

Background and atmosphere: The school foundation has its origins in the parish of St Dunstan's-in-the-East, established on St Dunstan's Hill in the City, the location of one of five schools ordained by the Archbishop of Canterbury and Bishop of London in 1446. By 1865 it was agreed to relocate the school to parish land elsewhere, where there could be playing fields and to be accessible by rail. The school was duly opened in its present location next to Catford Bridge in 1888. The school maintains its links with St Dunstan's-in-the-East, more commonly known as All Hallows by the Tower, and students take part in services and ceremonies such as the wonderfully curious 'beating the bounds'.

This relocation for more green space seems incongruous now as one approaches the school from the ever-congested stretch of the south circular between Forest Hill and Catford. The school shelters behind its red-brick gates next to DIY sheds, a railway station and inner city grot somewhat at odds with the pictures of children walking along a tree-lined grassy grove (the playing field presumably) on the website.

Inside, the red 'Hogwarts' building is at once impressive and in places shabbily homely. High ceilinged, metro-tiled corridors, lots of staircases with wooden handrails – no sliding – and a galleried Great Hall with stained glass windows, organ pipes and a multi-media desk for productions. Classrooms for year groups tend to cluster together, giving students a home base and possibly adding to the 'small' school feel. Sixth formers have their own shadowy domain which includes a large boarding school-style common room with sofas, snooker tables, study spaces and hot food from the dining room.

Parents speak of a change of pace: 'We are very happy that our children are aiming higher than before. It certainly isn't too intense'

The already large and well-equipped library has almost doubled in size, retaining the wooden panelling, but introducing two soundproof modern pods with a teaching capacity of six for tutorials, adding a flexible lecture theatre and incorporating learning support and enrichment. The librarian inducts all year 7s into the resources available for their studies, which include 6,000 e-books. Interns from London universities will become subject mentors, helping with research skills or providing careers inspiration.

We observed a happy and relaxed atmosphere. One parent told us: 'our daughter describes the school as busy, lively, noisy and feels confident, with many friends. Our son describes the school as friendly, very informative and very sporty and active with lots of good trips.' 'Down to earth, practical, energised and caring' seems to sum it up.

A new Sixth Form Centre and STEM building will go into production and will open in 2021

Pastoral care, well-being and discipline: A parent confided: 'the pastoral care for the children has always been and continues to be excellent', but the head wants no room for complacency and so has appointed a new deputy head pastoral. There are four houses named after the first headmasters. Uniform rules are fairly stringent and students look smart. No mobiles on during the day. No beards in the sixth form. And ties at the conventional length: hear, hear. Hoodies are specifically forbidden, perhaps in case of inner city associations.

Pupils and parents: Pupils come from the immediate but also extensive south east London neighbourhood stretching across Lewisham to Greenwich, from the west such as Dulwich and further south to Bromley and Croydon. Fleets of coaches but also independent train travel.

The school welcomes international students and the numbers of Chinese students in the sixth form are visible; we wondered at integration when a student was unsure where they lived during term. A new head of inclusion and enrichment might consider issues like this alongside the remit to create a school that 'teaches to individuality'. In the future, international students will not comprise more than 10 per cent of the student body.

The community is one of hard-working families, many of whom are first-time buyers: 'down to earth, friendly and appro[...] of her peers. Creative types [...] good company too. Old Dunston[...] politicians, businesspeople, sportspe[...] tists. Professor Sir Martin Evans, Nobel Pr[...] for genetics, the very Rev Dr John Hall, D[...] Westminster and Lord Grade of Yarmouth, form[...] chairman of the BBC and ITV, are among them.

Entrance: Whilst once upon a time the school was struggling for numbers, that is no longer the case. Year 7 is full and applications are up by 40 per cent. We believe this still makes it a gentle option compared with many. The head would love to lead on something truly radical with regards to 11+ entrance testing; year 7 applicants are currently tested in English, maths, verbal reasoning and abstract reasoning. Successful candidates are invited to return for an interview with a teacher and to meet either head or deputy head. No need for any nerves regarding parental interviews: it's simply time for a frank chat about the particular quirks of St Dunstan's offer and vision for the future. Testing takes place in January the year prior to entry. Unusually, there is an 11+ preparation scheme in place (for a fee), preparing candidates from all schools for the exams across three Saturdays. Far more entering from the local state primaries than is often the case – pupils come from Lewisham and Dulwich primaries, but also Heath House Prep, Oakfield Prep, Rosemead Prep and the Pointer School.

A small group of 13 or so enter at 13+, after taking English, maths and verbal reasoning papers. Prospective sixth formers are also required to sit papers in English, maths and verbal reasoning. Same interview process and references but the offer is conditional to the GCSE grades.

Exit: Most exit to university, with around 80 per cent to Russell Group. An interestingly diverse list of subjects being taken up for further study as befits the curricular offer here, recent range included biomedical science, design engineering, architecture, film practice, chemical engineering and neuroscience.

Money matters: There are academic, music, drama, art and design and sporting scholarships available at 11+ and academic and musical scholarships at 16+. Pupils who perform well in the entrance tests may be invited for an academic scholarship interview.

Potential scholars for the co-curricular awards must jump through a variety of hoops from one minute monologues (drama) to a colour study in oil pastels (art). Bursaries are generous and could run up to 100 per cent of fees for the right candidates.

dest but by no

those pupils and
tting on potential.

As the head says: 'we're not the finished article'. This location has to be a bit of a stumbling block but we expect parents looking for an effective and inspiring coeducational experience in south London to find themselves sorely tempted.

...n's College Junior School

Stanstead Road, London SE6 4TY

020 8516 7225 | info@sdmail.org.uk | www.stdunstans.org.uk

Independent	Pupils: 300
Ages: 3–11	Fees: £10,485 – £16,839 pa

Linked school: St Dunstan's College, 378

Head: Since 2015, Paul Cozens BA (40s). Degree in education studies with music and French from Exeter. Describes himself and the head of the senior school as a Venn diagram with a 50 per cent overlap of core values. He brings much to the party, including music and mindfulness. Previously deputy of St Paul's Cathedral School, his first posts were at South Hampstead High junior dept and the Beacon School before being appointed as director of studies at Newton Prep. He is an ISI inspector.

Parents enthuse: 'He is dynamic, interested, brave... he is open-minded and interested in new ideas'; 'he manages to uphold the college's traditions while keeping up with the current times'; 'just right for the age group – visible, involved, friendly and approachable towards the children yet also minded to get the very best from them he can.' Our guides were somewhat amazed: 'He's friendly: not what you think a headmaster will be like!'

Entrance: For 3+ nursery places, informal assessment and interview with parents. At 4+, small group assessments with tasks such as listening to a story and discussing shapes and colours. At 7+, assessment includes brief English and maths papers followed by drama and science activities.

Exit: Whilst most children move to the senior school, around 20 per cent historically head to local state grammar schools.

Remarks: Children and parents very appreciative of the teaching: an 11 year old reported: 'It is great to be able to work with fantastic teachers who are able to explain things in a way that you can understand.' A parent: 'I have always been impressed by how quickly each new teacher gains an understanding of our child'. Another: 'The teachers in the pre-prep were absolutely brilliant at devising lesson plans that engaged very young children, expanded their minds...and made learning absolutely fun.'

Despite these bright spots, Mr Cozens found plenty of scope for improvement. A new focus on a joined up subject leadership from nursery to sixth form benefits the junior and senior school curricula. Year 6 pupils moving on to the senior school find Mr Cozens teaching some ICT in year 7. Maths is taught creatively and memorably: designed a shopping centre whilst learning about area; creating and drinking 'mocktails' to understand units of measurement. Spanish is taught from nursery to year 1, French in years 2 and 3 and French, German and Spanish in years 4, 5 and 6. Latin is offered by way of co-curricular 'classics'. Mandarin is taught as a club. The maximum size of classes is 20.

Testing is more in the style of continuous assessments – children take it in their stride. Homework is deliberately light with little or nothing in the holidays. Some choose the school because of a relative lack of pressure, one parent feeling it 'would suit a child who thrives in a less competitive academic environment.' Those who need stretching are thought of too, however: the most able in years 5 and 6 have English and maths lessons with year 7 from time to time. We hear some year 6 children did feel under pressure, however, come the run up to the 11+ entrance testing.

All of the usual core sports take place on the extensive fields to the rear of the school – great to see the girls doing everything, even rugby. There's a newish head of sport who is redressing the balance: more time on skills, less time on matches. Some individual stars with a couple of county players.

A functional music block, with delightful sounds emanating; ensembles for everything, plus chapel choir, chamber music, big band and rock band. Music scholars perform at St John's Smith Square. As the children rise through the school dramatic opportunities grow in ambition. Pupils performed in a Shakespeare festival at Greenwich Theatre. One delighted parent said of her son: 'He went from preferring to be backstage when he first arrived to taking a central part in his year 6 school production.'

Given this inner city locale, the residential trips with an outdoorsy focus are a particular high. Junior school children take part in the college's Forder programme of extracurricular activities three times a week. Clubs could be music ensembles or opportunities to try new things such as debating or animation but also simply down-time pursuits like knitting and yoga.

Part Victorian red-brick, part Portakabin and part wooden 60s block. A whole new junior school building is in the pipeline, and architects have been appointed. In our opinion it can't come too soon, though with plenty of play equipment, a good art space, large ICT suite and bright, well-organised, clean classrooms pupils seem oblivious.

Children struck us as happy and relaxed. We witnessed reception boogying to Move It, Move It, year 2s in quiet concentration and those on the move holding doors open for each other politely. Parents say: 'It is a place where every parent feels comfortable leaving their child knowing that they will be looked after, they will be happy and they will prosper'; there is 'a huge emphasis on making them stand tall, but also stride out into the world with questions to ask' and 'most importantly, the children are given lots of opportunities to be children, to do fun things and enjoy their lives at school.'

Pets lend a family atmosphere. We met Fluffy 'the slightly evil hamster' and children eagerly awaited Marley the rescue rabbit. Come lunch time they troop to the senior school dining hall for a lunch which bears no re[...]ners'. Extraordinarily fresh.[...]

Parents speak highly of pa[...] said: 'My daughter is able to discus[...] concerns very easily with her form teach[...] is so at ease in the school environment[...] totally happy with any member of staff.' Young children can approach house captains as well as form teachers, and 'worry boxes' are a starting point. Years 1 to 4 have reading buddies. On a year 4 DT day each child created a pop-up book for their buddy based on the younger child's interests. Head aims that children should 'understand the notion of being competitive, but realise that if you work hard and well together that will reap rewards'.

We witnessed reception boogying to Move It, Move It, year 2s in quiet concentration and those on the move holding doors open for each other politely

The mother of a dyslexic daughter told us: 'She loves her teachers, she feels very safe and nurtured there' and that when extra help was needed the classroom teachers more than rose to the challenge (no one-to-one help so for mild needs only). Overall, parents feel: 'It's a caring school and children know each other by name over their year groups.' Any bullying 'is stopped very quickly and sorted out.'

A parent provided a pen portrait of peers: 'usually hardworking dual income families drawn from a range of communities'.

Before and after school care. 'Very welcoming' events organised by the PTA, called the Family Society.

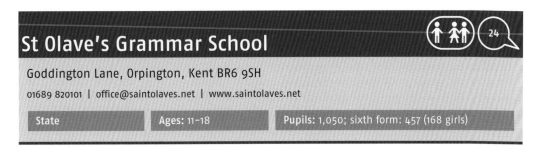

St Olave's Grammar School

Goddington Lane, Orpington, Kent BR6 9SH

01689 820101 | office@saintolaves.net | www.saintolaves.net

| State | Ages: 11–18 | Pupils: 1,050; sixth form: 457 (168 girls) |

Headmaster: Since September 2018, Andrew Rees, previously assistant and acting head. A chemist, he had been holding the fort since the resignation of Aydin Önaç. The school hit the headlines in 2017 as parents threatened legal action when their children were told to leave after failing to get three Bs at AS level.

Olave's results
of GCSE results
rly strong. At A
t A*/A and 92 per
ery highest aspira-
that translates into
ns. It's a given at St
e describe the staff as
and 'enthusiastic'.
to go well beyond the
There's a focus here on
going fu... ...urriculum, on exploring
and expanding y... ...wledge,' said a very personable sixth form girl. Boys from years 7-11 confirmed
that the teachers were 'really good at spotting where
you might need help.' 'St Olave's promotes independent learning, it has done from the beginning,'
reported a satisfied parent. 'Our son can structure
his own time without needing any input from us.'
'The academic rigour of lessons is great: our son is
challenged, and he has the opportunity to share his
ideas in a supportive atmosphere,' said another.
'High-achieving in a relaxed learning environment,'
said a third. 'Our approach can be summed up in
one word: scholarship,' affirmed the previous head.
Although those parents whose children had been
denied entry to year 13 because their year 12
summer exam results weren't deemed good enough
– a practice condemned in a damning recent independent report – might sum up the Olave's previous
approach in two words: 'weeding out'.

We have the very highest aspirations for all our students, and that translates into having the highest expectations. It's a given at St Olave's

Very broad curriculum, encompassing everything you'd expect, and a few things you wouldn't:
we were particularly pleased to see the new food
technology room, and to hear that cookery was a
popular part of the lower school curriculum. Lots
of emphasis on computing, and robotics has taken
off in a big way. Latin is compulsory in year 7, and
Greek, Japanese and Mandarin are all offered as
extracurricular options, but a recent decision to
axe (school prefers the phrase 'phase out') Spanish
and drama from the curriculum has ruffled the
waters somewhat. The previous head urged us not
to dwell on the matter, but parents and pupils alike
told us they were disappointed about it (or, in the
words of one, 'annoyed and angry'). We put these
concerns to the previous head, who responded
that the school had had to cut its cloth because of

forthcoming government cuts, 'and we just haven't
the numbers to fill a GCSE set.' According to the
website, both subjects were popular and successful, so this struck us as a little odd.

School has now moved to a three-year KS4, so
that students will choose their GCSEs in year 8 and
begin their courses in year 9. At sixth form level,
the school remains wholly committed to A levels
(as opposed to the IB or Cambridge Pre-U). 'We
prefer the depth,' said the director of studies, 'and
complemented by a vibrant extracurricular provision, they suit our students best.'

Games, options, the arts: There can't be many state
schools where rugby and Eton fives are the main
sports. Fives is hugely popular, with many boys
playing it every day ('It's quick and easy, and you
can play it in your uniform!') – and they recently
trounced many public schools to emerge national
champions in three age groups. The school's
rugby teams regularly win success at both local
and national level (1st XV reached final of NatWest
Bowl competition). Cricket is also big here – the
school toured recently to South Africa. Broad range
of other sports, including tennis, hockey, football
(1st XI winners of North Kent U18 league), swimming, basketball, squash, badminton and athletics.

The arts are also strong. 'The jazz band is
terrific,' said one parent, remembering a recent
concert in Croydon's Fairfield Halls. Lots of choral
singing, with all tastes catered for – 'I sing in six
choirs!' one boy told us, proudly – and the school
supplies all the choristers for the Queen's Chapel
of the Savoy (one of them recently won BBC Radio
2's Chorister of the Year). Children can learn almost
any instrument here, including the organ in the
school hall, and take their skills into the school's
many orchestras and bands. We're pleased to report
that drama is also strong. A few years ago, there
was just one annual production, and that was for
sixth formers; now there are plenty for everyone,
several of them directed by the students themselves. Lots of wonderfully cerebral stuff going
on in clubs: we saw a superb English version of
a German children's classic, translated and published by the students themselves, plus erudite
student-produced journals for the law society, the
history society, the medics' society, and more. Boys
report being made to feel welcome in all the activities they tried. Ambitious and enticing programme
of trips and excursions: in recent months, students
have had the opportunity to visit Iceland, New York,
Paris, Greece, South America, central Africa – the
list goes on.

Background and atmosphere: Originally located
in Tooley Street, Southwark, St Olave's received
its royal charter in 1571: display cases in the corridors show treasures from its archive collection, and

Fives is hugely popular, with many boys playing it every day ('It's quick and easy, and you can play it in your uniform!')

watercolours show the school at its various stages. It moved to its present spacious site, complete with beautiful modern chapel, in leafy Orpington in 1968, in quest of more space and its own playing fields – also, perhaps, to get away from the threat of being turned comprehensive. Long and proud history of being academically selective, with which the previous head was completely in tune: 'I believe this country neglects its brightest youngsters at its peril. They are the wealth creators and the job creators of the future. I spent 22 years in the comprehensive sector and I remain dedicated to its aims, but I'm also completely committed to giving these students the education they deserve.'

And yet, with all that was going on, and every reason for the Olave's air to be full of buzz and liveliness, we can only comment on what we found, which was a curious guardedness whenever we hove into view, not least in a reluctance to let us talk to the students without a member of SMT present; although, on our pressing the matter, they did agree. All staff, from the previous head downwards, reacted with surprise and displeasure when we passed on parental criticisms (perhaps, like some other high-achieving and oversubscribed schools, they don't often hear them), and a couple of the older staff simply refused to talk to us, actually getting up and walking away when we tried to ask them questions. One parent, whose son was doing very well at St Olave's, described the school as 'incredibly defensive', to which the previous head's response was, 'We don't have anything to be defensive about!' Others, however, have described a very different experience. 'On the few occasions I have needed to contact staff by email, their response has been prompt and helpful,' wrote one mother. 'Our sons have been incredibly happy at the school and we cannot fault it,' wrote another. We will watch with interest developments under the new head, who has unfortunately proved unwilling to meet the Guide.

Pastoral care, well-being and discipline: Mixed responses from parents, with some praising the school's 'very caring ethos', and others saying that bullying issues took too long to be resolved. Strong prefect system ensures older boys take responsibility for leading and mentoring the younger ones, and highly selective intake plays its part in developing the very strong work ethic apparent in lessons.

'It's almost unheard of for behaviour to be poor here,' said the previous head.

Pupils and parents: From all over the borough and beyond; nearly 50 per cent from ethnic minorities. Less diverse socially, with only two per cent of students on free school meals. Extremely supportive and active parents' association, which works tirelessly to raise funds for equipment, facilities and travel opportunities.

Entrance: Roughly 1,100 boys apply for 124 places, and an additional four places are offered to choral scholars who must pass the same stringent entrance tests.

New admissions policy for entry into year 7. First stage is logic, maths and English test in September. Those who pass invited to sit second stage English and maths test later in the autumn. First and second stage marks combined to give final score and the first 124 applicants in rank order offered places.

Around 500 boys and girls apply each year for the 110 sixth form places on offer to students from other schools. Grade point requirement for sixth form entry for internal as well as external candidates has been upped to 63, including at least 6 in English and maths and 7 in A level subjects. Those external candidates whose predicted grades meet these requirements will be asked to take written tests in their four chosen A level subjects; internal candidates who make the grades get automatic entry.

Exit: At 16, the great majority to St Olave's sixth form, although between four and eight per cent of Y11 students don't get the grades needed and have to leave. Those failing to get three Bs in Y12 have also been eased out in order to keep results high, but in 2017 some threatened legal action and the school backed down and agreed to readmit them. At 18, everyone goes to university: majority to Russell Group destinations. In 2019, 22 to Oxbridge and 24 off to study medicine or dentistry.

Money matters: State-funded grammar school, supported by Bromley education authority and the Diocese of Rochester. Parents invited to pay around £500 pa in voluntary contributions to help pay for facilities, etc. Accused of misleading parents by hiding considerable financial reserves in recent years.

Remarks: For the bright, motivated boy who is prepared to knuckle down, St Olave's is an excellent fit. As one parent put it, 'Very good, very impressive, very supportive. And we haven't had to pay for it.'

Sydenham High School

15 & 19 Westwood Hill, London SE26 6BL

020 8557 7000 | admissions@syd.gdst.net | www.sydenhamhighschool.gdst.net

| Independent | Pupils: 414; sixth form: 62 |
| Ages: 11–18 | Fees: £17,325 pa |

Headmistress: Since 2017, Katharine Woodcock BA. Studied French and Russian at Bristol University, followed by a PGCE at St Mary's College, Twickenham. Coming from a long line of teachers, her first teaching post was as a languages teacher and resident tutor at a co-educational boarding school in the Midlands. During her career, she has been a housemistress at Oakham School and most recently senior deputy head at Queen's College London.

We meet Mrs Woodcock two years into her tenure. We imagine her rather bare office is testament to the fact that from the moment she arrived she wasted no time on interior design, preferring to get her sleeves rolled up about the school. Parents agree and are wholehearted in their approval: 'Mrs Woodcock is outstanding. I don't say this lightly. I thought Mrs Pullen, the previous head, was great and I was so disappointed when she retired'; 'she has brought an elevated sense of achievement that the school desperately needed'; and 'She models resilience, hard work and fearlessness to the girls as well as being friendly and approachable.'

Drawn to the GDST by her passion for girls' schools and in particular for Sydenham's broad intake of girls with spark and potential, she feels girls here exhibit 'a real sense of purpose, ambition and knowing what they want from life'. Unlike some pupils, polished beyond belief with pure marketing copy flowing from their lips, the girls we met were down to earth and quietly happy here, making space for their enthusiastic teachers (who clearly knew them well) to prompt them out of their modesty and share their accomplishments.

With her family established in north London, Mrs Woodcock makes light of her cross-London commute. An early bird, she arrives with the dawn in time to find the school already awake, with ensembles warming up and rowers heading off to the water. Dogs are two a penny in heads' offices but Mrs Woodcock is more likely to bring in her pet Henry, a tortoise of which she is very fond. Dogs are very welcome, though, and she has her eyes on the well-being dogs found in other GDST schools. During the holidays she enjoys heading to the Jurassic coast with her family. 'I haven't looked back once. I'm the luckiest person in the world,' she concludes.

Academic matters: GCSE and A level results are on an upward trend. In 2019, 70 per cent 9-7s at GCSE. Excellent performances in the three sciences, RE, and English literature but room for improvement in other areas. At A level 57 per cent A*/A and 91 per cent A*-B in 2019.

A level results are a long way behind the particularly strong cohort of 2016 and very different to some of the local heavy-hitters, as noted by a couple of parents we spoke to who felt that the sixth form is something of a weak spot. The head has academic results firmly at the top of her agenda (has made changes to the tracking and reporting of assessment behind the scenes) but feels the results reflect girls doing brilliantly for who they are.

As a rule, girls take 10 GCSEs although sometimes nine or 11. Sciences taught separately from year 8. The maths top set take GCSE statistics in year 10. Almost all take one modern language to GCSE. French in year 7 and then German, Italian or Spanish are added in year 8.

Lessons aim to confront challenges and develop leadership abilities. Years 7 and 8 take part in an accelerated reading programme. Every pupil takes part in the UKMT maths challenges. One year 13 pupil awarded bronze in UK linguistics Olympiad. Separate computing lessons. Mixed ability teaching apart from maths and science. The Socrates programme aims to inspire creativity and a love of learning: it's designed for scholars in years 7 to 9, but any girl can attend.

In the sixth form, most take three, some four, A levels, plus the EPQ. Economics was added in 2018 and history of art in 2019. A year 13 pupil recently achieved a silver award in the UK chemistry Olympiad; year 12 physicists came third in a national talent 2030 engineering competition.

Careers prep starts early with 'take your daughter to work day'; then, work experience for year 11s; termly events focused on careers in anything from the creative industries to biomedical professions, law and finance, with the message that 'everything and anything is possible'. Recent speakers include a female EasyJet captain and a member of the London Fire Service.

Some 14 teachers have been with the school for over 10 years. A mother told us: 'The teachers are all willing to go out of their way to provide support for my daughter in overcoming issues and to come up with new approaches if she does not understand.'

Inevitably, with a newish head there have been staff room changes. New heads of department bring a fresh energy, particularly the highly-talented head of art. A new director of music is organising new concerts and recitals from prominent musicians. The head is proud of the efforts put into staff development through CPD.

Average class size is 22. Parents are united in the view that homework and pressure is well-handled and manageable. One told us: 'As a parent, it is great that they are in an environment where they are interested, enjoy the lessons and are self-motivated, rather than spoon-fed and endlessly tested.'

Those needing additional support are identified by baseline testing in the first month of year 7. Some 93 pupils have additional learning needs, quite a significant proportion, perhaps finding a warmer welcome here than at other local independent senior schools without any such provision.

Any child with SEND is placed on the SEND register and in some cases the learning support team will then create a learning plan. Support is in place for speech and language difficulties, hearing, ASD and social, emotional and mental health needs. Only a couple of girls with EAL requirements. All year 7 pupils receive a study skills class. Some one-to-one support developing individual strategies, which may be slotted in instead of Latin or library lessons. From speaking to staff there is clearly excellent communication between the SENCo and class teachers, who might notice any down-turn in a girl's work and flag up additional support being needed. One delighted parent shared: 'My daughter has dyslexia and started year 7 not very confident in her own academic ability. At the last parents' evening all the teachers were praising her hard work, and how much braver and more confident she is now.'

Teachers plan for those needing more stretch in lessons too. One mother described her daughter as 'challenged to push herself beyond her comfort zone and has a wonderful sense of self-belief that will stand her in good stead.'

Games, options, the arts: Sport is for all, not just the elite. There are squads for netball, hockey, swimming, athletics, cricket, badminton, rowing, football and trampoline. Also on offer: tennis, cross-country, volleyball, fencing and gymnastics. There is an eight-acre playing field in Lower Sydenham and girls also make use of nearby Crystal Palace National Sports Centre.

Everyone seems proud of the new foray into rowing, sharing the Dulwich College boathouse at Putney, competing in regattas and practising on the bank of rowing machines. Plenty of individual sporting stars: one year 7 pupil is fifth in the UK for BMX racing; another was third in the Brighton and Hove triathlon in her age group; a year 11 swimmer is the second fastest in the country for her age; and a year 8 girl achieved gold in diving at Plymouth.

Better than many schools in getting behind the climate emergency. Pupils have written to their MP, and on Switch Off Fridays keep energy consumption as low as possible

Performing arts centre includes a 90-seat recital hall with professional recording equipment. 'Drama and dance are remarkable,' said a parent. Dance – including street dance -is very popular, with an annual show and contemporary groups taking part in local and national competitions. Year 7 ended the year with a trip to see Wicked, their favourite musical. More distinctions and merits than passes in the LAMDA exams.

A third of girls play an instrument from beginner to diploma level – 200 lessons a week. The brick-built music block features graphic art of famous musicians and composers. One year 11 musician has recently been offered a place at the Guildhall School of Music and Drama. A wide range of choirs and ensembles of all abilities from jazz band to chamber choir. There is a lunch time concert series and the opportunity to compete for the title of GDST young musician of the year. Parents speak of performances at the Albert Hall and Southwark Cathedral.

An appealingly raw art space, perfect for getting creative, under the eaves at the top of the school with views across London. Girls were quietly absorbed in their projects, with displays of paper-engineered fashion from year 9 and year 10's industrial landscapes and sculptures taking inspiration from the local gasometers.

A relatively small DT workshop but with all of the gear. Mood lights and elaborately designed chairs on show. Sweet dreams in store for the year 7s whose dream-catchers and wind-chimes we admired, made by a variety of cutting and modelling techniques in mixed materials.

Wings are spread with national and international trips, including skiing. World Challenges have recently taken in Ecuador and Borneo. Girls raise funds for a sister school in Nepal which they visit in the sixth form. Year 10s can take the opportunity of an exchange with St Hilda's School, Australia. Good showing for DofE with 50 girls completing bronze, and the girls recently took home two of 15 prizes at a Model UN conference held at St Paul's boys' school. The school is more energised than many in really getting behind the climate emergency. Pupils have written to their MP, and on Switch Off Fridays keep energy consumption as low as possible.

An appealingly raw art space, with displays of paper–engineered fashion from year 9 and industrial landscapes and sculptures by year 10s inspired by the local gasometers

Enrichment for years 7 and 8 includes cookery, arts and mindfulness; in year 12 there's rock-climbing, sign language, first aid, political awareness and anatomical studies. Lower down the school girls take part in at least two extracurricular activities a week. Technical theatre, trampolining, debating, robotics, digital leaders, ultimate Frisbee, musical theatre and Bananagrams caught our eye, but the usual sporting, musical – choirs and chamber groups – are all there.

Background and atmosphere: Founded in 1887 and located on Westwood Hill, Crystal Palace, Sydenham High was one of the final schools founded by the Girls' Day School Trust, after a petition by a local resident appalled by the 'snobbery' of local schools in the area.

Housed in a rather grand converted hydropathic hotel, the forerunner of today's spa hotels, the grandeur now somewhat hidden, but visible from netball courts, once extensive lawns. Mrs Woodcock has her eye (and budget) firmly on the estate. The high boundary wall flanking the road will soon be replaced by something more open; there will be a new e-learning suite; an eco-zone with garden, greenhouse and pond; a new library; the sixth form centre, currently pretty unappealing, will get a major overhaul and one of the things we've always rather objected to, the drab breeze-block corridors, will be plastered to create a more polished learning environment. Let's hope that wonderful art displays will follow to brighten what currently feel like unloved spaces.

The central old part of the school, with a panelled hallway, art nouveau copper fireplace and grand staircase thrillingly complete with the ghost of an old headmistress, is charming. In contrast the glassy, modern dining hall looks out over the courts (all food is cooked from scratch on site).

Asked to describe the school's atmosphere, a mother said of her daughter's experience: 'cheerful and fun, with a feeling that everyone is important and that her teachers treat her needs seriously.'

Pastoral care, well-being and discipline: A strong structure is in place and girls report feeling that they know exactly who to turn to and that they are listened and responded to. The heads of lower, middle and upper school have pastoral responsibilities, with praise for the approachable deputy head pastoral reaching our ears more than once. A year 8 pupil said: 'The majority of the girls are really nice – everyone is really approachable and friendly. There can be some mean girl behaviour, which thankfully the teachers often sort.' However, staff also coach girls to manage low level friendship issues themselves. Very on point with regards to mental health issues; there are new 'sense of self' weeks inspiring bounce-backability and mental fitness, plus regular talks. There is a full-time school nurse and a counsellor and the school is unfazed by and supportive of girls choosing to transition whilst at school. The school motto is 'fear nothing'.

A parent told us: 'As a working mother of both girls and boys I love the great opportunities they have become well-rounded, caring and thoughtful individuals rather than simply high performing academic achievers.' There is a culture of giving back via outreach, volunteering and partnership with a local primary school.

Sixth formers wear their own clothes with the stipulation of 'smart': hard to tell just how smart this is as it was the exam period during our visit, but comfort seemed more the order of the day.

Year 7 pupils start the school year a day ahead of other pupils; they have attended a summer induction day and the first half of the autumn term is focused on this big step up to senior school, whilst the head spreads the word that 'it's still ok to play', introducing balls and hoops onto the Astroturf at break-time.

Pupils and parents: Pupils are mostly local, travelling from Dulwich, Herne Hill, Beckenham, Crystal Palace and Streatham. Small percentages from further afield: Croydon, Greenwich, Peckham or Camberwell. School bus services run across south London. The school describes itself as a diverse community but 'white British' is the box most frequently ticked (52 per cent) with equal clusters of girls from Indian, African and Caribbean families.

Alumnae include: Margaret Lockwood (actor), Philippa Darbre (scientist), Sophie McKenzie (author), Sandy Powell (Oscar-winning costume designer), Claire Bennett (fencing champion) and Bianca Miller (businesswoman and The Apprentice runner-up).

Parents, giving the inside scoop on each other, say: 'friendly, seem ambitious for their daughters and supportive of the school'; 'down to earth professionals that are looking for a school that focuses on their daughter's ability.'

Entrance: Broadly selective, but the ability range is wider than elsewhere locally. Although there are 3.5 applications for every place, the odds of a place are much higher than at the best local state schools. Open days and taster days throughout the school year. Examinations in maths and English, together with a satisfactory report from primary school. Thoughtful concessions such as the use of a laptop, additional time or a smaller testing venue for those with SEN. Assessments for other year groups where space allows. The main feeders for the school are Sydenham High Prep School, Oakfield, Rosemead, Rosendale and Dulwich Hamlet.

Exit: Some 65 per cent stay on to the sixth from. Of these, nearly half to Russell Group universities. A broad range of subjects pursued, with the straightforwardly academic – history, chemistry, philosophy/ethics/religion – mixed in with the more professionally orientated – law, criminology, events management, jewellery and silver-smithing, sport and exercise science. Plenty heading off to art school.

This isn't a school with a regular clutch of Oxbridge offers, but one offer in 2019. The new Oxbridge programme may assist, beginning in year 10 when girls are encouraged to consider elite universities, medicine or veterinary science. At sixth form there is interview practice with other GDST students and Dulwich College. One mother commented approvingly: 'As a university academic I consider the school to offer exactly the sort of preparation for success in higher education which one would hope to see.'

Money matters: Most recently some 11 per cent of pupils are in receipt of a means-tested bursary and 10 per cent of pupils have a scholarship. Realistically girls will need to perform well in the entrance test to be in with a chance of a bursary. As a guide, higher value bursaries are on offer for families with a household income of less than £40k. Scholarships are available for academia, music, drama, art and sport.

Remarks: With a fair wind, a determined head at the helm and the backing of the GDST, Sydenham HIgh School's evolution could deliver just the alternative independent choice this area is crying out for.

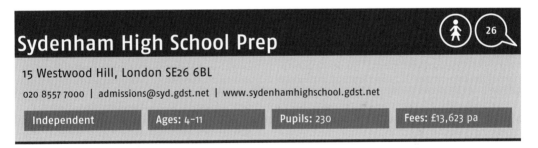

Sydenham High School Prep

15 Westwood Hill, London SE26 6BL

020 8557 7000 | admissions@syd.gdst.net | www.sydenhamhighschool.gdst.net

| Independent | Ages: 4–11 | Pupils: 230 | Fees: £13,623 pa |

Head: Since September 2019, Victoria Goodson BA, MA from Durham in educational leadership and management. Previously head of pre-prep at Newton Prep, as a girl she attended Norwich High, another GDST school. Very warm and sincere, she wants parents to feel she is really approachable and will be on the school gate every morning. She has two primary school age children and enjoys family time, reading, baking and bike riding. Her focus will be on developing 'fearless learners' and her first initiative a regular lecture series with a STEM focus drawing on the talents of the school community.

Entrance: At 4+ there are now two reception classes with entrance assessed by girls take place in a playgroup session with teachers for an hour. Staff are considering numeracy skills, early phonics, handwriting, conversation skills, plus interaction with staff and other pupils. School also requests a report

from any nursery. Any SEN needs may be discussed with the school prior to the day. Demand has never been higher, with three applicants for every place. Main feeders are Dulwich Prep London, The Villa and DUCKS.

At 7+ things become more formal with assessments in maths, reading, writing, plus a team-building and collaboration exercise. Four applicants for every place at this point with Herne Hill, The Villa and state primaries the feeder schools.

Exit: On average 85 per cent of girls transfer to the senior school. Nearly all the leavers go to other London day schools such as JAGS, Alleyn's, or City of London Girls' School with some 20 per cent gaining scholarships, a few to local state schools.

There has been a gear shift in 11+ prep. As a mother told us: 'the preparation for 11+ I know has improved immensely.' Another said approvingly:

'structured and effective without being overly pressurised or hothousey.' The aim is the prep school girls will arrive at the High 'top of the pile' with skills on a level with external candidates without sacrificing well-being.

Remarks: The school's value-added is now the best in the GDST for maths and English. There has been a real drive for staff to evolve their teaching practice, engaging with the latest educational research, and an expectation that they will evaluate everything new for its likely impact on the girls. A parent approved: 'We have consistently been impressed with the teaching staff, who seem to know our daughter really well. She has thrived since being there and is constantly being inspired by the breadth of topics taught.' Pupils enthuse: 'really friendly'; 'always helpful, really easy to talk to. They go slowly through things.'

Arriving at the school, you are currently greeted by tall metal giraffe sculptures rising from the lawn – which girls tell us reminds them to 'stick our necks out'

So far, so ordinary, we think as we take a walk across the playground with a pirate ship, hard court and shaded seating until we reach a little plot of land converted into an outdoor classroom where a tiered fire is burning well, and children are writing and exploring their responses to life as a Tudor – a good example of the school's creative, cross-curricular approach in action.

The science lab is large, orderly and complete with stick insects. Girls have enjoyed watching chicks hatch via a live web link on Twitter. Year 6s have been learning about genetics and the school attends GDST events such as junior science conferences.

Times-tables competitions are a school-wide battle with classes, rather than individuals, competing against each other. The library is large and light, with racks of iPads as well as books. The girls have been recently encouraged to buy a book for the library on their birthdays rather than bringing in cupcakes. 'I'm very fond of Greek myths,' piped up our guide. Year 6s have a go at debating with boys from Dulwich College.

In one classroom a teacher describes how carefully year 1 manages the transition from reception's focus on play to more formalised learning of year 2. In reception, one group of girls are cheerfully baking, whilst others play outside in their own walled playground, overlooked by the occasional

lorry, but well stocked with activities from a cupboard full of zoo animals, water-play, a shaded area and track for wheelie toys.

Average class size is 22. Pupils with SEN are supported by one-to-one support where necessary. Some 20 per cent of pupils arrive with EAL needs, mostly supported by in-class strategies. Those who need stretching are sometimes offered additional lessons: 'they really push you,' said one.

There are two PE sessions a week. Everyone plays netball, hockey, football in the winter with athletics, cricket and swimming at Crystal Palace sports centre in the summer. Some 20 fixtures a term, plus inclusive GDST rallies; gymnastics and dance are popular. One year 5 pupil is hoping to make the GB diving team and various programmes link the school with professional athletes. There is limited outdoor space here, but from year 3 the girls use the senior school's playing field.

There's a new focus on the teaching of art and on cross-curricular creativity. A lovely large art and DT room displays meticulous projects: paper-engineered clothing inspired by 1960s fashion particularly caught our eye.

Drama is a real highlight with three major productions a year. 'My youngest daughter's production of The Iron Man – told through puppetry and the girls' creation of a giant Iron Man sculpture – and my eldest daughter's year 6 play Suffragette were both incredibly powerful and emotional experiences, where the excellence and commitment of the teaching staff really shone.' The latest performance was A Midsummer Night's Dream. There are opportunities on stage and behind the scenes; year 6 prepped by visiting The Globe and we heard lovely singing from smiling girls as they rehearsed.

'I do think the music teaching has improved dramatically with the inclusion of another prep school music teacher,' volunteered a parent. All pupils from year 3 up learn the recorder, with nearly half playing another instrument too. There is a large, not terribly inspiring hall for performances and assemblies, but the girls also have access to the senior school's professional Westwood theatre and recital hall, where we saw them rehearsing.

A really tempting co-curricular programme of clubs and activities runs before and after school and at lunchtimes. Girls can choose from calligraphy, debating, ukulele, drumming, mini-coders, yoga bugs, fencing, 'thunk club' – which develops debating and analysis skills – and gardening. Year 6s participate in an enterprise project – coming up with product and service ideas to go on sale at the summer garden party. The school has a passion for eco projects and climate action, getting stuck into the current upturn in global focus. A group of eco warriors were on a high at the time of our visit, having recorded a song and appeared on Blue Peter to talk about it, gaining a commendation from Greta Thurnberg.

Trips make the most of London and the community: it might be Tate Modern, the National Maritime Museum or visiting a local care home. Year 5 have a PGL adventure. There's skiing for years 5 and 6 to Austria, whilst year 6s have a more sombre end to the year, with a trip to the battlefields of the Somme.

One mother shared, 'It's such a nurturing environment, my daughter is very sad to leave.' Another told us: 'Girls feel very comfortable about reaching out if they are not happy about something' and this empowerment certainly rings true. The girls we met were very engaged with the SPIRE peer mentoring scheme, which encourages girls to help each other to take a reflective approach to difficulties.

Mentions of unkindness amongst girls at times did reach our ears from parents. One, whose daughter relocated here, needed to speak to the head before her daughter's unhappiness was successfully resolved. Another told us: 'on emailing the school re the matter, I was incredibly impressed at the way the form teacher and head of year dealt with the issue, with no detrimental impact on the friendship group.' The girls we talked to were unfazed by the occasional 'mean behaviour', seeing it as part of school life, keen to find solutions themselves to 'figure it out' and respond empathically to what may be a difficulty at home. The school is clear that there is a robust approach to pastoral care: 'There

will always be bumps in the road. You might not feel happy every day in school. We address that and are very open'.

Still very much an all-through school, the name change from 'junior' to 'prep' reflects a GDST-wide switch recognising that the school's curriculum and specialist teaching place it firmly in the independent rather than state sector.

Arriving at the school, a large Victorian brick villa set alongside the busy Westwood Hill, a pleasant residential road with mature trees, you are currently greeted by tall metal giraffe sculptures rising from the lawn – which girls tell us reminds them to 'stick our necks out'. The giraffe theme continues inside with a new giraffe mural rising above the staircase. A few years ago, the school felt like Victorian villa without and within, but it now feels fresh and bright, with a glass-sided main staircase and ground floor classrooms with high-pitched ceilings. Everywhere art and meticulous classroom displays.

Younger girls will now wear navy cardigans with lilac trim, older ones graduate to navy pullovers. Our guides were some of the most delightfully enthusiastic and irrepressible we've encountered. Mothers told us: 'It is a small school and everyone knows everyone. I have myself been witness to the support the girls give each other independent of what year they might be in,' and 'each girl is allowed to evolve and develop into a confident, spirited, creative individual.'

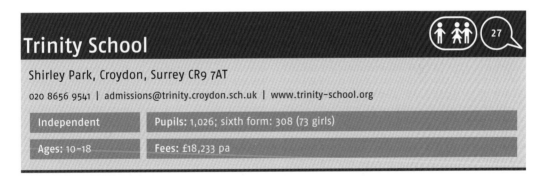

Trinity School

Shirley Park, Croydon, Surrey CR9 7AT

020 8656 9541 | admissions@trinity.croydon.sch.uk | www.trinity-school.org

| Independent | Pupils: 1,026; sixth form: 308 (73 girls) |
| Ages: 10–18 | Fees: £18,233 pa |

Headmaster: Since 2016, Alasdair Kennedy (early 40s). He read engineering at Cambridge, but realised well before finals that what he really wanted was to teach maths and physics. Independent schools are woven deep into his DNA: his father was head of science at Fettes in Edinburgh. 'My early birthday parties were spent running around all-weather pitches,' he remembers. 'I loved that feeling that activity was going on all around me'. He did big stints at Rugby and Sevenoaks, before becoming head of physics at Dulwich, and latterly

academic deputy there. He is married (his wife is in business) with three boys.

Despite the blue-chip schools which have made up so much of his life, he doesn't come across (nor does he seek to) as an obviously public school type. His manner is confident and engaged, but he communicates a strong sense that, whoever he is with, and wherever he may be, everyone is equally important in his eyes. 'The social elitism which coloured much of the public school tradition,' he says simply, 'is alien to me, and to my values. At Trinity, I believe we are bound up, wholeheartedly, in the pursuit of excellences of all kinds, but not in grandstanding.'

Academic matters: This is a selective school, but not preposterously so. The results, says the head, reflect 'plenty of hard work as well as natural talents'. At A level in 2019, 61 per cent A*/A (87 per cent A*-B) and at GCSE 89 per cent 9-7. A broad base of subjects with the accent, as one would expect, on traditional academic ones. Maths, English and history are very strong, and there is notably good biology. Modern languages seem a trifle subdued by comparison. The drive to STEM subjects impacts here as everywhere and, as the head acknowledges, other subjects feel the effect of that.

'Pupils are challenged academically,' said one parent with two children at the school. 'But they're enthused. The prospect of homework can lead them to huff and puff a bit, but that's normal. What's pretty consistent is that they're bowled over by all they are learning in the classroom.'

The buildings are beautifully maintained, if not aesthetically memorable – light, spacious and in every way perfect for all the very best kinds of learning

Special needs are taken seriously. 'It's entirely normal for boys in their early years to struggle with organisation,' says the head. 'We want to help them find ways to help themselves.' The school has a learning support team, which sees pupils, right through to sixth formers, on an individual basis. It also offers specialist help with maths and sciences for anyone struggling, and there are spelling clubs and unlimited assistance for anyone battling to get on top of exam techniques.

Games, options, the arts: 'The school's music is so good,' said one parent, 'that it defies any easy description'. Famous for the Trinity Boys' Choir, there are also superb opportunities for instrumentalists. Every new boy who does not already play a musical instrument is offered free lessons on an orchestral instrument of their choice and over half the boys in the school regularly take part in a musical activity. Ensembles include numerous orchestras, bands and chamber groups. Pupils participate in a dizzying array of national choirs and orchestras. The London Mozart Players coach the senior orchestra and Trinity Boys' Choir appears regularly at The Royal Opera House and at Glyndebourne. Recording studios, a 500-seat concert and no less than 26 Steinways help nurture

the musical education of pupils of every level. 'So many schools alienate both top musicians and the apathetic,' said a parent. 'That isn't the case here.'

A fine reputation for sport: 'Participation is all,' said head. Some 65 per cent of pupils are in school teams so 'everyone who wants to represent the school can do so'. Trinity has worked hard and fast to integrate the new sixth form girls into its sports programmes. Boys do rugby in the autumn term, then hockey and switch to cricket in the summer; girls' hockey dominates the autumn term, followed by netball in spring and rounders in the summer. Tennis and athletics for both and there are any number of other choices: football, water polo, swimming, indoor hockey, rugby 7s, squash, golf, basketball – ad infinitum. The facilities are all on hand to support such choice, with two all-weather pitches, two sports halls, a climbing wall, a swimming pool and tennis and squash courts.

The DofE is flourishing, and there is a 150 strong CCF contingent, comprising both Trinity students and those from the local academy. Occasional mutterings can be heard that the pressure of sport and music can build up unduly in some pupils. 'To be fair,' commented a parent, who had felt their child had been overloaded, 'when the problem was aired, it was rapidly dealt with. It's inevitable, I guess.'

The vibrancy extends to drama and the arts. There is a dedicated theatre space, flexible enough to stage both large scale and studio productions, and junior and senior drama clubs perform both at school and across London. The school has close links with the National Youth Music Theatre and other theatre companies.

Background and atmosphere: Trinity is one of the Whitgift Foundation schools. It opened, in 1858, specifically designated the Poor School – an allusion to the economic circumstances of its pupils and not an aspersion on its talents. Moved to its present site in 1965, and while the facilities are stupendous, it is sometimes hard to find many kind things to say about institutional architecture of that period. But the buildings are beautifully maintained, if not aesthetically memorable – light, spacious and in every way perfect for all the very best kinds of learning.

The school has turned a potential drawback into an opportunity: the normality of the place has made it brilliantly successful in allowing it to pitch itself as, first and last, a local school. In socioeconomic terms, Croydon and its hinterland is an area which veers between great suburban affluence and significant deprivation. 'There is no doubt,' AK says, 'that we are there for everyone', and there is close liaison with local state primary as well as independent prep schools. A strong sense of social awareness reaches beyond the locality, and the school has extensive links – including a feeding

'The school's music is so good,' said one parent, that it defies any easy description. Famous for the Trinity Boys' Choir

programme and placements for gap students – with a school in Malawi.

Their ambition has played off handsomely, not just in terms of demand for the school. Insofar as it's possible to generalise about 1,000 children and their teachers, they seem overwhelmingly appreciative of what the school does and is, and actively relieved that the school never tries to claim any social cachet. 'My mother was really relieved about that,' one girl said. 'I haven't found myself cut off from any of my old friends because of the new ones I've made here.' Men and women are both fully represented in senior positions in the school.

Pastoral care, well-being and discipline: Year heads take responsibility for each age group and the annual intake is small enough for them to deliver on their commitment to know each pupil personally. Up to GCSE, the forms have about 20 pupils, each overseen by a tutor, and these are the axis of the whole system, working closely with the pupils and the first point of contact with parents. In the sixth form, tutor groups have about a dozen students. Induction is carefully thought through: all new pupils and parents come to the school several times before the first day, and meet their form mentors. Every form in the younger years has a couple of sixth formers attached to it – 'much liked by all,' said one parent of a younger pupil.

Discipline is low-key, and relationships feel calm and cordial. Teenagers in any society can be unkind to each other, but both pupils and staff have confidence and this is quickly picked up. 'Having good structures is essential,' says one teacher, 'but it's even more important that it's seen, even by young pupils, as inherently wrong to pick on people.' Older pupils vociferously agreed. 'If you have a worry,' said one boy, 'there are so many teachers here who mind about that and are ready to help'. Of course, no school is immune to the complexities of the internet and the social challenges it may present. 'It nearly always comes down to helping people to identify moments of choice,' says the head 'and how to confront them. And that needs a culture of honest conversation – at home and school. We set out to do this.'

Uniform for all pupils up to GCSE. They look tidy, but not irritatingly scrubbed. Sixth formers have more freedom, 'so long as it's smart,

coordinated and tailored,' says the head. 'It's not a big source of controversy,' he adds

Pupils and parents: Close links with parents are fostered, but in a usefully businesslike way. Grades are sent out every half term, recording progress and effort, and there are two parents' evenings annually, as well as a full school report. It's evident the school wants parents reassured (they are even given the chance to try out the school food, says the head, 'which they seem uniformly to find excellent').

The catchment stretches from Wimbledon in the west to Bromley and Beckenham in the east, with school buses easing the daily commute. Yet the feel is local. Parents are making the investment gladly, but also unsentimentally: the overwhelming sense is that they want their children to grow up into successful citizens, but not grasping ones, nor to indulge in airs and graces. 'That matters a great deal,' said one parent. 'We love opportunity and we hate entitlement. Just now, we can see our children living in gratitude.'

Entrance: About 40 per cent of pupils come from other independent schools, and 60 per cent from state primaries. Given the different constituencies, the school has entry points for boys aged 10, 11 and 13, as well as at sixth form for boys and girls. An entrance examination (centred around English, maths and verbal reasoning) is set to all applicants, who are also given an interview. At sixth form, in addition to the tests and interviews, all incoming pupils must have achieved at least six 7s at GCSE.

Exit: The overwhelming majority go on to Russell Group universities. There were eight secured places for Trinity pupils at Oxbridge in 2019 and six places for medicine and dentistry. Two went to study in the US, with school commenting that 'the best of them value the whole person, in a way which presents a closer alignment with our sense of education at Trinity than with the approach of some UK universities'.

Money matters: Fees are considerably lower here than at local rivals (eg Whitgift and Dulwich). Lunch and transport are extras, as are most music lessons and the bigger trips, but the school is conscious it doesn't want to price anyone out. One way and another, some 50 per cent of students are receiving some kind of financial support, and about half of these are on bursaries.

Remarks: There is a sense in which Trinity is a real standard-bearer: its students leave school with a respect and appetite for learning; its commitment to arts, music and sport seems to delight almost every pupil, and to reassure many parents who, often justifiably, worry that 21st century living involves no stimulus other than that achieved at the end of an iPhone. Its strong investment the local community helps to ensure that Trinity boys and girls leave the school emotionally intelligent and socially grounded. This is a school committed to practising the essence of good citizenship as well as to nurturing personal success.

Whitgift School

Haling Park, South Croydon, Surrey CR2 6YT

020 8688 9222 | admissions@whitgift.co.uk | www.whitgift.co.uk

Independent	Pupils: 1,490; boarders: 61 full, 54 weekly/flexi (from age 13); sixth form: 358
Ages: 10–18	Fees: Day £20,640 pa; Boarding £33,081 – £40,140 pa

Headmaster: Since 2017, Christopher Ramsey (50s). With two headships already under his belt (King's Taunton and Chester), Mr Ramsey could be described as a 'career head' in some ways, but he also enjoyed a successful career as a modern languages teacher at the Leys, Shrewsbury and Wellington. Arriving here, he has faced the formidable challenge of succeeding an exceptional and long-serving (26 years) head, Dr Christopher Barnett, but is full of calm praise for his predecessor. 'I was lucky: not merely did I take over an excellent school, but it was one which Dr Barnett had acclimatised to accept change as part of the inevitable drive towards excellence'.

With nearly 1,500 pupils and 200+ teaching staff, Mr Ramsey might look at a glance like the supreme technocrat, but he's personally approachable and low-key. 'A headmaster has a licence to be nosey,' he muses – he is certainly trying to be visible in all areas. 'He comes to lunch,' said one pupil, matter-of-fact. 'Often he says hello; sometimes he tells us to tuck in our shirts.' Married with three children (teens and early 20s), he still somehow tries to find some time to enjoy theatre and football – these days as a spectator.

Academic matters: A place rich in ability and steeped in high endeavour. All-out effort seems to be the default setting, and this is reflected amply in the results. In 2019, 82 per cent of all I/GCSE grades were at 9-7. The A*-B rate for A level was 94 per cent, 66 per cent A*/A. In the IB, boys achieved an average points total of 39 out of 45. 'Unlike some', said one parent, 'this school has really integrated IB into the life of the school.'

Delving below these very strong performances, it's possible to detect hints of the underlying academic culture. Competence and hard work abound: pupils and staff are ambitious for success and share in the prevailing ethos that academic attainment is a huge part of school life, but emphatically not the whole deal. Great care is taken of those needing learning support, with five specialist staff catering for them – at no extra cost in the normal way.

Those who join the Section Française follow the French Ministry of Education curriculum in French lessons, and must be more-or-less fluent French speakers.

'The work ethos is excellent,' says the head, 'and the school has for long tried to maximise its pupils' potential to deliver: good teaching, enough homework, proper marking – all that'. He is also clear that, by taking careful incremental steps, the school must encourage its pupils to become ever more independent learners. 'It's tantalising,' says the head; 'we all want them to have that independence. But, of course, that involves loosening the reins a bit. Naturally, that can feel scary. So, we'll just move at a sensible pace, learning as we go.'

It's hard to believe Whitgift won't confront the challenge with its customary energy and integrity – a description which applies as much to the staff as pupils. School is, famously, a nursery for future heads. About 15 are doing teacher training at any one time. 'The only downside,' says the head, 'is that they then get a promotion and leave us'. Mainly a young staff body, with 12 old pupils currently teaching.

Games, options, the arts: Big numbers have helped to make Whitgift a home of serious schoolboy sport, but participation and teamwork run right through the school's DNA. Teams have won more than 120 national titles in the past five years: stalwart rugby and football, hockey and cricket – with nearly 30 school teams fielded in each. The participation levels are impressive, with more than 1,200 boys playing in 2,000+ fixtures annually. Over 40 sports are available, including superb athletics, modern pentathlon, tennis and golf. The sports facilities are magnificent – top-of-the-range everything: fitness centre, squash courts, indoor Olympic swimming pool, indoor and outdoor pitches of every kind. Only rowers are forced to take a coach ride. 'We can offer many things,' head acknowledges, 'but not our own river'. Many boys represent their country in a wide variety of sports, or go on to top-level sporting careers.

This same thoroughness and ambition shapes the school's cultural life: breath-taking music, with a symphony orchestra and a concert orchestra. There's also the Whitgift Chamber Orchestra, an ensemble composed of both Whitgift pupils and other talented boys and girls from the London area, which performs regularly at major national venues alongside the Royal Philharmonic Orchestra. There are two big choirs: the Whitgift Chamber Choir and Minster Choristers. Orchestras and choirs tour internationally, and play at major venues, including the Royal Albert Hall, Royal Festival Hall and Cadogan Hall.

Cracking drama, and a lot of it. 'It's as good, at least, as its sport,' said one parent, whose children have experienced both. The main assembly hall converts to a tiered-seating theatre for major productions; there is also a separate performing arts centre and concert hall for smaller productions. Very democratic feel: opportunities for boys of all ages, with some productions confined to particular year groups. Informal links with film companies have seen Whitgift boys take leading roles in TV productions and the West End. Some boys are also members of the National Youth Theatre. Recent plays include The Government Inspector, The Lion, the Witch and the Wardrobe and Doctor Faustus. The school sponsored a boy in his last year to run his own theatre company. 'We try to make everything possible,' says the head, 'if that seems consistent with good sense'.

More than 80 clubs meet at different times during the week. As well as over 200 pupils engaged at any time in DofE, there is also a CCF with over 400 pupils in its ranks. Worth mentioning that two local state schools take part in this – a very natural way to achieve outreach. One recent trip involved boys spending a week at a marine commando training centre. Service culture runs deep within the school's DNA: there are currently 38 Old Whitgiftians serving in the army. The school also pioneered an exceptional (surely unique) exhibition Remembering 1916 – Life on the Western Front: a homage to the sacrifice of lives (of old pupils among others) made during the First World War, brilliantly showcasing its social sensitivity, historical skills and an acute awareness of its own past.

Boarding: Whitgift's decision to open a boarding house in 2013 was an eloquent statement of self-belief. Many established boarding schools have come to rely increasingly on overseas boarders to make their existing establishments viable, but Whitgift has catered for a versatile market – over 50 per cent of whom live in the UK. The house is superbly comfortable and well-equipped (top flight IT equipment, study areas, en-suite bathrooms and spacious, communal social areas with kitchen facilities), but feels a considerable social success as well. Full boarding for some (mainly from overseas) but also weekly boarding, which between them account for over 100 pupils, of whom about half stay over the weekends. There's also flexi-boarding for interested day pupils between 13 and 18. As well as the housemaster and tutors, there's also a head of boarding who represents boarders' interests within the school's senior leadership team.

A home of serious schoolboy sport. Teams have won more than 120 national titles in the past five years: stalwart rugby and football, hockey and cricket

A strong sense of identity and conviviality seem to have evolved over the past years in this fledgling boarding community. This has no doubt been helped by the school's determination to ensure that its facilities are made available for boarders out-of-hours, and to exploit the endless resources of London: the result has been to foment a palpable energy and excitement.

Background and atmosphere: Strong sense of a place at ease with itself. Great investment of time and energy from all constituencies for local causes – visits to primary schools, elderly and disadvantaged – as well as energetic fundraising. Pupils and staff communicate an aura of being glad to be here, but no grand public school airs and graces. 'That was what sold us,' said one father. 'We wanted our son to have a busy and fulfilling life, but the sense of entitlement one sees in some schools was completely alien.' Manners are easy, with evident fondness as well as respect for others. All staff we met emphasised the diversity of the intake – socially and ethnically: middle-class affluent children from the Surrey and Sussex borders, but plenty from south London who are anything but. Nearly 50 per cent of the children here are being financially supported.

Excellent concentration by pupils evident in each of the classes visited, but with a style of comfortable interaction that made it all believable. Head is currently two-thirds of the way through marathon one-to-one interviews with all teaching staff and says, 'one theme recurs, time and time again. I ask them "What should I change?" And they, virtually every time, say "don't change the kids".'

Pastoral care, well-being and discipline: Form tutors are the everyday go-to teacher, especially for the younger pupils. These feed concerns into heads of year who work alongside heads of upper and lower school. It's a tried and trusted structure, but what really seems to make it work is the calibre of pupil-staff relationships. Head is quick to praise his predecessor who was 'way ahead of the game in pastoral matters, and a big support of counselling, long before it was fashionable'. The school currently has three counsellors. All pupils are also members of a house which has come to be a vehicle for much more than just competitive sports. 'Increasingly,' says the head, 'it's a focus of all kinds of activity – plays, concerts and so forth – but also of identity.' One or two parents wondered out loud at the intensity of life. 'Mainly I'm delighted,' said one, 'but there is a cost: my children are pretty often exhausted.'

A conservative society – no doubt about that. Zero-tolerance on drugs and, the head adds, 'we make it perfectly clear that, when you're a member of Whitgift, you're a member seven days a week, 365 days a year. Boundaries are important at any time.' As he acknowledges, that tough line can risk 'the chop falls on someone more unlucky than anything else'. No recent exclusions, however. There is a 'headmaster's detention' on Saturdays for medium-serious infractions – something which, Mr Ramsey admits, with a twinkle in his eye, he is not called to supervise.

Pupils and parents: Full communication between home and school: termly reports, and at least one major parents' evening annually for each year group. In a school with a much broader socioeconomic constituency than some independent schools, the accessibility and approachability of staff is much valued.

Screeds of distinguished old pupils – Chris Cook, previously editor of Newsnight, is a recent notable, and also Martin Jarvis and Derren Brown. Back in the day, Sir Bernard Crick and Lord Tedder also attended.

Entrance: Notwithstanding the huge numbers on the pupil roll, Whitgift is a highly selective school. Around 800 applicants at 11+ last year for the 180 places on offer. It evidently welcomes boys who are able, but likes them to be willing to contribute in a whole raft of activities. Entrance process inevitably emphasises the academic and the school is equally glad to receive pupils from independent or state schools. Main entry points are at 10+, 11+ and 13+ but a limited number of places are also available to boys at 12+ and 14+. The entrance examination concentrates on mathematics, English and verbal

reasoning for younger applicants, while older ones sit papers in mathematics, English and science. Section Française applicants will also sit a test in French. Some overseas applicants may take EAL exams. If all goes well enough, they then come for an interview. For 13+ entry from 2022, pre-test in year 6 for prospective day and boarding students, with offers subject to continuing 'satisfactory academic progress'.

Despite the peacocks parading on the lawn, nobody round here is preening

Prospective sixth form entrants need seven GCSE passes at grades 9-7 and sit the entrance examination in two of their subjects choices for A level or higher level IB.

Exit: There is no formal bar for getting into the sixth form for internal pupils; however, some do decide to move elsewhere at this point.

In 2019, 14 to Oxbridge and five medics. Whitgift boys, once launched in life, often do exceptionally well – often far outstripping those pupils from schools with results even glitzier than theirs. Maths and chemistry results seem particularly strong, with a slight but perceptible bias among students towards STEM subjects – so often the default setting for ambitious pupils these days.

Money matters: The school allocates significant resources for means-tested bursaries. These are targeted at day pupils, but the school has made boarding awards available for boys of exceptional talent who might benefit from boarding. There are art/design/engineering and music and drama awards, as well as academic scholarships. Nearly 50 per cent of the students here are on some form of financial support – a consequence of generations of philanthropy and of the massive contribution of school luminaries and well-wishers.

Remarks: An outstanding school, through and through. Despite the peacocks parading on the lawn, nobody round here is preening. We happened to bump into a great throng of pupils at the local train station and were struck by their combination of energy, cheerfulness and calm courtesy. The head's confidence in them, the staff and parents is a good augury. Yet he is also alert to the irreducible truth that the school is massively privileged. 'We do need to keep helping them see the extent of the privilege they enjoy,' he admits, 'so that we help them become more automatic givers.'

Schools for special educational needs

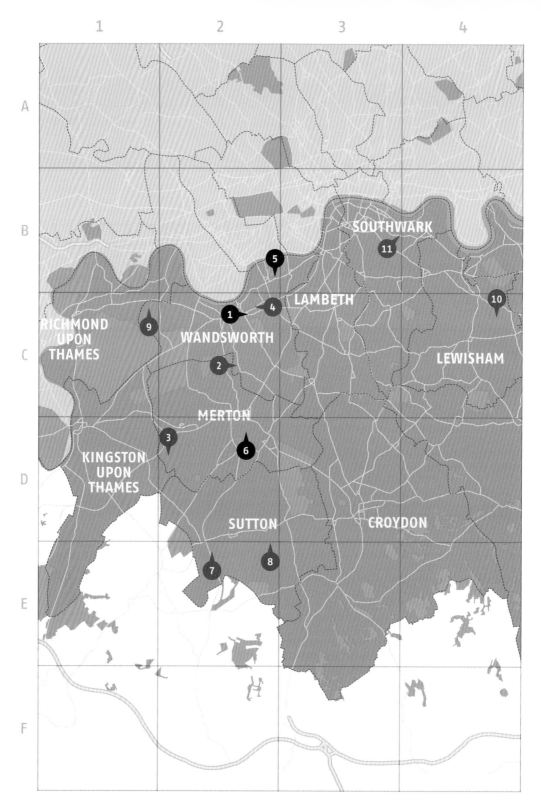

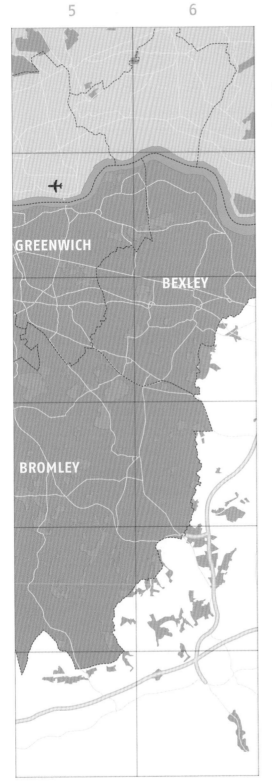

SCHOOLS FOR SPECIAL EDUCATIONAL NEEDS

Schooling for children with special educational needs

The scramble for London places has an extra layer of complexity when your child has additional needs. It's not just the decision between state and independent, but also between mainstream and specialist. And the financial considerations are greater – learning support is usually charged as an extra in mainstream independents, and specialist school places are expensive, meaning you may have to fight for state funding. And while state mainstream schools will all talk the talk about inclusive education, finding those that truly do well by special needs children is another matter.

How do I know whether my child has special needs?

If your child has a difficulty that makes learning harder for them than most children of the same age, then they may have a special need. Sometimes the difficulties are apparent from early childhood, but other conditions such as mild autism spectrum disorders, auditory processing difficulties or dyslexia may not become clear until well into their schooling. And other factors outside of any disability can affect a child's ability to learn, and can be counted as a special educational need – such as mental health disorders, or the after-effects of early trauma in adopted children.

Signs of an undiagnosed special need include:
- poor school performance which does not tally with the child's general ability
- frequent reports of misbehaviour or failing to pay attention in class
- a dislike of going to school, or onsets of headaches/tummy aches when it is time to go to school
- refusal to put pen to paper, even though articulate
- regular clashes over homework

- poor handwriting, presentation and pencil grip
- difficulties in understanding the nuance in language, social expectations, or making friends
- clumsiness or lack of spatial awareness
- and feelings of frustration or anxiety which may manifest as angry outbursts.

A common problem

If your child needs extra help at school they will be far from alone. Between 15 and 20 per cent of all children have some form of additional need. Around three per cent have more significant needs, and this is the group that qualifies for an Education, Health and Care plan (EHCP), which can provide the funding for a special school place or additional help within a mainstream school, and priority in school admissions. Those who do not qualify for an EHCP receive support from the school's own resources under a system known as SEN Support, and they are subject to the same admissions criteria as other children.

Where do I go for help?

For a young child, your GP or health visitor can advise on specialist assessments, for example from a speech therapist where there are possible issues with speech and language, or an occupational therapist for concerns over co-ordination. Waiting times to see NHS therapists are lengthy, and if you can possibly afford it, it will be worth organising one privately.

For a school age child, your first port of call should be the class teacher or the school's special educational needs co-ordinator (SENCo). Outline your concerns, and ask what they can do to help. If they dismiss your concerns, start to keep a record of instances which demonstrate your child is struggling – things your child tells you about their school day, occasions when the child has been upset and reluctant to go to school, any times the class teacher calls you in to report some problem that day. Then demand a meeting with the headteacher, and present your documentary evidence. We hear of too many occasions when parents are fobbed off – stick to your guns if you suspect things are not right.

Schools may then suggest organising an educational psychologist's (EP) report which will be able to identify any difficulties. However with current cutbacks and the shortage of EPs, we hear that schools are becoming increasingly reluctant to pay for these, while the wait to see a local authority EP can now be up to two years. Again, if you can possibly pay, it's worth commissioning one privately (our SEN team can provide details of EPs in your area).

State or independent?

You have a right to name any state school for your child with an EHCP (although for a selective school, they would still need to pass the entrance exam) in conjunction with your local authority. The LA is likely to be less receptive to naming one outside your own borough, as this is more costly for them. All schools are required by law to make any necessary adjustments, or to supply extra provision, that your child may need. The only grounds on which they can refuse a place to your child is where this would interfere with the efficient education of other children, or would not be an efficient use of resources. The schools' application of this premise varies hugely, from those who just toe the legal line, to those where the head truly embraces the idea of inclusive education, and is supported by a well-qualified and enthusiastic SENCo. Winkling out these gems is no easy task, and schools that aren't welcoming will use subtle ploys such as having no

SENCo available at an open day, or generally making you feel so unwelcome that you won't bother applying.

Independent schools have more freedom to select pupils. If they don't want to accept your child there is little you can do – even if you have grounds to challenge this decision under equality law, you are likely to be disinclined to do so when a school has taken this attitude. A few are genuinely welcoming to children with special needs, but they tend to have a quota on how many they admit in order not to overwhelm the special needs staff, and any such London places are usually snapped up at reception entry. Others will look at each child on merit, but the reality is there is little chance of a place for anything beyond mild needs.

It is possible, but rarely achieved, to get state funding for an independent school. Parents have successfully argued for this on grounds of school size/class size/peer group.

Mainstream or special school?

Most parents start with an inbuilt reluctance to contemplate a special school; but equally they can feel a huge sense of relief when their child has been placed in a specialist setting.

The right option for your child will depend very much on their individual circumstances. The biggest misconception is that a special school will somehow quash any potential – in fact a child who has floundered in mainstream can suddenly make huge leaps when the teaching is properly tailored to their needs, or when their self-esteem is restored. And behavioural problems can disappear overnight when children find themselves in a setting which understands their frustration and has the means to break through. It is possible to take a full range of GCSEs in a special school; they should enable a pupil to work to the best of their ability.

Any additional therapies needed will be more readily

available in a specialist school, and it can make all the difference that staff at these schools have specifically opted for special needs teaching. The downside is that these places are more costly, so you need to ready yourself for a fight, and may need to take the LA to Tribunal.

Conversely, some children with milder or transient needs will be better within a mainstream school. But the quality of support available can be extremely variable, so it is important to do your homework about exactly what provision there will be, and how inclusive it is. At primary school in particular, inclusion can mean the child spends their days working separately in the corner with a teaching assistant. Therapy provision will be delivered by external agencies, can be patchy, and will be an add-on, instead of infused through every part of the day as in a specialist school.

Be sure to have an individual meeting with the head and SENCo – are these people you will be able to deal with readily if there is an issue? Are they enthusiastic about the idea of taking your child, do they have knowledge and experience of their condition? Look for evidence of understanding across all teaching and support staff, rather than an attitude that this is a matter for the learning support department. And beware the well-meaning but inexperienced – it can become wearing when you have to keep close tabs on everything.

Can we help?

The Good Schools Guide website has informative features covering the various types of special needs, your legal rights, how to get an EHCP, family issues plus reviews of special schools across the country. See www.goodschoolsguide.co.uk/advice-service/special-educational-needs-service for individual help.

BeyondAutism Park House School

48 North Side, Wandsworth Common, London SW18 2SL

020 3031 9700 | parkhouseschool@beyondautism.org.uk | www.beyondautismschools.org.uk/parkhouse

Independent	Ages: 4-13	Fees: All funded by LA

Head: Since 2016 Kieran Bird BSc PGCE (30s). Studied psychology (planning to be an educational psychologist) but then took a PGCE at London South Bank and taught at several mainstream and special schools, finally working as head of a primary pupil referral unit before joining Park House School. A firm believer that 'everyone has a right to an education' and troubled by the trend of 'inclusion for exclusion' – which is what he fears happens when children with special needs are taught in mainstream environments.

An enthusiastic and professional, but modest, head who appears to empower his numerous staff to take responsibility. The reducing annual staff turnover must be in part thanks to his engaging and friendly style, as well as a result of providing them with space for continuing professional development which has enabled a dozen to take a Masters, and others to undergo ABA training and school direct teacher training.

He is backed by some long-standing staff, including a deputy head who has been there for eight years and works on developing the curriculum and the complicated timetabling of each school day 'with every child's personalised and realistic curriculum plan' as well as weekly assemblies, special events and trips away, and sharing the school's expertise with other schools and the local community.

Parents say head is there to welcome them at the gate and leaves his door open all day. 'I can talk to the head if there are any issues – I see him most days as he is normally around at drop off and collect' one told us. He has multiple examples of how the school makes a marked difference to both pupils and families by providing multiple opportunities to learn functional skills, which enable pupils to eat out, to travel, to be toilet trained, to communicate – either verbally or using an iPad, PECS or Makaton.

Academic matters: Scattered over two sites in Wandsworth, the school offers primary and secondary classes for children with a diagnosis of ASD or severe social communication disorder. All children enter with a statement or EHC plan from their LA. A handful appears in the two youngest classes and more arrive at year 7, often after a period of difficulty at a local mainstream or special school. A fledgling sixth form completes the school, currently making links with local colleges for vocational studies for 18-25s, as the school population matures. Seven classes in the whole school – mixing conventional year groups and named after colours of the rainbow. Class sizes are small (maximum eight). Boys outnumber girls four to one, but classrooms well-populated as each child has their own one-to-one tutor, as well as a class teacher. In addition an ABA supervisor and full time OT and SLTs are hands-on in the room. Now in its second year of post-19 provision in partnership with Lambeth College and based in Yarrow Housing. 'The first year has been a huge success and we are delighted with the progress and provision in place.'

You can't miss the pervading philosophy behind the teaching. Applied Behaviour Analysis, a programme taken from Skinner's behaviour modification findings of the 1920s, uses a system of motivators, rewards and positive reinforcement to effect change in the child's behaviour. Teaching takes the form of an individual timetable, often of 15-minute tasks, differentiated to suit the child's needs. The tutor combines intensive interaction with verbal requests to work towards a specified target. Each goal is a tiny step towards a social or functional end (eg indicating a piece of clothing) as a first step on the journey to dressing yourself. 'Everything with my child takes forever,' sighed one mum. 'The patience and resilience is unbelievable.' Tasks include table-based learning, sensory play, physical games and more traditional, academic subjects, reading, writing and numeracy. Earnest and strictly structured it may seem from the outside, but the outcome in social and verbal progress is a huge relief for parents. 'ABA is an intense and precise programme and that's part of its success,' said a mum. Another added: 'We thought ABA might be a way into our daughter's world. It opened the door so wide, we couldn't believe our luck.'

Class leaders take responsibility for academic curriculum, while ABA supervisors design programmes to enable the child to learn with carry-over for the parent at home; 'It doesn't work unless the parent gets involved,' the ABA supervisor told us. Each child has a one-to-one tutor for a term, then moves to a new one – 'it gives tutors a range of experiences and the children get variety and learn something new'.

Phonics and speech is a goal – though not all achieve speech, they do achieve a functional communication system. Read, Write Inc programme introduces children to literacy. In the sixth form, ASDAN curriculum offers students more vocational studies, like horticulture, animal care and catering. The oldest students had set up a canteen project, planning, buying and cooking lunch for 50 members of staff each week. Staff enthused about eating it too.

There is a strong belief in 'just enough support' allowing pupils to try for themselves every time before helping – even if the resulting holding back results in breakages

The teaching emphasises functional skills in an individual timetable. 'Generalisation is the thing the kids have most difficulty with,' said the head. Supervisors liaise with parents, including visits to the home, to design practical targets to help with day-to-day living, such as boiling a kettle or making a cheese sandwich. 'They really think about the child functioning in everyday things, that we all take for granted,' we were told. One parent was delighted her son's fussy eating was being targeted, another that her child's refusal to wash at home was tackled head-on in his IEP. Parents are expected to carry on the ABA tasks at home, in addition to more traditional homework, such as reading and spelling.

Games, options, the arts: Two playgrounds at the primary site and three at the secondary take learning out into the open. Frequent trips to the park and sports day on Wandsworth Common afford some green relief, while some children get the chance to learn to ride a bike. Fortnightly swimming at Latchmere Leisure Centre or Ernest Bevin College is offered to all, as well as weekly yoga classes. Riding for the Disabled at Vauxhall for the youngest has combined treat of tube journey. Fulham Football Club sends an outreach coach for the older ones. There is some integration with a local secondary school for PE, but one parent felt this was an area that could be expanded. A cricket coach from The Change Foundation (funded by Thomas's School Foundation) visits for indoor cricket sessions and a recent grant has sent some children sliding down the Hemel Hempstead ski slope.

Little in the way of art around the school but music bonds the children and favourite songs are used as rewards. We witnessed a high-energy assembly with singing and signing; remarkably, none of the children appeared hypersensitive to the whooping choruses. One boy sang solo and another played a tune on the piano, learned outside school (individual music lessons are on the head's to do list). A song club rehearses for harvest festival and the annual Christmas show. Oliver! was a recent success, performed at Thomas's theatre down the road, with every child and tutor participating. As one mum said: 'It was a triumph for some kids just to sit on the stage in their costume and not freak out – a real result.'

Using public transport (a painstaking learning task in itself), the children explore the local area on school trips – shopping at nearby Clapham Junction, using cafés and the public library. Unfazed by the exacting health and safety measures, groups have been taken to the Houses of Parliament and the London Eye. The fearless head led a group on a residential trip to Tenerife for a week. 'Even I, as a mum, would balk at that,' said one parent. No holiday club provision 'yet,' says school (watch this space).

Background and atmosphere: Founded in 2000 by the dynamic Karen Sorab, who was seeking ABA provision for her daughter. The school moved from its original location in a hut in the playground of Beatrix Potter School to Tram House, a tiny building once used as a shed for Edwardian trams coursing up and down Garratt Lane to Earlsfield. This has now been rebuilt as a brand new home for the upper school. The lower school has moved into the double fronted Victorian villa that used to house the upper school: an elegant blend of traditional and modern. Facing Spencer Park at one end of leafy Wandsworth Common, it comprises four storeys of whitewashed classrooms with a Scandinavian-style annex of timber boarding and jolly porthole windows.

A central stairwell courses through the building – made safe by ingenious wire 'harp strings' from ceiling to floor. There is a sense of 'architect-designed' interior, with clean walls and beechwood trim. Fenestrated classroom doors add light and transparency to the design. One parent praised the design, not for the obvious aesthetics – 'I don't think my daughter would care if it were laminated floor or mucky old floorboards' – but for the thoughtful inclusion of quiet rooms, for times of stress.

BeyondAutism, the charity behind the school's success, is based on the top floor of Spencer Park. A compact team of staff plan quiz nights, marathon runs and coffee mornings with the parents to raise funds for the school. They will tell you

'We thought ABA might be a way into our daughter's world. It opened the door so wide, we couldn't believe our luck'

the calculated cost of an autistic child to society (£4.7 million over a lifetime), and one mum said that without the provision at this school 'the state would have ended up paying for residential care for my son for the rest of his life'.

Pastoral care, well-being and discipline: Managing difficult behaviour, including self-harming, is not a separate issue here. The head confided that many of the children have arrived with challenging behaviour from other schools. 'It happens,' sighed one mum. 'I've seen him kick his tutor.' To manage behavioural issues, a child with emotional needs is sometimes afforded an extra tutor, subject to local authority funding, until they have settled and can return to one-to-one or a small group. We saw children gathered happily in groups for lunch – packed lunches only, due to the dizzying number of dietary requirements.

Rewarding good behaviour is inherent in the ABA philosophy. Many tutors carry tuck boxes for instant edible rewards and other children are given the chance to choose a favourite play activity. Gold star assembly each week celebrates individual successes – these may be as specific as 'passing on a phone message correctly to his teacher'.

A revamped home/school book communicates progress with the parents in great detail, with every half-hour of the child's school day accounted for and targets for home explained. One mum said: 'The home/school book is very technical. There could be a humanistic approach to parents' concerns.' Although there's no PTA parents were happy with the channels of contact – one parent said: 'I speak to his tutor every day.' A monthly coffee morning with a speaker (recent talks have covered e-safety, sleep and EHC plans) gives the parents a chance to meet the teachers informally. The head is fine about parents phoning or popping in. A welcoming notice on her wall says 'too blessed to be stressed'.

Pupils and parents: The children come from all over south and west London, with the exception of the local borough. The population is diverse, and on the day we visited they were dressed in eclectic blue mufti, emphasising their personalities. On a normal school day the uniform is a practical polo and navy sweatshirt, with dark trousers or grey skirt (an optional gingham summer dress for the girls). Tutors are identifiable by their 'STAFF'

hoodies. Most arrive by bus or taxi from 15 different London boroughs, as far afield as Croydon and Kingston. Parents who collect their children know each other and swap news over informal coffees, but as usual with the SEN bus system others from further afield only meet up on sports day, when they enjoy a picnic on the common. One mum put a more positive spin on it. 'Parents are confident, so there's less need to come in,' she said.

Entrance: All pupils have a diagnosis of autism spectrum disorder and have additional learning disabilities. Around 80 per cent are pre-verbal when they start the school, and few will work beyond national curriculum level 1. The admission process starts with a consultation with the local authority who send through the pupil's papers. The pupil attends an informal assessment with parents, then attends for an extended assessment to see whether the pupils' needs can be met and especially whether they would fit within the class cohort. 'They really worked with us as a family to help my child get a place' according to one parent. We observed assessments being positive experiences for the young people who were checking out the school space, whilst staff noted exactly what they liked doing and what they were able to do. Home visits before pupil starts sets off good school-home links. There is a sibling priority criterion for admissions. Pupils would not be offered a place if their behaviour is considered too challenging for the school to accommodate, or if their academic ability is too high for the peer group.

Exit: All pupils last year moved up to the school's secondary department, Tram House School, though there is the occasional move to different provision – possibly residential care (eg Prior's Court) or schools for moderate learning disability (eg Garratt Park School, Highshore, Southwark) or mainstream schools with a hub for SEN pupils.

Remarks: Pupils are visited at home or in their previous schools and then on entry are assessed for six weeks to get a baseline view of their core skills, and in particular to learn the best motivators for use as rewards in the Applied Behavioural Analysis (ABA) method of teaching (which uses a pupil's own motivation to work towards their learning goals and to increase socially acceptable behaviours). Children follow their own individual programme which is broken into 15 minute sessions; each might be with their individual tutor, in small groups, or in class.

Pupils are in year appropriate classes as far as possible with eight pupils per class. Each class has a lead ABA supervisor who develops the pupil's individual programme and collects data to monitor progress; an ABA instructor; and the pupils' one-to-one tutors who work on individually planned skills. Pupils are encouraged to manage noise and disturbance and situations that reflect the real world – pupils all work in the same space albeit on different activities and the pupils seemed to be used to the busy school atmosphere.

Reception to year 3 are in a modern separate early years building with a sensory garden for outside play. We noted cheerful bright room with trays of activities, and pupils with their individual tutors interacting all the time, even while waiting the two minutes for the bus to take them to swimming lessons.

Older classes are based in the main school building, a beautiful house facing Spencer Park off Wandsworth Common, which is well adapted and feels spacious and bright. In the basement is a soft play room, a medical room, and a sensory room – the latter we were told is 'some pupils' favourite space to choose to be in, and not used as a space to calm down in but a place to explore and enjoy'.

There is a showering block where pupils can be taught personal hygiene and getting used to water and washing. A kitchen is used for weekly food tech lessons, though pupils bring in their own packed lunch, or food to be prepared at school if that is part of their skills programme. Years 3 to 7 have English lessons and maths lessons according to their ability, both using intensive teaching through repetitive table based instructions to teach skills in a highly structured setting, and also by incorporating teaching opportunities in activities the pupil enjoys, thereby generalising skills to a natural setting – in school, over lunch, or wherever possible in the community.

'The sensory room is "some pupils" favourite space to choose to be in, it's not used as a space to calm down in but a place to explore and enjoy'

Other topics are linked into the skills learning – some geography when they go outside school, some science when they are preparing food for the mini-enterprise when they make lunch for staff and pupils. The ABA method of using motivation and reward to teach underpins all learning – rewarding pupils with the thing that motivates them most, for example, time on the iPad, music, time in the soft play room.

Each child has a tutor who works with them all day, though the tutors rotate to ensure pupils are able to work with different people. Despite constant input by tutors, there is a strong belief in 'just enough support' allowing pupils to try for

themselves every time before helping – even if the resulting holding back results in breakages ('three screens were broken in one episode but if we are too fearful we will never let our pupils extend themselves'). Parents raved about 'excellent, passionate and knowledgeable staff'. We were impressed by the orderliness and good repair ('that is thanks to our site manager who keeps things just so'). Yoga teacher teaches all pupils in the school, but they also go outside for snowmobility, horseriding for younger pupils at Vauxhall, weekly swimming, to the park and to the shops.

Skills are taught more than subjects – how to listen and how to communicate or make requests ('manding') so that pupils are able to express their needs, reducing frustration and difficult behaviour. A dog is brought in weekly to help children overcome fears, to learn about caring and for therapeutic intervention. Pupils are expressly taught how to share, working with siblings, peer interaction and ways of understanding and expressing their own and other people's feelings. 'We teach our vulnerable pupils how to say no when needed to keep them safe and comfortable,' head said. One parent told us: 'My son is learning how to be safety conscious so we can prepare him for walking to school and crossing roads safely.'

Tutors were seen constantly updating data sheets to show just how many minutes a child was able to sit, how many times they were able to initiate or make a request, watching for progress so that steps towards a goal could be adjusted. Super tight monitoring and assessing at every stage help inform planning, making sure every child is gently pushed on. The intensity of the work, and the fact that many young staff are gaining experience results inevitably in staff moving on. 'I would love there to be less turnover of staff, but it is a hugely demanding job I suppose,' said one parent.

Clubs on Friday afternoons expose pupils to new activities each half term eg music, pamper club (several of the girls had beautifully coloured nails), Spanish, basketball, hip hop.

Parents' afternoons twice a year as well as an open day when parents are encouraged to watch classes and lessons. A home-school book goes back and forth each day for communication and to ensure transferable skills are used outside school. We saw these well used books with appreciative comments from parents sharing achievements.

One full time speech and language therapist based at Park House, and a second shared with Tram House School and similarly one full time occupational therapist and one shared, who work in the classrooms or in the soft play room in the basement, with the pupil's tutor always present so the practice can be continued outside the therapy session. There was little divide between therapy and the rest of the school day which must be so much better for real integration and purposeful learning. 'My child is such a happy boy now – they really get what he needs,' summed up one parent.

We didn't see any child sitting alone or in their own world – they were busily engaged all the time supported by young, enthusiastic yet hugely patient tutors. The staff appear to support each other with good humour and there was an upbeat, positive atmosphere that spread to pupils who we saw

laughing and smiling frequently. Pupils are taught 'to like new things' – a joyous approach of teaching curiosity to children who might otherwise fear the unknown. This school feels buzzy and full of active learning without any overt stress. Parents need to buy into the ABA methodology, which they need to maintain at home; but for those whose children gain skills of communication, toilet training, or coping out in the community, it is life changing.

BeyondAutism Tram House School

520 Garratt Lane, Earlsfield, London SW17 0NY

020 3031 9707 | | www.beyondautismschools.org.uk/tramhouse

| Independent | Ages: 14–19 |

Headteacher: Since 2018, Jon Ascot (40s). Studied geography and sports, and took his PGCE at Exeter in geography and IT. He first worked in mainstream secondary comprehensive schools, but soon moved to special schools and children's support services. After working at Quadrant Children's Support Service in West Essex for a year he set up his own education consultancy business and worked in Haringey as a consultant head to a PRU, and then with the Priory Group in Devon, where he had a three year stint as head of Chelfham Bere Alston School for complex learning difficulties and autism.

His special area of interest is strategy and data, and several posts involved advising on alternative provision. He was brought in as a consultant to help this school transform from what was previously Rainbow School, as it developed its new site and transitioned to distinct lower (Park House) and senior (Tram House) schools. After two months as consultant, Ascot was made head of Tram House which caters for pupils aged 14-19. Parents appreciate that his office is at the front entrance, and all parents we spoke to said access and communication with head was easy.

Academic matters: Children here have a diagnosis of ASD or severe social communication disorder, and all need to have an EHCP. Teaching is based around Applied Behaviour Analysis (ABA), which uses a system of motivators, rewards and positive reinforcement to effect change in the child's behaviour. Each child has their own IEP with learning goals, which might be the ability to sit still for five minutes, to make requests, to select a piece of clothing. Goals can be social and functional (such

as dressing yourself) as well as academic, such as reading and writing.

Pupils are taught in groups but always with one-to-one tutors for each child working alongside the class teacher. Each child has an individual time-table, and one parent explained: 'They are always coming up with a next step and don't coast or rest on their laurels, so whenever my child has reached one goal, another useful skill is being taught.' The ABA system is intense and precise, and tutors constantly and meticulously track all achievements and progress made.

Timetables include structured teaching based on national curriculum objectives. English is taught using phonics, maths using number world, science in half termly topics. We watched a maths/science teacher giving a lesson on the moon and the sun, using an interactive whiteboard and worksheets, who told us: 'The concept of time is difficult for our pupils, we are starting with looking at day and night activities.' ICT is a specific target in pupils' IEPs, geography and history are covered both in themed weeks during the term, but also generalised during class outings. Science is incorporated in food tech (a weekly session encouraging independence and curiosity about new foods, as well as teaching cookery skills).

Alongside the academic learning are social interaction and emotional regulation lessons (using Lego therapy and practising turn taking). There are also sessions called 'attention autism' where pupils explore sight, sound and smell, and curiosity is encouraged.

Much learning is about breaking down fears and barriers, and the school works at this in a myriad of ways – getting pupils used to having their hair cut, first at school and then at the hairdressers; taking them to the library and involving them in the community wherever possible; outings to local businesses; and trips, such as a recent one to the London Wetland Centre. These outings are also a chance to generalise learning – something all the children struggle with.

We saw pupils fully engaged in every room we entered – every opportunity was taken to make it a learning experience – in the dining room, the classrooms, the shower room.

Year 9 pupils and above can access ASDAN accreditation by building up Personal and Social Development portfolios evidencing learning. Entry level maths and English exams are offered.

A preparation for adulthood curriculum has been created based around functional life skills. Pupils are supported on work experience placements by their individual tutors, at organisations including The Gate community cafe, the Trussell Trust food bank, local gardening projects (Roots and Shoots), and businesses like Holiday Inn.

The gym in the basement is set up like a public gym – very appropriate for teenagers who will then hopefully feel at ease when they join gyms outside school

Though not all of the pupils achieve speech, they do achieve a functional communication system. Parents are expected to carry on the ABA tasks at home, and staff will design programmes to address daily living skills such as washing or making a sandwich.

Games, options, the arts: The gym in the basement has several machines and is set up like a public gym – very appropriate for teenagers who will then hopefully feel at ease when they join gyms outside school. Pupils also go to a local sports centre where they are encouraged to swim and to maintain fitness. Groups go to the local park for cycling and football and the school has a link with Fulham football club, which provides an outreach coach. There are horse riding lessons and we saw one pupil practising yoga (there is a school yoga teacher who works with all the pupils).

There was some evidence of art on the walls but there is no dedicated art room – materials are brought to the classroom. We saw an electric piano and some percussion instruments in the basement room, and we were told that music lessons happen daily in class. Music and drama are incorporated during the winter production – a whole school performance – while the song club meets weekly and performs in school assemblies and in the community. Clubs on Friday afternoons (no after school clubs due to problems with transport) include pamper club, hair and make-up club, hip-hop club, Spanish club – the range changing regularly depending on staff interest and strengths.

Background and atmosphere: Originally founded by a parent seeking ABA provision for her daughter, the school started life in a garden shed in another school playground, before moving to the tiny building on Garratt Lane in Earlsfield. This has now been rebuilt as the senior school for pupils from 14+. Tram House is on a main road with almost no outside space, but it is like a tardis inside with open, airy spaces and whitewashed classrooms. Two security gates access the ground floor with generous reception area and the head's office, and a dining room giving onto the tiny outside space. The school classrooms are on the upper floors with the gym, showers and staff rooms in the basement. All wood and glass with huge windows, the building feels fresh, clean and comfortable, lit up by sunlight pouring in. Early days but the move from the original building (now the early years and junior years department) seems a big improvement and allows for a more grown up atmosphere. This is very much the senior school, pupils have more group lessons and there is a great emphasis on academic as well as functional skill learning.

Pastoral care, well-being and discipline: Rewarding good behaviour is an inherent part of the ABA method. It focuses on positive reinforcement and teaching a range of skills, including communication, with the aim to reduce the frustration which might result in problem behaviour, and to enable pupils to learn in more depth and with more focus. Rewards are given for achieving their goals – a minute on the iPad after having completed three accurate responses for example. Every response is recorded to plot progress or success, this is then analysed to check and adapt timetables and goals. Staff aim to give just enough support to build resilience and allow for calculated risk, then gradually reduce the intensity of support so that pupils can, for example, eat lunch together in groups of four without their one-to-one tutor.

Parents have mostly chosen this school specifically for the ABA framework which they say results in visible, if painstaking, progress. 'It took six months of gradual steps to teach my child to self-inject for diabetes, and that has been great for us all and will be literally a life saver for him,' one said.

Pupils and parents: As in many autism schools, the pupil body is almost entirely male. Around 30 per cent of pupils are verbal, for others communication

All wood and glass with huge windows, the building feels fresh, clean and comfortable, lit up by sunlight pouring in

often involves using an iPad (Proloque2go), Makaton and PECS. iPads are provided by the school, and occasionally by parents. We saw pupils sitting together to eat and learn, and all seeming to manage the hubbub (none was using ear defenders, which one parent thought was an achievement, saying 'Out in the world, he has to be able to manage noise and life going on').

There is a communication book with notes for the 95 per cent of parents who do not collect or deliver. There are parents evenings when parents help with goal planning for their children. A fledgling parent forum has started but it is typically hard to get parental involvement when families are spread across such a wide area – they come from all over south and west London. A parent video portal is being planned and will be welcomed by parents.

Entrance: All pupils have an EHCP (or are in the process of getting one) and have diagnosis of ASD and/or communication difficulties. Pupils also have significant learning disabilities. The school can accept pupils with some behavioural difficulties if they believe they can manage them and that using ABA methodology can teach new behaviours and communication. A behaviour analyst assesses pupils before a place is offered to identify their communication needs and to see whether they can be supported by ABA.

All seven year 8 pupils from Park House School moved up to Tram House when it first opened, along with other pupils who had previously been excluded, home schooled or were in alternative provision. Referrals are made by the local authorities (up to 17 LAs represented in the school); this is followed by a parents' tour, and informal and then an extended assessment. The school is frequently named on the EHCP and where needed, Tram House is able to support the LA in preparing the EHCP. The school does not accept self-funded pupils.

Exit: After school some pupils move on to residential care or to further education at provisions including Ambitious College, Jigsaw, and Orchard Hill. Links are being built with South Thames College and other local colleges to try to create hubs supporting pupils within the colleges.

Money matters: The school is run by the charity BeyondAutism which gets involved in a large amount of fundraising to complement income from school fees. Parents told us they were keen to support the charity – taking a table at the annual quiz for example. The charity accounts show healthy reserves.

Remarks: Pupils appear well managed and engaged here in this bright and attractive purpose built school. The high staffing ratios help to ensure that every child is busy and actively engaged in learning or doing. 'They teach for the real world and do not cosset pupils' according to one parent. It's intense stuff and you need to be prepared to buy into and play your part in ABA therapy, but for those whom it suits, parents report great progress and strides made that were never thought possible.

Blossom House School

Station Road, Motspur Park, New Malden KT3 6JJ

020 8946 7348 | admin@blossomhouseschool.co.uk | www.blossomhouseschool.co.uk

Independent	Pupils: 230
Ages: 3–19	Fees: £38,250 – £44,550 pa

Principal: Since 1983, Mrs Joanna (Joey) Burgess. A speech and language therapist by profession, she founded the school, initially with four pupils, in her grandmother's house. Trails a wake of swooning parents pinching themselves at their luck in

finally finding a school which understands their children and knows how to teach them. 'Love it. I feel like I've won the lottery,' said one. 'From the first moment of stepping into the school, the focus was all about what my son could do and how he could develop, given the right support and challenge,' said another.

Her understanding of parents' experiences has been sharpened by the arrival of a grandson with special needs, and watching the pain her daughter has gone through in the diagnosis and local authority battle mill. He is now a pupil at the school. One parent told us with gratitude of a day when they had to wrestle their son into school, and both parents were on the floor. 'We were in quite a state. She took us into her office, and looked after us.'

She has that personal warmth and skill at creating a rapport which finds you unwittingly telling her your life story. She was miffed to be referred to as 'diminutive' by a previous reviewer, so we'll add a parent's qualifying statement – 'only in stature'. The sharp focus, the attention to detail, the keenness to be personally on top of everything is evident; but there's apparently none of the monster that can accompany that.

Work experience opportunities have been boosted by the school's own café just outside the school gates; students cook for it and learn cash desk and customer service skills

'Really is as good as she seems – I've never seen her without a smile on her face,' one mother said. Another summed up: 'Always seems to have time for everyone, students, staff and pupils, but is also clearly a leader. Despite the growth of the school and a change of location in the last few years, the ethos and nurturing approach have remained in place. She is highly visible and accessible and always there at concerts, performances and end of year prom.'

Looks after staff with a weekly feast lunch on Fridays (we witnessed the delivery van unloading). One daughter teaches in the school, another runs the new café (more on this later).

Academic matters: Children need to be within the broad average cognitive range; but Joey acknowledges 'sometimes it is difficult to be specific about what is a result of cognitive impairment, and what is the impact of communication difficulties and anxiety'.

A good proportion of the children have autism, but the school is careful not to say it can take all children with autism. 'We are a modified mainstream, and for some the physical environment is too much,' head says. 'It's a case of can they cope with change and movement? If they get anxious with too much stimulation, or if they need an individual work station, then they might not manage.'

In the primary department there is a separate provision, Robin House, for children with more complex communication difficulties and autism. Some are able to transfer into the main school at the end of key stage 1, some aren't. The latter group have previously gone elsewhere at the end of key stage 1, but Robin House newly expanded into key stage 2 from September 2018. Some children in Robin House are non-verbal, and the focus is on communication first before academic learning.

In the main school classes are typically six to 10 pupils, with a teacher or therapist as group leader, which are then broken into smaller ability based groups. Secondary is taught in age groups, but in primary they mix ages, and group by social skills and ability. All follow the national curriculum, adapted as necessary. Some children will take GCSEs, some will do a combination of GCSEs, BTecs and entry level qualifications, and some will take functional skills and entry level courses only. There is a broad academic spread and while one or two parents might wish for more academic stretch, others note that the push has to be tempered by their child's fragility where stress is concerned. Most felt that the spread of ability is inconsequential, as one parent said: 'Because of the small class sizes and ratio of staff to pupils, there is room to challenge each child and to help them access learning in the way that best meets their needs.'

There is a visual timetable for each half day, which the class teacher will go through at registration. Before every lesson starts the teacher will write on the board what is going to happen, and cross it off as it's done.

It is effective, parents say. 'I can see during holidays that he misses the routines and his class. I can see he truly understands that they are there to help him with his emotions and find ways to make him feel better as well as teach him new things. He gets very excited about the new topics coming and he wants to learn.'

We watched the start of a year 5 science lesson, on the theme 'To find out about Isaac Newton'. As a teacher explained what they would cover, a boy reminded his classmate 'no talking'. Inside the classrooms we saw pupils with sensory cushions and wobble boards to help them focus. Outside the classroom there's a pull-up bar in the wall, the pulling up exercise apparently helpful to keep children regulated.

Another class was being led by an OT, and children were scampering around finding bits of a puzzle which would complete a picture of what they were doing that day. OTs work with the children on classroom skills such as cutting, using a ruler, and keyboard skills, and daily living skills such as tying shoelaces.

Before every lesson starts the teacher will write on the board what is going to happen, and cross it off as it's done

The staff are noticeably youthful, and all go by their first names, which some parents say is appreciated by their youngsters.

Some post-16 students take college link courses, spending two or three days out at college, and the remainder of the week at Blossom House, where they continue with therapy as well as English and maths, and work skills BTec qualifications. One staff member from Blossom House supports the students at each college (Nescot, South Thames, and Kingston Art College) but these pupils need to be able to cope with this low level support and with travelling independently.

A new parallel pathway was introduced in 2018, with all teaching at Blossom House for those who will not cope with going out to college.

Work experience opportunities have been boosted by the acquisition of the school's own café. It sits just outside the school gates, and students cook for it and learn cash desk and customer service skills. It's also a handy networking spot for school run parents.

Games, options, the arts: All the usual sports, with matches arranged against both other special schools and mainstreams. 'My son is really interested in sport and he has been given the opportunity to represent his school at five-a-side matches with other schools as well as being able to do a football club as an after school activity. His year group had the opportunity to go to a workshop run by Ballet Rambert and to perform with other schools at their studio at The National Theatre,' a parent told us.

There's a great range of overseas and off-site trips – recently students have jetted off to Barcelona and Valencia. There's a year 6 trip to an activity centre, and students can take the DofE award. 'My son has loved the opportunities he has had at the school – camping in Devon every year and getting involved in outward bound activities, going to Paris and Barcelona, getting work experience, doing Duke of Edinburgh, visiting all sorts of places both cultural and sporting, doing drumming lessons...' commented a parent.

Background and atmosphere: When it outgrew the grandmother's house, the school moved twice before finally moving in 2015 to the Motspur Park site. You'll be struck immediately by how spacious and perfectly presented it is. It was redeveloped from a former office block, which enabled them to start from the drawing board and purpose-design everything for the school cohort.

A train buff will be in their element; not only might you have to wait at the level crossing outside on the school run, you can also see trains running past the school windows.

Primary are downstairs, secondary fittingly on the second floor, and sixth formers have their own wing. It has everything you'd expect to see in a mainstream – the computer rooms, DT rooms with fancy equipment, home economics room, science labs complete with gas taps and lab benches, where we saw a white coated group of post-16s at work on their level 3 in applied science.

The outside space will surely lure in a reluctant child – there are climbing frames and other colourful play equipment, an outdoor gym, and a little stepped theatre.

Some parents bemoan the lack of a canteen – you'll have to pack sandwiches.

Pastoral care, well-being and discipline: The slippery process to getting this type of specialist provision means that inevitably many children arrive here after a torrid time in mainstream, convinced that they are stupid and unworthy, and feeling stressed and angry.

There's a separate area in the school known as The Zone, where a few pupils arriving in a fragile state might first spend time if they are not ready to go into the main school. Here they get more one-to-one input, and therapeutic work to address anxiety which may have become entrenched.

A train buff will be in their element; not only might you have to wait at the level crossing outside on the school run, you can also see trains running past the school windows

Throughout the school you will see 'star of the week' notices on classroom doors, and walls of fame in the corridors, highlighting individual students' achievements. 'We go over the top, with lots of positive language, these children need to feel they have come up from the bottom of the pile,' Joey says.

It has worked, according to one parent, who says that in mainstream her daughter used to say 'I'm rubbish. I can't write.' Now, 'she has her head held high. She used to be terrified of maths, now she loves the maths teacher.'

There are a lot of mental health problems among the school cohort, which are dealt with through collaborative working across the speech and language therapy, art therapy, music therapy, and psychotherapy teams. 'I think we would have had a school refuser if we hadn't found Blossom House. They are so understanding of him,' noted a parent.

Anxiety typically emerges in the older children. Sixth form students can self-refer to the therapy team, and they have three dedicated speech and language therapists.

It is not a school for children with behavioural difficulties, however meltdowns as a response to anxiety or frustration are all in a day's work. You won't see behavioural outbursts though, Joey says, because everything is well managed. You might instead see a child sitting on the stairs taking time out, or having pressure therapy with a ball. They have calm spaces and sensory diets, and every lesson has a break in the middle when all of the children do exercises developed by the OT department to help with regulation.

Pupils and parents: The school is heavily weighted to seniors, with only one-third of pupils in the primary department; the result of lengthy struggles to get children into this type of provision. Families cover all socio-economic backgrounds – but with a leaning towards those with the grit to battle LAs for a place here. 'It takes a certain sort of person to put up the fight for their child,' Joey says.

'I really appreciate the thoroughness of their approach. They didn't offer him a place until they were sure that it was going to be the right place for him'

The school has its own family support team, which some families find helpful. One mother said: 'Being a parent of someone with autism is an everyday challenge and sometimes a struggle. I know I always have them to talk to. They are always forthcoming with ideas for me if I need help with him. There is just so much experience and skilled expertise there. They understand. They have seen it all. We share funny moments, impressive improvements and any sadness.'

Others remarked on the mutual support between parents. 'I have made great friends with other parents there. It is a relief to have friends who fully understand the difficulties that we all face. There are plenty of opportunities for parents to meet, either at coffee meetings at the school or at the social events like quiz nights.'

Communication is good, we were told – concerns dealt with promptly and effectively, and parents given frequent updates on progress and how a child's day has been.

Entrance: The biggest entry point is in year 7, 'after a primary has made clear this child is not going to cope in mainstream'. There is also a steady stream joining in years 8 and 9 after a mainstream secondary has proved a disaster.

A lot of families face tribunals en route, or at least the threat of one. Joey will support the family's case at tribunal, and she says that on occasions when they haven't succeeded in getting the LA to fund the child at the school, they have at least been able to beef up the child's EHCP to ensure more support will be made available.

The entry process is rigorous – an initial informal assessment then a three-day assessment followed, for some, by a trial six week period to ensure the child will be in the right place. One parent described her experience: 'Apart from the battle to get funding from the local authority, my son also had to come to two or three in-depth assessment periods prior to him being accepted as suitable for the school. I really appreciate the thoroughness of their approach. They didn't offer him a place until they were sure that it was going to be the right place for him. By the time the place was offered, I was confident that they knew who they were dealing with and that they could provide the appropriate support.'

Exit: The majority stay on from the primary into the secondary school, although a few will go to a specialist residential school. Previously some children who couldn't manage to go out to mainstream colleges for 16+ courses have moved on to other specialist schools, but more are likely to stay on now with the addition of in-house 16+ courses.

Money matters: It is possible to self-fund, but around 90 per cent of children are local authority funded.

Remarks: If your child has communication difficulties, it's highly likely that you will be putting gains in speech and language higher on your wish list than a GCSE certificate, because when language is compromised, so is all learning. In comparison with other schools, this one offers the riches of Croesus in terms of speech therapy provision. The school building is a pleasant environment and has bang up to date facilities. Complete the picture with a head who has used a speech therapist's vision to create an education model that really works for these kids, who is on top of every detail, and who is even nice to deal with – it's like you've pulled a three line match on a one armed bandit.

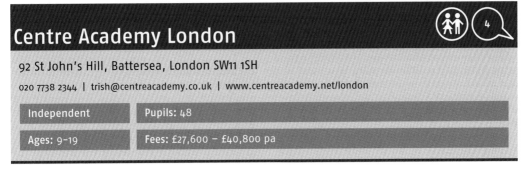

Centre Academy London

92 St John's Hill, Battersea, London SW11 1SH

020 7738 2344 | trish@centreacademy.co.uk | www.centreacademy.net/london

Independent	Pupils: 48
Ages: 9–19	Fees: £27,600 – £40,800 pa

Head of school: Since 2017 Miss Rachel Maddison, who joined in 2014 to teach maths, later overseeing assessments. Psychology and cognitive science degree at University College London led to 10 years in human resources before she brought her calm, friendly approach to teaching. Miss Maddison has an in-depth knowledge of the school and a clear commitment to the care and education of the pupils. Previous head and now principal and CEO Dr Duncan Rollo oversees both the London and East Anglia schools, particularly applications and exits.

Academic matters: A small special school with 45 ethnically-mixed students (four boys to every girl). Pupils are predominantly on the autistic spectrum (60 per cent ASD) but as most now come with more than one diagnosis, school accepts a broad range of additional needs, mainly dyslexia, ADHD, dyspraxia and speech and language difficulties. While some, often school refusers, present with behavioural difficulties arising from previous school experiences, the school would not accept pupils where this is their primary diagnosis.

There are two academic pathways: functional skills levels one and two, and GCSEs. While most study one or the other, a blended pathway is possible. Both groups follow the national curriculum studying English, maths and science plus there is a GCSE in humanities (history and citizenship) and options for film and drama. A science lesson in progress was surprising in taking place with no other facilities to differentiate it from the other classrooms than a sink – however, there is a second classroom in the annex with gas taps, a fume cupboard and stored equipment. Laptop-use is a normal way of working, with touch-typing learned in school.

School hours are 8.15am-3.45pm (3pm on Fridays). Teachers mostly have qualified teacher status (apart from a couple whose experience was gained teaching adults, outside the maintained schools system). Unusually there are no classroom assistants. Class size averages four to six – a reason commonly given for choosing the school by parents whose children would not succeed in a mainstream class of 30. Classes are not set in year groups but are an amalgamation of abilities; for example in a foundation-level class we saw a mix of six key stage four and five 15-18-year-olds studying for the film element of their creative media and performing arts entry level diploma. ASDAN life skills qualifications are also taken. Homework is done in school, during three weekly supervised sessions – a relief to many parents, although one would have liked his son to learn the discipline of completing work at home.

Displays included the products of a workshop where parents and children painted each other in the style of Picasso

In the sixth form there are again two pathways: to college for level one, two or three courses in music, sports, hospitality and vocational skills; or staying in-house for the American High School Diploma covering art or current affairs, English, history (US and world), maths, ICT and science. Dr Rollo explains how his own experience at the London School of Economics led to the latter choice: 'I saw students from around the world who could come to university in the UK without A levels, so 17 years ago we started the American High School Diploma here as we had found our students couldn't do A Levels, not because they weren't bright enough but due to anxiety over their exams'. Having this option of continuous assessment without final exams, students can go on to further education. Rollo says that 131 UK universities, including Oxbridge, accept this system and he says it 'is much fairer to our kids – we've got children with high IQs who'd not survive in a class of 30.' He advises on UCAS applications and gives a projected grade based on averaging the years' termly grades: 'We've not had a single child studying the American Diploma who wanted to go to university and didn't get in.' Parents are hugely grateful for the opportunity this gives their academically-able SEN children to go to university. External students can apply to join the sixth form where they can stay until they are 19, benefiting from an extra year of study. Both Miss Maddison and Dr Rollo continue to teach, so they know the students well.

Each lesson we saw had a quiet atmosphere with pupils clearly encouraged to give their views and contribute to a discussion. We heard a coherent and impassioned contribution to an English lesson on the point of education; the English teacher is also a dyslexia specialist. There is not the busyness of some school classrooms nor the buzz of learning often present, perhaps due to the deliberate creation of a low-pressure learning environment. One parent summed up a general view: 'Actually academics were the last thing on my mind because mental health is most important.' Another thought 'school pushes each to their ability.' A parent of an academically-able child told us that her daughter's wish to set up a parliamentary petition against the removal of course work from GCSEs, because this disadvantages SEN students, was organised as part of her citizenship GCSE and is now live.

Games, options, the arts: The art room is a great can-do place: 'All students are able to do art', says Miss Maddison. The students with dyspraxia and sensory issues are helped to work by the occupational therapist and, as they practise, their gross and fine motor skills improve without the need to be taken out of lessons for therapy. Displays included the products of a workshop where parents and children painted each other in the style of Picasso – lovely colourful portraits emerging from this parent-child engagement.

'She has a great group of friends who are direct and authentic with a joyousness about them, whereas she had no friends at all at her last school'

Outside space is limited to a small yard with a basketball hoop. There are weekly trips to Battersea sports centre and Latchmere pool, plus the local parks for daily activities – 'movement helps, especially with ADHD', says Miss Maddison.

A music teacher works four days a week giving both class and one-to-one lessons, also running choir club. Tuesdays are club afternoons, with a choice from books, disco, fashion and beauty, film and singing. Recent visits included some London museums and galleries plus a trip to Bletchley Park. There is an annual residential for the middle school to East Soar, a National Trust farm property on the South Devon coast, perfect for sea-crabbing.

Background and atmosphere: Epitome of a lovely small Grade II-listed red-brick school, which could now do with an up-to-date science lab and a transformation of its Nissan hut. The stairways display English and drama work: their production of Macbeth, poetry and a poppy collage commemorating the centenary of the First World War. The students are well-presented in their uniform of navy blue jacket and tie.

Privately UK-owned since 2002, along with a sister school in East Anglia.

Pastoral care, well-being and discipline: We saw lively school photographs of the mentor groups, each having four to six pupils. An early start to the school day allows 25 minutes' time with a mentor, going through homework, books, lunch, how a pupil is feeling; then a further 10 minute session after lunch to prepare for the homework period. These mentor sessions are seen as essential in how school supports pupils. There is also the option for another teacher of a child's choice to be mentor if needed.

A parent spoke of the balance to be found with behaviour – her well-behaved son can become scared if too restricted and close down whereas she would like him to be able to be more himself at school, letting his personality out as he does at home, this being best for his mental health – however, she feels fortunate that school is able to work individually with each child to try to find this balance. In the last five years there have been just three exclusions: Ms Maddison says 'We try hard not to exclude a child who may already feel they have failed.'

Pupils and parents: Communications with parents are by the mentor, plus termly reports, parents' evenings, a yearly conference and the student's annual review. One parent though said more feedback would be helpful, owing to having a child with communication difficulties.

A parent who takes and collects their child remarked: 'I am really impressed by the older students, by their behaviour, conversational skills and independence – they are fine young adults.'

Another gave a heartfelt comment on her son's change of attitude: 'He sings every morning now as he gets ready for school. He was bullied in mainstream primary where the others didn't understand him but now he has friends – they're on a level playing field and all in it together. It feels less cruel.'

Entrance: 'A well-kept secret' was how a parent described Centre Academy after their child attended three primary schools, was home-schooled and they had visited 15 potential secondaries. The in-school assessment which stretches over two or three days was praised: 'It's a bit like a marriage – it's so important that each side knows what they're signing up for', said a relieved parent who described feeling 'extremely lucky' to find this school. Another's entrance was helped by her son's clinical psychologist at CAMHS (Child and Adolescent Mental Health Services) writing that he wouldn't cope in mainstream, stressing the need for a small special needs school. For one it was not about choosing between schools but between home-schooling and Centre Academy because their child's mental health was most important. One family had a 20-mile commute but has since moved to Wandsworth after their son said, 'I fit in here'. Another child had managed only three hours a day in an SEN unit of a mainstream secondary whereas he's full-time at Centre Academy and, from having LA transport, now makes his own way to school by bus.

A couple of students join in year six, to help with their anxiety about changing school. A further nine or 10 join in the combined years seven and eight, while others can enter later if places are available. One mother told us that prior to diagnosis with Asperger's Syndrome her daughter was at an independent academically-selective mainstream – she started secondary and hit puberty and depression. Now she tells how school is helping her rewrite her narrative: 'she's extremely bright but she's doing six rather than ten GCSEs and has a great group of friends who are direct and authentic with a joyousness about them, whereas she had no friends at all at her last school.'

One child, offered a place in September, was refused local authority funding so did a term in mainstream before becoming a school refuser; following a successful appeal to the SEND tribunal he started here. 'It took five-to-six weeks to get him back to where he had been when he came for his assessment, gradually, one or two lessons at a time,' head says.

Exit: Dr Rollo: 'What we want for each student is a pathway and that they know where they are on that path.' From the most recent leavers, all those who wanted to go to university did so, while others started apprenticeships and one left for a gap year. Dr Rollo steers students towards universities where school thinks they will cope, often to four-year courses which include a foundation year. He talked of one student who, he felt, could have done anything, choosing photography and he showed us with pride and pleasure his award-winning photographs.

Money matters: £27,600–40,800 pa. The majority are local authority (LA) funded, a third now by Wandsworth plus eight other LAs.

Remarks: This school especially suits those who are debilitated by anxiety, who will benefit from the almost individual attention and support and come to thrive in this secure, small-school environment where they will be well looked-after. For some – bullied or ostracised in mainstream – it's also a place where they can first experience friendship.

The Dominie

55 Warriner Gardens, London SW11 4DX

020 7720 8783 | info@thedominie.co.uk | www.thedominie.co.uk

| Independent | Ages: 6–12 | Pupils: 31 | Fees: £28,050 pa |

Principal: Since 2007, the hugely experienced Anne O'Doherty BA Dip SpLD Dip Montessori. Previously co-ran Kensington Dyslexia Centre, has taught at The Dominie since 2001. A potent combination of charisma, expertise, approachability and good sense: you can see why she is called 'inspirational'. Loves theatre, music, dance and reading. Parents can make an appointment to see her at any time to discuss their child, plus termly parent-teacher meetings and reports. Organises annual drinks party for parents and staff, enthusiastically described as 'the best parent party in London'.

Secret weapon is Maisie the cairn terrier, who multi-tasks as school dog/school mascot/alternative school counsellor and sometimes sits on parents' knees at their first meeting. Much in evidence during our visit until picked up by her dog walker.

Deservedly something of a legend in the dyslexia world, it is Miss O'D's understanding of what children coming to The Dominie need that sets her apart. She cultivates excellent communication and mutual trust with London day school feeders. Firmly on the side of her pupils, understanding that most have had a rough time. 'Anne really does look after each individual. She likes all of them in their different ways,' said happy parent report. Parents united about her genuine passion for rebuilding self-esteem in order to learn, and focus on turning around previously negative school experiences. 'My child is a different person, in all the right ways' is a not uncommon theme.

Entrance: School is focused on children with specific learning difficulties: dyslexia, dyspraxia, dyscalculia, dysgraphia, speech, language and communication and associated learning difficulties. Miss O'D takes children who will fit in with The Dominie way of working because they are the children for whom the school can make the most difference. Our instincts were confirmed that this is definitely not a school for children with more serious difficulties who need more help than it can provide.

Secret weapon is Maisie the cairn terrier, who multi-tasks as school dog, school mascot and alternative school counsellor

Entry process starts with phone call followed by initial meeting with Miss O'D. Parental expectations managed with assertive charm born of years of experience. Potential pupils undergo three day assessment and observation by teachers and therapists. Children seem to enjoy them and school is looking for potential and not worried about spellings at this stage. More interested in children's learning methods, approach to school work and crucial compatibility with existing peer group. If no place offered, and she understands that parents find this hard, Miss O'D explains her reasons and guides towards a more suitable school, providing some integrity for often traumatised parents.

Exit: Majority to mainstream schools like More House in Knightsbridge, Broomwood Hall, Bethany School and Thames Christian College, with learning support structure and good pastoral care in place. Some to more specialist environments to meet particular needs. Leavers are grateful for the difference that Dominie made and for believing in them and giving them the skills to move on.

Remarks: Classwork and homework are individualised and teacher/therapist to pupil ratio is high,

but no culture of ongoing one-to-one support. Maximum 32 pupils, who tend to stay three or four years, and class sizes about eight. Children are engaged, and some very outgoing and chatty, especially the girls we met. There seemed to be more girls than boys, but this changes year on year.

On arrival, children's levels are rich and varied. The aim is to raise each child to age-appropriate levels in spite of their spiky profiles common to SpLD. Innovative learning includes a much talked about specialist philosophy teacher and school Question Time for 9-11 year-olds three times a week, with support of speech and language therapy, to develop public speaking and comprehension skills.

All teachers are fully qualified and have additional dyslexia qualifications, with high quality teaching assistants who are generally graduates, supported by team of SLTs and very experienced physio Sally Wright, who works across classes on handwriting, posture for learning etc. You get the impression that they really know the individual strengths and weaknesses of each of the children.

Parents report that even by half term of the first term the difference in their child's learning, confidence and progress can be 'unbelievable, as the first thing they do is to work on the main cause of the child's learning anxiety'. There is no pretence that children will outgrow their learning difficulties, but focus is on teaching strategies, resilience and confidence. Children are taught tricks for learning times tables which are 'really functional and help them understand multiplication once and for all'. Teachers react fast to lack of confidence/enthusiasm observed or reported by parents. Home-school communication is good, and during parents' evenings they 'actually explain how our children learn'.

Therapy input works alongside class teaching without being intrusive. Most work is small group or whole class, with occasional one-to-one work. Clear acknowledgement that learning is hard for the children within the context of high but realistic expectations. It feels purposeful and organised. Lessons capture learning opportunities and develop working memory and processing speeds. One class was loving playing a game jumping on word meanings with their speech and language therapist. Children are given learning strategies to encourage them to progress as independently as possible.

Based in a converted shoe-polish factory in an affluent residential street near Battersea Park. Clever use of indoor space, but packed lunches have to be eaten in classrooms. Interior is bright and cheerful with pupils' artwork liberally applied.

School has been kept small, which parents and pupils appreciate. Flip side of this is no lunch hall or outdoor space, so possibly not suitable for very physical, energetic children. Daily play time and

Much enjoyed Christmas play written by the drama teacher where every child has a real part. Children were rehearsing with gusto

weekly sports afternoon in Battersea Park (three minute walk) dependent on weather conditions, but Latchmere Leisure Centre is the indoor alternative. Options include two cooking clubs, guitar club, drama club, and not one but two homework clubs for the older children to build up their stamina for working independently. Surely a dream for parents exhausted by the battle ground of homework. Much enjoyed Christmas play written by the drama teacher where every child has a real part. Children were rehearsing with gusto. Limited space in the school hall make this the hottest ticket in south west London.

Miss O'D is in charge of pastoral care and knows her pupils well. She and Maisie have a kindly, no nonsense approach. Effort and motivation wildly celebrated alongside progress and achievement. Praise is highly valued. Everyone has difficulties so no one is different. As it is a specialist school, children come from wide geographical areas, and play-dates are more likely at weekends. Parents have to make more of an effort to connect their children. Often extra staff training days are good opportunities for play-dates, but complicated for working parents.

The benefits of being a very small school generally outweigh any social and geographical disadvantages for the children. It is expensive, and many parents self fund. This is a self-confident school that knows its market. Parents are very supportive: 'Being able to go to The Dominie was like coming home for my child'. Many children achieve beyond what they, and previous schools, believed was possible. Many even learn to love reading, which says it all, really.

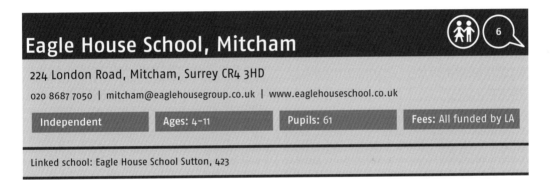

Eagle House School, Mitcham

224 London Road, Mitcham, Surrey CR4 3HD

020 8687 7050 | mitcham@eaglehousegroup.co.uk | www.eaglehouseschool.co.uk

| Independent | Ages: 4–11 | Pupils: 61 | Fees: All funded by LA |

Linked school: Eagle House School Sutton, 423

Head of education: Since 2016, Katherine Walker. Began teaching in mainstream primary and became increasingly interested in the learning of children with autism and how these children might be supported to lead a better life. She first joined the school as deputy head, becoming head within the year. 'I love seeing how we can help children of all abilities learn new skills and develop their individual natures, and start to become who they want to be.' Katherine is most pleased with the three learning pathways, developed to meet the broad range of ability in the school, and also the development of a new curriculum blending functional and academic learning, with therapists and teachers working collaboratively.

Academic matters: All follow highly adapted national curriculum that tries to link skills to life and looks for coherence rather than skills learned in isolation. Groups children by age and ability but each child has own specific objectives, with work differentiated to ensure an individualised approach within the group setting (maximum seven). Aims for a group emphasis and flexible thinking as these mirror the outside world, but offers one-to-one where appropriate. Tries to ensure lessons are multi-sensory and have an element of 'predictable surprise', with every lesson summarised using a memory board. ICT suite, plus interactive whiteboards in some rooms. One group of older children are working towards qualifications, with some life skills and functional learning.

Staff team includes two speech and language therapists, an occupational therapist plus assistant and two assistant psychologists. Speech and language sessions mainly integrated and used to help deliver literacy and numeracy as well as social and sometimes physical/motor skills. OT runs fun, engaging circuit activities designed to minimise the impact of sensory processing difficulties. Pot pourri of strategies, picks out best bits from a variety including: sensory integration therapy,

TEACCH, PECs, Makaton, social stories, drama and elements of SCIP (strategies for crisis intervention and prevention), aims to take a pro-active approach. Seeks to make school a dynamic place for both students and staff, saying they want people banging on the door, whether to work or place their child here. Keen to develop a nurturing, learning environment where everyone puts their best in and gets the best out. Doesn't force children to join in, but they always try something because curiosity gets the better of them.

Lots of staff training – mix of in-house and external expertise. Good male role models provided by the numerous men on the staff, parents unanimous that staff are genuinely enthusiastic and resourceful. One commented, 'They love my child as though he were a relative. They've given him a real sense of self-worth; they make them feel happy and secure. Not only is he happy with who he is – he has accepted his autism, likes the world and has good relationships with other people.'

Efforts made to ensure lessons are multisensory and have an element of 'predictable surprise', with every lesson summarised using a memory board

Games, options, the arts: Plenty on offer: riding, swimming, gymnastics sessions, football with Fulham FC, PE, plus relaxation as appropriate. High focus room and soft play area. Shakespeare for kids a regular event, plus annual creative arts week which includes belly-dancing, drumming, puppet-making etc. Christmas performance and sports day enable parents to share in and celebrate their child's achievements. Staff throughout the school tell stories – we sat in on a session with lots of animation, repetition, visual prompts, voice intonation and turn-taking. High-quality art work evidenced with some canvasses worthy of sale. Music via visiting specialist and therapist; dedicated music therapy room. Weekly Princess club provides craft and jewellery-making opportunities for the girls, boys' clubs tends to focus on team games, sometimes joined by children from local schools.

Background and atmosphere: Situated in a magnificent, Georgian, Grade 1 listed building, on a busy high street – somewhat incongruous in this area, but no cappuccino bars lining the permanently-congested thoroughfare: you can't get much more 'in the community' than here. Yet somehow the school, designed to keep anxiety levels down so children can think clearly, achieves

this with great aplomb. A rear playground, in need of an upgrade but providing enough space to run around or play on bikes, bounce on the trampoline etc. To the front, a well-thought-out lawned area with low-level activity equipment and space for contemplation. Younger pupils are taught in the adapted manor house, older ones in a sympathetically-designed school to the rear.

The school, the brainchild of Paul Conrath who, as an SEN lawyer, realised provision for ASD was limited, was founded in 2004 with a handful of children. Eagle House Group has grown steadily, adding sister schools in Sutton, Crouch End and nursery provision via the Little Group, currently seeking to build relationships with local mainstream schools.

Pastoral care, well-being and discipline: Good communication with parents seen as paramount – all have access to staff outside of school hours as well as during. Has started a termly 'get to know your teacher', very much guided by parents and providing opportunities to examine curriculum topics, plan activities for the term, plus socialise, have fun or even a good old moan. Home-school photo diary proving a great success – shows parents what's been happening at school and serves as visual prompt/reminder for the child. 'It's always so positive – even if he's had a difficult day, they don't blame him, but look to see how they can improve things for him.' Offers home visits to help work through strategies and give practical help. Recently worked with a child who was having problems dressing in the morning, now sorted; parents can relax and child comes to school happy and ready to face the challenges of the day. Family matters too – runs 'a day in the life of' for siblings. Tries hard with all, especially the little but important things – has managed to find a local barber happy to work with the school, encouraging youngsters to get their hair cut, and keen to foster good relations with other store keepers in the area.

All bring packed lunch; will help with heating food if required (this the only grumble from parents, who say it would be nice to have a dining facility). Uses snack time to reinforce the curriculum – we observed a session where youngsters were sentence-making to request a number of crisps, counting them out and, importantly, taking turns, communicating and learning to be patient and mindful of others.

Pupils and parents: From across the social spectrum and a range of London and outlying authorities (1.30pm finish on Friday helps with travel issues). Recognises every parent is different, operates an open door policy aiming not only to meet parents' needs but where possible their wishes too. 'Sometimes seemingly small things create anxiety.

One child was finding it hard to understand that his granny was going on holiday, so we created a social story.' One parent told us, 'My child had a terrible experience at his previous specialist school – he had become aggressive and uncooperative. Within weeks of his placement here we not only got our child back but, by half-term, he was so calm we managed a family holiday.'

Entrance: Pupils are aged 5-11 and have a primary diagnosis of autism; some additionally diagnosed with ADHD, dyspraxia or dyslexia. All pupils have an EHCP and are local authority-funded, coming to Mitcham in Surrey from 15 authorities. Most are brought by an LA funded school bus or taxi, with several sharing transport.

Children are assessed by both a home visit and a school one if currently in education, and also by a trial visit to the school. Part of the assessment involves looking at the existing peer group, to fit each child in the right space.

School does not usually cater for those with oppositional defiant disorder (ODD) or pathological demand avoidance (PDA).

Exit: Two-thirds of leavers continue on to Eagle House Sutton secondary school.

Remarks: A well-trodden path to this beautiful Queen Anne mansion is a mainstream start, followed by failure – on a scale varying from one child sent home each day after 40 minutes, to another being told he had the devil inside. There follows a period while a tribunal is sought if the local authority declines placement, aided by Eagle House not only visiting the current setting but offering in-school assessment which, if appropriate, shows the difference in how the child's needs can be met. Most parents who prepared for a tribunal found their local authority settled before the date, but not all.

Eleven classes each have four to six children, a teacher and three assistants; pupil capacity of 60 is matched by an equal number of staff. Children start in reception (no nursery), with only a couple aged four in early years.

The range of abilities is wide, with three learning pathways corresponding to 'extended P levels' (performance attainment targets for pupils working below or within the standard of the national curriculum): blue for those non-verbal with fleeting attention and with toileting needs; green for those becoming more verbal; and orange which is closer to the national curriculum for those with high-functioning autism but who often have anxiety.

The day starts with breakfast – helpful for those who left home early for a long journey to school. All sit, say hello and tell how they feel, using the school's four coloured 'zones of regulation': blue for low, tired; green for calm, ready to learn; yellow for happy, perhaps with some anxiety; red equals on the way to a meltdown; facial-expression cards are used by non-verbal children. Walker says these colours work well, giving school the chance to see who needs help. Children are taught to ask 'What do I need to help regulate myself?', choosing from a range of weighted jackets, breaks, or a sensory circuit. Staff know what each likes best from their pupil profile.

Tries hard with the little but important things – has managed to find a local barber happy to work with the school, encouraging youngsters to get their hair cut

All bring packed lunches (which can be heated at school), eaten together around a horse-shoe table, so lunchtime is another opportunity to learn social skills, such as using cutlery. In the emerging-verbal group we saw one boy with ear-defenders, another who rose between mouthfuls to dance around the room, returning to offer the TA a share of his lunch; afterwards the work was on teeth-brushing, choosing from a range of flavoured toothpastes so each child picks one they can tolerate. Occupational therapists run a weekly 'fun with food' session where children with restrictive diets can be referred.

Positive Behaviour Support (PBS) is key: what behaviour is wanted, rather than what is not. As behaviour is a form of communication, if it's inappropriate children are taught how to replace this with more suitable options, practising in a calm atmosphere, not when having a meltdown.

PODD (Pragmatic Organisation Dynamic Display) is the main communication tool rather than the frequently used PECS (Picture Exchange Communication System). PODD, initially developed in Australia for those affected by cerebral palsy, is a pictorial system used with language, a way of organising words and symbols in a communication book; the books show question words plus people, home, school and emotions, which the children become adept at flipping through.

Eagle House primary is a member of and accredited by the National Autistic Society. The Autism Education Trust framework is used for all, designed to support staff in identifying learning priorities and measuring progress. Staff communicate with a cluster of special schools, not only to share best practice but also to moderate learning levels.

The majority of the pupils are boys with circa 10 per cent girls, for whom there is a girls' club, which included an outing where the female deputy head took the male driver's place. Early-onset puberty was mentioned as an ASD trait so school teaches pupils how to handle such changes with dolls, before it happens.

The school environment is clearly well thought-out: pegs have visual labels, designed both for recognition and to reduce anxiety by removing choice. Children have visual timetables as a reminder and a reassurance – Velcro-backed laminated photographs of all children and staff can be placed and moved within the coloured zones. For the handful of students needing one-to-one support there is a separate block including a 'break-out' space, the latter repeated throughout the school. The IT suite is equipped with protected screens and blinkers around each workstation; the children are taught internet safety.

School will use physical intervention only if necessary; one mother, describing how her son can run off and endanger himself, spoke approvingly of the minimum necessary force used, saying her son understood why, that he knows who is in charge, and gets on well with staff.

A pleased parent told of the weekly trip to the supermarket where her son buys groceries for his cooking lesson and has learned not only how to pay the bill himself but also necessary road safety involved.

Housed in a stunningly beautiful 1705 Queen Anne Grade I listed building, with eight–foot–high doors (apparently to accommodate lofty wigs of the day)

Teachers are all qualified and TAs benefit from a comprehensive training programme. A mother of a six-year-old, recalling that her local authority wanted to place her non-verbal son in a mainstream base despite his difficulty coping in large groups, says he still struggles in crowds and if out of routine but that Eagle House is helping. Now he can have a small conversation and he is excelling at maths. He still has a meltdown on some mornings but school is working on this, for example his class teacher made a social story to help with the change of routine a holiday brings.

In-house therapists are assigned to classes where activities are jointly planned, delivered and assessed with teachers. The team consists of two-and-a-half speech and language therapists, two occupational therapists and a part-time music therapist. Occupational therapy makes use of a swing room, which also contains what looks like a mangle

– a squeeze machine loved by the children – plus a sensory room.

A part-time music therapist visits. An older boy wrote to the head that he'd like to teach younger children to play the guitar but that while one of the guitars was good, 'the other is rubbish, so could we have a new one?' The result was that we saw two newly-arrived guitars, in kit-form, being assembled by the boys with their class teacher.

Outside are two play areas with soft surfaces, a safe spring-less trampoline, trike and basketball areas plus a marvellous climbing frame and a spinning seat, used both in staggered break times and for therapy.

Activities include swimming, cycling, riding – even if it takes that half-term to don hat and sit on the horse. Clubs include trains, authors, dance, music, arts and a girls' club, all within the school day as journey times and transport-sharing preclude after-school activities.

Housed in a stunningly beautiful 1705 Queen Anne Grade I listed building, with eight-foot-high doors (apparently to accommodate lofty wigs of the day) the school, now incongruously surrounded by busy Mitcham roads, started here in 2004. Walls are lined with photographs of the children's activities and work produced in conjunction with a local artist who visits regularly.

Uniform is casual: yellow polo shirt and trousers, with an even more relaxed version for those with sensory issues of T-shirt and tracksuit trousers.

The school council is elected from all ability streams and the opportunity is taken to teach democracy, using ballot boxes, to make clear that every voice matters.

Staff include a parent liaison officer and a parent support officer; it is not uncommon to learn that staff had children in the school – as one said, 'I liked it so much I came to work here'.

Each child has a home-school book, read on arrival at school, written in before leaving. The therapy team runs a series of seven weekly 'getting started' workshops covering communication, feeding, gaining attention, sensory issues, play and independence. We met staff who had just been to the home of a child having difficulties with transport. Parents told of school advice they had found useful, such as how to talk to their child to encourage communication.

Reports record achievement levels and for a child's annual review detailed accounts are written by each therapist involved. Parents, remembering previous traumatic annual reviews in mainstream, tell how at Eagle House these reviews are happy, sometimes tearful occasions, as they discuss their children's progress. One mother, speaking of her eight-year-old son, said 'I had no idea he had that much ability in him. We used to cry every day and had no hope. Within a term, just a term, he flew:

attention was much better, speech started coming in and, for the first time, he held a pencil.' She described how previously in mainstream he would arrive home stressed but that she sees the results of him learning to cope in his new environment and now he can read and write and is relaxed at school – 'a boy who couldn't hold a pencil!'

A father of another eight-year-old told how his son's mainstream school reported that he had no reading, writing or apparent comprehension – 'yet we thought he could read but was unable to express himself. Now he had a reading age of twelve and a vast general knowledge. Previously when stressed he was made to suppress that distress, now he's learning to express and deal with it. You just won't learn if you're under great anxiety. He's now developing his interests, talking of wanting to save animals and asking what he will need to do to succeed in that – all born out of managing anxiety.'

This school is run by people who know what it's like to have an autistic child, where children learn self-regulation, without which they previously failed to thrive. A parent whose child travels 21 miles to the school says 'When he started, he knew nothing: he didn't speak more than 'yes' and 'no'. Now I can't believe the change: he is reading and writing and we have conversations about what work he's doing and what he likes.'

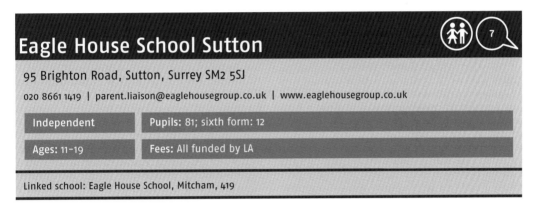

Eagle House School Sutton

95 Brighton Road, Sutton, Surrey SM2 5SJ

020 8661 1419 | parent.liaison@eaglehousegroup.co.uk | www.eaglehousegroup.co.uk

Independent	Pupils: 81; sixth form: 12
Ages: 11–19	Fees: All funded by LA

Linked school: Eagle House School, Mitcham, 419

Head of education: Since February 2018, Francesca Arocas. Qualified as a primary and early years teacher in 2000, training in a mainstream primary with an unusually large percentage of children with autism and moving with this cohort from nursery through reception and year 1. Then on to work in an all-though special school as teacher, key stage leader and deputy-head where 'there was nothing we didn't learn'. However, she hadn't trained in autism so an MA followed, from the 'huge motivation' of having her own autistic son. 'Many of the senior leaders have autistic children, including the owner, yet with different experiences as each child is different.' A short spell with the Priory Group ended with her realisation that she wanted to effect change more quickly than she thought possible in a large organisation.

Trim, short-haired and keen-eyed, Arocas is energetic and purposeful. Parent consensus is that she has put together a strong team and turned the school around.

Academic matters: Pupils have a primary diagnosis of autism, with an increasing number of co-morbidities such as mental health issues, ADHD, dyspraxia, dyslexia, Tourette's and some with medical conditions, for example epilepsy.

A wide range of ability is accommodated in classes for a maximum of six pupils. Pupils are grouped according to key stage, ability and peer group.

Each pupil has an individual pathway planned up to leaving age and beyond to 25. There are three pathways – sensory, middle and upper. The sensory pathway is aimed at pupils who will always need to be fully supported and would not be expected to live or work independently. In the middle pathway pupils are semi-supported, having a degree of independence in education, living skills and work placements but always requiring some degree of assistance to access these. In the upper pathway pupils show a greater degree of independence and are expected to aspire to live independently, continue studying and have paid work without support; these pupils have developed self-awareness and self-regulation skills.

There is a huge demand for children with pathological demand avoidance (PDA) according to Arocas, so school is running a pilot nurture class for a group of four students, with five staff.

Along with national curriculum subjects, in KS4 school now offers a wide range of accredited courses including John Muir Award for conservation, DofE, Arts Award, sport leader, first aid, food hygiene, entry level qualifications, BTec and GCSE, taking the latter only when ready.

School uses the Autism Education Trust framework and the Ziggurat Model, so all the student's needs are considered and planned for. Accreditation is a stepped approach, where the steps can be as small as is necessary, including life skills accreditations, such as travel training.

The most recent Ofsted was 'only' good. Arocas said: 'I knew the school's then assessment system was flawed but now it marries closely with our accreditation system, we have a new leadership team and a holistic approach – for example, we have an individual plan for the student who is great at maths but lacks functional skills.'

A preferred communication tool is PODD (Pragmatic Organisation Dynamic Display); a means of organising words and images which they carry on from the primary school. Students can take PODD booklets with them on trips to communicate.

We observed a science lesson for four students taking the middle pathway, of slightly mixed ages (roughly year 11) all verbal and of similar ability, donning overalls and protective eyewear with two helpers and the teacher; one student left, accompanied by his LSA, to de-escalate outside so as not to disrupt others, returning 10 minutes later to join in a practical using a balloon, propeller, burner, matches and a kettle. The lesson lasted 30 minutes – 'We experimented and this lesson-length proved optimal,' Arocas said. All appeared engaged and to be learning, the teacher checking at the end which of the learning targets had been understood and met.

Strawberry Lodge encourages independence and living skills: worn PE kit doesn't get taken home to Mum but laundered by the students in the utility room

In another classroom we saw a maths lesson for four boys, teacher and two LSAs. Another LSA was working one-to-one with a boy transitioning in and out of the class, working on ending a negative cycle of attention-seeking behaviour by joining for the practical parts of lessons with which he found it easier to engage. The lesson work was to draw around their hands in order to make 'additional fingers' for counting more than 10, learning left from right, with help for those who find cutting difficult, and sharing the glue (or not, but not a problem if that didn't work out). Noteworthy was the atmosphere of calm encouragement: one wanted to be 'teacher' and asked to wipe the board – response: 'Yes, when the task is finished';

another completed his 'hands' and was told enthusiastically, 'Your mother will love that'. There were reward tokens as each pupil has a chart for a task achieved or well-tried. Even in this small class there was a range of abilities.

Classrooms are designed on the principles of TEACCH (Treatment & Education of Autistic & related Communication-handicapped Children), focusing on individual strengths to enable development of independent learning skills, support weaknesses and reduce stress. There's a central table for group collaborative work, set times for individual work at separate work stations facing walls or away from each other, and individual numbered trays of work. It's an individualised approach, even down to the seating, a mixture of sizes and designs, including wheeled balance ball chairs to meet sensory integration needs, a touchingly 'three bears' approach.

One parent, pleased her child's reading and writing were progressing well, remarked 'I had wondered how much school could offer academically but the students are so engaged in the learning that my son doesn't seem to realise he's being taught – and with a maximum of six to a class, the teachers really get to know the students.'

In addition to school's post-16 department, Strawberry Lodge opened in Autumn 2018 on a separate site in nearby Carshalton. A beautiful light space in a newly-converted church, it caters for a growing cohort of sixth-formers capable of greater independence and is a bridge between special school and the outside world. The Lodge started with 12 on the roll (11 from the Sutton site), has a capacity of 32 with more transitioning and is aspirational for younger students from the upper and middle-upper streams who successfully master techniques of self-control and de-escalation.

Following the successful set-up and running of school's in-house Café Bleu at Sutton, which provides not only lunches but cookery lessons and enterprise work experience – planning, budgeting, shopping, preparing, cooking and selling – the Lodge café aims for something similar. The Strawberry Lodge set-up encourages independence and living skills: worn PE kit doesn't get taken home to Mum but laundered by the students in the utility room; pupils were involved in the garden area mosaic-making and will be designing and making their own table and chairs (one is taking a carpentry course at Carshalton College). Safe use of online banking is a new life skill being taught and practised.

Strawberry Lodge offer students a mixture of improving GCSE maths and English, and taking supported BTec and Level 1-3 courses; four students at Strawberry Lodge were taking BTec sports, with others going out to vocational courses at Carshalton College and NESCOT (North East Surrey College Of

Technology), learning animal care, ICT, carpentry, mechanics, hair and beauty, as well as life skills.

With the Lodge open, there is room at Sutton for a home area in the sixth form centre where students practise life skills, such as how to put a duvet in its cover – certainly a skill worth having. The two full-time occupational therapists advise on skills such as using cutlery, dressing/choosing outfits, teeth-cleaning and handwriting.

Games, options, the arts: Half-termly 'challenge weeks' covering creative, outdoor, STEM (science, technology, engineering and maths), poetry, healthy lifestyle and international give students a challenging experience within their comfort zone. Recent activities included a 'Jackson Pollock' paint spray, drama, dance, music, art, and mud sculpture with the head challenging herself too, joining students in climbing.

There are weekly trips to an outdoor education centre plus an annual residential trip for all (spread over three weeks).

Large numbers take the DofE bronze award (school having two DofE leaders), plus there is a forest school described as 'an irresistible invitation to learn' – heading for the day into woodland using map-reading, to do maths around a campfire with charcoal, testing insulating properties of natural findings following classroom experiments, all of which Arocas uses to build resilience and stamina, plus skills in communication, self-control and tool-using.

A gym, although small, can accommodate a whole class (of six). Clearly, available money has gone not on the building but on equipment: weights, treadmills, step machine, cycle, rocker plus a circuit programme and accompanying music.

Outside space is limited but well-used for staggered play on the MUGA (multi-use games area) plus trampoline (spring-less for safety), soft space, balance and a climbing area, with wall-mounted PODD symbols.

Two music teachers lead half the school in the Trinity College Rock & Pop exam and the four school bands. 'Music is a language, as are the arts and drama and our students can use them on a level playing field,' says Arocas. One student's grade 8 pass was celebrated, as was another's grade 1 piano exam, an achievement for each. We saw a lower/sensory pathway music lesson for four students with a teacher and two assistants, the teacher using visual reminders: on the carpet were large named pictures, 'piano' then 'drums', then 'ukulele', 'singing' and 'goodbye'.

Thoughtful planning of an accessible range of art work. We saw an example of 'art and enterprise': each student made their own pack of cards, having four designs, of professional appearance for sale to parents and each was appealing – we would have

liked to buy them. Designs were produced across the range of ability, from hand-drawn, to coloured-in, or use of foam stickers, while some were made with a die cutting machine; a favourite was a 'Van Gogh' A3-size pasta picture, reduced to an A5 card. The music in the art room certainly made us want to stay in such a welcoming, creative environment.

There is a forest school with map-reading, maths around a campfire with charcoal, testing insulating properties of natural findings following classroom experiments

Friday afternoon and lunchtime clubs give opportunities to pick from music, drumming, yoga, zumba, drama, ICT, art, photography and board games.

Background and atmosphere: The Ziggurat Method is the foundation, starting immediately on entry: is breakfast needed, or talking, energy-release or calming, an independent teaching task or sitting and reading? It's an individually-tailored approach.

We admired the lovely Victorian front of school, less so the Portakabins behind – yet one student told how he doesn't like the old, preferring the perfectly straight walls of the new and another's parent told how it benefited her son to have fresh air while moving between classrooms.

Uniform is a royal blue sweatshirt worn over a polo shirt, usually but not rigidly enforced – we saw one student without socks and another wearing his favourite wellies, while a third was out of uniform but not prevented from accessing education, rather receiving continued encouragement to conform. Staff now asking to be identified with school are looking to wear a similar uniform with a white logo on blue.

Pastoral care, well-being and discipline: 'Punishment doesn't work', says Arocas, 'Positive Behaviour Support does'. We twice saw a student struggling to cope and the situation being well-handled using Team Teach techniques, described as 95 per cent de-escalation, five per cent containment, with the latter not necessarily a restraint, it can be a support in self-regulation.

A parent described how the previous year her son had been with impeccably-behaved peers but this year some had challenging behaviour – and that he was now doing even better, being the quiet one, realising he can choose not do the same or be a ring-leader, not be an alpha male. 'He's learned more about self-regulation and his own boundaries from being with others; he needs strong boundaries. The staff know the children so well, they mix and change them round, according to need.'

Regarding exclusions, some are temporary, where there is a debrief and a student returns; permanent exclusion is rare, having happened twice to ensure the safety of the other pupils. One student told us that school is 'friendly but demanding, with high expectations'.

On the day of our visit, a student was diagnosed with diabetes and the school's family support swung into action, preparing a social story so that the child would go home at the end of school with resources explaining the new necessary daily routine.

Pupils and parents: Communication with parents is by home-school books, emails, telephone calls, annotated memory books, the annual review and end-of-year report plus two parents' evenings.

Local authority transport brings the majority by bus or taxi but we spoke with two families who chose a half-hour walk or a train journey, because it was enjoyed, as both a good time to spend together, helping a sense of wellbeing and a daily opportunity to see the LSA.

Some travel independently to an off-site college, work experience or Strawberry Lodge.

Entrance: All have an EHCP and enter via the SEN department of their local authority. After the initial paperwork has been completed, the current school (if any) is visited, followed by a 1-3 day 'sit-in' at school to assess suitability. Of the last intake of 22, only seven moved up from the group's junior school, Eagle House Mitcham; the rest are from other special or mainstream schools. Often pupils joining are older than 11, following the breakdown of mainstream placements and a time out of school.

Prospective parents can visit on twice-termly open days, with students in situ, for a tour with the head, parent liaison and therapists present. If a place is deemed appropriate but a local authority doesn't agree funding, some parents then prepare for SEND tribunals.

Those entering the two post-16 departments are mostly moving up from the school but there is external intake for years 12-14 where students attend full-time with a mixture of local college and in-house courses in English, maths, PSHE, life and living skills and work-related learning.

Students with profound and multiple learning difficulties would not be suitably placed here, while the school's facilities preclude those with some physical difficulties.

Exit: Last year there were no NEETS (Not in Education, Employment, or Training), with leavers heading for colleges (both mainstream and special needs), apprenticeships and work.

School facilitates work experience for all students both internally – the cafe or in head office administration – and externally in local garden centres, riding stables, salons and charity shops.

Both upper and upper-middle pathways now have the opportunity to stay for sixth form at either Sutton House or Strawberry Lodge, with students supported in their transition to Carshalton College and NESCOT.

Money matters: EHCP-funded by 14 local authorities (plus one from overseas).

Remarks: Unusually, school now covers the whole autistic spectrum, including PDA. A comprehensive range of therapists and teachers emphasise the acquiring of self-awareness and then self-regulation, to enable learning both of life skills and academics. Would suit those able to cope with moving to and fro between classrooms and to flourish in this can-do atmosphere.

Orchard Hill College of Further Education

Old Town Hall, Woodcote Road, Wallington, Surrey SM6 0NB

020 8254 7820 | enquiries@orchardhill.ac.uk | www.orchardhill.ac.uk

| Independent | Pupils: 350 |
| Ages: 16-25 | Fees: All funded by LA/EFA |

Head of college: Since 2015, Ashley Jordan-Diaper BA MA PGCE. Ashley has more than 20 years' experience of teaching in a variety of special schools and colleges. A personable and articulate man with lots of energy, commitment and a pioneering spirit ideally suited to the college. Parents, students and staff have all given excellent feedback: utterly wonderful and a great leader, a group of parents told us. Others highlighted his continued openness, care and support to improve the college. He also works at Chelsea football club on match days and has been coaching at the club's foundation disability project. In his spare time he enjoys entertaining party-goers playing music with his band. He lives in Thames Ditton with his wife, a social worker, and two daughters, one at university, one at secondary school.

Dr Caroline Allen OBE is the group principal of the academy trust. She maintains a strong presence within the college and gets to know the students through her monthly tea parties where students are presented with achievement awards.

Academic matters: Orchard Hill is a non-residential college offering a range of full and part-time courses for young people from 16 to 25 with a range of learning difficulties and/or disabilities (LDD). Students who attend full time mainly have profound, complex and severe LDD needs which may include physical difficulties, communication disorders and/or challenging behaviour. The college has a specialist unit based in Carshalton for those with autism spectrum disorders; learners follow vocational progression courses in partnership with Carshalton and Kingston FE colleges. Alongside the vocational courses, learners follow accredited qualifications in English, communication and maths. Where appropriate, they complete accredited vocational and community awards. Full-time students are also offered a Building Skills for Independence course; we saw students enjoying a communication workshop about going shopping. Part-time students can attend accredited specialist work and traineeship programmes for entry and level 1 learners, which leads to supported employment and work within local communities.

Typically, courses are one and a half days in college and two and a half days in the workplace; students can choose to train in catering, hairdressing, retail, customer services, horticulture and media. Some have one-to-one support in the college, community and work related projects. Parents commented that the college is very good at progressing learners from one-to-one support to small group settings. We saw students engage well with tutors during their weekly session to update their individual learning programmes and visual timetables and discuss personal goals with tutors.

The college has an excellent record of helping learners to find jobs after completing courses. Students design and update their own interactive CVs. They use tablets or iPads to film group work and voice recorders as an alternative to making a written record of their work and activities. Life and work skills programmes are part of the daily routine: students are encouraged to develop community living skills and learn about health, well-being and basic first aid. Life skills programmes are based around a range of accredited and non-accredited programmes. Full-time students currently follow the Ascentis personal progress and development entry level 1 awards for core areas of study, part-time learners follow the employability award at entry levels 1-3 and level 1. 'My son is so proud of his certificates,' said a cheerful parent.

Full-time students are also offered a Building Skills for Independence course; we saw students enjoying a communication workshop about going shopping

Classrooms are bright and spacious with access to kitchens so students can learn to prepare their own drinks, snacks and lunches. Much interaction was evident between staff and students choosing recipes and making menus. Life skills curriculums include food hygiene, kitchen safety and preparing simple meals. There are also specialist programmes for older students who are preparing for assisted living schemes and community PA projects.

Specialist teachers and support staff help students who have specific additional learning support needs within literacy and numeracy, usually dyslexia or dyscalculia and English as a second language.

Games, options, the arts: Orchard Hill College and Academy Trust has become well known for developing and expanding community links and partnerships, working with more than 40 SEN groups across its campuses. Strong community links are central to the ethos and lead to students being able to access many additional facilities and activities. The model is so successful other local authorities are keen to work with them and set up similar good practice in their own areas.

Students who want to get involved in expressive or creative arts have a wide range of opportunities. The college has partnership links with all the big LDD performing arts groups in SW London: The Baked Bean Company in Wandsworth, Gary Mason Charity's percussion group and Sutton Mencap's drama and arts programme. Has set up a specialist cinema group at Brook Coffee House in Wallington, and a community choir with two local special schools in Kingston. For live arts or access to local leisure services, links have been developed with a number of specialist personal assistance schemes. This includes Nikkel support, Sutton Mencap and

Club Soda, a club run by people with learning disabilities.

In college, students can volunteer to help run the on-site shop, select films for cinema club, or join clubs for cookery, gardening, art and craft projects. A student told us, 'I like college as I have learnt to do things for myself and I can go out with people I know.'

There are great opportunities to develop sporting skills. There are links with Crystal Palace Foundation and Surrey FA for football, plus bespoke keep fit and swimming/hydro activities at Phoenix's Sutton, Camberwell and New Malden's Leisure centres. Each year, the college runs a festival of sport with other local schools and colleges and more than 15 specialist sport and heath groups assisting the day. Last year 350 students took part.

With their own allotment and polytunnels, students get lots of horticultural experience and sell their produce at local farmers' markets. Sensory gardens have been incorporated into smaller outdoor spaces in all centres. Visitors from other community groups are always welcome to run workshops; recently students have enjoyed learning about, playing and listening to Indonesian music and watching birds of prey, and had fun playing with furry friends from Battersea Dogs' and Cats' home.

The college has been particularly innovative in its approach to supporting students to maintain and develop friendships using social media from home and college. Share Spare is an internal social networking website, similar to Facebook, specially designed with an easy-to-use visual and read aloud format. Students can have their own page where they can put their photographs and send messages. There are tabs for jobs and employment, student forums and a radio station. All the centres link together on Fridays for the weekly Orchard Hill radio show, which is run and produced by students.

Being part of an academy trust has enabled the college to build on and extend the scope of community links. A number of Orchard Hill students link with pupils within its academy schools to enable more group activities, art projects and sports festivals.

Background and atmosphere: Orchard Hill Centre was established within Orchard Hill Surrey Hospital site in 1983. In 1987 it became a college and moved to new premises. Today it has five centres and 350 students. The centres are all non-residential; everything has been adapted and designed for young people who would not be able to cope in larger further education colleges. The college has developed and grown steadily in response to parental demand for community-based day provision. Orchard Hill is now part of a wider academy trust which aims to promote excellence for children and young people with SEN and other barriers to learning.

Strong community links are central to the ethos and lead to students being able to access many additional facilities and activities

Premises are well kept with welcoming atmospheres and friendly receptionists. The main centre is housed in the Old Town Hall at Wallington, the other centres are close by in Hackbridge, Carshalton, Kingston and New Malden. Orchard Hill has a partnership with the Peabody Trust and has leased the BedZed building in Hackbridge designed by the architect Bill Dunster, famous for his eco-friendly buildings. The buildings have won many awards for design and sustainable living and are particularly well known in Japan. The site has large gardens and a café which the students can use. However, because of its design, it is the only centre which is not fully accessible for wheelchairs. A further branch of Orchard Hill College has opened in Hillingdon.

Pastoral care, well-being and discipline: Each student has a health and well-being plan matched to their weekly timetable. A main aim of the college is preparing students for independent living and occupations. Parents say the pastoral care is excellent.

Inter-agency planning for independence means that each person has personal plans for home living, community and work, including visual prompts and checklists. They also have a Hospital Passport, a personal booklet containing information for medical staff in case of accident or emergency. Practical advice for travel, staying safe and what to do if there's a problem is provided through links with the police, local businesses and the Surrey Advocacy Group. Students are made aware of and taken to visit local businesses and take part in the Safe Havens scheme: where to go and ask for help should the need arise. Parents feel that the college does very well in helping to ensure student safety both in and out of college.

Specialist behavioural therapists help with challenging behaviour and where necessary referrals can be made to CAMHS or similar organisations. Staff, including administrative staff, attend professional training sessions to ensure skills are updated.

Pupils and parents: Students come from a range of backgrounds. Most are local families from south west London and Surrey with a few from the borders of neighbouring boroughs. Friends of Orchard Hill was set up to help parents support learners and encourage everyone to get involved in fundraising activities. The Friends group has helped to set up vocational resources and enrichment activities. They also support decisions for the future with transition fairs providing information on the options for young people with disabilities at 25+.

Entrance: From 16+ and 19+ most come from specialist state schools, a few from independent provision. The college likes students and parents to attend an open day or make an appointment to visit before completing the application form. Each applicant is assessed to see whether Orchard Hill has the right provision and which courses they will be best suited to.

Exit: Most students are supported to progress into supported living home schemes, community well-being activities and a range of work or voluntary

work placements. Job coaches and mentors can be provided through Access to Work and other adult support through the charity Balance. Occasionally some students move to residential colleges, St John's Brighton being a popular choice.

Money matters: Students are funded through local authorities and the Education Funding Agency.

Remarks: Students gain greatly in self-esteem, communication and confidence. Their life and educational skills improve vastly, with the majority of them moving on into the workplace and some to independent living. The college really stands out for its work in the wider community and the links it has made to enable all the young people to get a tremendous social and extracurricular life. A remarkable place delivering remarkable outcomes,

The Priory Lodge School

Priory Lane, Roehampton, London SW15 5JJ

020 8392 4410 | theprioryfodgeschool@priorygroup.com | www.priorychildrensservices.co.uk

Independent	Pupils: 72; sixth form: 30
Ages: 10–19	Fees: Basic fee £59,571 pa

Head Teacher: Since December 2016, Jane Straw. Originally trained as a music teacher but swiftly moved into specialist teaching, and a long career in SEND includes posts as interim deputy head at Kisimul School, Surrey; head of education at Cambian Southwick Park School in Gloucestershire; assistant headteacher at Cantonian High School Cardiff; and headteacher of LVS Oxford. Parents say she is hard working and dedicated to the pupils.

Academic matters: Pupils at Priory Lodge have varying degrees of autism and associated conditions; most are high functioning with mild to moderate ASD. The school can accommodate a broad range of cognitive abilities, the emphasis is on meeting the needs of individuals. Different pathways are created to suit each pupil and support them in reaching their personal targets and potential. While some study functional skills, others take GCSEs, BTecs and A-levels in the sixth form. Apart from modern foreign languages, a full range of subjects is offered although it varies depending on demand and the needs of a particular year group.

The school has 12 small classes of up to eight pupils – some are mixed age group, pupils are placed where they fit socially, emotionally and academically. The youngest class is for key stage 3, although it sometimes includes junior age pupils if they are able to fit in with the group. Each pupil has an individual timetable covering academic subjects, therapies and exercise. Multisensory methods and support strategies are embedded into the curriculum.

Sparkling new science lab with nice touches, eye-catching posters, anti-glare screens and pod chairs with tennis balls on the feet to stop nasty squeaking sounds on the floor. Well organised, light and comfortable classrooms with class rules and code of conduct clearly displayed. There are also single study and therapy rooms and two ICT suites. Homework is set although a flexible approach is taken by teachers as some pupils can manage this better than others. Homework club is optional which parents say is useful for those who are not able to complete school work at home.

The aim across the school is to work towards independence, avoiding the need for constant one-to-one supervision. Teachers are aware that what suits one pupil is not necessarily going to work for another, hence the individual approach. Parents report that the staff are flexible, with a good understanding of how to address anxiety issues and emotional problems as they arise.

Pupils told us they love the sensory room with swing chairs and soft lighting, it is a place to go when they want a movement break, are feeling anxious or just need somewhere calm and quiet. Sixth formers have a separate area with a kitchen where they can make drinks, snacks and relax.

Games, options, the arts: There are 40 different clubs to choose from throughout the week which run at lunch times. There are no after-school clubs as many children are collected by taxis and so are not able to stay beyond the end of official school day at 3:40pm. The school also runs a good variety of trips and outings all over London throughout the school year.

Pupils love the sensory room with swing chairs and soft lighting – a place to go when they want a break, are feeling anxious or just need somewhere calm and quiet

Reasonable sized outdoor area which has been recently refurbished to include a quiet area with seating, basketball/tennis/badminton courts, gazebo and an outdoor gym. An area has been allocated to the sixth form which can be closed off from the main recreation area providing further seating, a trampoline and table tennis. As with many inner-city schools, outdoor space is limited but has been made the most of. Sports on offer are cycling, swimming basketball and football – pupils can choose what suits them. There is a multi-purpose hall for indoor exercise and preforming arts. Sixth formers use the Roehampton sports centre and get the opportunity to go swimming at Putney Leisure Centre.

Art is a popular choice at GCSE – we saw a well-stocked art studio with good, colourful displays of the pupils' work. Exciting looking woodwork room – we were particularly impressed with the pupils who told us about what they were making and the equipment that they needed to use. Pupils were well versed and trained in health and safety when using large and sharp equipment.

Drama and music are both popular, with several students choosing to do the Performing Arts Award comprising music, drama and creative writing. Individual instrumental lessons can be arranged with private tutors. Largish cookery room for food tech, up-to-date equipment and delicious smells. Everyone follows 'skills for independent living' which includes cookery, everyday finances and using public transport. Some older students travel independently to and from the school by bus or via train to nearby Barnes station

Background and atmosphere: The school was purpose-built in 2010 in the grounds of the Priory Hospital, a secluded location neighbouring Richmond Park. Tucked discreetly behind security gates, the school has an efficient in-and-out driveway which allows for easy drop-off and collection by parents and local authority taxis. The design of the building is utilitarian with a modern outlook creating light and cheerful rooms neatly spaced along streamlined corridors.

Pastoral care, well-being and discipline: Well-being and happiness remain a top priority, the student well-being leader is on hand to ensure pupils get the support and therapies they need to manage any anxieties. Good communications are considered essential, parents, teachers and therapists all work together as a team. Every week there are thinker and worker awards and embedded across the school are its five values – fairness, teamwork, learning, independence and purpose. Staff teams meet regularly to discuss pupils' progress and EHCPs are regularly updated. Any deterioration in a pupil's behaviour is seen as a cause for concern to be investigated and resolved including through therapy.

Pupils are always encouraged to be more independent and take on small responsibilities; in turn this helps them build up confidence. They can get involved in a variety of roles throughout the school by becoming a student mentor, joining the student council or fundraising and charity projects.

Pupils and parents: Families come from all over London and surrounding counties, the school works with around 16 local authorities. Many of the pupils at Priory Lodge have managed well at junior schools; however when they move to secondary schools they are often not able to cope and become overwhelmed in these large and busy environments. So, although there are a handful of younger pupils, the majority enter the school from 12/13 years. Several parents have had quite a battle to get their children into a specialist school and are happy to have found a small, caring environment where their child can be happy, start to learn again and rebuild their self-esteem. Boy heavy – only around one-quarter of pupils are girls.

Entrance: A small number of primary school age children are included in the youngest class. Most

A haven for autistic children, particularly for anxious, emotionally fragile pupils with good underlying cognitive abilities

arrive from 11 years and upwards. The school will ask to see prospective pupils' reports, EHCP and any other relevant paperwork. Following this, if the school feels there is a suitable match, the pupil will be invited for a taster day. This provides a good opportunity for the pupil to meet teachers and therapists to ensure Priory Lodge is going to be an appropriate placement for their future education. Support is available for those with heightened anxiety issues who may require the type of therapies the school provides. The school is not resourced to support pupils who are violent or in crisis.

Exit: Pupils are advised on the most suitable future pathway for them, through targeted educational guidance and careers advice. A popular move is to one of the London further education colleges including the South Thames Group and Richmond College. Others choose apprenticeships, some go to Capel

Manor or Merristwood to do agricultural apprenticeships. If they are academically able, students go on to take university courses. Occasionally ones go to another specialist college in the Priory Group.

Money matters: Parents can self-fund, although most pupils are funded by their local authority. The school has autonomy over what they consider a generous budget from the Priory Group and is well resourced with good quality staff and equipment. Back up from the Priory Group is in terms of governance, management, marketing and sharing good practice within their schools. The high staff ratio and London location go some way to explaining the top fees, which can make it an expensive option for privately funded pupils.

Remarks: A haven for autistic children who have often had unhappy experiences in mainstream schools. The education, emotional support and therapies are carefully designed to fit around the individual. Well-organised and caring, the school can turn round the lives of vulnerable children and assist them on the road to becoming balanced young adults enabling them to make good life choices. Particularly good for anxious, emotionally fragile pupils with good underlying cognitive abilities.

Riverston School

63-69 Eltham Road, Lee Green, London SE12 8UF

020 8318 4327 | office@riverstonschool.co.uk | www.riverstonschool.co.uk

Independent	Pupils: 206; sixth form: 19
Ages: 5-19	Fees: £11,781 – £15,483 pa

Head: Since 2001, Mrs Sarah Salathiel (50s), who started as a PE teacher at Riverston 38 years ago shortly after graduating from Dartford College London, and has worked her way from the girls' PE teacher via various roles to become head. She still teaches PE and is a force to be reckoned with as she races round the school teaching, handing out awards and running assemblies, meeting with parents and now working on the 'Riverston Group', since the owners of Riverston School have acquired a second school in the north of England. Her husband, Phillip, is now the deputy head and SENCo. Her personal drive and determination must be a large part of the growing success of the school, of which she is fiercely protective – there are even

plans afoot to develop another school abroad. 'We were most impressed by the head – she sold the school to us,' according to the parent of a young boy on the autism spectrum.

Academic matters: The infant department is slowly being phased out. There will be no reception entry from September 2019; current children will continue through years 1 to 4, but eventually intake will be from year 5 only.

In the junior school the children move from an amalgamated class to separate year groups with some separate subject teachers (music, PE and French) and there are very small classes, which attract parents who want their children to have more individual teaching. There is evidence of purposeful teaching and real learning in all the junior school. We watched a class involved in role play and a freer style of learning than may be possible in larger classes. The junior school also makes much use of the outside space (perhaps having an ex-PE teacher as a head encourages this enjoyment of the external space and physical activity?) and there is an a forest school with its own wood hut for exploratory learning from nature. There is an influx of (mostly special needs) pupils at year 5 who move then to avoid having the stress of the year 6 exam entry into a secondary school. This lower entry point is also due to the fact that children are getting earlier diagnoses and assessments allowing parents to choose private special schools over mainstream primary schools.

The senior school feels more serious than the junior school, as appropriate. There is a much-needed full timetable for students, many of whom are not good at organising their own learning. There are several ability groups within each small year group, so students are taught at their own level. High expectations are evident from the fact that all the students have qualifications when they leave. There is a choice of 12 BTec subjects, as well as a reasonable range of GCSEs (including entry level where needed) – maths, English, science (science teacher keen to promote a move to separate sciences eventually for those who are keen), French, ICT, business studies, computer science.

School also caters for quirky types – one parent we spoke to said that the school has given her daughter space to be herself, with her own individual manner

In the sixth form the 20 or so students (half girls) see this a good stepping stone to prepare for further education or the outside world. Students are not expected to do private studying but are building their study skills and confidence. As well as A levels with almost one-to-one tuition, students get careers guidance, work experience (including in the school's own nursery), interview practice and life skills teaching such as transport and travel planning, cooking and money. Students also continue with additional literacy and numeracy. The sixth form is growing and one pupil has stayed on for a year 13+, something the school thinks will expand as the students may still not be ready to leave school at 18.

Games, options, the arts: Outside there are separate areas for the early years and younger junior school pupils with colourful equipment and wooden tables and a new playground for the senior school. Physical activity is promoted in the school and all the pupils partake in sports – football, netball, rounders, hockey, cross-country and athletics, with extracurricular rugby, karate, trampoline and dance. Competitive sports encouraged. Forest school takes place in a grass area at the front of the school or at the local park. Swimming at public pool for those in the junior school, with swimming club once a week for those who want to continue to pursue this activity. Sports leadership qualification is encouraged as an ideal practical course to help sportspeople to build towards a career.

Background and atmosphere: Riverston was started by Elizabeth Lewis, and continued by her son Michael Lewis and his wife who are the current owners and governors. There is a sense of history and continuity and tradition despite the fact that it has changed from a mainstream school to having a student body that now largely (80 per cent of senior school) has special needs. The building is made up of three large Victorian townhouses joined through in a slightly maze-like manner. Classrooms in this part of the building are small and inevitably feel like being in a bedroom or sitting room – cosy for the junior school students. There are more modern extensions and additional buildings perched on the side for senior school classrooms – science labs, libraries, a modern kitchen. Teenagers in uniform slouch in common rooms, jumping to open the door politely for visitors. When you move round the school, it does not feel like a special needs school – routines very much like in any school with students waiting outside classrooms to be let in for lessons, moving around the school chatting and laughing. Only the very small numbers in the classes and the differentiated groups give a hint of the fact that education is very much tailored to the students. The sixth form, now known as Riverston College, is growing apace.

Pastoral care, well-being and discipline: This is the selling point of the school – it has always had a reputation for good pastoral care and this has led to the school filling a niche market for those pupils who need more support than most. There are also regular multi-disciplinary meetings which give space for communication about individual children. Each child has a tutor and they are the point of contact first thing in the morning and after lunch. They check on homework and personal issues and are the first point of call for parents. There are subject teachers who attend the multi-disciplinary meetings together with therapists. This is the heritage of a small school when

A wide range of subjects is taught but they make it achievable. There's a very full timetable and all take qualifications; school ensures that each child has a bespoke education

communication would have taken place in the staff room; it is gradually changing to more formal systems of communicating as the school grows. One parent we spoke to felt that the head did not delegate to teachers and that all decisions had to go through her – it can not be easy working for a husband and wife leadership team, with a husband and wife ownership team, but it does mean that the school has a strong sense of direction.

Pupils and parents: The school has more than 200 pupils, of which two-thirds are boys. It has a mixed intake of local pupils whose parents choose this independent school over their local primary – partly perhaps because they have a nursery and extended hours are possible. Quite a few pupils are not native English speaking (20 EAL pupils) and from a refreshing mix of ethnic and social backgrounds. The upper school has increasing numbers of special needs pupils – about 50 per cent of the whole school, and 80 per cent of the senior school have EHCPs and their places are paid for by local authorities.

Around 50 per cent of pupils are on the autism spectrum. Pupils are mixed also in terms of ability – and there is a range of pathways for different needs. School also caters for quirky types – one parent we spoke to said that the school has given her daughter space to be herself, with her own individual manner. The sixth form is still very small, but with its own space and growing need, this is beginning to attract pupils who do not want to go to larger sixth form colleges and appreciate the individual care and support they get here. 'Most of the kids are very nice' was the comment we got from pupils.

Entrance: Very flexible – the school says it welcomes visits and is aware that the experience needs to be kept comfortable for both parents and pupils. In our experience, it is necessary to speak directly to the head if you want to arrange a visit. If the school feels it can provide, the child is given a three day trial assessment – or up to a whole week if necessary. In particular, school looks for behaviour it will not be able to manage in order to protect the existing cohort. Staff work hard to explain and justify to parents (and, as required, by local authorities) exactly why they cannot take any child, and will

make suggestions of other schools that might be a better fit.

There will be no reception intake in September 2019, no reception or year 1 in September 2020, and so on until the school will admit from year 5 only. Nursery and pre-school will continue.

Exit: Pupils leave from the junior school to local secondary schools, and some leave the senior school to go to local mainstream schools (Kent grammar schools or local state schools). On the whole the pupils with special needs stay on as long as possible – hence the sixth form which even has a year 13+. The last years of senior school are preparation for further education or employment. In the main pupils go on to further education – eg Eltham College, Greenwich College – or on to apprenticeships. Employment helped by sixth form careers guidance and two weeks' work experience. Work links with local nurseries, the Co-op or with Greenwich Council. In 2017, three-quarters left after year 11 and 30 per cent after year 12. Others went to the University of East London and Greenwich University, with one off to Rice University in the US to study business management and economics.

Money matters: Pupils who have special needs, and an EHCP, have their fees paid by local authorities. Fees for mainstream pupils are paid by parents. The school says that money is stable now that so many students are paid for by local authorities, with regular income and the steady growth in student numbers. But this is a private school and accounts are kept private too. There is a dedicated financial director as well as a director who is responsible for appraisal. The head is on the board of governors too, so this is a close knit arrangement. That may be to the school's strength and has clearly allowed for 90 years of continuous growth.

Remarks: This would be a good school for a child who wants to be in a cohort of understanding children with learning differences. The school has high expectations – very full timetable, all take qualifications, wide range of subjects taught – but they make it achievable by ensuring that each child gets a bespoke education. Very small classes at all sorts of levels of ability, a good amount of therapy and extra support, counselling, drama and pastoral care. Large enough to have the feel of a mainstream school – assemblies, mentoring between years, prefects etc – but small enough to give each child the support they need. A real ethnically, socially and ability mixed London school for the child who needs a little more attention.

Spa School

Monnow Road, London SE1 5RN

020 7237 3714 | headteacher@spa.southwark.sch.uk | www.spa.southwark.sch.uk

State	Ages: 11–19	Pupils: 100

Head: Since 2006, Simon Eccles (50s). He has developed this school in a quiet and gentle way, making it a haven of calm for pupils with a diagnosis of autism. It has grown in size since he has been there, and a new sister school in Camberwell is in development. He trained in Australia (primary diploma in teaching) and then moved to the UK where he first taught at a primary school in Tower Hamlets, working with children with EBD while studying for an MA in psychoanalytic psychotherapy at the Tavistock Clinic. These developed his interest in special needs and autism and he worked for four years at Bridge House, a state school in Islington, where he ended up heading the autism provision in Islington. In order to develop what was becoming his specialist area of interest, he moved to TreeHouse School, first as a senior teacher and then rapidly becoming head.

His time at the school has seen improvements both in its buildings and facilities, and in the quality of the teaching and monitoring. He is self-effacing and no publicist, but well able to plug into the many wonderful resources London has to offer, getting involvement of others: PWC pays for pantomime tickets each year, the Oval hosts their cricket lessons, Millwall their football training, the Globe their theatre outings. He is clearly enormously engaged and proud of the school, and well loved by all the pupils, who spoke fondly of and to him. Parents said they can contact him at any time – 'no restrictions' – and they know their opinions and concerns will be dealt with respectfully and effectively. A down to earth, practical head, cycling to school, joining in all school events, visiting classrooms daily and setting an example to both pupils and staff of gentle, purposeful action.

Academic matters: The head has a deputy and four assistant heads who meet daily, and the assistant heads monitor planning of learning objectives and teaching, giving training and development points to teachers – creating, head says, 'a constant emphasis on improving the quality of teaching and learning'. Teaching assistants stay for daily after-school meetings so they can all review lessons and make plans for the following day. These systems help to ensure that teaching and learning are effective and the pupils are getting the benefit of lessons that have a clear focus.

IEPs have three goals – communication, independence and aspirations – and pupils also have weekly targets in literacy, numeracy, reading and speaking and listening. Small classes of between six and nine pupils, several with individual teaching assistants, ensure that learning matches a child's ability. This is further enhanced by having vertical groupings according to needs rather than age. One tutor group was for girls only when we visited – 'It worked better for them that way' – but no hard and fast rules: the pupils' needs lead the teaching and organisation, rather than the other way round. Parents said, 'It is really inclusive, no child is left out, they all do the same lesson but at different levels'.

School will take pupils with complex and challenging behaviour because the sensory and visual support here can help so much

Each day starts in the tutor group – so that if a child arrives late, they are not rushing between classes – making sure everyone knows the plans for the day with plenty of visual timetables and visual cues. Maths in the morning, then a lesson followed by a break, then a further hour's lesson followed by lunch. This means not too many room or subject changes, reducing transitions and thereby reducing stress levels. Even lunch time is structured – half an hour eating time (most children have lunch cooked on the premises in the canteen) and then half an hour for clubs or set activities. After lunch there is half an hour reading and shared attention time before afternoon lessons. As well as daily maths and English, there are science lessons in the science lab and computing in the IT lab (though this is not a school that relies on technology – newsletters sent in paper form, not emailed, parents phone rather than sending messages, limited use of voice activated technology, relying instead on PECS and Makaton). 'These pupils participate in games which are repetitive and safe, we want them to be involved in practical doing learning, not screen time'. Having said that, one of the students recently gained an Oscar in a national competition for a short film they had made.

There is an emphasis on communication and those skills are reinforced in lessons all through the day as well as having specific social communication lessons – how to stay safe, how to be polite, how to look at people when you are speaking to them, how to complete forms for independent living. Uses a benchmarking system to compare the progress of Spa School pupils against other similar level pupils and thereby ensure that Spa pupils are making better than average progress. Qualifications include ASDAN, entry level and foundation level accreditation. It is not unknown for pupils to take GCSEs – though it is not common – and the school can link with mainstream schools for teaching and exams. Students we spoke to said that one of the things they liked about Spa School was 'the chance to work and get levels', and parents also spoke about the 'steep learning curve' they observed in their children.

Games, options, the arts: There's a well planned playground with climbing equipment, a scooter path, covered sitting areas, a chicken run and raised vegetable beds, as well as a stream and generous grassed areas, fully grown apple and cherry trees, planted beds and a rambling vine. Not at all bad for a central London school. Space to be alone but safe, and space to run a little wild when you need to. We liked seeing pupils using the playground for their horticulture lessons, and kids collecting eggs from the chickens for the canteen or use in their cooking lessons.

PE popular with students we spoke to – and plenty of options for those who don't like team sports too. Cricket (at the Oval cricket ground), football, fitness (a generous suite for working out), BMX bike training, martial arts. Plenty of gymnastics, table tennis and trampolining in the school gym, trapeze in the local sports centre. Ballet Rambert involved in some dance workshops on top of weekly dance lessons. The need to stay fit has been emphasised recently at school while obtaining their Healthy School status, which means that pupils are aware of the need to eat healthily and also to keep active, and this new drive has pupils eating fruit at break time and doing more fitness work, with a consequent reduction in obesity. 'My daughter loves trampolining – not only in PE lessons but also at other times to use up some energy and to help her feel better'.

Drama important to help students gain confidence and hone speaking skills. Specialist drama teacher gets pupils to perform in end of term plays – whilst we were there pupils were acting as children during the Nazi occupation of France, where they were hunting out acts of kindness. Parents felt there was evidence of inclusion here too: 'even though my son is non-verbal and was reluctant, he has been in school plays, dancing and playing instruments'. Role play encouraged in weekly communication lessons as well as during drama classes – two drama studios, but also theatre trips as part of drama curriculum to the pantomime and the Globe, Young Vic and Southwark theatres.

Older pupils gain work experience in the School House Café in an adorable Victorian cottage adjoining the school, helping with cooking, serving and cleaning

Food tech in dedicated and well-equipped kitchen where we saw pupils tucking into chicken pizzas that they had made. This is a weekly class for the whole school as it also helps to encourage independence – how to use a knife, how to make a hot drink. Many pupils achieve food hygiene qualifications this way. Older years have their own common room and can use the small flat that helps to prepare them for independent living as well as preparing meals for them to eat at the dining table. These older pupils also gain work experience in the attached School House Café in an adorable Victorian cottage adjoining the school. Pupils get to help with cooking, serving and cleaning in this community café. Whilst enjoying a coffee there, we saw other local groups coming to have good food at reasonable prices and the general interaction between the pupils and the public is clearly of benefit to all.

The art room a well used generous space with a wide range of art techniques – we saw model making, ceramics, collage, painting and printing. We watched a class of boys totally immersed in the pinch pots that they were creating and decorating, and explaining how they intended using them. Design technology is mostly wood but also some plastic modelling.

Horticulture with specialist teacher, so pupils can grow vegetables for the school's café and gain further employment skills.

Weekly music lessons with keyboards and instruments – chances for performing in the weekly assemblies.

Background and atmosphere: The traditional red-brick Victorian building in a residential setting makes this feel like a community school. The solid feel, high ceilings and wide corridors create space and light, with room to breathe and spread out. The heart of the school may be the open plan library with sofas that is used in break times as well as for lessons. Classrooms have high windows which help keep distraction down. Enough wall displays to give information and share good work, without creating visual overload. Things feel controlled and orderly – everything immaculately clean, from the toilets to the dining room. Parents say that 'my child walks into school and feels secure. It is safe for him here'. And 'my child is happy to get on the bus to school and always says he has had a good day at school'.

Plans well on their way for a new school in Camberwell for 120 pupils from 5-16 years, to be run by the existing deputy head; there are also hopes for a new college for 19-25 year-olds to provide better value vocational training than currently available to pupils after leaving Spa School.

Pastoral care, well-being and discipline: Individualised teaching and learning possible thanks to small classes and high teacher to pupil ratio. Main emphasis on structured time – both inside and outside classes. Break out rooms available for students needing time alone as well as several sensory rooms. Large amounts of communication between the school and parents to ensure that issues dealt with very quickly. 'If something has upset my child, the school deals with it straight away, they sort it out and find solutions. For example, when my child found it difficult to go in to school with the other children, they agreed that he could go straight to the classroom a little later to avoid the stressful transition.' Phone calls a routine method of quick communication, but parents also appreciate the communication book 'so I can say how he has slept and to give some idea of his emotions'. All staff trained in restraint techniques, but mostly there is a great deal of respect between all the school community, and this feeds down to pupils, who know not only that they will be treated with care, but that they should treat others likewise.

Pupils and parents: There are 14 classes of six to nine pupils each. All locals, some 25 per cent white British, with a ratio of 80:20 boys to girls. A full-time family liaison member of staff helps parents to negotiate state bureaucracy for transport, funding, support and ways to work with their children, and also ensures good parent/school communication. 'They always help you out,' said one parent gratefully. Only one parental complaint in the last 10 years. We saw a parents' meeting to explain about a residential trip where parents were encouraged to voice their concerns. 'Our son, who had never been away from us, went on a two night residential last year and is happy to go again this year'. 'My daughter has gained confidence and has learned so much.' Parents said they feel the school keeps their children safe, and helps them to gain independence and communication skills as well as learning. 'They are so considerate' and 'they know each child really well and are so involved in their learning'.

Entrance: Pupils all have a diagnosis of autism and moderate or severe learning difficulties. All pupils have an EHCP and since the school is over-subscribed, pupils come from an ever-narrowing catchment area within Southwark. This reduces the need for transport for pupils and ensures a more local intake. The school says that 'Southwark is supportive and helps us choose 20 pupils from the 40 applications.' It will take pupils with complex and challenging behaviour because the sensory and visual support here can help so much. 'Often problems in behaviour are reduced once they come here, though if a pupil's main needs are behavioural, Spa might not be the right place.'

Exit: Almost none leave at 16; a few move on to mainstream Lambeth or Lewisham Colleges, or to specialist Orchard Hill or Aurora Centre, with plenty of help with transition. When pupils leave, they all have some accredited qualifications, and all will have had work experience in the School House Café next door.

Money matters: The school has a steady income from the LA and seems to manage its budget effectively, allowing for building plans and a high staff ratio.

Twelve governors, including ex-parents, help raise the profile of the school as well as actively monitoring and being helpfully involved.

The School House Café only covers costs as it is a community cafe, and the school does not do big fundraising amongst parents, who are not expected to pay for any extras – even clubs.

The school is expected to become part of a multi academy trust because it is opening a second school in Camberwell and hoping to open a college for post-19 students.

Remarks: Spa School is growing in reputation and size, thanks to really solid educational practice led by a calm and kind head. No gimmicks here but planned teaching, purposeful lessons and reflective teachers building on the quality of their teaching. This is paying off, with a school where pupils are safely moving forward and growing in independence, confidence and well-being. Teachers, parents and pupils are all well supported – that is why this is such a good school community. Clever Southwark to have nurtured this haven and no longer having to send these pupils out of borough.

THE GOOD SCHOOLS GUIDE

Moving abroad?

☑ Tickets

☑ Passports

☑ Visas

❓ Schools

Still need to sort your schooling?

Go straight to The Good Schools Guide International.

The first class guide to world class schools.

goodschoolsguide.co.uk/international

YES, IT'S A
CRYING SHAME...

...that she left it too late to apply for Hurtwood House because it's simply the best for acting, dancing, singing, film-making – "A utopia for creative minds" – as the Good Schools Guide says.

And crucially, this exciting school is equally successful academically. In fact, it's statistically one of the top co-ed boarding schools in the UK.

So, if you're looking for a really exciting and rewarding change of school at 16 – don't leave it too late.

Contact Cosmo Jackson or visit our website for more information.

HURTWOOD HOUSE

T: 01483 279000   E: info@hurtwood.net
hurtwoodhouse.com

City slippers – boarding schools for Londoners

Boarding, like sheep herding, polytunnelling and plume scrumpling, is something many Londoners assume to be a predominantly rural activity. Whether this adds or detracts from its appeal is down to the individual but boarding, especially weekly boarding, is an increasingly popular option. It's no coincidence that boarding schools whose yield per hectare, if not quite a match for top cash crops, comes close, hit greatest density levels within easy reach of London's top postcodes – no more than a sonic boom's echo from Heathrow or Gatwick.

Some families who have never before considered the idea of boarding wonder whether the bracing two-hour trek across London to and from that excellent day school (and in the dark both ways during winter) really is as character forming as they'd hoped. For such families, boarding can seem life-enhancing, making it possible for their children to start early and stay late with food and friends provided – and without a punitive journey at the beginning and end of the day

Full boarding

Most famous of the lot are Eton, Harrow, Radley and Winchester. While other schools have not just rolled over in response to parental requests for part-time boarding but also offered to juggle a couple of hoops with their front paws, there are no such concessions here. When boys-only full boarding for all has worked for centuries, you can't really blame them.

It's the same story for the girls at schools such as Downe House, Wycombe Abbey and Tudor Hall, which although they take a handful of day pupils are essentially full boarding in ethos. Parents who don't buy in to the idea of boarding the traditional way are gently – but firmly – advised to look elsewhere.

Weekly and flexi-boarding

Many schools make a virtue – and success – of combining education with what can feel like a large-scale bed and breakfast operation: some pupils day only, some there pretty much full time, others opting for in-school sleepovers because of parental commitments, exam revision, late night play rehearsals or early morning training.

Girls-only establishments offering boarding and day places within or close to the M25 include Woldingham in Surrey, Marymount in Kingston-upon-Thames and St George's Ascot to the south and south west, while the Royal Masonic School for Girls and Queenswood fill a similar niche north of the river. Boy boarders, meanwhile, can opt for St Paul's School, Whitgift or Dulwich College, though day pupils predominate at both.

Those in search of a co-ed environment are, if not spoiled for choice close to London, far from being deprived, with Mill Hill School in north London and, farther afield, Aldenham and Haileybury in Herts, Sevenoaks in Kent and Epsom College and City of London Freemen's School in Surrey, among others.

Schools for skills

Then there are the specialists – such as the Purcell School (music) and Tring Park (performing arts) – where boarding helps the super talented to hone their skills in and out of hours, free from tube strike blues and similar aesthetic lows; the different (eg St Christopher in Letchworth, set up by the Theosophists); and the new (flushed with the success of its first boarding house, Whitgift School, in the non-plush territory of south Croydon, is already mulling over a second).

Even costs don't necessarily need to be sky high if you opt for a state boarding school such as Cranbrook (selective), St

"Excellence is evident in all aspects of school life"
ISI Inspection 2018

Godstowe

An independent day and boarding school for girls aged 3-13 and boys aged 3-7.
An unrivalled academic reputation and non-selective entry.

Just minutes from the M40 in High Wycombe, Buckinghamshire

Girls can be full, weekly or flexi boarders from the age of seven, and enjoy school, clubs and supervised homework all under one roof.

Godstowe Preparatory School, High Wycombe, Buckinghamshire HP13 6PR
01494 529273 registrar@godstowe.org

www.godstowe.org

George's Harpenden (church-goers) or Gordon's (all-comers), where parents pay for accommodation while teaching comes courtesy of the ever-generous taxpayer.

For any dyed in the wool Londoners who come over all faint at the prospect of breathing air outside the congestion zone, no longer enhanced with flavoursome carcinogens, it's hard to beat boarding, literally, on your doorstep. Westminster School, with 185 or so boarders (including girls, admitted in the sixth form), is pretty much as close as you can get to total immersion in the beating heart of the city without squatting in Big Ben. 'You get that sense of community,' says a former Westminster parent. 'You have more time to get involved and people tend to stay late anyway.'

For some London parents, day places will always be the educational black, the only goal worth pursuing, with boarding the reserve choice when all other options have been exhausted. Others, relishing the out of hours opportunities, from extra tuition to drama, debate, music and sport, feel very differently. Costs permitting (and boarding is, undeniably, costly) it could well be worth taking a look at both.

For detailed information and reviews of the UK's best independent and state boarding schools, including those outside London, see Good Schools Guide Boarding Schools or visit our website (www.goodschoolsguide.co.uk).

Tutors and tutoring – a Londoner's view

Tutoring is endemic in the UK these days, and nowhere more so than in the capital, where the top agencies have parents queuing up to pay £80+ an hour to buy their child an advantage. They'd have you believe that without a tutor your toddler will miss the academic boat, but keep your head – there's still plenty of time.

Two is too early

Seriously, there are folks out there offering to tutor children as young as 2, but don't be taken in. Spend the money at one of London's wonderful bookshops and read to your child instead. What pre-school-age children need is not tutoring and angst, but time and love from the grown-ups who care for them. If you're reading this article, you are by default an educated, thinking parent who wants the best for your child, so give her the treasures of your mind, your vocabulary, your tastes; they will far out-class anything a tutor can provide.

A clear reason

When do you need a tutor? Put simply, when there is a clear and specific reason for using one. Your child may need help with the 11+ or 13+ entry to an academically selective senior school, particularly from a state school. Or perhaps he's struggling with a particular GCSE/A level subject. Or she may be falling behind at school. Or he may have missed school through illness or some other crisis. Where there is a known goal to work towards, or a genuine problem to address, tutoring comes into its own.

For a shy child who's underperforming, a friendly tutor can be a godsend. Free from the distractions of the classroom and other pupils, he or she can sit quietly with your child and concentrate solely on whatever's confusing her, filling in gaps in her knowledge and building up her confidence. Grades start to improve, and the child becomes a happier learner, keener to put her hand up in class and more relaxed about going to school. For a teenager who's struggling with maths, demoralised by always coming last in his set and stressed about approaching exams, quality one-to-one teaching from someone with no preconceptions about him can make the difference between failure and success; between giving up and keeping on.

Or it could be that you're putting your child through the state system to begin with while you save up for the independent senior school you hope he'll attend. But an over-stretched primary school teacher, with 30 children to get ready for their Sats, will have no interest in helping Harry prepare for independent school entrance, and even mention of the local grammar school is unlikely to get a sympathetic response. After all, from her perspective, selective education isn't what school's about. No matter how bright your child is, he'll be up against other children who have been intensively coached so tutoring is pretty much essential unless you are confident about your ability to fill in gaps.

A real need

Perhaps you feel your child needs a tutor even though he's already at a good preparatory school. Well, maybe. Be very sure, though, that the need is real. You are already paying a fair whack for his education at a school whose job it is to prepare him for secondary school exams. Depending on where he is, a year's tutoring in the run-up to common entrance may make sense, if only because it'll bring you peace of mind. But to have your tutored 7-year-old win a place at a high-achieving prep, and then immediately start having him tutored some more just because everyone else is doing it, will only exhaust him and your bank account. Wave him off to St Brainiac's with a proud smile, and let the school do its work.

On the other hand, if you've just relocated to the UK from overseas, using a tutor is an excellent way to get your kids up to speed with the English system and help them to feel more assured and comfortable in lessons. This in turn will help them to make friends, and the whole settling-in process will be smoother. For a child in a new country, confidence is key.

Where to look

If you want a tutor for your child, how do you find one? The best way should be word of mouth, of course. However, tutoring is one of those things parents usually do in secret, either because they don't choose to tell it around that their child struggles at school, or because they've no wish to increase the opposition's chances in the race for places. Try asking a friend with an older child, who won't begrudge your using what they no longer need. If this doesn't bring results, don't worry. This is London, and you have plenty of options.

Tutor companies

The first of these is to approach a tutor company. We review many of the best of these on the Good Schools Guide website, and using them has a number of benefits. They'll be skilled at matching your child to the right person, and will give you redress if you're not happy. The work of looking will be taken off your hands, and, since the tutors usually come to you, the whole process becomes very straightforward. This is the most expensive way of employing a tutor, however. Almost all companies will charge you a registration fee, which can be anything from a few quid to a hair-raising £180, and the hourly rate for tuition will be high (be prepared for at least £45), because the company will take a cut before paying the teacher.

Some of the really big tutorial companies cover too wide a geographical area to interview all their tutors in person, but they will have interviewed them by phone, and checked their references and DBS record.

Online search

A cheaper option is finding a tutor online. There are a number of websites on which tutors can advertise, and whose contact details you buy, usually for around £20, after you've had an exchange of messages with your selected tutor to see if they're the right fit. Tuition rates vary from around £16 ph – probably an undergraduate trying to earn a bit of extra cash – to £45+ ph for an experienced and qualified teacher. The website companies run checks to ascertain whether the tutor advertising is who they claim to be, but otherwise it's down to you to judge people's suitability. Use your common sense. If a person's replies to your messages are semi-literate, don't engage them as an English tutor.

Do your homework

Whether you're paying top whack for Kensington's finest hand-picked Oxbridge scholars, or searching through the online jungle with only your five wits to guide you, there are some measures it's sensible to take. After all, this is your child. Self-employed individuals are unlikely to be DBS-checked, because the law prevents them from running a check on themselves, so ask to see references or to speak to previous clients. In fact, do this even if they are DBS-checked. Interview the tutor on the phone before fixing a first date, and don't feel pressured into accepting someone who doesn't sound right. Don't be afraid to sit in on the first lesson, and afterwards ask your child what she thought. If the tutor is travelling to you, check that they can get there easily. Don't believe them when they say they can get from Wood Green to Putney in half an hour; they absolutely can't. Lastly – and this wisdom comes from years of weary experience – insist on punctuality. A tutor who is routinely late will soon drive you up the wall.

In short, if you do your homework your child's tutoring experiences should be happy, productive and affordable. Good luck.

A word on child protection

If you are preparing to entrust your child to a school – whether day or boarding – you will most likely assume that your child will be safe and that all members of the school's staff will take the greatest care to ensure that this is always the case. The chances are that your expectations will be fulfilled, but unfortunately in a sad minority of cases that is not what happens.

We have all read news reports of bullying and abuse and may have shuddered at the thought that those very people who smilingly welcome our children into their care may be the last people to whom we would entrust them, if we knew all.

A flood of historical allegations against schools, court cases, mobile phones, flexi-boarding, more parental involvement, the internet, sex education and heightened awareness have together helped usher in some sunlight and fresh air. Schools are now a less than perfect setting for paedophiles and bullies. Child protection policies, found on every school website, usefully make plain the possibility of abuse at schools – something rarely contemplated a generation ago.

Abuse can occur at any school, anywhere. Fame is no protection, and nor is obscurity. Some kinds of school, though, need to take particular care – and whether they do should be obvious to you when you visit. International schools have transient pupil populations, and teachers whose histories may be overseas and hard to research. Specialist music teaching necessarily involves a good deal of physical contact with the teacher and the pupil alone in a closed room. Religious schools can have a system of authority that keeps abuse concealed. Boarding schools can become very closed worlds. Special schools may have to deal with a large range of communication and emotional difficulties.

What can you do?

Parents do well to warn their children – gently but seriously – of the dangers, however remote these may be, so they feel that it is easy to speak to you should they meet them. It is worth pointing out that abuse can come from anyone – including a teacher or an adult they know well, or from another child at the school.

Raise your own antennae at any school you may be considering. You can inquire about the steps taken to safeguard children in the same way you might ask about bullying or learning support. As always, much can be gleaned from the head's attitude when questions about child protection are asked. Is he or she ill at ease? Defensive? Or happy to engage, and proud of the steps their school has taken? Openness is what you're looking for.

How easy is it for a child, or a parent for that matter, to report an incident? Schools make this possible in a variety of ways; what matters is that passing on concerns is a routine thing (children and parents do it about lots of things all the time), and is welcomed by the school, and is low-stakes: the person registering the concern knows that they are not putting their relationships within the school at risk, let alone threatening someone's place in the school. That may seem an odd thing to say, but if you fear to report, say, careless management of a museum trip because it will harm an otherwise much-loved teacher, you probably choose to stay mum. Your concerns have to cross a high threshold before you communicate them, so you never pass on those troubling observations that may be the outward indication of serious problems. To be safe, schools need to hear the little voices, not just the shouting.

Do not think less of a school because a case of abuse has been brought to light there. Tabloid coverage can be the price the school has to pay for handling a case of abuse or bullying

449

openly. It is inevitable that abuse will occur somewhere. What matters is how well the school deals with it, how well it performs in bringing the abuse to light and how open it is on the subject with current and future parents.

Further reading

The Good Schools Guide

Features independent and unbiased views of over 1,200 state and independent schools throughout Britain, written by parents for parents.

The Good Schools Guide Boarding Schools

Reviews 350+ boarding schools across Britain, independent and state, with advice on when to start boarding, applying from abroad, sex and drugs and homesickness, boarding for a child with SEN.

The Good Schools Guide online subscription

All the reviews plus details of every school in Britain, with exam data, catchment maps, university entrance information. Advice on choosing a school, SEN, tutors, talented children and much more.

Uni in the USA

Written by students who have been through the US system, features in-depth descriptions of 65 US universities, plus the inside track on getting in and preparing for life across the pond.

Uni in the USA and Beyond online subscription and ebook

Also includes unis in Europe and the East, from Alberta to Abu Dhabi, and advice from SATS to visas.

The Good Schools Guide International online subscription

The one-stop educational shop for expats, it reviews the best state and independent schools round the globe, plus insider knowledge on life overseas.

All available via www.goodschoolsguide.co.uk/shop-online

London South school index

School	Section	Page

List of advertisers

House ads

Notes

Notes

Notes

Notes